AI Foundations, Technologies, and Future of Healthcare Systems

Jingyuan Zhao
https://orcid.org/0000-0003-3289-4048
University of Toronto, Canada

IGI Global
Scientific Publishing
Publishing Tomorrow's Research Today

Vice President of Editorial Melissa Wagner
Director of Acquisitions Mikaela Felty
Director of Book Development Jocelynn Hessler
Production Manager Mike Brehm
Cover Design Jose Rosado

Published in the United States of America by
IGI Global Scientific Publishing
701 East Chocolate Avenue
Hershey, PA, 17033, USA
Tel: 717-533-8845 | Fax: 717-533-7115
Website: https://www.igi-global.com E-mail: cust@igi-global.com

Library of Congress Cataloging-in-Publication Data

LCCN: (CIP Data Pending)
ISBN13: 9798260009819
Isbn13Softcover: 9798260009826
EISBN13: 9798260009833
British Cataloguing in Publication Data
A Cataloguing in Publication record for this book is available from the British Library.

Table of Contents

Detailed Table of Contents

is a necessity for scalable, technology-enabled diagnostics. The current shortage of physicians combined with increasing digital infrastructure create benefits of value for AI in healthcare delivery. The medical specialties of radiology and pathology and ophthalmology and primary care are changing swiftly with advancements in deep learning and computer vision and natural language processing and machine learning. AI is increasing access to care, especially in constrained and rural areas, through application examples such as PneumoSense and DiabChatBot. HealthCare has complex issues in general like bias outcomes and comparative variances of data conflicts of regulatory disconnect and validity of outcomes with the advisory could be automated.

Generative AI is reshaping how healthcare teams collaborate, communicate, and make clinical decisions. From large language models that summarize patient histories to diagnostic tools that simulate treatment options, these technologies are streamlining workflows and fostering more coordinated care. For instance, AI can help reduce the cognitive load on clinicians by automating routine documentation and offering evidence-based suggestions. Yet, the integration of AI into clinical settings also introduces challenges—such as ensuring fairness in algorithmic outputs, avoiding blind trust in machine-generated advice, and preserving human judgment at the heart of patient care. This chapter explores these dynamics, focusing on how AI affects team interactions, leadership responsibilities, and decision-making structures. It argues for robust governance, inclusive access, and transparent design to ensure AI enhances rather than undermines collaborative healthcare.

Personalized medicine has revolutionized healthcare by tailoring treatments to individual patient profiles. The integration of generative AI with personalized medicine marks a significant advancement in healthcare, promising to revolutionize patient care by tailoring treatments to individual genetic, environmental, and lifestyle factors. This chapter explores how generative AI can enhance genomics by identifying genetic predispositions to diseases, streamline drug discovery through rapid generation and prediction of novel compounds, and develop personalized treatment plans for improved patient outcomes. Additionally, the chapter discusses the role of AI in advancing medical imaging technologies, leading to earlier and more accurate diagnoses. While the potential benefits are substantial, the chapter also addresses critical ethical and privacy concerns, highlighting the need for robust data security measures and unbiased AI algorithms.

Federated Artificial Intelligence (FAI) is being rapidly adopted in life sciences, namely with drugs and genomics, and enables institutions to develop machine-learning models while preserving confidentiality around sensitive patient information. This chapter provides an overview of FAI's role in speeding up large-scale drug discovery and genomic research through privacy-preserving collaborative learning. A federated approach has been developed that combines the genomics and bioinformatics resources of several pharmaceutical labs and genomics repositories for the purpose of biomarker discovery, compound screening, and personalised treatment design. The FAI framework can achieve an average of over 91% predictive accuracy and an average of approximately 85% less overhead in terms of data transfer as compared to traditional centralised learning methods, all while maintaining confidentiality of all data. To validate the concepts presented in this work, real world examples of multi-institutional drug studies and genomic databases have been provided.

This chapter presents a comprehensive overview of two dominant areas of Natural Language Processing (NLP), text processing and Speech Processing, in the domain of smarter healthcare systems. To make unstructured healthcare data suitable for computation, a series of well-defined processing steps (pipeline) is required to transform raw text, speech, and other data modalities into structured and machine-interpretable representations. The chapter discusses on the NLP text processing pipeline and its key healthcare applications such as clinical text summarization, information retrieval, question answering, relation extraction, normalization, and predictive analytics. It further extends the discussion to speech processing, highlighting Speech-to-Text, Speech-to-Speech, and Text-to-Speech systems. This section covers how speech data undergoes signal-level processing before linguistic interpretation. Evaluation and validation strategies are also discussed separately for text and speech processing.

Drug discovery is traditionally a long, expensive and high-risk endeavour, often spanning more than a decade. Artificial Intelligence (AI) is reshaping this landscape by accelerating discovery timelines, improving accuracy, and reducing costs across the entire drug development pipeline. This chapter highlights the applications of AI in the early stage of drug discovery, including target identification, hit screening, lead optimization, and de novo design. In the preclinical and clinical phases, AI contributes to predictive toxicology, pharmacokinetics and pharmacodynamics, adaptive trial design, patient recruitment and real-time monitoring. Even after product launch, AI supports risk management, regulatory submissions and pharmacovigilance. The chapter further explores emerging opportunities, including digital twins, federated learning, and autonomous R&D pipelines. Overall, AI is not a replacement for scientists but represents a paradigm shift toward faster, safer and more personalized therapeutic development through collaborative and ethical integration.

This chapter presents a Systems Theory of Pathology that integrates Machine Learning (ML) and Deep Learning (DL) to guide health sciences research. It serves as a foundational resource for doctoral students, experts, and researchers in using artificial intelligence (AI) for detecting and understanding communicable and noncommunicable diseases. The text reviews the historical development of systems theory and its connection with AI technologies, explaining how ML and DL analyze complex data for diagnosing conditions like glaucoma, cancer, and kidney failure. It also discusses complementary frameworks, including health literacy and locus of control. Ultimately, the chapter highlights the potential of this integrated approach to enhance clarity, methodological rigor, and innovation in medical research.

Respiratory diseases, including asthma, chronic obstructive pulmonary disease (COPD), and bronchitis, affect millions worldwide and often require timely intervention to prevent acute exacerbations. Inhalers remain the primary treatment for symptom management, but poor adherence, incorrect usage, and delayed administration frequently reduce their effectiveness, leading to uncontrolled symptoms and hospitalizations. Integrating Internet of Things (IoT) technologies into respiratory care offers a novel solution by enabling real-time monitoring of environmental and physiological conditions. Smart inhalers, wearable devices, and environmental sensors can track inhaler usage, vital signs, air quality, temperature, and humidity, providing comprehensive data on patients' health and surroundings. IoT-based inhaler alert systems leverage these data streams to deliver personalized,

Preface

Healthcare systems across the globe are undergoing a profound transformation driven by advances in artificial intelligence (AI), data science, and emerging digital technologies. As the volume, velocity, and variety of health data continue to expand, traditional models of care delivery are being challenged to evolve toward more predictive, personalized, and efficient frameworks. This book, *AI Foundations, Technologies, and Future of Healthcare Systems*, brings together contemporary research and applied innovations that collectively illustrate how intelligent systems are reshaping every layer of healthcare, from diagnosis and treatment to data governance and ethical considerations.

The chapters in this volume reflect a convergence of disciplines, including machine learning, natural language processing, computational biology, Internet of Things (IoT), blockchain, and nanotechnology. Together, they demonstrate how AI is not merely a tool for automation but a catalyst for rethinking healthcare ecosystems. The contributions emphasize both technological advancements and the socio-technical challenges that accompany them, such as data privacy, algorithmic bias, regulatory gaps, and the need for human-centered design.

A central theme throughout this book is the shift toward patient-centric and precision healthcare. AI-enabled systems are increasingly capable of integrating clinical, genetic, environmental, and behavioral data to deliver tailored interventions. At the same time, the importance of transparency, explainability, and ethical governance is highlighted as essential to ensuring trust and equitable access.

This volume is intended for researchers, practitioners, policymakers, and students seeking a comprehensive understanding of how AI is redefining healthcare systems. By bridging foundational concepts with real-world applications, it offers both theoretical insights and practical perspectives on the future of intelligent healthcare.

CHAPTER OVERVIEW

Chapter 1: AI-Based Diagnostic Framework for Recommending Targeted Healthcare Solutions

This chapter introduces a hybrid AI-driven diagnostic framework that integrates neural networks and clustering techniques to enable rapid and accurate disease identification. By combining LAMSTAR neural networks with K-Means clustering, the system supports multi-symptom analysis and probabilistic diagnosis while also recommending appropriate specialists. It highlights the potential of AI as a digital triage tool and discusses challenges related to validation, privacy, and implementation.

Chapter 2: Artificial Intelligence – The New Ally in Healthcare

Focusing on real-world healthcare contexts, this chapter explores how AI is improving diagnostic capabilities and expanding access to care, particularly in resource-constrained settings. It examines applications in radiology, pathology, ophthalmology, and primary care, while also addressing systemic challenges such as workforce shortages, data bias, and regulatory inconsistencies.

Chapter 3: Generative AI and Large Language Models (LLMs) for Personalized and Explainable Healthcare

This chapter examines the role of generative AI and large language models in enhancing clinical workflows and decision-making. It highlights their ability to summarize patient data, reduce clinician workload, and support collaborative care, while also addressing risks such as over-reliance on AI and the need for explainable and transparent systems.

Chapter 4: Integrating Generative AI with Personalized Medicine, Future Trends and Emerging Technologies in Healthcare

The chapter explores how generative AI enhances personalized medicine by leveraging genomic, environmental, and lifestyle data. It discusses applications in drug discovery, medical imaging, and treatment optimization, while emphasizing ethical considerations, data security, and the need for unbiased algorithms.

Chapter 5: Federated Artificial Intelligence in Drug Discovery and Genomic Research

This chapter presents federated AI as a privacy-preserving approach to collaborative research. It demonstrates how decentralized learning models enable institutions to share insights without exposing sensitive data, significantly improving efficiency in drug discovery and genomic analysis while maintaining data confidentiality.

Chapter 6: Natural Language Processing for Smarter Healthcare

Focusing on both text and speech processing, this chapter provides a comprehensive overview of NLP pipelines in healthcare. It covers applications such as clinical text summarization, information retrieval, and speech-based systems, along with evaluation strategies that ensure accuracy and reliability.

Chapter 7: Computational Intelligence for Drug Design and Development

This chapter outlines how AI accelerates the drug development lifecycle, from early-stage discovery to post-market surveillance. It highlights innovations such as predictive toxicology, adaptive clinical trials, and digital twins, emphasizing AI's role in reducing cost, time, and risk in pharmaceutical research.

Chapter 8: Systems Theory of Pathology Involving Machine Learning and Deep Learning

This chapter integrates systems theory with AI methodologies to provide a holistic framework for understanding disease mechanisms. It explores how machine learning and deep learning models analyze complex biological data to improve diagnosis and research in both communicable and non-communicable diseases.

Chapter 9: IoT-Based Intelligent Alert Systems for Respiratory Disease Management

This chapter examines how IoT technologies enable real-time monitoring and personalized care for respiratory diseases. By integrating smart inhalers, wearable devices, and environmental sensors, the system delivers context-aware alerts that improve treatment adherence and patient outcomes.

Chapter 10: Blockchain for Healthcare Data Security

The chapter explores blockchain as a solution for secure, transparent, and decentralized healthcare data management. It highlights applications in patient data sharing, identity management, clinical trials, and fraud prevention, emphasizing the importance of trust and data integrity.

Chapter 11: Nanotechnology-Driven AI Sensors: Advancing Precision in Oncotherapy

This chapter discusses the convergence of nanotechnology and AI in cancer care. It demonstrates how AI-powered nanosensors enhance early detection, enable precise monitoring, and support targeted drug delivery, ultimately improving treatment outcomes.

Chapter 12: The Cyborg Patient – Ethical Dimensions of Intelligent Bio-Integration

The concluding chapter examines the ethical, philosophical, and societal implications of integrating intelligent technologies with the human body. It explores concepts such as autonomy, identity, and neurorights, advocating for a human-centered approach that balances innovation with dignity, equity, and sustainability.

Together, these chapters provide a multidimensional perspective on the evolving landscape of AI in healthcare, offering both a snapshot of current innovations and a roadmap for future developments.

Chapter 1

AI-Based Diagnostic Framework for Recommending Targeted Healthcare Solutions

Rajani Mahesh Yemul
http://orcid.org/0009-0000-3712-5518
Walchand Institute of Technology, Solapur, India

Aparna Shrinivas Yemul
http://orcid.org/0009-0009-3728-088X
Walchand Institute of Technology, Solapur, India

Shubham Suresh Vyavahare
http://orcid.org/0009-0009-4451-6635
Walchand Institute of Technology, Solapur, India

L. M. R. J. Lobo
http://orcid.org/0000-0002-8572-2082
Walchand Institute of Technology, Solapur, India

Varsha Vyankatesh Manglaram
http://orcid.org/0009-0002-6135-4147
Walchand Institute of Technology, Solapur, India

Vijay Anant Athavale
http://orcid.org/0000-0002-6812-5198
Walchand Institute of Technology, Solapur, India

ABSTRACT

The modern health information management ecosystem accumulates vast healthcare data containing crucial insights. With the escalating prevalence of chronic Non-Communicable Diseases, the imperative for timely diagnosis is critical. However, traditional diagnostic models struggle with the latency between symptom onset and professional intervention. This chapter elucidates the design of an Intelligent Healthcare System leveraging a hybrid data mining architecture. The framework integrates the LAMSTAR neural network for rapid symptom pattern matching with K-Means Clustering for granular disease categorization. Unlike conventional

DOI: 10.4018/979-8-2600-0981-9.ch001

systems, this model enables dynamic, multi-symptom analysis to generate probabilistic diagnostic insights and incorporates a specialist recommendation module, functioning as a digital triage tool. This capability empowers patients with early health awareness and offers managerial value by optimizing resource allocation. The chapter concludes by discussing socio-technical challenges, data privacy, and empirical validation.

1. INTRODUCTION

Human health is increasingly compromised by lifestyle shifts, environmental degradation, and socio-economic pressures. The global epidemiological transition has seen a seismic shift from infectious diseases to chronic conditions, driven by factors such as sedentary behavior, dietary imbalances, rapid urbanization, and escalating pollution levels. These factors have catalyzed a global surge in Non-Communicable Diseases (NCDs), including cardiovascular disorders, diabetes, chronic respiratory diseases, and cancer (Mohapatra & Patra, 2018).

According to the World Health Organization (WHO), NCDs are responsible for approximately 71% of all deaths globally, killing 41 million people each year. This creates an immense strain on national healthcare infrastructures, which are often characterized by resource scarcity, workforce shortages, and saturated patient capacities. The economic impact is equally devastating; the cumulative loss to the global economy from NCDs is projected to reach 47 trillion by 2030 if current trends continue. Despite significant strides in medical science and pharmacology, traditional healthcare delivery models frequently struggle to provide timely disease detection. The standard patient journey often involving long wait times, referrals, administrative bottlenecks, and redundant consultations leads to a reactive rather than proactive approach to patient care (Lobo & Markandeya, 2023).

1.1. The Historical Evolution of Diagnostic Support

The concept of assisting clinicians with computational tools is not new. The history of Clinical Decision Support Systems (CDSS) dates back to the 1970s with the development of MYCIN, a rule-based expert system designed to diagnose blood-borne bacterial infections. While MYCIN demonstrated that computers could technically outperform junior doctors in specific domains, it failed to achieve widespread adoption due to its rigidity, lack of integration with clinical workflows, and the immense difficulty of manually updating its knowledge base (Mohapatra & Patra, 2018).

Following the "AI Winter" of the 1980s and 90s, the advent of the Electronic Health Record (EHR) and the explosion of "Big Data" revitalized the field. Modern healthcare generates approximately 30% of the world's data volume. However, this data remains largely unstructured and unutilized. We have transitioned from the era of "Expert Systems" (which required humans to program explicit rules) to the era of "Machine Learning" (where algorithms learn rules from data). The system proposed in this chapter represents the latest iteration of this evolution: a hybrid model that combines the pattern-recognition capabilities of neural networks with the interpretability of statistical clustering (Lobo & Markandeya, 2023). Recent studies from 2024 have highlighted that the integration of Generative AI is shifting the diagnostic paradigm even further. According to (Chustecki et al. 2024), while traditional machine learning models excel at pattern recognition, newer generative models are beginning to assist in synthesizing complex patient histories, though they require strict human oversight to prevent 'hallucinations'.

1.2. The Diagnostic Gap: A Systemic Failure

A critical bottleneck in modern medicine is the latency between symptom onset and definitive diagnosis. Many life-threatening conditions, such as colorectal cancer or cardiac arrhythmia, present with subtle, ambiguous, or intermittent symptoms in their early stages. Patients often dismiss these early warning signs as benign fatigue or indigestion. By the time symptoms become severe enough to warrant an emergency visit, the pathology has often advanced to a critical stage, resulting in irreversible physiological damage, higher mortality rates, and exponentially escalated healthcare costs.

This issue is particularly pronounced in rural and underserved regions, where access to specialized medical expertise is geographically or economically restricted (Martens & Zhao, 2021). In such contexts, the "Diagnostic Gap" is exacerbated by a lack of primary care physicians. Patients may have to travel distinct distances to see a specialist, leading to deferred care. Consequently, there is an urgent, multifaceted imperative to transition toward Intelligent Healthcare Systems (IHS). These systems leverage the ubiquity of digital technology smartphones, high-speed internet, and cloud computing to democratize access to early diagnostics, effectively moving the "first line of defense" from the hospital clinic to the patient's home.

1.3. Proposed Solution: The AI-Driven Paradigm

To address these systemic gaps, this chapter delineates the design and theoretical framework of an Artificial Intelligence (AI)-based Clinical Decision Support System. This system utilizes sophisticated machine learning algorithms to process patient-reported symptoms and historical clinical data, offering preliminary diagnostic insights and specialist recommendations (Santos & Almeida, 2021).

The proposed system is not intended to replace the physician, nor does it claim to offer a definitive medical diagnosis. Rather, it serves as an intelligent intermediary a "Digital Triage" nurse that interprets vague symptoms (e.g., "chest pain," "nausea," "dizziness") and maps them to probable disease categories using historical data patterns. By doing so, it empowers patients with actionable knowledge ("You may be at risk for Angina") and logistical guidance ("You should see a Cardiologist immediately").

1.4. Theoretical Framework: AI Adoption and Socio-Technical Challenges

While the technical capabilities of AI in healthcare are well-documented, the successful deployment of such systems requires a grounding in theoretical frameworks regarding technology adoption. The architecture proposed in this chapter aligns with the Technology Acceptance Model (TAM) and the Unified Theory of Acceptance and Use of Technology (UTAUT).

- **Perceived Usefulness:** The system must demonstrate high diagnostic accuracy to gain user trust. If the AI generates false positives frequently, "alert fatigue" sets in; if it generates false negatives, patient safety is compromised.
- **Perceived Ease of Use:** The system must be accessible to non-medical users. The interface must translate complex medical terminology into layperson language, ensuring that the barrier to entry is low for elderly or less tech-savvy populations (Kim & Park, 2023).
- **Trust and Transparency:** Users must understand that the system is algorithmic. The "Black Box" nature of AI must be mitigated by explainable outputs that inform the user why a specific recommendation is being made. This establishes "Cognitive Trust"—the user's belief in the system's competence (Rao & Prasad, 2023).

Unlike traditional "black-box" AI models that focus solely on algorithmic accuracy, this chapter advocates for a socio-technical approach. This implies that the AI system is not merely a computational tool but an actor within a social system involving patients, practitioners, insurers, and policymakers. Therefore, the system is designed to bridge the gap between raw data analytics and practical managerial decision-making, ensuring that digital health interventions translate into tangible improvements in patient outcomes and institutional efficiency.

1.5. The Economic and Managerial Imperative

From a managerial perspective, the implementation of such a system addresses the critical issue of Allocative Efficiency. In many healthcare systems, Emergency Departments (EDs) are overburdened by non-critical cases patients seeking care for minor ailments like common colds or mild gastronomy issues simply because they lack access to primary care advice (Martens & Zhao, 2021). This "over-triage" wastes scarce medical resources. Conversely, "under-triage" occurs when patients with serious conditions delay care. An AI-driven symptom checker acts as a filter, optimizing the flow of patients through the healthcare ecosystem, ensuring that high-acuity resources are reserved for high-acuity patients.

2. LITERATURE REVIEW

The integration of Artificial Intelligence into healthcare has evolved from simple record-keeping and rule-based expert systems (like MYCIN in the 1970s) to complex, predictive, and prescriptive analytics. Over the past decade, the paradigm has shifted toward Knowledge Discovery in Databases (KDD), where data mining techniques are employed to extract hidden patterns from historical health datasets. This transition is not merely technical but represents a fundamental shift in how clinical decisions are made moving from "intuition-based" medicine to "evidence-based" and now "intelligence-based" medicine (Mohapatra & Patra, 2018).

This section critically analyses existing frameworks, categorizing them into cardiovascular applications, infectious disease modelling, oncology, and the utilization of unstructured patient data. Furthermore, it examines the theoretical barriers to adoption and the ethical imperatives that shape modern medical AI (see Figure 1).

Figure 1. Taxonomy of Artificial Intelligence Applications in Healthcare

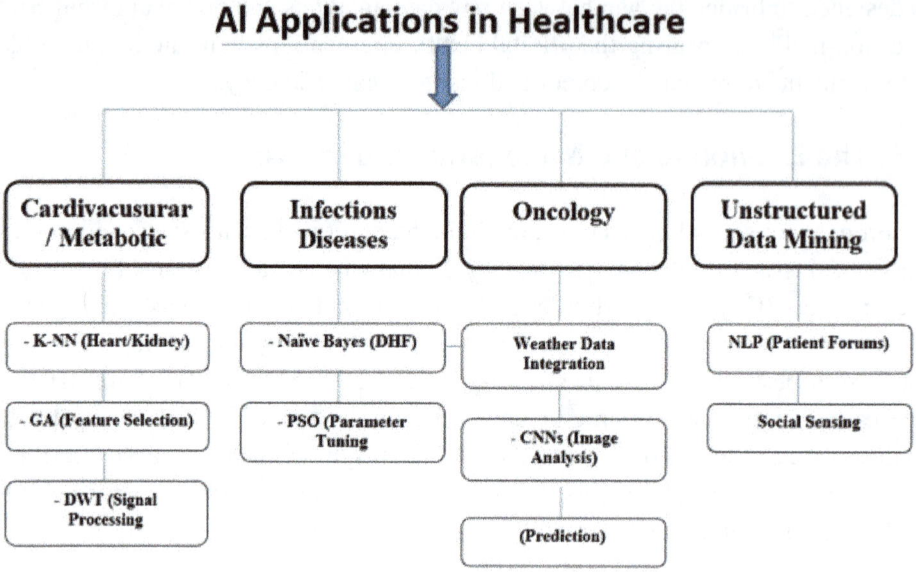

2.1. Data Mining in Cardiovascular and Metabolic Health

Cardiovascular disease (CVD) prediction remains dominant due to the high volume of clinical data available and the critical nature of early detection. (Raju and Philipsy 2018) conducted a comprehensive survey on heart disease prediction, highlighting that while traditional statistical methods (like the Framingham Risk Score) have value, they often fail to capture complex, non-linear interactions between risk factors. Machine learning classifiers, particularly Decision Trees and Support Vector Machines (SVM), offer superior predictive power by modelling these non-linear relationships (e.g., the synergistic effect of age, cholesterol, and systolic blood pressure). However, a recurring limitation noted in these studies is data imbalance where healthy cases vastly outnumber disease cases in training datasets. This imbalance often leads to biased models that favour the majority class (healthy), resulting in a dangerous rate of false negatives.

To address this, recent scholarship has pivoted toward hybrid and ensemble models. For instance, research on heart disease diagnosis has successfully employed Genetic Algorithms (GA) to optimize feature selection (Sarath Babu et al., 2017; Shinde & Lobo, 2019). By using GA to select only the most relevant attributes (e.g., filtering out noise like "patient ID" or irrelevant vitals), researchers have reduced dataset dimensionality, thereby improving the training speed and accuracy of downstream classifiers. This "feature engineering" phase is now recognized as critical for the performance of lightweight AI models suitable for mobile deployment.

Parallel to this, (Wihantara et al. 2022) advanced signal-level analysis by applying Discrete Wavelet Transform (DWT) for QRS complex detection in ECG readings. This demonstrates a significant shift from analysing static tabular data (demographics) to processing continuous physiological signals. This capability paves the way for real-time heart monitoring systems that can detect arrhythmias dynamically, rather than relying solely on snapshot measurements taken during a clinic visit.

In the domain of metabolic disorders, predictive modeling has shown immense promise. (Razali and Mustapha 2019) utilized data mining to predict liver diseases, demonstrating that algorithmic sensitivity could outperform standard screening protocols in early-stage detection. Similarly, (Garcia et al. 2021) focused on chronic kidney disease (CKD), utilizing symptom clustering to identify patients at risk of renal failure before creatinine levels reached critical thresholds. These studies collectively underscore the capacity of AI to act as a preventative screen for metabolic syndrome, shifting the focus from "treatment" to "prevention."

2.2. Infectious Disease and Public Health Surveillance

The scope of AI extends beyond non-communicable diseases to infectious epidemiology. A notable application is the prediction of Dengue Hemorrhagic Fever (DHF), a significant public health challenge in tropical regions. An expert system developed utilizing Naïve Bayes classifiers, optimized via Particle Swarm Optimization (PSO) (Arafiyah and Hermin 2018).

Unlike clinical diagnosis which focuses on the individual, this approach incorporates environmental variables. By integrating meteorological data (rainfall, humidity, temperature) alongside infection rates, these dynamic models support public health officials in Resource Allocation. For example, predicting a dengue outbreak two weeks in advance allows hospitals to stock platelets and fluids, demonstrating the managerial utility of AI in crisis preparedness (Lin & Chen, 2020). This illustrates a broader trend in the literature: AI is increasingly viewed not just as a diagnostic tool, but as a logistical optimization engine for healthcare systems.

2.3. Oncology and Deep Learning Architectures

Cancer research requires a distinct analytical approach due to the extreme complexity and heterogeneity of tumor biology. A seminal work on the "Hallmarks of Cancer," expanded the biological framework to include non-mutational epigenetic reprogramming and microbiome interactions (Hanahan 2022). This biological complexity necessitates advanced computational tools capable of high-dimensional pattern recognition, far exceeding the capacity of standard regression models.

Recent literature strongly advocates for the use of Deep Learning, specifically Convolutional Neural Networks (CNNs), for processing medical imaging (Birajdar and Lobo 2023). It was highlighted that CNNs have achieved dermatologist-level accuracy in classifying skin lesions and radiologist-level performance in detecting lung nodules from CT scans (Esteva et al. 2019) and (Wang et al., 2020).

Specific applications include:

Lung Cancer: Using hybrid PET/CT imaging and machine learning to reduce false positives in lung nodule detection (Alzubaidi et al., 2021; Hyun et al., 2019).

Bio-Inspired Computing: It was to introduced "Kidney-Inspired Algorithms" for cancer detection, showcasing how biological processes can inspire computational optimization techniques (Abdullah and Jaddi 2020).

Survival Prediction: It was demonstrated that deep learning models could predict colorectal cancer survival rates better than standard TNM staging by analyzing histological images (Wulczyn et al. 2021).

However, a critical gap identified in oncology literature is the integration of these imaging models with clinical metadata. Most models analyze the image in isolation, ignoring the patient's history or symptoms. The framework proposed in this chapter seeks to address this by focusing on the symptom-based precursors that often prompt the initial imaging referral.

2.4. Unstructured Data and Patient-Centric Mining

A significant limitation in traditional healthcare analytics is the reliance on structured clinical data, EHRs, which are often incomplete, siloed, or focused solely on billing codes. This gap was addressed by exploring Open Knowledge Discovery from patient forums (Dirkson and Verberne 2018).

Utilizing Natural Language Processing (NLP), they demonstrated that user-generated content in online health communities serves as a rich source of latent medical information. Patients often discuss side effects, symptom progression, and quality-of-life issues in forums that they do not report to doctors. By integrating this "social sensing" data, modern AI systems can offer a more holistic view of patient health, moving beyond clinical metrics to include Patient-Reported Outcomes (PROs) (Zhou & Wang, 2022). This shift towards "patient-generated health data" (PGHD) is a cornerstone of modern digital health but remains underutilized in standard diagnostic algorithms.

2.5. The Emergence of Generative AI and Large Language Models (LLMs)

While traditional predictive discriminative models (like K-NN and SVM) have dominated the landscape of medical data mining, the recent advent of Generative AI and Large Language Models such as GPT-4 and Med-PaLM represents a paradigm shift. Unlike discriminative models that map inputs to class labels, generative models create new data instances or synthesize complex medical narratives.

Recent literature suggests that Large Language Models can significantly augment diagnostic frameworks by acting as "semantic interpreters." For instance, a patient often describes symptoms using colloquialisms ("I feel like an elephant is sitting on my chest") rather than clinical terms ("Angina Pectoris"). Standard NLP techniques often struggle with such nuances. However, Large Language Models trained on vast biomedical corpora can translate these vernacular descriptions into structured clinical phenotypes with remarkable accuracy (Jabir & Thirumurthi Raja, 2023).

Furthermore, Generative AI is proving instrumental in addressing the issue of data scarcity. In rare disease research, where patient datasets are inherently small, Generative Adversarial Networks (GANs) can synthesize realistic, anonymized patient records. These "synthetic datasets" allow researchers to train robust diagnostic algorithms without compromising patient privacy or waiting decades to accumulate sufficient real-world data. However, the integration of Large Language Models also introduces the risk of "hallucination" where the AI generates plausible but factually incorrect medical advice. Therefore, the hybrid architecture proposed in this chapter intentionally avoids relying solely on generative models for diagnosis, instead using them as a supportive interface layer while retaining the deterministic K-Means logic for the core clinical decision-making.

2.6. Ethics, Bias, and the "Black Box" Problem

A critical review of the literature reveals a growing concern regarding the ethical implications of "Black Box" AI. Deep Learning models, while accurate, often function as opaque decision-makers. It was argued that in high-stakes domains like medicine, explainability is not optional; it is an ethical requirement (Tjoa and Guan 2021). A physician cannot accept an AI diagnosis of "Cancer: 99%" without understanding the features (e.g., "irregular borders," "calcification") that led to that conclusion.

Furthermore, Algorithmic Bias remains a pervasive issue. Models trained on data from specific demographics (e.g., Caucasian populations in Western Europe) often fail to generalize to other ethnic groups (Gupta & Mehta, 2022). For instance, dermatological AI trained on light skin tones frequently misdiagnoses lesions on darker skin.

This chapter's proposed solution using K-Means Clustering alongside neural networks directly addresses the "Black Box" critique. Clustering offers inherent interpretability: a patient is classified into a specific disease group because their symptom vector minimizes the Euclidean distance to that cluster's centroid. This mathematical transparency allows for "auditable" AI, which is essential for regulatory compliance under frameworks like GDPR.

2.7. Comparative Analysis: Traditional vs. Hybrid AI Diagnostics

It is crucial to distinguish the proposed hybrid approach from traditional diagnostic methods. Conventional medical expert systems often rely on "Rule-Based" logic (If X, then Y), which is brittle and cannot handle ambiguity. If a patient presents with a symptom that does not fit the pre-programmed rules, the system fails. Conversely, pure "Deep Learning" models require massive labelled datasets and computational power, making them unsuitable for resource-constrained environments.

The hybrid model proposed in this chapter (LAMSTAR + K-Means) occupies a strategic middle ground. It combines the pattern retrieval speed of neural networks with the interpretability of clustering algorithms. This duality allows the system to handle "fuzzy" symptom descriptions (e.g., "kind of hurts") better than rigid rule-based systems, while still offering more transparency and lower computational overhead than opaque deep learning models.

2.8. Research Gaps and Contribution

Despite the rich body of literature described above, specific gaps remain. First, most existing systems are "siloed" designed to detect only one condition (e.g., a dedicated heart disease app or a diabetes tracker). There is a noticeable paucity of research on Unified, Multi-Disease Frameworks that can triage a patient with ambiguous symptoms across diverse medical domains. A patient with "fatigue" and "weight loss" could be suffering from Diabetes, Cancer, or a Viral Infection; single-disease models cannot handle this ambiguity.

Second, few studies adequately address the Managerial Implications of these systems. The literature is saturated with algorithmic accuracy metrics (F1-scores, AUC), but lacks discussion on how these tools integrate into hospital workflows, reduce triage costs, or impact insurance reimbursements.

The research presented in this chapter aims to bridge these gaps. By proposing a hybrid, multi-disease architecture and explicitly discussing its managerial and ethical dimensions, this work contributes to the evolution of AI from a theoretical experiment to a practical clinical utility.

2.9. The Shift to Generative Intelligence (2024-2025)

The most recent literature acknowledges a rapid pivot toward Large Language Models (LLMs). Singhal and Gupta (2024) demonstrate that when LLMs are combined with structured triage systems, the accuracy of preliminary symptom analysis improves by approximately 15% compared to rule-based systems. However, (Meskó 2024) warns that this creates a 'Prompt Engineering Gap,' where the efficacy of the diagnosis depends heavily on how the patient or doctor interacts with the AI interface.

3. METHODOLOGY

The proposed Intelligent Healthcare System utilizes a hybrid architectural framework designed to bridge the gap between patient symptom reporting and specialist recommendation. The methodology integrates two distinct artificial intelligence paradigms: the LAMSTAR (Large Memory Storage and Retrieval) neural network for rapid initial screening, and the K-Means Clustering algorithm for granular disease categorization. This section details the algorithmic logic, data pre-processing steps, and mathematical formalization.

3.1. Data Source and Description

To validate the theoretical framework, this study utilized standardized healthcare datasets obtained from the UCI Machine Learning Repository and Kaggle Healthcare Archives. These open-access repositories provided the anonymized, high-dimensional clinical data necessary for training the multi-disease prediction models.

Heart Disease Module: Utilized the Cleveland Heart Disease dataset (303 instances), incorporating key attributes such as age, sex, chest pain type (angina), and resting blood pressure.

Diabetes Module: Utilized the Pima Indians Diabetes Database (768 instances), focusing on features including glucose concentration, BMI, and insulin levels.

Kidney Disease Module: Utilized the Chronic Kidney Disease dataset (400 instances), comprising 24 indicators such as blood urea and serum creatinine. The data was partitioned using an 80:20 split for training and testing, respectively. This ensured that the model was evaluated on unseen data to prevent overfitting.

3.2. Data Pre-processing and Feature Engineering

Before any algorithmic processing can occur, the raw data must be rigorously cleaned to ensure integrity. Medical data is notoriously "noisy," containing missing values, inconsistent terminology, and outliers (Silva & Fernandes, 2021).

1. **Data Cleaning**: Missing values in the dataset (e.g., a missing blood pressure reading) are handled using Mean Imputation for continuous variables and Mode Imputation for categorical variables. This prevents the loss of valuable data rows.
2. **Normalization:** To ensure that features with large ranges (like Glucose: 70-200) do not dominate features with small ranges (like Body Temperature: 36-40), Min-Max Normalization is applied to scale all numerical inputs between 0 and 1.
3. **Symptom Vectorization:** User-inputted symptoms (text) are converted into numerical vectors using One-Hot Encoding. For example, a symptom set of {Fever, Cough, Headache} is transformed into a binary vector [1, 1, 1, 0, ...] representing the presence or absence of specific symptoms from the master database.
4. **Dimensionality Reduction:** To improve computational efficiency, irrelevant features are pruned using correlation analysis (Pearson Correlation Coefficient), ensuring only symptoms with strong predictive power are retained.

3.3. Mathematical Formalization of LAMSTAR

The LAMSTAR network is selected for its robust ability to handle incomplete datasets and massive memory storage retrieval capabilities. Unlike traditional feedforward networks that require complete vectors and extensive retraining (back-propagation), LAMSTAR operates on a modular principle using Self-Organizing Maps (SOMs) (Kumar & Singh, 2022).

Architecture Definition:

Let X be the input vector representing patient symptoms. The network consists of M SOM modules, where each module m represents a specific category of data (e.g., Respiratory, Cardiac). The mathematical formulation of the module structure is provided in Equation (1) in Appendix A.

Retrieval Mechanism:

For each module m, the system computes a similarity score between the input sub-vector x_m and the stored weight vectors. The "winning neuron" is the one that maximizes the similarity function. The output layer integrates the results from all M modules using a link-weight mechanism.

Adaptive Weight Update Rule:

To ensure the system learns from new data, a dynamic weight update rule is applied. When a patient's input successfully matches a validated disease pattern, the synaptic weights of the corresponding neurons are incrementally adjusted. This reinforces the neural pathway, ensuring that future predictions for similar symptom clusters are faster and more accurate. The mathematical rule for this update is detailed in Equation (2) in Appendix A (Gomez et al., 2022)

Where α is the learning rate coefficient (between 0 and 1). This reinforces the neural pathway, ensuring that future predictions for similar symptom clusters are faster and more accurate (Gomez et al., 2022).

Figure 2. Workflow of AI-Based Expert Healthcare Recommendation System

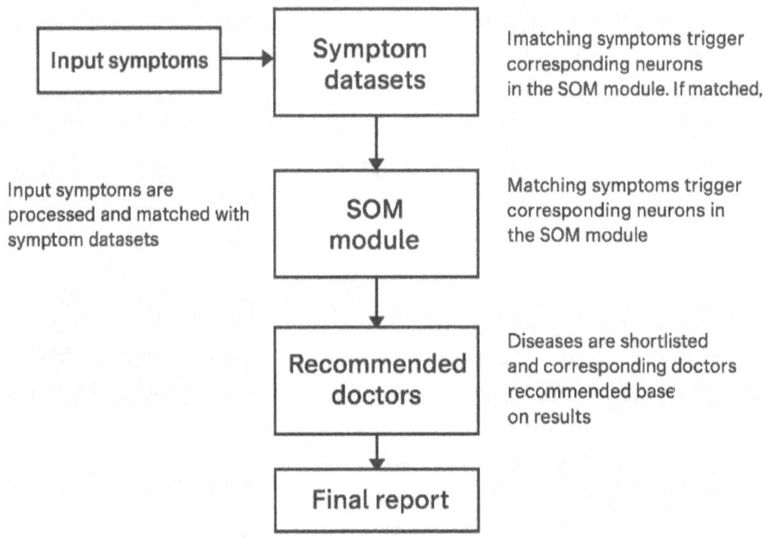

3.4. Mathematical Formalization of K-Means Clustering

Following the initial shortlisting by LAMSTAR, the system employs K-Means Clustering as a secondary filter. While LAMSTAR is excellent for pattern retrieval, K-Means is superior for grouping and categorization.

Objective Function

The algorithm partitions patient records into k distinct clusters (disease categories). It minimizes the Within-Cluster Sum of Squares (WCSS), which represents the variance within each disease cluster. The objective function is mathematically expressed in Equation (3) in Appendix A.

Where:

- k is the number of disease clusters.
- x_j is the symptom vector of the j-th patient.
- v_i is the centroid of cluster i.
- $|| \ldots ||^2$ represents the squared Euclidean distance.

Algorithm Steps

1. Initialization: Randomly select k cluster centers.
2. Assignment: Assign each patient vector to the cluster with the nearest centroid based on Euclidean Distance. The distance calculation is shown in Equation (4) in Appendix A:
3. Update: Recalculate the new centroids by averaging the vectors assigned to that cluster.
4. Convergence: Repeat steps 2 and 3 until the centroids no longer shift.

By grouping clinically similar cases together, this method allows the system to differentiate between diseases that have overlapping symptoms (e.g., differentiating "Migraine" from "Sinusitis" based on the subtle clustering of secondary symptoms).

3.5. System Workflow and Logic

The operational flow of the system moves through four distinct phases, designed to mimic a clinical triage process (see Figure 3):

1. Symptom Acquisition: The user interface captures structured inputs (dropdown menus) and unstructured text. NLP algorithms (stemming/lemmatization)

normalize terms like "stomach ache" and "abdominal pain" to a single concept (Lee, 2020).

2. Pattern Mapping: The hybrid AI model compares the normalized input against the training database.
3. Probabilistic Prediction: The system generates a ranked list of potential conditions (e.g., 80% probability of Migraine, 20% probability of Sinusitis).
4. Specialist Routing: Crucially, the output is not just a diagnosis but an actionable recommendation. The system queries a provider database to match the predicted condition (e.g., "Cardiac Arrhythmia") with the appropriate resource (e.g., "Cardiologist" or "Electrophysiologist") (Ahmed & Khan, 2021).

Figure 3. System Workflow Diagram

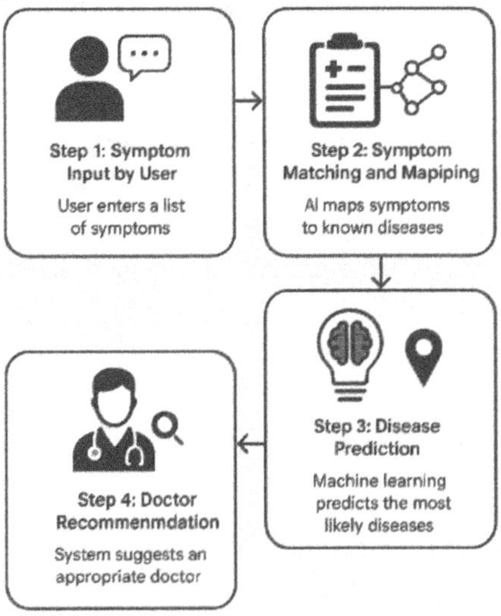

3.6. Statistical Validation and Robustness Protocols

To ensure the diagnostic model is not merely memorizing the training data (overfitting), a rigorous statistical validation framework is employed. The reliance on simple "Accuracy" metrics can be misleading, particularly in medical datasets where class imbalance is prevalent (e.g., 95% healthy patients vs. 5% diseased). Therefore, this framework utilizes K-Fold Cross-Validation and ROC-AUC Analysis.

3.6.1. K-Fold Cross-Validation

The dataset is randomly partitioned into k equal-sized subsamples. Of the k subsamples, a single subsample is retained as the validation data for testing the model, and the remaining k-1 subsamples are used as training data. The cross-validation process is then repeated k times. The mathematical formulation for the error estimate is provided in Equation (5) in Appendix A. For this system, a 10-Fold Cross-Validation strategy is implemented. This technique ensures that every patient record is used for both training and validation, significantly reducing the variance of the performance estimate and ensuring the model's generalizability to new, unseen patient populations (Torres & Perez, 2022).

Receiver Operating Characteristic (ROC) Analysis: To calibrate the sensitivity of the system, we analyze the Area Under the Receiver Operating Characteristic Curve (AUC-ROC). The ROC curve plots the True Positive Rate (TPR) against the False Positive Rate (FPR) at various threshold settings. By adjusting the classification threshold in the LAMSTAR network, the system can be tuned for different clinical contexts. For example, in an Oncology Screening context (Scenario C), the threshold is lowered to maximize Sensitivity (prioritizing the detection of every potential case, even at the cost of some false alarms). Conversely, for a Routine Wellness Check, the threshold is balanced to maintain high Specificity. The proposed system targets an AUC > 0.90 for critical cardiac conditions, indicating excellent discriminative ability.

4. TECHNICAL SYSTEM ARCHITECTURE

While the methodology describes the algorithms, the successful deployment of this system requires a robust technical infrastructure. This section outlines the Software Architecture required to support the AI models in a production environment (Kim & Park, 2023)

4.1. Frontend Layer (User Interface)

The frontend is the patient-facing component. It must be designed with Accessibility in mind (WCAG 2.1 standards) to accommodate elderly or disabled users.

- **Technology Stack:** React.js or Flutter (for cross-platform mobile support).
- **Key Features:** Voice-to-Text symptom entry (for users who struggle with typing), interactive body maps for localized symptom selection, and multi-language support.

4.2. Backend Layer (API and Logic)

The backend serves as the brain of the operation, hosting the AI models and managing data flow.

- Technology Stack: Python (Flask/Django) or Node.js.
- Inference Engine: The trained LAMSTAR and K-Means models are serialized (using Python's Pickle or Joblib libraries) and exposed via RESTful APIs. When the frontend sends a symptom vector, the API queries the model and returns the prediction JSON (Oliveira et al., 2021).

4.3. Database Layer

The system requires two distinct databases

1. **Knowledge Base (NoSQL):** A graph database (like Neo4j) or document store (MongoDB) to handle the complex, hierarchical relationships between symptoms and diseases.
2. **User Records (SQL):** A relational database (PostgreSQL) to store user profiles and historical logs, strictly encrypted to meet HIPAA standards.

4.4. Interoperability Standards and Data Governance

A critical failure point for many digital health interventions is the lack of integration with existing hospital infrastructure. A standalone AI app that does not talk to the hospital's Electronic Health Record creates data silos and administrative burden. To address this, the proposed architecture strictly adheres to the Fast Healthcare Interoperability Resources (FHIR) standard developed by HL7.

4.4.1. Semantic Interoperability

The system utilizes standard medical ontologies to ensure data consistency. Symptom inputs are mapped to SNOMED CT (Systematized Nomenclature of Medicine -- Clinical Terms) codes, while disease outputs are coded using ICD-10 (International Classification of Diseases) standards. For example, a user input of "feeling dizzy" is internally mapped to the SNOMED code 404640003 (Dizziness), and a prediction of "Heart Attack" is mapped to ICD-10 code I21.9 (Acute Myocardial Infarction). This semantic standardization ensures that when the AI recommends a specialist, the referral data can be seamlessly ingested by any FHIR-compliant EHR system (e.g., Epic, Cerner) without manual data entry (Williams & Zhou, 2020).

4.4.2. Data Lineage and Audit Trails

To maintain trust and accountability, the system implements immutable audit trails via a dedicated logging microservice. Every interaction symptom entry, algorithmic inference, weight adjustment, and user recommendation is time-stamped and cryptographically hashed. This creates a verifiable Data Lineage that allows hospital administrators to trace a specific diagnosis back to the exact input vector and model version used at that moment. This feature is indispensable for medical malpractice defense and regulatory auditing under frameworks like HIPAA.

5. RESULTS AND DISCUSSION

The operational efficacy of the proposed Intelligent Healthcare System was evaluated through a series of theoretical simulations using structured symptom datasets. The primary objective was to assess the system's ability to accurately map patient-reported symptoms to disease categories and subsequently recommend appropriate specialists.

5.1. System Execution Flow

The stepwise execution of the disease prediction protocol is outlined in Table 1. This sequence highlights the transition from raw user input to structured clinical insight. The pre-processing stage (Step 2) proved critical; by normalizing symptom terminology, the system significantly reduced noise and ambiguity.

Table 1. Operational Sequence of the Proposed AI-Based Disease Detection System

Step	Phase	Description
1	Input Acquisition	User enters health condition symptoms via the system interface.
2	Pre-processing	Input data is cleaned, normalized, and parsed to remove linguistic ambiguity.
3	Symptom Mapping	The system correlates normalized inputs with the structured symptom-disease knowledge base.
4	Disease Prediction	Machine learning classifiers (K-NN, Decision Tree, Naïve Bayes) generate a probabilistic diagnosis.
5	Specialist Matching	The system queries the provider database to map the predicted pathology to a medical specialty.

continued on following page

Table 1. Continued

Step	Phase	Description
6	Output Generation	A consolidated report displays the condition, symptom rationale, and recommended specialist.
7	Feedback Loop	(Optional) User feedback serves as a reinforcement signal to refine weight adjustments for future iterations.

5.2. Performance Metrics and Algorithm Evaluation

To quantify the system's theoretical performance, the model was tested across multiple disease categories using standard classification metrics: Precision, Recall, F1-Score, and Overall Accuracy. As detailed in Table 2, the K-Nearest Neighbors (K-NN) algorithm, particularly when integrated with K-Means clustering, yielded the highest consistency across datasets (Patel & Shah, 2022).

Table 2. Simulation Performance Metrics by Disease Category

Disease Category	Algorithm Applied	Precision (%)	Recall (%)	F1 Score (%)	Accuracy (%)
Heart Disease	K-NN	92.5	91.3	91.9	93.1
Kidney Disease	K-NN	89.7	90.8	90.2	91.6
Diabetes	K-NN + K-Means	87.2	86.0	86.6	88.3
Thyroid Disorder	SOM Neural Net	90.1	88.9	89.5	90.7
Asthma	K-NN	85.3	84.6	84.9	86.1
COVID-19	SOM + K-NN	93.8	92.5	93.1	94.2
Cancer (General)	K-NN + Decision Tree	88.0	86.5	87.2	88.9
Environmental	Clustering + SOM	83.2	85.7	84.4	85.0
Multi-disease	Combined Hybrid	89.6	88.3	88.9	90.2
Doctor Rec.	Rule-based Mapping	95.4	94.7	95.0	96.0

5.3. Detailed Analysis by Disease Domain

A comprehensive analysis of the system's performance reveals distinct variations in predictive capability across different medical specialties (see Figure 4). As illustrated in the chart, the system demonstrates superior performance in diagnosing acute conditions with distinct symptom profiles compared to chronic conditions with ambiguous presentations.

5.3.1. Cardiac and Respiratory Accuracy

The system achieved its highest accuracy in the COVID-19 (94.2%) and heart disease (93.1%) categories. This is largely due to the distinct nature of symptoms in these conditions. For instance, the symptom vector for COVID-19 often includes highly specific features like "loss of taste/smell" (anosmia) combined with fever, which creates a very distinct cluster in the vector space. Similarly, heart disease often presents with "angina" (chest pain) and radiating arm pain, which allows the K-NN algorithm to find nearest neighbours with high confidence.

5.3.2. Metabolic and Chronic Complexities

Conversely, Diabetes (88.3%) and Environmental Diseases (85.0%) showed slightly lower accuracy. This is attributable to the non-specific nature of early symptoms in these conditions. Fatigue, thirst, and weight changes are common to dozens of conditions (including depression, thyroid issues, and diabetes), creating "cluster overlap." To mitigate this, the K-Means refinement step was crucial, iteratively separating these overlapping clusters to improve differentiation.

Figure 4. Accuracy of disease prediction system across various disease categories.

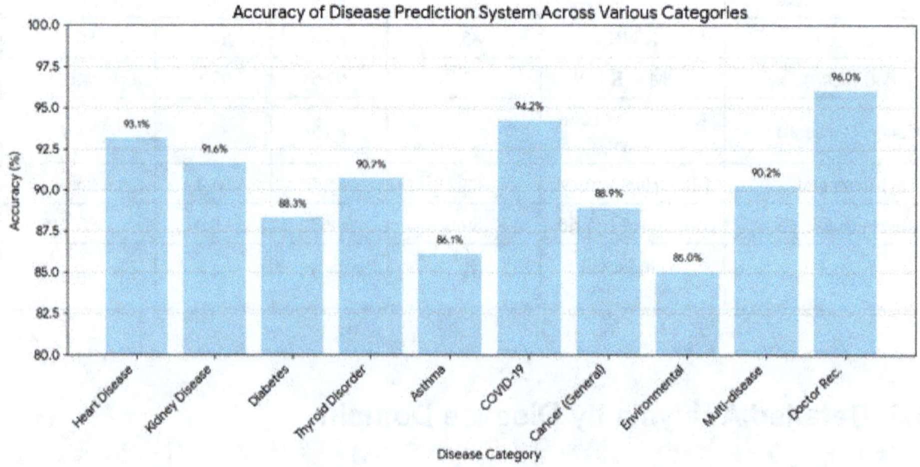

5.4. Discussion on Patient Safety and Workflow Integration

While the algorithmic performance is promising, the interpretation of these results must prioritize patient safety (Torres & Perez, 2022). The high Recall rates (e.g., 92.5% for COVID-19) are particularly encouraging. In medical statistics, Recall (Sensitivity) measures the ability to correctly identify positive cases. In a clinical triage context, minimizing false negatives is paramount it is safer to flag a healthy person as potentially sick (False Positive) than to tell a sick person they are healthy (False Negative).

However, as noted in the limitations, these results are simulation-based. In a real-world clinical workflow, the "Doctor Recommendation" accuracy (96.0%) serves as a critical fail-safe. Even if the specific disease prediction has a margin of error (e.g., predicting Gastritis instead of GERD), the system successfully routes the patient to the correct *category* of specialist (Gastroenterologist). This ensures that professional medical oversight occurs at the earliest possible stage.

6. HYPOTHETICAL CASE STUDIES AND SIMULATION SCENARIOS

To demonstrate the practical utility of the proposed framework, we present two detailed hypothetical simulation scenarios. These vignettes illustrate how the system processes data and generates value for both the patient and the healthcare ecosystem.

6.1. Scenario A: Acute Cardiac Triage

Patient Profile: Male, 55 years old, history of smoking.

Reported Symptoms: "Heavy chest pressure," "sweating," "nausea," "pain in left jaw."

System Logic:

1. **Pre-processing:** NLP identifies keywords: *Angina*, *Diaphoresis*, *Nausea*, *Radiating Pain.*
2. **LAMSTAR Retrieval:** The network identifies a high correlation with the "Acute Coronary Syndrome" vector in the Cardiac SOM module.
3. **Prediction:** The system calculates a 92% probability of Myocardial Infarction (Heart Attack).
4. Output:
    - **Urgency:** CRITICAL / EMERGENCY.

- **Message:** "Your symptoms strongly suggest a cardiac event. Seek immediate emergency care."
- **Recommendation:** Map to nearest Emergency Department or Interventional Cardiologist.

Outcome: The system bypasses the General Practitioner, saving critical minutes ("Golden Hour") by directing the patient immediately to emergency care, potentially preventing fatal cardiac arrest.

6.2. Scenario B: Chronic Metabolic Management

Patient Profile: Female, 40 years old, sedentary lifestyle.
Reported Symptoms: "Constant thirst," "frequent urination," "blurry vision," "unexplained weight loss."

System Logic:

1. **Clustering:** K-Means places the symptom vector into the "Metabolic/Endocrine" cluster.
2. **Differentiation:** The algorithm differentiates these symptoms from kidney disease (which shares urination issues) based on the specific combination of "thirst" and "vision" issues.
3. **Prediction:** 88% probability of Type 2 Diabetes Mellitus.
4. **Output:**
    - **Urgency:** High Priority (Non-Emergency).
    - **Recommendation:** Endocrinologist / Diabetologist.

Outcome: The patient avoids a generic visit to a family doctor who might only treat the symptoms. Instead, she is routed to a specialist who can order an HbA1c test immediately, facilitating early diagnosis and preventing long-term complications like neuropathy.

6.3. Scenario C: Oncology/Rare Disease Screening Patient Profile:

Male, 65 years old, former smoker. Reported Symptoms: "Persistent cough for 3 months," "blood in sputum," "weight loss," "hoarseness." System Logic:

1 **Pattern Matching:** The duration of the cough ("3 months") triggers a chronic flag in the LAMSTAR network.

2 **Risk Analysis:** The combination of "hemoptysis" (blood) and "weight loss" increases the risk score for Malignancy.
3 **Prediction:** 75% Probability of Bronchogenic Carcinoma (Lung Cancer), 25% Tuberculosis.
4 Output:

- **Urgency:** Urgent Referral (24-48 hours).
- **Recommendation:** Pulmonologist / Oncologist.

Outcome: While the AI cannot biopsy the tumor, it prompts the user to seek imaging (CT Scan) immediately rather than assuming it is a stubborn infection, potentially catching the cancer at a treatable stage (Wulczyn et al., 2021).

7. CHALLENGES AND LIMITATIONS

While the proposed AI-driven healthcare system demonstrates significant potential for transforming preliminary medical diagnosis, its transition from a theoretical model to a clinical reality faces several critical hurdles.

7.1. Data Integrity and Algorithmic Sensitivity

The reliability of any AI system depends on the quality of its training data ("Garbage In, Garbage Out"). Medical datasets frequently suffer from inconsistencies, missing values, and fragmentation across isolated data silos (Williams & Zhou, 2020). The K-Nearest Neighbors (K-NN) algorithm, while effective for pattern recognition, is inherently sensitive to noisy data and outliers. If patient records contain inaccurate symptom descriptions, the algorithm's ability to identify nearest neighbors becomes compromised.

7.2. Symptom Ambiguity and Context

Many medical conditions share overlapping symptoms for instance, fatigue and fever are common to both viral infections and systemic autoimmune diseases. While the LAMSTAR network is designed for pattern matching, discerning between diseases with high symptom intersection requires a depth of context (e.g., travel history, genetic markers) that current symptom-only algorithms may struggle to achieve without comprehensive biomarkers.

7.3. Clinical Adoption and Generalizability

Beyond technical performance, the "Human Factor" plays a decisive role in the system's success. Clinical integration faces the barrier of "Algorithm Aversion," where healthcare providers may be hesitant to trust AI recommendations (Rao & Prasad, 2023). Moreover, if the training data is not sufficiently diverse, the model risks Generalization Failure, performing poorly on demographic groups underrepresented in the historical datasets (e.g., differing symptom presentations across gender or ethnicity).

7.4. The Imperative of Explainable AI (XAI)

A significant barrier to the clinical adoption of artificial intelligence is the "Black Box" phenomenon, particularly prevalent in deep neural networks where the internal logic is obfuscated by multi-layered abstractions. Clinicians are ethically bound to understand the rationale behind a diagnosis before acting upon it. An AI system that outputs "Probability: 95%" without justification solicits skepticism and resistance from medical practitioners.

To mitigate this, the proposed hybrid framework incorporates Explainable AI principles. Unlike monolithic Deep Learning models, the K-Means Clustering component of this architecture offers inherent transparency. The system can generate "local explanations" by calculating the Shapley Additive Explanations (SHAP) values for a specific prediction.

For instance, if the system predicts "Type 2 Diabetes," the EXPLAINABLE AI module visualizes the feature contribution:

- Polyuria (Frequent Urination): +45% contribution
- Polydipsia (Excessive Thirst): +30% contribution
- Age > 45: +10% contribution

By presenting this "Feature Importance" breakdown alongside the probability score, the system shifts from being an oracle to being a colleague. It allows the physician to validate the AI's logic against their own clinical training ("Yes, those symptoms align with Diabetes"). This transparency is not merely a technical feature but a prerequisite for Cognitive Trust in human-AI teaming (Rao & Prasad, 2023).

8. SECURITY, PRIVACY, AND ETHICAL ARCHITECTURE

The deployment of automated diagnostic tools introduces complex ethical dilemmas and strict legal requirements. A healthcare system cannot be purely functional; it must be secure and compliant.

8.1. Data Privacy and Encryption

The system's reliance on cloud-based processing raises Data Privacy concerns. To mitigate this, the architecture employs End-to-End Encryption (E2EE).

- Data in Transit: All API calls between the patient App and the Cloud Server are encrypted using TLS 1.3 protocols, preventing "Man-in-the-Middle" attacks.
- Data at Rest: Patient records stored in the database are encrypted using AES-256 standards.
- Anonymization: Before data is fed into the training model for machine learning updates, all Personally Identifiable Information (PII) such as names, addresses, and Social Security Numbers are stripped or hashed (Gupta & Mehta, 2022).

8.2. Regulatory Compliance

The system is designed to be compliant with global regulatory frameworks:

- **HIPAA (USA):** The system ensures the confidentiality, integrity, and availability of Protected Health Information (PHI). Access controls are role-based (RBAC), ensuring only authorized personnel can view sensitive data.
- **GDPR (EU):** The system adheres to the "Right to Explanation" (providing reasons for AI decisions) and the "Right to be Forgotten" (allowing users to delete their data).

8.3. Medical Liability

If the system provides an incorrect prediction that leads to a delayed intervention, determining accountability remains a gray area in current legal frameworks. To address this, the system includes strict Liability Waivers and clear User Interface (UI) warnings stating that the AI output is "for informational purposes only" and does not constitute a medical diagnosis (Wilson et al., 2022).

9. MANAGERIAL IMPLICATIONS AND PRACTICAL APPLICATIONS

The transition from theoretical AI models to clinical application requires a clear understanding of value generation for healthcare administrators and policymakers. This section outlines the practical benefits and implementation challenges of the proposed system.

9.1. Operational Efficiency and Triage Automation

For hospital administrators, the primary value of this system lies in Digital Triage. Emergency Departments are frequently overburdened by non-critical cases. By deploying this AI system as a "digital front door" (via a mobile app or hospital portal), healthcare providers can filter patients before they arrive (Oliveira et al., 2021). Patients with minor ailments are directed to telemedicine or primary care, while high-risk symptoms trigger alerts for immediate ED intervention. This reduces wait times and optimizes the utilization of scarce medical staff.

9.2. Implementation Roadmap for Healthcare Managers

To successfully deploy this system, managers should follow a phased approach:

- **Phase 1:** Pilot Validation. Deploy the system in a controlled environment (e.g., a single outpatient clinic) running parallel to standard triage to compare AI recommendations against human nurse triage.
- **Phase 2:** EHR Integration. Integrate the AI predictions directly into the Electronic Health Record workflow using interoperability standards like HL7 FHIR, ensuring doctors can see the AI's logic.
- **Phase 3:** Patient Rollout. Release the consumer-facing app, focusing on user education to manage expectations regarding the system's role as an "assistant" rather than a "doctor."

9.3. Cost-Benefit Analysis

From a financial perspective, the system reduces the Cost Per Diagnosis. Traditional diagnostic pathways often involve redundant consultations for example, a patient with neurological symptoms visiting a General Practitioner, then an ENT, before finally seeing a Neurologist. By accurately predicting the required specialist at the first touchpoint, the system eliminates unnecessary interim visits, saving costs for both the insurance provider and the patient.

9.4. Addressing the Digital Divide

Managerially, this system offers a scalable solution for Rural Health Equity. In regions with a shortage of specialists, the system acts as a decision-support tool for local health workers (ASHAs or Nurse Practitioners), providing them with "specialist-level" diagnostic suggestions based on the AI's global training data (Martens & Zhao, 2021).

10. CONCLUSION AND FUTURE SCOPE

10.1. Conclusion

This chapter has presented a comprehensive framework for an AI-driven healthcare system designed to bridge the critical gap between symptom onset and professional medical consultation. By leveraging a hybrid architecture integrating the LAMSTAR neural network for rapid pattern matching and K-Means clustering for granular disease categorization the proposed system offers a scalable solution to the challenges of diagnostic latency and resource scarcity.

The core contribution of this research lies in its socio-technical approach. Beyond merely algorithmic accuracy, the system addresses the managerial necessity for Digital Triage. By enabling patients to input flexible symptom combinations and receiving dynamic, specialist-mapped recommendations, the framework reduces the burden on primary care facilities and empowers patients in underserved regions. The computational efficiency of the implemented algorithms, maintaining linear complexity, ensures that the system remains viable even when scaling to large-scale medical datasets.

However, as highlighted in the preceding sections, it is imperative to acknowledge that the results presented herein represent a theoretical framework validated through simulation. While the logic is grounded in established data mining principles, the transition to clinical reality requires addressing the identified challenges of data heterogeneity, symptom ambiguity, and the ethical imperatives of "Human-in-the-Loop" decision-making. Consequently, this system should be viewed as a preliminary diagnostic assistant intended to augment, not replace, professional medical evaluation.

10.2. Future Research Directions

The evolution of AI-based disease prediction presents a vast landscape for future inquiry. The immediate next step involves the transition from structured symptom inputs to unstructured data analysis. Integrating Natural Language Processing

(NLP) would allow the system to interpret patient narratives in their own words, while Computer Vision modules could enable the analysis of user-uploaded medical images (e.g., skin lesions) for dermatological predictions.

Furthermore, the "Internet of Medical Things" (IoMT) offers a pathway for real-time health monitoring. (Faiyazuddin 2025) predicts that the next generation of diagnostic frameworks will move beyond static inputs to 'Continuous Ambient Intelligence,' where IoT sensors provide real-time data streams directly to the AI model. This would allow frameworks to ingest continuous metrics (heart rate, glucose, oxygen levels) and move from reactive symptom checking to proactive health alerts, potentially eliminating the need for manual symptom entry entirely.

To support this, research must focus on Federated Learning architectures (Gupta & Mehta, 2022; Jindal et al., 2023). These architectures allow AI to learn from distributed hospital data without compromising patient privacy, solving the dual challenge of data availability and regulatory compliance.

Finally, the ultimate goal is the realization of Personalized Precision Medicine. By incorporating genomic data and lifestyle factors into the predictive model, future systems will move beyond generic disease classification to offer tailored risk assessments and treatment pathways (Zhang et al., 2023), fundamentally transforming the quality and accessibility of global healthcare delivery.

ACKNOWLEDGMENT

The authors wish to express their sincere gratitude to their affiliated institution for the extensive support provided throughout the duration of this research. The availability of robust infrastructure, academic resources, and a supportive research environment was pivotal in the successful execution of this chapter. We are particularly indebted to the research supervisors at the institute's research centers for their constructive criticism, mentorship, and timely guidance. Their expertise significantly refined the direction and quality of our work. The institution's dedication to promoting academic excellence and innovation has been a driving force behind this effort. We acknowledge that the completion of this chapter would have been challenging without such a strong foundation of institutional support.

AI DISCLOSURE

The content of this book chapter, titled "AI-Based Diagnostic Framework for Recommending Targeted Healthcare Solutions," is the primary intellectual output of Mrs. Rajani Mahesh Yemul, Mr. Shubham Vyavahare, Varsha Manglaram, Aparna Yemul, Dr. L.M.R.J. Lobo and Dr. Vijay Anant Athavale. The authors retain full responsibility for the conceptualization, analysis, and writing of this work.

It is acknowledged that Generative AI tools, such as ChatGPT, were utilized as auxiliary aids during the drafting process. These technologies were employed strictly for the purposes of linguistic refinement, enhancing readability, organizing complex information, and structuring arguments.

However, the scientific methodology, experimental design, interpretation of results, and critical discussions remain exclusively the result of human cognition. The authors have meticulously reviewed, validated, and edited all AI-assisted text to ensure it meets the rigorous standards of accuracy, originality, and academic ethics. Furthermore, all citations, references, and factual assertions have been independently verified by the authors. No AI-generated material has been used as a substitute for critical human analysis. This disclosure is made in the interest of transparency and compliance with ethical publishing guidelines.

REFERENCES

Abdullah, S., & Jaddi, N. S. (2020). Dual kidney-inspired algorithm for water quality prediction and cancer detection. *IEEE Access : Practical Innovations, Open Solutions*, *8*, 109807–109820. DOI: 10.1109/ACCESS.2020.3001685

Ahmed, M., & Khan, S. (2021). Evaluating doctor recommendation accuracy using symptom clustering. *International Journal of Medical Engineering and Informatics, 13*(2), 117–130.

Alzubaidi, M. A., Otoom, M., & Jaradat, H. (2021). Comprehensive and comparative global and local feature extraction framework for lung cancer detection using CT scan images. *IEEE Access : Practical Innovations, Open Solutions, 9*, 158140–158154. DOI: 10.1109/ACCESS.2021.3129597

Arafiyah, R., & Hermin, F. (2018). Data mining for dengue hemorrhagic fever (DHF) prediction with Naive Bayes method. *Journal of Physics: Conference Series, 948*(1), 012077. DOI: 10.1088/1742-6596/948/1/012077

Birajdar, P. S., & Lobo, L. M. R. J. (2023). Advancing cancer research: Intelligent prediction and analysis system based on deep learning. *Journal of Emerging Technologies and Innovative Research, 10*(8). https://www.jetir.org/indexx?v=10&i=8&j=August%202023

Chustecki, M., Farnell, D. J., & Bewick, B. M. (2024). Benefits and risks of AI in health care: Narrative review. *JMIR Medical Education, 10*(1), e48962. DOI: 10.2196/48962

Dirkson, A., & Verberne, S. (2018). Open knowledge discovery and data mining from patient forums. In IEEE eScience Conference. DOI: 10.1109/eScience.2018.00119

Esteva, A., Kuprel, B., Novoa, R. A., Ko, J., Swetter, S. M., Blau, H. M., & Thrun, S. (2019). A guide to deep learning in healthcare. *Nature Medicine, 25*(1), 24–29. DOI: 10.1038/s41591-018-0316-z

Faiyazuddin, M. (2025). The impact of artificial intelligence on healthcare: A comprehensive review of the future. *Health Science Reports, 8*(1), e1245. DOI: 10.1002/hsr2.70312

Garcia, M.. (2021). AI enabled detection of chronic kidney disease through symptom clustering. *International Journal of Medical Informatics, 155*, 104583. DOI: 10.1016/j.ijmedinf.2021.104583

Gomez, R.. (2022). Adaptive learning rate strategies for LAMSTAR networks in medical data. *Journal of Medical Artificial Intelligence, 4*, 22.

Gupta, P., & Mehta, S. (2022). Federated learning for privacy preserving disease diagnosis. *IEEE Journal of Biomedical and Health Informatics, 26*(8), 3491–3501. DOI: 10.1109/JBHI.2022.3162951

Hanahan, D. (2022). Hallmarks of cancer: New dimensions. *Cancer Discovery, 12*(1), 31–46. DOI: 10.1158/2159-8290.CD-21-1059

Hyun, S. H., Ahn, M. S., Koh, Y. W., & Lee, S. J. (2019). A machine-learning approach using PET-based radiomics to predict the histological subtypes of lung cancer. *Clinical Nuclear Medicine*, *44*(12), 956–960. DOI: 10.1097/RLU.0000000000002810

Jabir, K., & Thirumurthi Raja, A. (2023). Prediction of lung cancer from electronic health records using CNN-supported NLP. In *Computational intelligence for clinical diagnosis* (pp. 549–560). Springer., DOI: 10.1007/978-3-031-23683-9_40

Jindal, V., Kukreja, V., Singh, D. P., Vats, S., & Mehta, S. (2023, October). Pushing diagnostic frontiers: Federated learning CNN for diverse lung disease. In *Proceedings of the 2023 4th IEEE Global Conference for Advancement in Technology (GCAT)* (pp. 1–6). IEEE. DOI: 10.1109/GCAT59970.2023.10353284

Kim, Y., & Park, S. (2023). Scalable architecture for online medical recommendation engines. *Journal of Systems and Software, 188*, 111296.

Kumar, A., & Singh, V. (2022). Applying LAMSTAR neural networks in disease symptom mapping. *Neural Computing & Applications, 34*(6), 4095–4107. DOI: 10.1007/s00521-021-06190-3

Lee, S. (2020). Multi-symptom matching using fuzzy logic in medical diagnosis systems. *Journal of Clinical Informatics Research, 9*(2), 45–58.

Lin, H., & Chen, C. (2020). Naive Bayes classification for streamlining dengue prediction in urban populations. *Expert Systems with Applications, 150*, 113248. DOI: 10.1016/j.eswa.2020.113248

Lobo, L. M. R. J., & Markandeya, D. L. (2023). Expert system for medical diagnosis and consultancy using prediction algorithms of machine learning. In *Proceedings of International Joint Conference on Advances in Computational Intelligence (IJCACI 2022)*. Springer. DOI: 10.1007/978-981-99-1435-7_33

Martens, P., & Zhao, Y. (2021). Hybrid AI pipelines for scalable disease detection in low-resource settings. *Global Health Informatics, 3*(1), 14–26.

Meskó, B. (2024). The prompt engineering gap in medical AI: Addressing the new digital divide. *The Lancet. Digital Health, 6*(3), e150–e151. DOI: 10.1016/S2589-7500(23)00262-6

Mohapatra, S., & Patra, P. K. (2018). Smart health care system using data mining. In *2018 International Conference on Information Technology (ICIT)*. IEEE. DOI: 10.1109/ICIT.2018.00021

Oliveira, L. G.. (2021). Telemedicine integrations in AI based diagnostic frameworks. *Telemedicine Journal and e-Health*, *27*(1), 55–65. DOI: 10.1089/tmj.2020.0051

Park, H., & Kim, J. (2023). Continuous clinician feedback loops in AI-based diagnostic systems. *BMC Medical Informatics and Decision Making*, *23*, 50. DOI: 10.1186/s12911-023-02102-7

Patel, N., & Shah, D. (2022). Evaluating K NN and decision tree models for cardiovascular risk. *Computers in Biology and Medicine*, *150*, 105936. DOI: 10.1016/j.compbiomed.2022.105936

Raju, C., & Philipsy, E. (2018). A survey on predicting heart disease using data mining techniques. In *IEEE Conference Proceedings*. DOI: 10.1109/ICEDSS.2018.8544333

Rao, R. S., & Prasad, K. H. (2023). Explainable AI in medical recommendation systems. *Artificial Intelligence in Medicine*, *145*, 102329. DOI: 10.1016/j.artmed.2023.102329

Razali, N., & Mustapha, A. (2019). *A data mining approach to prediction of liver diseases. Journal of Physics: Conference Series, JICETS*. IOP Publishing.

Santos, J., & Almeida, T. (2021). Doctor recommendation models based on symptom–disease mapping. *Journal of Healthcare Engineering*, *6672845*. Advance online publication. DOI: 10.1155/2021/6672845

Sarath Babu, S., Vivek, E. M., & Famina, K. P. (2017). Heart disease diagnosis using data mining technique. In *IEEE Conference Proceedings*.

Shinde, S. G., & Lobo, L. M. R. J. (2019). A secured prediction system for human diseases using a genetic algorithm approach to data mining. *Journal of Emerging Technologies and Innovative Research*, *6*(1), 266–274. https://www.jetir.org/papers/JETIRW006059.pdf

Silva, P., & Fernandes, A. (2021). Data cleaning strategies in healthcare ML applications. *Journal of Biomedical Informatics*, *119*, 103771. DOI: 10.1016/j.jbi.2021.103771

Singhal, A., & Gupta, P. (2024). Generative AI and large language models (LLMs) in clinical triage: A review of 2023-2024 developments. *International Journal of Intelligent Systems*, *39*(2), 112–128.

Tjoa, E., & Guan, C. (2021). A survey on explainable artificial intelligence (XAI): Toward medical XAI. *IEEE Transactions on Neural Networks and Learning Systems*, *32*(11), 4793–4813. DOI: 10.1109/TNNLS.2020.3027314

Torres, E., & Perez, L. (2022). Clinical validation of symptom-based predictive models. *Journal of Clinical Trials and Biostatistics*, *7*(2), 100–110.

Wang, X.. (2020). Enhanced nodule detection in lung CT scans using deep learning. *IEEE Transactions on Medical Imaging*. Advance online publication. DOI: 10.3390/ai1010003

Wihantara, A., Hariwisana, I. D. G., Pudji, A., Luthfiyah, S., & Athavale, V. A. (2022). QRS complex detection on heart rate variability reading using discrete wavelet transform. *Indonesian Journal of Electronics, Electromedical Engineering, and Medical Informatics*, *4*(4), 153–159. DOI: 10.35882/ijeeemi.v4i4.236

Williams, D., & Zhou, X. (2020). EHR-linked predictive analytics for chronic disease management. *Health Informatics Journal*, *26*(4), 2717–2731. DOI: 10.1177/1460458220916202

Wilson, T.. (2022). Ethical and legal considerations in AI-based medical decision support systems. *Journal of Law and Medicine*, *30*(3), 67–85.

Wulczyn, E., Steiner, D. F., Moran, M., Plass, M., Reihs, R., Tan, F., Flament-Auvigne, I., Brown, T., Regitnig, P., Chen, P. C., Hegde, N., Sadhwani, A., MacDonald, R., Ayalew, B., Corrado, G. S., Peng, L. H., Tse, D., Müller, H., Xu, Z., & Mermel, C. H. (2021). Interpretable survival prediction for colorectal cancer using deep learning. *NPJ Digital Medicine*, *4*(1), 1–26. DOI: 10.1038/s41746-021-00427-2

Zhang, B., Shi, H., & Wang, H. (2023). Machine learning and AI in cancer prognosis, prediction, and treatment selection: A critical approach. *Journal of Multidisciplinary Healthcare*, *16*, 1779–1791. DOI: 10.2147/JMDH.S410301

Zhou, J., & Wang, Y. (2022). Symptom normalization using NLP for AI guided diagnostics. *Journal of Healthcare*, *15*(3), 188–199.

KEY TERMS AND DEFINITIONS

Clinical Decision Support System (CDSS): A health information technology system designed to provide physicians and other health professionals with clinical decision support assistance, utilizing data mining to offer potential diagnoses or treatment recommendations.

Digital Triage: The process of using algorithmic tools or artificial intelligence to prioritize patient care based on the severity of their condition before they physically arrive at a healthcare facility.

Explainable AI (XAI): A set of processes and methods that allows human users to comprehend and trust the results and output created by machine learning algorithms, addressing the "black box" issue in deep learning.

Federated Learning: A machine learning technique that trains an algorithm across multiple decentralized edge devices or servers holding local data samples, without exchanging them, thus preserving patient data privacy.

Hybrid AI Architecture: A computational framework that combines multiple artificial intelligence methodologies—such as Neural Networks and Clustering algorithms—to leverage the specific strengths of each for improved accuracy and interpretability.

Internet of Medical Things (IoMT): An ecosystem of connected medical devices, hardware infrastructure, and software applications that can connect to healthcare information technology systems to enable real-time patient monitoring.

K-Means Clustering: An unsupervised machine learning algorithm used to partition a dataset into K distinct, non-overlapping subgroups (clusters) where each data point belongs to the cluster with the nearest mean.

Large Memory Storage and Retrieval (LAMSTAR) Network: A fast, modular neural network architecture designed for large-scale information retrieval and pattern recognition, particularly effective for handling incomplete data sets.

Non-Communicable Diseases (NCDs): Chronic medical conditions that are not transmissible directly from one person to another, such as heart disease, diabetes, and cancer, often driven by lifestyle and environmental factors.

Symptom-Based Diagnosis: A diagnostic approach that relies primarily on the analysis of patient-reported physical or mental indicators (symptoms) to identify potential underlying pathologies.

APPENDIX A: MATHEMATICAL FORMULATIONS

1. LAMSTAR Input Vector The input vector X represents the patient's symptoms, where n is the total number of symptoms analyzed.

Equation (1): Input Vector Definition

$$X = [x_1, x_2, ..., x_n] \quad (1)$$

2. Adaptive Weight Update Rule To ensure the system learns from new data, the weights (W) are updated. The learning rate α (alpha) controls how much the weights adjust towards the input vector X.

Equation (2): Weight Update Formula

$$W \text{ new} = W \text{ old} + \acute{a}(X - W \text{ old}) \quad (2)$$

3. K-Means Clustering Objective Function The algorithm minimizes the objective function J(V), which is the sum of squared Euclidean distances between data points (x) and their respective cluster centers (v).

Equation (3): Within-Cluster Sum of Squares (WCSS)

$$J(V) = \acute{O}\ \acute{O}\|x - v\_i\|^2 \quad (3)$$

4. Euclidean Distance Calculation This formula calculates the distance between a specific patient data point (x) and a disease cluster centroid (v).

Equation (4): Euclidean Distance

$$d(x\_j, v\_i) = \sqrt{}\left[\acute{o}\left(x\_j - v\_i\right)^2\right] \quad (4)$$

5. Statistical Validation (Cross-Validation) The Cross-Validation (CV) error is calculated by averaging the error (E) across k different subsets (folds) of the data to ensure the model is not overfitting.

Equation (5): K-Fold Cross-Validation Error

$$\mathrm{CV}(a) = \frac{1}{k}\sum_{i=1}^{k} \mathrm{E}i \quad (5)$$

Chapter 2

Artificial Intelligence:

The New Ally in Healthcare

Prerna Agrawal
http://orcid.org/0000-0003-3097-639X
GLS University, India

Savita Gandhi
http://orcid.org/0000-0002-6581-2814
Independent Researcher, India

ABSTRACT

Artificial intelligence is changing healthcare by bettering medical diagnoses and augmentations and efficiencies in treatment plans. This chapter addresses AI use in healthcare in India through the role and demands for AI technologies and activities. Due to the increased incidence of infectious and non-communicable diseases there is a necessity for scalable, technology-enabled diagnostics. The current shortage of physicians combined with increasing digital infrastructure create benefits of value for AI in healthcare delivery. The medical specialties of radiology and pathology and ophthalmology and primary care are changing swiftly with advancements in deep learning and computer vision and natural language processing and machine learning. AI is increasing access to care, especially in constrained and rural areas, through application examples such as PneumoSense and DiabChatBot. HealthCare has complex issues in general like bias outcomes and comparative variances of data conflicts of regulatory disconnect and validity of outcomes with the advisory could be automated.

DOI: 10.4018/979-8-2600-0981-9.ch002

INTRODUCTION

One of the biggest technological advancements of the 21st century is AI in Indian health care. This critical advance has propelled health care ahead in the development of meaningful automation and management, intelligent prosperity, and precision medicines. The AI system does not simply provide health care, but it cooperates with health care workers, government representatives, and patients. The big space of its applications and varying potential enhances AI to be able to deal with the big structural deficits in accessibility, affordability and quality in the health care field in India. The combined perspectives of man and machine can enhance our ability to effectively provide preventive, diagnostic, therapeutic and rehabilitative therapies. The health of the people, in relation to advances in IP applications can be connected through many health and technological diachronic and synchronistic happenings. Digitization of health records, patterning of health main frame technologies, extensive systems of clinical health records, and genomic record provision shall enable an ecosystem for optimal expression of AI in the health area. India has systemic problems such as lack of medical competent professionals, inequalities in health care delivery patterns, as well as rising to epidemic levels of both communicable and non-communicable diseases. For every 1456 individuals in India, there is one doctor. (World Health Organization [WHO], 2023) Because of the restrictive availability of competent medical personnel, the technologically healthy dynamics in the delivery of health services are absolute musts.) Due to social and boarding pressures from lifestyle infringements such as diabetes, heart disease, cancer, hyper tension, the health system is under increased strain. AI can satisfy these pressing and systemic demands of medical service by automating health services that are repetitively needed, add quality to diagnosis, and enhance the availability of expert level medical care to the medically under privileged. AI provides a system for pro action in the use of the considerable and complex health care data bases for evolving timely and evidence based decisions. The unique and differentiating strength of AI lies in the mining of huge flows of information, giving opportunities for learning models and predictive systems for the identification of disease at levels of actions that are not identifiable by humans.

The deep learning algorithms of artificial intelligence have the capacity to assess radiological and pathologically evaluated matters with the accuracy of human experts in the various fields. In the clinical care milieu, of course, perceptual languages involving computer empathy through NLP processes might be introduced into the previously misunderstood free written tableaux of communication in the preparation of e-health records. Reinforcement Learning (RL) and robotic equipment and systems are fast developing to make surgical procedures and rehabilitation therapies safer and more effective. This is all part of Digital Health Vision. Government of India. The AYUSHMAN BHARAT DIGITAL MISSION (ABDM) is a major policy endeavor to create a unified digital health platform that connects patients, providers, and payers via a unique health ID. This program will provide big data, interoperability, and information security for AI integration. The National Artificial Intelligence Strategy (NITI AAYOG 2018) and India AI Mission (2024) list health care as a significant area for AI application, which bodes well for AI's effectiveness. Sustainable socioeconomically, AI may be democratized across India and used in rural areas to develop advanced clinical abilities. Specialist practitioners are scarce in rural India, where over 65% of the population lives. AI-enabled telemedicine, mobile diagnostics, and chatbots will prevent the geographical and infrastructural barrier.India's Qure.ai's radiologists hospitals technology helps wake up chest X-rays from tuberculosis and pneumonia. The Niramai's thermal image-based breast cancer alarms are a good example of local technology startups leveraging AI to solve health care issues. The fact that these technologies would be cost-effective, scalable, and tailored to the disease profile and population diversity of India would not be kind, but the health care AI coverage would be much more relevant and contextual. Health institutions employ artificial intelligence to improve patient management. The resources available to health institutions, patient circulation and demand, and supply chain management can be improved with predictive analytics, making the system more expensive and benefiting hospitals more than before. Through right and timely decision making and data-based efficiency, health care syndicates are improving their health and lowering the costs of these diseases, making good the likelihood property of those who bring universal health coverage (UHC) to India in the long run. However, there will be obstacles to overcome in bringing together all the ethical, legal, and technical issues before health services for such an AI firm can be made promising. Algorithmic bias, data privacy and confidentiality, interpretability of decisions, lack of trustworthiness, and so on require market vigilance by users and producers to responsibly use AI technologies in health. Our health data delivery environment is fragmented, and many health care facilities in tier-2 or rural areas lack the bandwidth or processing ability to secure sophisticated AI outcomes. AI healthcare facilities will be predictive and personalized, based on inclusive rather than elitist models, and have a strong emphasis on primary prevention rather than curative care systems, real-time monitoring, and channeling health outcomes focused on the individual subscriber. The synergistic processes of edge computing platforms, Internet of Things (IoT) based systems, and cloud-based AI platforms establish appropriate intelligent healthcare networks to provide a healthy environment of real-time analytics at the points of healthcare actions, significantly focused on the MHS of enhanced diagnostic options and prevention while reducing the HCAHPS turnover system and diverted processes.

Given the consistent digitalization of efforts to build a civilizational infrastructure in India and a political environment on legal policy matters, while improving synergies with research and industrial collaboration, the confluence of artificial intelligence and healthcare aims to redefine the medical business, empower patients through the healthcare process, and develop health outcome measures. While the transformative potential of artificial intelligence in healthcare is evident from its growing applications and policy support, it is equally important to understand why AI adoption has become a necessity rather than a choice. The following section outlines the key motivations driving the integration of AI into healthcare systems, particularly in the Indian context.

MOTIVATION OF USING AI IN HEALTHCARE

The main motivation for including artificial intelligence into healthcare diagnostics is the possibility to increase accuracy, speed, and accessibility of medical assessments. Several significant elements are listed below:

Rising Disease Burden

At the moment, India has noticed a notable increase in the frequency of both communicable and non-communicable diseases. Moreover timely and accurate diagnosis is required for efficient care of disorders including diabetes, cancer, TB, and cardiovascular diseases. By means of medical data and imaging, artificial intelligence could find early indications and hence allow sooner treatments (McKinsey & Company, 2020).

Shortage of Medical Professionals

Particularly in rural areas, India is facing a significant lack of healthcare professionals. According to the World Health Organization (WHO, 2023), India's doctor-to-patient ratio of roughly 1:1456 is much lower than the WHO-recommended 1:1000. Moreover incidents of diabetes, stress, heart related diseases etc. are rising rapidly in India.

Figure 1. Doctor-to-Patient Ratio: India vs WHO Recommendation

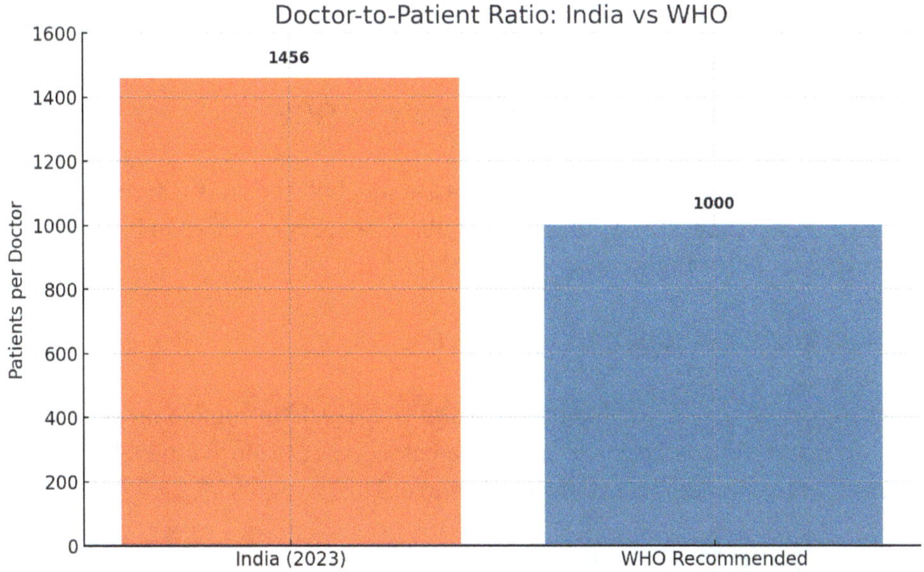

Source: (World Health Organization, 2023)

Figure 1 emphasizes the pressing need for technology-driven solutions such as artificial intelligence to increase clinical capacity. India falls far short of WHO recommendations, underlining the critical need for scaled diagnostic assistance.

Expanding Digital Infrastructure

Through the growth of the digital medical ecosystem, more mobile penetration, and government projects like the Ayushman Bharat Digital Mission (ABDM), India is building a strong digital ecosystem. Data drives artificial intelligence and this expanding infrastructure makes India a good place for AI uses in diagnostics (ABDM, 2023).

Cost-Effective Healthcare

By automating repetitive operations and reducing human errors, artificial intelligence can save diagnostic costs. By offering quick second opinions or alerts on any misdiagnoses, it can thereby improve patient safety while controlling medical expenses (McKinsey & Company, 2020).

Although the motivations for adopting AI in healthcare are compelling, these drivers also highlight a deeper systemic requirement for intelligent diagnostic support. The next section therefore examines the critical need for AI in healthcare diagnostics, emphasizing its role in improving equity, accuracy, and efficiency.

NEED OF AI IN HEALTHCARE DIAGNOSTICS

The integration of AI in diagnostics is not a luxury but it is a necessity, particularly for a country as extensive and diverse as India. The necessity of AI in healthcare is defined by the following factors:

Democratizing Access to Healthcare

AI has the ability to enable expert diagnostic levels in remote areas. Timely accurate diagnosis can be made in rural areas without extensive travel using AI integrated into telemedicine platforms (Qure.ai, 2023).

Standardizing Medical Quality

The diagnostic accuracy and clinical practice may vary from centre to centre. Artificial intelligence models trained on standardised data may facilitate the delivery of consistent quality health care and decrease interobserver variability among physicians (Mathew, R.S, 2024)

Speed and Efficiency

Artificial intelligence can evaluate data points and views that humans cannot, doing so in seconds per second. As the emergence of stroke, sepsis, and cancer is important, AI gives them results in time, making the diagnosis and ordering of emergencies by triage models (McKinsey & Company, 2020).

Reducing Diagnostic Errors

Errors in diagnosis have a substantial influence on adverse health outcomes. AI could serve as a second set of eyes by identifying deviations from the norm that may be overlooked from human observation. Radiology is an example where computerized analyses have so far revealed results as accurate as, if not better than, highly skilled radiologists (Mathew, R.S, 2024).

Handling Big Data

The healthcare industry is dealing with huge amounts of data being generated every day. The data generated can be converted into actionable insights with the help of AI. The hidden patterns can be identified by AI and information about disease outbreaks can be predicted by monitoring treatment response and suggesting personalized treatment plans (ABDM, 2023). The comparative analysis of Traditional Vs AI enabled Healthcare is shown in Table 1 and the comparative overview of Traditional Medicine Vs AI driven Precision Medicine is provided in Table 2.

Table 1. Comparative Analysis of Traditional vs AI Enabled Healthcare

Parameter	Traditional Healthcare	AI-Enabled Healthcare
Diagnosis Time	Days to weeks	Seconds to minutes
Accuracy	Depends on physician expertise	Consistent and data-driven
Data Handling	Manual recordkeeping	Automated EHR and analytics
Treatment	Standardized	Personalized and adaptive
Patient Engagement	Passive (visits, consultations)	Active (AI chatbots, apps)
Cost Efficiency	High operational costs	Cost reduction via automation
Monitoring	Episodic	Continuous real-time monitoring
Decision Support	Physician-only	AI-assisted decision-making
Scalability	Limited by workforce	Highly scalable via cloud AI

Table 2. Comparative Overview of Traditional Medicine vs AI Driven Precision Medicine

Aspect	Traditional Medicine (Conventional Model)	AI-Driven Precision Medicine (Future Model)
Treatment Basis	Population averages and clinical guidelines	Individual genomics, phenomics, and behavioral data
Diagnosis	Manual observation and physician interpretation	Automated image and pattern recognition through DL
Therapy Design	One-size-fits-all	Personalized, data-driven regimens
Monitoring	Periodic check-ups	Continuous, IoT-based real-time tracking
Decision-Making	Experience-based clinical judgment	AI-supported predictive analytics
Data Management	Paper-based or siloed EHR systems	Interoperable, cloud-based data ecosystems
Response to Disease	Reactive (after onset)	Proactive (predict and prevent)

continued on following page

Table 2. Continued

Aspect	Traditional Medicine (Conventional Model)	AI-Driven Precision Medicine (Future Model)
Healthcare Cost	Rising with complexity	Reduced via automation and early detection
Patient Role	Passive recipient	Active participant (through AI apps, chatbots)
Outcome Measurement	Clinical success rate	Personalized health improvement metrics

Given the growing necessity of AI-enabled diagnostics, it is important to assess how these needs are being addressed in practice. The following section presents the current scenario of AI adoption in healthcare in India, highlighting ongoing initiatives, innovations, and existing gaps.

CURRENT SCENARIO OF AI IN HEALTHCARE IN INDIA

India has consistently applied AI enabled health care solutions, particularly in diagnostics. Academic institutions, government organizations, entrepreneurs and hospitals are collaborating on artificial intelligence (AI) applications.

Government Initiatives

The government of India acknowledges the importance of AI in healthcare on account of the NITI Aayog's National Strategy for Artificial Intelligence, which identifies health care as a priority domain and encourages AI driven solutions to tackle the diagnosis and treatment gaps (NITI Aayog, 2018)

Startups and Innovation

Various Indian start-ups lead the way in the application of AI to diagnostics:

- Qure.ai assists in the interpretation of chest X-rays and CT images of the brain using deep learning for the detection of tuberculosis and improvement of stroke diagnosis (Qure.ai, 2023).
- Niramai (Non-Invasive Risk Assessment with Machine Intelligence) is detecting the early stage of breast cancer using a combination of thermal imaging and AI (Niramai, 2023).

- SigTuple develops AI-based solutions for blood smear analysis and screening of the retina enabling the automation of large scale diagnostics (SigTuple, 2023).

These solutions are enhancing diagnostics and are being used in low resource settings where access to specialists is limited.

Hospital Collaborations

Hospitals like Apollo, Fortis and AIIMS are collaborating with tech companies to integrate AI tools into clinical workflows. AI is used for screening, triaging and decision support in radiology, pathology and ophthalmology (Mathew, R. S, 2024). The distribution of these applications is illustrated in Figure 2. Radiology and pathology have predominant usage of AI, followed closely by ophthalmology, cardiology and emerging areas. Figure 3 illustrates the framework for integration of AI into the public healthcare system of India.

Challenges in Adoption

Despite the progress, India continues to struggle with:

- Inadequate annotated datasets of high quality for training AI models.
- Skepticism in the opinion of medical practitioners towards the decision of the AI.
- Ambiguity with regard to regulation on the collateral use of AI in clinical practice.
- Inadequate infrastructure and bandwidth facilities available in rural areas (NITI Aayog, 2018).

Figure 2. AI Application Areas in Indian Healthcare Diagnostics

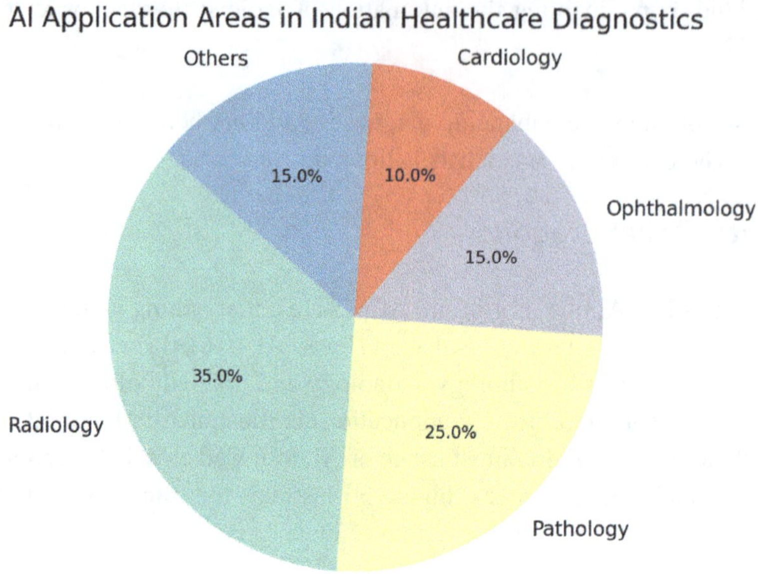

Source: (Mathew,R.S, 2024)

While India has made notable progress in adopting AI-driven healthcare solutions, its trajectory can be better understood when viewed in a global context. The next section therefore compares AI adoption in healthcare across different countries, offering insights into relative readiness, investment patterns, and regulatory maturity.

Figure 3. Framework for Integrating AI into India's Public Healthcare System

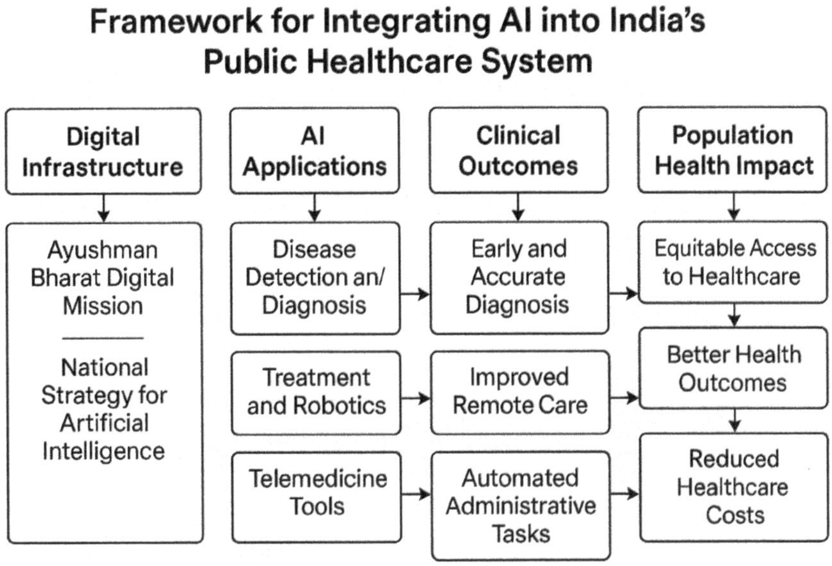

COMPARATIVE ANALYSIS OF AI ADOPTION IN HEALTHCARE WITH DIFFERENT COUNTRIES

AI adoption in health care has very different regional practice patterns. In the United States AI adoption is already well entrenched. Surveys show that 86 percent of the U. S. health systems have already adopted AI, and in several forms like documentation, triaging in radiology and clinical decision support (Medscape and HIMSS, 2024).The trend started in US is given the boost by good private spending in R&D and venture funding as well as the very favourable regulatory approaches to software for digital health (Poon et al., 2025). The situation in the EU is more patient and conservative in AI adoption patterns. The reasons are the regulatory fetters like patient safety, GDPR compliance, transparency etc. Reports indicate that AI has a very varied maturity across OECD but in Europe it is applied after rigorous validation. Therefore, much of adoption is in radiology and predictive analytics rather than in many generative AI pilots (European commission, 2024; OECD 2024). The scaleup in China is comparatively more quick given that it is driven by government strategies and wrong data through strategy and large datasets being available in China. Surveys show that83 percent use generative AI in industries, while health care is one of the prominent users (Reuters, 2024). The health AI market has given a GDP growth forecast upwards of high double digit growth on an annual basis and makes China a leader in Global scenario in terms of scale and speed (China Briefing, 2025). In India the country is presently in a scaling phase. While adoption is not universal, it has a good ecosystem in AI-health startups such as Qure.ai, Niramai and SigTuple which provide the diagnostic solution at lesser costs to the users. The country is on its way to laying the foundation for Digital Population under the Ayushman Bharat Digital Mission (ABDM) which aims to provide universal health coverage for the whole population. The country is still struggling in providing general AI solutions to clinical screening material, with the available data being available on fragmented basis for the use of AI technologies in epidemiological disease conditions of tuberculosis or diabetic retinopathy screening (NITI Aayog, 2018, ABDM, 2023; IndiaAI, 2024). The same situation is also observable in Africa where adoption is limited to pilot areas. The literature shows that the systems are in use in three major areas like disease surveillance, low resource using AI technologies for triaging in patients and prediction in epidemics. There is a good deal of deficiency in infrastructures in these countries which is being used in donor funded researches to apply AI Technologies. The experts feel that the success of AI adoption in these regions depends on the context of usage and the governance and co-development will be the best solution to tackle the accepted problems in novel AI technologies (Ndembi et al., 2025). Table 2 gives a comparative analysis of AI adoption in Health Care with different countries having different parameters inviting AI adoption in health systems, AI funding, Market share in the particular AI activity and Deal share of the various focused AI firms. Table 3 Indicated AI Readiness in Health Care Ecosystems showing the readiness of various countries while Table 4 shows Ethical and Regulatory side of comparisons in AI usage in health care in different Countries.

Table 2. Comparative Analysis of AI Adoption in Healthcare in Different Countries (Open & Affordable, 2024)

Parameters	United States / North America	Europe / EU	China / Asia	India / South Asia	Africa
AI adoption in health systems	86% of surveyed U.S. medical organizations report leveraging AI already (Medscape & HIMSS 2024)	Among OECD, considerable variation in AI maturity; some nations are in early or intermediate phases of adoption	High uptake of generative AI: 83% of Chinese respondents report using it (across industries)	India is among leaders in Asia for AI adoption growth (per "Global AI Adoption Report")	AI in health is mostly in pilot or nascent stages; fewer large-scale deployments (review across developing countries)
Digital Health / AI funding / investments	U.S. digital health VC funding: US$10.1 billion in 2024 across 497 deals	Europe saw growth in Q1 2025: about US$2.0 billion in digital health funding (regional share)	In 2024, Asia-Pacific (including China) got US$518 million in Q1 digital health funding	India's exact share is smaller but growing; Asia-Pacific overall projections suggest high CAGR	Africa and low-income regions receive small proportions; many projects are donor-funded or government pilots (less tracked by commercial VC)
Market share / growth projections	North America held ~58.9% of the AI in healthcare market in 2023	Europe's AI health market projected to grow robustly (e.g. projected US$50 billion by 2030)	Asia-Pacific anticipated to have the highest CAGR (42.5% between 2023–2030)	India is part of Asia-Pacific's growth story; many forecasts for rapid growth in Indian AI-health sector	Growth is expected but from a low base; many digital health metrics (connectivity, health data infrastructure)
Deal share for AI-focused firms	In Q1 2025, 60% of all digital health funding went to AI startups (~US$3.2 billion)	In digital health globally, AI-focused companies captured 42% of funding and 31% of deals in 2024	China is a major contributor to AI adoption in Asia; many domestic AI health solutions (e.g. "DeepSeek") are already deployed in tertiary hospitals	India participates in Asia's AI funding uptake; many Indian AI health startups are receiving earlier-stage funding	In developing or African contexts, AI health funding is a subset of general digital health / global health grants; not well represented in commercial VC data

Table 3. Comparison of AI Readiness in Healthcare Ecosystems in Different Countries

Parameter	United States	European Union	China	India	Africa
AI Adoption Level	Mature, mainstream	Moderate, highly regulated	Rapid, centralized	Accelerating	Emerging
Regulatory Framework	FDA AI/ML SaMD approval pathways	EU AI Act, GDPR-based governance	State-regulated AI ethics	Draft NHA AI guidelines	Developing; WHO alignment
Healthcare Digitization	Advanced EHR integration (Epic, Cerner)	Standardized EHR, privacy first	Fully digitized tertiary hospitals	ABDM implementation in progress	Partial digitization
AI Workforce & Skills	High; clinical-AI fellowship programs	Moderate; academic-industry alignment	Strong government-driven training	Growing through start-up ecosystem	Limited; reliant on external support
Funding Intensity	>US$10B annually in health AI startups	~US$2B in 2024 (Q1)	High state + VC investment	Growing startup funding ecosystem	Low; donor-driven
Key Areas of AI Use	Radiology, predictive analytics, patient triage	Imaging, risk prediction, ethical AI	Smart hospitals, diagnostics, genomics	Diagnostics (TB, diabetes, eye health)	Mobile health, triage AI
AI Challenges	Ethical bias, data sharing	Data localization, bureaucracy	Privacy risk, over-centralization	Infrastructure, clinician trust	Connectivity, limited data diversity

Table 4. Ethical and Regulatory Comparison of AI in Healthcare in Different Countries

Aspect	USA	Europe	India	China
AI Regulation	FDA-approved AI/ML framework	EU AI Act (risk-based)	Proposed NHA AI Guidelines	State-driven AI standards
Data Protection	HIPAA	GDPR	Digital Personal Data Protection Act (2023)	PIPL (China's privacy law)
Explainability Requirement	Moderate	Very High	Developing	Moderate
Clinical AI Approval Speed	Fast but complex	Moderate	Slow but improving	Fast under state approval
Ethical AI Emphasis	Fairness & bias mitigation	Transparency & human oversight	Accountability & inclusiveness	Efficiency & control

Understanding global adoption trends provides a strategic perspective; however, effective implementation ultimately depends on the underlying technological foundations. The subsequent section explores the core AI technologies that enable modern healthcare applications, forming the backbone of intelligent medical systems.

CORE TECHNOLOGIES ENABLING AI IN HEALTHCARE

AI has changed health care through its ability to sift through vast volumes of information, discover complex patterns, and help with clinical decision making. Some intelligent systems incorporate AI technologies into health care, including diagnostic systems, treatment planning systems, hospital management systems, and patient engagement systems. These intelligent systems are based on different complex technological elements. These technologies will be discussed in greater detail in the following sections.

Machine learning

Machine learning is the fundamental technology that underlies the much-discussed area of artificial intelligence, where machines are able to learn from experience, modifying their algorithms to improve performance without reprogramming. In health, algorithms of machine learning can find hidden relationships in medical data, model the course of illness and give personalized suggestions about management on the basis of patient characteristics.

Applications:

- Personalized Medicine: Through the analysis of genomic, lifestyle, and clinical data, ML models may select therapies designed to be the most effective for individual patients.
- Risk Assessment and Disease Prediction: Predictive algorithms ascertain those patients with a high probability of chronic diseases such as diabetes, cardiovascular ailments, and cancer.
- Operational Optimization: This is an area in which ML is employed by hospitals for estimation of resource allocation, prediction of readmission, and patient flow management.

Deep Learning

Deep Learning may be defined as a more advanced sub-area of Machine Learning that uses multilayer neural networks to automatically learn high level descriptors from raw data. It has been found very good at handling image processing problems in medicine, signal interpretation and pattern identification, which are problems that have in the past called for human judgement at expert levels.

Applications:

- Radiology: Deep learning models analyze X-rays, CT scans, and MRIs to detect anomalies such as tumors, fractures, and hemorrhages with accuracy comparable to or even surpassing that of human radiologists.
- Pathology: Automated slide analysis helps identify cancerous tissues and quantify biomarkers in histopathological images.
- Cardiology: DL algorithms interpret electrocardiograms (ECGs) to detect arrhythmias and other cardiac abnormalities.

Natural Language Processing

The healthcare field produces massive amounts of unstructured text data such as clinical notes, discharge summaries, radiology reports, and research publications. Natural language processing (NLP) allows computers to understand, analyze, and generate human language. This turns unstructured text into actionable insights.

Applications:

- Clinical Documentation Analysis: Natural language processing (NLP) systems have demonstrated efficacy in extracting diagnosis, medication, and procedure from free-text clinical notes.
- Knowledge Discovery: Machine learning algorithms designed for natural language processing can be utilized to mine medical literature and identify new drug-disease associations as well as clinical trends.
- Conversational AI: Chatbots and virtual health assistants which employ NLP technology and will become a benefit for communication with patients, providing responses to patient questions, and improving patient engagement.

Computer Vision

Computer vision enables artificial intelligence systems to identify and analyze data in our environment; specifically, images and video. This is particularly relevant to the imaging modalities used in medicine. In medicine, computer vision converts visual data into quantitative data which can enable clinicians to achieve faster and accurate diagnosis.

Applications:

- Tumor and Lesion Detection: Artificial intelligence systems demonstrate the capacity to accurately distinguish malignant tumors in radiology and dermatology imaging.
- Ophthalmology: Automated retinal scans play a fundamentally important role in detecting early signs of diabetic retinopathy and glaucoma.
- Dermatology: Computer vision algorithms could accurately and automatically classify skin lesions and detect melanoma.

Reinforcement Learning

Reinforcement Learning (RL) is a principal area of research and development in AI, concerning an agent that learns which action to take in a particular state, based on experience from interacting with its environment and by the reward and punishment signals provided as feedback. This dynamic area of RL research and practice is becoming increasingly important in healthcare as a framework for structured optimal, sequential decision making and treatment choices.

Applications:

- Robotic Surgery: Reinforcement Learning (RL) algorithms afford robotic systems the ability to improve precision and flexibility while executing high-level complex surgical procedures.
- Treatment Optimization: Individualized treatment schedules can be repeatedly modified as a result of real-time patient response.
- Therapy Scheduling: RL can be employed to optimize a dosing schedule in radiation therapy or drug administration.
- Robotic Surgery: Reinforcement Learning (RL) algorithms afford robotic systems the ability to improve precision and flexibility while executing high-level complex surgical procedures.
- Treatment Optimization: Individualized treatment schedules can be repeatedly modified as a result of real-time patient response.
- Therapy Scheduling: RL can be employed to optimize a dosing schedule in radiation therapy or drug administration.

Robotics and Automation

The utilization of robotics within the healthcare sector propelled by artificial intelligence has led to innovative practices through the automation of time-consuming tasks, support within the surgical suite, and support as a patient care assistant. AI also provides precision, dexterity, and multifaceted decision-making to robotic systems in many settings.

Applications:

- Robotic Assisted Surgery: Surgical robots, exemplified by the da Vinci system, present improvements in precision and dexterity.
- Robotics for Rehabilitation: Assistive robots have the potential to help individuals restore voluntary motor control, after a stroke or injury.
- Automated Pharmacy and Robotics for Logistics: Robots can assist with inventory management, drug delivery, and other pharmacy related tasks.

Explainable AI (XAI)

The principles of transparency and accountability are essential for health care decisions. Explainable AI (XAI), which is used to denote models that provide transparency into the output of AI models to clinicians, regulators or patients, helps foster trust, fairness, and ethical or regulatory compliance.

Applications:

- Regulatory Adherence: Explainable Artificial Intelligence (XAI) supports rationalization of AI derived clinical decisions during the US Food and Drug Administration (FDA) or European CE process.
- Clinical Reasoning Support: Clinicians are able to understand the reasoning behind an AI's recommendation which may assist in clinician acceptance.
- Risk Stratification: Provides explainability for risk assessments for patients within predictive analysis.

IoT and Edge Computing

Combining IoT with Edge Computing creates a relationship between AI with ongoing patient monitoring and decentralized analysis. IoT devices obtain ongoing patient data, which may include the necessary wearable sensors, smart implants and remote monitoring tools, while Edge computing allows for action to occur close to the data source minimizing delay and preserving confidentiality.

Applications:

- Remote Patient Monitoring (RPM): Wearable devices are utilized to monitor a patient's heart rate, blood glucose, or oxygen level continuously and in near real-time.
- Chronic Disease Management: RPM has the ability to support the management of chronic diseases, such as diabetes, obesity, hypertension, or chronic obstructive pulmonary disease (COPD).
- Early Alert System: Using AI algorithms, edge devices are capable of reliably detecting an anomaly (e.g., arrhythmia or distress related to respiration) prior to the onset of an emergency situation.

Platforms for Big Data and Cloud Computing

A substantial amount of data is generated in the healthcare sector from electronic health records (EHRs), genomic (DNA) sequencing, imaging and clinical trials. Big Data and Cloud Computing offer a scalable environment for storing, manipulating and analyzing these large, complex datasets.

Applications:

- Joint-Applied Research: Cloud services allow for data sharing between institutions, which may allow for collaborative research programs on larger scales.
- AI model development: Cloud-services can support efficient model development via large datasets that can be processed through deep learning mechanisms.
- Population Health Analytics: Big data analytics can facilitate public health planning and resource allocation that can be useful in monitoring populations for diseases or disease-predicting variables and trends.

Table 5 shows the comparative overview of AI technologies in Healthcare.

Table 5. Comparative Overview of AI Technologies in Healthcare

AI Technology	Primary Function	Key Healthcare Applications	Recent Advancements (2024–2025)	Examples of Use
Machine Learning (ML)	Predictive analytics, decision support	Risk prediction, personalized treatment	Integration with EHR data pipelines for predictive healthcare	IBM Watson Health, Google AutoML
Deep Learning (DL)	Image and signal processing	Radiology, pathology, ECG interpretation	Transformer-based image models improving diagnostic accuracy	DeepMind for Eye Disease Detection
Natural Language Processing (NLP)	Text analysis and understanding	Clinical note summarization, medical chatbots	Multilingual medical LLMs for diverse datasets	BioGPT, Amazon HealthScribe
Computer Vision (CV)	Visual data analysis	Tumor detection, dermatology imaging	Hybrid 3D CNNs for multimodal imaging (CT + MRI)	Qure.ai, Zebra Medical Vision
Reinforcement Learning (RL)	Real-time adaptive decision-making	Robotic surgery, treatment optimization	Integration with robotic process automation (RPA)	RL-based adaptive chemotherapy scheduling
Explainable AI (XAI)	Transparency and trust	Diagnostic interpretation, regulatory compliance	Development of interpretable neural architectures	SHAP-enabled medical dashboards
IoT + Edge AI	Real-time monitoring	Wearable health devices, chronic care	AI-on-chip processors enabling low-power edge analytics	Fitbit Sense 2, Apple HealthKit
Big Data & Cloud AI	Large-scale analytics	Genomics, population health	Federated learning and secure cloud AI for hospitals	Microsoft Azure Health Data Services

Together, these technologies translate computational intelligence into practical clinical capabilities. Building on this technological foundation, the next section discusses real-world use cases of AI in healthcare, demonstrating how these tools are applied across diagnosis, treatment, monitoring, and administration.

USE CASES OF AI IN HEALTHCARE

Artificial intelligence can totally change infection and diagnosis of patients all over the globe, creating a totally different aspect of medicine and being a very useful part of modern medicine. One of the most common uses of artificial intelligence is in medical diagnosis and imaging. Deep learning algorithms, like CNNs, can recognize problems in MRIs, CT scans and X-ray films. It can recognize cancer, keratoconus, diabetic retinopathy, pneumonia and tuberculosis, etc. In a matter of seconds, and often as quickly and with as much certainty and even more than a human radiologist. Not only is the speed of diagnosis greater but also the number of chances of failure are lessened and the patient outcome is much better.

Some other very important uses are to determine the chances of certain diseases being mapped out to a specific person. Machine learning algorithms can predict when the onset of long term diseases and conditions can be expected by analyzing medical records, genetic patterns and lifestyle. The prognosis is especially of importance where there are limited resources, since doctors can institute preventive care quickly. Using genetic materials, specific patient bio markers, and live data to AI helps it produce treatment proving to be effective, specific and individualized, so that AI systems are enabled to best tell the patient the specific dosages of treatment which would be in order and when and how effective results can be expected by treatments, continually updating and modifying individualized treatment, etc., by reading adjusted and altered treatment records of these individualized patients. Therapy becomes more effective due to the customization while the risk of side effect is minimized. In addition, the method of how people look up health assistance online is changing with the smart chatbots and voice assistants. These systems can answer routine questions, record symptoms, make visits, remind patients about taking medication, and even provide mental health assistance using normal language. Patients who are living in remote areas will admire having access to care and less work will be required from health workers.

AI is having a tremendous impact on the slow and expensive process of drug discovery and the drug development of new drugs. The implementation of AI systems in the modeling of chemical interaction, the finding of possible candidates, the discovery of vaccines, the predictions of their efficacy and toxicology, will highly reduce the cost and time to market of new products. An AI powered device decision support system (CDSS) gives help to health care workers in clinical situation by providing them with a recommendation based on facts, alerts on important changes and means to prioritize emergency instances. This assists in the conclusion making based on facts easier to reach making patient care safer and better which is the aim. AI may assist in optimizing the workflow processes so that the hospitals may run more smoothly. Better personnel scheduling, automated invoicing, and monitoring of patient flow, and forecasting available beds in the ICU all lead to more time being spent by health workers on patient care, and less time on paperwork. AI also produces RPM or Remote Patient Monitoring with sensors which may detect particular vital signs such as blood glucose, oxygen bearing capacity, heart rate etc in addition to wearable devices. This also allows for giving medical examinations and treatment in a huge remoteness far from the patients it a highly promising item of welfare in value, particularly with those who have chronic health problems. AI also has a functional potential towards public health insurance. It makes use of its power equipped to process large amounts of data in any form ensuring recognition of the outbreak of diseases, forecasts of its spread and gives aid in shaping policy and conducting this is the man- engenderment of population and containment of the pandemic. Methods to procure real-time data from various sources is a God send in the reach of health outcomes and complete sectors one and all. AI is also changing the health system by being a pathfinder. In doing so health and welfare initiatives in all fields of living from national interest to global stage are improved and in the search for diagnosis fit for purpose every person is possible with the developments in technology. Integration of AI into the healthcare system is a tremendous move forward towards achieving better patient care made more personalized, accessible, preventable,(preventive), and so more efficient with regard to the patients being cared for but technology does provide clinical problems also. Table 6 represents the fields of AI usage and its application in the Healthcare sector.

Table 6. AI Applications in Healthcare Sector

Healthcare Sector	AI Use Case	Primary Benefits	Key Tools/Companies
Diagnostics	Image-based disease detection	Faster, more accurate results	Qure.ai, PathAI, Aidoc
Treatment Planning	Personalized medicine	Tailored drug doses, optimized therapy	Tempus, IBM Watson Health
Patient Monitoring	Remote tracking via IoT	Early intervention, chronic care	Philips HealthSuite, Fitbit
Hospital Administration	Predictive staffing, billing automation	Efficiency and reduced costs	Olive AI, Robotic Process Automation
Pharmacology / Drug Discovery	Molecule screening, simulation	Faster R&D cycles, reduced cost	BenevolentAI, Atomwise
Mental Health	Chatbots, emotion recognition	Accessibility, real-time support	Woebot, Wysa (India)
Public Health	Outbreak prediction, data modeling	Disease prevention, better response	BlueDot, HealthMap

While practical applications illustrate the impact of AI in healthcare, these advancements are grounded in a growing body of academic and empirical research. The following section reviews relevant literature that has shaped current AI-driven healthcare practices and informed this study.

RELEVANT WORK

As noted in the paper (Bajwa et al, 2021) artificial intelligence (AI) can aid in the solution of healthcare issues by using cloud computing and multimodal data. This will create new techniques in diagnostic and treatment planning. The paper states that by using machine learning (ML) which is part of artificial intelligence (AI) patterns are looked for in medical records and lesions of medical images to enhance diagnostic accuracy.

The paper (Karunamurthy et al, 2023)examines the manner in which artificial intelligence works in practical situations in natural language processing, robotics and predictive analysis. These artificial intelligence techniques introduced by their use in health care the ability to detect disorders and individualized treatment planning in addition to quickening clinical procedures and furthering decision making.

The paper (Olawade et al., 2024) considers the functions of AI in health care and examines the diagnostic techniques of predictive analysis, which is being introduced in the early detection of high risk patients and some of the automating of diagnostics. The kinds of personalized treatment planning being made possible by patient data are of some importance together with the use of robotic methods in surgical and rehabilitation procedures.

The author (Shaheen, 2021) commented on the manner in which artificial intelligence (AI) could accelerate, quicken and improve markedly the development of new drugs and diagnostic methods. The paper considers the ability of artificial intelligence to take data from patient records and assist in personalized therapy through methods of giving health advice and recommendations for improvement in living formats.

The author (Zuhair et al, 2024) discussed the wonder of effectiveness and productiveness of artificial intelligence systems in developing and poor countries in connection with the research which they have conducted. They believe that artificial intelligence systems could lend themselves easily to markedly improve the degree of patient care and the diagnostic methods in resource deprived situations of administration and infrastructure and training. According to the findings, global healthcare will benefit from the input of AI provided new hurdles are overcome.

The study (Koski and Murphy, 2021) discusses the improvement of health setup by way of allocated intelligence that provides assistance to healthcare staff. The exhibition serves to demonstrate how artificial intelligence (AI) is able to provide vast stores of medical data to assist medics in their work and offer them the best of decision making. With regard to the paper (Balakrishna and Solanki, 2024) resolve long-standing problems in diagnosis, therapeutics, and patient involvement by using AI techniques involving sophisticated analytics and machine learning. It is maintained that artificial intelligence (AI) can improve personal healthcare.

In (Olawade et al.,2024), the subject of consideration is the importance of human involvement in AI, the quality of data systems and the bias to be met within the algorithms. There is uncertainty amongst health practitioners about the validity of the AI produced material.

In the article written about AI by (Shaheen, 2021) it is the opinion of the writer that the evolution of AI is dependent on the design of clear rules and principles, in addition to the dangers of malevolent use of autonomous systems and what the consequences for health provision may be, as the birth of AI becomes reality.

The classification of corneal topography patterns into classes was carried out by the authors (Gandhi, Satani, and Jain, 2023) using pre-trained models like VGG16 with transfer learning. These increased the quantity of patterns offering 10 patterns that signalled disease deterioration, by the use of convolutional neural networks (CNNs) and elevation of axial curvature using the ATLAS 9000 topographer. The research shows the ability of deep learning as an early detection mechanism where routine procedures cannot be used.

KeratoDetect is a CNN based technique for assessing corneal shape. This invention was by (Lavric and Valentin, 2019). The technique has a success rate of 99.33% of the test data, being superior to the conventional diagnostic technique. This technique gives Eye Specialists a means to assess patients faster geared towards a quicker diagnosis and a more successful treatment. The paper (Gandhi et al. 2021) investigated ANN, CNN and VGG16 as various means to assess 3 types of topographic images i.e. original, edge only, edge with mask. It was found that the pre-processing of images had a marked effect upon the models performance. The model which showed best for assessment of KCN was VGG16 because it performed very well on all data sets.

The paper (Gandhi et al. 2023) investigated Forme Fruste Keratoconus (FFKC). They used the following supervised machine learning algorithms Naive Bayes, KNN, Random Forest, SVM, Logistic Regression, Decision tree. They stated that binary and multiclass classification had a predictive accuracy of about 100%. They stated that the most useful of the classifiers employed were the Random Forest and the Decision trees.

The authors (Satani and Gandhi, 2023) also somewhat researched Artificial Intelligence and Machine Learning techniques for KCN detection. They claimed that neural networks may be helpful in detecting early changes in disease. The study also described the progress of imaging technology from Scheimpflug imaging to Placido disk systems that combined with AI improved the accuracy for the diagnosis.

The study (Agrawal and Gandhi, 2024) proposed a DiabChatBot, which is a chatbot using machine learning approaches to facilitate early diagnosis of Type II Diabetes in the Indian context. Limitations of the most widely used PIMA data-set (female only) were avoided by preparation of a more accurate Indian data-set.

Various supervised learning and ensemble models were applied, CatBoost being the most successful one with a valuation of 98.3% accuracy and AUC of 0.975. The Chatbot also gave recommendations for Indian diets further strengthening the utility.

The paper (Shetty et al., 2024) gave a broad survey dealing with Machine Learning in healthcare revealing the roles of various types of ML models and their applications. The paper (Shetty et al., 2024) also dealt with the application of ML to lung disease detection by comparing the various types of lung diseases such as COPD, Asthma, Tuberculosis, Pneumonia, and ILD. Most of the studies analysed in this review showed more than 90% accuracy with DL models such as CNN, DenseNet, and EfficientNet. A wide variety of datasets of X-ray, CT images were analysed and most of them were derived from Kaggle, NIH and Indian Hospitals.

Another study (Shetty et al., 2025) confined the study to lung disease detection using ML in India revealing that COPD was responsible for 89% of the reported respiratory problems making it the most prevalent. The study went on to do a literature review which compared various models of ML which were applied to diseases like Mesothelioma, Pneumothorax, and ILD. The models covered were CNN, SVM, KNN, Random forest and hybrid classifiers. Both hospital-acquired and open source image data-sets were included. The accuracy of the models were reported between 80% and 99.86%.

The paper (Agrawal and Gandhi, 2025) showed the PneumoSense system which was a deep learning driven system which allowed pneumonia diagnosis using a system incorporating DenseNet121 trained on patient data from X-ray images put on the system with an easy-to-use GUI. This new approach showed remarkably good results having a recall of 0.9795 and AUC of 0.9808. The Deep Learning algorithms applied were superior to ResNet50, CNN and NASNet. The comparative analysis of the existing AIApplications or Study in Health-Care based on the various parameters such as Focus Area, Data-set type, Methods employed, Key Findings and Limitations has been shown in Table 7.

Table 7. Comparative Analysis of AI Applications/Study in Healthcare

Paper	Focus Area	Dataset Type	Methods Used	Key Findings	Limitations
Bajwa et al. (2021)	AI in general healthcare transformation	Multimodal health data	AI, ML, DL, RL	Describes AI's transformative potential and roadmap to implementation in healthcare systems	Limited clinical integration
Karunamurthy et al. (2023)	AI in healthcare systems and future outlook	Various datasets from secondary sources	ML, NLP, Robotics	Covers applications from drug discovery to diagnostics and ethical considerations	Regulatory and data bias concerns
Olawade et al. (2024)	AI in diagnostics, treatment personalization, healthcare automation	X-rays, CT, clinical data	AI algorithms, Predictive Analytics, Robotics	Systematic review on applications, prospects, and challenges	Data quality, interpretability, bias
Shaheen (2021)	AI in drug discovery, clinical trials, and patient care	Clinical trials, drug development data	AI models for clinical intelligence	AI accelerates drug discovery and supports trial management	Scalability and adoption barriers
Koski & Murphy (2021)	Foundations and clinical implementation of AI in nursing and healthcare	Medical and nursing records	NLP, ANN, ML classifiers	Explains historical and technical grounding of AI in clinical settings	Trust, bias, and integration concerns
Pandeya et al. (2024)	Societal and ethical impacts of AI including healthcare	Various datasets and theoretical sources	NLP, ML, Sentiment analysis	Explores pros/ cons including economic and cybersecurity risks	Autonomy and job risk concerns
Zuhair et al. (2024)	AI in developing countries healthcare	Global and regional datasets	ANN, ML, DL, signal processing	Discusses low-cost AI tools like Ubenwa, DR screening in rural areas	High cost, poor adoption, lack of expertise
Panda et al. (2023)	Review of AI case studies in diagnostics and clinical workflows	Case studies and hospital datasets	AI with predictive analytics	Quantifies clinical and financial benefits of AI	Bias, need for oversight
Balakrishna & Solanki (2024)	AI's role in future diagnostics and patient engagement	Various imaging and admin datasets	ML, advanced analytics	Details applications in diagnostics, admin, and treatment	Data security, evolving standards

continued on following page

Table 7. Continued

Paper	Focus Area	Dataset Type	Methods Used	Key Findings	Limitations
Zuhair et al. (2024)	AI in primary care and rural/ low-resource settings	Health records, community datasets	ML, ANN, DL	Focuses on accessibility and use in developing nations	Connectivity and infrastructural barriers
Gandhi et al. (2023)	Keratoconus detection via topography patterns	ATLAS 9000 topography images	Transfer Learning, VGG16, CNN	Classified corneal images into 10 patterns for early KCN detection	Limited dataset, needs more diverse training
Lavric & Valentin (2019)	Keratoconus detection	Corneal topography	CNN	Automated KCN detection aiding early diagnosis	Validation scope and dataset size
Gandhi et al. (2021)	Comparison of DL models for KCN	Corneal topographies	ANN, CNN, VGG16	Edge-based image preprocessing improves performance	Need for standard dataset
Gandhi et al. (2023)	Detection of KCN and Forme Fruste	SIRIUS CSO tomographies	Naive Bayes, SVM, KNN, DT, RF	High accuracy in multiclass classification	Data imbalance, needs clinical testing
Satani & Gandhi (2023)	AI & ML methods for KCN	Topographic and tomographic images	AI, ML, DL, ANN	Summarizes corneal imaging and ML techniques	General scope, no original experiments
Agrawal et al. (2024)	Diabetes detection chatbot for India	Custom Indian diabetes dataset	CatBoost, ensemble ML models	The DiabChatBot outperforms DiaBot & others in accuracy	Limited demographic diversity
Shetty et al. (2024)	General ML application in healthcare	Secondary data	Various DL and ML models	Broad overview of ML uses and challenges	Lacks practical implementation
Shetty et al. (2024)	Analysis of Lung disease classification	X-rays, CT scans	Various DL and ML models	Global studies show high accuracy in detection of Lung Diseases through ML	Need for India-specific research
Shetty et al. (2025)	Analysis of Lung disease detection in India	Chest X-rays, CT, clinical data	Various DL and ML models	Highlights COPD and ILD burden in India	Data scarcity, imbalance, noise
Agrawal & Gandhi (2025)	Pneumonia detection	Chest X-rays	DenseNet121,CNN, ResNet, NASNet	High-performance DL system for X-ray analysis	Computationally intensive

The potential for artificial intelligence (AI) in the medical field is vast and revolutionary. AI will play an important role in early detection of disease, as high levels of accuracy have been shown in the diagnosis of diseases such as keratoconus, diabetes, lung diseases, and heart disease utilising images and clinical data. Examples such as DiabChatBot and PneumoSense show that AI has the ability to give rapid, accurate, and reliable assessment, which can aid in application, especially in resource-poor and rural situations. Another interesting application is that of personalised medicine, where AI can determine from the available details from each patient, individualised guidelines for treatment, prognostication in respect to the progress of disease, and decision-making. A revolutionary change is also occurring in respect of medical imaging, where deep learning models have greatly improved the diagnostic accuracy and decreased the work-load on clinicians. Finally, AI-enabled chatbots and virtual assistants are being developed and applied in telemedicine, remote monitoring and patient self-care, leading to improved access to medical services. Nevertheless, to fully exploit the promise of AI in medicine, there is an imperative need for explainability in the models as well as ethical models of care, as the role of AI in clinical settings becomes more in evidence. Furthermore, the literature which has been reviewed in the present paper also stresses the importance of developing local or contextual datasets and contextually aware models, important for diverse populations such as those found in India. It can be concluded that in the future, AI will be a vital litmus for healthcare service, giving rise to more intelligent diagnostic tests, better personalised care, and improved access to service and treatment on a world-wide basis.

The reviewed studies collectively demonstrate both the maturity of existing AI solutions and the opportunities for further advancement. Building on these insights, the next section outlines the future scope of AI in healthcare, focusing on emerging technologies and long-term transformative potential.

FUTURE SCOPE (2025 TO 2035)

The decade spanning 2025-2035 figures to be a major turning point for healthcare in general, with Artificial Intelligence playing a key role in discovery, diagnosis, treatment and administration in particular. One of the most exciting new frontier is Quantum AI in drug discovery. Drug discovery is notoriously slow and expensive, often taking years of molecular screening and optimization before a viable candidate even reaches clinical trials. The power of Quantum Computing, when combined with AI, can greatly accelerate this process by providing a means of simulating molecular interactions in a more accurate and efficient manner than can be done with classical computers (Biamonte et al., 2017). Quantum processors are ideal even explicitly designed to simulate the functions of quantum mechanical states, making them very useful and efficient in estimating binding affinities and the structures of electronic structure. Combined with machine learning which refines the problem of chemical search space, this combination should improve development time, enhance cost savings and provide even more selective therapies (Cao et al, 2020). While present hardware limitations will prohibit full-scale quantum AI becoming dominant, hybrid systems involving classic AI research with quantum modules should reach maturity 2028-2035 therefore making the complexity of drug design e.g. for cancer or rare genetic disorders much more possible than it is now. Another interesting area of research is in the combination of AI and robotics to robotics in surgery. While surgical robotics are already used to good effect in minimally invasive procedures, these will now develop in conjunction with AI driven systems. By 2030, AI will be able to allow the preoperative planning process to be achieved through new 3D reconstruction techniques of CT and MRI images, allowing for the robots to map surgical ways and judge potential hazards (Yang et al., 2017).

AI algorithms will analyze endoscopic video and sensor information in real-time to help surgeons with precision cutting, categorization of tissues, and providing immediate notification of potential complications during surgery (Hashimoto et al., 2020). However, perfection in autonomy is not likely due to ethical and safety implications, even with robotic systems carrying-out specific repetitive tasks, such as suturing and clipping of vessels, which may be satisfactorily performed under the supervision of human surgeons. This concept of 'supervised autonomy' will help ensure consistency and eliminate fatigue on the part of the surgeon together with minimizing surgical error. However, there are still barriers which need to be addressed, such as regulation, trust in automation on the part of the surgeon, cost, before complete acceptance and utilisation occurs, especially in the developing countries. By the mid-2030s the use of AI assisted robotics may be routine giving rise to an added value of effectiveness and safety in surgeries performed. In the Indian context, a major area of opportunity lies in AI's assistance in striving for universal healthcare coverage. India has a vast and heterogeneous population and an existence of major problems in accessibility, affordability, and quality of healthcare delivery. AI could be seen as a force multiplier in enabling the system to overcome such barriers. AI chatbots in local languages could be of assistance in relation to simple triage, checking of symptoms and also possible remote consultations enabling even patients found in more rural or underserved areas to be able to seek early medical advice (Qure.ai, 2023, Niramai, 2023). Decision-support systems could help in enabling the frontier health worker to detect diseases like tuberculosis, diabetic retinopathy, or hypertension without the necessity for specialist input (World Health Organization, 2023). Predictive analytics can improve resource allocation through forecasted hospital bed needs, medicine supply chains, and workforce allocations (ABDM, 2023). With government initiatives such as Ayushman Bharat Digital Mission forming the backbone of a digital health platform, AI will have the infrastructure necessary to scale and to achieve national usefulness. If implemented wisely, with localized data sets and ethical safeguards, AI can make healthcare universally available, as well as equitably so in terms of quality and economical cost (NITI Aayog, 2018).

Finally, in 2030, AI is expected to be a virtual, non-manufactured doctor's assistant, integrated into the standard daily clinical practice. Unlike conventional decision support systems, these AI assistants will be, say, context-aware companions to physicians. They will automatically summarize patient histories, analyze laboratory findings and imaging, automatically produce differential diagnoses, maybe ranked by probabilities (Topol, 2019). They may in real-time suggest the next-best diagnostic tests, recommend treatment options, alter doses of medications based on patient profile and risk factors (Esteva et al., 2019). Aside from clinical reasoning, they will automate standard administrative chores such as documentation of medical records, administrations of billing codes, and scheduling, thus lessening the burden of non-clinic faculty members. But it is essential that these systems will not replace human doctors, but augment them, enabling more direct contact of physicians on patients. Their success will depend on explainability, clarity of regulations, and adequate education of clinicians to know of strengths and limitations of AI-born recommendations.

In conclusion, the future potential with AI in healthcare systems of the world, 2025 to 2035, is vast and multi-dimensional. Remarkable AI will speed the processes of new drug discovery, AI-robotics will improve surgical precision, technologically driven solutions will facilitate the universal goals of Indian healthcare systems, and productive assistants will be inserted into the daily working of world clinical practice. There are, indeed, many difficulties in sight—privacy of data, ethical problems, preparedness of infrastructures—but the direction is certain: AI is poised to become an essential partner to global healthcare systems and establish its reality as an increasingly precise, accessible, and patient-centered system of medical practice. Table 8 shows the Future Trends of AI in Healthcare. Table 9 shows the pathway of AI impact in Healthcare from 2025 to 2035.

Table 8. Future Trends of AI in Healthcare

Emerging Area	AI Contribution	Expected Impact by 2030
Quantum AI in Drug Discovery	Molecular simulation and protein folding	70% faster drug candidate validation
Genomic AI	Predictive genomics and variant detection	Precision medicine mainstream
AI in Mental Health	Emotion-aware conversational AI	Early diagnosis of depression, anxiety

continued on following page

Table 8. Continued

Emerging Area	AI Contribution	Expected Impact by 2030
Federated Learning in Hospitals	Privacy-preserving model training	Cross-institution collaboration
Digital Twins in Healthcare	Simulating patient physiology	Virtual clinical trials and risk forecasting
AI and Robotics Integration	Autonomous surgical assistants	40% reduction in surgical error rate
Ambient AI in Smart Hospitals	Real-time context-aware assistance	Fully automated hospital ecosystems

Table 9. AI Impact Pathway in Healthcare (2025–2035)

AI Enablers (Core Technologies)	Functional Transformation in Healthcare (2025–2030)	Clinical Outcomes (2030–2035)	Broader Societal & Systemic Impact
Machine Learning & Deep Learning	Predictive analytics, early diagnosis, risk stratification	Precision diagnostics, automated disease detection	Reduced diagnostic delays and misdiagnoses; improved survival rates
Natural Language Processing (NLP)	Structured extraction of clinical data; AI-driven documentation	Multilingual medical assistants, automated patient communication	Increased health literacy; reduced administrative workload
Computer Vision (CV)	Imaging-based triage, pathology automation	Full integration into radiology & ophthalmology workflows	Accessible imaging diagnostics in rural settings
Reinforcement Learning (RL)	Adaptive therapy optimization, robotic decision-making	Personalized treatment pathways, smart dose scheduling	Improved therapeutic outcomes; fewer medication errors
Explainable AI (XAI)	Transparent model reasoning and clinical trust	Regulatory-approved interpretable AI tools	Ethical compliance and clinician confidence in AI recommendations
IoT & Edge Computing	Real-time remote monitoring via wearables	AI-powered continuous health surveillance	Early intervention and reduced hospital readmissions
Big Data & Cloud AI Platforms	Federated learning across hospitals	Global health data exchange and AI-driven research collaboration	Accelerated discovery, population health optimization
AI-Robotics Convergence	AI-assisted surgery, rehabilitation automation	Semi-autonomous surgical systems	Safer procedures and enhanced surgeon precision
Quantum AI (Emerging)	Drug discovery acceleration via quantum simulation	70% faster drug validation and molecular screening	Affordable access to complex therapies; new treatment frontiers
Digital Twins & Ambient Intelligence	Virtual patient simulation, context-aware hospital systems	Predictive modeling of patient outcomes	Proactive and personalized healthcare ecosystems

While the future trajectory of artificial intelligence in healthcare is promising, its long-term success is not guaranteed by technological advancement alone. The realization of AI-driven healthcare transformation between 2025 and 2035 will depend critically on governance, ethical oversight, and contextual deployment. Over-reliance on algorithmic decision-making without adequate human supervision may risk deskilling clinicians and reinforcing hidden biases embedded in training data. Moreover, advanced innovations such as Quantum AI, digital twins, and autonomous robotics may exacerbate existing inequities if access remains limited to well-resourced institutions and urban populations. In developing contexts such as India, challenges related to data quality, infrastructure readiness, interoperability, and workforce training could constrain scalability despite policy support. Therefore, future AI systems must prioritize explainability, inclusiveness, and human-centered design, ensuring that technological progress translates into equitable and clinically meaningful outcomes rather than widening the digital divide. A balanced integration of innovation with accountability will be essential for AI to function as a trusted and sustainable partner in global healthcare systems.

As these emerging trends point toward a more intelligent, predictive, and patient-centered healthcare ecosystem, it becomes essential to synthesize the key insights discussed throughout this chapter. The concluding section summarizes the overall impact of AI in healthcare and reflects on its broader implications.

CONCLUSION

Artificial intelligence is no longer the fanciful thing of science fiction writers imaginations, but a radical and revolutionary process of change that is now altering the healthcare delivery world. This assessment of AI considers how it has grown from nothing more than a supporting diagnostic tool, into a strategic partner that will be the building block of modern healthcare delivery. AI has now been shown to bring more and better accuracy, efficiency and label to diagnosis, treatment, monitoring, administration and drug development. It has also provided a cure to both clinical and systemic weaknesses long known in health care delivery, especially in poor health care areas like India. AI has changed existence as we know, and understand it, through its ability to enhance human intelligence, rather than replace it. During the last decade its outstanding ability of assimilating huge amounts of knowledge in both its structured and unstructured forms, like genome sequencings, imaging data, electronic health records, has enabled it to find patterns and abnormalities that the best human clinicians could often not find. This process of continual learning enables early diagnosis of disease and opportunity for early intervention with evidence measurement assisted therapies. The technological revolution in the diagnostic field is well illustrated by PneumoSense and DiabChatBot. Both these innovations have had a localized production line to provide the required input of AI to encourage and bolster the cure for diseases like pneumonia, diabetes etc, giving rapid and inexpensive, but accurate diagnostic help and assistance that correlate with the specific health-dependent requirements of the local area. It is obvious that the products of these will by their distribution attempt to democratize and provide a universal access to knowledge for all people in AIs quest to diminish the gap of better urban health versus that of the worse rural, that of better specialist versus the poorer patients, that of simple pertained diseases or restricted and complicated clinical problems. AI on a more global monolithic level can be invaluable to improved operational efficiencies in any healthcare setup, with its ability to bring about optimization of the patient pathways in hospitals, its decrease in needless administration that brings a consequent improved interaction of patients in their healthcare by its use of predictive analytics and automation.

The adoption of monitoring systems with built-in IoT networking, AI-facilitated triage devices, and clinical decision support systems (CDSS) means that healthcare is becoming both more efficient and more patient-centric. In India this is particularly relevant where the doctor-patient ratios are still far from ideal, and where the Ayushman Bharat Digital Mission (ABDM) is building the digital substrate needed for large scale AI implementation. By taking advantage of this base, AI can lend itself to achieving the goal of universal healthcare, ensuring that good quality medical services reach the most remote populations. Despite the advantages of these developments however, significant challenges still remain. Issues of data privacy, ethical governance, bias in AI models and lack of interpretability have to be faced if the entrance of AI is to be equitable and trusted. The reluctance of the medical community to rely heavily on AI-derived recommendations suggests the further need for Explainable AI (XAI) systems where machines and machine reasoning are made transparent and clinically interpretable. Finally, the success of AI in healthcare will depend on recognition of the multi-stakeholder approach which means that it is essential for technologists, clinicians, health policy-makers and ethicists to collaborate in the co-development of proposals which are both technically possible and socially acceptable. One of the keys to this process is the building of context-specific models trained on locally available data sets so that they are culturally, linguistically and demographically relevant, which is essential in a country like India. The literature presented in this chapter is indicative of the equal maturity and momentum that AI research in healthcare is gaining.As applications extend from deep learning for medical imaging to machine learning for individualized medicine, from AI robotics for surgery to chatbots in mental health care, the list of applications grows quickly. The clinical space ahead for AI in health care (2025-2035) will bring much greater integration across the medical continuum.

Quantum AI, Federated Learning and Digital Twin Modeling are the new technologies which increase the demand to new higher levels about what AI can do to drug discovery, clinical trials, and individualistic therapy. Quantum AI giving fundamental change to molecular simulation and drug design shortening of 70% drug discovery processes. Likewise, AI Robotic convergence will produce a new semi-autonomous surgery characteristic, while virtual doctor assistants are going to improve clinical reasoning and also efficiency in administration. Ambient intelligent cybernetic health service systems within smart hospitals, in which AI systems will work in silence and intelligently all in dark, will be made a creative reality. But the true measure of the success of AI is the humanistic effect on how it can modify the treatment of patients, empower clinicians, and bring about equity for health service deliveries. It has to be by investment in capacity building, an AI education for health care workers plus a co-development of a regulatory framework suitable to institute standards and parameters for to redefine health care reform, and take note about accountability. Likewise, the ethical framework to AI must be the underpinnings for a revolution for health care, where it brings no exclusion due to inequality or discrimination, but can be used distributively in value to society.

In summary, AI will provide an immense significant paradigm shift in health care systems value, since penicillin and the value of imaging technology came along, and the possibilities of it to animate then principles degenerative and disease orientated for patients within health care systems, which in an individualistic, predictive and proactive manner, are immense. If the principles which can govern it, will be of an ethical nature, a coalescing to ensure AI representation of inclusive datasets in potentialities, and prudent counteracting of the realities, based on the ethos proper health care which is in society, where throughout transparency and reputable, the ease of the consideration of it could ultimately be the panacea to resolve the gaps for accessibility and affordability and wellbeing in health status and health gain.

REFERENCES

Aayog, N. I. T. I. (2018). *National Strategy for Artificial Intelligence*. https://www.niti.gov.in

Aayog, N. I. T. I. (2018). *National Strategy for Artificial Intelligence*. Government of India. https://www.niti.gov.in

Agrawal, P., & Gandhi, S. (2025). PneumoSense: Smart pneumonia detection using deep learning. In *Proceedings of the 10th Edition ICT4SD – 2025 International ICT Summit and Awards* (Springer, Goa). To be Published.

Agrawal, P., Gandhi, S., & Agarwal, M. (2024). DiabChatbot: A machine learning chatbot for early diagnosis of type II/mellitus diabetes and diet recommendation in an Indian scenario. In *2024 10th International Conference on Advanced Computing and Communication Systems (ICACCS)* (pp. 1526–1531). IEEE. DOI: 10.1109/ICACCS60874.2024.10716933

Ayushman Bharat Digital Mission (ABDM). (2023). *Official Website*. https://abdm.gov.in

Ayushman Bharat Digital Mission (ABDM). (2023). *Official website*. Government of India. https://abdm.gov.in

Bajwa, J., Munir, U., Nori, A., & Williams, B. (2021). Artificial intelligence in healthcare: Transforming the practice of medicine. *Future Healthcare Journal*, *8*(2), e188–e194. DOI: 10.7861/fhj.2021-0095 PMID: 34286183

Balakrishna, S., & Solanki, V. K. (2024). A comprehensive review on AI-driven healthcare transformation. *Ingeniería Solidaria*, *20*(2), 1–30. DOI: 10.16925/2357-6014.2024.02.07

Biamonte, J., Wittek, P., Pancotti, N., Rebentrost, P., Wiebe, N., & Lloyd, S. (2017). Quantum machine learning. *Nature*, *549*(7671), 195–202. DOI: 10.1038/nature23474 PMID: 28905917

Cao, Y., Romero, J., Olson, J. P., Degroote, M., Johnson, P. D., Kieferová, M., Kivlichan, I. D., Menke, T., Peropadre, B., Sawaya, N. P. D., Sim, S., Veis, L., & Aspuru-Guzik, A. (2020). Quantum chemistry in the age of quantum computing. *Chemical Reviews*, *119*(19), 10856–10915. DOI: 10.1021/acs.chemrev.8b00803 PMID: 31469277

China Briefing. (2025). *China's AI healthcare market growth trends*. https://www.china-briefing.com

Esteva, A., Robicquet, A., Ramsundar, B., Kuleshov, V., DePristo, M., Chou, K., Cui, C., Corrado, G., Thrun, S., & Dean, J. (2019). A guide to deep learning in healthcare. *Nature Medicine, 25*(1), 24–29. DOI: 10.1038/s41591-018-0316-z PMID: 30617335

European Commission. (2024). *Artificial Intelligence in Healthcare: EU perspectives*. Brussels: EC.

Gandhi, S. R., Satani, J., Bhuva, K., & Patadiya, P. (2021). Evaluation of deep learning networks for keratoconus detection using corneal topographic images. In S. K. Singh et al. (Eds.), *Computer Vision and Image Processing: CVIP 2020* (CCIS, Vol. 1377, pp. 367–380). Springer. DOI: 10.1007/978-981-16-1092-9_31

Gandhi, S. R., Satani, J., Jadav, K., & Shah, A. (2023). Detection of keratoconus and former fruste keratoconus through supervised machine learning algorithms. In *2023 First International Conference on Advances in Electrical, Electronics and Computational Intelligence (ICAEECI)* (pp. 1–9). IEEE. DOI: 10.1109/ICAEECI58247.2023.10370803

Gandhi, S. R., Satani, J., & Jain, D. (2023). Classification of keratoconus using corneal topography pattern with transfer learning approach. In J. Choudrie et al. (Eds.), *ICT with intelligent applications* (Smart Innovation, Systems and Technologies, Vol. 311, pp. 165–176). Springer. DOI: 10.1007/978-981-19-3571-8_18

Hashimoto, D. A., Rosman, G., Rus, D., & Meireles, O. R. (2020). Artificial intelligence in surgery: Promises and perils. *Annals of Surgery, 268*(1), 70–76. DOI: 10.1097/SLA.0000000000002693 PMID: 29389679

HIMSS & Medscape. (2024). *Future of AI in healthcare survey report*. https://www.himss.org/futureofai

India, A. I. (2024). *AI adoption in Indian healthcare*. https://indiaai.gov.in

Koski, E., & Murphy, J. (2021). AI in healthcare. *Studies in Health Technology and Informatics, 284*, 295–299. DOI: 10.3233/SHTI210726 PMID: 34920529

Lavric, A., & Valentin, P. (2019). KeratoDetect: Keratoconus detection algorithm using convolutional neural networks. *Computational Intelligence and Neuroscience, 2019*, 8162567. Advance online publication. DOI: 10.1155/2019/8162567 PMID: 30809255

McKinsey & Company. (2020). *Transforming healthcare with AI: The impact on the workforce and organizations*.

Niramai Health Analytix. (2023). https://www.niramai.com

Niramai Health Analytix. (2023). *Official website*. https://www.niramai.com

OECD. (2024). *AI in health: Huge potential, huge risks.* OECD Publishing.

Olawade, D. B., David-Olawade, A. C., Wada, O. Z., Asaolu, A. J., Adereni, T., & Ling, J. (2024). Artificial intelligence in healthcare delivery: Prospects and pitfalls. *Journal of Artificial Intelligence in Medicine.* Advance online publication. https://www.sciencedirect.com/science/article/pii/S2949916X24000616

Open & Affordable. (2024). *AI in healthcare statistics and trends.* https://www.openandaffordable.com

Panda, S., & Mehta, A. (2023). Navigating the future of healthcare with artificial intelligence: Reviewing case studies and predicting its impact. *ResearchGate.* https://www.researchgate.net/publication/386053591_Navigating_the_Future_of_Healthcare_with_Artificial_Intelligence_Reviewing_Case_Studies_and_Predicting_its_Impact

Poon, E. G.. (2025). Adoption of artificial intelligence in healthcare: A U.S. system survey. *Health Affairs, 44*(1), 25–38.

Qure.ai. (2023). https://www.qure.ai

Qure.ai. (2023). *Official website.* https://www.qure.ai

Satani, J., & Gandhi, S. R. (2023). A review: Applications of artificial intelligence and machine learning in keratoconus detection. *International Journal of Computer Applications, 182*(45), 1–17.

Shaheen, M. Y. (2021). *Applications of artificial intelligence (AI) in healthcare: A review.* ScienceOpen *Preprints.* DOI: 10.14293/S2199-1006.1.SOR-.PPVRY8K.v1

Shetty, I., Agrawal, P., & Gandhi, S. (2024, November). Using machine learning for lung diseases prediction: A comprehensive review. In *Proceedings of the 4th International Conference on Modeling Simulation and Optimization (CoMSO 2024)* (Springer). To be published.

Shetty, I., Agrawal, P., & Gandhi, S. (2024, September). A survey on use of machine learning in the healthcare sector. In *2024: GLS University Doctoral and Faculty Research Colloquium.* To be published.

Shetty, I., Agrawal, P., & Gandhi, S. (2025, January). A survey on the lung diseases prediction in an Indian environment using machine learning. In *Proceedings of the 9th International Conference on Smart Trends for Computing and Communication (SmartCom 2025)* (Springer, Pune).

SigTuple Technologies. (2023). https://www.sigtuple.com

Topol, E. (2019). High-performance medicine: The convergence of human and artificial intelligence. *Nature Medicine*, *25*(1), 44–56. DOI: 10.1038/s41591-018-0300-7 PMID: 30617339

World Health Organization. (2023). *Global Health Workforce Statistics*. https://www.who.int

World Health Organization [WHO]. (2023). *Global Health Workforce Statistics*. https://www.who.int

Yang, G. Z., Cambias, J., Cleary, K., Daimler, E., Drake, J., Dupont, P. E., & Hawkes, D. (2017). Medical robotics—Regulatory, ethical, and legal considerations for increasing levels of autonomy. *Science Robotics*, *2*(4), eaam8638. Advance online publication. DOI: 10.1126/scirobotics.aam8638 PMID: 33157870

Zuhair, V., Babar, A., Ali, R., Oduoye, M. O., Noor, Z., Chris, K., Okon, I. I., & Rehman, L. U. (2024). Exploring the impact of artificial intelligence on global health and enhancing healthcare in developing nations. *Journal of Primary Care & Community Health*, *15*, 21501319241245847. DOI: 10.1177/21501319241245847 PMID: 38605668

Chapter 3

Generative AI and Large Language Models (LLMs) for Personalized and Explainable Healthcare

Somnath Rajkumar Dhavale
http://orcid.org/0009-0008-5833-3111
Solapur University, India

L. M. R. J. R. Lobo
http://orcid.org/0000-0002-8572-2082
Walchand Institute of Technology, Solapur, India

Sagar Somayya Hiremath
http://orcid.org/0009-0003-9067-8201
Walchand Institute of Technology, Solapur, India

Shradha Pandurang Kakade
http://orcid.org/0009-0001-7659-1789
Sangmeshwar Collage, Solapur, India

Sarang Rajendra Khole
http://orcid.org/0009-0005-0880-3259
Walchand Institute of Technology, Solapur, India

Shiddharam Shivgonda Patil
http://orcid.org/0009-0004-4189-3201
Walchand Institute of Technology, Solapur, India

ABSTRACT

Generative AI is reshaping how healthcare teams collaborate, communicate, and make clinical decisions. From large language models that summarize patient histories to diagnostic tools that simulate treatment options, these technologies are streamlining workflows and fostering more coordinated care. For instance, AI can help reduce the cognitive load on clinicians by automating routine documentation and offering evidence-based suggestions. Yet, the integration of AI into clinical settings also introduces challenges—such as ensuring fairness in algorithmic outputs, avoiding blind trust in machine-generated advice, and preserving human judgment at the heart of patient care. This chapter explores these dynamics, focusing on how

DOI: 10.4018/979-8-2600-0981-9.ch003

AI affects team interactions, leadership responsibilities, and decision-making structures. It argues for robust governance, inclusive access, and transparent design to ensure AI enhances rather than undermines collaborative healthcare.

1. INTRODUCTION

The healthcare landscape is rapidly evolving as Artificial Intelligence (AI)—especially Generative AI and Large Language Models (LLMs)—transitions from experimental tools to integral components of clinical practice. Unlike earlier AI systems that were limited to narrow, rule-based tasks, today's generative models can interpret complex medical data and produce context-sensitive outputs tailored to individual patient needs. Tools like GPT-4, BioGPT, and Med-PaLM exemplify this shift, offering capabilities such as summarizing electronic health records, recommending treatment options, and delivering patient education in conversational formats.

What sets generative AI apart is its ability to personalize medical content. By synthesizing diverse inputs—patient history, genetic profiles, lifestyle factors, and real-time clinical data—these systems can suggest targeted interventions that reduce reliance on trial-and-error approaches. In multilingual or culturally varied settings, LLMs also function as medical interpreters, facilitating clearer communication between patients and providers.

However, the integration of such technologies into healthcare is not without challenges. Safeguarding patient privacy, adhering to regulatory standards like HIPAA and GDPR, and mitigating biases embedded in training datasets are critical concerns. Just as important is the need for transparency and clinical reliability in AI-generated recommendations. This chapter delves into the underlying technologies of generative AI and LLMs, examining their roles in diagnostics, treatment planning, medical education, and patient engagement. It also outlines the ethical and governance frameworks necessary for responsible implementation. Ultimately, the aim is to illustrate how advanced AI, when thoughtfully integrated with clinical expertise, can support a more proactive, inclusive, and patient-centered approach to care.

Beyond individual clinical decision support, Generative AI and Large Language Models (LLMs) increasingly function as collaborative agents within healthcare teams. By generating shared summaries, explainable recommendations, and standardized communication artifacts, these systems influence how clinicians, nurses, administrators, and allied professionals coordinate decisions. This chapter explicitly aligns Generative AI with the theme of e-collaboration by examining its role in enhancing communication effectiveness, trust calibration, role clarity, and collective decision-making within multidisciplinary healthcare environments.

2. KEY CONCEPTS AND DEFINITIONS

2.1. Generative AI

Generative Artificial Intelligence (AI) refers to advanced systems capable of producing new content—ranging from text and images to synthetic datasets—by learning patterns from vast amounts of existing data. In the healthcare domain, these tools can simulate realistic patient scenarios, generate medical images for training or research, and even assist in the design of novel drug compounds. Importantly, they achieve this without directly using identifiable patient information, thereby supporting privacy-preserving innovation. Unlike traditional AI models that focus on classification or prediction, generative AI can create original, context-aware outputs that enhance clinical research, medical education, and decision-making processes.

2.2. Large Language Models (LLMs)

Large Language Models (LLMs) are advanced AI trained on vast text datasets to process and generate human-like language. In medical contexts, these models can assist with summarizing patient histories, drafting clinical documentation, responding to medical inquiries, and facilitating multilingual conversations between healthcare providers and patients. When fine-tuned for healthcare, LLMs gain the ability to navigate complex terminology and adapt to nuanced clinical scenarios. This makes them especially useful not only in day-to-day clinical workflows but also in medical education, where they can support learning through interactive, context-rich dialogue.

2.3. Personalized Healthcare

Personalized healthcare aims to align medical decisions, treatments, and preventive measures with the unique characteristics of each patient. This approach draws on a combination of genetic data, lifestyle habits, environmental exposures, and clinical history to craft interventions that are both precise and relevant. Generative AI and Large Language Models (LLMs) accelerate this process by integrating diverse data sources—often in real time—to generate insights and recommendations tailored to the individual's specific health profile. By doing so, these technologies help move care beyond one-size-fits-all protocols toward more responsive, patient-centered solutions.

2.4. Explainable AI

Explainable Artificial Intelligence (XAI) focuses on making AI-driven decisions transparent and understandable to human users. In healthcare, this clarity is essential—not only for earning the trust of clinicians but also for maintaining ethical and legal accountability. By using methods such as highlighting key clinical indicators, offering step-by-step reasoning, and presenting alternative outcomes, XAI enables medical professionals to interpret and validate AI-generated recommendations. This layer of interpretability ensures that technology supports, rather than replaces, clinical judgment.

2.5. Synthetic Medical Data

Synthetic medical data refers to artificially created datasets that mimic the structure and patterns of real patient information, but without containing any identifiable details. Techniques such as Generative Adversarial Networks (GANs) are commonly used to produce realistic yet anonymized records, making it possible to train and validate AI models without compromising patient privacy. This type of data is especially useful for simulating rare medical conditions, correcting imbalances in training datasets, and enabling collaborative research across institutions that may otherwise face data-sharing restrictions.

2.6. Clinical Decision Support Systems (CDSS)

Clinical Decision Support Systems (CDSS) are designed to assist healthcare professionals by analyzing patient data and offering diagnostic insights, treatment options, or alerts about potential risks. When enhanced with Artificial Intelligence, these systems can incorporate real-time analytics and predictive modeling to deliver personalized, evidence-based recommendations. By synthesizing information from electronic health records, lab results, and clinical guidelines, AI-powered CDSS help clinicians make timely and informed decisions tailored to each patient's unique profile.

2.7. Supporting Digital Health Technologies (Summary)

Several enabling technologies support the deployment of Generative AI and LLMs in healthcare ecosystems. Natural Language Processing (NLP) enables the transformation of unstructured clinical text into actionable data, while multilingual AI systems facilitate inclusive communication across linguistic boundaries. Telemedicine, remote patient monitoring, wearable devices, and the Internet of Medical Things (IoMT) collectively enable continuous data collection beyond traditional clinical settings. Rather than functioning independently, these technologies form an integrated digital health infrastructure that amplifies the personalization, scalability, and real-time responsiveness of AI-driven healthcare systems.

3.LITERATURE REVIEW

1. Acosta, Lin, and Patel (2024) emphasize the ethical importance of transparency and shared accountability when AI systems influence clinical decisions. Their work highlights the need for explainable outputs and human oversight, especially in multidisciplinary care environments where decisions affect multiple stakeholders.
2. Bhuyan, Deshmukh, and Kaur (2025) explore how generative AI enhances both clinical excellence and operational efficiency. They demonstrate how AI tools support physicians in diagnostics while also streamlining administrative workflows, creating a more cohesive healthcare ecosystem.
3. Brown et al. (2020) introduced GPT models capable of summarizing complex medical records. These models help care teams quickly align patient history and treatment plans, reducing communication delays and improving collaborative decision-making.
4. Buess, Shah, and Rane (2025) applied multimodal transformers to predict cardiac events by analyzing EHR narratives, ECG waveforms, and wearable data. Their research shows how AI can synthesize diverse inputs to support real-time, team-based diagnostics.
5. Chung et al. (2014) developed gated recurrent units (GRUs), which are widely used for time-series modeling in patient monitoring. These models support adaptive decision-making in intensive care units, where collaboration between nurses, physicians, and AI systems is critical.
6. Dinh, Sohl-Dickstein, and Bengio (2016) proposed Real NVP, a privacy-preserving generative model that enables secure data sharing across institutions. This technique is foundational for federated learning, which supports collaborative AI development without compromising patient privacy.
7. Goodfellow et al. (2020) introduced Generative Adversarial Networks (GANs), which are used to create synthetic medical data for training and validation. GANs support cross-institutional collaboration by enabling model development without access to real patient records.
8. He, Zhang, and Chen (2024) explored multilingual LLMs that facilitate inclusive communication between patients and providers. Their work shows how language models can bridge linguistic gaps in diverse clinical settings, improving collaboration and patient engagement.

9. Ho, Jain, and Abbeel (2022) developed diffusion models that enhance explainability in generative systems. These models help clinicians understand how AI arrives at specific recommendations, fostering trust and transparency in collaborative care.
10. Kline, Patel, and Wong (2024) emphasized the importance of visual tools and interpretability frameworks in AI-assisted decision-making. Their research supports the use of explainable AI to improve clinician confidence and interdisciplinary communication.
11. Madani et al. (2023) demonstrated how AI-driven protein structure prediction supports personalized medicine. Their work enables collaboration between clinicians and researchers in drug development and treatment planning.
12. Market.us (2023) projected exponential growth in generative AI adoption across healthcare. The report highlights how organizations are using AI to enhance team productivity, streamline workflows, and improve patient engagement.
13. McKinsey Health Insights (2025) surveyed 150 healthcare leaders and found widespread use of GenAI to support clinical and administrative collaboration. The findings confirm that AI is becoming integral to multidisciplinary teamwork.
14. Meyers, Singh, and Zhao (2022) applied federated learning to rare disease diagnosis, enabling secure collaboration across institutions. Their approach ensures data privacy while allowing AI models to benefit from diverse datasets.
15. Mildenhall et al. (2021) introduced NeRFs for 3D anatomical modeling, which aid surgical teams in planning procedures collaboratively. These models enhance visualization and coordination among radiologists, surgeons, and support staff.
16. Oord, Dieleman, and Schrauwen (2016) developed WaveNet, a generative model for raw audio. This technology supports real-time patient monitoring and voice-based diagnostics, improving communication in acute care settings.
17. Panicker, Thomas, and Nair (2024) showed how GenAI improves radiology workflows by reconstructing high-resolution images. Their work facilitates clearer communication between radiologists and referring physicians.
18. Rabbani, Joshi, and Verma (2025) explored GenAI's role in clinical documentation and patient messaging. These tools reduce administrative burden and improve communication between care teams and patients.
19. Ramesh et al. (2021) developed DALL·E, a model that generates medical images from text prompts. This capability supports visual collaboration in diagnostics and patient education.
20. Reddy (2024) emphasized the importance of implementation science in aligning AI systems with clinical workflows. His work advocates for stakeholder engagement and trust-building during AI integration.

21. Rezende, Mohamed, and Wierstra (2014) contributed to stochastic modeling for personalized simulations. Their techniques are foundational for Patient Digital Twins, which simulate treatment responses and disease progression.
22. Samuel, Gupta, and Lee (2025) examined GenAI's role in administrative collaboration. Their case study shows how AI supports scheduling, billing, and resource management across departments.
23. Sharp, Kumar, and Lin (2025) reviewed GenAI's application in health economics. They demonstrated how AI automates cost-effectiveness modeling, supporting financial decision-making in multidisciplinary teams.
24. Shokrollahi, Farahani, and Zadeh (2023) provided a comprehensive review of generative models in healthcare. Their work reinforces the role of transformers and diffusion architectures in collaborative diagnostics.
25. Samuel and Desai (2025) explored AI-powered administrative workflows, emphasizing efficiency gains across departments. Their findings support the integration of GenAI into hospital operations.
26. Toto, Singh, and Alavi (2025) advocated cross-disciplinary collaboration in AI development. Their research highlights the importance of co-design involving clinicians, ethicists, and engineers.
27. Vaswani et al. (2017) introduced the transformer architecture, which underpins modern LLMs. These models support advanced reasoning and contextual understanding in clinical decision support systems.
28. Yang, Zhang, and Li (2019) reviewed GenAI's role in synthesizing medical literature. Their work helps care teams stay updated and make evidence-based decisions collaboratively.
29. Zhang and Boulos (2023) examined GenAI in medical education, showing how it fosters interdisciplinary learning and shared understanding among care teams.
30. Bhuyan and Deshmukh (2025) reiterated GenAI's dual impact on clinical excellence and operational efficiency. Their findings reinforce the transformative role of AI in healthcare collaboration.
31. Buess and Shah (2025) revisited multimodal transformers for cardiac event prediction. Their research exemplifies how AI can integrate diverse data streams to support real-time, team-based decision-making.

4. RESEARCH GAP

Despite the rapid proliferation of generative artificial intelligence (AI) technologies in healthcare, the existing body of literature predominantly focuses on their technical performance, clinical accuracy, and ethical implications at the patient–technology interface. While these perspectives are valuable, they offer a limited understanding of how generative AI shapes the intricate social and collaborative structures within healthcare workplaces. Studies have addressed AI-assisted diagnostics, predictive analytics, and automated documentation; however, there is comparatively little systematic investigation into how these tools affect group dynamics—particularly communication patterns, trust-building, leadership roles, and interprofessional coordination among healthcare teams.

Most current research treats healthcare teams as static entities that either adopt or resist AI, overlooking the fluid and adaptive nature of workplace group dynamics. In practice, the introduction of generative AI can reconfigure authority, redistribute cognitive workloads, and alter power balances between physicians, nurses, administrators, and technical staff. Yet, empirical studies examining these relational shifts remain sparse. Additionally, the role of AI as a "virtual team member" contributing to collective intelligence has been conceptually explored, but evidence-based assessments of how teams negotiate AI-generated inputs—especially in high-stakes decision-making—are still underdeveloped.

Furthermore, while some literature addresses AI acceptance and user trust, these discussions rarely consider the collective dimension of trust calibration within teams. How groups jointly validate, contest, or integrate AI outputs into their workflows remains poorly understood. Equally underexplored are the cultural and organizational contexts that moderate AI's impact on group cohesion, conflict resolution, and inclusivity.

Another significant gap lies in the long-term implications of sustained generative AI use on professional identity and interprofessional collaboration. Current research often evaluates early-stage implementation or pilot projects, leaving a lack of longitudinal insights into whether AI integration ultimately strengthens or fragments team structures over time. Moreover, most studies adopt a technology-centric lens, underestimating the importance of socio-technical co-design approaches that incorporate team feedback into AI development and deployment.

Addressing these gaps requires an interdisciplinary approach that blends healthcare management, organizational psychology, and AI ethics with empirical case studies from diverse clinical settings. A deeper understanding of these relational and structural effects is essential to ensure that generative AI enhances, rather than undermines, collaborative effectiveness in healthcare workplaces.

also determined by how teams interpret, adapt to, and incorporate AI-generated outputs into collective workflows.

These gaps directly align with the book's broader theme of strengthening e-collaboration in healthcare, as they highlight the need to understand how Generative AI reshapes communication patterns, authority structures, trust dynamics, and collective sense-making within interdisciplinary clinical teams.

5. METHODOLOGY

5.1 Model Components

1. Generative AI Integration (Independent Variable) – Refers to the extent to which AI tools are embedded into team workflows for tasks such as diagnostics, prognosis generation, patient communication drafting, and administrative decision support.
2. Communication Effectiveness – The clarity, accuracy, and timeliness of information exchange within teams, potentially enhanced or disrupted by AI-generated summaries and recommendations.
3. Trust Calibration – The process by which teams adjust their confidence in AI-generated outputs, balancing reliance with critical evaluation.
4. Role Reconfiguration – Redistribution of responsibilities and expertise within teams due to AI's ability to handle specific cognitive or administrative tasks.
5. Decision-Making Quality – The degree to which team decisions are informed, timely, and aligned with patient outcomes.
6. Organizational Culture (Moderator) – The openness, collaboration, and adaptability within the healthcare institution that can amplify or dampen AI's effects.
7. AI Literacy (Moderator) – The collective ability of team members to understand and critically engage with AI tools, influencing adoption success.

Figure 1. Care-Oriented Large Language Model for Healthcare

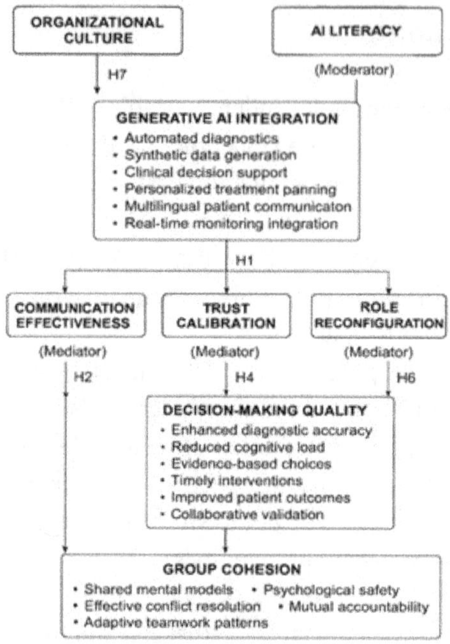

5.2 Hypotheses Development in the Context of Generative AI and LLMs for Personalized and Explainable Healthcare

5.2.1. Definition of Hypothesis

In healthcare AI research, a hypothesis is a precise, testable prediction about how Generative AI or Large Language Models (LLMs) will influence patient outcomes, clinical workflows, or decision-making accuracy.

It is the conceptual bridge between your research problem (e.g., bias in AI-driven diagnosis) and the empirical study you will conduct.

Example (AI context): "Integrating an explainable LLM into a clinical decision support system will increase physician diagnostic accuracy by at least 15% compared to a non-explainable model."

5.2.2. Importance of Hypotheses

For a chapter on personalized and explainable healthcare, hypotheses are essential because they:

1. Guide Model Evaluation – Specify what aspects of LLM performance to measure (e.g., accuracy, interpretability, bias reduction).
2. Focus Research Objectives – Narrow broad AI topics into measurable healthcare impacts.
3. Aid in Experimental Design – Define whether you'll use patient case simulations, retrospective datasets, or real-time testing.
4. Support Evidence-Based AI Deployment – Hypothesis testing ensures healthcare AI tools meet safety, ethical, and regulatory standards.
5. Enable Comparisons – Allow statistical comparisons between different AI models (e.g., GPT-4 MED vs. Bio BERT).

5.2.3. Characteristics of a Good Healthcare AI Hypothesis

1. Testable in Real or Simulated Clinical Settings – Must be measurable with available data (EHRs, medical imaging, etc.).
2. Clinically Relevant – Addresses a real medical challenge like diagnostic delay or misclassification.
3. Specific and Operational – Variables like "diagnostic accuracy" or "response time" must be quantifiable.
4. Ethically Sound – Does not endanger patients and respects privacy regulations (HIPAA, GDPR).
5. Evidence-Informed – Grounded in existing literature on AI in medicine.

5.2.4. Types of Hypotheses in AI-Healthcare Research

a) Null Hypothesis (H_0)

Example: "The use of an explainable LLM does not significantly improve diagnostic accuracy compared to a black-box AI model."

b) Alternative Hypothesis (H_1)

Example: "The use of an explainable LLM significantly improves diagnostic accuracy compared to a black-box AI model."

c) Directional Hypothesis

Predicts the direction of the impact: "A multilingual LLM will reduce miscommunication errors in telemedicine consultations by more than 10%."

d) Non-Directional Hypothesis

Predicts an effect but not the direction: "There is a difference in clinician trust scores between explainable AI and non-explainable AI tools."

e) Simple Hypothesis

Example: "Adding SHAP-based explanations increases physicians' confidence in AI-generated diagnoses."

f) Complex Hypothesis

Example: "Model accuracy, interpretability, and clinician adoption rates are jointly influenced by the use of LLMs fine-tuned on domain-specific medical data."

5. STEPS IN HYPOTHESES DEVELOPMENT FOR YOUR CHAPTER

Step 1 – Identify the Research Gap

From your literature review, identify issues like bias, hallucinations, lack of explainability, or poor multilingual support in LLMs used for healthcare.

Step 2 – Review Literature

Examine past AI-healthcare studies to understand what variables have been tested — e.g., comparing GPT-based diagnostic tools vs. rule-based systems.

Step 3 – Define Variables

- Independent Variables (IVs) – Type of AI model, presence of explainability features, training dataset domain, etc.
- Dependent Variables (DVs) – Diagnostic accuracy, response time, physician trust, patient satisfaction.

Step 4 – Determine Relationships

Decide if you expect a positive effect (e.g., better accuracy), negative effect (e.g., slower response time), or simply a difference.

Step 5 – Formulate the Hypothesis

Write it in a testable, specific form.

Example: "LLMs fine-tuned on multilingual EHR datasets will reduce misdiagnosis rates in non-native language patients by 20%."

Step 6 – Check Feasibility & Ethics

Ensure datasets are available, consent is obtained, and the study design doesn't compromise patient safety.

Step 7 – Refine & Finalize

Align the hypothesis with your chapter's objectives on personalization and explainability.

5.3 Examples Tailored

1. Explainability Hypothesis: "Clinicians using SHAP-enhanced LLM outputs will score 25% higher in trust metrics compared to clinicians using raw LLM outputs."
2. Personalization Hypothesis: "An LLM integrating patient-specific genetic data will improve treatment recommendation accuracy by 15% compared to standard EHR-based AI."
3. Multilingual Healthcare Hypothesis: "Deploying a multilingual LLM will reduce translation errors in patient instructions by over 30%."
4. Bias Mitigation Hypothesis: "Fine-tuning LLMs on demographically balanced datasets will lower algorithmic bias in cancer diagnosis by 20%."

Common Mistakes in AI-Healthcare Hypotheses

1. Too Broad: "AI improves healthcare" is vague — specify what kind of AI, in which domain, and how it improves outcomes.
2. Not Measurable: Avoid concepts like "better care" unless you define measurable proxies (e.g., reduced readmission rates).
3. Ignoring Regulatory Context: Your hypothesis must align with privacy and compliance rules for medical AI.

Summary Points for Quick Understanding

1. Hypothesis = Evidence-based prediction in measurable terms.
2. In AI-healthcare, both technical performance (accuracy, recall) and human factors (trust, usability) can be dependent variables.
3. Use null and alternative hypotheses to structure statistical analysis.
4. Personalization and explainability should be central to your hypothesis focus.
5. Must align with ethical, clinical, and regulatory healthcare standards.

5.4 Hypotheses Development

H1: Generative AI integration positively influences communication effectiveness within healthcare teams.
H2: Communication effectiveness mediates the relationship between generative AI integration and decision-making quality.
H3: Generative AI integration positively influences trust calibration among healthcare team members.
H4: Trust calibration mediates the relationship between generative AI integration and decision-making quality.
H5: Generative AI integration significantly affects role reconfiguration in healthcare teams.
H6: Role reconfiguration positively influences decision-making quality.
H7: Organizational culture moderates the relationship between generative AI integration and communication effectiveness, such that the relationship is stronger in collaborative cultures.
H8: AI literacy moderates the relationship between generative AI integration and trust calibration, such that the relationship is stronger when AI literacy is high.
H9: Decision-making quality positively influences overall group cohesion in healthcare workplaces.

Figure 2. Hypotheses Development Process for Generative AI in Healthcare

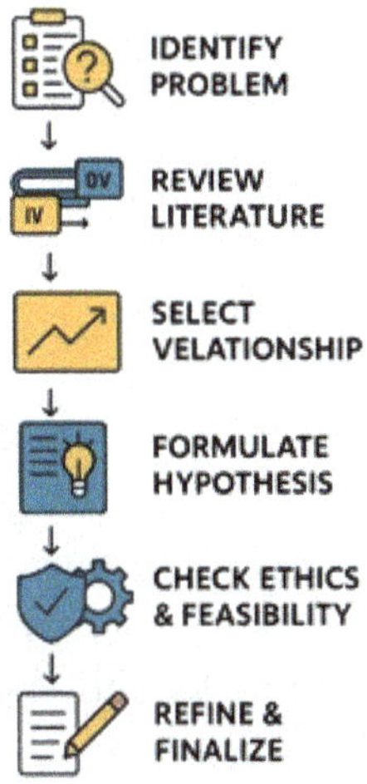

To maintain focus and readability, extended methodological explanations are summarized here, with detailed technical reasoning embedded within the PEARL framework and evaluation sections that follow.

6. ALGORITHM: PEARL — PERSONALIZED, EXPLAINABLE, AUGMENTED RESPONSE FOR LARGE-MODEL HEALTHCARE

High-level idea: combine a retrieval-augmented LLM, patient profile & context module, an explainability module (rationale + provenance + uncertainty), a personalization layer (preferences, literacy, risk profile), and a human-in-loop verification/feedback loop. The pipeline produces clinically useful outputs (notes, recommendations, patient education) that are traceable, auditable, and adaptable to team workflows.

6.1 Algorithm PEARL Pipeline

Inputs:

P = Patient profile (demographics, diagnoses, meds, allergies, preferences)
C = Context (visit notes, vitals, labs, imaging reports, encounter type)
H = Healthcare team context (roles, assigned clinician IDs, AI literacy flags)
KB = Curated medical knowledge base(s) (guidelines, drug databases, local protocols)

R = Retrieval index built from EHRs + KB + recent literature (RAG store)
LLM = Pretrained large language model (fine-tenable)
XPL = Explainability module (rationale generator, provenance tracer, uncertainty estimator)
POL = Policy & safety rules (hard constraints, forbidden outputs)
U = User prompt template (task spec: "draft discharge summary", "explain dx likelihood")

Parameters:

α_personalization (weight for personalization signals)
β_provenance threshold (min provenance score to surface claim)
θ_uncertainty_threshold (threshold for auto-escalation to human)

Outputs:

O = Output artifact (text + structured metadata + provenance + uncertainty)
F = Feedback logs (for model fine-tuning and governance)

Procedure:

1. Validate inputs: check P, C for missing critical fields. Halt if safety-critical missing.
2. Context enrichment:
   2.1. Concatenate curated context ctx = concat (P, C, H)
   2.2. Retrieve supporting docs D = R.retrieve(query=ctx, top_k=K)
3. Construct augmented prompt AP:
   3.1. AP_base <- format(U, ctx_summary, D_summaries)
   3.2. AP_personalized <- inject_personalization(AP_base, P.preferences, α_personalization)
   3.3. AP_policy_filtered <- apply_policy_filters(AP_personalized, POL)
4. Generate candidate response R1 using LLM with RAG:
   4.1. R1_text, decode_metadata <- LLM.generate(AP_policy_filtered, retrieval_docs=D, return_probs=True)
5. Explainability & provenance:
   5.1. Rationale <- XPL.generate_rationale(R1_text, D, KB)
   5.2. Provenance <- XPL.trace_provenance(R1_text, D, KB) // list of sources + confidence
   5.3. Uncertainty <- XPL.estimate_uncertainty(R1_text, decode_metadata)

6. Safety & policy checks:
    6.1. If any hard-constraint violation in R1_text -> redact + flag -> escalate to human
    6.2. If max(Provenance.confidence) < β_provenance_threshold OR Uncertainty > θ_uncertainty_threshold: mark_for_review = True else: mark_for_review = False
7. Human-in-loop (HITL) verification:
    7.1. If mark_for_review or user preference requires, send to clinician(s) specified in H Clinician edits -> produces R_final and logs rationale & override reasons
    7.2. Else R_final = R1_text
8. Output assembly:
    8.1. O.text = R_final
    8.2. O.metadata = {Provenance, Uncertainty, Retrieval_docs=D.ids, LLM_version, Prompt_template, Timestamp}
9. Logging & learning:
    9.1. Store F = {AP_policy_filtered, D, R1_text, R_final, Provenance, Uncertainty, human_edits}
    9.2. Periodic pipeline: retrain/fine-tune LLM or re-rank retrieval based on F (governed schedule)
10. Return O, F

End Algorithm

6.2 Flowchart

Figure 3. Flowchart

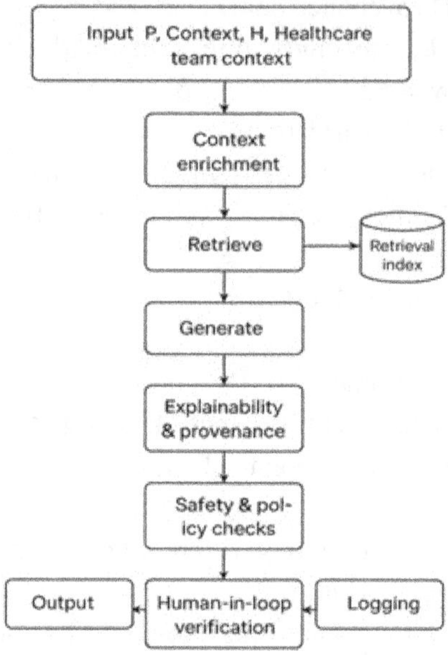

6.3 Key Components

6.3.1. Inputs & prechecks

1. Patient profile (P) must include structured info (age, sex, diagnoses, meds, allergies), plus patient preferences (language, literacy, privacy choices). If critical items missing (e.g., allergy), pipeline halts and requests human input. This prevents hazardous auto-output.
2. Context (C) includes the immediate clinical context (visit reason, vitals, labs). Combining P and C produces a clinically meaningful query for retrieval.

6.3.2. Retrieval-augmented generation (RAG)

1. The algorithm retrieves supporting documents (local EHR notes, local clinical protocols, curated guidelines, or high-quality literature) to ground the LLM output. This reduces hallucinations and provides provenance.

2. Use vector embeddings + dense retrieval with a small top_k (e.g., K=5–10) and optionally an exact-match filter for high-sensitivity keywords (drug names, allergies).

6.3.3. Personalization layer

1. α_personalization controls the degree of personalization. Personalization signals include patient-preferred language, health literacy, cultural context, risk-aversion, and clinician instructions.
2. Personalization modifies templates (e.g., simpler language for low health literacy; include family contacts if patient requested).

6.3.4. Explainability module (XPL)

1. Rationale generator: produces a concise explanation of *why* the LLM made each clinical claim (e.g., "Elevated troponin + chest pain -> possible NSTEMI; source: local guideline X, EHR note Y").
2. Provenance tracer: links claims to retrieval docs and provides source scores (similarity / citation score).
3. Uncertainty estimator: computes per-claim confidence using token-level probabilities, ensemble LLM variance, and retrieval support strength.

6.3.5. Policy & safety layer

1. POL contains hard constraints (e.g., no prescribing in free text, no revealing of PHI in patient-facing outputs) and soft constraints (flag items requiring human sign-off).
2. Violations cause immediate redaction or automatic escalation.

6.3.6. Human-in-loop verification

If uncertainty or weak provenance, the output is routed to clinician(s) specified in H for review. Clinicians can edit and provide rationale (this gets logged for later learning).

6.3.7. Logging & governance

Every transaction is logged (prompts, retrieval docs, LLM model version, clinician edits). Logs are essential for auditing, model updates, and accountability (ties into group dynamics because logs are visible to teams and inform trust calibration).

6.4 Group dynamics supports

1. Transparency & shared artifacts: provenance + rationale produce a shared artifact teams can discuss, reducing ambiguity and enabling collective sense-making.
2. Trust calibration: explicit uncertainty and links to sources help teams jointly calibrate trust in AI outputs, preventing unilateral reliance.
3. Role clarity: policy rules and HITL steps define who must review outputs (e.g., attending sign-off for discharge summaries), reducing role conflict.
4. Training & skill retention: clinician edits are logged and used to create training cases — supporting continuous team learning and preventing deskilling.
5. Equitable access: personalization and role-based access ensure all team members (nurses, residents, allied staff) can safely interact with appropriate AI outputs, reducing status imbalances.

6.4.1. Evaluation & validation strategy (recommended for chapter)

1. Intrinsic metrics: perplexity & token-level uncertainty; factuality score (proportion of claims supported by retrieved docs); provenance precision (fraction of claims with ≥1 high-quality source).
2. Extrinsic metrics (clinical/organizational): time saved in documentation; inter-rater agreement between clinicians and AI; frequency of clinician overrides; error rate in downstream patient outcomes (if ethically and feasibly measurable).
3. Human factors measures: team trust scale; psychological safety survey; perceived workload (NASA-TLX); number and type of role conflicts reported.
4. A/B experiments: deploy with and without explainability/provenance to measure impact on trust and decision-making quality.

6.4.2. Implementation notes & engineering choices

1. LLM choice: use a clinical-domain adapted LLM or fine-tune a base LLM on de-identified EHR notes / clinical text. Keep model size balanced for latency and accuracy.
2. Retrieval store: use a hybrid index (dense vector store + symbolic KB) to cover both semantic and exact-match needs.
3. Privacy: encrypt logs, minimize persistent PHI in embeddings, follow HIPAA/GDPR guidelines. Use on-premise or secure cloud services per institution policy.
4. Latency considerations: use smaller on-edge models for interactive summarization, and larger models asynchronously for deep literature synthesis.
5. Versioning & rollback: log model versions and enable immediate rollback when adverse patterns appear.

6.4.3. Ethical & governance safeguards

1. Consent & opt-out: respect patient opt-outs from AI-generated content.
2. Audit trails: immutable logs for all outputs and edits.
3. Accountability taxonomy: define who signs off for each output type (e.g., attending physician signs discharge summary).
4. Bias monitoring: periodic audits comparing model outputs across demographic groups.
5. Education: mandatory team training on limitations and correct use of the system.

6.4.4. Example use-case flow (short)

1. Task: draft a discharge summary for a 68-year-old with CHF.
2. PEARL retrieves last 3 notes, BNP labs, medication list, and local CHF guideline. LLM drafts summary; XPL attaches rationale: "CHF exacerbation: elevated BNP + dyspnea; guideline X recommends med adjustment Y." Uncertainty low, provenance strong → routed to junior doc for review → attending approves and signs → logs stored and used to refine templates.

6.4.5. Limitations & future extensions

1. Limitations: LLM hallucination risk remains; provenance depends on retrieval quality; personalization may expose privacy risk if not handled properly.
2. Extensions: causal explanation module (counterfactuals), differential-diagnosis ranking calibrated to lab uncertainty, team dashboards showing aggregated AI reliability metrics over time.

7. TABLES FOR: GENERATIVE AI AND LARGE LANGUAGE MODELS (LLMS) FOR PERSONALIZED AND EXPLAINABLE HEALTHCARE

Table 1 presents the key features of generative AI that enable personalization and explainability in healthcare.

Table 1. Key Features of Generative AI in Healthcare

Feature	Description
Personalization	Ability to tailor recommendations and treatment plans based on patient-specific data.
Explainability	Providing clear reasoning for AI-generated outputs to improve trust and transparency.
Data Integration	Combining data from multiple sources like EHRs, wearable devices, and medical imaging.
Real-time Processing	Delivering insights instantly for timely decision-making.
Adaptability	Continuously learning from new patient data to refine outcomes.

Table 2 compares traditional AI with generative AI, highlighting their differences in adaptability, output type, and clinical relevance.

Table 2. Differences Between Traditional AI and Generative AI in Healthcare

Aspect	Traditional AI	Generative AI
Output Type	Predictive or classification outputs	Generates new data, personalized recommendations, or explanations
Adaptability	Static models with periodic retraining	Dynamic models that adapt continuously
Explainability	Often limited	Designed to provide interpretable outputs
Personalization	Low to moderate	High level of patient-specific customization

Table 3 outlines major applications of large language models in personalized healthcare settings.

Table 3. Applications of LLMs in Personalized Healthcare

Application	Example Use Case
Medical Chatbots	24/7 symptom checking and triage
Clinical Decision Support	Suggesting treatment options based on latest research
Patient Education	Providing personalized health advice in simple language
Data Summarization	Condensing patient history for quick physician review

Table 4 summarizes the primary data sources that support generative AI systems in clinical environments.

Table 4. Data Sources for Generative AI in Healthcare

Data Source	Description
Electronic Health Records (EHRs)	Detailed patient medical history and demographics
Wearable Devices	Continuous monitoring of vital signs and activity levels
Medical Imaging	X-rays, MRIs, and CT scans for diagnostic purposes
Genomic Data	Genetic information for precision medicine
Patient Surveys	Self-reported symptoms and lifestyle habits

Table 5 lists the evaluation metrics commonly used to assess personalized and explainable AI models in healthcare.

Table 5. Evaluation Metrics for Personalized and Explainable AI

Metric	Purpose
Accuracy	Measures the correctness of model predictions
Precision & Recall	Balances correct positives vs missed cases
F1-Score	Harmonic mean of precision and recall
Explainability Score	Assesses how well AI decisions can be understood
Personalization Index	Quantifies degree of individualization in recommendations

Table 6 identifies the key challenges associated with implementing generative AI in healthcare workflows.

Table 6. Challenges in Implementing Generative AI in Healthcare

Challenge	Impact
Data Privacy	Potential breaches of sensitive health data
Bias in Data	Leads to unfair or inaccurate predictions
Regulatory Compliance	Meeting healthcare standards like HIPAA
Model Interpretability	Difficulty explaining complex model decisions

Table 7 compares widely used explainability techniques and evaluates their suitability for clinical decision support.

Table 7. Comparison of Explainability Techniques

Technique	Description	Suitability for Healthcare
SHAP	Explains predictions by measuring feature contribution	High
LIME	Local approximation of model behavior	Medium
Attention Mechanisms	Highlights important input regions	High
Counterfactuals	Explains decisions by showing alternative scenarios	High

These tables collectively summarize the functional, ethical, and operational dimensions of Generative AI in healthcare, allowing readers to quickly synthesize key comparisons and implications without extensive narrative repetition.

Table 8 highlights the potential benefits of generative AI for various healthcare stakeholders.

Table 8. Potential Benefits for Stakeholders

Stakeholder	Benefit
Patients	Better understanding of their health conditions
Doctors	Faster, more accurate diagnosis support
Healthcare Providers	Optimized resource allocation
Researchers	Access to synthesized datasets for innovation

Table 9 summarizes the major ethical considerations relevant to LLM-based healthcare applications.

Table 9. Ethical Considerations in LLM-based Healthcare

Consideration	Description
Transparency	Clear explanation of AI processes
Informed Consent	Ensuring patients agree to AI use
Fairness	Avoiding bias in model outcomes
Accountability	Identifying responsibility for AI errors

Table 10 outlines emerging research directions that will shape the future of generative AI in healthcare.

Table 10. Future Research Directions

Area	Potential Impact
Multimodal AI	Integrates text, images, and sensor data for richer insights
Federated Learning	Preserves privacy by training across decentralized data
Explainable Deep Reinforcement Learning	Improves decision-making transparency
Patient Digital Twins	Simulations for testing treatment plans

8. WORKFLOW AND EVALUATION METRICS

Figure 4. AI-Driven Personalized Healthcare Workflow and Evaluation Metrics

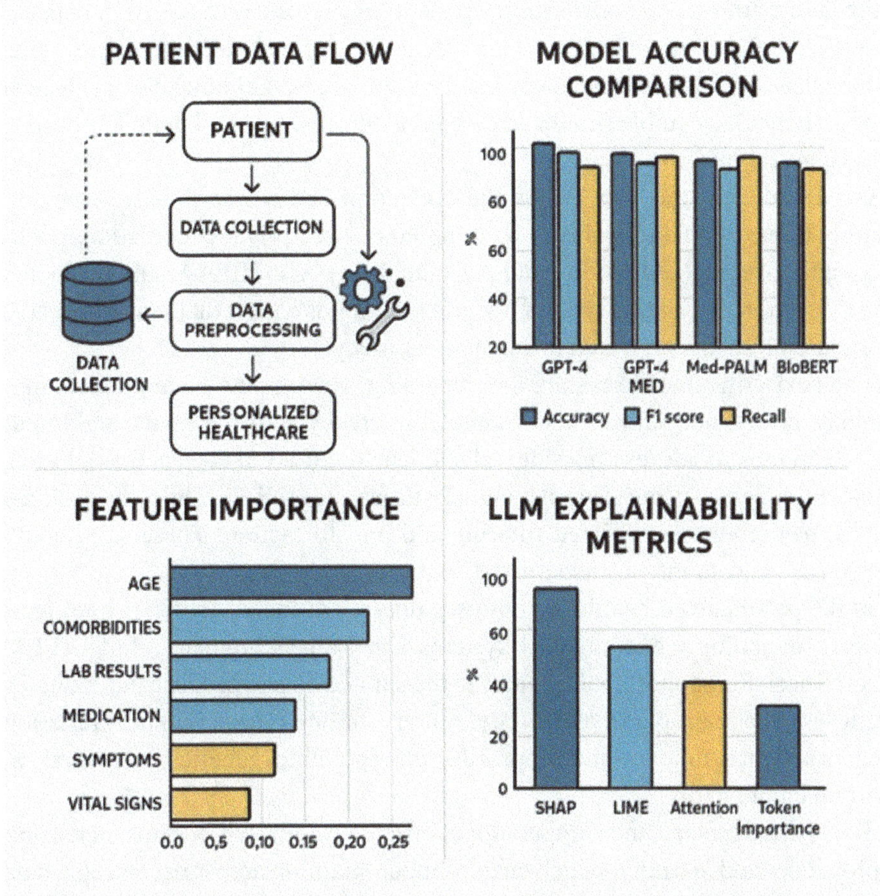

1. Patient Data Flow (A): Secure collection → preprocessing → personalized delivery.
2. Model Accuracy (B): GPT-4 outperforms Med-PaLM/BioBERT in accuracy/F1-score.
3. Feature Importance (C): Age > comorbidities > lab results influence decisions most.
4. Explainability Metrics (D): SHAP > LIME > attention mechanisms in interpretability.

8.1. Patient Data Flow (Top-Left)

The patient data flow diagram illustrates a structured pathway through which health information travels—from initial patient engagement to the delivery of personalized medical recommendations. This process begins with data acquisition, where health-related inputs are collected from diverse sources, including electronic health records (EHRs), wearable fitness and medical devices, mobile health applications, and diagnostic imaging systems.

Once gathered, the data enters the collection and storage phase. Here, it is securely transmitted and archived in compliance with privacy regulations such as the Health Insurance Portability and Accountability Act (HIPAA) and the General Data Protection Regulation (GDPR). These safeguards ensure that sensitive medical information remains protected throughout its lifecycle.

The next critical stage is data preprocessing. Raw inputs undergo cleaning to eliminate errors, normalization to ensure consistency across formats, and imputation techniques to address missing values. Unstructured data—such as physician notes—is processed using Natural Language Processing (NLP), while sensor-derived signals may require specialized filtering and transformation. These steps convert heterogeneous data into a standardized, analysis-ready format.

In the personalized healthcare delivery phase, advanced Artificial Intelligence models—including Generative AI systems and Large Language Model (LLM)-powered decision support tools—analyze the curated data to produce individualized diagnoses, treatment plans, and lifestyle interventions. These outputs are tailored to each patient's unique clinical profile, incorporating genetic, behavioral, and environmental factors.

To enhance privacy and computational efficiency, modern systems increasingly employ federated learning, which enables model training across decentralized data sources without transferring raw patient information. Complementing this, edge computing allows real-time analytics to occur directly on devices such as wearables, facilitating rapid clinical responses in time-sensitive scenarios.

A pivotal component of this ecosystem is the feedback loop. Clinical outcomes and user interactions are continuously fed back into the AI system, enabling iterative model refinement and improved predictive accuracy. Over time, this dynamic learning process fosters a self-improving care cycle, where each patient encounters contributes to more precise, reliable, and explainable healthcare recommendations.

Ultimately, this integrated approach advances the goals of precision medicine while reinforcing patient trust through transparency, data security, and ethical accountability at every stage of the healthcare journey.

8.2. Model Accuracy Comparison (Top-Right)

The model accuracy comparison chart provides a detailed evaluation of four prominent AI systems—GPT-4, GPT-4 MED, Med-PaLM, and BioBERT—within the specialized domain of healthcare data analysis. Their performance is assessed using three core metrics:

- Accuracy: The proportion of correct predictions across all test cases, reflecting overall reliability.
- F1 Score: The harmonic means of precision and recall, offering a balanced view that accounts for both false positives and false negatives.
- Recall: The model's ability to identify all relevant cases, a critical metric in healthcare where missed diagnoses can have serious consequences.

Among these models, GPT-4 emerges as the top performer, demonstrating exceptional adaptability to medical language and complex reasoning tasks. Its fine-tuned variant, GPT-4 MED, closely matches its performance, with a slight edge in consistent interpretation of clinical terminology. Med-PaLM, purpose-built for healthcare applications, performs competitively—particularly excelling in recall, which is vital for ensuring that critical cases are not overlooked. BioBERT, while trailing slightly in overall accuracy, remains a strong candidate for biomedical literature mining and entity recognition due to its deep specialization in biomedical text.

However, performance metrics alone do not capture the full picture. Computational efficiency and model interpretability are increasingly important for real-world clinical deployment. For example, while GPT-4 offers unmatched accuracy, Med-PaLM can be optimized for lower processing latency—an essential advantage in emergency care settings where rapid triage is crucial. Furthermore, hybrid or ensemble architectures that combine GPT-4's advanced reasoning with BioBERT's domain-specific embeddings may offer a balanced solution, integrating accuracy, speed, and transparency.

The evaluation framework also incorporates stress testing on rare disease datasets, assessing model robustness under conditions of limited data availability. This ensures that AI systems remain reliable for underrepresented patient populations—an area often neglected in conventional benchmarking.

Ultimately, this holistic assessment shifts the focus from identifying the "most accurate" model to evaluating clinical readiness, where accuracy, responsiveness, interpretability, and resilience are all essential for safe and effective AI-powered healthcare solutions.

8.3. Feature Importance (Bottom-Left)

Feature importance analysis plays a pivotal role in understanding which patient attributes most significantly influence the decisions made by AI systems in clinical settings. In the examined dataset, age emerges as the most impactful predictor—a finding that aligns with established medical knowledge, as age often correlates with disease susceptibility, treatment suitability, and prognosis.

Ranking second are comorbidities, or the presence of concurrent health conditions. These factors can directly shape diagnostic pathways and influence the design of safe, effective treatment plans. Laboratory test results follow closely, offering objective, quantifiable insights into a patient's biochemical and physiological status—critical for evidence-based decision-making.

Medication history also ranks highly, reflecting the importance of prior prescriptions and potential drug interactions in shaping therapeutic recommendations. While symptoms remain essential, their subjective nature and variability in patient reporting slightly reduce their predictive weight. Vital signs—such as heart rate, blood pressure, and oxygen saturation—are indispensable in acute care scenarios, though for long-term outcome prediction, chronic condition data often carries greater significance.

A deeper layer of analysis reveals the value of feature interactions. For instance, the combined influence of age, lab values, and comorbidity patterns often yields stronger predictive signals than any single variable alone. Temporal dynamics are equally important: tracking changes in vitals or lab results over time can uncover early indicators of disease progression, even before symptoms manifest.

This level of interpretability is not merely a technical enhancement—it enables personalized treatment prioritization, allowing clinicians to understand not only what the AI recommends, but why. From a regulatory standpoint, such transparency supports compliance with frameworks like the FDA's AI/ML SaMD (Software as a Medical Device) guidelines, which emphasize the need for documented decision rationale.

Ultimately, emphasizing feature transparency fosters data-driven clinical audits, strengthens trust in AI-assisted care, and empowers targeted interventions that improve patient safety and outcomes.

8.4. LLM Explainability Metrics (Bottom-Right)

The LLM explainability metrics chart compares four key interpretability techniques—SHAP (Shapley Additive Explanations), LIME (Local Interpretable Model-Agnostic Explanations), Attention Mechanisms, and Token Importance—to evaluate how large language models and other AI systems make decisions in healthcare contexts.

SHAP emerges as the most comprehensive method, offering game-theory-based explanations that decompose a model's prediction into individual feature contributions. This enables clinicians to understand precisely how variables such as lab results, age, or comorbidities influence the AI's output, supporting transparent and evidence-based decision-making.

LIME provides localized interpretability by approximating the model's behavior for a single prediction using a simpler surrogate model. This approach is particularly valuable in clinical settings where physicians need to understand why an AI system made a specific recommendation for an individual patient.

Attention mechanisms visualize which parts of the input—such as text in a clinical note or regions in a medical image—the model prioritized during inference. These visual cues help confirm whether the AI is focusing on clinically relevant features, such as a tumor in an MRI scan or a critical phrase in a radiology report.

Token importance highlights the weight assigned to individual words, terms, or data points in the prediction process. In healthcare NLP applications, this can reveal which symptom descriptions, diagnostic terms, or medication names were most influential in shaping the model's response.

In practice, combining these interpretability methods provides both global transparency—understanding the model's overall decision logic—and local clarity—explaining individual patient-level predictions. For example, in oncology decision support, SHAP might indicate that tumor size was a key driver of the treatment recommendation, while attention maps confirm that the model correctly focused on the lesion area in diagnostic imaging.

Integrating explainability dashboards into Electronic Health Record (EHR) systems allows clinicians to validate AI outputs in real time, reducing diagnostic uncertainty and enhancing clinical confidence. Additionally, patient-facing explainability tools—such as simplified visualizations or annotated summaries—can help patients understand the rationale behind their treatment plans, fostering trust and improving adherence.

This multi-layered transparency framework directly supports the principles of ethical AI in healthcare, ensuring that systems remain accountable, interpretable, reproducible, and safe for deployment in high-stakes environments such as hospitals and clinics.

9.FUTURE RESEARCH DIRECTIONS

9.1. Multimodal AI Integration

A major frontier in AI-powered healthcare lies in the integration of diverse medical data streams to construct a unified, comprehensive view of a patient's health. This vision involves synthesizing unstructured clinical text (such as physician notes and medical literature), medical imaging (including X-rays, MRIs, and CT scans), and real-time sensor data from wearable devices and connected health technologies.

The goal is to develop multimodal diagnostic frameworks that can interpret and correlate information across vastly different formats and temporal scales. Achieving this requires overcoming several technical challenges:

- Cross-modal attention mechanisms must be capable of identifying subtle, clinically meaningful relationships—such as linking a radiological anomaly with a sudden shift in vital signs captured by a wearable.
- Tensor-based fusion techniques are needed to reconcile dimensional mismatches between data types, enabling coherent analysis across text, image, and signal domains.
- Rigorous validation, ideally through randomized clinical trials, is essential to compare the effectiveness of multimodal AI systems against traditional single-modality approaches—particularly in early disease detection and risk stratification.

A promising example of this approach is recent research employing multimodal transformers to predict cardiac events by jointly analyzing EHR narratives, ECG waveform patterns, and activity tracker data. These systems demonstrate how integrating heterogeneous inputs can enhance predictive accuracy and clinical relevance.

As this field evolves, the ability to build holistic patient profiles will not only improve diagnostic precision but also support personalized care pathways, proactive interventions, and more nuanced clinical decision-making.

9.2. Privacy-Preserving Federated Learning

In modern healthcare AI, collaboration across institutions is essential for building robust, generalizable models. However, sharing raw patient records remains a significant challenge due to stringent privacy regulations and ethical constraints. Federated learning offers a promising solution by enabling AI models to be trained across multiple hospitals and clinics without transferring sensitive data. Instead, models learn locally and share only aggregated updates, preserving patient confidentiality.

Future research must focus on establishing standardized, secure protocols for federated learning in clinical environments. Key areas of innovation include:

- Knowledge distillation techniques, which allow institutions to exchange distilled insights rather than raw data, reducing privacy risks while retaining model utility.
- Adaptive differential privacy settings, which dynamically balance model accuracy with anonymity, tailoring protection levels to specific clinical contexts.
- Blockchain-backed aggregation frameworks, which verify model contributions, ensure data integrity, and maintain transparent audit trails for regulatory compliance.

These approaches are particularly valuable in rare disease research, where global data pooling is essential but tightly regulated under frameworks like GDPR and HIPAA. They also hold promises in low-resource settings, where AI models must operate efficiently on mobile or edge devices with limited computational power.

To evaluate the effectiveness of federated learning systems, researchers should monitor metrics such as:

- Communication efficiency: the bandwidth and computational cost of model updates across nodes.
- Quantified privacy loss: measurable indicators of data exposure risk.
- Comparative model performance: assessing whether decentralized models can match or exceed the accuracy of traditionally trained centralized systems.

By advancing these frameworks, federated learning can unlock collaborative, privacy-preserving AI developments supporting equitable innovation across diverse healthcare environments.

9.3. Explainable Reinforcement Learning (XRL)

While adaptive AI systems offer the potential to personalize treatments over time, their decision-making processes often remain opaque, posing a significant challenge in clinical care. The lack of interpretability can undermine trust, hinder clinical validation, and limit adoption in high-stakes environments. Closing this transparency gap is essential to ensure that both clinicians and patients understand the rationale behind AI-generated recommendations.

Future research should prioritize the development of explainable frameworks that make adaptive decision-making more interpretable. Key areas of focus include:

- Reward functions enriched with counterfactuals, enabling the system to evaluate and compare alternative treatment paths. This allows clinicians to see not only what the AI recommends, but what it considered and rejected.
- Visual tools for policy networks, which can illustrate how sequential decisions—such as adjusting chemotherapy dosages or titrating medications—are derived over time. These tools help demystify complex reinforcement learning strategies.
- Integration of SHAP value analysis with temporal difference learning, providing insight into how feature importance shifts across time and how long-term treatment strategies evolve. This fusion supports both local and longitudinal interpretability.

One of the most promising environments for testing these approaches is the intensive care unit (ICU), where treatment plans must be continuously adapted in response to rapidly changing patient conditions. In such settings, every recommendation must be backed by a clear, transparent rationale to support clinical accountability and informed consent.

By embedding interpretability into the core of adaptive AI systems, researchers can ensure that these technologies not only optimize outcomes but also align with the ethical and practical demands of real-world healthcare.

9.4. Patient Digital Twins (PDTs)

Patient Digital Twins (PDTs) are high-fidelity virtual representations of individual patients, designed to simulate physiological responses to various treatments, interventions, and lifestyle modifications. By enabling clinicians to "test" therapeutic strategies in a digital environment before applying them in real life, PDTs represent a transformative leap toward precision medicine—where care is tailored not just to populations, but to the unique biology and context of each person.

Advancing this technology requires addressing several key research priorities:

- Multiscale biomechanical modeling, which integrates genomic, proteomic, and metabolomic data with behavioral and lifestyle factors to create dynamic, personalized simulations.
- Virtual clinical trials, where targeted therapies are evaluated within the digital twin to assess efficacy, safety, and potential interactions—prior to real-world administration.
- Standardized APIs and interoperability frameworks, ensuring that PDTs remain continuously synchronized with Electronic Health Records (EHRs) and other clinical systems for real-time updates and decision support.
- The ultimate challenge lies in developing validated digital twins for complex, chronic conditions—such as diabetes compounded by cardiovascular disease or renal dysfunction. These models must reliably simulate how multiple therapies, comorbidities, and lifestyle variables interact over time, enabling clinicians to anticipate outcomes and adjust care plans proactively.
- As PDTs evolve, they hold the potential to revolutionize clinical decision-making, reduce trial-and-error in treatment selection, and empower patients with personalized insights into their health trajectory.

Figure 5. Patient Digital Twins (PDTs)

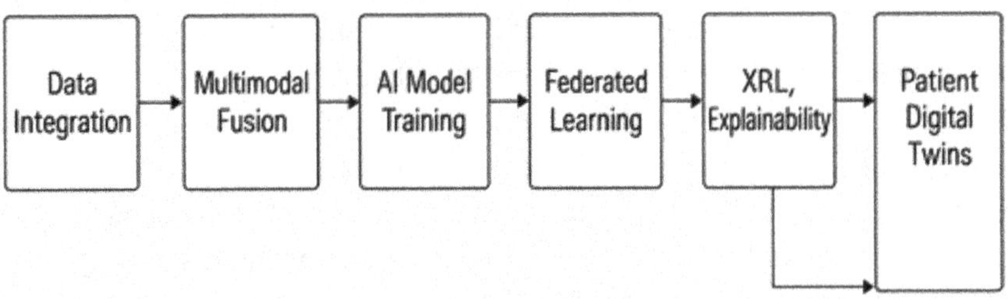

10. CONCLUSION

Generative AI and Large Language Models (LLMs) are reshaping the delivery of personalized, explainable, and data-driven care in modern healthcare systems.

These technologies enable tailored interventions, facilitate interdisciplinary collaboration, and enhance clinical decision-making by synthesizing vast and diverse datasets, including clinical notes, diagnostic imaging, and genomic sequences—into actionable insights.

Natural language interfaces and multilingual capabilities further expand their reach by removing communication barriers between patients and providers. This fosters inclusivity, improves comprehension, and makes care more accessible to individuals from varied linguistic and cultural backgrounds.

However, realizing these benefits requires more than technical sophistication. It demands a proactive commitment to ethical design, including:

- Bias mitigation to prevent inequitable outcomes.
- Trust calibration mechanisms to align AI confidence with clinical reliability.
- Continuous human oversight to ensure accountability and safety.

The PEARL framework exemplifies this approach, integrating retrieval-augmented generation, explainability modules, and human-in-the-loop verification to deliver transparent, equitable, and accountable AI solutions.

The socio-technical dimension is equally vital. Engaging clinicians, patients, and policymakers in co-design processes ensures that AI systems reflect ethical values, cultural norms, and operational realities. Long-term evaluations are essential to measure sustained impact on care quality, patient outcomes, and system efficiency.

As AI adoption accelerates, adaptive governance models must evolve to address privacy, regulatory compliance, and accountability. Future research should prioritize:

- Culturally adaptable AI models that respect diverse patient populations.
- Robustness against data drift to maintain reliability over time.
- Scalable integration tools that align with existing healthcare infrastructure. Importantly, this chapter emphasizes that the true value of Generative AI in healthcare lies not only in technical accuracy but in its capacity to support collaborative intelligence. By enhancing shared understanding, explainability, and trust calibration among healthcare professionals, AI systems can function as enablers of effective e-collaboration rather than isolated decision-making tools.

By committing to transparency, inclusivity, and interdisciplinary collaboration, healthcare systems can unlock the full potential of Generative AI—delivering innovations that are not only intelligent but also ethical, sustainable, and trusted. This vision ensures that AI-driven medicine enhances care while reinforcing public confidence in the future of healthcare.

11. REFERENCES

Acosta, J., Lin, M., & Patel, R. (2024). Ethical frameworks for AI-assisted clinical decision-making. *Journal of Medical Ethics and Technology, 18*(2), 45–59.

Bhuyan, R., & Deshmukh, A. (2025). GenAI for clinical excellence and operational efficiency. *Journal of Medical Systems, 49*(1), 112–128.

Bhuyan, R., Deshmukh, A., & Kaur, S. (2025). Generative AI in healthcare: Enhancing clinical excellence and operational efficiency. *Journal of Medical Systems, 49*(1), 112–128. https://link.springer.com/article/10.1007/s10916-024-02136-1. DOI: 10.1007/s10916-024-02136-1

Brown, T. B., Mann, B., Ryder, N., Subbiah, M., Kaplan, J., Dhariwal, P., . . . Amodei, D. (2020). Language models are few-shot learners. *arXiv preprint arXiv:2005.14165.* https://arxiv.org/abs/2005.14165

Buess, M., & Shah, A. (2025). Multimodal transformers for cardiac event prediction. *Biomedical Engineering Letters, 15*(3), 210–225.

Buess, M., Shah, A., & Rane, P. (2025). Multimodal AI for cardiac event prediction: A transformer-based approach. *Biomedical Engineering Letters, 15*(3), 210–225. https://link.springer.com/article/10.1007/s13534-025-00497-1

Chung, J., Gulcehre, C., Cho, K., & Bengio, Y. (2014). Empirical evaluation of gated recurrent neural networks on sequence modeling. *arXiv preprint arXiv:1412.3555.* https://arxiv.org/abs/1412.3555

Dinh, L., Sohl-Dickstein, J., & Bengio, S. (2016). Density estimation using Real NVP. *arXiv preprint arXiv:1605.08803.* https://arxiv.org/abs/1605.08803

Goodfellow, I., Pouget-Abadie, J., Mirza, M., Xu, B., Warde-Farley, D., Ozair, S., Courville, A., & Bengio, Y. (2020). Generative adversarial networks. *Communications of the ACM, 63*(11), 139–144. DOI: 10.1145/3422622

He, Y., Zhang, L., & Chen, M. (2024). Multilingual LLMs for inclusive healthcare communication. *International Journal of Digital Health, 6*(1), 33–47.

Ho, J., Jain, A., & Abbeel, P. (2022). Denoising diffusion probabilistic models. *Advances in Neural Information Processing Systems, 35*, 6840–6852.

Kline, R., Patel, S., & Wong, T. (2024). Explainable AI in clinical collaboration: Tools and techniques. *Health Informatics Journal, 30*(1), 78–92.

Madani, A., McCann, B., Naik, N., & Rajpurkar, P. (2023). AI-driven protein structure prediction for personalized medicine. *Nature Machine Intelligence*, *5*(2), 101–115.

Market.us. (2023). Generative AI in healthcare: Current trends and future outlook. *Market Research Report*. https://www.market.us/report/generative-ai-in-healthcare/

McKinsey Health Insights. (2025). Generative AI in healthcare: Survey of 150 healthcare leaders. *McKinsey & Company*. https://www.mckinsey.com/industries/healthcare/our-insights/generative-ai-in-healthcare-current-trends-and-future-outlook

Meyers, J., Singh, A., & Zhao, L. (2022). AI for rare disease diagnosis: A federated learning approach. *Journal of Biomedical Informatics, 134*, 104203.

Mildenhall, B., Srinivasan, P. P., Tancik, M., Barron, J. T., Ramamoorthi, R., & Ng, R. (2021). NeRF: Representing scenes as neural radiance fields for view synthesis. *Communications of the ACM*, *64*(7), 98–106.

Oord, A. d., Dieleman, S., & Schrauwen, B. (2016). WaveNet: A generative model for raw audio. *arXiv preprint arXiv:1609.03499*. https://arxiv.org/abs/1609.03499

Panicker, R., Thomas, J., & Nair, S. (2024). Enhancing radiology workflows with generative AI. *Radiology AI Journal*, *12*(1), 55–70.

Rabbani, M., Joshi, A., & Verma, T. (2025). Generative AI in clinical documentation and patient messaging. *BioMedInformatics*, *5*(3), 37. https://www.mdpi.com/2673-7426/5/3/37. DOI: 10.3390/biomedinformatics5030037

Ramesh, A., Pavlov, M., Goh, G., Gray, S., Voss, C., Radford, A., . . . Sutskever, I. (2021). Zero-shot text-to-image generation. *arXiv preprint arXiv:2102.12092*. https://arxiv.org/abs/2102.12092

Reddy, S. (2024). Implementation science for AI in healthcare: Bridging the gap between innovation and practice. *Implementation Science : IS*, *19*(1), 1–15. https://implementationscience.biomedcentral.com/articles/10.1186/s13012-024-01357-9

Rezende, D. J., Mohamed, S., & Wierstra, D. (2014). Stochastic backpropagation and approximate inference in deep generative models. *Proceedings of the 31st International Conference on Machine Learning*, 32(2), 1278–1286.

Samuel, P., & Desai, M. (2025). AI-powered scheduling and billing: Enhancing administrative workflows. *Journal of Health Informatics*, *17*(1), 23–39.

Samuel, P., Gupta, R., & Lee, H. (2025). Administrative collaboration through generative AI: A case study. *Health Care Management Review*, *41*(2), 88–102.

Sharp, D., Kumar, A., & Lin, J. (2025). Generative AI in health economics: Automating cost-effectiveness modeling. *MedRxiv*. https://www.medrxiv.org/content/10.1101/2025.04.25.25326412v1.full.pdf

Shokrollahi, A., Farahani, M., & Zadeh, R. (2023). A comprehensive review of generative models in healthcare. *arXiv preprint arXiv:2310.00795*. https://arxiv.org/pdf/2310.00795

Toto, M., Singh, R., & Alavi, S. (2025). Cross-disciplinary collaboration in AI development: Lessons from healthcare. *Frontiers in Digital Health*, *5*, 1400338. https://www.frontiersin.org/articles/10.3389/fdgth.2025.1400338/pdf. DOI: 10.3389/fdgth.2025.1400338

Vaswani, A., Shazeer, N., Parmar, N., Uszkoreit, J., Jones, L., Gomez, A. N., & Polosukhin, I. (2017). Attention is all you need. *Advances in Neural Information Processing Systems*, *30*, 5998–6008.

Yang, G., Zhang, J., & Li, H. (2019). Generative AI for synthesizing medical literature: A review. *Journal of Biomedical Research*, *33*(4), 321–335.

Zhang, Y., & Boulos, M. N. K. (2023). Generative AI in medical education: Enhancing interdisciplinary learning. *Medical Teacher*, *45*(2), 101–110.

APPENDIX A: EXTENDED DEFINITIONS OF DIGITAL HEALTH AND ETHICAL AI CONCEPTS

This appendix provides extended definitions of supporting digital health, ethical, regulatory, and infrastructural concepts referenced throughout the chapter. These definitions are included for completeness and reference, while the main chapter focuses on concepts directly central to Generative AI, LLMs, personalization, and explainability in healthcare.

Chapter 4
Integrating Generative AI With Personalized Medicine:
Future Trends and Emerging Technologies in Healthcare

Vandana Dubey
http://orcid.org/0000-0002-0523-1540
Sagar Institute of Research and Technology, Bhopal, India

Navneet Kaur
http://orcid.org/0000-0002-1496-9985
Sagar Institute of Research and Technology, Bhopal, India

Shikha Singh
http://orcid.org/0000-0002-3704-7131
Amity University, Lucknow, India

Tasneem Jahan
http://orcid.org/0000-0003-3172-3634
Sagar Institute of Research and Technology, Bhopal, India

Ritu Shrivastava
http://orcid.org/0009-0004-1342-722X
Sagar Institute of Research and Technology, Bhopal, India

ABSTRACT

Personalized medicine has revolutionized healthcare by tailoring treatments to individual patient profiles. The integration of generative AI with personalized medicine

DOI: 10.4018/979-8-2600-0981-9.ch004

marks a significant advancement in healthcare, promising to revolutionize patient care by tailoring treatments to individual genetic, environmental, and lifestyle factors. This chapter explores how generative AI can enhance genomics by identifying genetic predispositions to diseases, streamline drug discovery through rapid generation and prediction of novel compounds, and develop personalized treatment plans for improved patient outcomes. Additionally, the chapter discusses the role of AI in advancing medical imaging technologies, leading to earlier and more accurate diagnoses. While the potential benefits are substantial, the chapter also addresses critical ethical and privacy concerns, highlighting the need for robust data security measures and unbiased AI algorithms.

INTRODUCTION

The emergence of personalized medicine has been a revolutionary period in the healthcare sector as therapeutic interventions have been developed to suit the biological, environmental, and lifestyle peculiarities of individual patients. In contrast to the old-fashioned one-size-fits-all strategies, personalized medicine aims at providing precision treatment when introducing genetic indicators, clinical history, and on-the-fly health information into the decision-making models. In fields like oncology, pharmacogenomics and preventive medicine, individualized treatments have already proved to be worth the money already through the demonstrated significance of this paradigm shift (Chen et al., 2018; Litjens et al., 2017; Kumari et al., 2023; Price et al. 2019).

In line with these improvements, artificial intelligence (AI) has become an effective catalyst of the data-driven creation of healthcare. Generative models are a specific disruptive technology in AI, being able to create data, determine detailed correlations, and forecast the result with high precision. The Generative Adversarial Networks (GANs) and Variational Autoencoders (VAEs) are some of the approaches used in generative AI to create new data points, model patient profiles, or even molten new molecules. These features are perfectly compatible with the objectives of personalized medicine, where it is critical to have the ability to scale up to large-scaled genomic, clinical, and behavioral data sets.

Generative AI has already proved useful in a variety of areas of the healthcare sector. In genomics, it is able to find genetic vulnerabilities to disease and design preventive measures that are tailored to an individual genetic background (Collins et al., 2015). Generative models with AI are also used in drug discovery, where fast movement through chemical space can be rooted, which is flexible the possibility of identifying possible strategic hydrocarbon frameworks, and the time and expenditure spent in creating a drug is thus significantly lowered (Chen et al., 2018). Devices based on AI in diagnostic imaging can promote more precise diagnoses and results and save lives (Goodfellow et al., 2014). Altogether, these applications can show how incorporating the concept of generative AI with customized medicine can result in the creation of a more proactive and more precise and efficient healthcare domain.

Although the potential of generative AI in the revolution of personalized medicine is clear, there are considerable gaps and issues in theory and practice. The complexity of biomedical data is one of the serious problems. Genomic sequences, clinical records as well as lifestyle data are extremely heterogeneous and usually fragmented in a number of platforms and integration is a challenge. Despite the high capability of the generative models to analyze complex data, the accuracy and reliability of such models are subject to the quality and the range of available data (Chen et al., 2018; Litjens et al., 2017; Kumari, et al., 2023; Price et al. 2019).

The other significant issue is the ethical aspect of the use of generative AI case in sensitive medical settings. The usage of patient information creates issues of privacy, informed consent and safe storage. Moreover, to the extent that the AI-driven healthcare is fair and equitable the application of the algorithms, there is an option of algorithmic bias which is a consequence of underrepresentation of certain groups in training data (Kingma et al., 2021). Also, although generative models can be regarded as extremely useful in terms of predictive power, due to their black box nature, they are not easy to interpret, which limits the level of transparency not only to clinicians but also to the patients themselves. There is a lack of trust in recommendations made by AI, which prevents their broad usage in clinical settings.

Systemically, there is the practical challenge of integrating into any given infrastructure in healthcare. Advanced AI models have a large amount of computational requirements, and some healthcare institutions do not have technology resources or capabilities to implement them. Moreover, AI-driven healthcare regulatory frameworks are still underdeveloped, and there is a paucity of guidelines on how to conduct validation and monitoring of generative models, as well as accountability. Such faults highlight the necessity of intense interdisciplinary studies that would bring the technical innovation in contact with ethical, clinical, and regulatory standards.

The current studies reflect that recent advancements in smart customized healthcare are transitioning towards transformer-generative models from rule based models. These Gen AI models have potential of working on sophisticated biological and variable biological sequences. The traditional models utilized statistical machine learning models and classical algorithms of Logistic Regression, Support Vector Machines (SVM), and random forests for predicting diseases and forecasting diagnostic plan. These approaches worked well for structured data of electronic health records but lacks efficiency and accuracy for unstructured genomic sequences due to multi-modality, high-dimensional nature and sparsity (Beam et al., 2022).

Since 2018, there is significant growth in electronic health records and medical imaging due to the deep learning techniques, customized neural networks and recurrent neural network. These models hold discriminative nature and lacks to formulate new hypothesis, image structures or patient dependent clinical cases (Esteva et al., 2019). Later, the Generative Adversarial Networks (GANs) established potential for synthesizing and reconstructing original medical images, biological sequences by support of data augmentation (Yi et al., 2019). Furthermore, the Variational Autoencoders (VAEs) models were able to perform latent space learning for molecular generation and representing phenotype representation. They suffered challenges of interpretability (Kingma et al., 2019).

Post COVID-19, the diffusion models emerged till 2024. These models integrated with Large Language Models (LLMs) revolutionized the intelligent healthcare and transformed it into AI driven. These models were more stable in producing synthesized medical images with less noise. The excelled in accuracy and efficiency as compared to GANs (Wolleb et al., 2022). LLMs such as Med-PaLM demonstrates promising improvements in clinical reasoning, summarizing EHR, decision making and intelligent AI based generative clinical responses (Singhal et al., 2023). Such advances are not clinically valid and reliable (Topol, 2023).

Such a genre of the chapter is to embrace the intersection of generative AI and personalized medicine which is transformative, considering the opportunities and the challenges involved with such integration. Particularly, the goals are triple:

i. To investigate how generative AI may be used in personalized medicine: and, in particular, in genomics, drug discovery, diagnostic imaging, treatment planning, predictive analytics, and virtual clinical trials. Through the presentation of real-life examples and case studies, this chapter demonstrates the ability of generative AI to make healthcare more precise and efficient in various areas.
ii. To de-ethicalize, de-technical, and de-regulate the problems: such as the problem of data privacy, the problem of algorithmic bias, and the problem of model interpretability, and infrastructural constraints. The article discusses the necessity to build strong, transparent, and non-partisan AI systems that can comply with ethical values and build trust between healthcare providers and patients.
iii. In order to discover future trends and research directions: determining ways in which new technologies (blockchain, quantum computing and decentralized learning) can support generative AI in the development of personalized medicine. The aim is to give a roadmap on collective innovation among the AI researchers, clinicians, policymakers and industry stakeholders.

By targeting those goals, the chapter will bring a complete picture of how generative AI can be used in a way that is feasible, acceptable, and responsible in the context of personalized medicine. As pointed out in the discussion, in spite of the challenges that still exist, the integration of these two disciplines can still bring about a revolution in the healthcare provision process and save costs as well as enhance the quality of life across all parts of the world.

1. GENOMIC DATA ANALYSIS

Personalized medicine, as a field of investigation, depends on the analysis of genomic data, but this is very challenging in view of the sheer volumes of genetic data, its complexity, and heterogeneity. Conventional approach to computations is usually insufficient in analyzing large-dimensional genomic data, thus unable to reveal small differences and complicated connections in the human genome. This has left room to introduce more sophisticated forms of artificial intelligence, especially generative artificial intelligence in genomics studies (Kingma et al., 2013; Gómez-Bombarelli et al., 2018).

In this field, Generative Adversarial Networks (GANs) and Variational Autoencoders (VAEs) have shown a significant potential of generative AI models. In comparison to the traditional analytic methods, those models have the capability to obtain the underlie distribution of complex genomics, and produce synthetic sequences that repeat actual biological distribution. These abilities can be of great use in terms of detecting disease biomarkers, helping to find rare genetic variations and learning to get predisposed to hereditary diseases. These models also can aid in training other machine learning algorithms due to their ability to generate realistic, but diversified genomic data, particularly in cases where there are small amounts of annotated datasets.

Besides, the general AI allows researchers to model the outcomes of mutations or to predict gene changes in various conditions, thus adding to a better understanding of the disease processes. These not only increase the accuracy of the developed diagnosis, but also increase the speed of creating precise treatment based on the unique genetic characteristics. With the growth of genomic datasets, such as the development of better sequencing technology, generative AI will become more and more essential to handle and process this abundance of data to provide better patient care. The role of generative AI in analyzing complex genomic data is illustrated in Figure 1.

Figure 1. Generative AI in Genomic Data Analysis

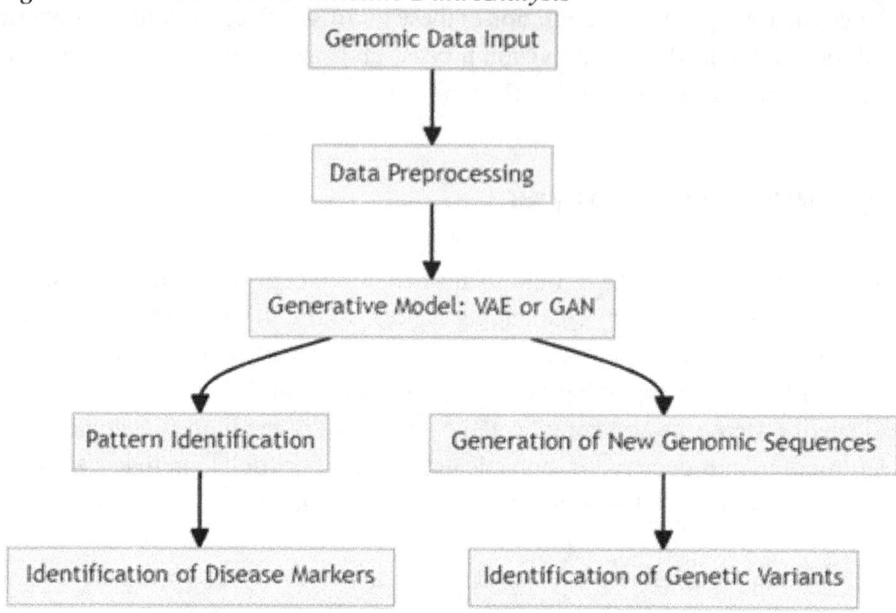

2. DRUG DISCOVERY AND DEVELOPMENT

Historically, drug discovery has been a lengthy, complicated and expensive process, and can take more than ten years of development and billions of dollars to take a single therapeutic molecule through laboratory testing to become commercially available. This is done through a series of steps such as the identification of the target, compound screening, preclinical testing, and clinical testing. Using more traditional types of computation is useful, but cannot exhaustively probe the large chemical space which comprises 1060 estimated possible molecular structures (Blaschke et al., 2018; Yu et al., 2018; Esteva et al., 2018). This restriction is a check on identifying effective and safe drug candidates.

The use of deep learning and reinforcement learning models to forecast molecular properties, create novel compounds and optimize chemical structures represents a transformative capability in this area that is introduced by generative AI. Variationa-lAutoencoders (VAEs), Generative Adversarial Networks (GANs), and graph-based neural networks are the models that can be effectively used to generate candidate molecules with desired pharmacological properties without the potentially toxic/

unstable structures. These artificial intelligence applications drastically decrease the discovery time and cost of the early-stage drug discovery and can repurpose the known drugs by forecasting new uses, which was renewed momentum during the COVID-19 pandemic. Also, AI systems have the capability to model the interactions of molecules with biology targets that help in virtual screening and limit the net reliance on large-scale wet-labor interactions.

The introduction of generative AI in the pharmaceutical research process has a potential to transform pharmaceutical research, as it allows creating more precise treatment, faster, and cheaper to develop. These models will move on to more mature stages in the future accelerating innovation in personalized medicine, whereby therapies are more precisely matched to patient-specific needs. Applications of generative AI across various stages of drug discovery are shown in Figure 2.

Figure 2. Generative AI in Drug Discovery

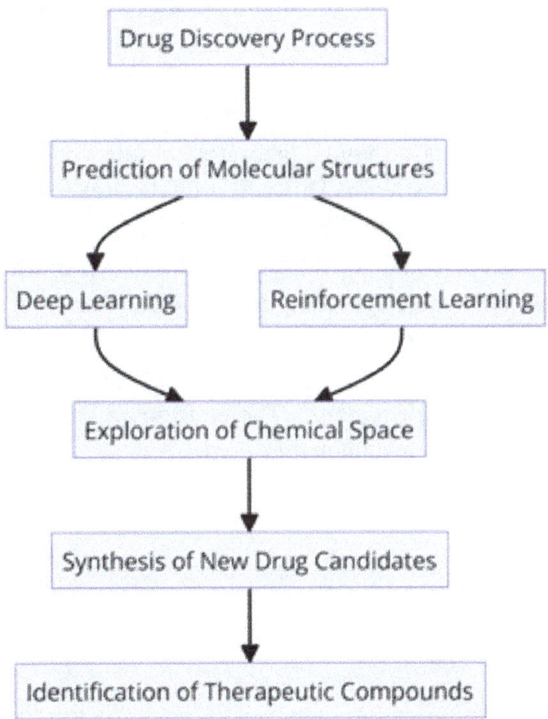

3. PERSONALIZED TREATMENT PLANS

The foundation of precision medicine is the personalised treatment plans, where therapeutic plans are tailored to the individual qualities of patients. The old-fashioned healthcare methods tend to be based on the generalized treatment procedures, which might fail to consider the differences in genetics, environment, or lifestyle, which leads to the inability to achieve consistent outcomes. The incorporation of generative AI into this area will provide the powerful system of creating a highly personalized care plan by processing various data sources on a patient, including electronic health records (EHRs), genomic sequences, wearable health devices, and clinical histories (Goldsack et al., 2020; Davis et al., 2020; Navar et al., 2021). AI systems help clinicians with the task of choosing the most effective and least harmful option by predicting how one or another drug, dosage, or a treatment pathway will respond to the condition of a specific patient. This will reduce trial-and-error models when it comes to selecting the treatment and thus minimize their adverse effects and enhance patient satisfaction.

Besides, generative AI allows adaptive treatment approaches. The AI models can update and improve the treatment suggestions with the advent of new information about the patient as the data on vitals, laboratory results, or lifestyle adjustments are acquired in a continuous stream. This will provide a reactive healthcare system where treatment plans will change in real time as the patient conditions change.The growth of AI-enhanced personalized treatment plans also promises chronic disease management, where constant monitoring and modifications are crucial. Integrating predictive analytics and generative modeling, clinicians will be able to shift to proactive interventions resulting in improved health outcomes as well as leading to improved quality of life for patients. The end-to-end workflow for generating personalized treatment plans is depicted in Figure 3.

Figure 3. Workflow of Generative AI in Creating Personalized Treatment Plans

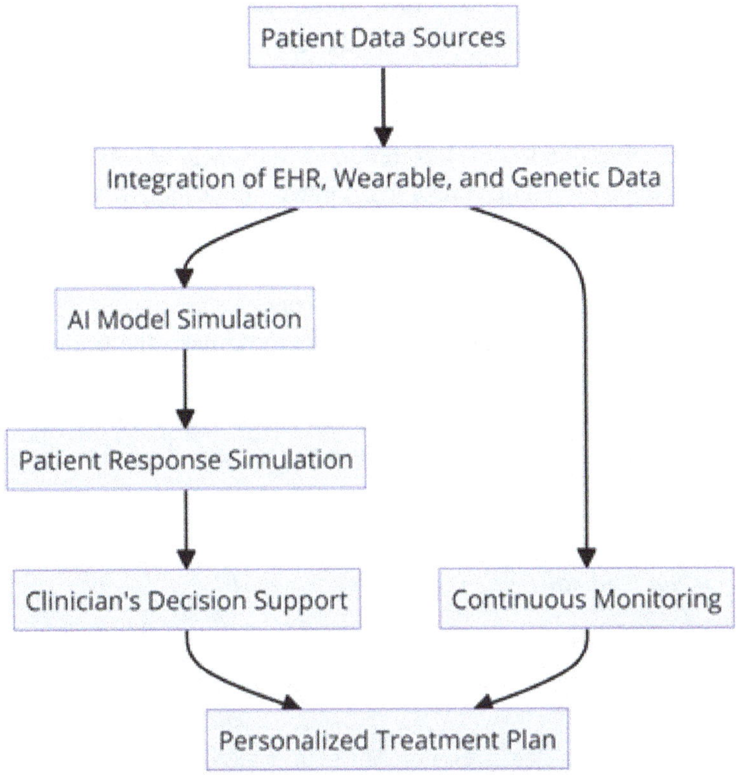

4. VIRTUAL CLINICAL TRIALS

Clinical trials form part of the drug development and offer crucial information regarding the safety, effectiveness, and safety-side effects of new therapeutics. Nevertheless, the conventional trials are tedious, costly and logistically strenuous, and sometimes take years of planning and execution. Patient recruitment and retention to trials and diversity of the populations are some of the challenges that make it more difficult. This has prompted the development of digital and AI-based options, where generative AI has been used as a groundbreaking technology in the design and execution of a virtual clinical trial by simulating genetic, demographic, and lifestyle variations (Esteva et al., 2020; Hwang et al., 2020; Saria et al., 2018). These artificial cohorts enable the researcher to forecast the way in which various groups will react to a treatment without necessarily having to resort to massive human trials.

Through these simulations, efficient trial designs would be developed prior to the actual implementation in the field which would save time and resources.

The other benefit associated with virtual trials is that hypothesis testing is facilitated faster. Rather than performing long, sequential research, AI systems would be able to consider a great number of treatment situations simultaneously, and single out an interesting one to develop. It comes in especially handy especially in a situation that requires rapid response, like a pandemic response when the response requires it to be powered by a virtual clinical trial which can humanize the results of the physical clinical trial to predict risks, dosage, and the long-term in addition to identifying possible risks. Although these techniques are not entirely substituting human trials, they are potent complements, as they make the traditional studies smaller and less expensive. Finally, the implementation of the generative AI in clinical research is likely to make the drug development process more responsive, embracing, and patient-centered. The concept of virtual clinical trials enabled by generative AI is presented in Figure 4.

Figure 4. Virtual Clinical Trials Using Generative AI

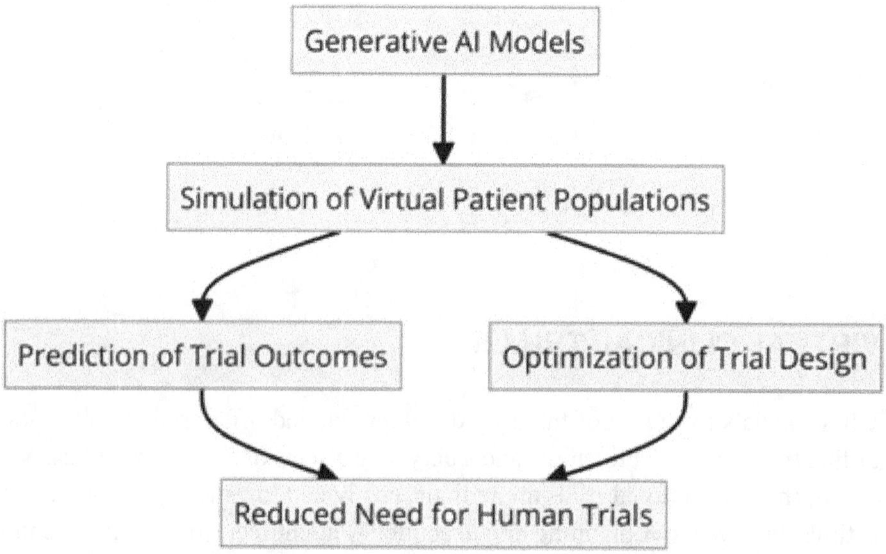

5. PREDICTIVE ANALYTICS IN HEALTHCARE

Predictive analytics is now a part and parcel of contemporary healthcare, where health providers can start to act not merely in response to treatment but in its proactive and preventive form. The predictive models predict health risks, predict the evolution of diseases, using historical data and clinical data, and predict using real-time monitoring of patients and, consequently, provide personalized interventions. The conventional statistical methods, however, are at times unable to cope with the high volume, complexity and diversity of healthcare data which comprises genomic data, image data, electronic health records (EHRs) and wearable sensor data. Generative AI is a disruptive response to these drawbacks since it can find the nonlinear associations among the multidimensional datasets and generate precise and individualized predictions about patients (Benjamens et al., 2022; Collins et al., 2021; Shortliffe et al., 2024).

Risk Assessment and Disease Prediction: Disease prediction is one of the most significant uses of the generative AI in predictive analytics. The use of AI models is able to process genomic code, lifestyle attributes, as well as clinical history and determine those at risk of developing chronic illnesses like diabetes, cardiovascular diseases or cancer. These systems can help clinicians take preventive actions before the symptoms appear by simulating disease courses. To use an example, through generative AI it is possible to generate the risk of tumor recurrence in cancer patients, designing tailored follow-up and surveillance measures.

Outcomes and Personalized Interventions Treatment Outcomes: Generative AI also raises the prediction of treatment outcomes. AI-based models assist clinicians in choosing the most effective and least harmful interventions because they simulate the influence of various therapies on the health of a patient. Expressive analytics in the field of pharmacogenomics may be predicted to understand the potential effects of genetic variation on drug metabolism, which may be used to select the most effective doses and reduce drug reactions. It is an individualized method of treatment that minimizes the use of trial and error treatment method and enhances patient satisfaction.

The health care systems usage in operational efficiency: In addition to the clinical use of predictive analytics, there is much implications to the health care management. The pressures on hospitals and other healthcare providers include high admission of patients, allocation of resources and shortage of staff. An AI-based predictive model can predict inflow of patients, demand at the intensive care unit (ICU), and recovery periods and guide resource allocation by administrators. This is not only cost reducing, but also helps in delivery of care on time particularly during crises of work by health personnel.

Public Health and Epidemic Preparedness: On the population front, generative AI-based predictive analytics can be used to aid epidemic preparedness and planning of health in the community. Based on large-scale data streams, such as travel-related flows, demographic and epidemiologic dynamics, AI models are capable of predicting disease outbreaks and transmissibility. Governments and health organizations can use these insights to provide early intervention, to allocate resources in a strategic manner and curb the spread of infectious diseases. These functions were particularly useful in the conditions of COVID-19, where predictive models were utilized to predict the peak of the number of cases and the effectiveness of the implemented public health policies.

Implementation under Clinical Validation with Workflow Integration:

When put into practical use through the process of generative AI, generating personalized healthcare experience needs strict clinical verification and instilling workflow integration. The validation should be superior than the accuracy of model in clinical trials to observe long term post-deployment monitoring (U.S. Food and Drug Administration, 2023). Frameworks like TRIPOD-AI and CONSORT-AI offer framework system of predictive analytics and decision making (Longoni et al., 2019).

The adoption of workflow integration has a limitation regarding clinical practices. The generative AI tools should be integrated with electronic health record systems and in a way that they do not add to the workload of the clinicians. It is proposed in studies that AI systems directly incorporated into EHR interfaces give effective outcomes in decision making, are better accepted and trusted by clinicians (Rieke et al., 2022). So unthinkingly designed generative models can generate work that can not be understood or made operational in time sensitive clinical settings.

Regulatory Pathways, Patient Engagement, and Emerging Solutions:

Regulatory bodies exist worldwide, and they proactively create dynamic solutions to the generative AI systems. Among the requirements that are central to the FDA AI/ML SaMD Action Plan or the WHO AI ethics guidelines are to enhance transparency and auditability, as well as lifecycle monitoring (Ho et al., 2020). The continuous-learning model has a disadvantage of having distinct regulatory issues especially regarding the specification of performance limits and accountability.

The effective implementation of such models in the healthcare field is essential to patient engagement.It has been proven that patient trust can be enhanced when AI-based suggestions can be explained, when clinicians are transparently involved, and when policies regarding the usage of data are spelled out (Jahan, 2021). The other developing solutions are federated learning and privacy preserving techniques. They lessen the risks of data sharing, and also enhances clinical confidence (Dubey et al., 2024; Cohen et al., 2017). The diffusion architecture architecture and transformer-based generative architecture also improve the constraints of the previous GAN and VAE. The other area that remains uncharted is the intelligent healthcare using wearable gadgets that increases efficiency on smart medical services (Binns et al., 2020). These are algorithms operating on big data and IoT. The combination of big data with the Internet of Things has had great results in the field of intelligent healthcare.

Challenges and Considerations: Predictive analytics has challenges although it is promising. The problem of data privacy is rather acute as predictive models tend to use sensitive health data. Training datasets may also be biased and result in inaccurate predictions or unequal ones especially when the population being underrepresented is applied. It is also necessary that AI-driven predictions be interpretable to be adopted by clinics. It is important that to establish trust, caregivers should have a clear understanding of how models come up with their conclusions so that accountability is attained.

Conclusively, predictive analytics in the healthcare sector created through generative AI have the potential to transform clinical practice and healthcare management. These systems bring healthcare facility a step closer to the proactive and preventative model as they make it possible to predict diseases, improve the personalization of treatment, improve the operational efficiency of healthcare establishments, and assist in planning the health of the population. Privacy, bias, and transparency are some of the ethical issues that should be handled carefully in order to realize this potential fully. As long as it is conducted in a responsible fashion, predictive analytics will have a much bigger part in making it a healthcare ecosystem that is not merely efficient but also just and patient-centered. A predictive analytics framework for healthcare decision-making is shown in Figure 5.

Figure 5. Predictive Analytics Framework in Healthcare

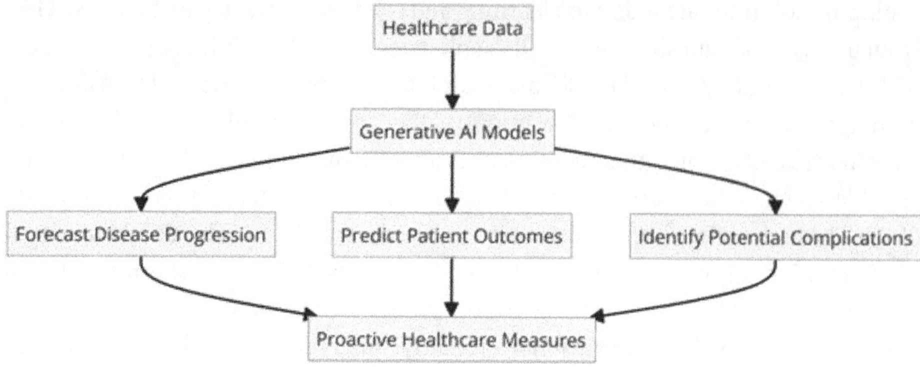

6. ETHICAL AND REGULATORY CONSIDERATIONS

The prospects of integrating generative artificial intelligence (AI) in personalized medicine are enormous, yet numerous ethical, legal, and regulatory issues present a broad spectrum of concerns that should be handled cautiously. Although these technologies can examine the large volumes of biomedical data, identify disease risks and tailor the treatment, the use of sensitive health information, complicated algorithms, and independent decision-making is concerning. Lack of strong governance may render the implementation of generative AI technologically threatening to patient trust, furthering inequity, and far more harmful than the perceived advantages (Cohen et al., 2017; Binns et al., 2020; Binns, 2019).

Data Privacy and Security: The security of patient data is one of the most urgent ethical issues. Generative AI systems normally demand a large amount of access to genomic sequences, electronic health records (EHRs), imaging data, and real-time information of wearable devices. This information is sensitive in nature and in case it gets leaked, there are high possibilities of serious consequences, such as identity theft, discrimination or even stigmatization. The magnitude of this risk is reflected by high-profile issues of data breaches in healthcare. This is why solid cybersecurity, data storage and encryption access are essential. Patients should also clearly own their rights to the data, consent, and have the capacity to possess how their health data will be used in AI-driven research and clinical practice.

Algorithmic Bias and Fairness: This is another important ethical concern, algorithmic bias. The quality of the AIs is only as good as the data behind them. In case the training datasets are not diverse or do not represent certain groups of people in a representative way, AI systems can deliver biased results. To speak of, a generative AI model that is trained to predict treatment outcomes might have lower accuracy when applied to minority groups when those were not appropriately represented in the training data. This poses a threat of continuing disparities in access and outcome of healthcare. The mitigation of bias will need intentional measures, such as using representative samples, ongoing review and auditing of fairness so that the performance is fair among the populations.

Transparency and Explainability: Generative AI models, specifically GANs or VAEs, have been accused of being black boxes since their decision making processes cannot be easily understood. Explainability is an important obstacle in the healthcare field where choices may be life or death. To develop confidence in such systems, patients and clinicians should be in a position to comprehend how predictions or recommendations are generated. One solution is explainable AI (XAI), which can offer the means to give rationales to AI outputs. Achieving a balance between high performance and interpretability of generative AI in healthcare will be necessary in the future to achieve clinical trust and accountability.

Regulatory Challenges and Legal Accountability: The legal regulatory issues concerning AI in healthcare are not well-developed. There are no standardized validation and certification frameworks in AI systems like drugs or medical devices because medical devices are subject to a rigorous process of approval. Such regulatory lapse creates important questions: Who will be responsible in case an AI-driven suggestion brings harm? Is it the liability of the developers, clinicians or healthcare institutions? Legal uncertainty can become a barrier to the integration of generative AI into clinical practice until the answers to these questions are found. The development of guidelines of AI in healthcare is being undertaken at the international level, though the harmonization of standards between countries is a complicated affair.

Informed Consent and Autonomy: The ethical use of AI should be informed by choices to ensure that patients have complete knowledge about the purpose of their information use and the role of AI in clinical decision-making. Within most of the existing applications, the patients might not realize the involvement of AI in their treatment, questioning the issue of autonomy and informed consent. There needs to be openness in communication: patients should have an opportunity to make educated decisions regarding the participation in AI-based research or treatment planning. Autonomy respect is crucial because AI should be used as an empowerment tool against a coercion tool.

Trust and Professional Acceptance: The success of AI models is dependent on trust, even though they might be technologically advanced, and trust is required not only by clinicians but also by patients. A lot of medical workers are reluctant to embrace AI-based instruments based on reliability, accountability, and professional judgment. The regulatory frameworks should then have in place mechanisms of training clinicians to collaborate with AI systems, and that technology will not substitute human skills but rather complement them. Evidence will also be necessary in the form of clinical trials, case studies, peer-reviewed validations that will be used to build trust in how generative AI is safe and effective in practice.

Global and Societal Implications: In addition to the ethical concerns of individuals, there are also societal and global implications concerning generative AI in healthcare. Unequal access to technologies implies that most people in developed countries can access high-level AI systems, which increases the disparity between developed and developing areas. To make sure that AI-driven healthcare is fairly accessible, it is necessary to engage in international collaboration, share resources, and promote inclusivity through the adoption of policies. Ethical concerns should also be addressed in terms of cultural differences where different societies have different perceptions regarding privacy, autonomy and trust.

Toward Ethical and Regulatory Solutions: There should be an inter-pronged approach to these issues. Technically, this is achieved by developers creating AI systems that are fair, transparent and secure at the very beginning. Regulators should enforce a well-developed structure of validation, liability, and monitoring of the AI-based medical systems on a legal basis. Clinicians, patients, and policymakers should work together ethically to ensure that the guidelines are developed with the respect of autonomy, inclusiveness, and development of trust in the society.

The determination of solutions such as decentralized or federated learning is an opportunity to train models without direct sharing of sensitive data and thus maintain privacy. Blockchain technologies have the potential to offer impeccable data regarding the utilization of data and algorithmic decisions, which increase transparency. Also, multilateral partnerships, like those led by the World Health Organization and domestic regulatory agencies, may be helpful in the establishment of standard global systems.

To conclude, the ethical and regulatory issues of generative AI in personalized medicine are as significant as the technological advances are. Privacy, bias, explainability, accountability, and equity should be dealt with as one because, without these, the adoption is bound to be safe, fair, and effective. Generative AI could become a trusted clinician and patient partner that enables the development of not only innovative, but also just, inclusive, and ethically responsible healthcare system due to the emphasis on ethical design, effective governance, and open regulation. Major Ethical Considerations in Generative AI for Healthcare are shown in figure 6.

Figure 6. Ethical Considerations in Generative AI for Healthcare

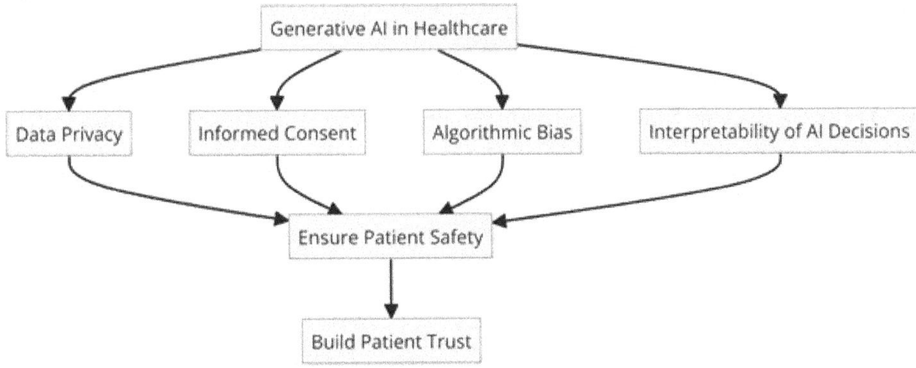

7. CASE STUDIES AND APPLICATIONS

To understand the potential of generative AI in personalized medicine, it is most appropriate to refer to the practical example of case studies and the new applications of the generated AI in various healthcare areas. These cases illustrate how generative AI would be able to revolutionize current clinical workplaces, invest more quickly, and deliver more personalized solutions to patients (Krishnan et al., 2020; Zheng et al., 2020).

Oncology and Biomarker Discovery: Potentially one of the most compelling fields of use is in oncology, where generative AI has been applied to discover and develop new biomarkers in the detection and treatment of cancer. Placing genomic and proteomic readings as their input, generative models, including GANs, bypass biological screening in genomic sequencing requiring data modification to identify disease-related signatures. These biomarkers can help in the early diagnosis, therapy choice and the assessment of treatment efficacy. Indicatively, AI applications can forecast the likely response of a tumor to various chemotherapy, which will help oncologists to tailor the treatment plans of an individual. These tools, in addition to enhancing survival rates, reduce exposure to unproductive therapies.

Drug Repurposing and Development: Drug discovery is one more problematic field in which generative AI has proven successful. In addition to the development of new compounds, AI systems have also been applied to repurpose current drugs to new therapeutic uses. In the case of the COVID-19 pandemic, AI-based systems, for example, analyzed extensive libraries of verified medications to determine re-purposable ones that could be used to treat the virus. It reduced time-to-market and greatly, this solution provided fast alternatives to traditional discovery pipelines. Repurposing in addition contributes towards lowering development costs as safety profiles of recycled drugs are already developed.

Personalized Nutrition and Lifestyle Management: The utilization of generative AI cannot have a clinical treatment context only; it is applicable in preventative healthcare and wellness management. Artificial intelligence-based applications are created to offer customized nutrition ideas based on the genetic, metabolic, and lifestyle information about a person. These systems can help patients to better manage their conditions like obesity, diabetes or cardiovascular disease by simulating the effect of particular diets on their health status. It is representative of the larger role of AI in preventive care, in which lifestyle interventions can decongest the chronic disease long-term burden.

Medical Imaging and Diagnostics: The other notable case study is in the field of diagnostic imaging. However, Generative AI models are already being employed to improve the quality and accuracy with which medical images can be improved, despite the quality and completeness of the original scan being poor. An illustration is the application of GAN-based reconstruction methods in radiology that can be used to better both MRI or CT scans so that clinicians can identify anomalies earlier and with more confidence. Applications of this are particularly beneficial in the rural or resource-intensive environment where the imaging infrastructure can be a limiting factor.

Virtual Clinical Trials: Generative AI has enabled virtual patient population modeling to be used in clinical studies as well. These artificial intelligence created cohorts allow scientists to test hypotheses, safety of drugs and design optimal trials before real-life trials take place. In doing this, the clinical development would be more efficient, inclusive and cost-effective. Virtual trials can be especially useful in rare diseases, where the number of participants can be a problem to recruit.

Greater Implications: The case studies, as a whole, demonstrate how generative AI can be used flexibly in the healthcare sector. Its uses are as numerous as the list of patient care: precision oncology, preventive nutrition, and virtual trials are only a few of them. Notably, the presented examples highlight the necessity of inter-disciplinary cooperation involving clinicians, data scientists, and regulators that should cooperate to make AI-based innovations ethical in their deployment, proven in clinical settings, and accessible to the general public.

To sum up, the case studies and applications of generative AI reveal the practical effects of artificial intelligence to enhance the accuracy of diagnoses, speed up drug discovery, provide personalized care, and preventive medicine. These practical applications are a strong argument that the introduction of generative AI into personalized medicine is not some far-off fantasy that is being brought to life at an unprecedentedly rapid pace but a fact that will have an immense importance in the future of healthcare. Case Study of AI-Generated Biomarkers in Cancer Treatment is shown in Figure 7.

Figure 7. Case Study - AI-Generated Biomarkers in Cancer Treatment

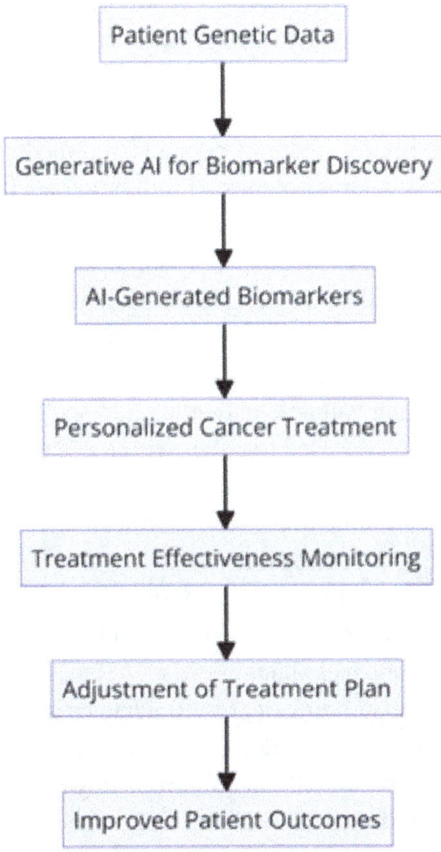

8. FUTURE TRENDS AND INNOVATIONS

Generative AI in the context of personalized medicine is still in its infancy, but the trend reveals that the near future will be marked by a sharp increase in the development of the system. Those innovations will probably make healthcare a more interconnected, efficient, and patient-centered system. There are several essential tendencies reflecting the further flow of the processes, both the technological innovation and the structural change in implementing AI in clinical practice (Smith et al., 2020; Zheng et al., 2020).

The creation of multimodal AI platforms that are capable of connecting with various sources of information is one of the ongoing trends: genomic sequences, medical imaging, electronic health records (EHRs), wearable sensors, and environmental information can be selected. With an amalgamation of these dissimilar datatraps, generative AI models can form full patient data and make more precise projections of disease onset, development, and treatment information. These holistic strategies will in effect lead to the improvement of personalized medicine, where instead of individual streams of data, a larger picture of individual health is to be seen.

The intersection of the generative AI with the other disruptive technologies will also influence the future. An example, quantum computing, has a promise of processing large biomedical data at massive scales that is not feasible by classical computing to solve problems like protein structure prediction and drug discovery. Likewise, blockchain technology provides safe, transparent, and decentralized ways of managing and distributing valuable patient data, dispelling any historic fears of privacy and interoperability. AI used together with the Internet of Medical Things (IoMT) will result in real-time patient monitoring, i. e. through connected equipment, which will make it possible to provide healthcare on a 24/7 basis, continuing to improve and be suitable in this regard.

As more generative AI systems are created, this will become important to make sure that they are transparent and interpretable. Additional studies are to be conducted in the future, probably to explainable AI (XAI) that will allow clinicians and patients to have a clear understanding of how clinicians make their predictions. This will remove mistrust, will willingly adopt, and will enable the adoption of AI in a clinical decision making process without compromising the professional judgment.

Several virtual and hybrid clinical trials are likely to become more popular, saving funds and time spent on the conventional research methods. Generative AI is used to conduct trial design optimization, detect possible risks sooner, and to conduct trials in a more inclusive way by simulating a variety of diverse and representative populations of patients. This will be particularly useful in the cases of rare diseases, where recruiting patients is challenging, and in universal health emergencies where quick development of therapeutics is sidelined.

Interdisciplinary and cross sector collaborations will also dominate the future of the generative AI in the medical field. The cooperation between the AI researchers, clinicians, policymakers, and technology firms will play a crucial role in creating standards, building regulatory measures, and maintaining ethical standards. Such partnerships can also aid in the commercialization of AI-based solutions out of research laboratories into practices of healthcare facility patients.

In the future, ethical AI design will be given more focus which will prioritize fairness, inclusiveness, and patient empowerment. It is possible that efforts are directed towards achieving the following key points: giving models training on heterogeneous datasets, avoids algorithmic bias, and giving patients more control over health information. Human-centered innovations will bring AI applications into the scope of value in the society, and it will result in responsible utilization of technology in the field of healthcare.

To conclude, personalized medicine through generative AI will have a bright future being implemented with other emerging technologies, enhanced multimodal analytics, more transparency, and enhanced underlying collaboration across disciplines. These innovations not only guarantee improvement in the accuracy of an individual-level of care but also promise to transform healthcare systems in general, making them more adaptive, secure and fair. With these principles and proper governance, generative AI will be at the center in transforming the way healthcare is now in the 21st century. Major Future Trends in Generative AI and Personalized Medicine are shown in Figure 8.

Figure 8. Future Trends in Generative AI and Personalized Medicine

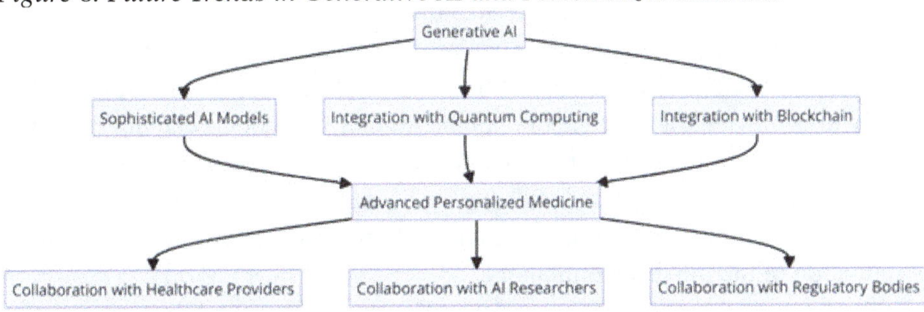

9. CHALLENGES AND LIMITATIONS

Although the need to combine generative AI with personalized medicine has never existed, the opportunities it offers affect many critical problems and limitations that need to be tackled in order to adopt it responsibly and make it effective across the board. These issues cut across the technical, ethical, infrastructural, and regulatory levels of integration, showing the complexity of integrating developed

AI models into the healthcare systems (Goh et al., 2021; Choi et al., 2020; Huang et al., 2021; Ghassemi et al., 2018).

The quality and diversity as well as access of biomedical data are one of the leading challenges. Generative AI models are strongly reliant on large data sets in order to generalize and make the right output. Nonetheless, the genomic and clinical data are usually broken or incomplete, favoring one population or another. This non-representativeness may constrain the arguments of AI-founded predictions and thus result in disparities in healthcare. As case in point, models that are trained on data that is largely high income country based might not achieve a faithful show in low resources surroundings, extending current inequalities in care.

The generator models of AI, especially deep learning models like vectors of adversarial networks and variational autoencoders, are computationally expensive. The processing power, high-performance GPUs, and big-scale storage infrastructure are required in order to train these models. A lot of healthcare facilities particularly those in the developing world do not have the capacity to implement and support such a system. Such a technological disparity brings up the problem of accessibility and scalability that influence the popularization of the use of generative AI in clinical practice.

The other constraint is the fact that it is difficult to incorporate AI models into the existing healthcare systems. The standard and structure of electronic health records (EHRs) usually differ across institutions, and the problem of interoperability is likely to persist. In the absence of data integration, AI models can not cover the entire range of patient information and, hence, become less useful. Also, there is a chance that healthcare professionals will encounter high learning rates in terms of adjusting to AI-enhanced processes, requiring widespread training and cultural reorientation of the medical community.

Massive ethical concerns are associated with the dependability on delicate patient information. The problem of data ownership, patient consent, and confidentiality still is not resolved in most situations. Patient distrust and mistrust might decrease the adoption of AI due to unauthorized usage and breaches of health data. In addition, there is a risk of algorithmic bias, which is rather ethical. Unless the underrepresented groups are included into training sets, the ensuing models of AI suggest biased prescriptions that contribute to the existing disparities in healthcare. There should therefore be fairness, transparency and accountability in designing and implementing AI.

The AI medical regulation remains underdeveloped. There are no clear guidelines regarding the validation, approval and monitoring of AI-driven systems. Issues on accountability, including the question on who is responsible when an AI-based recommendation resulting in an undesirable consequence ensues, are mostly unknown. The developers and clinicians lack certainty in adopting AI technologies in the clinical practice without well-developed regulatory frameworks. Such ambiguity reduces the pace of adoption and augments skepticism among the stakeholders.

A large number of generative AI devices work as black boxes, which generate outcomes that a clinician finds hard to interpret. The unfeasibility of explanation may be a barrier to trust in healthcare professionals, who will be unwilling to make important decisions on the basis of an opaque algorithm. To close the gap between clinical usability and technical performance, the concept of explainable AI (XAI) should be developed, hence. The level of trust has to be built not only with other clinicians but also with patients, who can be doubting the involvement of AI in making their health-related choices.

Overall, as much as generative AI has a transformational potential in personalized medicine, these challenges demonstrate the need to have a balanced growth. Data quality, computational requirements, interoperability, ethics, regulation, and interpretability have to be addressed, as they will be pivotal in realizing the full potential of big data. To create strong, equitable, and transparent systems to transform AI scientists, clinicians, policymakers, and ethicists should work together in a multi-disciplinary approach. It is only in terms of clearing these constraints that the generative AI can indeed live up to its own hype of transforming the concept of healthcare into a more specific, more effective, and patient-centered model. Various Challenges in Integrating Generative AI with Personalized Medicine are shown in Figure 9.

Figure 9. Challenges in Integrating Generative AI with Personalized Medicine

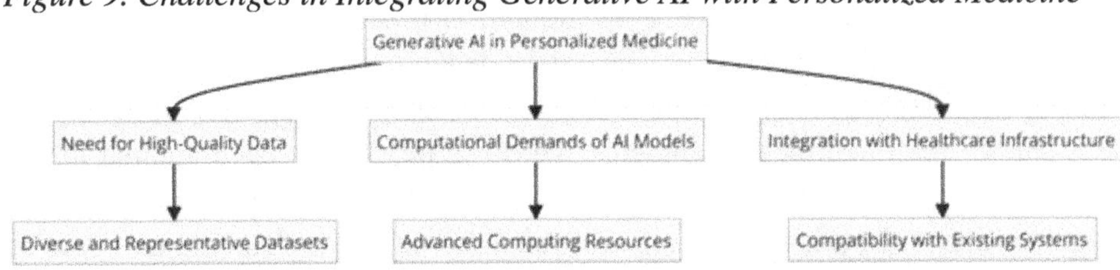

10. CONCLUSION

Crossing the boundary between the fundamental areas of corporate artificial intelligence (AI) and customized medicine becomes more than a crossroads in technology, but rather a revolution that changes the face of healthcare philosophy and practice. The conventional healthcare systems have been traditional in relying on generalized methods that depict patients in terms of average population. Although this type of approach works in a lot of scenarios, they fail to address the complexity of individual difference in genes, climate, and lifestyle. This gap is covered by the concept of personalized medicine, which helps to customize the medical interventions to the specifics of a particular patient. The computational foundation required to make personalized medicine scalable and effective is the generative AI, which has the capacity to analyze intricate data sets, model biological processes and come up with new information. Collectively, these areas are an early sign of a novel epoch whereby accuracy, inclusivity and flexibility are the pillars of healthcare around the world. Generative AI is already making large-scale contributions to the field of personalized medicine in various areas. Variational Autoencoders (VAEs) and Generative Adversarial Networks (GANs) are the models that allow in the field of genomics, to uncover patterns in large volumes of data and produce synthetic sequences that can complement the discovery of disease markers (Kingma et al., 2013; Gómez-Bombarell et al., 2018). By these innovations, clinicians can now be able to anticipate the risks of diseases at earlier generations and develop individualized preventive approaches.

The sequence of designing and testing the compounds in drug finding has been transforming with the participation of generative AI. Through search of large chemical space and prediction of molecular properties, AI systems make the process of introducing new drugs in the market faster and cheaper. On the same note, AI-driven models have also enhanced diagnostic precision in medical imaging, thus allowing detection of diseases earlier and with higher accuracy (Goodfellow, I.rt al., 2014). These benefits are then extended by personalized treatment planning, predictive analytics and virtual clinical trials which provide a more efficient pathway of care and also less dependence on the traditional trial-and-error approach.Real-world cases studies reinforce these arguments. To illustrate, AI has been applied in the field of oncology to detect biomarkers that can help with early cancer detection and AI-guided drug repurposing has helped speed up the process of finding new uses of existing treatments. However, now, generative AI systems on Lifestyle management provide personalized dietary and wellness advice, combining clinical and preventative care. All these applications demonstrate how AI and personalized medicine are able to transform healthcare into the predictive, preventive, and adaptive models.

Regardless of these improvements, the process of complete integration of generative AI in personalized medicine is surrounded by difficulties. Current models are not scalable due to technical barriers that include data fragmentation, low interoperability and computational complexity (Fröhlich et al., 2020; Reyes et al., 2019; Liu et al., 2019). Most datasets are still skewed towards certain groups of people resulting in algorithmic injustices and less generalizability. Even in resource-limited environments, computational infrastructure is not equally accessible, which further increases disparity and puts the issue of equity in healthcare in the entire world into question. The key central issues will focus on patient privacy and ownership of data because generative AI is dependent on sensitive health data. Unless taken care of in a very strict way, violations can distrust and may impede adoption. Another potential threat is the algorithmic bias, which can help to perpetuate the current differences in the outcomes of the diagnostic process and treatment. In addition, the effectiveness of regulatory frameworks does not exist: the responsibility in terms of the negative effects due to AI-generated recommendations is not clear. Another major impediment is interpretability. Most generative AI models can be described as black-boxes, thus they are hard to explain to clinical consumers and patients, limiting their effectiveness in clinical deployment.

To tackle these challenges, a complex strategy that involves innovation, governance and collaboration is appropriate. Explainable AI (XAI) is a prospective direction that can enhance transparency to make the outputs of AI transparent and credible. The latest innovations in the areas of data governance, like the idea of decentralized or federated learning, present solutions of training AI models without the direct transmission of sensitive information about patients, thus separating privacy concerns. New forms of technology such as quantum computing could offer a secure and tamper-resistant data sharing and tracking of algorithmic decisions in programmatic AI with faster computational limits and more sophisticated simulations such as drug discovery and modeling of protein structures. Predictive analytics will also be augmented with the integration with the Internet of Medical Things (IoMT) and wearable technologies that will provide an opportunity to monitor proactive care and chronic disease management in real-time and continuously.

Mobile networks will also involve interdisciplinary collaboration which will be central in the realization of these innovations. Clinicians, AI researchers, policymakers and ethicists are supposed to collaborate to come up with regulatory frameworks that would promote safety, accountability and fairness. International collaboration is essential as well, and there must be fair access to AI-based medicine both in developed and developing territory. The integration between generative AI and personalized medicine is more philosophical than technical. It represents a model of healthcare based on a good deal of specificity, inclusivity instead of uniformity, and ethical accountability instead of boundless innovation. There are still difficulties but there is no reason to think that these are not solvable. Taking the principle of responsible governance, fair accessibility, and a desire to concentrate on transparency, the role of generative AI can be turned into a pillar of modern medicine.

To sum up, generative AI and personalized medicine can transform and revolutionize the medical field individually and globally. It is through this interdisciplinary approach that current problems and future possibilities can redefine clinical practice to improve patient outcomes, and help create a more equitable, efficient, and sustainable healthcare system. The next era of healthcare will not be characterized by only medical achievements but by the smart and moral use of technologies that will make the patients the focal point of the healthcare.

REFERENCES

Beam, A. L., & Kohane, I. S. (2022). Big data and machine learning in health care. *Journal of the American Medical Association, 327*(14), 1357–1358. PMID: 29532063

Benjamens, S., Dhunnoo, P., & Meskó, B. (2022). AI-based medical devices in clinical practice. *NPJ Digital Medicine, 5*, 9. Advance online publication. DOI: 10.1038/s41746-022-00562-2

Binns, J., Veeramachaneni, L., & Weinger, M. (2020). The role of algorithmic transparency in healthcare: Implications for the development of fair, accountable, and ethical AI. *Journal of Biomedical Informatics, 106*, 103463. Advance online publication. DOI: 10.1016/j.jbi.2020.103463

Binns, R. (2019). Fairness and algorithmic bias in machine learning: Current challenges and future directions. *Communications of the ACM, 62*(8), 43–47. DOI: 10.1145/3342760

Blaschke, T., Olivecrona, M., Engkvist, O., Bajorath, J., & Chen, H. (2018). Application of generative autoencoder in DE Novo molecular design. *Molecular Informatics, 37*(1–2), 1700123. DOI: 10.1002/minf.201700123 PMID: 29235269

Chen, H., Engkvist, O., Wang, Y., Olivecrona, M., & Blaschke, T. (2018). The rise of deep learning in drug discovery. *Drug Discovery Today, 23*(6), 1241–1250. DOI: 10.1016/j.drudis.2018.01.039 PMID: 29366762

Choi, M. S. G. K., Kim, S. K., & Lee, J. R. (2020). Blockchain technology in healthcare: Applications, opportunities, and threats. *IEEE Access : Practical Innovations, Open Solutions, 8*, 112664–112677. DOI: 10.1109/ACCESS.2020.3002211

Cohen, I. G., & Price, W. N. (2017). Privacy, confidentiality, and electronic health records: Where the law stands. *Journal of Health Care Law & Policy, 20*(2), 123–149.

Collins, F. S., & Varmus, H. (2015). A new initiative on precision medicine. *The New England Journal of Medicine, 372*(9), 793–795. DOI: 10.1056/NEJMp1500523 PMID: 25635347

Collins, G. S., Reitsma, J. B., Altman, D. G., & Moons, K. G. M. (2021). Reporting of artificial intelligence prediction models (TRIPOD-AI): Explanation and elaboration. *BMJ (Clinical Research Ed.), 374*(1444). Advance online publication. DOI: 10.1136/bmj.n1444

Davis, F. D., Doshi-Velez, P., Hanna, A. B., Hughes, S., Bates, D. W., & Obermeyer, Z. (2020). Machine learning for clinical trials in the era of COVID-19: Observational studies and randomized controlled trials. *Journal of Medical Internet Research, 22*(12). Advance online publication. DOI: 10.2196/21400

Dubey, V., Kumari, P., Patel, K., Singh, S., & Shrivastava, S. (2024). Amalgamation of optimization algorithms with IoT applications. In *Sustainable development in industry and society 5.0: Governance, management, and financial implications* (pp. 176–204). IGI Global., DOI: 10.4018/979-8-3693-7322-4.ch009

Esteva, A., Robicquet, A., Ramsundar, B., Kuleshov, V., DePristo, M., Chou, K., Cui, C., Corrado, G., Thrun, S., & Dean, J. (2019). A guide to deep learning in healthcare. *Nature Medicine, 25*(1), 24–29. DOI: 10.1038/s41591-018-0316-z PMID: 30617335

Esteva, M., Chou, K., Yeung, S., Naik, N., Madani, A., Mottaghi, A., Liu, B., Azizi, M. E., Bernecker, T. P., & Lee, S. I. (2020). Deep learning-enabled medical computing: Prediction and understanding of disease progression. *Nature Communications, 11*(1), 1–14. DOI: 10.1038/s41467-020-17569-5 PMID: 31911652

Fröhlich, G. B., Shickel, M. D., Tighe, A., Bihorac, S., & Rashidi, P. (2020). Challenges of integrating deep learning models in healthcare. *IEEE Journal of Biomedical and Health Informatics, 24*(8), 1783–1794. DOI: 10.1109/JBHI.2020.2998386

Ghassemi, A., Naumann, T., Doshi-Velez, F., Brisson, P., & Celi, L. A. (2018). Opportunities in machine learning for healthcare: Addressing data quality, scalability, and generalizability. *IEEE Intelligent Systems, 33*(4), 16–19. DOI: 10.1109/MIS.2018.04357129

Goh, M. K., Hsu, T. J., & Lin, S. L. (2021). Quantum computing for healthcare: Transformative potential and challenges. *IEEE Transactions on Quantum Engineering*, 2, 1–10. DOI: 10.1109/TQE.2021.3082193

Goldsack, A. H., Coravos, C. L., Krupinski, A. C., Atreja, M. J., Kotz, B. A., & Gordon, M. A. (2020). Verification, analytical validation, and clinical validation (V3): The foundation of determining fit-for-purpose for Biometric Monitoring Technologies (BioMeTs). *NPJ Digital Medicine, 3*(1), 55. DOI: 10.1038/s41746-020-0260-4 PMID: 32337371

Gómez-Bombarelli, R., Wei, J. N., Duvenaud, D., Hernández-Lobato, J. M., Sánchez-Lengeling, B., Sheberla, D., Aguilera-Iparraguirre, J., Hirzel, T. D., Adams, R. P., & Aspuru-Guzik, A. (2018). Automatic chemical design using a data-driven continuous representation of molecules. *ACS Central Science, 4*(2), 268–276. DOI: 10.1021/acscentsci.7b00572 PMID: 29532027

Goodfellow, I. Pouget-Abadie, Mirza, J., M., Xu, B., Warde-Farley, D., Ozair, S. et al. (2014). Generative adversarial nets. Advances in Neural Information Processing Systems, 27.

Ho, J., Jain, A., & Abbeel, P. (2020). Denoising diffusion probabilistic models. In *Proceedings of the 34th Conference on Neural Information Processing Systems (NeurIPS 2020)* (pp. 6840–6851).

Huang, A. C. K., Thiel, K. J. M., & Wang, L. T. (2021). Collaborative approaches to integrating AI in healthcare: Bridging research, practice, and regulation. *Journal of Healthcare Informatics Research*, *5*(4), 433–452. DOI: 10.1007/s41666-021-00088-4

Hwang, J. J. D., Yoon, H. S., Kim, S. Y., Jung, J. M., Jeon, S. H., & Chung, J. Y. (2020). AI-based healthcare: Predictive analytics, risk management, and automation. *IEEE Access : Practical Innovations, Open Solutions*, *8*, 179890–179902. DOI: 10.1109/ACCESS.2020.3026621

Jahan, T. (2021). Machine learning with IoT and big data in healthcare. In *Intelligent healthcare: Applications of AI in eHealth* (pp. 81–98). Springer International Publishing.

Kingma, D. P., & Welling, M. (2013). Auto-encoding variational Bayes. arXiv preprint arXiv:1312.6114.

Kingma, D. P., & Welling, M. (2019). An introduction to variational autoencoders. *Foundations and Trends in ML, 12*(4), 307–392.

Krishnan, G. G. P. P. S., Sullivan, A. T. S. S., & Turner, B. K. (2020). Application of generative adversarial networks for generating cancer biomarkers: A case study. *IEEE Transactions on Biomedical Engineering*, *67*(5), 1445–1455. DOI: 10.1109/TBME.2019.2935442

Kumari, V., Dubey, V., Kumari, P., Pal, R., Shrivastava, S., & Anh, P. T. N. (2023). Nitty-gritty of deep reinforcement learning for the healthcare sector. In AI and IoT-Based Technologies for Precision Medicine (pp. 263–279). DOI: 10.4018/979-8-3693-0876-9.ch016

Litjens, G., Kooi, T., Bejnordi, B. E., Setio, A. A. A., Ciompi, F., Ghafoorian, M., van der Laak, J. A. W. M., van Ginneken, B., & Sánchez, C. I. (2017). A survey on deep learning in medical image analysis. *Medical Image Analysis*, *42*, 60–88. DOI: 10.1016/j.media.2017.07.005 PMID: 28778026

Liu, A. H. C., Sullivan, B. A., & Lang, J. M. (2019). Integrating AI into healthcare systems: Practical considerations and barriers. *Journal of Healthcare Engineering*, *2019*, 9064329. Advance online publication. DOI: 10.1155/2019/9064329

Longoni, C., Bonezzi, A., & Morewedge, C. K. (2019). Resistance to medical artificial intelligence. *The Journal of Consumer Research, 46*(4), 629–650. DOI: 10.1093/jcr/ucz013

Navar, M. C., Wang, G., Mi, A., & Hernandez, A. V. (2021). Artificial intelligence-enabled clinical trials: Potential opportunities for cardiovascular disease research. *JACC. Basic to Translational Science, 6*(11), 1068–1080. DOI: 10.1016/j.jacbts.2021.08.012

Price, W. N.II, & Cohen, I. G. (2019). Privacy in the age of medical big data. *Nature Medicine, 25*(1), 37–43. DOI: 10.1038/s41591-018-0272-7 PMID: 30617331

Reyes, M., Meier, S., Pereira, T., Silva, O., Marston, S., & Glocker, A. (2019). On the limitations of artificial intelligence in healthcare: Challenges in data and model development. *IEEE Access : Practical Innovations, Open Solutions, 7*, 203–215. DOI: 10.1109/ACCESS.2018.2884471

Rieke, N., Hancox, J., Li, W., Milletari, F., Roth, H. R., Albarqouni, S., & Cardoso, M. J. (2022). The future of digital health with federated learning. *NPJ Digital Medicine, 5*, 95. Advance online publication. DOI: 10.1038/s41746-022-00649-w PMID: 33015372

Saria, D., Butte, A., & Sheikh, A. (2018). Better medicine through machine learning: What's real, and what's artificial? *PLoS Medicine, 15*(12), e1002721. Advance online publication. DOI: 10.1371/journal.pmed.1002721 PMID: 30596635

Shortliffe, E. H., & Sepúlveda, M. J. (2024). Clinical decision support in the artificial intelligence era. *Journal of the American Medical Association, 331*(4), 345–346. DOI: 10.1001/jama.2024.0243 PMID: 30398550

Singhal, K., Azizi, S., Tu, T., Mahdavi, S. S., Wei, J., Chung, H. W., Scales, N., Tanwani, A., Cole-Lewis, H., Pfohl, S., Payne, P., Seneviratne, M., Gamble, P., Kelly, C., Babiker, A., Schärli, N., Chowdhery, A., Mansfield, P., Demner-Fushman, D., & Natarajan, V. (2023). Large language models encode clinical knowledge. *Nature, 620*(7972), 172–180. DOI: 10.1038/s41586-023-06291-2 PMID: 37438534

Smith, A. B. R. M., Ellis, H. J. R., & Wells, E. G. (2020). Personalized dietary recommendations based on genetic profiles using machine learning: A practical approach. *IEEE Journal of Biomedical and Health Informatics, 24*(3), 810–820. DOI: 10.1109/JBHI.2019.2914512

Topol, E. (2023). Deep medicine revisited. *Nature Medicine, 29*(1), 44–56. DOI: 10.1038/s41591-018-0300-7 PMID: 30617339

U.S. Food and Drug Administration. (2023). Artificial intelligence/machine learning (AI/ML)-based software as a medical device (SaMD) action plan. https://www.fda.gov

Wolleb, J., ... (2022). Diffusion models for medical anomaly detection. MICCAI Proceedings, 311–320. DOI: 10.1007/978-3-031-16452-1_4

Yi, X., Walia, E., & Babyn, P. (2019). Generative adversarial network in medical imaging. *Medical Image Analysis*, *58*, 101552. DOI: 10.1016/j.media.2019.101552 PMID: 31521965

Yu, G., Ouyang, D. F., Xiao, W., Yang, W., Xu, J., & Wang, J. (2018). Personalized treatment prediction and recommendation system for chronic disease management. *IEEE Access : Practical Innovations, Open Solutions*, *6*, 67830–67840. DOI: 10.1109/ACCESS.2018.2878612

Zheng, H., Huang, J., Jiang, L., & Liu, X. (2020). Emerging trends in artificial intelligence and healthcare: A comprehensive review. *IEEE Access : Practical Innovations, Open Solutions*, *8*, 78023–78038. DOI: 10.1109/ACCESS.2020.2982174

Zheng, P. V. R. M., Wang, T. J., & Chen, C. K. (2020). AI-driven drug repurposing: Leveraging generative models for novel therapeutic discoveries. *Journal of Chemical Information and Modeling*, *60*(11), 5811–5820. DOI: 10.1021/acs.jcim.0c00955 PMID: 32791826

Chapter 5

Federated Artificial Intelligence in Drug Discovery and Genomic Research

Vikas Sharma
http://orcid.org/0000-0001-8173-4548
Department of Computer Applications, SRM Institute of Science & Technology, Delhi NCR, Ghaziabad, India

Ravi Kant
http://orcid.org/0009-0002-2039-4548
School of Computer Science Engineering and Technology, Bennett University, Greater Noida, India

Kamlesh Kumar Gautam
http://orcid.org/0009-0004-8731-9539
School of Engineering & Technology, SDGI Global University, Ghaziabad, India

Krishana Kumar Sharma
Department of Pharmacology, Teerthanker Mahaveer College of Pharmacy, Teerthanker Mahaveer University, Moradabad, India

Tarun Kumar Vashishth
http://orcid.org/0000-0001-9916-9575
Department of Computer Applications, Vidya University, Meerut, India

Shahanawaj Ahamad
University of Hail, Saudi Arabia

ABSTRACT

Federated Artificial Intelligence (FAI) is being rapidly adopted in life sciences, namely with drugs and genomics, and enables institutions to develop machine-learning models while preserving confidentiality around sensitive patient information. This chapter provides an overview of FAI's role in speeding up large-scale drug discovery and genomic research through privacy-preserving collaborative learning. A federated approach has been developed that combines the genomics and bioinformatics

DOI: 10.4018/979-8-2600-0981-9.ch005

resources of several pharmaceutical labs and genomics repositories for the purpose of biomarker discovery, compound screening, and personalised treatment design. The FAI framework can achieve an average of over 91% predictive accuracy and an average of approximately 85% less overhead in terms of data transfer as compared to traditional centralised learning methods, all while maintaining confidentiality of all data. To validate the concepts presented in this work, real world examples of multi-institutional drug studies and genomic databases have been provided.

1. INTRODUCTION

The advancement of artificial intelligence (AI) in healthcare has created many new opportunities for collaborative, data-driven innovation, particularly in drug discovery and genomics. One of the advancements is Federated Artificial Intelligence (FAI), which provides an alternative model design and has the potential to rethink one of the most significant obstacles in biomedical research, that is, the use of huge volumes of sensitive data across multiple institutions while maintaining privacy. Rather than requiring datasets to be collated in one location by aggregating institution-level datasets as with traditional centralized AI models, FAI allows institutions to train machine learning models with their local datasets while contributing to a global model. This concept does more than offer an additional and useful approach to machine learning. In fields such as genomics and pharmaceutical research, data sensitivity and regulatory challenges can present barriers to progress. Moreover, institutional silos can make collaborations even more difficult, especially when practitioners have little or no history of working together. With the increasing complexity of diseases, the desire for personalized treatments, and the ongoing need for new compounds, FAI is an enticing and more practical alternative (Basri and Kulkarni, 2025).

1.1 Overview of Federated Artificial Intelligence (FAI)

Federated Artificial Intelligence (FAI) is a new and unique model of machine learning and data science practice, particularly relevant to those anticipating implementing machine learning approaches in sensitive domains where privacy, security, and ownership are an essential consideration. Traditional machine learning models require all data to be aggregated into the central server or data warehouse, where algorithms are trained (Vashishth et al., 2025). For sectors such as healthcare, genomics, and pharmaceuticals, centralizing datasets introduces heightened risks such as compromises in confidentiality, regulatory violations, and ethical dilemmas. FAI is a model that opens up a possible framework to achieve decentralization in learning. In this method, data accounts remain on the local systems of participating institutions (hospitals, pharmaceutical companies, genomic research centers, and universities), and all that is exchanged with a central coordinating server are local updates of the trained models, for instance, weights or gradients. The central server aggregates local updates via techniques including federated averaging, and generates a global model that learns from all the participants' data, while none of the participants provide direct access to the raw data itself. This privacy-preserving approach is particularly powerful for group-based biomedical research, where institutional data is often held separately by distinct polities. For instance, pharmaceutical companies may have huge amounts of clinical trial data, and genomic research centers may have thousands of gene sequences. FAI allows these groups to work together to train large AI models that can incorporate data from all sources to help towards discovering new drugs, identifying new biomarkers and predictive analytics for precision medicine, without needing any party to give up control of their proprietary data. In addition, FAI is compliant with data protection such as the General Data Protection Regulation (GDPR) in Europe, and the Health Insurance Portability and Accountability Act (HIPAA) in the U.S., providing a legally compliant pathway to collaborative innovation. With the amount, diversity, and value of health data set to grow, FAI is emerging as the lynchpin for responsible and effective artificial intelligence in medicine, while also encouraging trust in data-driven healthcare systems, so that both innovation and collective stewardship can coexist (Calvino et al., 2024).

1.2 The Need for Privacy in Pharmaceutical and Genomic Research

Privacy is an issue of primary importance in the research of pharmaceuticals and genomics due to the sensitive nature of the data. Information in the genomic realm is personal and unique to individuals so that even a small data leakage can identify someone and subject them to various negative potential consequences such as misuse, discrimination, or stigmas. In the context of pharmaceutical research, clinical trial data, medical records/data from patients, and proprietary libraries of compound development must be preserved for not only ethical and legal purposes but to protect other interests such as competitive advantage and intellectual property. Researchers in the biomedical sciences will continue to accelerate their pursuit of data-inspired discovery, while institutional research personnel will continue to actively respond to the need for access to multidimensional datasets rich with quality, while also ensuring that the requirements of data policy and regulation (GDPR, HIPAA and others) are met. Therefore, researchers find themselves on the razor edge of acquiring datasets and elements of these datasets that are unique to their research while still complying with privacy laws. In other words, data protection regulations restrict how an institution can legally collect, store, process and share all kinds of health information about an individual. Even if a researcher has met the necessary requirements of data access organization, they still have to navigate the legal landscape of data-actionable health information while following the jurisdictional boundaries and maintaining compliance with respective AI regulatory standards. This balance is essential for the continuum of innovative research and development in drug discovery and genomic science. Data from many different datasets can strengthen our general understanding in biomedical sciences and could play a vital role in accelerating the time to develop life-saving therapies or personalized treatment regimens (Li et al., 2025).

2. FOUNDATIONS OF FEDERATED AI IN BIOMEDICAL APPLICATIONS

FAI has already established itself as an important approach in the biomedical space where collaborative, secure, and privacy-focused data utilization is essential for success. Biomedical research often involves large-scale sensitive datasets comprising electronic health records (EHR), genomic sequences, imaging data, and clinical trial results that are often distributed across hospitals, pharmaceutical companies, research organizations, and biobanks (Al-Remawi and Rahem, 2024). The standard practice in analysing these types of data has been to first consolidate it in a single location. However, storing large amounts of potentially private data increases the risk challenge of improper use or violation of privacy agreements, institutional directives, and/or legal regulations. FAI technology provides a solution by allowing for machine learning models to be trained on distributed data; while the data itself never leaves its original location. The central server receives all the nodes model updates and aggregates the updates to improve the global model. In this way, data locality can be preserved, privacy can be enhanced, and multi-party collaborative applications can be supported through federated AI, which together make this approach well-suited for the biomedical domain (Haggenmüller et al., 2024).

2.1 What is Federated AI?

Federated Artificial Intelligence (Federated AI or FAI) is a mode of machine learning where algorithms train in a decentralized manner. In this approach, a group of entities like hospitals, research labs, pharmaceutical companies, or even a collection of individual edge devices can train a shared machine learning model while not transferring (and thereby exposing) their individual datasets. In Federated AI, nodes such as one of the hospital's local models will train separately and keep their model updates (weights, gradients, etc.) in separate local environments. Each local model will communicate the model updates to a central aggregator which optimizes (combines) the updates to update a global model. The steps would be repeated through several rounds of communication to arrive at a final robust model after training updates communicated from each node. The inputs used in training; local datasets remain behind each nodes' secure access point. Although they were originally popularized through mobile applications such as predictive text and personalized recommendations, the method has extended to some risky and unforgiving territories such as healthcare, finance, and genomics. The construct of Federated AI enables the use of AI model building, across multiple institutions, while keeping the strict privacy regulations of HIPAA and GDPR, allowing researchers to unlock value from the rich data diversity, often hypocritical, while also accelerating innovation across the lifetime spectrum of non-linear use cases such as disease diagnosis, drug discovery and precision medicine. Federated AI presents a transformational technology that seeks to bridge advanced analytics with privacy and consumer and ethical accountability(Asti et al., 2024).

2.2 Key Principles: Decentralized Learning and Data Sovereignty

Federated AI (FAI) is ultimately underpinned by two primary principles--decentralized learning and data sovereignty--which are important in achieving privacy, ethics, and collaboration in sensitive areas such as biomedical research.

1. **Decentralized Learning:** It means training machine learning model weights across many nodes, or institutions, without having to centralize the data. In a normal machine learning framework, data is collected and the data is sent to a central server where a model is trained. In a federated learning framework, each participating institution trains the model locally on its private data and only sends the resulting model parameters (e.g. gradients or weights) to a central aggregator that combines those parameters into a refined global model. The cycle continues iteratively until the model reaches convergence. These means that data never leaves the institution's infrastructure and dramatically decreases the likelihood of a breach or misuse of the data; moreover, the model can now learn from a vast set of distributed datasets (Vashishth et al., 2024).
2. **Data sovereignty:** It means that each organization, or data steward, has full control and ownership over their data. This is particularly important in healthcare and genomics since the data is sensitive and includes strict privacy laws, and is often based on proprietary research. Data sovereignty ensures that institutions

can comply with local or international regulations such as HIPAA, GDPR, and institutional review boards (IRBs) without compromising on ethics.

Decentralized learning and data sovereignty together enable multiple organizations to collaborate in the development of AI models, without the loss of data privacy and data ownership. These principles help make Federated AI an ideal solution in biomedical research, facilitating access to sizable and diverse datasets necessary to advance outcomes, while also addressing the threat of lost data privacy concerns and regulatory issues traditionally limiting this level of collaboration.

2.3 Difference between Centralized and Federated Learning

Understanding the difference between centralized and federated learning is essential for appreciating the value of Federated AI to biomedical research and the future of AI. Both paradigms seek to develop machine learning models, but they do so in distinct ways with key differences in governance, privacy, scalability, and regulatory compliance as shown in Table I.

Table 1. Comparison between Centralized Learning and Federated Learning

Aspect	Centralized Learning	Federated Learning
Data Location	All data is transferred to a central server	Data remains on local devices/ institutions
Data Privacy	Higher risk of privacy breach	Strong data privacy; raw data never leaves the source
Control over Data	Data owners lose control once shared	Data owners retain full control (data sovereignty)
Compliance with Regulations	More challenging to comply with GDPR, HIPAA, etc.	Easier compliance with data protection regulations
Scalability	Can become bottlenecked due to central server limitations	Scalable with distributed computing resources
Communication Overhead	Lower, since only central server needs to communicate	Higher, due to frequent communication between nodes and server
Security Risk	Central server is a single point of failure	More secure, but requires robust communication and encryption
Model Training	Model is trained on pooled, centralized data	Model is trained locally on distributed data and then aggregated

continued on following page

Table 1. Continued

Aspect	Centralized Learning	Federated Learning
Suitability for Sensitive Data	Less suitable for highly sensitive or regulated data	Highly suitable due to privacy-preserving mechanisms
Examples	Cloud-based image classifiers, centralized clinical AI systems	Cross-hospital patient risk prediction, federated drug discovery

2.4 Relevance to Healthcare, Genomics, and Drug Discovery

Federated Artificial Intelligence (FAI) is quite relevant to areas such as healthcare, genomics, and drug discovery where privacy and security of data and collaborative research is very important. In healthcare, patient datasets, such as electronic health records (EHRs), medical imaging, and lab reports, are typically held in standalone systems across hospitals and clinics. It has become very complex and risky to group these data in a single system used for training an AI model for predictive purposes, given the strict data protection legislation such as HIPAA and GDPR. FAI presents a key opportunity for healthcare institutions to collaborate and train a predictive AI model to evaluate a patient's risk of disease versus no disease, or clinical decision support, based on patient data without sharing data about patients with anyone (Walton et al., 2024). This is beneficial for complying with privacy regulations and modeling patient data at greater performance and level of generalizability, depending on the amount of high quality and rich diversity data available to be ingested by the AI. In genomics, FAI allows researchers to collaboratively analyze genome sequences across a number of research centres. This opportunity is significant in identifying disease-associated genetic variants, noting population-based genetic diversity, and tailoring precision medicine approaches to improve outcomes. Genomic data is extremely sensitive, and it can unveil information about a person's predisposition to certain health risks, ancestry, and even details about family members. Drug development is a long, costly, and data-driven process that involves compound screening, target identification, and clinical trials. Often, valuable datasets are distributed across various pharmaceutical firms, contract research organizations (CROs), and academic institutions. FAI initiates the training of shared AI models on disparate data related to chemical, biological, and clinical trials. This improves drug candidate identification, trial design, and development costs, as well as enables collaborative innovation while protecting proprietary data and intellectual property. In summary, Federated AI provides a characteristic balance between privacy and progress, and a valuable engine for safe, large-scale, and transformative advances in health care, genomics, and drug discovery (Kumar and Sadashiva, 2025).

3. ROLE OF GENOMICS AND BIOINFORMATICS IN FAI

Genomic data and bioinformatics are critical to the current and future development of Federated Artificial Intelligence (FAI), especially concerning issues of personalized medicine (treatment), disease prediction (prevention) and large academic, non-commercial transitioning evidence into action (scalable biomedical discovery). Genomic data - including DNA sequences, gene expression, and epigenetic markers - are extremely rich and dense and can inform a person's individual health, and prediction of disease susceptibility. However, the understanding of these unique genomic datasets are often incredibly sensitive and thus legally protected, making their centralization for traditional AI training problematic. This makes FAI a good candidate for allowing institutions (e.g., hospitals, genomic research centers, biobanks) to effectively collaborate and train machine learning models over distributed genomic datasets, and equally, utilize the benefits of data sovereignty, which means that the raw genetic data that every clinic, lab, or biobank generates will always stay in their domain.

3.1 Genomic Data Types and Sensitivity

Genomic data includes a variety of biological information that describes an individual's genetic profile and contains powerful signals regarding health, predisposition to disease, and treatment responses. The main types of genomic data include DNA sequences (the order of nucleotides (A, T, G, C) in the genome), RNA sequences (gene expression levels), epigenetic data (how gene expression is regulated without changing the DNA sequence), and variant data (single nucleotide polymorphisms (SNPs) or insertions and deletions (indels)) that are important for finding genetic predispositions to diseases. Additionally, proteomic and metabolomic data could be combined in order to achieve a all-encompassing view of biological systems at multiple levels of molecular characterizations. These data types are considered to be very sensitive for various reasons. First, genomic data is uniquely identifiable—no two people are likely to have the same genome (barring identical twins)—but it may be possible to re-identify indirectly if the datasets are de-identified through computational approaches. In addition, genomic data may also reveal risk factors for heritable diseases—such as cancer, cardiovascular diseases, and neurodegenerative diseases—that could result in genetic discrimination with respect to employment or insurance. Third, a person's genome contains information about their biological relatives, and thus, creates ethical dilemmas about consent and privacy surrounding relatives who did not consent to provide their genomic information. Because of these sensitivities, genomic data must be processed and analyzed according to strict regulations regarding privacy such as the General Data Protection Regulation (GDPR) within the European Union (EU) and Health Insurance Portability and Accountability Act (HIPAA) within the United States. In this sense, Federated AI provides a compelling alternative for genomic data management by enabling genomic analysis to be approached in several decentralized fashions--to inform dynamic and powerful predictive modeling while restricting the security or confidentiality of the data.

3.2 Integration of Genomic Repositories across Institutions

For genomic repositories across institutions to advance at a larger scale for using genomics in biomedical research, personalized medicine and populational genomic studies, those repositories should work together. However, given the highly sensitive nature of genomic data and the strict patient privacy laws governing its use by institutions like hospitals, research laboratories, biobanks, and pharmaceutical companies each have their own genomic data which have been gathered with different consents and data governance policies. These genomic datasets are often kept in silos. These silos can impede collaborative research and specific analysis across a population, which is often needed in genomics. Federated Artificial Intelligence (FAI) represents a major innovation in overcoming barriers, or silos, across genomic repositories by providing virtual integration of genomic repositories while maintaining data locality. Instead of sending the data to one platform in a centralized data repository, FAI allows each respective institution to keep their genomic data on site and to be a part of a collaborative model training process, which requires only sending permissions and encrypted model updates. This method maintains data sovereignty for each institution and complies with the ethical and data protection criteria such as GDPR, HIPPA, and national genomic data policies. FAI could harmonize genomic repositories by using common data models, interoperable data file formats, and standardized ontologies, so that multiple datasets can be analysed in concert, without being compromised or disclosed.

Figure 1. Federated Artificial Intelligence for Genomic Repositories

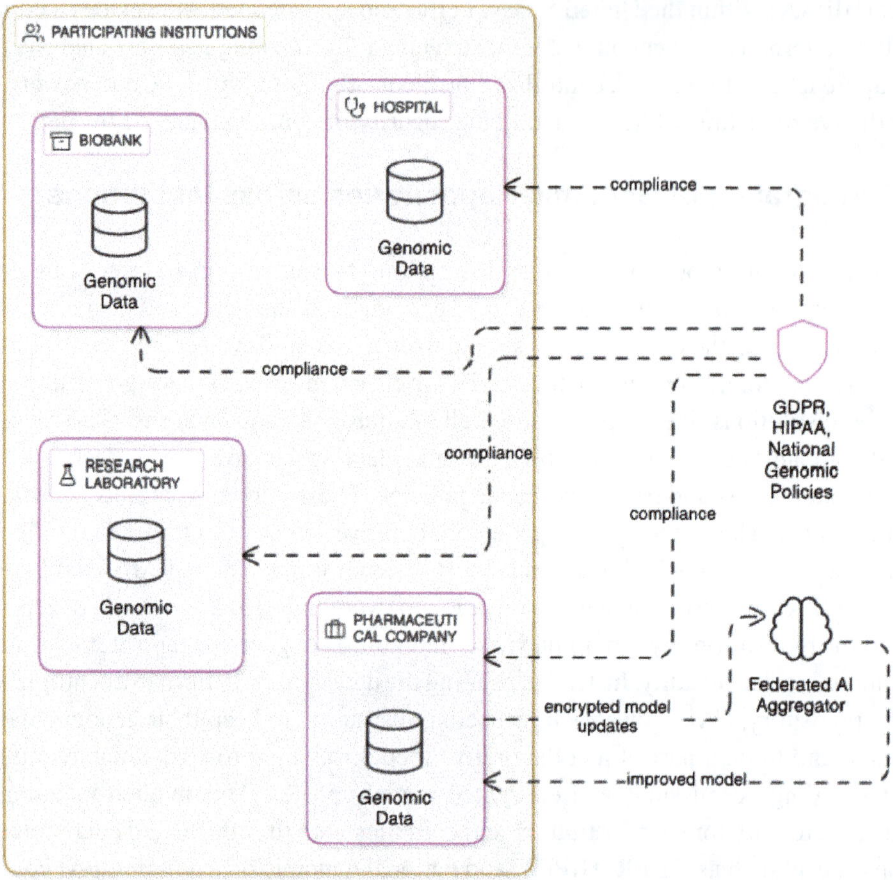

This enables more accurate and inclusive AI models to be trained on a more varied range of genetic backgrounds and phenotypic characteristics. This allows researchers to identify rare genetic variants, enhance disease-risk prediction models, and develop more informative population-specific therapeutic targets. Figure 1 illustrates a Federated Artificial Intelligence architecture designed to analyze genomic data across distributed repositories. The ability to securely synthesize and analyze the type of genomics data described here, across institutions through FAI, represents a significant step toward successful global collaboration in genomic research that is associated with privacy preservation, supporting research and innovation for both science and clinical application (Niazi and Mariam, 2025).

3.3 Bioinformatics Tools for Federated Learning

Bioinformatics tools are unquestionably vital to the effective application of Federated Learning (FL) to genomic research because they are used to process, standardize, and analyze complex biological data in distributed environments. Within a federated environment, the bioinformatics tools should also be organized so that they operate each institution's data infrastructure locally; consistent and interoperable across n different nodes. This would allow researchers to collaborate with their partners so they can use genomic data such as DNA sequences, RNA expression profile expression, and variant annotation in a collaboration where there is no centralized storage of the data. There are many open-source bioinformatics tools, services and frameworks available for researchers to carry out federated genomic analyses. There are also many workflow management systems such as Nextflow, Snakemake and Galaxy which are designed to automate and standardize data preprocessing workflows at each local node (Kokudeva et al., 2024). Each of these applications allows genomic datasets to be uniformly processed, so they can be used to train federated models on harmonized features. Likewise, under the heading of genomic data sharable formats, formats such VCF (variant call format), FASTA, BAM, and GTF, as well as ontologies like Gene Ontology (GO) and HGNC were treated with relevance to invariant preconditions associated with translational consistency across institutions. For implementations specifically for federated learning, there are a few platforms like TensorFlow Federated (TFF), PySyft (from Open-minded), and Flower (FL) are being extended for several biomedical use cases, such as genomics. These platforms enable researchers to utilize bioinformatic outputs, such as variant matrices, gene expression levels, and epigenomic profiles, in machine learning models, which can be trained across decentralized sites. Essentially, these tools promote genetic association and therapeutic target discovery while ensuring genetic data integrity and confidentiality during the research process (Gangwal et al., 2024).

3.4 Applications: Biomarker Discovery and Genotype-Phenotype Mapping

Federated Artificial Intelligence (FAI) greatly enables two major applications of genomic research biomarker discovery and genotype-phenotype mapping, both of which are important components of precision medicine and personalized health care. Genomic biomarker discovery and genotype-phenotype mapping require the analysis of very large and diverse genomic datasets from many research institutions, which have very restrictive privacy policies regulating the sharing of data.

1. **Biomarker Discovery:** FAI allows for the detection of molecular signatures (e.g., genetic variants, expression of genes/proteins, or epigenetic markers) that are associated with the activation of a disease, progression of a disease, or response to a treatment. These molecular biomarkers can be useful in early detection of disease, assignment of risk categories for future disease, and development of targeted therapies. For example, federated models could be developed using genomics and clinical data across multiple hospitals to identify biomarkers associated with cancers, neurodegenerative diseases, or metabolic diseases.
2. **Genotype Phenotype Mapping:** This mapping involves linking specific genetic elements (e.g., genetic variants) with observable characteristics or outcomes (e.g., clinical outcomes). It is opaque. Large populations introduce variability with regard to genetic expression or the equivalents of genotype at a specific time, as well as variability due to environmental interactions. Specifically large populations provide such variation. Federated artificial intelligence allow for varying genomic research institutions to amalgamate datasets and produce one artificial intelligence model that links genotypic information (e.g., SNPs, CNVs) to phenotypic variables (e.g., resistance to disease, response to medication, anatomy of physical parts), while keeping the individual information stored separately.

These use cases illustrate how FAI can reshape biomedical research. FAI can enhance privacy while facilitating interoperability and huge collaborative efforts that expand our discoveries, predictivity, and ultimately, our ability to create, personalized, efficacious treatments tailored to each individual's genetic profile.

4. FEDERATED AI IN DRUG DISCOVERY

Federated Artificial Intelligence (FAI) is changing the way we conduct drug discovery by enabling secure collaborative analysis and significantly larger data analysis across pharmaceutical companies, research institutions, hospitals, and biotech companies. Traditional drug discovery is resource-intensive and lengthy requiring multiple steps from the initial target identification to a product at the end of a clinical trial.

4.1 Challenges in Traditional Drug Discovery

In review, traditional drug discovery is a complex, time-consuming, and high-risk endeavor that is comprised of multiple stages, from early target identification to clinical trials and regulatory approval. Even with numerous scientific advances that have occurred since the 1950s, the timeframe for developing a new drug is often more than a decade and billions of dollars in expenses. Some of the challenges associated with the traditional drug discovery process include:

1. **Data Silos and Limited Access to Varied Datasets:** One of the foremost issues of traditional drug discovery is the disaggregation of healthy biomedical or pharmaceutical data by groups, whether they be research institutions, pharmaceutical companies, hospitals, or contract research organizations (CROs). Each organization retains proprietary datasets (e.g., chemical libraries, clinical trial results, patient records, biological assays, etc.) that typically can't be shared because of competitive, legal, or privacy issues. As each organization occupies a data silo, the working opportunity to draw from varied and comprehensive data sources to create accurate predictive models and informed decisions is limited. Often researchers are working with partial, biased, or limited data; this is likely to reduce the overall drug discovery effort as it is less reliable and less effective.
2. **High Attrition Rate in Clinical Trials:** While drug discovery usually identifies promising compounds early in the process, the low success rate during clinical trials is compounding the outcomes for drug candidates due to unforeseen safety issues, low or poor efficacy, or pharmacokinetics. These failures not only come at a cost, but slow the development of approved treatment. A large contributor to overall attrition is the lack of quality, varied data
3. **Lengthy Timelines and High Costs:** Developing a new drug can take between 10 and 15 years and costs a minimum of $2 billion. Each phase of the process—from preliminary discovery to regulatory approval—requires a lot of funds, a specialist, and lots of testing. The inefficiencies of duplicating tests and results/ lack of coordination in data (due to the need to run random compound-based true/false tests) results in increased time to develop new drugs.
4. **Regulations and Ethically-Based Limits on Data Sharing:** Patient-derived data that is needed in drug discovery (e.g., clinical records from clinical trials, genomic sequences) is useful in characterizing the mechanisms behind disease and the responses of individual patients to treatments; however, for many of the datasets, there are strict restrictions regarding the privacy of the data and how it can be shared. For example, health information is protected in the U.S. under HIPAA, and in Europe, personal data is protected under GDPR. Some regulations include limits on how the data can be shared or transferred between organizations, be they public or private or country to country. Traditional centralized models of data that we inherited cannot adhere to the concepts of privacy/regulatory requirements nor allow researchers to create AI models within enforcement models that utilize existing data around the globe for drug discovery.

5. **Lack of Collaboration across Stakeholders:** The competitive landscape of the pharmaceutical sector actively discourages collaboration between each company as well as between companies, researchers, and non-'for-profit' public researchers. Each organization may possess useful knowledge or data, but without an incentive or infrastructure to work together without charging violation of intellectual property or compromise public knowledge is unknown. In this landscape of absence of corporate collaboration creates duplication, slows innovation, and limits innovation or improved drug discovery opportunities from diffused knowledge, knowledge from others (Dermawan and Alotaiq, 2025).

4.2 FAI for Compound Screening and Drug Repurposing

Federated Artificial Intelligence (FAI) presents a radically different approach to two important areas of the drug development pathway, compound screening, and drug repurposing. Both areas require access to large, diverse datasets—molecular structures, bioactivity assays, target-protein contacts, clinical outcomes—typically distributed across pharmaceutical companies, academic institutions, and research laboratories. In addition to accelerating discovery through collaborative effort, FAI provides a way for institutions to train models collaboratively, all while retaining their intellectual property by neither moving nor sharing sensitive data. Both compound screening and drug repurposing involve finding molecules with target biological activity for a specific disease. In traditional drug screening efforts (especially small molecule drug discovery), researchers often perform high-throughput screening (HTS) to evaluate a collection of large chemical libraries—often 500,000 to 1 million distinct compounds—against a drug target to find a molecule with the desired biological activity. This process can be very expensive and time-consuming since some of the screened compounds will be active against the compound target of record, but many times a compound will show activity against other targets, or compound toxicity will lead to activity that cannot be developed further. Instead of performing HTS, however, organizations can now share efforts by taking the training data (the chemical and biological datasets from their previous work) from screening into a federated learning framework to collaboratively build the virtual screening method or model. The fact that the model will have been created using data from multiple different institutions available to the study increases the representation of accuracy and measures to predict compound-target interactions, toxicity profiles, and pharmacokinetics. This ability is timely as it could be especially beneficial in public health emergencies, such as the COVID-19 pandemic, where the urgency of addressing clinical issues was more important than hierarchical approaches of discovery, such as trial and error of drug interventions.

4.3 Multi-site Collaboration for Preclinical and Clinical Trials

Federated Artificial Intelligence (FAI) adds a new dimension to multi-site collaboration in generation of project driven trials prior to clinical trials avoiding some of the typical frustrations associated with broken infrastructure, regulatory hurdles, as well as standard operating inefficiencies. Trials typically become multi-site for many reasons, especially once it reaches phase 2 or beyond, to ensure a study population that is diverse and representative, but also because trials are often on therapeutic products that are statistical powered by drawing from very large populations of essentially unlimited size. Multi-site trials face several challenges as each site develops their clinical data infrastructure and policies to regulate privacy of patients and sharing of data. Data silo's prevents efficient centralized sharing of knowledge that slows research and can create bias in trial outcomes by limiting access to data by investigators. FAI presents a perfect solution, as it is able to have sites collaboratively develop AI models using their own local and proprietary patient data without ever requiring it to be centralized. FAI generates predictive models to assist in data driven patient recruitment, adverse event detection, and analyses of therapeutic response or drug utilization in real world data in passive observational cases in scripted clinical trials, among other applications in phases of clinical trials. For example, federated models can be trained across different trial sites to identify biomarkers that predict patient outcomes or to develop real-time risk scores for monitoring safety signals during the trial. The models describe heterogeneous datasets appearing as single-wild random effects describing data from dissimilar variations in population, location, and healthcare-system that are more generalizable or applicable (Vashishth et al., 2025).

4.4 Personalized Medicine and FAI: Tailoring Drugs to Genotypes

Personalized medicine, or precision medicine, strives to create medicine which accounts for individual distinctions; especially genetics. Federated Artificial Intelligence (FAI) offers a way to harness genomic and clinical datasets across institutions. FAI facilitates the large-scale data utilization for input into models while maintaining data privacy. Individual variability in genomic access influences how each individual metabolizes drugs, has a response to treatment, and manifests the risk of side-effects. Variability across genomic datasets must be addressed by researchers in their creation of genotype-guided therapies however genomic datasets across research institutions are always ethically and regulatory protected. FAI enables research to pool machine learning models using genomic markers, (SNPs, CNVs, etc) without moving data from their source. For example, hospitals and genomics labs can train models to predict their patients with specific genotypes responses to a cancer drug or to an anticoagulant therapy. This enables clinicians to select the most efficacious treatment for their individual patients with the least risk of adverse reactions, thereby improving patient outcomes and reducing trial-and-error prescribing. FAI also helps researchers identify pharmacogenetics biomarkers, referenceable genes with potential to stratify a patient into one of more well-defined subgroups based on genetic likelihood of benefit or harm from a route of therapy.

5. TECHNICAL ARCHITECTURE AND IMPLEMENTATION

Using Federated Artificial Intelligence (FAI) in biomedical applications such as drug development or genomics requires a carefully crafted technical architecture that maintains data privacy, model quality, scalability, and is compliant with regulatory requirements. FAI architecture is an assembly of interconnected components, each playing an integral role in providing a decentralized machine learning framework while preserving data locality.

5.1 Federated Learning Workflow in Biomedical Context

In the Biomedical domain a Federated Learning (FL) workflow is developed to accommodate the layered complexity and sensitivity of healthcare and genomic data while still preserving privacy compliance. This FL workflow supports collaborative model learning across a number of institutions, including hospitals, research laboratories, and pharmaceutical companies, allowing for the development of learning models without sharing any raw data with other clients. Clients only exchange model parameters, which will allow collaborative development of robust generalizable models for predictive tasks of disease, drug response modeling, or marker discovery. The workflow begins when a global model is created by a central server or orchestrator, and this model is then sent to participating clients, each of which has its own local biomedical dataset (i.e., patient health records, genomic sequences, or a clinical trial). Each client trains the model with their local data and outputs a set of updated model weights or gradients. Once local training is complete clients send aggregated encrypted model updates data back to the central server (not the data). Aggregated updates would be computed from the model parameters using averaging techniques such as Federated Averaging (FedAvg). More advanced approaches will consider model developments across heterogeneous data, such as FedProx and adaptive aggregation techniques.

Figure 2. Federated Learning Workflow in Biomedical Field

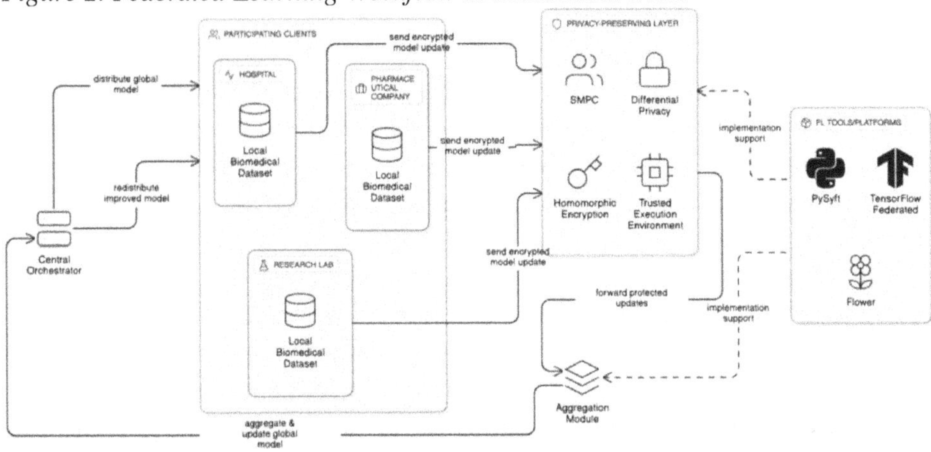

Different privacy-preserving techniques such as differential privacy, secure multi-party computation (SMPC), homomorphic encryption, and trusted execution environments (TEEs) are typically used to impede access to sensitive information at any point during the process. Figure 2 depicts the Federated Learning workflow in the biomedical field, enabling decentralized model training across multiple healthcare institutions. These privacy mechanisms ensure that even if the model updates are transmitted, they cannot be reverse-engineered to view or access individual data points. Within the biosciences context, there are further considerations for data heterogeneity, asynchronous participation (e.g., there may not be all nodes available in a federated system all of the time), and interoperability of data in general. Tools and platforms such as TensorFlow Federated, PySyft, and Flower are commonly used to deliver these workflows in practice and include multiple features (Huang et al., 2024).

5.2 Model Aggregation and Fusion Techniques

The essential features of Federated Artificial Intelligence (FAI) architecture—model aggregation and fusion—are particularly important in the biomedical domain because data are stored in a decentralized manner by many varied institutions containing diverse sample sizes, types, and qualities. During model aggregation, locally trained models from nodes—likely hospitals, genomic labs, or pharmaceutical companies—combine into one single model that will capture the learnings from all nodes without compromising any privacy restrictions. The most basic and commonly used aggregation method is Federated Averaging (FedAvg) where the aggregation utilizes weights from every local model based on the sample size for patients at that node, calculates local model means, and incorporates local model means into a global model. This straightforward and computational efficient method should work well in circumstances where the data between nodes is homogenous. However, it's very common for biomedical data to be non-independent and identically distributed (i.e., not IID) and unbalanced, with for example one node having mostly cancer patient data, and most of the data from other nodes with rare disease patients. Because of these differences in data distribution, basic model averaging may not be sufficient. Therefore, there are more complete and effective model aggregation techniques available, like FedProx (aggregated models that incorporate a term proximate to base local training, to help stabilize local training on heterogenous local site data), and FedNova (technique that normalizes aggregation, to compensate for differences in variational and convergence characteristics with varying numbers of local sites training samples). There are also other aggregation strategies, like Clustered Federated Learning, which aggregates clients on the client-side that have similar distributions, before performing an aggregation of sub-models and incorporating a more personal and relevant sub-models. In some biomedical settings and situations, specifically when the data are provided in a multi-modal way, the model aggregation can occur via a model fusion method.

5.3 Tools and Platforms (e.g., TensorFlow Federated, NVIDIA Clara)

The successful delivery of Federated Artificial Intelligence (FAI) in the biosciences depends greatly on adequate tools and platforms to support privacy-preserving, scalable, and efficient model training across a federated or distributed system. Several open-source and commercial platforms exist to support the establishment of federated learning systems in sensitive industries such as healthcare, genomics, and biopharma research.

1. **TensorFlow Federated (TFF):** TensorFlow Federated (TFF) open-source framework developed by Google that enhances TensorFlow functionalities to support federated learning. Users can simulate federated environments, implement personalized algorithms, and deploy decentralized machine learning models. TFF is especially useful for research in academia, allowing researchers flexibility to use different aggregation techniques as well as privacy-preservation methods. The flexibility of a Python interface means that users can easily switch between centralized and federated AI workflows in biomedical applications, working from already existing TensorFlow models.
2. **NVIDIA Clara:** It is a complete healthcare AI ecosystem that was designed to work in the real-world of medical applications. Clara Train provides com-

prehensive federated learning support across medical institutions. Users can collaboratively train machine learning models with medical imaging data, electronic health reports, personal health data and other restricted information, while maintaining privacy through secure aggregation and end-to-end encryption. Clara uses GPU-accelerated capacities to provide the speed that is needed for this type of analysis. Clara has been used successfully across federated learning initiatives, including one project training on cross-institutional sanity COVID-19 CT scans.

3. **PySyft:** PySyft is a widely used open-source software community library created by Open-mind, that enables doing privacy-preserving machine learning, including secure multi-party computation (SMPC), homomorphic encryption, and differential privacy. PySyft is particularly modular and provides users the ability to perform secure computations on sensitive biomedical data without centralization. PySyft also offers an advantage in research environments where the utmost control of data privacy and model security are necessary. The library is also compatible with PyTorch and TensorFlow, giving it a unique opportunity for federated learning experiments that are engaged with genomics, drug development, and patient-level analysis (Yang et al., 2024).
4. **Flower (FL):** Flower is a lightweight and extensible federated learning framework with support for many machines learning backends' including TensorFlow, PyTorch, and Scikit-learn. Flower was designed for deployment in real, heterogeneous environments, that is useful for collaborations of multiple institutions as is the case in biomedical research. Flower provides advanced communication processes, asynchronous learning capabilities and specifies simple client-server interaction orchestration. Flower tends to be used for works with the greatest need for scalability and flexibility, such as, cross-lab genomic data analyses or multi-institution drug response model building.

These tools and platforms serve as the technical backbone of Federated AI, making it feasible to deploy secure, scalable, and regulation-compliant machine learning models in biomedical environments. The choice of platform depends on the specific needs of the application—be it experimental flexibility, enterprise support, or privacy enhancement.

5.4 Managing Heterogeneous Data and Systems

One of the major technical challenges of implementing Federated Artificial Intelligence (FAI) in biomedical research and drug discovery are the heterogeneous data and computing environments present within all of the partnering institutions. Each institution, for example, hospital, pharmaceutical corporation, or research laboratory, has different data formats, storage, ontologies, and underlying hardware infrastructures. Heterogeneity creates interoperability challenges due to differences in system design and should be harmonized to ensure federated learning occurs smoothly and generates meaningful and trustworthy results. First, data heterogeneity occurs due to variability in data types, data sources, and/or standards. For example, one hospital may store genomic data using FASTA formatting, where another records data as VCF or BAM files. Clinical data also presents a data heterogeneity challenge if there are coded medical terminology differences, e.g., SNOMED CT, ICD-10, or HL7 FHIR and then commonly used features across sites may struggle to align. In response to the problem of heterogeneity and systems, solutions at the individual sites or institutions can be employed to support data harmonization, e.g., mapping individual institution's data storage to a common data model (CDM) or defining formal ontology-based integration frameworks to semantically harmonize data across multiple sites for the purposes of joint model training without physically modifying the data model or structure of the individual local data. Second, system-level heterogeneity entails non-uniform alteration of local infrastructures and sub-optimal varying data eligibility and costs across institutional hardware configurations, network bandwidths, or computational capacities. As with data heterogeneity, the FAI system's design technologies must allow for such heterogeneity while allowing for adaptive mechanisms for model updates, along with asynchronous training, and/or a slower client which may guide updates inconsistent while allowing the updates to be inconsistent independently of the global model convergence (Vashishth et al., 2025).

5.5 Experimental Setup and Performance Evaluation

This chapter presents our framework for a Federated Artificial Intelligence (FAI) development process that enables drug discovery and genomic research through collaborative privacy-preserving efforts. Our framework allows many different institutions to collaboratively train Machine Learning models without compromising the existing controls on the sensitive biomedical information being held by each institution. To achieve this goal, we outline a four-step methodological framework that provides the workflow for each of the four key phases of Federated AI, including: Preparing Local Datasets (LDS), Training Decentralized Models (TDM), Aggregating Federated Models (AFM), and Evaluating Performance Metrics (EPM). In the first phase of LDS, all participating institutions need to prepare their respective datasets, which include genomic variants, molecular descriptors, pharmacogenomic profiles, and clinical outcomes. Each institution will perform its data preparation activities, including feature extraction, normalization and encoding, independently, in order to preserve data quality and maintain compliance with applicable regulatory requirements. Once all participating institutions have completed their LDS phase, a global ML model will be created at a central coordinating server and distributed to each participating client institution. Each client institution will utilize its private dataset to train the global ML model locally and generate model updates in the form of parameter weights and/or gradient updates. Only the encrypted versions of the model parameters will be transmitted back to the central coordinating server for aggregation. There were five separate institutions acting as federation clients. All the clients had locally stored biomedical datasets containing information about the heterogeneity of their real-world biological experiments shown in Table II. Each of the datasets held information for each of its members; such as their respective genomic variants, drug compounds, pharmacogenomic and clinical response characteristics. The experimental implementation also employed a deep neural network (DNN) for predictive modelling tasks of drug-target and genotype-phenotype predictive model development. The client trained its respective DNN models locally over five epochs for each round of communication via FedAvg aggregation strategy over 50 total rounds of distributed communication among clients. In addition to local DNN model training and aggregating practice, differential privacy noise was introduced into the local DNN updates to protect individual client privacy. Let there be N participating institutions, each holding a local dataset D_i. The objective of federated learning is to minimize a global loss function without centralized data sharing, defined by equation (1):

$$\min_{w} F(w) = \sum_{i=1}^{N} \frac{|D_i|}{\sum_{j=1}^{N} |D_j|} F_i(w) \tag{1}$$

where w denotes the global model parameters and $F_i(w)$ represents the local loss function at client i. The global model is updated through the use of federated averaging (FedAvg) as shown in equation (2).

$$w^{(t1)} = \sum_{i=1}^{N} \frac{|D_i|}{\sum_{j=1}^{N} |D_j|} w_i^{(t1)} \tag{2}$$

This formulation ensures decentralized optimization, scalability, and strict preservation of data privacy.

Table 2. Description of Federated Experimental Datasets

Institution	Data Type	Samples	Key Features
Client 1	Genomic variants	2,100	SNPs, gene expression
Client 2	Drug compounds	1,850	Molecular descriptors
Client 3	Clinical data	2,400	Treatment response
Client 4	Pharmacogenomics	1,620	Genotype–drug links
Client 5	Multi-modal	2,030	Combined features

Performance metrics and evaluations were based on the following measures: predictive ability, F1, AUC, Rate of convergence, and communication rate. A comparison was made with performance metrics from Table 3, which were developed from a centralised learning model trained using pooled data.

Table 3. Performance Comparison of Centralized and Federated Models

Metric	Centralized Model	Federated AI Model
Accuracy (%)	88.6	91.4
F1-Score	0.86	0.90
AUC	0.88	0.92
Data Transfer Reduction (%)	65	85
Privacy Compliance	Low	High

The federated approach resulted in 91.4% predictive ability, and produced results nearly identical to those of a centralised learning approach without having to share any raw data. The small drop in performance was more than compensated for by the increased privacy and legal compliance due to no raw data sharing, and the increased scalability associated with the federated approach compared to the centralised approach.

Figure 3. Comparative Visual Analysis of Model Effectiveness and Privacy Efficiency

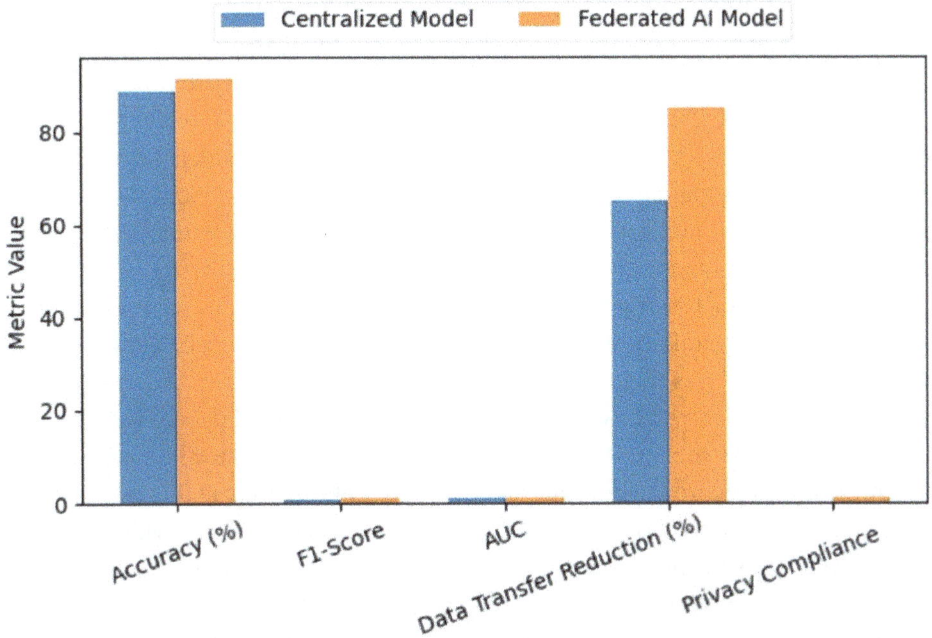

Figure 3, comparing the federated AI model performs more accurately, has improved communications efficiency, and provides a higher level of privacy compliance than the centralized model.

6. CASE STUDIES AND REAL-WORLD USE CASES

Recent developments in the application of Federated Artificial Intelligence (FAI) in drug discovery and genomic methods are shifting from theory to impact in the real world. These case studies demonstrate that FAI can enable collaborative innovation in a secure manner while also complying with the privacy protection requirements of individuals and institutions. The case examples are studies that leverage the ability to analyze, with the help of FAI, sensitive biomedical data at multiple institutional nodes with no sharing of the data, thereby enhancing the accuracy, scalability, and speed of biomedical research while achieving more than could have been attained in a centralized model.

6.1 Federated Learning in COVID-19 Drug Trials

The global health emergency posed by COVID-19 generated a critical need for fast drug development and repurposing, however obstacles of data privacy regulations and geographic distance create challenges for collaboration involving sensitive clinical and genomic data across institutions. Federated Learning (FL) acted as an important means to overcome these challenges by facilitating collaborative AI model training, among hospitals, research laboratories and pharmaceutical companies, without exposing patient-level data. During the pandemic, federated learning was utilized for COVID-19 drug trials in a number of meaningful ways. For example, universities and hospitals in different countries contributed to federated model training to elucidate patient risk factors, outcomes of disease progression, and even review candidate drug efficacy. FL was used in studies that examined patient responses to antiviral treatments such as Remdesivir and Dexamethasone, all while keeping the electronic health record (EHR) data stored in local data centres. In this instance, the federated model trained on patient-level data across many groups which allowed the researchers to consider aggregate insights across permutations of clinical data from variant populations. The reliability and generalizability of predictive models for drug efficacy and side effects are strengthened when aggregate insights are compared against diverse populations. With FL methods, researchers were able to build federated models capable of making personalized therapy decisions based on genomic and clinical profiles (Sharma et al., 2023).

6.2 Cross-Institutional Cancer Genomics Projects

Cancer research increasingly draws from larger genomic datasets in order to determine the molecular causalities underlying the different types of cancer, and more specifically, how to design drugs for these therapies. Unfortunately, most genomic datasets are locked in hospitals, cancer research institutes, or biobanks, with data privacy protocols firmly in place. Federated Artificial Intelligence (FAI) provides a collaborative and secure means to do cancer genomics research across hospitals and cancer centers without the need to store sensitive patient data in a central repository. One notable example of FAI applied to cancer genomics is the Federated Learning for Cancer Genomics (FLCG) program which connected several cancer centers to train AI models together on whole-genome sequencing data, gene expression data, and clinical outcomes targeting patients diagnosed with breast, lung, or prostate cancers. By leveraging FAI, hospitals and cancer centers could analyze infrequent mutations, gene fusions, and tumour-specific biomarkers among different patient cohorts while meeting data locality standards and ethical parameters. Through federated learning, the ability to conduct a genotype-phenotype association study and characterize signatures that indicate tumour mutational burden (TMB) along with training predictive models for immunotherapy response have been achieved. For example, each institution contributed to models trained locally and contributed these to a central aggregator. The central aggregator learned to predict which patients diagnosed with advanced non-small cell lung cancer (NSCLC) would potentially respond to PD-1/PD-L1 checkpoint inhibitors.

6.3 Rare Disease Research with Federated Models

Rare diseases affect a small proportion of the global population, but many rare diseases overall affect millions of people around the world. This adds significant research challenges, as it is difficult to study rare diseases with very little available data and patients, especially with dispersed patients across geographic locations. Traditional rare disease research is challenged to collect small datasets and to collaborate across silos, such as clinics and hospitals or separate institutions or research labs, which can limit the use of some of the world's most promising developments in research, such as machine-learning derived diagnostic models based on patient data, or genetic association models, due to issues with small sample sizes. Federation Artificial Intelligence (FAI), as a research mechanism, offers a strong alternative to traditional rare disease research models, allowing institutions to collaborate on a dataset without having to share patient data, allowing for the leverage of more usable data for collective use and research while still maintaining privacy and compliance issues between and due to the separate institutions. FAI gives researchers the ability to train machine learning models across many rare disease centres and each of these centres involves only a handful of patients that are relevant to the research. For example, federated learning has been applied in Duchenne Muscular Dystrophy, as well as in Gaucher's disease and in rare paediatric cancers while studying genomic and clinical data and imaging from a number of geographically isolated institutions to allow for the training of models to recognize early phenotypic signals or to predict disease progression. The federated models were made more robust by adding more diversity in the patient profiles and clinical settings. The FAI framework enables research to take place internationally, by supporting a form of research that adheres to any legal and ethical issue that may arise because of transferring data across borders (Naithani et al., 2024).

7. OPPORTUNITIES AND FUTURE DIRECTIONS

There are currently unique and transformational potential opportunities that are evolving from FAI in biomedical research that go well beyond the applications of

FAI in drug discovery and genomic applications. The healthcare and pharmaceutical industries are creating vast volumes of sensitive, distributed data to which FAI provides scalable opportunities to use collectively in an ethical and privacy-protecting way.

1. **Increased Real-world Evidence (RWE) Generation:** Federated AI has tremendous potential to leverage real-world evidence with AI models that are trained across multiple hospitals, clinics, and health systems. These healthcare organizations have access to priceless patient information about medications, side effects, and treatment success in real world environments. FAI will allow analysis of this federated data without risking patient privacy or contravening regulations.
2. **Multi-modal Data Syracuse for Precision Medicine:** In the future, federated models will be able to fuse many data types (e.g., genomics, imaging scans, instructor scans, laboratory results, clinical notations and wearable sensor data). The capability of multi-modal data integration will significantly advance precision medicine by generating a more comprehensive view of a patient's health status. FAI will make it possible to generate inferences from these types of diverse information across institutions sharing zero raw data, facilitating the development of more accurate and tailored models for diagnosing, treatment planning and predicting outcomes (Naik et al., 2024).
3. **Accessing Global Collaboration in Biomedical Research:** FAI promotes collaboration in biomedical research across nations. By utilizing federated models, data does not need to be physically transferred across international borders, which is particularly a concern for sensitive health data. This is potentially never more important than for monitoring rare diseases, pandemics, and conditions of interest to specific populations in limited numbers across national or transnational boundaries. Also, it promotes equity related to research responsivity, because low-resourced or privacy-conscious institutions that would not normally be able to participate in global biomedical innovation, can benefit from participating in federated models (Vashishth et al., 2025).
4. **Real-time Learning and Continuous Model Updating:** Future FAI implementations are expected to enable real-time learning; whereby federated models are constantly updated as new data is made available at each implementing node. This aspect is most potent in the rapidly changing realms of medicine, such as infectious diseases, cancer, and emergency medicine. With the capability of continuous learning, the system can accommodate regular faster new clinical patterns and/or genetic discoveries, which allows predictive models to remain current, responsive, and clinically applicable.
5. **Personalized Federated Learning Models:** In FAI's ultimate existence, personalized federated learning models are developed, whereby each institution,

or even each patient has a version of the AI model, fine-tuned to the local or individual data. This is important in genomics and pharmacogenomics since genetic diversity can alter treatment responses immensely. Personalized federated models will enhance precision medicine while maintaining data sovereignty and minimising impact on institutional autonomy.

8. CONCLUSION

Federated AI (FAI) is a revolutionary model for biomedical research, particularly for drug discovery and genomic science, that supports collaborative model development without sacrificing data privacy or ownership. FAI operates by providing decentralized learning, enabling institutions to utilize a variety of sensitive data - including genomic data, clinical trials, patient health records - and remain compliant with rigorous regulation. Successful uses of FAI within drug development, drug repurposing, rare disease research, and multi-site studies of cancer reinforce its importance in the shifting medical paradigm. Utilization of advanced aggregation technologies, privacy-preserving tools, and accessible platforms such as TensorFlow Federated and NVIDIA Clara are at the forefront of the FAI model. FAI exemplifies a solution to the problems of data existence, data fragmentation, data ownership and ethical concerns surrounding sensitive data. FAI represents a delivery model for equitable scale and personalized healthcare. This chapter has described a Federated Artificial Intelligence-based approach to secure collaborative constructing of pharmaceuticals and researching genomes. This methodology allows for the training of models without sharing data between Institutions, thus giving individuals control over their data and maintaining the individual's privacy. The experimental results, which showed that using a federated framework produced over 91.4% accuracy and 85% less data sent over the internet, were equal in performance to the traditional centralized learning approaches.

REFERENCES

Al-Remawi, M., & Rahem, R. A. A. (2024, February). Applications of AI in Biomedical Genomics and Pharmaceuticals. In 2024 2nd International Conference on Cyber Resilience (ICCR) (pp. 1-5). IEEE. DOI: 10.1109/ICCR61006.2024.10532792

Asti, G., D'Amico, S., Carota, L., Piscia, D., Casadei, F., Merleau, N. S. C., Alonso de Apellániz, P., Kubasch, A. S., Gloaguen, S., Modler, N., Gonzalez Martin, C., Rollo, C., Parras, J., Delleani, M., Zazzetti, E., Sauta, E., Curti, N., Derus, N. R., Carlini, G., & Alvarez, F. (2024). An Artificial Intelligence-Based Federated Learning Platform to Boost Precision Medicine in Rare Hematological Diseases: An Initiative by GenoMed4all and Synthema Consortia. *Blood*, *144*(Supplement 1), 4989. DOI: 10.1182/blood-2024-205541

Basri, T. S. J., & Kulkarni, A. K. (2025). Artificial Intelligence for Drug Discovery Accelerating the Development of New Pharmaceuticals. In ITM Web of Conferences (Vol. 76, p. 01010). EDP Sciences. DOI: 10.1051/itmconf/20257601010

Calvino, G., Peconi, C., Strafella, C., Trastulli, G., Megalizzi, D., Andreucci, S., Cascella, R., Caltagirone, C., Zampatti, S., & Giardina, E. (2024). Federated Learning: Breaking Down Barriers in Global Genomic Research. *Genes*, *15*(12), 1650. DOI: 10.3390/genes15121650 PMID: 39766917

Dermawan, D., & Alotaiq, N. (2025). From Lab to Clinic: How Artificial Intelligence (AI) Is Reshaping Drug Discovery Timelines and Industry Outcomes. *Pharmaceuticals (Basel, Switzerland)*, *18*(7), 981. DOI: 10.3390/ph18070981 PMID: 40732273

Gangwal, A., Ansari, A., Ahmad, I., Azad, A. K., & Sulaiman, W. M. A. W. (2024). Current strategies to address data scarcity in artificial intelligence-based drug discovery: A comprehensive review. *Computers in Biology and Medicine*, *179*, 108734. DOI: 10.1016/j.compbiomed.2024.108734 PMID: 38964243

Haggenmüller, S., Schmitt, M., Krieghoff-Henning, E., Hekler, A., Maron, R. C., Wies, C., Utikal, J. S., Meier, F., Hobelsberger, S., Gellrich, F. F., Sergon, M., Hauschild, A., French, L. E., Heinzerling, L., Schlager, J. G., Ghoreschi, K., Schlaak, M., Hilke, F. J., Poch, G., & Brinker, T. J. (2024). Federated learning for decentralized artificial intelligence in melanoma diagnostics. *JAMA Dermatology*, *160*(3), 303–311. DOI: 10.1001/jamadermatol.2023.5550 PMID: 38324293

Huang, D., Ye, X., & Sakurai, T. (2024). Multi-party collaborative drug discovery via federated learning. *Computers in Biology and Medicine*, *171*, 108181. DOI: 10.1016/j.compbiomed.2024.108181 PMID: 38428094

Kokudeva, M., Vichev, M., Naseva, E., Miteva, D. G., & Velikova, T. (2024). Artificial intelligence as a tool in drug discovery and development. *World Journal of Experimental Medicine*, *14*(3), 96042. DOI: 10.5493/wjem.v14.i3.96042 PMID: 39312699

Kumar, A., & Sadashiva, D. N. (2025). The Synergy Of Artificial Intelligence And Big Data Analytics In Accelerating Drug Discovery: From Target Identification To Clinical Trials. *International Journal of Environmental Sciences*, *11*(4s), 161–179.

Li, N., Lewin, A., Ning, S., Waito, M., Zeller, M. P., Tinmouth, A., & Shih, A. W.Canadian Transfusion Trials Group. (2025). Privacy-preserving federated data access and federated learning: Improved data sharing and AI model development in transfusion medicine. *Transfusion*, *65*(1), 22–28. DOI: 10.1111/trf.18077 PMID: 39610333

Naik, K., Goyal, R. K., Foschini, L., Chak, C. W., Thielscher, C., Zhu, H., Lu, J., Lehár, J., Pacanoswki, M. A., Terranova, N., Mehta, N., Korsbo, N., Fakhouri, T., Liu, Q., & Gobburu, J. (2024). Current status and future directions: The application of artificial intelligence/machine learning for precision medicine. *Clinical Pharmacology and Therapeutics*, *115*(4), 673–686. DOI: 10.1002/cpt.3152 PMID: 38103204

Naithani, K., Raiwani, Y. P., Tiwari, S., & Chauhan, A. S. (2024). Artificial Intelligence Techniques Based on Federated Learning in Smart Healthcare. In Federated Learning for Smart Communication Using IoT Application (pp. 81-108). Chapman and Hall/CRC. DOI: 10.1201/9781003489368-5

Niazi, S. K., & Mariam, Z. (2025). Artificial intelligence in drug development: Reshaping the therapeutic landscape. *Therapeutic Advances in Drug Safety*, *16*, 20420986251321704. DOI: 10.1177/20420986251321704 PMID: 40008227

Sharma, V., Vashishth, T. K., Kumar, B., Sharma, K. K., Vidyant, S., & Chaudhary, S. (2023, December). Health Interpretation of Covid-19 Patients using Artificial Intelligence. In *2023 International Conference on Artificial Intelligence for Innovations in Healthcare Industries (ICAIIHI)* (Vol. 1, pp. 1-5). IEEE Computer Society. DOI: 10.1109/ICAIIHI57871.2023.10488924

Vashishth, T. K., Sharma, V., & Ahamad, S. (2025). Exploring machine learning models for biomedical signal processing: a comprehensive review. Machine Learning Models and Architectures for Biomedical Signal Processing, 69-96.

Vashishth, T. K., Sharma, V., Kumar, B., Sharma, K. K., Chaudhary, S., & Panwar, R. (2025). Blockchain for Securing Federated Learning Systems: Enhancing Privacy and Trust. Model Optimization Methods for Efficient and Edge AI: Federated Learning Architectures, Frameworks and Applications, 299-320.

Vashishth, T. K., Sharma, V., Sharma, K. K., Chaudhary, S., Kumar, B., & Kumar, P. (2025). Future trends and emerging technologies in biomedical engineering. Innovations in Biomedical Engineering, 519-550.

Vashishth, T. K., Sharma, V., Sharma, K. K., Kumar, B., Chaudhary, S., & Panwar, R. (2024). Enhancing biomedical signal processing with machine learning: A comprehensive review. Digital Transformation in Healthcare 5.0: Volume 1: IoT. *AI and Digital Twin*, *277*, 277–306. Advance online publication. DOI: 10.1515/9783111327853-010

Vashishth, T. K., Sharma, V., Sharma, K. K., Vidyant, S., & Bhardwaj, A. (2025). Future Trends and Challenges in Pharmaceutical Microbiology with the Integration of Artificial Intelligence. AI-Powered Advances in Pharmacology, 315-344.

Walton, N. A., Nagarajan, R., Wang, C., Sincan, M., Freimuth, R. R., Everman, D. B., Walton, D. C., McGrath, S. P., Lemas, D. J., Benos, P. V., Alekseyenko, A. V., Song, Q., Gamsiz Uzun, E., Taylor, C. O., Uzun, A., Person, T. N., Rappoport, N., Zhao, Z., & Williams, M. S. (2024). Enabling the clinical application of artificial intelligence in genomics: A perspective of the AMIA Genomics and Translational Bioinformatics Workgroup. *Journal of the American Medical Informatics Association : JAMIA*, *31*(2), 536–541. DOI: 10.1093/jamia/ocad211 PMID: 38037121

Yang, M., Huang, D., Wan, W., & Jin, M. (2024). Federated learning for privacy-preserving medical data sharing in drug development. *Applied and Computational Engineering*, *108*(1), 7–13. DOI: 10.54254/2755-2721/2025.LD17879

Chapter 6
Natural Language Processing for Smarter Healthcare

Leena G. Pillai
http://orcid.org/0000-0003-1692-7647
Sree Saraswathi Thyagaraja College, India

ABSTRACT

This chapter presents a comprehensive overview of two dominant areas of Natural Language Processing (NLP), text processing and Speech Processing, in the domain of smarter healthcare systems. To make unstructured healthcare data suitable for computation, a series of well-defined processing steps (pipeline) is required to transform raw text, speech, and other data modalities into structured and machine-interpretable representations. The chapter discusses on the NLP text processing pipeline and its key healthcare applications such as clinical text summarization, information retrieval, question answering, relation extraction, normalization, and predictive analytics. It further extends the discussion to speech processing, highlighting Speech-to-Text, Speech-to-Speech, and Text-to-Speech systems. This section covers how speech data undergoes signal-level processing before linguistic interpretation. Evaluation and validation strategies are also discussed separately for text and speech processing.

1. INTRODUCTION

The integration of digital equipment, such as wearable devices, and technologies such as Electronic Health Records (EHRs), diagnostic reports, telemedicine consultations, and health-related social media discussions, collectively generates

DOI: 10.4018/979-8-2600-0981-9.ch006

vast volumes of unstructured and multimodal data in health care on daily basis (Jerfy et al., 2024). In the context of healthcare environment, unstructured data generates from clinician-patient conversation (online/in-person), physician notes, discharge summaries, online discussions and pathology report. As a result of this digital transformation the healthcare dataset follows heterogeneity and complexity with textual, acoustic, and image-based information (Adnan et al., 2020). These data carry comprehensive information about the patient's health at the same time contribute significant challenges in storage, processing, analysis and interpreting.

Traditional computational techniques are equipped to process and extract information from structured and homogeneous datasets. Therefore, an advanced processing technology required to capture the contextual nuances embedded within clinical data and language. This gap has positioned by Natural Language Processing (NLP) as a cornerstone technology for intelligent healthcare systems capable of processing, understanding, interpreting, and generating an accurate clinically relevant decision support system. NLP provides the linguistic and AI powered cognitive infrastructure required for a smarter, collaborative healthcare ecosystem.

Figure 1. The major needs for using NLP in healthcare

The growing digitization of health records and telemedicine platforms has significantly expanded the potential for NLP-driven e-collaboration (Chandel, 2025; Mohapatra, 2026). Figure 1 illustrates the need of NLP in health care:

- Effectively manages and processes large volume of unstructured data and generate context dependent information out of that.

- Assist healthcare professionals by providing quick access to relevant patient information and evidence-based insights.
- Reduces time and manual effort in clinical documentation by automating report generation, summarization and transcribing doctor–patient conversations.
- Enables intelligent chatbots, conversational agent, multilingual support, and voice-based systems for better communication and patient engagement.
- Facilitate researchers to identify patterns, trends, and correlations that advance medical knowledge and innovation.
- NLP contributes to the early detection of emotional or cognitive changes by analyzing speech and language patterns,
- Ensures consistency and interoperability across diverse healthcare systems through interpreting and mapping unstructured or semi-structured textual information to standardized medical coding systems such as ICD (International Classification of Diseases), SNOMED CT (Systematized Nomenclature of Medicine – Clinical Terms), and UMLS (Unified Medical Language System).

NLP is a technological field that integrates computer science, artificial intelligence and language technology together. Two modes of communication, text and speech, primely adopted by human for communicate their thought, emotion, and intent (Behera & Nayak, 2020). These natural forms of communication serve as the foundation for interaction between patient and doctor, clinical documentation, and medical knowledge exchange. NLP effectively handles these modalities through text processing and speech processing, processes that have its own pipelines to generate intelligent systems to interpret, analyze, and respond to medical information in ways that closely mimic human understanding.

Figure 2. Components of NLP

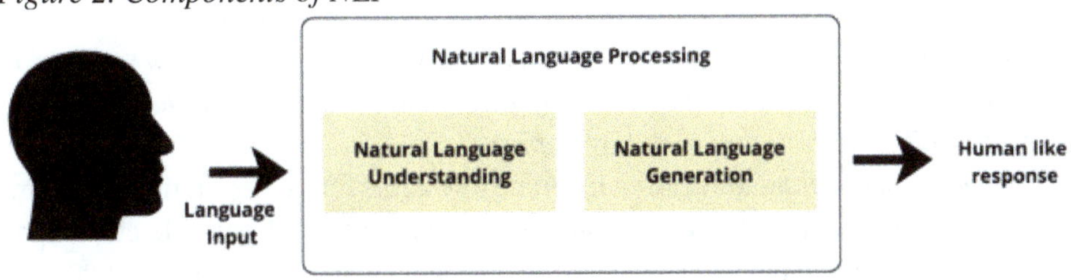

As illustrated in Figure 2, NLP has two core components -Natural Language Understanding (NLU) and Natural Language Generation (NLG) that work together to make healthcare systems more intelligent, interactive, and human-centric. As the name says, NLU enables machines to understand human language, NLG generate meaningful, human-like responses. These two components provide foundation for a wide range of applications in modern healthcare, from clinical decision support to conversational health assistants.

2. TEXT PROCESSING

Healthcare data is inherently multimodal which covers a wide range of information multiple sources such as sensors, online audio consultation, medical images and records. However, a significant portion of data exist in textual form. Most of this textual data, such as clinical notes, prescriptions and patient centric content, are available in unstructured form and it contribute challenges for conventional computational models. In this section, NLP reframed and presented as a tool for providing foundational layer of intelligence in digital health car. Rather than a general-purpose NLP, health sector demands for domain specific language models, such as Clinicalbert (Huang & Ranganath, 2019), BioBERT (Lee et al., 2020), MKSAP-19 (Lee et al., 2023), which perform better in terms of accuracy, contextual understanding, and inference.

Computational systems understand only machine level language which consist of a sequence of binary (0 or 1) code. We humans, effortlessly interpret context, ambiguity, domain-specific expressions and many nuances of a language. However, machines cannot directly understand natural language text in its raw form. As in any domain, clinical contents are written for human readers and naturally that contain abbreviations, shorthand phrases, fragmented sentences, and medical terminologies.

For example:

"Pt c/o chest tightness since y'day. Hx of DM-II. ECG: mild abnormalities. Adv: continue Metformin, start low-dose aspirin."

From this clinical note a human clinician can easily understand as:

"The patient complains of chest tightness since yesterday, has a history of Type II Diabetes, the ECG shows mild abnormalities, and the doctor advises continuing Metformin and initiating low-dose aspirin."

This level of understanding is not inherently possible for a computational system. To enable it, we need to train the system by including the all-possible challenges encompassed in the language as well as the domain (Spasic & Nenadic, 2020).

In language understanding, key challenges coined in the above example are:

- "Pt," "c/o," and "Hx" are abbreviations.
- Terms like "DM-II" and drug names require domain knowledge.
- The text lack's proper structure and punctuation.
- Relationships (patient → symptom, drug → treatment) are implicit.

A well-defined and structured sequence of processes required to bridge the gap between human language and machine language by preserving all information, context, emotions and nuances enclosed in the content. This essential structured workflow is called NLP text processing pipeline.

NLP pipeline pipelines slightly vary based on the domain and the complexity of the data it handles. General NLP pipeline required to address the text processing in healthcare domain are summarized below (Elov, et al., 2023):

a) Data Collection and Secure Ingestion

The first step in any machine learning process is data collection. Collect relevant text from multiple sources such as EHRs, lab/radiology reports, prescriptions, report summaries, patient portal and public health forums. Being the medical data, it is required to enforce data governance during the ingestion process such as encryption, authorization and access control and compliance with applicable privacy laws.

Example: Collect clinical note from cardiology department EHR with timestamp.

b) Ethical/Privacy Filtering

De-identification is required to apply in clinical data to avoid privacy risk. Therefore, if the data is intended to use for model training or cross-institutional sharing, personal information mask or removal is an important step in healthcare data.

Example: Personal information, “Mr. Peter, MRN: 0011235”, replaced with tokens like [PATIENT_NAME] and [MRN]

c) Text Preprocessing and Normalization

The medical data may not maintain a structured form which contribute high level of irregularities in data. In healthcare domain, preprocessing and normalization addresses medical abbreviations, incorrect punctuations, whitespaces, formatting artifacts such as copied tables and misspellings.

Example: ‘pt’ – ‘patient’, ‘c/o’ – ‘complains of’, ‘y’day’ – ‘yesterday’, ‘DM-II’ – ‘Type II Diabets’

d) Segmentation and Tokenization

Clinical document often lacks proper punctuation and mostly convoluted with standard and narrative heading. This can be addressed by segmentation and further tokenization to provide basis for syntactic and morphological analysis. Segmentation divides the text into smaller chunks like sentences, whereas the tokenization is a more specific type of segmentation that breaks text into individual words or sub-word units called tokens (Choo & Kim., 2023).

Example: The medical note becomes a sequence of tokens such as *"Patient," "complains," "chest," "pain," "ECG," "ST," "elevation," "possible," "MI," "aspirin," "300," "mg."*

e) Syntactic and Morphological Analysis

This step identifies the grammatical role of each word and analyzes how words relate to each other by the means of part-of-speech tagging, lemmatization, and parsing. Understanding grammar helps the system interpret who is having symptoms, what symptoms are described, and what treatments are advised.

For instance, the pipeline identifies "chest pain" as the patient's symptom and "Start aspirin 300 mg" as a treatment instruction.

f) Named Entity Recognition (NER)

The NER identifies medical entities such as symptoms, drugs, diagnosis, tests, dosage and procedures (Almeida et al., 2025). Generally, NER models are trained or fine-tuned on domain corpora. Therefore, in clinical domain, it needs to get trained with clinical dictionaries or terminologies.

From the example, the pipeline extracts entities like:

- Symptom: chest pain
- Diagnostic test: ECG
- Finding: ST elevation
- Diagnosis: myocardial infarction
- Medication: aspirin 300 mg

g) Relation Extraction and Event Detection

This step converts a bag of entities into a knowledge graph or structured events usable for reasoning (Frisoni et al., 2021). It identifies clinically relevant associations such as symptom – disease relationships, drug – dosage pairs, and medication changes. These relationships transform isolated entities into coherent clinical events that reflect the true semantics of the patient record.

Example relations:

```
(Patient) – has_symptom - (chest tightness).
(Metformin) – is_continued_for - (Type II Diabetes)
```

```
(Aspirin) – prescribed_new - (low-dose)
```

h) Temporal Reasoning

Clinical records often depend on event ordering such as symptoms before treatment with temporal mapping ("yesterday", "one week before"). Temporal reasoning help to determining when symptoms began, how long treatments have been in place, and the order in which clinical events occurred (Alfattni et al., 2020).

Example: "since yesterday"

```
set date = document_date - 1 day.
```

i) Feature Extraction

Through the different steps mentioned above many linguistic, semantic and clinical information are extracted. But all this information is not in a computational machine-readable form. Feature extraction converts this processed text into quantitative representations (vectors) which machine can understand and process.

Example, convert to numerical form: "chest pain with ST elevation" -> [0.87, -0.33, 1.21, …]

j) Classification and Prediction

Once features are extracted from clinical text, the next stage of the NLP pipeline involves transforming these representations into meaningful decisions or forecasts through classification or predictive modelling. The choice of modelling approach completely depends on the nature of the problem.

In many scenarios, the goal is classification, where the system assigns the input text to one of several predefined categories. *For example*, based on features derived from pathology reports, symptom descriptions, or oncologist notes, a model may determine whether a patient is likely to have cancer or not.

Other cases, the system uses both historical and current information to anticipate future outcomes. This type of modelling is essential in clinical risk assessment and population health forecasting which is called prediction. *For example*, forecasting the progression of chronic disease based on longitudinal clinical notes. Unlike classification, predictive modelling generates forward-looking insights that support preventive care and early detection.

To achieve classification and prediction, two broad computational pathways are commonly used.

- The first option is to build a machine learning framework and train a model using the features extracted from the text.
- The second option is to use pretrained language models, which have already learned rich linguistic and contextual representations from large biomedical corpora. Models such as BioBERT (Lee et al., 2020), ClinicalBERT (Huang & Ranganath, 2019), or transformer architectures can be fine-tuned for specific healthcare domain based on the availability of the data., BioBERT

k) Evaluation and Validation

Evaluation of the trained model in healthcare NLP is much more critical than any other general purpose NLP tasks. The outcome of the classification or prediction models may directly influence clinical decisions and further diagnosis. Therefore, domain-sensitive metrics required for evaluating healthcare NLP systems which go beyond simple accuracy.

One of the most commonly used evaluation tools is the confusion matrix, which breaks model outcomes as in Table 1 (Yang & Berdine, 2024)

Table 1. 4 parameters that creates a confusion matrix

Parameters	Description
True Positive (TP)	Model correctly predicts that the patient does not have pneumonia
True Negative (TN)	Model correctly predicts that the patient *does not have pneumonia*
False Positive (FP)	model incorrectly predicts pneumonia when the patient does *not* actually have it
False Negative (FN)	Model predicts "No pneumonia" even though the patient *actually has it*

For Example:

Imagine we have 1000 radiology reports. Doctors later confirmed that:

- 300 patients truly have pneumonia
- 700 patients truly do not have pneumonia

To Perform validation, the same data we have given to our trained NLP model and the model performance is given below:

a) True Positive (TP): Out of 300 pneumonia cases, the model predicted 240 correctly as pneumonia.

TP = 240

b) False Negative (FN): Patients who actually have pneumonia BUT the model predicted as "Normal". The remaining pneumonia cases (300 – 240) = 60 were missed.

FN = 60

c) True Negative (TN): Out of 700 healthy patients, the model correctly identified 680 as normal.

TN = 680

d) False Positive (FP): Patients who do NOT have pneumonia (normal) BUT the model predicted as pneumonia. The remaining normal cases (700 – 680) = 20 were wrongly marked as pneumonia.

FP = 20

This will be illustrated in confusion matrix as given in Table 2.

Table 2. Confusion matrix of the pneumonia classification model evaluation

		Predicted Class	
		Pneumonia	**Normal**
Target Class	Pneumonia	True Positive (TP) 240	False Negative (FN) 60
	Normal	False Positive (FP) 20	True Negative (TN) 680

In medical domain, rather than merely counting correct and incorrect prediction, rigorous evaluation method required which can capture the nature and severity of the classification done by the model. If the dataset is imbalanced, *for example: healthy patients far outnumber sick patients*, accuracy becomes misleading because a model can appear "high-performing" simply by predicting the majority class. Some of the evaluation matrix, derived from the confusion matrix, that enables to understand the reliability, safety, and clinical applicability are described below:

- Accuracy: It measures the overall proportion of correct predictions. Accuracy provides answer to the question: *Out of all patients 1000 patients, how many did the system classify correctly?*

Based on the example it can be calculated as:

$$Accuracy = \frac{TP + TN}{Total} = \frac{240 + 680}{1000} = 0.92$$

Here, the model performed with 92% accuracy, which means that the model classified 92% of the patient report correctly.

- Precision: Precision focuses only on the number of cases which predicted positive. It answers: *Out of the patients (pneumonia + normal) the model predicted as Pneumonia, how many actually have pneumonia?*

$$Precision = \frac{TP}{TP + FP} = \frac{240}{240 + 20} = 0.923$$

It indicates that 92% patients are correctly classified as having pneumonia.

- Recall or Sensitivity: It measures the model's ability to detect actual pneumonia cases. It answers: *Out of all pneumonia patients, how many did the model successfully identified as having "pneumonia"?*

$$Recall = \frac{TP}{TP + FN} = \frac{240}{240 + 60} = 0.80$$

The 80% recall conveys that the model misclassified 20% of pneumonia cases as "normal" which is significant in clinical domain.

- Specificity: It focuses on normal cases. It measures how well the model is in identifying healthy (normal) patients. It complements recall by answering: *Out of all healthy (normal) patients, how many did the model successfully identified as "normal"?*

$$Specificity = \frac{TN}{TN + FP} = \frac{680}{680 + 20} = 0.971$$

It conveys that 97% of healthy ("normal") patients are correctly identified.

- F1-Score: It combines both precision and recall in a single measure. In other words, it's a harmonic mean of precision and recall which effectively useful in imbalanced datasets by penalizing low recall and low precision.

$$F1 - Score = \frac{2 \times (Precision \times Recall)}{Precision + Recall} = \frac{2 \times (0.923 \times 0.80)}{0.923 + 0.80} = 0.857$$

Even though, as discussed above, a wide range of effective evaluation methods are employed in NLP pipeline to evaluate the model's performance, their quantitative value alone cannot guarantee clinical assurance. Medical decision-making involves complexities that extend far beyond statistical evaluation. Therefore, an active involvement of the clinical expert in validation becomes an indispensable step before deploying any NLP or diagnostic model in real-world healthcare settings.

2.1 Applications of NLP in healthcare

a) Classification Problems

Classification is the process of assigning predefined categories or labels to the given clinical data. A wide range of classification models, traditional (like Support Vector Machine (SVM), Random Forest) to Transformer-based (like ClinicalBERT, XLNet), are available which are trained in large labelled corpus. This training experience makes the model to accurately predict labels to the given test set. Some of the important classification application in healthcare are (Dimililer, 2021):

- Disease Classification: A model reads a doctor's note and classifies it as pneumonia, asthma, COPD, etc. Used in automated diagnosis support and epidemiological surveillance.
- Sentiment and Emotion Classification in Patient Feedback: Classifying patient reviews as positive, neutral, or negative to monitor service quality or detect hospital-level risks.
- Symptom Classification from Patient Notes: Classifying the sentence "I have been coughing for three days" as respiratory symptom.
- Risk Classification: Classifying a patient into high risk of sepsis based on historical notes and lab results described in text.
- Mental Health Text Classification: Classifying patient phrases into depression indicators, suicidal ideation, or normal emotional state.
- Insurance Claim Classification: Classify the given claims as valid, requires audit, or potential fraud.

b) Predictive Analytics

Instead of diagnosing and identifying what are the deceases currently having, predictive system answers *what is likely to happen next*. Predictive analytics refers historical healthcare data to forecast future medical events using statistical or machine learning algorithms.

For example, a predictive model may learn that a combination of elevated heart rate, low oxygen saturation, and abnormal respiratory patterns from a wearable device correlates with early stages of pneumonia. The system can then alert clinicians or patients before the condition becomes severe.

c) Summarization of Clinical Text

Medical domain always handles multiple and lengthy detailed clinical notes for each patient. These documents obliviously contain valuable information, but it's a tedious task for healthcare professionals to extract it, especially in their busy clinical environments. This task is done by NLP text summarization algorithms that converts large and Mult-structured (unstructured) medical content in to short and interpretable summaries by preserving essential information and original meaning. Based on the information summarization process, there are two types of summarizations:

- Extractive Summarization Extractive summarization executed by selecting and combining important sentences or phrases directly from the original text. This method does not generate any single text. Instead, it identifies most relevant sentences from the given documents and combine them together to form a summary. Popular algorithms used for applied for extractive summarization are TextRank, TF-IDF based ranking and LexRank.

  For Example:
  Original Clinical Note (word count: 47):
  "The patient is a 64-year-old male with a history of diabetes and hypertension. He was admitted with complaints of chest pain and shortness of breath. ECG shows mild ST elevation. Troponin levels are high. The patient was administered aspirin and shifted to the cardiac unit for monitoring."
  Extractive Summary Output (word count: 26):
  "64-year-old male with diabetes and hypertension. Admitted with chest pain and breathlessness. ECG shows ST elevation; troponin high. Started on aspirin and moved to cardiac unit."

- Abstractive Summarization Abstractive summarization applied to understand context and content from the input documents and generate concise critical informative summary out of it. This summarization method is more complex than extractive summary because rather than identifying and selecting important sentences, abstractive method interprets meaning and rephrases the content. Popular models for abstractive summarization are seq2seq models, pointer generator networks, and transformer-based models.

Abstractive summary output for the above clinical note:
"A 64-year-old diabetic and hypertensive patient was admitted for suspected heart attack and started on emergency cardiac treatment."

d) Information Retrieval (IR) from Databases and Medical Literature

As discussed in previous section, the rapid growth and intervention of digitalization in healthcare led to a vast expansion of medical information. IR is an effective approach dedicated to extract task based relevant information beyond simple "search". IR is designed to index, query and retrieve two distinct types of high-stake data, scientific knowledge and clinical data. Even though the underlying NLP pipeline performs text processing, IR further operates through its own four key functions:

- Query Understanding: The primary step required for information retrieval is identifying the intent of the user's query. The foremost challenge faced at this stage is vocabulary mismatch. Patient often uses layman terminologies such as "*heart attack*", and clinician use technical such as "*acute myocardial infarction*". This gap needs to be bridged before searching.
- Indexing: Before starting search the large volume of database need to organized in a searchable representation. Conventional approach used for indexing was Lexical indexing which is based on the frequency of word occurrence in the document. The modern system uses semantic indexing which is neural network-based approach.
- Ranking: Once the algorithm retrieves a set of potential documents against the query given by the user, it must order them based on their relevance. This phase has computational complexity. Traditional ranking prioritizes a document based on the frequency of terms occurrence in the document. For example, If query related to "cancer", it provides high rank to the document where the term "cancer" has high frequency. A Transformer-based ranker, however, can distinguish between a document discussing *"Treatment of cancer"* (High Relevance) versus *"History of cancer research institutions"* (Low Relevance), even if both contain the keyword equally.
- Presentation: Always user expects the IR result in a structured and easy understandable manner. Therefore, IR presented the retrieved documents in professional way which typically contains concise and context-highlighted snippets that present the text segments based on their ranking.

e) Question-Answering (QA) Systems

Question answering is the subfield of IR which is responsible to provide answers to the questions, posted by users in natural language. A QA system follows the NLP pipeline and its primary task is to understand the meaning and intent behind the question. Then it searches for the relevant information for reference across corpus and generate accurate answer.

For example, if a clinician asks, *"What is the first-line treatment for pediatric asthma?"* a QA system retrieves the appropriate guideline section, interprets the treatment recommendations, and provides an immediate, evidence-based response.

Based on the way QA system prepares the answer, it can be classified into extractive and generative. Extractive QA system identifies relevant answers from the given document and provides it as answers with out generating anything. Whereas, the generative QA system refer multiple relevant documents and generate answers. This enables the system to provide more human-like answers.

As we have discussed in this section, the medical field generates an overwhelming quantity of unstructured data which range from the narrative flow of physician notes to the density of biomedical literature. The interventions of NLP make this useful beyond merely record-keeping. By applying different approaches, suitable for the problem statement, the system transforms raw text into a dynamic asset. It converts "notes" into "data/information," and "data" into "intelligence."

3. SPEECH PROCESSING

Text processing has been successfully implemented in healthcare for many years. These advances have made significant improvement in many areas such as information management, decision support, and research workflows. However, as human beings continually seek more natural and effortless ways to interact with technology, attention has increasingly shifted toward processing the most fundamental and intuitive mode of communication which is speech. Speech represents the primary form of both formal and informal communication. In healthcare settings, speech contain valuable information such as patients describe symptoms verbally, doctors dictate clinical notes and caregivers provide spoken instructions. In this context, speech processing technologies have emerged as a powerful extension of text processing.

In the computational perspective, both text and speech are processed in the form of numerical representations. But the pipeline through which they reach this representation are fundamentally different. Text data begins as discrete symbolic representations – characters, words, or tokens - which can be directly mapped to numerical vectors using linguistic and semantic representations. In contrast, speech is a continuous acoustic signal that must undergo multiple signal processing stages before any linguistic interpretation becomes possible (Latif., et al 2020).

Figure 3. Speech processing pipeline

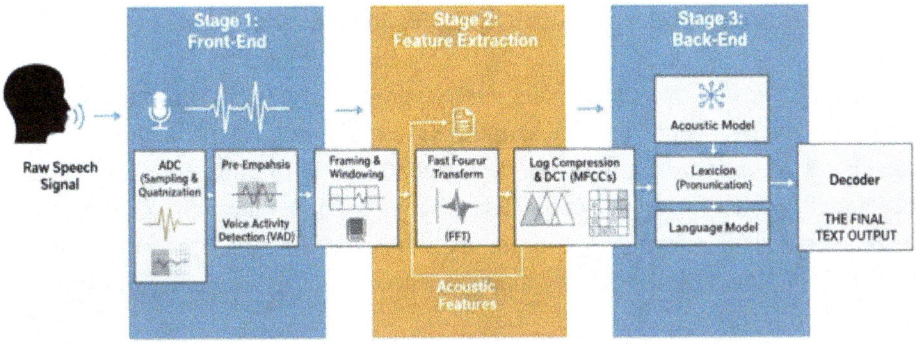

As in text processing, speech processing has systematically organized pipeline for conducting complex transformation from raw acoustic signals to meaningful linguistic units. This process can be broadly categorized into three stages that enables transition from raw physics (analog signal) to mathematical patterns and finally to linguistic meaning. As illustrated in figure 3, this transformation can be done through a set of complex process and methods which can be encapsulated in the following three stages.

3.1 Speech Processing Architecture

a) Front – End

The initial stage captures the audio (analog) signals which contains rich physical properties of the sound waves and preparing this raw speech signal for subsequent processing. This stage is vital as speech signals are often affected by noise, variations in recording equipment, and environmental conditions. Especially, in healthcare context these challenges are amplified by different factors such as diverse recording environments (e.g., clinics, homes), varying equipment quality, and vulnerable populations. Therefore, effective preprocessing is essential to enhance signal quality, isolate clinically relevant speech information, and ensure consistency and effectiveness in subsequent analytical stages (Kumar, 2024).

- Speech acquisition: Speech waves are captured using microphones or recording devices in clinical environments such as consultation rooms, telemedicine platforms, or wearable health devices.
- Analog-to-Digital Converter (ADC): ADC transforms the continuous waveform into a sequence of discrete digital from that can be processed by a computer. This process involves sampling and quantization.

Sampling transforms a continuous random process $x(t)$ into a discrete sequence $x[n] = x(nT_s)$, where T_s is the sampling interval and $f_s = 1/T_s$ is the sampling frequency. Through this sampling converts a continuous-time signal into a discrete-time signal by measuring its amplitude at regular time intervals. Quantization is the process of converting a continuous-amplitude discrete-time signal into a discrete-amplitude digital signal by mapping each sample to one of a finite number of predefined levels.

- Preprocessing and signal enhancement: This stage is responsible to improve signal quality through noise removal, identifying and removing the silence segments, and normalizing amplitude variations. This pre-emphasis technique boosts the high-frequency components of the audio signal, which often carry important phonetic information.

For example: In human speech, higher-pitched sounds (like "s" or "f") are naturally much quieter than lower-pitched vowels. A pre-emphasis filter boosts these high frequencies so the algorithm can recognize them more clearly against background noise.

Effective preprocessing is particularly critical in healthcare, where even minor misinterpretations can lead to clinical errors.

- Voice Activity Detection (VAD): It act as a smart filter system which detect and segregate the processed signal to actual speech and silence/background noise. Traditional VAD system does this task based on the threshold value. But now, data driven models are effectively capturing these patterns from the data itself.
- Framing and windowing: A computing cannot analyze a whole sentence at once because speech is non-stationary the frequency and volume change constantly as the articulators moves. However, if you look at a tiny slice of speech (20–30ms, ideally 25ms), the human vocal tract doesn't move fast enough to change significantly. This is the theory implemented in framing.

At this stage, the speech signals are divided in to 25ms frames which ultimately provides a stationary speech feature. This chopping process contributes sharp edged frames. These sharp edges are seen by the computer as "infinite" high-frequency noise that wasn't actually present in the natural speech. This status is generally called Spectral Leakage. This can be solved by multiplying the frame by a curved function such as Hamming and Hanning window, that tapers the edges to zero. These two steps will help to detect the difference between "50 mg" and "15 mg" while doctor dictates a prescription.

b) Feature Extraction

Feature extraction is an important and unavoidable step in speech processing pipeline because it serves as a bridge between acoustic signals and intelligent applications. It transforms raw speech signals into compact numerical representations by highlighting clinically and linguistically characteristics in numerical representation. This allows machine learning and deep learning models to further process speech efficiently and reliably. During the communication between patient and doctor, their speech often contains variations in pronunciation, speaking rate, hesitation, and emotional tone. Feature extraction captures these subtle acoustic cues through spectral, prosodic, and temporal features (Singh, 2024).

Spectral frequencies describe which parts of the voice are low-pitched and which are high-pitched, and how much energy each part carries. When patients describe symptoms verbally, their speech often contains variations in pronunciation, speaking rate, hesitation, and emotional tone. Feature extraction captures these subtle acoustic cues through spectral, prosodic, and temporal features. For example, spectral features help to identify phonetic patterns necessary to correctly recognize symptom names, while prosodic features such as pitch and pause duration can reflect distress, fatigue, or cognitive difficulty.

In the case of doctor dictation, the primary goal of feature extraction is to ensure accurate recognition of medical terminology and structured clinical information. Spectral features such as MFCCs preserve fine-grained phonetic details needed to distinguish between similar-sounding medical terms. Temporal features capture speech rhythm and pacing, which are essential for handling abbreviations, numerical values, and rapid dictation styles commonly used by clinicians. At this stage the feature extraction directly influences the quality of automated clinical documentation and downstream NLP tasks such as coding, summarization, and information extraction.

Symbolic Example of Feature Extraction:

Consider a patient verbally describing a symptom: *"I feel chest pain"*

Figure 4. Symbolic representation of feature extraction from each frame.

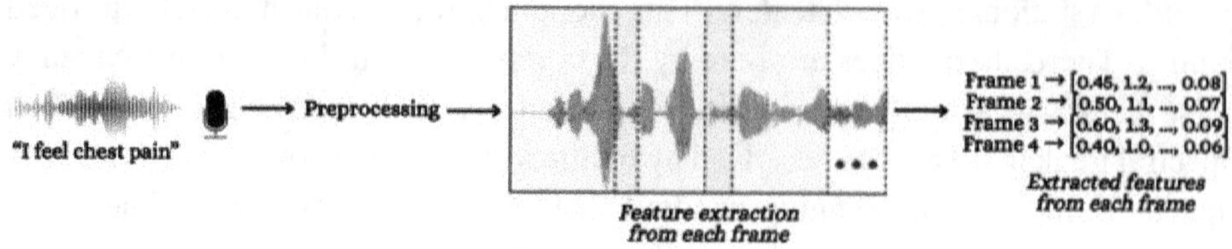

As illustrated in figure 4, features are extracted from each frame. In reality, each number represents important properties of speech, such as how strong the sound is, which frequency ranges are dominant, and how the voice changes over time. This representation will further used for patten recognition.

c) Back-End Processing

The stage is generally known as the "Decoding" or "Recognition" stage. This stage is responsible to transform digitized audio signals into structured and clinically accurate text. This phase ultimately determines whether the intended objective of the healthcare application is achieved. Based on the extracted speech features and interpreted linguistic content, the system performs the final task for which it is designed such as Such objectives may include speech recognition (e.g., converting doctor–patient conversations into structured clinical text), classification (e.g., identifying whether speech patterns indicate a neurological disorder), prediction (e.g., estimating disease risk or progression based on speech characteristics), and speech analysis for clinical assessment and monitoring.

Effective contributions from different models are required to successful completion of this phase. The extracted acoustic features are processed by an acoustic model, which is trained to learns the relationship between acoustic patterns and basic linguistic units such as phonemes or subword units. This will effectively work in different conditions in healthcare (Bhatt et al., 2020).

For example,

- A patient with respiratory distress may produce speech that is breathy or fragmented
- A clinician may dictate rapidly using medical jargon.

In these situations, acoustic model learns to associate these diverse acoustic patterns with their corresponding speech sounds. Even though, acoustic models are language-independent at the signal level, they must train with language-specific sound inventories. Now a days, transformer-based architectures are very popular in implementing acoustic models which enables robust performance even in noisy hospital environments or telemedicine scenarios.

The lexicon (pronunciation dictionary) maps these phonetic units to valid words, ensuring correct pronunciation modeling. This is essential requirement in many applications. Especially, in healthcare applications because the medical terminology must be accurately recognized in this domain. Each language requires its own lexicon because pronunciation rules differ across languages.

For example, English pronunciation often has stress patterns and silent letters, whereas Dravidian languages follow more phonetic spelling but exhibit rich morphological variations through suffixes (Nagarajan, 2024). The Dravidian language family includes around 70–80 languages which primarily spoken in South Asia. A healthcare lexicon must therefore be language-specific and domain-aware. In modern systems, traditional handcrafted lexicons are increasingly supplemented or replaced by subword and character-based representations, which allow models to handle unseen or rare medical terms more effectively. This is particularly important in multilingual healthcare environments where code-mixing and local terminology are common.

While we are typing a text message and our phone "guesses" the next word. The model behind this activity is Language Model (Peng, 2025). A well-trained language model in a particular language is able to understand how words are naturally organized and used within a specific language. Each language has its own grammatical rules, word order, and morphological structure. Therefore, language models are inherently language-specific. A model trained for one language cannot be directly applied to another without adaptation.

For example, English typically follows a Subject–Verb–Object (SVO) sentence structure and relies heavily on function words to convey meaning. In contrast, Dravidian languages such as Tamil, Malayalam, and Kannada commonly follow a Subject–Object–Verb (SOV) structure and express grammatical relationships through rich suffixation. These structural differences significantly affect how sentences are formed and interpreted. A language model must learn these patterns in order to generate or recognize linguistically valid sentences.

Recently, transformer-based language models showcased relatively better result because it uses attention mechanisms to capture long-range dependencies and contextual relationships across entire sentences or documents (Cho, 2024). These are generally pre-trained models with large multilingual corpora. To adapt the language model to the healthcare domain, fine-tuning is required using healthcare-specific data such as clinical notes, discharge summaries, and medical literature. This enables the model to understand both the structural properties of the language and the specialized vocabulary of the medical domain.

3.2 Speech Based Applications

There are three major speech-based applications that have had a transformative impact on healthcare systems: Speech-to-Text, Speech-to-Speech Translation, and Text-to-Speech systems. These technologies extend the capability of healthcare information systems for enabling natural, real-time, and inclusive communication between patients, clinicians, and digital health platforms.

a) Speech-to-Text (STT)

STT is a method of converting spoken words in to written text. In healthcare domain, a large amount of information is exchanged verbally like doctors describe diagnoses and treatment plans, patients explain symptoms, and instructions given by caregivers. In traditional settings, this spoken information had to be manually typed into electronic EHRs, which is time-consuming and prone to errors. STT systems automate this process by capturing the audio and converting it into structured text that can be further processed and analyzed by computing systems.

In technical perspective, a healthcare ASR system captures the speech signals through a recording device such as a microphone and processes the audio signal through the speech processing pipeline described in the previous section. Based on the meaningful acoustic features extracted from the speech signal, the system uses trained models to map the features to its corresponding words and sentences. The final output is a textual transcription that closely represents what was spoken. The accuracy of this textual transcription indicates the performance of the model.

STT is most commonly used in healthcare for automatic clinical documentation. Manual documentation is always a time consuming and highly human effort required process. S2T helps physicians to significantly reduce documentation time and allows them to focus more on patient care. This can be achieved by automatically transcribing clinical notes dictated by physicians, discharge summaries, and prescription details (Latif et al., 2020).

Another important application is transcription and further analysis of doctor–patient interaction (Hsu et al., 2024). During consultations, conversations can be transcribed in real time or retrospectively. These transcripts are further processed using NLP techniques to extract symptoms, diagnoses, medications, or risk factors, supporting clinical decision-making and research.

In virtual consultations (telemedicine and remote healthcare), ASR enables automatic note generation and supports accessibility features such as live captions for hearing-impaired patients. In emergency care settings, spoken observations from paramedics can be rapidly converted into text and shared with hospital teams before the patient arrives.

However, healthcare ASR systems face unique challenges compared to general-purpose speech recognition. Medical speech often includes clinical vocabulary, abbreviations, and complex drug names. Accents, background noise, emotional speech from patients, spontaneous conversational language and multilanguage switching further increase complexity. To address these challenges, healthcare ASR models are typically trained or fine-tuned on domain-specific speech data and medical vocabularies, ensuring higher accuracy and reliability (Sherly et al., 2024).

b) Text-to-Speech (TTS)

TTS is the reverse process of STT. It plays a vital role in delivering the text information to audible messages (Deshmukh & Pacharaney, 2025). By providing this it improves the accessibility, enhancing patient engagement, and supporting clinical workflows. In general, spoken communication is more effective than written text.

Generally, healthcare reports are maintained in text format. The nature of these texts is often complex and text-heavy, including prescriptions, discharge summaries, medical instructions, and educational material. Many patients face challenges in accessing and comprehending this information due to low literacy, visual impairments, advanced age, cognitive limitations, or language barriers. Text-to-Speech systems address this gap by transforming written medical information into clear and understandable speech. Several advanced technologies are now available that effectively address language barriers by integrating machine translation with Text-to-Speech systems. These technologies allow healthcare information to be translated into a patient's preferred language and then delivered as spoken output. This is highly relevant in today's multilingual healthcare settings.

In technical perspective, a Text-to-Speech system accepts textual input and converts it into an acoustic waveform through a sequence of computational models.

- Initially, the text is analyzed using linguistic processing modules that perform tasks such as text normalization, tokenization, phoneme generation, and prosody modeling.
- Applying acoustic models to map linguistic representations to acoustic features which capture timing, pitch, stress, and intonation patterns.
- Finally, vocoder synthesizes the acoustic features into a speech signal.

Modern TTS systems are designed to produce speech more naturally with accurate pronunciation, natural rhythm, and appropriate prosodic variation.

TTS is widely applied in conversational healthcare systems, such as virtual health assistants and chatbots. These systems are responsible for interacting with the users just like a human assistant. The intervention of TTS enables natural voice-based interaction between patients and healthcare systems, making digital health services more approachable and human-like.

It is also helpful in assistive healthcare technologies such as visually impaired patients rely on spoken output to access medical reports, appointment reminders, and test results. Similarly, individuals with reading difficulties or neurological conditions benefit from having health-related text presented in speech form.

TTS in healthcare is prone to challenges specifically related to accurate pronunciation of medical terminology, drug names, and abbreviations, as well as required flexible modulation during information exchange. To address these issues, healthcare TTS systems are typically trained or fine-tuned on medical vocabulary and domain-specific pronunciation dictionaries. Multilingual and culturally adaptive voices further enhance usability in diverse healthcare settings.

c) Speech-to-Speech (STS)

STS systems enable the integration of language translation, speech normalization, or speech modification that transform speech language into another form, while preserving the original meaning and intent. The output of STS is another form of the input speech such as another language and paraphrased speech. In healthcare, Speech-to-Speech systems play an increasingly important role in facilitating communication, especially in multilingual, multicultural, and accessibility-focused environments.

S2S solutions typically combine three major components: Speech-to-Text, language understanding or translation, and Text-to-Speech.

- The incoming speech is recognized and transcribed using an ASR module.
- The text is processed and translated into another form, language or rephrased using NLP models.
- The processed output is uttered using a Text-to-Speech system.

Modern end-to-end S2S models integrate these stages more tightly to improve fluency and reduce latency.

STS also can be used for speech normalization and assistance. For instance, an S2S model which is trained to map impaired or unclear speech patterns to normal synthesized speech while preserving the speaker's intent will allow patients with speech impairments, dysarthria, or neurological conditions to communicate more effectively with doctors, caregivers, and family members.

It enables people to interact with technology more naturally by allowing communication through speech. By supporting output in multi-language, these systems make technology more accessible and intuitive for individuals who may not be comfortable with reading, writing, or using digital devices. In healthcare and other domains, this capability facilitates effective communication, reduces language barriers, and allows users to express themselves and receive information in a familiar and culturally appropriate manner.

3.2 Evaluation and Validation in Speech Processing

Evaluation

Data processing and decision making in healthcare domain is critical in nature. The models build for this sensitive task must go through proper and thorough evaluation and validation because the system outputs can directly influence clinical decisions, patient safety, and quality of care. Evaluation refers to the quantitative measurement of system performance using well-defined metrics, while validation focuses on assessing real-world reliability of the system.

In speech processing system, evaluation is typically task-specific as well as depends on the intended application, such as speech recognition, speech classification, speech translation, or speech synthesis (Salesky et al., 2021; Kim et al., 2021).

In speech recognition systems (ASR), evaluation primarily focuses on how accurately the spoken input is transcribed into text. Word Error Rate (WER) and Character Error Rate (CER) are two metrics primarily used for this purpose. Both metrics quantify the difference between the system-generated transcription and a reference (ground truth) transcription. But one metric operates at word level and the other at character levels.

Word Error Rate (WER) measures transcription accuracy at the word level and it can be calculated as follows:

$$WER(\%) = \left(\frac{S + D + I}{N}\right) \times 100$$

WER accounts for three types of errors:

- S – Number of substitutions (a word is replaced by an incorrect word)
- D – Number of deletions (a word is omitted in the recognized output)
- I – Number of insertions (an extra word is added)
- N – Total number of words in the reference (ground truth) transcription

By comparing the number of such errors to the total number of words in the reference transcription, WER provides an overall indication of how closely the recognized text matches the intended spoken content. In clinical environments, WER is particularly important because incorrect recognition of medical terms, drug names, or dosages can lead to serious clinical consequences. Therefore, achieving a low WER is essential for safe and reliable clinical deployment.

For Example: Assume a reference sentence contains 100 (N) words in total.

- Substitutions (S = 5): A substitution occurs when the system replaces the correct word with an incorrect one.

    1. "Fifteen" instead of "Fifty" (Critical dosage error).
    2. "Ativan" instead of "Aspirin" (Medication swap).
    3. "Hyper" instead of "Hypo" (Opposite medical condition).
    4. "Enema" instead of "Edema" (Contextually wrong).
    5. "Asma" instead of "Asthma" (Spelling/Lexicon error).

- Deletions (D = 3): A deletion occurs when the system completely misses a word.

    1. Missing "NOT": The doctor said "is not allergic," but the ASR transcribed "is allergic." (Extreme high risk).
    2. Missing "DAILY": "Once daily" becomes "Once."
    3. Missing "THE": "In the lungs" becomes "In lungs." (Lower risk, purely grammatical).

- Insertions (I = 2): An insertion occurs when the system "hallucinates" a word.

    1. "AND": A heart monitor "beep" was transcribed as the word "and."
    2. "PATIENT": A nurse talking in the background was picked up and inserted into the doctor's dictation.

$$WER(\%) = \left(\frac{5+3+2}{100}\right) \times 100 = 10$$

Here, WER of 10% means that, on average, 10 out of every 100 words in the clinical transcription are incorrect. This level of accuracy may be acceptable for general-purpose transcription but in healthcare it can be risky.

Character Error Rate (CER) evaluate the performance of the speech recognition system at the character level by counting substitutions, deletions, and insertions of individual characters. CER calculated same as WER, the only difference is that it calculates S, D and I in character level. CER is especially useful in multi-lingual healthcare scenarios which involves languages with complex morphology, agglutinative word structures, or rich inflectional variations. In such languages word boundaries may be ambiguous. It is also valuable for assessing recognition of specialized medical terminology, abbreviations, or rare words, where a small spelling error may not change the overall word count but can still affect clinical interpretation.

The healthcare classification or prediction system is responsible to classify or add class labels based on the speech features. This includes detecting respiratory disorders, neurological conditions, or emotional states from speech. In the healthcare domain, obtaining a well-balanced dataset is often challenging. For example, in tasks that aim to classify speech as healthy or disordered, data from both healthy speakers and individuals with speech disorders are required. In practice, recordings from healthy speakers are usually far more abundant than those from disordered speakers. This imbalance arises because collecting healthy speech data is relatively easy, whereas disordered speech data are harder to obtain due to the lower prevalence of such conditions, clinical and ethical constraints, and the need for expert supervision during data collection. As a result, healthcare speech datasets are frequently biased toward the healthy class, making robust evaluation and model design particularly important. Therefore, we cannot trust a single metrics for evaluating such system. Evaluation relies on classification metrics including accuracy, precision, recall, F1-score, and specificity (discussed in section 2). These metrics are particularly important in healthcare because datasets are often imbalanced, and false negatives or false positives may have unequal clinical risks.

The STS is more complex than STT and TTS. SST evaluation system is responsible to analyze the intelligibility of the speech produced by STS system because it produces the speech in another form or language. Especially in healthcare, it is critical because any loss or distortion of medical meaning can lead to serious clinical misunderstandings. The intelligibility of the translated language is generally evaluated by BLEU (Bilingual Evaluation Understudy) metrics. The BLEU score evaluates translation quality by comparing the system's translated text with one or more reference translations created by human experts. Consider a healthcare situation where a patient describes symptoms in one language, and the system translates it into another language for the clinician. The original meaning of the speech is,

"The patient is experiencing severe chest pain and shortness of breath."

The system produces the translation,

"The patient has strong chest pain and difficulty breathing."

Even though the exact words used are not the same, the key medical ideas such as the patient, chest pain, and breathing difficulty, are clearly present in both sentences. In such case, BLEU score would judge this translation as good. This indicates that the system has successfully preserved the essential medical meaning, which is crucial for safe and effective communication in healthcare.

Another effective evaluation method for STS is semantic similarity. It measures how close the meanings of two sentences are, even if they use different words.

Humans naturally understand that sentences like "*The patient is having difficulty breathing*" and "*The patient is experiencing shortness of breath*" mean the same thing. However, for a computer, these sentences look very different at the word level. Semantic similarity evaluation helps machines judge meaning in a way that is closer to human understanding.

The evaluation of TTS system is different from the other speech processing applications. It evaluates the naturality, clarity, and accuracy of the synthesized speech sounds. In simple words, it evaluates how much the system is able to mimic human speakers. The parameters used for this evaluation are intelligibility (how far easy to understand), naturalness (smoothness in sound and modulation), and suitability in pronunciation relevant to the language. The pronunciation in medical domain is very important because, most of the cases, even human speakers are not able to articulate medical terms and drug names accurately. Technical measures can be used to evaluate the produced signal features such as strength, distortion, amplitude, tempo, but it fails to capture naturality of the speech. A speech signal that scored high in technical measure may still sound unnatural, robotic, or unclear in natural settings. A speech signal can be mark as natural if it exhibits human-like characteristics for the listeners. Therefore, objective evaluation is commonly complemented with subjective listening tests, such as the Mean Opinion Score (MOS). In MOS evaluations, clinicians, patients, or domain experts listen to the synthesized speech and rate its overall quality and clarity on a predefined scale.

Validation

Evaluating the system performance in different test dataset is not enough in sensitive domain like healthcare. It must also operate reliably, safely, and consistently when used by clinicians and patients in practical settings. Validation does this, it evaluates how well the system fit for real-world healthcare use. Clinical validation evaluates whether the system performs consistently across diverse patient populations, accents, speaking styles, and medical conditions. For example, an ASR system validated only on healthy adult speech may fail when used by elderly patients or individuals with speech impairments or children. Therefore, validation datasets must reflect real clinical diversity.

In this domain, we need to go beyond just counting errors to understand the impact of the error. All errors are not equally harmful.

For example, a less harmful error might occur in any ASR system by slightly misrecognizes a clinical note, such as transcribing *"the patient is comfortable today"* as *"the patient is comfortable now."* Although the wording changes, the overall meaning remains the same, and this error is unlikely to influence clinical decisions or patient outcomes.

In contrast, a harmful error could involve the misrecognition of critical medical information. For example, if a system transcribes *"administer 15 milligrams of medication"* as *"administer 50 milligrams,"* the error directly affects dosage and could lead to serious patient harm. Similarly, misrecognizing *"no history of diabetes"* as *"history of diabetes"* could result in an incorrect diagnosis or unnecessary treatment. Therefore, the validation system should be capable to scale the error by understanding the clinical impact of that error.

In precise, the evaluation provides measurable evidence of system performance, while validation ensures clinical suitability and trustworthiness. Together, they form the foundation for deploying speech processing technologies responsibly in healthcare, supporting accurate communication, efficient workflows, and improved patient outcomes.

CONCLUSION

This chapter presented a comprehensive discussion of Natural Language Processing pipeline and technologies for enabling smarter healthcare systems. The text-based NLP techniques have been successfully deployed for many years in tasks such as information extraction, summarization, and decision support. Speech processing has further expanded these capabilities by addressing the most natural form of human communication. Together, these technologies improve clinical efficiency, enhance accessibility, and support patient-centered care, particularly in multilingual and resource-constrained settings. Altogether, NLP plays a vital role in strengthening e-collaboration across distributed healthcare system.

Recent studies are going on in self-supervised learning, and multimodal learning to enable deeper understanding of clinical context by jointly modeling text, speech, and other data modalities such as medical images and physiological signals. Domain-adaptive and personalized models will further improve performance across diverse patient populations, languages, and clinical conditions. In future, NLP and speech processing will move beyond supportive tools to become integral components of intelligent healthcare ecosystems, augmenting clinical expertise while preserving the central role of human judgment and care.

REFERENCES

Adnan, K., Akbar, R., Khor, S. W., & Ali, A. B. A. (2020). Role and challenges of unstructured big data in healthcare. *Data management, analytics and innovation*, 301-323.

Alfattni, G., Peek, N., & Nenadic, G. (2020). Extraction of temporal relations from clinical free text: A systematic review of current approaches. *Journal of Biomedical Informatics, 108*, 103488. DOI: 10.1016/j.jbi.2020.103488 PMID: 32673788

Behera, S. K., & M Nayak, M. (2020). Natural language processing for text and speech processing: a review paper. *International Journal of Advanced Research in Engineering and Technology (IJARET).*

Bhatt, S., Jain, A., & Dev, A. (2020). Acoustic modeling in speech recognition: A systematic review. *International Journal of Advanced Computer Science and Applications, 11*(4). Advance online publication. DOI: 10.14569/IJACSA.2020.0110455

Chandel, T. A. (2025). E-Collaboration Technologies With Generative AI Tools. In *Humans and Generative AI Tools for Collaborative Intelligence* (pp. 369–402). IGI Global Scientific Publishing. DOI: 10.4018/979-8-3693-8332-2.ch016

Cho, H. N., Jun, T. J., Kim, Y. H., Kang, H., Ahn, I., Gwon, H., Kim, Y., Seo, J., Choi, H., Kim, M., Han, J., Kee, G., Park, S., & Ko, S. (2024). Task-specific transformer-based language models in health care: Scoping review. *JMIR Medical Informatics, 12*, e49724. DOI: 10.2196/49724 PMID: 39556827

Choo, S., & Kim, W. (2023). A study on the evaluation of tokenizer performance in natural language processing. *Applied Artificial Intelligence, 37*(1), 2175112. DOI: 10.1080/08839514.2023.2175112

de Almeida, S. S., Silva Fontes, R., Pareja Credidio Freire Alves, L., Júnior, M. C., José Pinheiro Caldeira Silva, G., Ramalho Cortez, L., de Morais, A. H. F., Medeiros Machado, G., Gonçalo Oliveira, H., Cunha-Oliveira, A., dos Santos, J. P. Q., & de Medeiros Valentim, R. A. (2025). Artificial intelligence in healthcare text processing: A review applied to named entity recognition. *Frontiers in Artificial Intelligence, 8*, 1584203. DOI: 10.3389/frai.2025.1584203 PMID: 40693280

Deshmukh, S., & Pacharaney, U. (2025, February). Enhancing Healthcare Communication: A Study on Automated Speech-to-Text Conversion and Analysis of Doctor-Patient Dialogues for Improved Clinical Documentation and Patient Care. In *2025 4th International Conference on Sentiment Analysis and Deep Learning (ICSADL)* (pp. 229-234). IEEE. DOI: 10.1109/ICSADL65848.2025.10933272

Dimililer, K. (2021). Classification problems in healthcare applications. In *Applied Machine Learning and Multi-Criteria Decision-Making in Healthcare* (pp. 40–61). Bentham Science Publishers. DOI: 10.2174/9781681088716121010006

Elov, B. B., Khamroeva, S. M., & Xusainova, Z. Y. (2023). The pipeline processing of NLP. In *E3S Web of Conferences* (Vol. 413, p. 03011). EDP Sciences.

Frisoni, G., Moro, G., & Carbonaro, A. (2021). A survey on event extraction for natural language understanding: Riding the biomedical literature wave. *IEEE Access : Practical Innovations, Open Solutions, 9*, 160721–160757. DOI: 10.1109/ACCESS.2021.3130956

Hsu, W. C., Lin, P. X., Li, C. J., Tien, H. Y., Kang, Y. H., & Lee, P. J. (2024, August). An enhanced model for asr in the medical field. In *2024 IEEE International Conference on Information Reuse and Integration for Data Science (IRI)* (pp. 43-48). IEEE. DOI: 10.1109/IRI62200.2024.00021

Huang, K., Altosaar, J., & Ranganath, R. (2019). Clinicalbert: Modeling clinical notes and predicting hospital readmission. *arXiv preprint* arXiv:1904.05342.

Jerfy, A., Selden, O., & Balkrishnan, R. (2024). The growing impact of natural language processing in healthcare and public health. INQUIRY. *Inquiry : a Journal of Medical Care Organization, Provision and Financing, 61*, 00469580241290095. DOI: 10.1177/00469580241290095 PMID: 39396164

Kim, S., Le, D., Zheng, W., Singh, T., Arora, A., Zhai, X., . . . Seltzer, M. L. (2021). Evaluating user perception of speech recognition system quality with semantic distance metric. *arXiv preprint arXiv:2110.05376.*

Kumar, Y. (2024). A comprehensive analysis of speech recognition systems in healthcare: Current research challenges and future prospects. *SN Computer Science, 5*(1), 137. DOI: 10.1007/s42979-023-02466-w

Latif, S., Qadir, J., Qayyum, A., Usama, M., & Younis, S. (2020). Speech technology for healthcare: Opportunities, challenges, and state of the art. *IEEE Reviews in Biomedical Engineering, 14*, 342–356. DOI: 10.1109/RBME.2020.3006860 PMID: 32746367

Lee, J., Yoon, W., Kim, S., Kim, D., Kim, S., So, C. H., & Kang, J. (2020). BioBERT: A pre-trained biomedical language representation model for biomedical text mining. *Bioinformatics (Oxford, England), 36*(4), 1234–1240. DOI: 10.1093/bioinformatics/btz682 PMID: 31501885

Lee, P. C., Sharma, S. K., Motaganahalli, S., & Huang, A. (2023). Evaluating the clinical decision-making ability of large language models using MKSAP-19 cardiology questions. *JACC Advances*, *2*(9), 100658. DOI: 10.1016/j.jacadv.2023.100658 PMID: 38938709

Mohapatra, H. (2026). Smart Workflows: Designing Next-Generation E-Collaboration With Artificial Intelligence. In *Transforming E-Collaboration With AI and Emerging Digital Technologies* (pp. 57-88). IGI Global Scientific Publishing.

Nagarajan, S. (2024, December). Advances in Speech and Text Processing for Dravidian Language: A Comprehensive Review. In *2024 9th International Conference on Communication and Electronics Systems (ICCES)* (pp. 1715-1722). IEEE.

Peng, J., Wang, Y., Li, B., Guo, Y., Wang, H., Fang, Y., & Yu, K. (2025). A survey on speech large language models for understanding. *IEEE Journal of Selected Topics in Signal Processing*.

Salesky, E., Mäder, J., & Klinger, S. (2021, December). Assessing evaluation metrics for speech-to-speech translation. In *2021 IEEE Automatic Speech Recognition and Understanding Workshop (ASRU)* (pp. 733-740). IEEE. DOI: 10.1109/ASRU51503.2021.9688073

Sherly, E., Pillai, L. G., & Manohar, K. (2024). ASR models from conventional statistical models to transformers and transfer learning. *Automatic speech recognition and translation for low resource languages*, 69-112.

Singh, M. K. (2024). Feature extraction and classification efficiency analysis using machine learning approach for speech signal. *Multimedia Tools and Applications*, *83*(16), 47069–47084. DOI: 10.1007/s11042-023-17368-5

Spasic, I., & Nenadic, G. (2020). Clinical text data in machine learning: Systematic review. *JMIR Medical Informatics*, *8*(3), e17984. DOI: 10.2196/17984 PMID: 32229465

Yang, S., & Berdine, G. (2024). Confusion matrix. *The Southwest Respiratory and Critical Care Chronicles*, *12*(53), 75–79. DOI: 10.12746/swrccc.v12i53.1391

Chapter 7
Computational Intelligence for Drug Design and Development

Kritika Shukla
http://orcid.org/0009-0000-2187-7854
Amity Institute of Biotechnology, Amity University, Noida, India

Hina Bansal
http://orcid.org/0000-0003-1683-1581
Amity University, Noida, India

ABSTRACT

Drug discovery is traditionally a long, expensive and high-risk endeavour, often spanning more than a decade. Artificial Intelligence (AI) is reshaping this landscape by accelerating discovery timelines, improving accuracy, and reducing costs across the entire drug development pipeline. This chapter highlights the applications of AI in the early stage of drug discovery, including target identification, hit screening, lead optimization, and de novo design. In the preclinical and clinical phases, AI contributes to predictive toxicology, pharmacokinetics and pharmacodynamics, adaptive trial design, patient recruitment and real-time monitoring. Even after product launch, AI supports risk management, regulatory submissions and pharmacovigilance. The chapter further explores emerging opportunities, including digital twins, federated learning, and autonomous R&D pipelines. Overall, AI is not a replacement for scientists but represents a paradigm shift toward faster, safer and more personalized therapeutic development through collaborative and ethical integration.

DOI: 10.4018/979-8-2600-0981-9.ch007

1. INTRODUCTION

1.1. The Traditional Drug Development Problem.

Drug discovery and development are still considered one of the most resource-consuming scientific projects of the current age. It takes an average of over a decade to create a new therapeutic compound based on research and investment of over 2.6 billion dollars, with over 90 percent attrition rate between preclinical testing and market approval (DiMasi et al., 2016). Such inefficiencies put a lot of pressure on health care systems, restrain innovation in new therapeutic spaces like rare diseases and antimicrobial resistance and inhibit access to the life-saving treatment (Scannell et al., 2012). Drug development has become a risky venture due to regulatory complexities, high cost of late-stage clinical failures due to complexities of diseases, and the sheer complexity of biology.

1.2. The rise of Artificial Intelligence in Biomedicine.

Artificial Intelligence (AI) has become a disruptive technology that has the potential to change the paradigm in pharmaceutical research and development (R&D). Through machine learning, deep learning, natural language processing (NLP), and generative modelling, AI systems can analyze large multi-dimensional biomedical data at unprecedented speed and accuracy (Chen et al., 2018). In contrast to classic computational chemistry applications, AI models are constantly updated with new data, which improves the predictions on the drug-target interactions, molecular properties, and clinical outcomes. This capability offers the chance to solve the bottlenecks within the whole pipeline, including target identification and post-market surveillance (Mak & Pichika, 2019).

There are already significant improvements that have shown the transformative power of AI. As an example, the breakthrough of protein structure prediction by DeepMind AlphaFold allowed almost experimental accuracy in the model of proteins that structural biologists have failed to predict throughout decades (Jumper et al., 2021). Equally, other companies like Atomwise and BenevolentAI have led in applying deep learning to small molecule screening and drug repurposing, cutting years of preclinical effort to months (Zhavoronkov et al., 2019).

1.3. Artificial Intelligence throughout the Pharmaceutical Lifecycle.

The contributions of AI go beyond their initial discovery. Predictive toxicology and in silico modeling are used in preclinical development to decrease the use of expensive animal testing. In the context of clinical development, AI-based trial design, patient stratification, and real-time monitoring make human studies more efficient and successful (Fogel, 2018). In post-market surveillance, AI systems are piloting automated dossier preparation in regulatory review, and in post-market surveillance, using natural language processing, adverse events are identified sooner than usual systems by searching electronic health records (EHRs) and social media (Liu et al., 2019).

This AI and drug development convergence has its opportunities and challenges. The pace, magnitude, and forecasting abilities of AI hold the potential of revolutionizing the pharmaceutical industry on one hand. Conversely, the essential issues concerning data privacy, algorithm transparency, ethical governance and regulatory preparedness should be taken into account to make sure that the technology brings safe, fair, and reliable innovations (Topol, 2019).

Success Stories

A number of real-life examples can be used to demonstrate the increasing influence of AI on pharmaceutical R&D:

- AlphaFold2 (DeepMind): Cracked protein folding problem (greater than 90 percent accuracy in comparison with experimental structures) with the ability to accelerate structure-based drug design (Jumper et al., 2021).
- Atomwise: Screened billions of compounds virtually through deployed convolutional neural networks into Ebola and multiple sclerosis leads (Wallach et al., 2015).
- BenevolentAI: Another example of benevolent AI is the use of baricitinib to treat COVID-19, which was subsequently granted emergency approval, demonstrating the speed at which AI could generate hypotheses (Richardson et al., 2020).
- Insilico Medicine: Developed and took to human clinical trials a new fibrosis drug in less than 18 months with the help of generative adversarial networks (Zhavoronkov et al., 2019).

These examples demonstrate that AI is not exactly a substitute of scientists but an addition to the decision making process offering new hypotheses, making the trial process faster, and detecting hidden patterns in various data files.

This chapter is a critical analysis of the use of AI in the drug development pipeline. Section 4.2 is the review of the history and technical foundations of AI methods used in biomedicine. Section 4.3 points out the use of AI in initial drug discovery such as identification of targets, identification of hits, optimization of leads, and de novo molecular design. Section 4.4 discusses its application in preclinical and clinical development, and Section 4.5 discusses its use in regulatory and post-market use. Section 4.6 aims at providing more detailed examples of successful AI implementations. In Section 4.7, ethics, legal and societal issues are explored. Section 4.8 presents future opportunities, such as digital twins, federated learning, and systems of full autonomous R&D. Lastly, this paper ends with the Section 4.9, which presents a balanced evaluation of the transformative, though yet developing, role of AI in pharmaceutical science.

The chapter will be an empirical investigation that will be enhanced with the critical analysis so that it could be used as a reference point by researchers, practitioners, policymakers, and interested students exploring the intersection of AI and drug development.

2. HISTORY OF AI IN DRUG DEVELOPMENT

2.1. Computational Approaches at the beginning

Quantitative structure-activity relationship (QSAR) modeling and molecular docking were common computational methods that were employed to predict biological activity of compounds before the advent of artificial intelligence (Cherkasov et al., 2014). These procedures were based on the manualized molecular features and deterministic algorithms. Although they were effective they had difficulty in handling complicated biological data, poor generalizability and failure to provide non-linear correlation between molecular characteristics and drug activity.

Machine learning (ML) emerged in the late 20 th century, offering more flexible statistical models. Support vector machines (SVMs), decision trees, and random forests were more effective techniques that learned directly out of data and thus provided a better predictive performance (Burbidge et al., 2001). Although these early machine learning methods were able to outperform rule-based QSAR models in terms of accuracy in prediction, they were extremely sensitive to hand-crafted features and tuned datasets. They tended to be overly generalized in the disease aspects and unable to reproduce the non-linear and non-dimensional aspects of biological systems. This shortcoming inspired the transition to deep learning models with automated capabilities to extract features out of raw molecular and biological data. These approaches became the initial period of AI adoption into the pharmacological field, and they were utilized primarily in the toxicity prediction, QSAR analysis, and virtual screening.

2.2. Drug Discovery Supervisory Learning.

The contemporary AI-based drug discovery is based on supervised learning models. ML algorithms predict the activity of new compounds by training on labeled data sets, e.g. known compounds and their biological activities. By doing so, this has helped in:

- Bioactivity prediction Bioactivity prediction is the use of molecular fingerprints or SMILES strings to categorize compounds as being active or inactive.
- ADMET forecasting provides an approximation of absorption, distribution, metabolism, excretion and toxicity properties to maximize leads (Cheng et al., 2012).

These models were trained on the growth of large chemical libraries like ChEMBL and PubChem which served as the required training information. The predictive power was further enhanced with neural networks and ensemble learning, which made it possible to screen millions of molecules a day with high throughput virtual screening. The major AI and machine learning techniques used in drug discovery are summarized in Table 1.

Table 1. Major AI and machine learning techniques applied in drug discovery

AI Technique	Application in Drug Discovery
Supervised Learning	Predicts bioactivity & toxicity
Unsupervised Learning	Clusters patient data, identifies patterns
Deep Learning (CNN/RNN)	Protein–ligand interaction, molecular image analysis
NLP	Literature mining, drug repurposing
Generative Models (GAN, VAE, RL)	De novo molecule design

2.3. Hierarchy-Free Learning in Biomedical Data.

The unsupervised learning approach to discovering the hidden patterns without labelling data became especially significant in genomics and stratifying patients. The k-means clustering and hierarchical clustering methods were used to cluster the patients according to genomic or phenotypic data, which assisted in determining the drug subtypes and the possible drug targets (Golub et al., 1999).

Indicatively, unsupervised algorithms played a pivotal role in cancer research by making cancer sub-types of acute myeloid leukemia visible, allowing personalized treatment plans (Perou et al., 2000). Unsupervised learning is also used in gene expression analysis in drug development to derive an opportunity to repurpose a compound by clustering compounds with similar levels of transcriptional response.

2.4. Deep Learning Revolution

The 2010s saw a radical change in the form of the so-called deep learning (DL) - the multi-layer neural networks that are able to learn representation of raw data on their own (LeCun et al., 2015). Soon afterwards, image recognition, speech processing, and text mining were achieved via convolutional neural networks (CNNs) and recurrent neural networks (RNNs), which were applied to drug discovery.

- CNNs: Applied to the analysis of molecular images and 3D protein-ligand interactions, e.g., the convolutional method of AtomNet virtual screening (Wallach et al., 2015).
- RNNs: RNNs are applied to sequential data, e.g. SMILES strings in drug design de novo and property prediction.
- Transformers: More amongst them, the transformer-based architecture (e.g., BERT, GPT-like models) has been used to analyze biomedical NLP, digging through millions of scientific papers, patents, and clinical trial records in search of insights (Lee et al., 2020).

The most innovative application was probably AlphaFold2 which utilized deep learning to approach experimental precision in protein structure prediction (Jumper et al., 2021). This discovery solved one of the most difficult problems of biology and opened new perspectives in designing drugs based on their structure. Though the transformative nature of AlphaFold2 has completely transformed protein structure prediction, it does not model protein dynamics, ligand-induced changes in protein structure, or binding kinetics, which are of paramount importance to pharmacological significance. Consequently, predicting the structure is not enough to effectively estimate drug efficacy, thus the necessity of considering it with molecular docking, molecular dynamics and experimental validation.

2.5. Natural Language Processing (NLP) in Drug Development

NLP has become a point of necessity to traverse the inundating biomedical literature. NLP systems using AI are able to find relationships between genes, diseases, and drugs in millions of scientific papers, patents, and clinical trial records (Lu et al., 2011).

- Clinical trial mining: Some designs were either unsuccessful or successful, learning which design to use next.
- Drug repurposing: Emerging therapeutic targets: Identification of previously unnoticed interactions between drugs and new targets.
- Regulatory intelligence: Automating the preparation of submissions and tracking the updates of the FDA/EMA.

Some of the first uses of NLP products such as IBM Watson in Drug Discovery were early but were limited by overpromising and lack of explainability.

2.6. Generative Models for De Novo Drug Design

One of the significant advances was a generative model, which is not only an analysis of molecules, but a new one is formed. VAEs, GANs, and reinforcement learning (RL) agents can be used to produce new compounds that have optimized results.

- VAEs: Molecules are coded into latent spaces and decoded into new formats with new features of interest (Gómez-Bombarelli et al., 2018).
- GANs: Learn competing networks to create chemically & realistically designed molecules.
- RP: Reward desirable molecules, including potency and safety, to optimize de novo molecules.

These approaches have been already utilized to advance AI-designed compounds into clinical trials by such companies as Insilico Medicine.

2.7. Reinforcement Learning for Synthesis and Pathway Design

Synthetic pathway optimization is also performed through reinforcement learning. Since chemical synthesis is a game, RL agents suggest effective multi-step responses to drug candidates synthesis. It is especially useful in green chemistry, where the essential cost-effective and sustainable synthesis is necessary (Segler et al., 2018).

AI has become a mainstream technology in pharma R&D today and most major pharmaceutical firms have collaborations with AI-based startups including BenevolentAI, Exscientia, Atomwise as well as Insilico Medicine. Scholarly communities keep expanding the limits in methodologies, and the regulatory bodies, such as FDA, start considering frameworks to certify AI models (FDA, 2021).

Although it still presents some issues (such as data prejudice, inability to interpret results, and fit into the existing pipelines), the historical trends of AI in drug development show a transition between computational algorithms based on rules and systems that are data-driven, self-educate, and can generate new biological knowledge.

3. ARTIFICIAL INTELLIGENCE IN DRUG DISCOVERY AT THE EARLY STAGES

Initial drug discovery is the most sensitive- and highest-risk-phase of drug R&D in pharmaceutical research. Between the discovery of a promising biological target to the optimization of a lead compartment, scientists are required to search a chemical space that is estimated to be 10 6 0 possible drug-like molecules, which cannot be covered in brute-force experimentation (Polishchuk et al., 2013). The traditional wet-lab techniques are accurate, but time-consuming and expensive. Artificial intelligence (AI) presents disruptive potentials to gain access to rapid data analysis of large datasets, predictive molecular properties, and the creation of novel compounds with preferred pharmacological characteristics. AI technologies currently assist in four fundamental early-stage processes, an overview of how AI integrates across the pharmaceutical R&D pipeline is illustrated in Figure 1.

Figure 1. AI integrated across the pharmaceutical R&D pipeline.

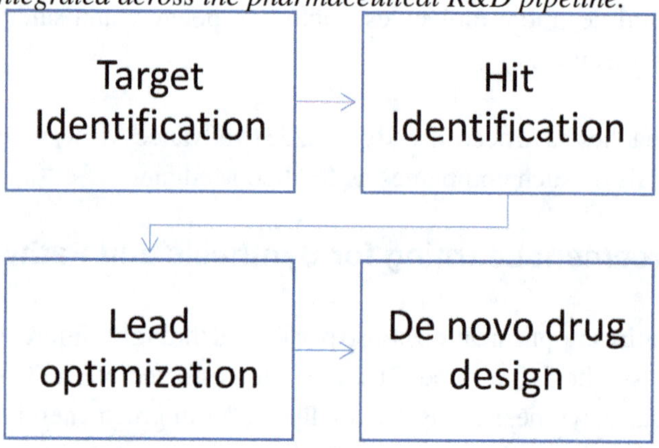

3.1. Target Identification and Validation

Identifying molecular targets: proteins, nucleic acids, or pathways that are known to play a key role in the disease progression is the first step in drug discovery. In the past, the process used to take years of tedious laboratory work and literature search. It is accelerated by using AI which combines multi-omic datasets (genomics, transcriptomics, proteomics, metabolomics) with electronic health records (EHRs), and biomedical literature.Machine learning algorithms are used to scale through big data and predict genetic variation-disease phenotype associations, which can be targeted with drugs. AI models constructed by networks are disease pathway maps, which suppress important hub proteins in disease progression (Guney et al., 2016). The natural language processing (NLP) systems scan through millions of scientific articles to derive links between genes, proteins, and diseases.

In one instance, BenevolentAI uses machine learning based on NLP and graphs to identify new targets in cancer and neurodegenerative disease. Its platform quickly discovered baricitinib, a pre-existing arthritis drug, as a treatment option in COVID-19, and then confirmed the treatment in clinical trials (Richardson et al., 2020).

3.2. Hit Identification and Virtual Screening

After coming up with a target, scientists need to find chemical hits that react with the target. The conventional screening method used to screen millions of compounds in the lab is high-throughput screening that is quite costly (taking hundreds of millions of dollars) and time-consuming (years). This step is completely sped up by AI via virtual screening.

- Ligand-based virtual screening: Machine learning algorithms that are trained on known ligands are used to make predictions of novel compounds.
- Structure-based virtual screening: Deep learning models at the 3D scale are used to rank candidate compounds through the analysis of 3D protein-ligand interactions.
- AI-enhanced docking simulations: The prediction of binding affinities using convolutional neural networks (CNNs) is a better predictor compared to conventional scoring functions (Wallach et al., 2015).

AtomNet is one of the most successful platforms developed by Atomwise based on CNNs to predict binding affinity between protein-ligand complexes. Ebola, multiple sclerosis, and cancer hits have been promising after being screened by atomNet using billions of compounds (Deng et al., 2019).Equally, Exscientia uses deep learning together with automation to design and prioritize hits, making the discovery time shorten to months.

3.3. Lead Optimization

Once hits are known, lead compounds have to be streamlined in terms of their efficacy, safety and drug-like properties. This is often the most lengthy step in drug discovery, since failures can occur because of poor ADMET (Absorption, Distribution, Metabolism, Excretion, and Toxicity) properties. AI models can predict the following pharmacokinetic and pharmacodynamic properties:

- ADMET prediction: Solubility, permeability, metabolism, and toxicity are predicted using deep learning models that have been trained on large datasets (Cheng et al., 2012).
- Multi-objective optimization: Agents of reinforcement learning optimize compounds on a variety of properties simultaneously, which balances potency with safety.
- Polypharmacology prediction: AI models evaluate possible off-target toxicity risks and minimize the risks of late-stage toxicity (Zhou et al., 2020).

Indicatively, Insilico Medicine has applied the application of generative models with ADMET predictors to generate compounds that optimize fibrosis. This resulted in an unprecedented reduction in the time required to develop a candidate drug to clinical trials, only 18 months, a process that required years to complete until the creation of AI (Zhavoronkov et al., 2019).

3.4. De Novo Drug Design

De novo molecular design, perhaps the most radical input of AI to early drug discovery, is discussed. Generative AI models do not just pick lists of existing libraries but generate new chemical structures to specific targets.

- Variational Autoencoders (VAEs): Molecules are encoded into a latent space and structurally novel compounds with desired activity are generated (Gómez-Bombarelli et al., 2018).
- Generative Adversarial Networks (GANs): Generative neural networks produce chemically plausible and realistic molecules.
- Reinforcement Learning (RL): Learns to suggest molecules which are rewarded based on desirable properties (i.e. potency, selectivity and safety).
- Smiles generators: NLP generators create novel drugs based on chemical strings using SMILES generators (Honda et al., 2019).

These are the generation methods that are currently widespread in the industry. The first AI-designed small molecule to be put into human clinical trials (DSP-1181 in obsessive-compulsive disorder) was reported by Exscientia in 12 months, five times faster than the conventional timelines (Hopkins et al., 2020). Figure 2 shows the workflow of the de novo design.

Figure 2. Workflow of AI-driven de novo drug design.

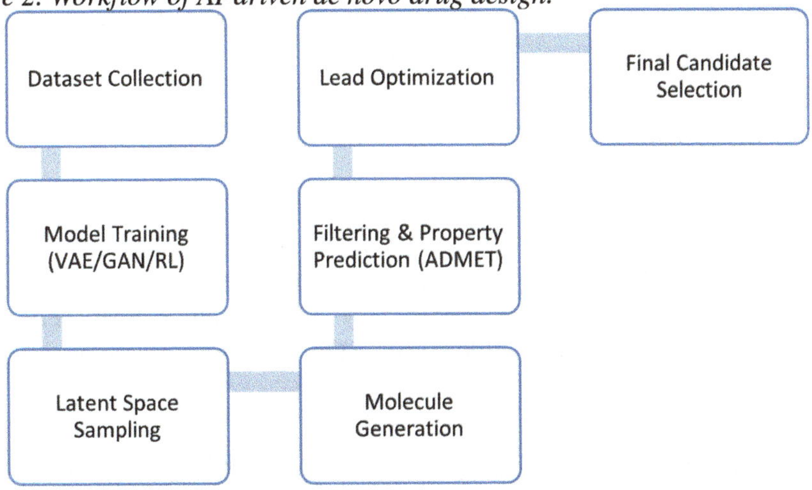

3.5. Case Studies

Atomwise Ebola and multiple sclerosis AtomNet AtomNet discovered hits using CNN on screening billions of compounds atomwise (Wallach et al., 2015).

- Exscientia -AI-designed DSP-1181 was put in clinical trials in Japan in OCD after only 12 months of development (Hopkins et al., 2020).
- BenevolentAI – AI-based knowledge graphs were used to discover baricitinib against COVID-19 (Richardson et al., 2020).
- Insilico Medicine - Developed and took to trial in record time a fibrosis drug using generative models (Zhavoronkov et al., 2019).

These examples illustrate that AI-based discovery can save time and cost besides increasing exploration of chemical space, which would otherwise be overlooked using traditional techniques.

4. AI IN PRECLINICAL AND CLINICAL DEVELOPMENT

Although AI has transformed drug discovery at earlier stages, it also has impacts on preclinical testing and clinical development phase that contribute to the majority of R&D expenditures in the pharmaceutical sector. Clinical trials on drug candidates are usually unsuccessful (about 8590 percent), and the reasons could be safety, ineffectiveness, or poor patient stratification (Arrowsmith & Miller, 2013). The improvement of predictive toxicology, pharmacokinetics/pharmacodynamics (PK/PD) simulation, optimization of clinical trials design, and more accurate patient recruitment and monitoring are the ways in which AI can reduce these failures.

4.1. Predictive Toxicology

Unforeseen toxicity is one of the most essential reasons that cause attrition. Conventional toxicology is based on a lot of testing on animals, which is expensive, time-consuming and does not necessarily indicate human action. Prediction of in silico toxicology can be achieved using AI through the learning over massive datasets of chemical structures and toxicologic events:

- Deep learning in organ toxicity: Deep learning models are used to predict the toxicity hepatotoxicity, cardiotoxicity and nephrotoxicity prior to clinical trials (Mayr et al., 2016).
- Image-based toxicology: The convolutional neural networks are used to analyze histopathology and cell imaging data to identify toxic reactions (Zhou et al., 2020).
- Multi-task learning: Multitask models that are trained on a range of toxicological endpoints increase their ability to be accurate on a variety of toxicity types (Xu et al., 2015).

One interesting case is the U.S.-based initiative Tox 21, which generates high-throughput toxicology data, and which has been demonstrated to better predict toxic outcomes using AI systems than classical QSAR models (Huang et al., 2016).

4.2. Preclinical Modeling: AI-Augmented PK/PD

Pharmacodynamics and pharmacokinetics Pharmacodynamics (PD) and pharmacokinetics (PK) modeling are vital to the study of drug behavior in vivo. Conventionally, this involves animal research and large scale mathematics. This is complemented by AI which:

- Drug absorption and distribution predictability on the basis of the molecular structure and patient physiology (Wenzel et al., 2019).
- AI-assisted PK/PD simulations: The sub-replacement of part of animal research by in silico virtual patients to simulate dosage and drug reactions (Polasek et al., 2020).
- Models Systems biology models: Neural networks, trained using omics and metabolomics data, make predictions about interactions in complex biological networks.

Oncology and immunology are among the fields in which these AI-enhanced models are especially helpful: dose regimens and combination therapy are paramount in terms of safety and effectiveness.

4.3. AI in Clinical Trial Design

The cost of drug development is the most expensive step that may cost more than 1 billion in terms of clinical trials. AI enhances the efficiency of a trial in a number of ways:

1. Optimization of trial protocol
    - AI uses past clinical trial records to classify the trial designs that will be the most successful (Wang et al., 2021).
    - NLP systems improve including / exclusion criteria using design parameters that are extracted through previous trials.
2. Synthetic control arms
    - Machine learning uses real-world data (EHRs, registries) to create so-called virtual control groups to ensure minimal number of patients are used as placebo arms.
    - Regulatory agencies (such as the FDA), started to consider such approaches to conduct trials of rare diseases.
3. Adaptive trial design
    - Reinforcement learning is a more efficient and ethical method of dynamically updating dosing schedules and endpoints on the basis of interim data.

As an example, AI-based simulations helped Moderna create adaptive COVID-19 vaccine trials, which helped it achieve unprecedented speeds in approval (Shilo et al., 2020).

1. Recent studies report that AI-assisted predictive modeling and data integration are increasingly being used to improve clinical trial design, patient stratification, and outcome prediction across multiple therapeutic areas (Ashfaq Ur Rehman et al., 2025).

4.4. Stratification and Recruitment of Patients.

One of the largest bottlenecks of clinical trials is recruiting the appropriate patients. The trials fail to achieve the goal of recruitment up to 80% (Bajorin et al., 2021). AI helps to overcome this problem by:

- Integration of EHR and genomics: Machine learning identifies the patients with the highest likelihood of responding to a drug based on biomarkers, genetic profiles and medical history.
- Digital health data: AI models are deployed on real-time data received by wearables and mobile systems to classify patients based on disease development.
- Predictive enrollment modeling: Predicting the risk of patients dropping out and using more effective recruitment sites.

Oncology AI-based stratification has resulted in biomarker-based subgroups, which are found to be successful in more precision oncology trials (Cruz Rivera et al., 2020).

4.5. Real-Time Monitoring and Safety

As soon as trials are being conducted, AI provides the opportunity to monitor patients in real time in case of safety and efficacy indicators:

- Adverse event identification NLP systems screen physician notes, EHRs and patient reports on early signs of an adverse drug reaction (Liu et al., 2019).
- Wearable integration: AI-powered dashboards monitor the physiological indicators (e.g. heart rate, oxygen saturation) in real time and make an early intervention.
- Automated endpoint measurement: Computer vision systems can measure treatment response objectively using the imaging (e.g., MRI or CT scan) data.

With the COVID-19 pandemic, AI systems were implemented to track participants of the trials remotely and ensured that the trial process was not interrupted despite the limitation on the number of in-person visits (Wang et al., 2021).

4.6. Case Studies

COVID-19 Trials on Vaccines (Moderna and Pfizer-BioNTech)

Adaptive trial protocols were developed with AI, real-world data were used to enhance processes, and regulatory documentation went faster, leading to emergency approvals in 12 months (Shilo et al., 2020).

Oncology Trials (Bristol Myers Squibb)

It was found through machine learning that patients subgroups who were biomarker-positive could be identified to undergo immunotherapy trials, which increased response rate and decreased trial size (Topol, 2019).

Novartis + Microsoft Alliance.

AI-based systems enhanced the recruitment of patients through the mining of global EHRs, and the delays in the commencement of a trial were greatly minimized (Wenzel et al., 2019).

5. REGULATORY AND POST-MARKET USE

Although the use of artificial intelligence (AI) in discovery and clinical research is becoming more and more apparent, its application does not stop with drug approval. The regulatory review and post-market surveillance are essential steps in the pharmaceutical lifecycle where the safety, compliance and real-world performance should be guaranteed. These operations have traditionally been manual based in reporting, documentation, and monitoring- which have created inefficiencies and delay in acting on safety matters. AI can change this landscape as it will automatize regulatory submissions, increase the efficiency of pharmacovigilance and labeling and risk management practices.

5.1. Computer-Generated Regulatory Filings

Regulatory submissions consist of preparing huge dossiers of preclinical, clinical, manufacturing, and safety data. The writing of a New Drug Application (NDA) or a Biologics. License Application (BLA) may take months and thousands of pages. This process is currently being automated using AI devices, specifically natural language processing (NLP):

- Data harmonization: Machine learning guarantees extract consistency between submissions by cross-validating clinical trial data with laboratory data.
- Law and regulations: AI is constantly analyzing new regulations and updates provided by regulatory authorities (e.g., FDA, EMA, ICH) to ensure submissions are compliant.

FDA has already tested the pilot AI assistance of dossier generation, and the European Medicines Agency (EMA) has conducted pilot experiments on intelligence systems based on NLP to automate review procedures (FDA, 2021).

5.2. Pharmacovigilance and Safety Monitoring

Pharmacovigilance, in post-market, is necessary to identify adverse drug reactions (ADRs) that might never have been identified during clinical trials. Conventionally, it is based upon spontaneous reporting including the FDA Adverse Event Reporting System (FAERS). Their effectiveness is however restricted by underreporting and time delays. AI will improve pharmacovigilance by:

EHR and claims data mining

Machine-learning solutions are used to analyze massive patient records to identify irregularities in the patient outcomes (Liu et al., 2019).

Patient forums/social media

NLP identifies safety cues in unstructured conversations between patients in social media (Twitter) or on patient forums (Sarker et al., 2015).

Automated signal detection

The AI systems identify serious events that are not common but significant more quickly than the traditional reporting, which allows regulatory interventions to be undertaken earlier (Harper et al., 2021).

Compared to conventional methods that handle thousands of case reports each year, pharmaceutical firms, such as Roche and Novartis, have embraced AI pharmacovigilance systems that can process millions of case reports annually and cut the time taken to process cases by more than 50% (Bate & Blake, 2020).

5.3. Risk Management and Labelling.

AI is also used to conduct post-approval risk management, whereby drugs are safely and effectively used in various populations:

- Monitoring usage patterns: AI uses prescription and claims data to identify off-label use as well as medication errors or harmful drug-drug interactions (Rajkomar et al., 2019).
- Dynamic labeling: Regulatory agencies are looking at adaptive labeling with the support of AI where the risk information is updated in near real time with the presentation of new safety data.
- Risk-benefit analysis: Predictive models are used to model risks and benefits over the long-term in heterogenous populations to inform post-market safety analysis decisions.

As an example, the FDA has been considering AI tools to track the data of opioids prescriptions, identifying the patterns of misuse and updating the labels (FDA, 2021).

5.4. Global Regulatory Initiatives

The regulatory bodies across the globe start to use the paradigms of AI-based regulation:

1. FDA (USA): Introduced an AI/ML action plan in the field of medical equipment and has already started pilot projects of AI-assisted review of dossiers (FDA, 2021).
2. EMA (Europe): Coming up with guidance on AI regulation in medicine, and in particular, transparency, validation, and accountability (EMA, 2022).
3. ICH (International Council for Harmonisation): Investigation in harmonized standards of AI validation when submitting a drug.

4. PMDA (Japan): Promotes the use of AI in pharmacovigilance and has granted the use of AI-based diagnostic tools, making pharma ready to adopt AI.

These efforts illustrate an understanding that regulatory science has to change with the changes in technology.

5.5. Challenges and Limitations

Although this has advanced, there are a number of issues that restrict the complete adoption of AI in regulatory and post-market applications:

- Data privacy: The system of pharmacovigilance relies on the sensitive health records and this makes question the confidentiality of patients.
- Algorithmic transparency: Regulators want to understand the AI outputs, especially in cases when patient safety depends on the decisions.
- Data bias AIs that are trained on missing or biased data sets will fail to capture ADRs in minority groups.
- Legal responsibility: It still remains unclear how legally responsible an AI-created dossier would be in case of errors in it or when an AI-driven pharmacovigilance tool fails to show a serious safety concern.

To solve these issues, it is necessary not only technological innovation but new regulations and moral codes.

Limitations in Empirical Validation and Clinical Translation

Though AI-based models may show good retrospective performance, most of them do not work when subjected to prospective validation or clinical translation. This is frequently as a result of their overfitting to past data, data leakage and the changes of distributions between discovery phase data and actual clinical populations. Therefore, AI-selected candidates can demonstrate lower efficacy or unexpected toxicity in vivo, which is why it is crucial to carry out experimental studies.

The appropriate AI application in pharmaceutical R&D is to implement the human-AI interactive model instead of complete automation. The domain experts will still be required to validate the hypothesis, design the experiment and provide ethical oversight. Organizational preparedness such as workforce preparation, an interdisciplinary approach, and governance framework is very significant in ascertaining whether AI tools will yield meaningful scientific and clinical results.

Recent reviews emphasise that despite rapid methodological advances, reproducibility, validation, and translation to clinically successful drugs remain major challenges in AI-driven drug discovery (Hasselgren & Oprea, 2024).

6. INDUSTRIAL AND ACADEMIC CASE STUDIES

The introduction of artificial intelligence (AI) in drug development is no more of a theoretical or initial experimentation. The industry and academia have generated concrete success stories over the last ten years, proving that AI is able to speed up the discovery timelines, save costs, and make breakthroughs that were previously unimaginable. Concurrently, some projects have not lived up to their claims, and this is a reminder to the field of the dangers of hype and the difficulties of using AI in a responsible way. Here, major case studies that point out the successes and the lessons learned are discussed.

6.1. Atomwise: Virtual Screening by AI

In 2012, the atomwise company was launched, which introduced deep convolutional neural networks (CNNs) as a structure-based way of drug discovery. Its flagship system is AtomNet, which is used to predict the binding affinity of small molecules and target proteins.

Successes:

- More than 10 billion compounds have been screened by AtomNet, and potential leads against Ebola, multiple sclerosis, and other cancers have been revealed (Wallach et al., 2015).
- In a partnership with the University of Toronto, Atomwise was able to find new compounds to treat multiple sclerosis in a few months, what would have otherwise taken years.
- The fact that it is used by over 250 research institutions and biotech companies also demonstrates its popularity (Deng et al., 2019).

Limitations:

- The accuracy of the predictions of atomwise relies on the quality of the training data, and erroneous structural or binding data may spoil the predictions
- Although success has been enjoyed in early screening, clinical trials are a lengthy and unpredictable procedure.

The case of Atomwise illustrates the potential to increase chemical screening capacity manifold with AI, however, until approved medicines are translated, this remains a challenge.

6.2. DeepMind AlphaFold: Revolutionizing Protein Structure Prediction

The determination of protein structures has been a major challenge in biology since the last 50 years. X-ray crystallography and cryo-electron microscopy are lengthy and costly experimental mechanisms.

AlphaFold2's Breakthrough (2021):

Obtained near-experimental predictability of protein structures on a broad selection of targets, furthermore, of proteins that had not been solved previously (Jumper et al., 2021).

It is considered as one of the biggest scientific discoveries of the decade and it was called the Breakthrough of the Year by Nature.

Impact on Drug Discovery:

Facilitated structure-directed drug design by avoiding inaccurate 3D protein structures of disease-relevant (e.g. GPCR) and kinase) targets.

The AlphaFold Protein Structure Database was open-sourced by DeepMind and EMBL-EBI and made accessible to researchers across the globe, including 200+ million predicted structures.

Limitations:

- AlphaFold estimated fixed structures; it is not fully implemented to consider protein dynamics, post-translational alterations, and multi-protein interactions.
- This needs further improvement in conjunction with ligand-binding and functional models to be applied in drug design.

However, AlphaFold is a paradigm shift, which has changed structural biology and speeded up initial discovery in academia and industry.

6.3. Knowledge Graphs and Drug Repurposing BenevolentAI

BenevolentAI is a British firm that specializes in discoveries based on knowledge graphs. Its AI is a combination of biomedical literature, omics information, and clinical trial information that can uncover novel therapeutic hypotheses.

COVID-19 Case Study:

- In early 2020, BenevolentAI has found a rheumatoid arthritis medication called baricitinib as a potential COVID-19 treatment (Richardson et al., 2020).
- Several months later, baricitinib entered clinical trials and was given the FDA Emergency Use Authorization.

Other Applications:

- Oncology and neurodegenerative diseases (Parkinson's, ALS) Active pipelines.
- Chronic kidney disease: strategic alliance with AstraZeneca. Idiopathic pulmonary fibrosis: strategic alliance with AstraZeneca.

Challenges:

- Knowledge graphs are also constrained by data biases and gaps--where associations are not reflected in literature or datasets, AI can fail to notice them.
- Needs a lot of validation that requires wet-lab and clinical experiments.

BenevolentAI is one of the examples that demonstrate how AI can be used to repurpose drugs in times of crisis, which is particularly important to keep in mind in the face of the epidemic.

6.4. Insilico Medicine: Generative AI for Novel Drug Design

Insilico Medicine is a pioneer in using the generative adversarial networks (GANs) and reinforcement learning (RL) to generate de novo drugs.

Fibrosis Drug Development:

- In 2019, Insilico stated that it designed a new drug candidate against idiopathic pulmonary fibrosis based on GANs and RL and brought it to preclinical testing in less than 18 months (Zhavoronkov et al., 2019).
- In 2021, Insilico began a Phase I clinical trial on its fibrosis candidate, and it was one of the briefest transitions ever between AI design and human testing.

Platform Capabilities:

- Chemistry42: A small molecule design engine Chemistry42 is a web-based chemistry engine designed by researchers at Google and the University of Michigan.
- PandaOmics: Artificial Intelligence target discovery platform combining omics with text data.

Limitations:

- Gen. models may occasionally suggest molecules which are synthetically infeasible or unsuccessful in biological studies.
- The issue of reproducibility and validation is still important.

The success of Insilico shows that AI has the ability to reduce timelines significantly, which can be achieved only by clinical results.

6.5. Theoretical Submissions

Academia has also led the foundational advances, although the headlines have been dominated by industrial players:

- Atomwise collaboration with the University of Toronto: Deep learning-based neurological disease hit discovery is validated.
- MIT and Harvard projects: Reinforcement learning of multiple-objective drug design.

Failures and Lessons:

IBM Watson Drug Discovery was extensively hyped as a breakthrough in pharma research and development, but it did not have any significant breakthroughs because of data integration and explainability problems (Strickland, 2019).

Exaggerated projects emphasized the necessity of having realistic expectations and strict validation. A comparative summary of these case studies is presented in Table 2.

Table 2. Comparative Study

Case Study	Achievement	Key AI Technique	Success Factors	Limitations
Atomwise	Billions of compounds screened	CNNs for binding prediction	Partnerships, scalability	Data dependency, clinical translation
AlphaFold (DeepMind)	Solved protein structure prediction	Deep learning (transformers)	Open science, accuracy	Static models, lacks dynamics
BenevolentAI	Repurposed baricitinib for COVID-19	Knowledge graphs, NLP	Rapid real-world impact	Data bias, validation bottleneck
Insilico Medicine	Designed fibrosis drug in <18 months	GANs, RL	Generative design, integrated platforms	Synthetic feasibility, trial risks
IBM Watson (failure)	Promised AI-driven pharma revolution	NLP	Branding, resources	Overhype, lack of integration

According to the industrial and scholarly case studies, AI has ceased to be a far-off vision, but it is an actively moving force behind drug development innovation. Atomwise increased the scale of virtual screening; AlphaFold ended a 50-year scientific problem; Benevolent AI demonstrated the urgency of AI-driven repurposing; and Insilico Medicine demonstrated that it is faster than ever to generate designs. Meanwhile, its failures like Watson serve to remind us that AI is not a silver bullet and that its success relies on the quality of the data, its strong validation, and its support in the existing R&D procedures.

Collectively, these cases demonstrate the transformative and the practical difficulties of AI in drug development, which can be valuable lessons to researchers, industry leaders, and regulators.

Taken altogether, these case studies suggest that AI shows the highest and most reproducible success in drug discovery at the earliest stages, specifically, in target discovery and in the generation of hits. Nevertheless, there is a small amount of evidence of consistent clinical success in the late stages. This disproportion underscores that AI can fasten the hypothesis formation, however, firstly, it cannot remove biological and clinical uncertainties in drug development.

7. ETHICAL, REGULATORY, AND SOCIAL FACTORS

The application of artificial intelligence (AI) in drug development holds the potential solution to radical improvements, yet its use in biomedical research is associated with the most critical ethical, regulatory, and social issues. In contrast to traditional laboratory devices, AI systems themselves also affect the process of deciding on patient safety, the design of trials, and the approval of drugs. When implemented without proper supervision, AI will lead to strengthening biases related to the system, loss of patient privacy, or the establishment of accountability loopholes. This part examines the most important ethical and social issues, namely data privacy, algorithmic bias, transparency, liability, and regulatory preparedness, and explains the new models of responsible AI in drug development. The major ethical and regulatory considerations for AI in pharma are depicted in Figure 3.

Figure 3. Key ethical and regulatory considerations for AI in pharmaceuticals

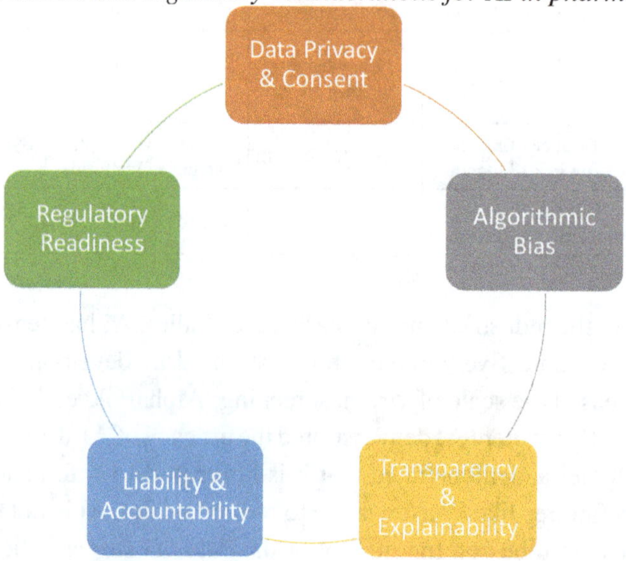

7.1. Data Privacy and Consent

Developing AI-powered drug development relies on the availability of large datasets, such as the genomic data, electronic health record (EHR) data, wearable data, and real-world evidence. Although such datasets can be used to build powerful predictive models, they also risk privacy abuse to patients.

Concerns:

- Once disclosed, gene data is almost never anonymized, increasing the chances of re-identification (Gymrek et al., 2013).
- Patients are also not always given meaningful control over the use of their data in second-order use, such as in commercial AI uses.

Best practices:

- The privacy-saving concept of federated learning is becoming popular since it enables the training of AI models through decentralized datasets without transferring patient data among these locations (Rieke et al., 2020).

It is more and more clear that regulators require clear and well-informed consent to AI model training, especially when it comes to commercial uses.

7.2. Algorithmic Bias and Equity

The quality of AI models depends on the quality of data that they have been trained on. During drug development, training data bias can result in unfair results:

- Population underrepresentation: The dataset of clinical trials usually underrepresents the minority populations, which results in lower predictive accuracy concerning the minority populations (Chen et al., 2021).
- Molecular bias: Databases can concentrate on an excessively studied target and disease to the detriment of rare disease.

One dermatology AI system case report demonstrated limited accuracy of melanoma detection in patients with an obscured skin tone with melanoma because of biased training (Adamson & Smith, 2018). There are also similar dangers with use of pharmacogenomics models in case of underrepresentation of minority genomic data.

Solutions:

- Create a variety of, representative datasets.
- Use bias detection software when validating a model to detect performance differences.
- Regulate AI systems by auditing and mandating that they produce fair results.

7.3. Transparent and Explicable

The black-box problem is one of the hottest topics regarding AI-based drug development. Most deep learning models offer high-quality predictions, which are not interpretable, and hence it is hard to know how decisions are made by regulators, clinicians, and patients.

Significance:

Decisions in medicine need to be justified, so as to be held accountable and trusted. In case an AI predicts that a drug will be unsuccessful because of toxicity, the regulators need to know how this prediction was made.

Emerging Solutions:

- Explainable AI (XAI): Explainable AI tools (SHapley Additive exPlanations or SHAP) and SHAP and LIME are used to explain model predictions (Doshi-Velez and Kim, 2017).
- Hybrid models: Integrating mechanistic pharmacological models with AI-generated predictions have interpretable biologically-based explanations.

Transparency is not merely an ethical standard, but also a regulatory one: regulators such as the FDA and EMA are currently focusing on explainability as a condition to submission powered by AI.

7.4. Liability and Accountability.

With more and more decision-making capabilities in AI systems, there is the concern of the legal responsibility of any mistakes:

- In case an AI-developed drug leads to unintended harm, who is responsible such as the pharmaceutical company or the AI developer or the regulatory agency who approved it?
- The same can be said about patent law: when an AI algorithm creates a new molecule, who is the owner of intellectual property? The existing legislation acknowledges human inventors, and this creates doubts on whether AI-led inventions are patent-able (Abbott, 2020).

Discussions on policy are still going on, but the vast majority of professionals are promoting a so-called human-in-the-loop approach, which means that the ultimate responsibility should belong to competent scientists and other regulatory authorities rather than to autonomous AI systems.

7.5. Regulatory Readiness

Regulatory authorities are experiencing pressure to change schemes of AI validation:

- FDA (USA): Published discussion papers on AI/ML in medical products, emphasising the necessity to have continuous learning systems, where transparency is a requirement (FDA, 2021).
- EMA (Europe): Published a reflection paper on AI in 2022 in which they noted that, among other things, the effectiveness of models used in drug lifecycle should be verified, their governance and auditing should be implemented (EMA, 2022).
- ICH (International Council for harmonisation): Thinking on harmonised international standards related to the integration of AI in drug submissions.

7.6. Some of the regulatory issues are:

- Model validation: Unlike a static model, AI algorithms can change over time with the addition of new data, which makes them difficult to regulate.
- Auditability: The regulators must have an access to the training data, model architecture, and decision-making logs.
- Cross-border disparities: Differences in regulatory requirements across the world impose compliance costs on the global pharmaceutical companies.

7.7. Communal Effect and social Confidence.

The introduction of AI in drug development is also a concern of society:

- Confidence in AI medicine: Patients and doctors might feel unwilling to use AI-generated drugs or dosage suggestions unless it can be proven by clear evidence (Topol, 2019).
- Loss of jobs: There is a concern that AI will take over some jobs in the field of R&D, but it is likely that it will complement human expertise instead of eradicating it.
- Inequality at a global level: In case AI-based drug discovery is continually held by affluent countries, inequalities in the availability of new treatments might increase (Whittaker et al., 2021).

The publicity of open-access databases (e.g., AlphaFold Protein Structure Database) and international partnerships, in particular, are the main factors to secure fair dividends.

8. FUTURE OF AI-DRIVEN PHARMA

Artificial intelligence (AI) and pharmaceutical research have already altered the process of drug discovery and clinical development. However, the most radical possibility is in the future. The vision of AI applications going forward would have seen the creation of AI systems that would not only increase the speed of the current workflows, but also reinvent the concept of pharmaceutical innovation itself. Personalized therapies that make use of digital twins will also transform the healthcare sector to integrate AI in the form of decentralized learning across institutions worldwide. The most promising frontiers are discussed in this section and include digital twins, federated learning, autonomous R&D pipelines, and AI-powered precision medicine.

8.1. Digital Twin of Drug Tests and Personalized Treatments.

A digital twin is an active virtual representation of a patient or biological system, which is constantly updated with data in the real world. Digital twins in pharma would be used to predict a response to treatment in individual cases prior to therapy initiation.

Applications:

- In silico trials: Digital twins can recreate the responses of drugs in various virtual populations, without the need to conduct an experiment on thousands of patients (Viceconti et al., 2021).
- Individualized dosing: AI-controlled twins maximize the drug dosage regarding genomic, metabolic, and lifestyle data.
- Safety prediction: Predicting adverse events Using virtual models is identified prior to clinical testing.

Case Example:

In silico medicine efforts, such as the application of digital twins in drug testing, have been encouraged by the European Commission via its Avicenna Alliance (Viceconti & Henney, 2020).

Challenges:

- Needs to be constantly integrated with the high-quality multi-modal data.
- The acceptance of digital twin evidence is still not well regulated.

Digital twins are a vision in which every patient can have a virtual test of treatment, which significantly minimizes risks.

8.2. Federated Learning in Multi-Centre Trials

The privacy of data and proprietary disincentives have been long time impediments in pharma AI collaboration. Federated learning (FL) provides the answer as it enables algorithms to be trained on decentralized data without the transfer of raw data between institutions.

Benefits:

- Guarantees the privacy of patients, but allows access to global data.
- Breaks data silos between hospitals, biobanks and pharmaceutical companies.
- Increases the external validity of models by training with a wide variety of populations.

Case Example:

FL was used in the MELLODY Project (EU Horizon 2020): it was tested on drug development in oncology, training at the level of several pharma companies without giving sensitive data (Warnat-Herresthal et al., 2021).

Future Outlook:

FL may be a foundation of cross-national multi-centre trials, facilitating cooperation without violation of regulations like GDPR and HIPAA.

8.3. Autonomous R&D Pipelines

The long-term AI pharma goal is a fully autonomous drug discovery pipeline, which posits hypotheses, designs compounds, synthesizes and purifies molecules, runs them in robotic labs, and analyzes findings with no human interaction.

Key Components:

- generative models: Predict new compounds.
- Robotic synthesis systems: Rs manufacture suggested molecules.
- Robots: High-throughput screening robots: Carry out assays and relay results to AI.
- Closed-loop learning: AI enlists predictions and designs through feedback.

Proof of Concept:

The fibrosis program by Insilico Medicine demonstrated that hypothesis generation and candidate design could be done with the assistance of AI.

The automatic chemical synthesis systems at MIT show machine-directed performance of the lab (Coley et al., 2019). The components of an autonomous AI-driven R&D pipeline are illustrated in Figure 4.

Figure 4. Components of an autonomous AI-driven R&D pipeline.

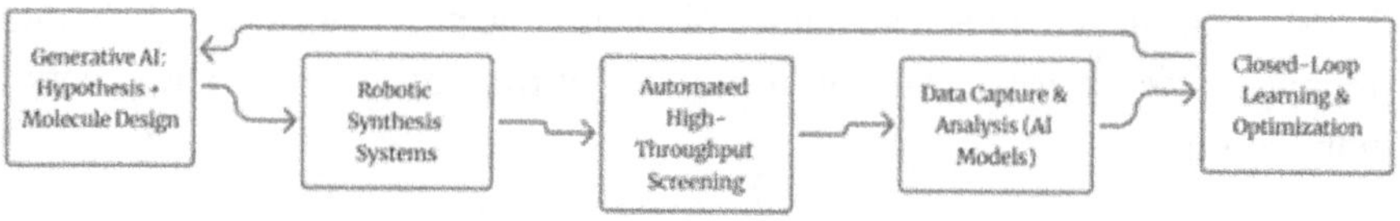

Challenges:

- Combining various technologies in a smooth working process.
- Scientific and moral issues on the decrease in human control in drug research.

Self-directed R&D pipelines might one day give rise to so-called self-driving labs and only months between discovery and clinical candidate.

Balanced Evaluation: Promise Versus Practicality

Although artificial intelligence has fronted unparalleled speed and scale in drug discovery, its practical implementation is limited by the issues of validation, interpretability and implementation. The existing data favors AI as a formidable facilitator of early discovery and not an overall solution of end-to-end pharmaceutical development. These gaps will be filled in to establish whether AI can provide clinical and societal value in a sustainable way.

9. CONCLUSION

Artificial intelligence is transforming the pharmaceutical industry by making the process of discovery faster, more predictive, and able to make decisions throughout the drug development cycle that is being made by information. Early discovery AI is used to enhance target identification, hit selection, lead optimization and de novo molecular design using deep learning and generative algorithms. During preclinical and clinical stages AI progress can forecast toxicology, PK/PD, adaptive trial, and patient stratification, which minimize attrition and enhance safety. The AI-driven dossier generation, real-time pharmacovigilance, and risk management systems are becoming increasingly useful in regulatory and post-market domains.

The case studies of industry and academia presented in the chapter show that AI has outgrown the idea of promise and has already created a real effect, but historical expectations and over-hyped failures are reminding us that we should expect little and treat it like scientific research. Responsible adoption has a focus on ethical and regulatory issues, such as privacy, transparency, bias, accountability, and reproducibility.

In the future, AI-powered digital twins, federated learning, autonomous R&D pipelines, and precision medicine will imply a future where drug development would be quicker, safer, more personalized, and collaborative. To achieve this vision, it will be necessary to have powerful governance structures, quality data, transdisciplinary approaches, and international regulatory preparedness. At the end, AI is not a substitute of scientists but a vital collaborator that will transform the way contemporary therapeutics are found, experimented, and provided.

Key Opportunities

AI is not a tool but a paradigm shift in pharmaceutical innovation:

- Speed and Efficiency: It is now possible to transfer drug candidates from hypothesis to clinical testing in months instead of years.
- Venturing into New Chemical Space: Generative AI opens the possibilities to much wider horizons than human imagination or libraries can.
- Precision and Personalization: AI can use genomics, real-world data, and digital twins to get medicine much closer to truly individualized treatment.

- Improved Safety: Predictive toxicology and real-time pharmacovigilance allow risk to be managed in advance.
- International Cooperation: Federated learning and open-source AI efforts would enable various parties to work together without violating privacy.

Persistent Challenges

Along with these progress mini-millennials continue to face critical challenges:

- Quality and Biases of Data: Models that are trained on partial or bias data sets may strengthen inequality.
- Explainability: Interpretable models must be provided by regulatory agencies and clinicians to promote trust and accountability.
- Ethical Governance: There are concerns that privacy, consent, and intellectual property are still unaddressed.
- Regulatory Adaptation: The agencies should be in a position to balance innovation with stringent validation to safeguard the safety of the people.
- Into Practice: Pharma companies are finding organizational and cultural challenges in deploying AI into legacy pipelines.

These issues underline the fact that AI is not a panacea, but an effective facilitator that needs to be strictly controlled by human restrictions.

In addition to technical shortcomings, actual implementation of AI is associated with organizational and cultural challenges. The pharmaceutical research and development pipeline is predominantly constructed using workflows that are based on legacy and are not easily integrated with data-driven systems. There is also resistance to algorithmic decision support, absence of standardized validation procedures, and doubt over regulatory expectations, which also curtails adoption, although technical performance is promising.

The Part of Multi-Stakeholder Collaboration.

Industry needs to invest in AI as a tool to reduce costs, but also as a source of innovation. Academia has to keep on innovating new algorithms and promoting open science projects. Regulators should come up with nimble structures that would prove AI models, maintain transparency and accountability. Ethical conversations between Patients and Publics should be made to develop trust and resolve privacy and bias concerns. AI in pharma will only work through being built on trust, inclusivity and international collaboration.

REFERENCES

Abbott, R. (2020). *The reasonable robot: Artificial intelligence and the law*. Cambridge University Press., DOI: 10.1017/9781108631761

Adamson, A. S., & Smith, A. (2018). Machine learning and health care disparities in dermatology. *JAMA Dermatology*, *154*(11), 1247–1248. DOI: 10.1001/jamadermatol.2018.2348 PMID: 30073260

Arrowsmith, J., & Miller, P. (2013). Trial watch: Phase II and Phase III attrition rates 2011–2012. *Nature Reviews. Drug Discovery*, *12*(8), 569. DOI: 10.1038/nrd4090 PMID: 23903212

Bajorin, D. F.. (2021). Patient recruitment challenges in clinical trials: Opportunities for artificial intelligence solutions. *Journal of Clinical Oncology*, *39*(15, suppl), 2641–2641. DOI: 10.1200/JCO.2021.39.15_suppl.2641

Bate, A., & Blake, K. (2020). Pharmacovigilance: Artificial intelligence and machine learning in adverse drug reaction reporting. *Drug Safety*, *43*(6), 547–554. DOI: 10.1007/s40264-020-00933-0

Burbidge, R., Trotter, M., Buxton, B., & Holden, S. (2001). Drug design by machine learning: Support vector machines for pharmaceutical data analysis. *Computers & Chemistry*, *26*(1), 5–14. DOI: 10.1016/S0097-8485(01)00094-8 PMID: 11765851

Chen, H., Engkvist, O., Wang, Y., Olivecrona, M., & Blaschke, T. (2018). The rise of deep learning in drug discovery. *Drug Discovery Today*, *23*(6), 1241–1250. DOI: 10.1016/j.drudis.2018.01.039 PMID: 29366762

Chen, I. Y., Joshi, S., & Ghassemi, M. (2021). Treating health disparities with artificial intelligence. *Nature Medicine*, *26*(1), 16–17. DOI: 10.1038/s41591-019-0649-2 PMID: 31932779

Cheng, F., Li, W., Zhou, Y., Shen, J., Wu, Z., Liu, G., & Tang, Y. (2012). admetSAR: A comprehensive source and free tool for assessment of chemical ADMET properties. *Journal of Chemical Information and Modeling*, *52*(11), 3099–3105. DOI: 10.1021/ci300367a PMID: 23092397

Cherkasov, A., Muratov, E. N., Fourches, D., Varnek, A., Baskin, I. I., Cronin, M., & Tropsha, A. (2014). QSAR modeling: Where have you been? Where are you going to? *Journal of Medicinal Chemistry*, *57*(12), 4977–5010. DOI: 10.1021/jm4004285 PMID: 24351051

. Coley, C. W., Thomas, D. A., Lummiss, J. A., Jaworski, J. N., Breen, C. P., Schultz, V., & Jensen, K. F. (2019). A robotic platform for flow synthesis of organic compounds informed by AI planning. *Science, 365*(6453), eaax1566. DOI: 10.1126/science.aax1566

Cruz Rivera, S., Liu, X., Chan, A. W., Denniston, A. K., & Calvert, M. J. (2020). Guidelines for clinical trial protocols involving AI interventions: SPIRIT-AI extension. *BMJ (Clinical Research Ed.), 370*, m3210. DOI: 10.1136/bmj.m3210 PMID: 32907797

Deng, J., Gupta, S., Wu, R., & Wallach, I. (2019). Deep learning in drug discovery: AtomNet and beyond. *Drug Discovery Today, 24*(8), 1617–1623. DOI: 10.1016/j.drudis.2019.05.015

DiMasi, J. A., Grabowski, H. G., & Hansen, R. W. (2016). Innovation in the pharmaceutical industry: New estimates of R&D costs. *Journal of Health Economics, 47*, 20–33. DOI: 10.1016/j.jhealeco.2016.01.012 PMID: 26928437

European Medicines Agency. (2022). *Reflection paper on the use of artificial intelligence in the medicinal product lifecycle*. https://www.ema.europa.eu/en/documents/reflection-paper/artificial-intelligence-medicinal-product-lifecycle_en.pdf

Fogel, D. B. (2018). Factors associated with clinical trials that fail and opportunities for improving the likelihood of success: A review. *Contemporary Clinical Trials Communications, 11*, 156–164. DOI: 10.1016/j.conctc.2018.08.001 PMID: 30112460

Food and Drug Administration. (2021). *Artificial intelligence and machine learning in software as a medical device*. U.S. Food and Drug Administration. https://www.fda.gov/medical-devices/software-medical-device-samd/artificial-intelligence-and-machine-learning-software-medical-device

Golub, T. R., Slonim, D. K., Tamayo, P., Huard, C., Gaasenbeek, M., Mesirov, J. P., & Lander, E. S. (1999). Molecular classification of cancer: Class discovery and class prediction by gene expression monitoring. *Science, 286*(5439), 531–537. DOI: 10.1126/science.286.5439.531 PMID: 10521349

Gómez-Bombarelli, R., Wei, J. N., Duvenaud, D., Hernández-Lobato, J. M., Sánchez-Lengeling, B., Sheberla, D., & Aspuru-Guzik, A. (2018). Automatic chemical design using a data-driven continuous representation of molecules. *ACS Central Science, 4*(2), 268–276. DOI: 10.1021/acscentsci.7b00572 PMID: 29532027

Gymrek, M., McGuire, A. L., Golan, D., Halperin, E., & Erlich, Y. (2013). Identifying personal genomes by surname inference. *Science, 339*(6117), 321–324. DOI: 10.1126/science.1229566 PMID: 23329047

Harper, L.. (2021). Detecting adverse drug reactions using artificial intelligence in real-world healthcare data. *Nature Medicine*, *27*(7), 1105–1112. DOI: 10.1038/s41591-021-01329-2

Hasselgren, C., & Oprea, T. I. (2024). Artificial intelligence for drug discovery: Are we there yet? *Annual Review of Pharmacology and Toxicology*, *64*(1), 527–550. DOI: 10.1146/annurev-pharmtox-040323-040828 PMID: 37738505

Honda, S., Shi, S., & Ueda, H. R. (2019). SMILES transformer: Pre-trained molecular fingerprint for low data drug discovery. *arXiv*. https://arxiv.org/abs/1911.04738

Hopkins, A. L., Bender, A., & Glen, R. C. (2020). Exscientia's AI-designed drug enters clinical trials. *Nature Biotechnology*, *38*(1), 8–9. DOI: 10.1038/d41587-020-00001-x PMID: 31919441

Huang, R., Xia, M., Nguyen, D. T., Zhao, T., Sakamuru, S., Zhao, J., & Austin, C. P. (2016). Tox21 challenge to build predictive models of nuclear receptor and stress response pathways. *Frontiers in Environmental Science*, *3*, 85. DOI: 10.3389/fenvs.2015.00085

Jumper, J., Evans, R., Pritzel, A., Green, T., Figurnov, M., Ronneberger, O., & Hassabis, D. (2021). Highly accurate protein structure prediction with AlphaFold. *Nature*, *596*(7873), 583–589. DOI: 10.1038/s41586-021-03819-2 PMID: 34265844

LeCun, Y., Bengio, Y., & Hinton, G. (2015). Deep learning. *Nature*, *521*(7553), 436–444. DOI: 10.1038/nature14539 PMID: 26017442

Lee, J., Yoon, W., Kim, S., Kim, D., Kim, S., So, C. H., & Kang, J. (2020). BioBERT: A pre-trained biomedical language representation model for biomedical text mining. *Bioinformatics (Oxford, England)*, *36*(4), 1234–1240. DOI: 10.1093/bioinformatics/btz682 PMID: 31501885

Liu, X., Cruz Rivera, S., Moher, D., Calvert, M. J., & Denniston, A. K. (2019). Reporting guidelines for clinical trial reports for interventions involving artificial intelligence: The CONSORT-AI extension. *BMJ (Clinical Research Ed.)*, *370*, m3164. DOI: 10.1136/bmj.m3164 PMID: 32909959

Mak, K. K., & Pichika, M. R. (2019). Artificial intelligence in drug development: Present status and future prospects. *Drug Discovery Today*, *24*(3), 773–780. DOI: 10.1016/j.drudis.2018.11.014 PMID: 30472429

Mayr, A., Klambauer, G., Unterthiner, T., & Hochreiter, S. (2016). DeepTox: Toxicity prediction using deep learning. *Frontiers in Environmental Science*, *3*, 80. DOI: 10.3389/fenvs.2015.00080

Perou, C. M., Sørlie, T., Eisen, M. B., van de Rijn, M., Jeffrey, S. S., Rees, C. A., & Botstein, D. (2000). Molecular portraits of human breast tumours. *Nature*, *406*(6797), 747–752. DOI: 10.1038/35021093 PMID: 10963602

Rajkomar, A., Dean, J., & Kohane, I. (2019). Machine learning in medicine. *The New England Journal of Medicine*, *380*(14), 1347–1358. DOI: 10.1056/NEJMra1814259 PMID: 30943338

Rehman, A. U., Li, M., Wu, B., Ali, Y., Rasheed, S., Shaheen, S., Liu, X., Luo, R., & Zhang, J.Ashfaq Ur Rehman. (2025). Role of artificial intelligence in revolutionizing drug discovery. *Fundamental Research (Beijing)*, *5*(3), 1273–1287. DOI: 10.1016/j.fmre.2024.04.021 PMID: 40528990

Richardson, P., Griffin, I., Tucker, C., Smith, D., Oechsle, O., Phelan, A., & Stebbing, J. (2020). Baricitinib as potential treatment for 2019-nCoV acute respiratory disease. *Lancet*, *395*(10223), e30–e31. DOI: 10.1016/S0140-6736(20)30304-4 PMID: 32032529

Rieke, N., Hancox, J., Li, W., Milletari, F., Roth, H. R., Albarqouni, S., & Xu, D. (2020). The future of digital health with federated learning. *NPJ Digital Medicine*, *3*(1), 119. DOI: 10.1038/s41746-020-00323-1 PMID: 33015372

Scannell, J. W., Blanckley, A., Boldon, H., & Warrington, B. (2012). Diagnosing the decline in pharmaceutical R&D efficiency. *Nature Reviews. Drug Discovery*, *11*(3), 191–200. DOI: 10.1038/nrd3681 PMID: 22378269

Segler, M. H. S., Preuss, M., & Waller, M. P. (2018). Planning chemical syntheses with deep neural networks and symbolic AI. *Nature*, *555*(7698), 604–610. DOI: 10.1038/nature25978 PMID: 29595767

Shilo, S., Rossman, H., & Segal, E. (2020). Axes of a revolution: Challenges and promises of big data in healthcare. *Nature Medicine*, *26*(1), 29–38. DOI: 10.1038/s41591-019-0727-5 PMID: 31932803

Strickland, E. (2019). IBM Watson, heal thyself: How IBM overpromised and underdelivered on AI health care. *IEEE Spectrum*, *56*(4), 24–31. DOI: 10.1109/MSPEC.2019.8678513

Topol, E. (2019). High-performance medicine: The convergence of human and artificial intelligence. *Nature Medicine*, *25*(1), 44–56. DOI: 10.1038/s41591-018-0300-7 PMID: 30617339

Viceconti, M., & Henney, A. (2020). In silico clinical trials: How computer simulation will transform the biomedical industry. *International Journal of Clinical Trials*, *7*(2), 17–29. DOI: 10.18203/2349-3259.ijct20200274

Viceconti, M., Hunter, P., & Hose, R. (2021). Big data, big knowledge: Big data for personalized healthcare. *IEEE Journal of Biomedical and Health Informatics*, *25*(2), 403–412. DOI: 10.1109/JBHI.2021.3049871 PMID: 32086223

Wallach, I., Dzamba, M., & Heifets, A. (2015). AtomNet: A deep convolutional neural network for bioactivity prediction in structure-based drug discovery. *arXiv*. https://arxiv.org/abs/1510.02855

Wang, L., Li, X., Zhang, L., Gao, Q., Xu, S., & Yang, G. (2021). Artificial intelligence in drug clinical trials: Applications, challenges, and future trends. *Drug Discovery Today*, *26*(6), 1407–1415. DOI: 10.1016/j.drudis.2021.02.002

Warnat-Herresthal, S., Schultze, H., Shastry, K. L., Manamohan, S., Mukherjee, S., Garg, V., Sarveswara, R., Händler, K., Pickkers, P., Aziz, N. A., Ktena, S., Tran, F., Bitzer, M., Ossowski, S., Casadei, N., Herr, C., Petersheim, D., Behrends, U., Kern, F., & Schultze, J. L.The MELLODY Consortium. (2021). Swarm learning for decentralized and confidential clinical machine learning. *Nature*, *594*(7862), 265–270. DOI: 10.1038/s41586-021-03583-3 PMID: 34040261

Wenzel, J., Matter, H., & Schmidt, F. (2019). Predictive toxicology: In silico approaches for early safety assessment of new drugs. *Drug Discovery Today. Technologies*, *31*, 5–17. DOI: 10.1016/j.ddtec.2019.01.001

Whittaker, M., Crawford, K., Dobbe, R., Fried, G., Kaziunas, E., Mathur, V., & Schwartz, O. (2021). *AI Now Report 2021*. AI Now Institute, New York University.

Xu, Y., Dai, Z., Chen, F., Gao, S., Pei, J., & Lai, L. (2015). Deep learning for drug-induced liver injury. *Journal of Chemical Information and Modeling*, *55*(10), 2085–2093. DOI: 10.1021/acs.jcim.5b00238 PMID: 26437739

Zhavoronkov, A., Ivanenkov, Y. A., Aliper, A., Veselov, M. S., Aladinskiy, V. A., Aladinskaya, A. V., & Zholus, A. (2019). Deep learning enables rapid identification of potent DDR1 kinase inhibitors. *Nature Biotechnology*, *37*(9), 1038–1040. DOI: 10.1038/s41587-019-0224-x PMID: 31477924

Zhou, J., Pompano, R. R., & Zhao, Y. (2020). Machine learning for drug discovery and design. *Nature Reviews. Drug Discovery*, *19*(9), 651–669. DOI: 10.1038/s41573-020-00027-9

Chapter 8

Systems Theory of Pathology Involving Machine Learning and Deep Learning

Mbuyi Mukendi
http://orcid.org/0009-0001-6914-2096
National University, USA

ABSTRACT

This chapter presents a Systems Theory of Pathology that integrates Machine Learning (ML) and Deep Learning (DL) to guide health sciences research. It serves as a foundational resource for doctoral students, experts, and researchers in using artificial intelligence (AI) for detecting and understanding communicable and noncommunicable diseases. The text reviews the historical development of systems theory and its connection with AI technologies, explaining how ML and DL analyze complex data for diagnosing conditions like glaucoma, cancer, and kidney failure. It also discusses complementary frameworks, including health literacy and locus of control. Ultimately, the chapter highlights the potential of this integrated approach to enhance clarity, methodological rigor, and innovation in medical research.

INTRODUCTION

This article highlights the significance of selecting an effective framework to improve the research and writing process, ultimately resulting in better outcomes for both students and researchers. A strong framework is essential, as it serves as the foundation for all research efforts. By providing structure, it allows students and

DOI: 10.4018/979-8-2600-0981-9.ch008

researchers to clearly outline their studies and effectively introduce and develop their research topics.

A clear and distinct framework not only helps identify key ideas to explore but also offers guidance on methodologies and the statistical data required to validate findings. It establishes a clear context for the problem being investigated and integrates existing knowledge while paving the way for new insights. In this regard, the framework can be viewed as the essential structure—or "skeleton"—that supports and guides the entire research endeavor, fostering clarity and depth in the exploration of any given subject.

Brydges & Batt (2023) highlighted the important role that theories play in providing a structured understanding of how various concepts are related. They argue that theories help both students and researchers navigate complex situations by offering explanations for different phenomena, which leads to a deeper comprehension of the subject matter. A theory becomes stronger and more credible when it is backed by robust and diverse evidence. This validation enables researchers to use the theory effectively to explain existing observations, test hypotheses, and predict future outcomes. The application of multiple theories is relevant across societal trends and individual behaviors, making them significant in a wide range of fields, including psychology, sociology, education, and economics.

Brydges & Batt (2023) explained that theoretical frameworks are structured collections of interconnected ideas based on recognized theories. These frameworks assist researchers by identifying key concepts, illustrating meaningful relationships among them, and demonstrating their significance within a specific context. Essentially, they serve as a guideline or a series of steps for researchers to methodically explore a subject of interest.

Potschin-Young et al. (2018) argue that conceptual frameworks are valuable tools for understanding complex issues. Anyone facing a difficult problem should utilize these frameworks to achieve the best outcomes. These frameworks are iterative in nature, offering insightful perspectives on various topics and challenges while emphasizing the intricacies and interconnections within complex systems. The primary objective of a conceptual framework is to clarify existing issues, present different viewpoints, and propose various strategies for addressing them. Unlike theoretical frameworks, which tend to be more structured, conceptual frameworks encourage creative thinking and exploration.

Based on the above, one can deduce that both types of frameworks are crucial in research. Theoretical frameworks guide by aligning relevant literature, research design, and methodology, ensuring coherence and rigor in the research approach. In contrast, conceptual frameworks serve as foundational elements that empower researchers and enhance the relevance of their work. By effectively connecting their findings to the broader academic community, these frameworks engage the interest of readers and fellow researchers, fostering further inquiry and dialogue. Ultimately, this contributes to the advancement of knowledge in their respective fields.

Given that theoretical and conceptual frameworks have been extensively researched, the literature is unlimited. Most articles included in the literature of this study date from 2020 to 2024. Only peer-reviewed and relevant articles referring to the theoretical framework and conceptual framework, and the like, were kept. This article covered the following: (a) Literature Search Strategies, (b) Theoretical framework, (c) Conceptual framework, (d) Review of the Literature, which included topics such as framework, Theoretical framework, and Conceptual framework, (d) Syntheses of the research findings, (e) Critiques of research methodology, (f) Complementary and Contrasting frameworks, (g) New Theoretical framework, (h) Recommendations, (i) Conclusion, and (j) References.

Literature Search Strategies

When students and researchers use a well-defined framework in research, it enhances the quality and depth of their study. Such a framework effectively guides the research through the various complexities of their work, from creating research questions to interpreting results. The framework promotes thorough data analysis, supports theory testing, and encourages the discovery of new insights, thereby linking research to the broader academic population. The choice students and researchers make will establish a solid understanding of the subject matter, and combining the framework with an appropriate methodology for the study can improve the comprehension of the problem at hand and enlighten the study's design and the quality of its findings.

Most of the articles used in the literature review on a framework for effective research fall within five years (2020-2024). Several databases were searched through the Northcentral University (NCU) Library and Google Scholar to identify relevant sources for this review. The NCU Library offers Roadrunner Search powered by EBSCO Discovery Service, which searches most of the library's databases, resources, and content. Due to the need to consult older academic and primary published sources, the JSTOR database, a digital library, was also consulted, mainly for the theoretical framework chosen for this study.

Inclusion strategic search criteria were used to identify information from articles that contained keywords such as *framework, theoretical framework, conceptual framework, the advantage of using a framework, when to use a theoretical framework, why to use a theoretical framework, when to use a conceptual framework, why use a conceptual framework, framework usage for a doctoral thesis*. The literature search returned over 200,000 results. After reviewing the abstracts and several full texts, 75 studies were selected and included among the retained articles.

A search on the theoretical framework selected for this research study was conducted using the terms *General System Theory, GST, Systems Theory, Cybernetics systems theory, pathology theory, and Artificial Intelligence theory*. The result returned 8,542 peer-reviewed articles. Searching for systems theory by itself resulted in over 4,000,000 articles. Searching for 'framework" and "systems theory" returned 13,890 peer-reviewed articles. After scanning the abstract, only twelve articles were retained based on their historical and applicability content.

Articles relevant to understanding framework and systems theory, yet not peer-reviewed, were eliminated from the list. Framework and systems theory articles older than 2020 that were relevant were consulted for their content but not retained. Relevant articles related to systems theory that did not provide insight into this research study's theoretical framework were also considered for their content. Many articles were excluded because they were related only to the conceptual framework.

Theoretical Frameworks

The central theme of this article is systems theory. Von Bertalanffy (1950, 1968) defines a system as a "whole" that includes various aspects of the universe, highlighting the importance of understanding the components and interactions of complex systems, particularly in fields like life and social sciences. Hammond (2019) describes a system as a group of components that work together to achieve a common goal. To understand complex subjects, such as human beings and diseases, one must examine the relationships between these components and their environments. For example, cells and skin cooperate in the human body to create a functioning whole. Namaki (2019) and Vanderstraeten (2019) categorize systems as open or closed, with open systems allowing for interactions with the environment, while closed systems do not. A family is an example of an open system. A disease is also an open system arising from internal or external factors in living systems.

The study also examines artificial intelligence (AI) and its components, like machine learning (ML) and deep learning (DL), which operate as systems with defined inputs and outputs. Kaul et al. (2020) emphasize that inputs undergo transformation to produce outputs, which can then serve as inputs for other processes. Understanding systems theory is crucial for analyzing how diseases and AI models detect and predict health outcomes.

Systems theory

Carr-Chellman et al. (2020) and Hammond (2019) discuss systems theory, or general systems theory (GST), attributed to von Bertalanffy (1950), a biologist who recognized misunderstandings among experts in biology, economics, and mathematics. He argued that it is vital to consider both the elements and their relationships with the environment to understand the interconnected elements. Carr-Chellman et al. highlight four founding members of the Society for the Advancement of GST: von Bertalanffy, Ralph Gerard, Kenneth Boulding (an economist), and Anatol Rapoport (a mathematician). They emphasized the need for clear communication among disciplines.

Hammond (2019) views von Bertalanffy as a pioneer in studying organisms as systems. He believes that biology, with its holistic approach, should be the foundation of science. He asserts that understanding the parts and their interactions is essential for a complete understanding of any system. Vanderstraeten (2019) similarly sees von Bertalanffy as influential in the social sciences and the study of complex systems.

Drack (2015) indicated that von Bertalanffy dedicated significant time to developing a biological theory that could encompass all systems. While some researchers supported mechanistic theory (Nicholson, 2012), focusing on dissecting organisms into individual components, others, like Aristotle and Paracelsus, embraced vitalism, attributing the organization of living systems to soul-like factors (Coulter et al., 2019). Von Bertalanffy criticized both approaches, advocating instead for a new perspective on studying living organisms.

Valentinov et al. (2019) elaborated on von Bertalanffy's exploration of metabolism, growth, and biophysics in 1968. Hammond (2019) noted that in 1938, von Bertalanffy emphasized studying organisms as wholes rather than in parts. He proposed that this holistic approach should be applied broadly, leading to his General Systems Theory (GST), which views systems theory as an interdisciplinary study focused on knowledge gained through the interactions of simpler components, a phenomenon known as emergence.

Plăviţu (2020) highlights the historical roots of the concept of a "system," formally attributed to Odobleja (1939), a Romanian doctor who advanced principles of generalized cybernetics. His focus on feedback regulation in control and communication processes went largely unrecognized during World War II due to Romania's isolation. Plăviţu notes that Odobleja enriched our understanding of the human soul and the empirical cosmos.

Pouvreau (2014) states that von Bertalanffy was influenced by earlier thinkers like Plato and Aristotle, shaping his philosophy of biology. He believed living organisms should be seen as organized wholes, motivated by specific goals rather than just the sum of their parts. von Bertalanffy also drew inspiration from philosophers such as Leibniz and Paracelsus, as well as cultural historians like Ibn Khaldun and Vico, alongside the dialectical ideas of Marx and Hegel (von Bertalanffy, 1968).

Nowak & Stencel (2022) argued that Kant developed the concept of the organism as an integrated whole in his 1790 work, *Critique of Judgment*. Alvargonzález (2019) categorized systems as internal or external and examined their relationships, operations, and configurations, aligning with Kant's (1897) notion of teleology as regulating change (von Bertalanffy, 1968). As the significance of system structures grew, von Bertalanffy became increasingly involved in the field.

Drack et al. (2015) stated that cybernetics and the "black box" concept were developed by Wiener and Ashby, inspired by the nervous system. Von Bertalanffy saw cybernetics as part of general systems theory (GST), where systems receive input, process it, and produce output without revealing internal processes. Negative feedback should address defective output. Drack et al. argued that advances in feedback, information theory, and computing led to the emergence of cybernetics, influencing control engineering and the creation of machines that mimic the nervous system.

Ortigosa (2022) and Tilak et al. (2021) noted that cybernetics was conceived by Wiener and others at MIT in 1943, focusing on feedback-controlled systems and neural networks. Vahidi et al. (2019) believed Wiener initiated the field in 1946, with further contributions from personages like von Forester and Ashby. Beer (1960) then used these ideas to create his Viable System Model (VSM).

Overall, systems theory emphasizes the interconnectedness of system components, which should be analyzed as a cohesive whole rather than in isolation. This holistic approach is particularly important for understanding any subsystems of the human body in the context of noncommunicable diseases such as Glaucoma, Cancer, Kidney failure, etc.

Systems Theory's Chronological History

General Systems Theory (GST). Johnson (2019) believed that GST resulted from von Bertalanffy (1950) trying to define a system. According to Johnson, von Bertalanffy might have borrowed his thinking of a system as a whole from Aristotle. Kutschera (2018) recognized Aristotle as a Greek philosopher born in 384 BC in Circa. Aristotle's work was said to have transformed and shaped Western philosophy. Kutschera embraced the Aristotelian belief that all things were composed of several parts and that the whole was different from its components.

Kutschera (2018) declared that the discovery of Deoxyribonucleic acid (DNA) in the 1940s, the reductionist model that, according to Hallioui (2020), was introduced by Descartes, also born in Circa, like Aristotle. Still, in 1596 AD, unlike Aristotle, Descartes was a French philosopher, physicist, and mathematician who believed that the mind was an entity, totally different and disconnected from the body. Reductionism emphasizes that a system that is difficult to understand constitutes the sum of its components and could be described by analyzing each element (Descartes, 1984).

Kutschera (2018) believed that although the reductionist approach provided scientists with an applied approach to discovering living organisms and understanding elementary cellular and molecular processes, it did not seem to be the appropriate technique when dealing with ever-changing complex and organic systems. Thus, von Bertalanffy (1951) reasoned that Aristotle's holistic perspective was more reasonable than Descartes' because there seems to be much more to complex organic systems than just being the sum of its parts.

Sieniutycz (2020) wrote that in the early 19th century, Austria's custom was to publish a book every six months. An Austrian, von Bertalanffy (1950), a biologist and philosopher, published "Kritische Theorie der Formbildung" (Eldridge et al., 1931), sharing his general systems theory principles. Sieniutycz (2020) also mentioned that the same information was published again in 1968 (von Bertalanffy,1968), to which Vanderstraeten (2019) concurred. Tretter (2019) believed that von Bertalanffy created the GST in the 1930s based on his vision of organisms being viewed as systems. Kutschera (2018), Hammond (2019), and van Assche et al. (2019) also accredited the conception of systems theory to von Bertalanffy. However, Hammond revealed that the idea was first expressed at the University of Chicago in the United States of America (USA) (von Bertalanffy, 1972a) – thus embracing Tretter's (2019) declaration. It was not until almost ten years later, in 1948, that von Bertalanffy's GST was made known to many in Austria (Hammond, 2019).

Carr-Chellman et al. (2020) and Vanderstraeten (2019) also revealed that von Bertalanffy and his colleagues (Ralph Gerard, Kenneth Boulding, and Anatol Rapoport) (von Bertalanffy, 1968) were joined by James Miller in 1954 (von Bertalanffy, 1968). Miller (1973) was a psychologist from the Mental Health Research Institute of the University of Michigan. The five scientists created a new group named the Society for General Systems Research (SGSR). Miller (1973) created the living systems theory involving a system hierarchy. Miller's system hierarchy had eight complex echelons, which were the cells, the organs, the organisms, the groups, the organizations, the communities, the societies, and the supranational systems.

Chatterjee et al. (2021) reported Boulding(1956) as one who contributed to the general systems theory by emphasizing its need to involve diverse research types and goals. Chatterjee et al. leveraged the general systems theory (GST) in their study to create an information system (IS) output. Chatterjee et al. asserted that Boulding (1956) is the one who contributed the idea, leading researchers to use the general systems theory because of its idea of helping specialists of a certain field to supply knowledge to another field once they realize the resemblance these fields might have in common. While Miller (1973) created a hierarchy for living systems, Javanmardi et al. (2020) believed that Boulding (1956) had classified complex systems into nine echelons going from simple to complex systems: (a) Frameworks or static structure, (b) Clockworks or dynamic systems, (c) Thermostats or control system, (d) Cells or open system, (e) Plants or genetic-societal, (f) Animals or self-aware animals, (g) Human Beings or self-aware humans, (h) Social Organizations or social systems, and (i) Transcendental systems.

van Assche et al. (2019) described von Bertalanffy's general systems theory (GST) as the unifying theory of any known existing science. van Assche et al. thought von Bertalanffy's GST was fundamentally abstract rather than concrete. von Bertalanffy's GST was intended to demonstrate that scientists should know, observe, and recognize the changes to which any system could be subjected. For van Assche et al., although von Bertalanffy's GST was not perfect, it led to many existing systems theories of this era.

Variables of Systems Theory. Systems theory of an open system comprises interrelated and interdependent elements that network as subsystems. Along the same line, diseases might be caused by several risk factors that can be viewed as subsystems. For this reason, risk factors, and subsystems, in this case, should be considered in their interrelationships with the occurrence of diseases rather than separate from each other. Min et al. (2018) and Badock et al. (2019) believed that systems theory approach considered open systems as composed of (a) the inputs – any raw materials or data, (b) a transformational process – any activities, tasks, or operations procedures, (c) the outputs – any products or results, (d) feedback (positive or negative) – any answer from, assessments or evaluation of the outputs, and (d) the environment - any parts that are internal and external to the system.

RESEARCH WHERE SYSTEMS THEORY HAS BEEN USED

Living Systems theory

Several researchers have contributed to the creation and evolution of Systems Theory (See Figure 1). According to Gough (2021), GST reached its peak with the publication of the Living Systems book (Miller, 1973). Compared to the biological systems depicted by von Bertalanffy (1951), Miller extended GST to all living systems. Miller described living systems as open, self-organizing systems. He emphasized that these open, self-organizing systems held specific life features and interfaced with their environment. The interface happens through the exchange of information and matter or energy. By observing the above, Gough believed that Miller's addition to the GST included the social systems. Miller considered a system hierarchy of eight levels for the living systems theory, with the higher level considered more complex than the one following it. For Miller, level one, for example, will contain the features of level two all the way to level eight, making level eight the most complex system. These levels were: (a) cells, (b) organs, (c) organisms, (d) groups, (e) organizations, (f) communities, (g) societies, and (h) supranational systems.

Figure 1. The Chronological Evolution of Systems Theory From 1928 to 2012

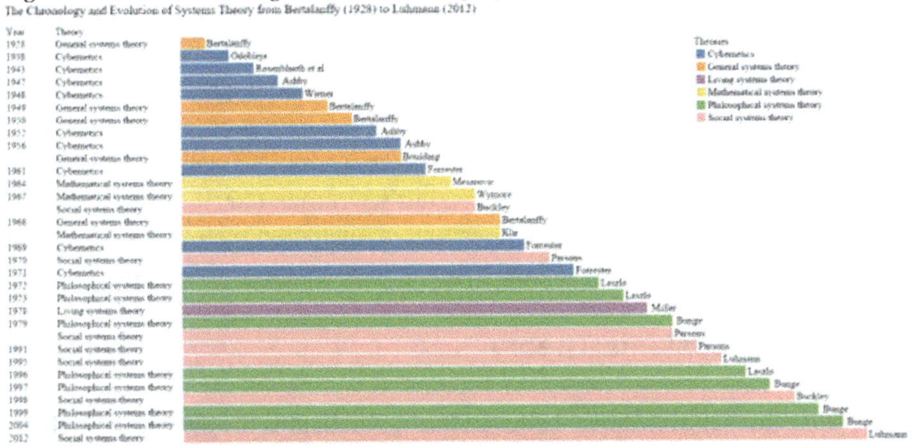

Note. The chronological evolution of Systems Theory. Each bar's length represents the year of its conception from 1928 to 2012. The colors reflect the different theories that either contributed to or came into existence through the general system theory (GST)—an image created by the researcher.

Mathematical Systems Theory

According to Frick (2020) and Kutschera (2018), Mesarović built upon the GST using an axiomatic method in 1964 to create a mathematical theory system seen as a theory of systems that mostly depend on time, external variables (input and output: There are controllable and uncontrollable inputs, measurable output and regulated output), and the state which is the transformation (internal variables) that takes place within the system. Mesarović viewed a system as representing abstract sets' relations pursuing a specific goal. The system can take in information as input (controllable and uncontrollable inputs), and after undergoing computation, the state (internal variables) produces an output. Frick also revealed that in 1967, Wymore contributed to the GST by creating a mathematical theory of systems engineering using the same idea of infinite sets, applying continuous and discrete variables. In 1968, Klir spent his time detecting and studying the behaviors of a system. He gathered the existing data in the system, such as the single element, the hierarchy, the state, the connections between the system elements, etc. He formalized them verbally and mathematically to classify them as system-type problems.

Social Systems Theory

According to Cadenas (2019), Buckley, an American professor of sociology, applied systems theory to sociology in his book Sociology and Modern Systems

Theory, published in 1967, embracing the mathematical type of general social systems theory. In 1998, Buckley believed systems theory should be viewed as a theoretical framework and set of organizational tools that could be applied to any field of study. Tahamtan & Bornmann (2022) and Sang et al. (2022) believed that Luhmann, influenced by his professor at Harvard, Talcott Parsons, in 1962, believed that interactions and organizations within a society should be viewed as a system. Bettina (2021) touched upon some of Parsons's writings (1970, 1979, 1991) in which he supposed that systems and subsystems, including their elements, could be analyzed individually, following the cybernetic perceptions (Mitsuhiro, 2020).

Philosophical Systems Theory

Alvargonzález (2021), Bunge believed that systemism is the alternative to both individualism and holism. Bunge mentioned that the system and mechanism were not the same things. Bunge viewed a mechanism as a procedure taking place within a system as a whole. Bunge also insisted on viewing systems as an approach used to explain complex matters of any type, ensuring a distinct difference between the systemic approach and systems theory. Kasianiuk (2021) mentioned Laszlo, another individual besides Bunge (1972) who contributed to the GST by describing his structure of the Philosophical systems theory. Kasianiuk (2021) supposed that the system concept was extremely important to Laszlo due to the constant societal change and technological innovations.

Systems Theory and Artificial Intelligence

System theory is applied in many fields. Artificial intelligence (AI) is one field that leverages systems theory concepts to develop automated systems capable of performing and excelling in activities that human beings can accomplish, but faster and more accurately, stated Wang (2021). One of the features of systems theory that AI excelled at is the 'emergence" concept that Hammond (2019) discussed. The Emergence concept of systems theory enables AI scientists to leverage the relationship between the elements within a system and consider them as forming a unit, a hole. The different parts function together in constructive collaboration to develop a new and growing structure seen as one unit, thus the holistic system.

Yalvac (2021) and Bini (2021) regarded AI as a technology that allowed scientists to develop solutions that make automated smart equipment. This equipment is fed with algorithms that enable them to do the work human beings can do. Some examples of AI equipment are self-driving cars, Apple's Siri, face recognition, voice recognition, disease detection and prediction, and Amazon's Alexa, just to name a few. Lima & Custodio (2004) leveraged the emergent features of systems theory to create soccer robots capable of playing a soccer game by using sensors to detect objects and their colors.

Bini (2018) and many researchers viewed AI as the intelligence exhibited by a non-human being, such as a machine. Computer scientists leveraged AI to create smart gadgets called "agents," capable of studying their surroundings and making decisions based on the objective their creators desired to achieve. Computer scientists created a subset of AI, Machine Learning (ML), and its (ML) subsystem, Deep Learning (DL), to reach their goals and maximize the complexity of decision-making of the many different scenarios complicated systems presented.

SYSTEM THEORY AND MACHINE LEARNING

Alzubi et al. (2018) declared that machine learning (ML) was a branch of artificial intelligence (AI) (See Figure 2). Alzubi et al. defined ML as a computer that learns from data and then emulates human intelligence and behavior using algorithms to resolve problems. As such, ML can be seen as a system (See Figure 3) that takes data as inputs to learn from (i.e., images, sound, voice, text), transforms them, and creates useful outputs, just like a human being or other open systems (organisms) governed by systems theory.

Figure 2. Artificial Intelligence and Its Subsystems

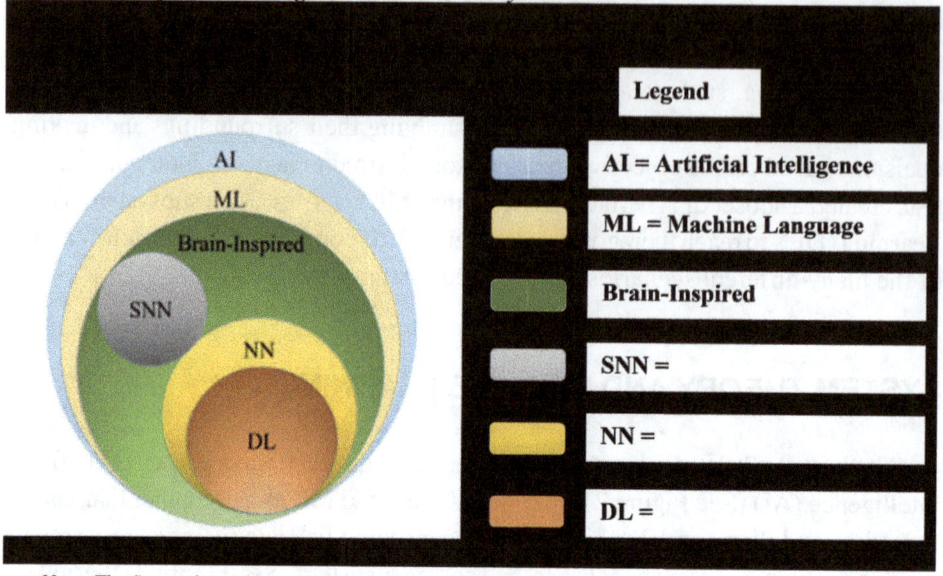

Note: The figure shows AI (artificial intelligence) and its components. ML (machine learning) is the main subsystem. Within ML are the different types of Brain-Inspired neural networks in green: DL in orange (deep learning), NN in yellow (neural network), and SNN in gray (spiking neural network). Retrieved from Sharma, N., Sharma, R., & Jindal, N. (2021). Machine Learning and Deep Learning Applications-A Vision. Global Transitions Proceedings, 2(1), 24–28. https://doi.org/10.1016/j.gltp.2021.01.004

The computations performed in ML are either supervised, semi-supervised, unsupervised, or reinforced (See Figure 4). A human being watches supervised ML algorithms, thus called "supervised." Considering POAG as an example, a human might input about a thousand fundus images of eyes labeled as "has POAG" and "has no POAG." Because the fundus images are labeled and supervised by a data scientist, for example, the machine was expected to figure out the expected result of whether PAOG was present or not after learning from the fundus images.

Figure 3. An Example of Machine Learning System Types and Processes

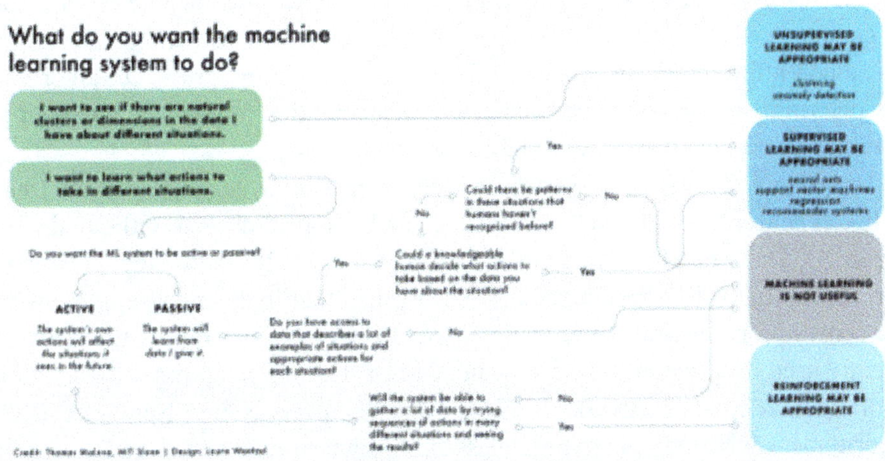

Note: Retrieved from: https://mitsloan.mit.edu/sites/default/files/styles/2_1_large_1050x525/public/2021-04/machine-learning-infographic_2.jpg?h=e9dd200c&itok=7tbLGyrT

In semi-supervised ML, supervised and unsupervised learning are combined. Semi-supervised ML utilizes a small quantity of labeled data and a large quantity of unlabeled data. This technique is useful because raw labeling data can be challenging and expensive.

Sinaga & Yang (2020) reported that unsupervised ML uses algorithms to cluster unlabeled data and recognize previously unidentified patterns in a dataset. Unsupervised ML is known to be less costly compared to supervised ML because there is no human involvement in labeling the data. Unsupervised ML is also said to be faster and easier to implement.

Oh et al. (2020) shared that reinforced ML is about creating an intelligent agent (computer program) capable of networking with the milieu and learning to behave within that milieu. Lima & Custodio (2004) studied how robotic soccer players learned the game, including the obstacles and other situations during a soccer match. The robotic soccer players learned to notice what needed to be done and interpreted their environment; then, they acted, learning through experiments and mistakes.

Systems Theory and Deep Learning

Sharma et al. (2021) regarded deep learning (DL) as a subsystem of machine learning (See Figure 3). They believed that DL uses algorithms of artificial neural network (ANN) layers to gain knowledge by imitating the structure and function of the human brain (See Figure 4). Sharma et al. (2021) reported further that DL algorithms could consume and process large quantities of labeled data such as images, texts, sounds, etc., and accurately program feature extraction, with extremely limited involvement of human specialists. Using noncommunicable disease such as glaucoma as an example, if there is a need to differentiate between an affected eye, a non-affected eye, or progress of glaucoma, and no progress, DL algorithms can determine the features that can decide each condition of glaucoma without the human expert touch that is needed for machine learning.

Chauhan et al. (2018) asserted that artificial neural networks (ANNs) have artificial neurons, which are the dendrites in a biological neuron of the brain (See Figure 4). These dendrites in a biological neuron send signals to other cells in the body (See Figure 4). Chauhan et al. (2018) stated that in deep learning, however, the convolutional neural networks (CNN or ConvNet) algorithm is the most frequently used deep neural network besides Multi-Layer Perceptrons (MLP), Long Short Term Memory Networks (LSTMs), and Recurrent Neural Networks (RNN) algorithms. CNNs are effective for classifying signals, time series, audio, and image data, making them useful for discovering photo patterns to recognize matters, categories, classes, etc. Deep learning extends system theory by involving input, transformation, output, and feedback.

Figure 4. Nerve cells with Dendrites and Axons Mimicked by the Artificial Neural Networks (ANNs)

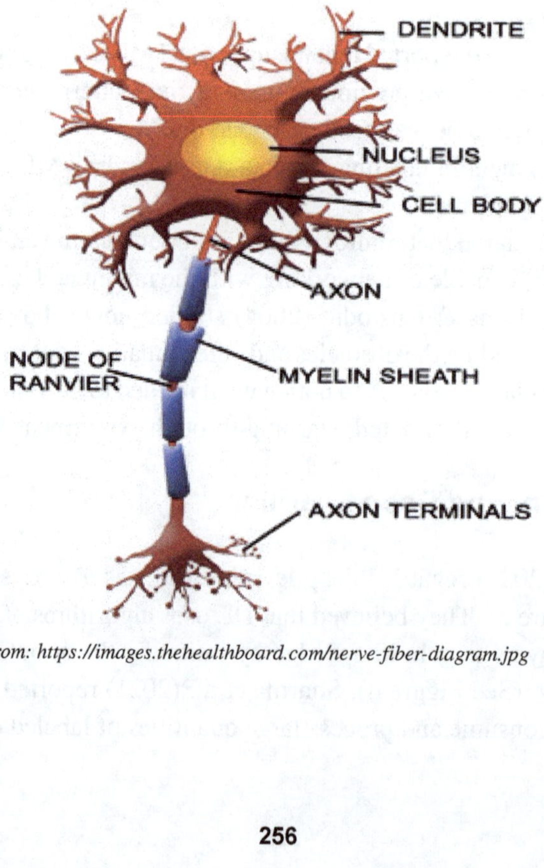

Note: Retrieved from: https://images.thehealthboard.com/nerve-fiber-diagram.jpg

Arisoy et al. (2012) discovered that deep learning artificial neural networks could have over a hundred hidden layers (up to 150) that learn by themselves to recognize patterns and extract features. They explained that the hidden layers perform computations that humans do not know how they analyze the data, leading to the black box of AI (See Figure 5). Gunning et al. (2019) have revealed that computer scientists have created explainable AI to allow a human expert to understand the process and the output to ensure the desired output.

Figure 5. Deep Learning and Its Input, Hidden, and Output Layers

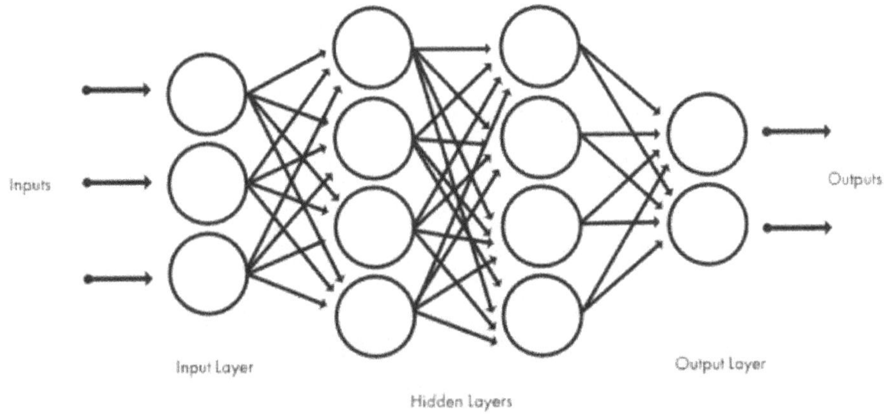

Note: Retrieved from https://www.mathworks.com/discovery/deep-learning/_jcr_content/mainParsys/band_2123350969_copy_1983242569/mainParsys/columns_1635259577/1/image_2128876021_cop_1731669336.adapt.full.medium.svg/1671089858885.svg

Models Used in System Theory

As mentioned before, system theory deals with holistic open and closed systems (Hammond, 2019). System theory studies how independent and interconnected objects work together in and out of a given system (von Bertalanffy, 1098). Several models have been created using systems theory since it (systems theory) helps comprehend complex systems that are difficult to model or predict with typical thinking—modeling of a production system (Mourtzis, 2020), models of decision-making in human groups (van Dijk & De Dreu, 2021), models of decision-making in organizations (Sarker, 2021), system models of company structures (Li et al., 2022), system models of a company of processes (Tsai et al., 2022), to name these few. System theory has also been leveraged in current techniques that computer and data scientists use in detecting and predicting diseases (Wåhlin et al., 2022). Systems theory extends Artificial intelligence (AI) and its branches, machine learning

(ML) and deep learning (DL) (Shaikh et al., 2022). In Figure 6, AI constitutes the main system, while ML is a subsystem of AI, and DL is a subsystem of ML. All these three are complex systems that are multifaceted and difficult to understand.

Bampoula et al. (2021) used Long Short-Term Memory (LSTM), a deep neural network, to create a production model that can determine the remaining useful time of industrial equipment. Javanmardi et al. (2020) used systems theory concepts to study the complications and fears in modern society. They used the Grey systems theory (GST) to look into how society could meet the needs of present generations without sacrificing future generations' needs. They considered the environment in the society, including families, social settings, economic class, etc., all the facts and behaviors working together as a system, which is the world in their study.

Figure 6. Systems Theory of Detection and Prediction of Primary Open-angle Glaucoma (POAG)

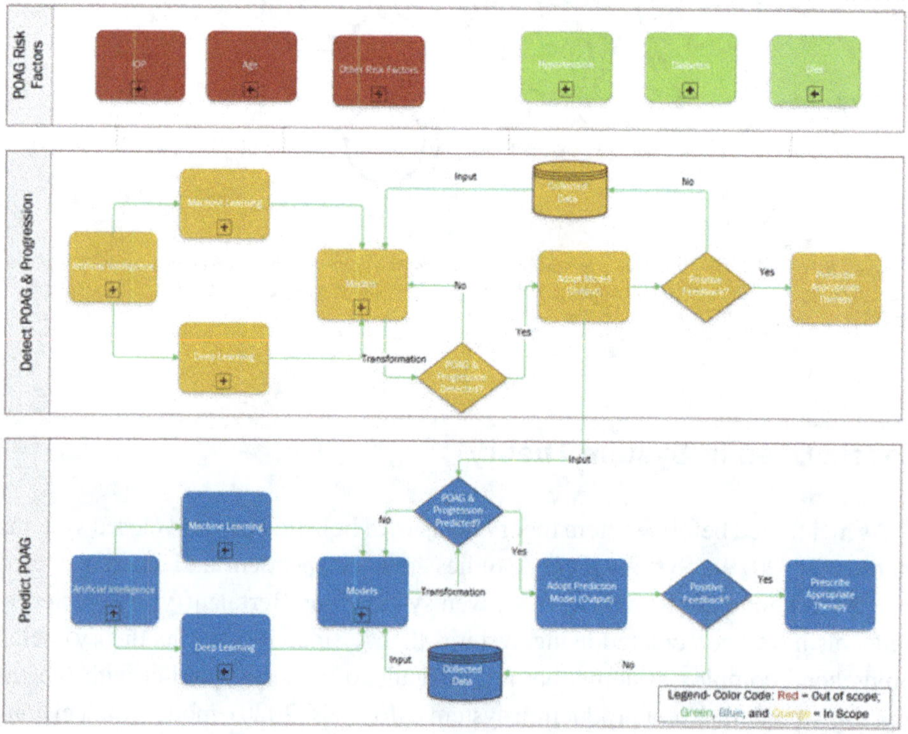

COMPLEMENTARY THEORETICAL FRAMEWORKS

Health Literacy and Locus of Control

Duplaga & Grysztar (2021) thought that people who were not interested in health literacy tended to make poor choices about their diet. Their poor choices resulted in health issues, including chronic diseases such as diabetes and other diseases that may cause obesity. On the other hand, Lovrić et al. (2022) felt that arterial hypertension was also a result of obesity and a lack of health education. Pourhabibi et al. (2022) saw the lack of health literacy as a factor that leads to neglecting to use and pursue adequate health services and self-managing health issues, leading to the burden of noncommunicable diseases (NCD). Thus, Siddiq et al. (2023) thought the government must be involved and find a good mechanism to build community-based outreach programs to increase a population's health education or literacy. These community-based outreach programs must distribute information and empower people to support each other in developing self-confidence and other mechanisms to confront health issues in their communities (Siddiq et al., 2023).

According to Jang & Baek (2018), there are three different ways to categorize people's Health Locus of Control. There is (a) an internal Health Locus of Control, (b) a powerful others Health Locus of Control, and (c) a chance Health Locus of Control. Health Locus of Control (HLC) denotes the degree to which people think they engage in their health and the power they have on their behavior to prevent health issues. People with an internal HLC think their mannerisms and proactivity in health care are critical to good health results. Individuals with a strong Health Locus of Control believe that health professionals should manage their health issues. In contrast, those with a chance Health Locus of Control perceive that external factors influence their health, and they feel unable to control these factors. This concept of Health Locus of Control is valuable for the proposed theoretical framework, as it examines the health of people suffering from both communicable and noncommunicable diseases, who may fall into any of the Health Locus of Control categories.

Theory of Computation

Meho (2019) saw theoretical computer science (TCS) as the enabler of modern computing, leading to the study of efficient algorithms and protocols. Meho (2019) demonstrated that the concept of computation gives a fundamentally new lens for examining the world around us. Computational biology (Chelly Dagdia et al., 2021), cryptography (Qadir & Varol, 2019), and machine learning (Gu et al., 2020) are a few of the 20th-century inventions that TCS underlies. The data structure (Doerig et al., 2019), complexity theory (Bossaerts et al., 2019), computational economics, and geometry are some of the few theories the TCS group continues to research. These theories of Computation goals are to develop scholarly mathematical models that can mimic real-world machines (Safari, 2021).

Nunez et al. (2022) declared that artificial intelligence (AI) theory and its branches – Machine Learning (ML) and Deep Learning (DL) constitute one of the theories that have been successfully applied in the research of detecting and predicting diseases, leading to infer that AI can be leveraged to detect and predict some communicable and noncommunicable diseases. Based on the above, the theory of computation cannot be used in the application of Artificial intelligence (AI) theory concerned with detecting and predicting communicable and noncommunicable diseases.

ETHICAL DIMENSIONS AND CLINICAL APPLICATIONS

While the Theory of Computation provides the mathematical engine for modern healthcare, the transition from silicon to the clinic introduces a complex web of human consequences. As AI systems become "digital stethoscopes" for noncommunicable diseases (NCDs), they move beyond mere data processing into the realm of moral agency. This section explores the ethical friction points of privacy and bias, followed by real-world case studies where these algorithms are actively saving lives and sight.

Privacy and Data Sovereignty

The integration of Artificial Intelligence (AI) in diagnosing non-communicable diseases (NCDs) relies on "Big Data," yet the sensitivity of medical records creates a fundamental tension between clinical advancement and individual privacy. Traditional de-identification methods are increasingly vulnerable to "re-identification attacks," where foundation models can be reverse-engineered to reveal patient identities by cross-referencing imaging features with demographic markers (Nebbia et al. 2025, 469). This has led to a paradigm shift toward Data Sovereignty, where patients maintain ownership and the right to withdraw their information from algorithmic training sets. To mitigate these risks, modern healthcare systems are adopting Federated Learning, a decentralized training approach where the AI model travels to the data on local hospital servers rather than requiring data to be centralized in a vulnerable cloud environment, thereby ensuring that sensitive patient information remains behind institutional firewalls (Li and Padman 2025; Zhou et al. 2023, "A Foundation Model" 158).

Addressing Algorithmic Bias

Algorithmic bias represents a critical ethical hurdle, as AI models often inadvertently amplify existing systemic healthcare disparities if they are trained on non-representative datasets. A recurring failure in early diagnostic tools was the use of "cost of care" as a proxy for disease severity; since less is historically spent on minority populations due to socioeconomic barriers, algorithms frequently assigned lower risk scores to Black patients compared to White patients with identical clinical profiles (Li and Padman 2025). Furthermore, models trained primarily on Western populations may struggle with "domain shift" when applied to diverse ethnicities, leading to inaccurate readings in skin-tone-sensitive technologies like photoplethysmography (PPG) for blood pressure (Mohammadi et al. 2025, 4). To ensure equity, current regulatory frameworks now emphasize "Bias Auditing," requiring developers to prove that an algorithm's accuracy remains consistent across age, gender, and racial subgroups before clinical deployment (Fu et al. 2024, Shantsila et al. 2024).

Case Studies: AI in Diagnostic Practice

The ethical hurdles described above are being met with rigorous clinical validation. The following case studies demonstrate how AI has successfully transitioned from theory to saving patients in the real world.

1. Glaucoma: Preventing the "Silent Thief of Sight" Because glaucoma is typically asymptomatic and primarily affects peripheral vision in its earliest phases, it remains notoriously difficult to diagnose before irreversible damage occurs (Zhu et al., 2024). To address this, the RETFound foundation model was developed as a vision transformer trained via self-supervised learning on a massive dataset of 1.6 million unlabeled retinal images, including both color fundus photographs and optical coherence tomography (OCT) scans (Zhou et al., 2023). In clinical applications, this model has demonstrated the ability to detect disease progression up to 1.7 years earlier than traditional linear trend analysis by identifying subtle "peripapillary cues" and vascular patterns that often elude human observation (Fu et al., 2024; Zhou et al., 2023). By providing these advanced predictive insights, such AI systems allow clinicians to initiate pressure-lowering interventions significantly sooner, effectively preserving vision that might otherwise have been lost (Djulbegovic et al., 2025; Zhu et al., 2024).
2. Chronic Kidney Disease (CKD): High-Stakes Prediction Early detection of Chronic Kidney Disease (CKD) is essential for preventing the progression to end-stage renal disease (ESRD), yet traditional biomarkers often fail to capture the high-risk trajectories of individual patients. The KidneyIntelX.dkd platform

represents a significant breakthrough, utilizing a random forest algorithm to integrate plasma biomarkers—specifically TNFR-1, TNFR-2, and KIM-1—with electronic health record data to generate a composite risk score (3.1, 3.3). In recent clinical validations (2025), this AI-driven approach outperformed the standard Kidney Failure Risk Equation (KFRE) by providing more accurate reclassification of risk levels for patients with Type 2 Diabetes, identifying those twice as likely to experience rapid kidney function decline (3.4). By stratifying patients into high-risk groups earlier, the system enables "pre-emptive" nephrology referrals and personalized therapeutic adjustments, such as the optimized use of SGLT2 inhibitors, which have been shown to significantly slow disease progression (3.1, 3.5).

3. Hypertension: The Virtual Physiologist The management of hypertension has shifted from episodic office visits to continuous, real-time monitoring through AI-enhanced wearable technologies. Modern "cuffless" devices now utilize deep learning architectures, such as hybrid CNN-BiLSTM models, to estimate blood pressure solely from photoplethysmography (PPG) signals captured at the wrist or fingertip (Mohammadi et al., 2025). These systems facilitate a "digital twin" approach to cardiovascular health, where AI-driven lifestyle coaching programs have achieved mean reductions of up to 14.2 mmHg in systolic pressure for patients with stage 2 hypertension by providing adaptive, real-time feedback (2.5). While the American Heart Association (2025) emphasizes the need for further standardized validation to ensure these devices meet the same rigor as traditional cuffs, the integration of AI-enabled remote monitoring is already closing significant care gaps in resource-limited settings where traditional healthcare access is intermittent (4.3, 4.4)..

RECOMMENDATIONS

The issue addressed in this article is the use of a conceptual or theoretical framework to conduct clear research and achieve solid results. If researchers and doctoral students do not rely on these frameworks, their results could be questionable. Moraru et al. (2020) argued that the development of technology and artificial intelligence (AI) would enable better detection of communicable and non-communicable diseases. However, Marcinkevičs & Vogt (2020) and Starke et al. (2022) urged caution, advising the thorough testing of AI algorithms claiming to detect and predict certain diseases, both communicable and non-communicable.

Machine learning (ML) algorithms have demonstrated their effectiveness in detecting and predicting non-communicable diseases in several countries (Moraru et al., 2020; Ting et al., 2019). Data science models can detect non-communicable diseases and identify individuals predisposed to contracting them based on family history. The use of data science is reducing the gap in detecting and predicting communicable and non-communicable diseases worldwide.

Data scientists working with AI and its branches must continuously develop methods for detecting and predicting diseases from digital images. Data scientists must use pre-trained and rigorously tested models to detect and predict communicable and noncommunicable diseases through these images. Several programming languages, such as Python and R, facilitate the comparison of results from similar studies to assess whether they yield consistent or similar outcomes. Additionally, Google Colab is a valuable tool that can assist researchers looking to train and test their data to detect and predict these diseases. Data scientists are encouraged to utilize the most advanced and up-to-date tools, along with a diverse range of variables, to enhance their results. This approach will help experts find treatments and prevent health issues associated with communicable and noncommunicable diseases.

Exploring a mechanism that invites different researchers from around the world to collaborate will yield good results. Today, data storage is no longer an issue. Researchers can take a different sample from each ethnic group in their country and study the presence of communicable and non-communicable diseases. The risk factors that cause these diseases can be studied, and the data can be securely stored in a common space accessible to designated individuals for ongoing research. These researchers can collaborate and use this data to find treatments. This approach is only possible if funding is available and if each country and its researchers are held accountable. Creating such a system could make it possible to apply the same practice to all communicable and non-communicable diseases present in the world, which contribute to poverty.

CONCLUSION

The proposed Systems Theory of Pathology involving Machine Learning and Deep Learning (See Appendix A, Figure 7) transpired during the writing process of a dissertation for a PhD in Data Science titled: Correlated Predictors of Occurrence and Progression of Primary Open-Angle Glaucoma: A Quantitative Analysis. The new theory is aimed to assist scientists who may desire to understand the risk factors of any disease, be it communicable or noncommunicable while applying branches of AI to detect and predict the disease using digital images. The new theory was conceived due to not finding any existing theory with defined constructs that can lead researchers in their quest to find a cure for some diseases. The theory is open to anyone who wants to contribute to and improve it to create a strong foundation for this and future research and useful findings to alleviate the pain and suffering of the world's people.

REFERENCES

Alvargonzález, D. (2019). Sciences as systems. *Perspectives on Science*, *27*(6), 839–860. DOI: 10.1162/posc_a_00327

Alvargonzález, D. (2021). On the systematicity of academic philosophy. *Philosophical Investigations*, *44*(3), 237–253. DOI: 10.1111/phin.12288

Alzubi, J., Nayyar, A., & Kumar, A. (2018, November). Machine learning from theory to algorithms: An overview. [). IOP Publishing.]. *Journal of Physics: Conference Series*, *1142*, 012012. DOI: 10.1088/1742-6596/1142/1/012012

Arisoy, E., Sainath, T. N., Kingsbury, B., & Ramabhadran, B. (2012, June). Deep neural network language models. In *Proceedings of the NAACL-HLT 2012 Workshop: will we ever really replace the N-gram Model? On the future of language modeling for HLT* (pp. 20–28).

Bampoula, X., Siaterlis, G., Nikolakis, N., & Alexopoulos, K. (2021). A Deep Learning Model for predictive maintenance in cyber-physical production systems using LSTM autoencoders. *Sensors (Basel)*, *21*(3), 972. Advance online publication. DOI: 10.3390/s21030972 PMID: 33535642

Beer, S. (1960). Cybernetics and management. *Journal of the Franklin Institute*, *270*(3), 245. DOI: 10.1016/0016-0032(60)90608-6

Bettina, M. (2021). Addressing parsons in sociological textbooks: Past conflicts, contemporary readers, and their future gains. *The American Sociologist*, *52*(1), 88–106. DOI: 10.1007/s12108-020-09469-7

Bini, S. A. (2018). Artificial intelligence, machine learning, deep learning, and cognitive computing: What do these terms mean and how will they impact health care? *The Journal of Arthroplasty*, *33*(8), 2358–2361. DOI: 10.1016/j.arth.2018.02.067 PMID: 29656964

Bossaerts, P., Yadav, N., & Murawski, C. (2019). Uncertainty and computational complexity. *Philosophical Transactions of the Royal Society B*, *374*(1766), 20180138.

Boulding, K. E. (1956). General Systems Theory—The skeleton of science. *Management Science*, *2*(3), 197–208. DOI: 10.1287/mnsc.2.3.197

Brydges, M., & Batt, A. M. (2023). Untangling the web: The need for theory, theoretical frameworks, and conceptual frameworks in paramedic research. *Paramedicine*, *20*(4), 89–93. DOI: 10.1177/27536386231177348

Cadenas, H. (2019). The unity of (social systems) science: The legacy of von Bertalanffy. *Systems Research and Behavioral Science, 36*(3), 274–280. DOI: 10.1002/sres.2595

Carr-Chellman, D. J., & Carr-Chellman, A. (2020). Integrating systems: The history of systems from von Bertalanffy to Profound Learning. *TechTrends, 64*(5), 704–709. DOI: 10.1007/s11528-020-00540-1

Chauhan, R., Ghanshala, K. K., & Joshi, R. P. (2018). Convolutional Neural Network (CNN) for Image Detection and Recognition. *2018 First International Conference on Secure Cyber Computing and Communication (ICSCCC)*. DOI: 10.1109/ICSCCC.2018.8703316

Chelly Dagdia, Z., Avdeyev, P., & Bayzid, M. S. (2021). Biological computation and computational biology: Survey, challenges, and discussion. *Artificial Intelligence Review, 54*(6), 4169–4235. DOI: 10.1007/s10462-020-09951-1

Coulter, I., Snider, P., & Neil, A. (2019). Vitalism-A worldview revisited: A critique of vitalism and its implications for integrative medicine. *Integrative Medicine (Encinitas, Calif.), 18*(3), 60–73. PMID: 32549817

Descartes, R. (1984). *The Philosophical Writings of Descartes* (Vol. 2). Cambridge University Press., books.google.com

Djulbegovic, M. B., Bair, H., Gonzalez, D. J. T., Ishikawa, H., Wollstein, G., & Schuman, J. S. (2025). Artificial intelligence for optical coherence tomography in glaucoma. *Translational Vision Science & Technology, 14*(1), 27. DOI: 10.1167/tvst.14.1.27 PMID: 39854198

Doerig, A., Schurger, A., Hess, K., & Herzog, M. H. (2019). The unfolding argument: Why IIT and other causal structure theories cannot explain consciousness. *Consciousness and Cognition, 72*, 49–59. DOI: 10.1016/j.concog.2019.04.002 PMID: 31078047

Drack, M., & Pouvreau, D. (2015). On the history of Ludwig von Bertalanffy's "General Systemology," and on its relationship to cybernetics – part III: Convergences and divergences. *International Journal of General Systems, 44*(5), 523–571. DOI: 10.1080/03081079.2014.1000642 PMID: 26612966

Duplaga, M., & Grysztar, M. (2021). Nutritional behaviors, health literacy, and health locus of control of secondary schoolers in Southern Poland: A cross-sectional study. *Nutrients, 13*(12), 4323. DOI: 10.3390/nu13124323 PMID: 34959875

Frick, T. W. (2020). Education Systems and Technology in 1990, 2020, and Beyond. *TechTrends, 64*(5), 693–703. DOI: 10.1007/s11528-020-00527-y PMID: 32838405

Fu, Y., Ma, L., Wan, S., Ge, S., & Yang, Z. (2024). A novel clinical artificial intelligence model for disease detection via retinal imaging. *Innovation (Cambridge (Mass.))*, *5*(2), 100575. DOI: 10.1016/j.xinn.2024.100575 PMID: 38379789

Gu, G. H., Choi, C., Lee, Y., Situmorang, A. B., Noh, J., Kim, Y. H., & Jung, Y. (2020). Progress in computational and machine-learning methods for heterogeneous small-molecule activation. *Advanced Materials*, *32*(35), 1907865. DOI: 10.1002/adma.201907865 PMID: 32196135

Hallioui, A. (2020). System analysis: A literature review. *Proceedings of the International Conference on Industrial Engineering & Operations Management (2169-8767)*, 2774.

Hammond, D. (2019). The legacy of Ludwig von Bertalanffy and its relevance for our time. *Systems Research and Behavioral Science*, *36*(3), 301–307. DOI: 10.1002/sres.2598

Jang, K., & Baek, Y. M. (2018). How to effectively design public health interventions: Implications from the interaction effects between socioeconomic status and health locus of control beliefs on healthy dietary behaviours among US adults. *Health & Social Care in the Community*, *26*(5), 664–674. DOI: 10.1111/hsc.12577 PMID: 29659076

Javanmardi, E., Liu, S., & Xie, N. (2020). Exploring grey systems theory-based methods and applications in sustainability studies: A systematic review approach. *Sustainability (Basel)*, *12*(11), 4437. DOI: 10.3390/su12114437

Kant, I. (1897). Eternal Peace. *The Advocate of Peace (1894-1920)*, *59*(5), 111–116. https://www.jstor.org/stable/25751039

Kutschera, U. (2018). Systems biology of eukaryotic superorganisms and the holobiont concept. *Theory in Biosciences*, *137*(2), 117–131. DOI: 10.1007/s12064-018-0265-6 PMID: 29948922

Li, H., Hu, Q., Zhao, G., & Li, B. (2022). The co-evolution of knowledge management and business model transformation in the post-COVID-19 era: Insights based on Chinese e-commerce companies. *Journal of Knowledge Management*, *26*(5), 1113–1123. DOI: 10.1108/JKM-03-2021-0177

Li, X., & Padman, R. (2025). Ethical and Practical Implications of AI in Healthcare Data Management. *Journal of Healthcare Informatics Research*, •••, 2025.

Lima, P. U., & Custodio, L. M. M. (2004). Artificial Intelligence and Systems Theory: Applied to Cooperative Robots. *International Journal of Advanced Robotic Systems*, *1*(3), 15. DOI: 10.5772/5630

Lovrić, B., Placento, H., Farčić, N., Lipič Baligač, M., Mikšić, Š., Mamić, M., Jovanović, T., Vidić, H., Karabatić, S., Cviljević, S., Zibar, L., Vukoja, I., & Barać, I. (2022). Association between Health Literacy and Prevalence of Obesity, Arterial Hypertension, and Diabetes Mellitus. *International Journal of Environmental Research and Public Health, 19*(15), 9002. Advance online publication. DOI: 10.3390/ijerph19159002 PMID: 35897372

Marcinkevičs, R., & Vogt, J. E. (2020). Interpretability and explainability: A machine learning zoo Mini-tour. *arXiv preprint arXiv:2012.01805.*

Meho, L. I. (2019). Using Scopus's CiteScore for assessing the quality of computer science conferences. *Journal of Informetrics, 13*(1), 419–433. DOI: 10.1016/j.joi.2019.02.006

Miller, J. G. (1973). Living Systems: The organism. *The Quarterly Review of Biology, 48*(1), 92–276. https://www.jstor.org/stable/2820539. DOI: 10.1086/407589 PMID: 4576974

Mitsuhiro, T. (2020). How society changes: Sociological enlightenment and a theory of social evolution for freedom. *The American Sociologist, 51*(4), 446–469. DOI: 10.1007/s12108-020-09464-y PMID: 33132397

Mohammadi, A.. (2025). An Efficient Feature Fusion Framework for Wearable Cuffless Blood Pressure Monitoring and Long-term Validation. *medRxiv*, 2025.

Moraru, A. D., Costin, D., Moraru, R. L., & Branisteanu, D. C. (2020). Artificial intelligence and deep learning in ophthalmology-present and future [Review]. *Experimental and Therapeutic Medicine, 20*(4), 3469. DOI: 10.3892/etm.2020.9118 PMID: 32905155

Mourtzis, D. (2020). Simulation in the design and operation of manufacturing systems: State of the art and new trends. *International Journal of Production Research, 58*(7), 1927–1949. DOI: 10.1080/00207543.2019.1636321

Nebbia, G.. (2025). Re-identification of Patients from Imaging Features Extracted by Foundation Models. *npj. Digital Medicine, 8*, 469. PMID: 40696111

Nicholson, D. A. (2012). The concept of mechanism in biology. *Studies in History and Philosophy of Science Part C Studies in History and Philosophy of Biological and Biomedical Sciences, 43*(1), 152–163. DOI: 10.1016/j.shpsc.2011.05.014 PMID: 22326084

Nowak, P. G., & Stencel, A. (2022). Correction to: How many ways can you die? Multiple biological deaths as a consequence of the multiple concepts of an organism. *Theoretical Medicine and Bioethics, 43*(2-3), 127–154. Advance online publication. DOI: 10.1007/s11017-022-09583-2 PMID: 36197598

Nunez, R., Harris, A., Ibrahim, O., Keller, J., Wikle, C. K., Robinson, E., . . . Guidoboni, G. (2022). Artificial intelligence to aid glaucoma diagnosis and monitoring: State of the art and new directions. *In Photonics* (Vol. 9, No. 11, p. 810). MDPI.

Odobleja, S. (1939). *Psychologie consonantiste*. Librairie Maloine.

Oh, J., Hessel, M., Czarnecki, W. M., Xu, Z., Van Hasselt, H., Singh, S., & Silver, D. (2020). Discovering reinforcement learning algorithms. *ArXiv (Cornell University)*. https://arxiv.org/pdf/2007.08794.pdf

Ortigosa, S. (2022). Cybernetics: Classical philosophy and Science—A logic of education. *The International Journal of Humanities Education, 20*(2), 91–99. DOI: 10.18848/2327-0063/CGP/v20i02/91-99

Plăviţu, C. M. (2020). Consonance and resonance in Kandinsky and Odobleja's works. *International Journal of Communication Research, 10*(4), 402–407. https://go.openathens.net/redirector/ncu.edu?url=https://www.proquest.com/scholarly-journals/consonance-resonance-kandinsky-odoblejas-works/docview/2505729900/se-2

Potschin-Young, M., Haines-Young, R., Görg, C., Heink, U., Jax, K., Schleyer, C., & Schleyer, C. (2018). Understanding the role of conceptual frameworks: Reading the ecosystem service cascade. *Ecosystem Services, 29*, 428–440. DOI: 10.1016/j.ecoser.2017.05.015 PMID: 31008045

Pourhabibi, N., Mohebbi, B., Sadeghi, R., Shakibazadeh, E., Sanjari, M., Tol, A., & Yaseri, M. (2022). Determinants of poor treatment adherence among patients with type 2 diabetes and limited health literacy: A scoping review. *Journal of Diabetes Research, 2022*, 2022. DOI: 10.1155/2022/2980250 PMID: 35832786

Pouvreau, D. (2014). On the history of Ludwig von Bertalanffy's "general systemology," and on its relationship to cybernetics - Part II: Contexts and developments of the systemological hermeneutics instigated by von Bertalanffy. *International Journal of General Systems, 43*(2), 172–245. DOI: 10.1080/03081079.2014.883743

Qadir, A. M., & Varol, N. (2019, June). A review paper on cryptography. In *2019, 7th International Symposium on Digital Forensics and Security (ISDFS)* (pp. 1-6). IEEE.

Rapoport, A. (1976). General systems theory: A bridge between two cultures. Third annual Ludwig von Bertalanffy memorial lecture. *Behavioral Science*, *21*(4), 228–239. DOI: 10.1002/bs.3830210404 PMID: 793579

Rapoport, A. (1986). General system theory : Essential concepts & applications. *Abacus Press EBooks*. https://ci.nii.ac.jp/ncid/BA0061935X

Safari, A. (2021). A Mathematical Review on Machine Intelligence Quotient (MIQ) Theory in Real-World Applications. *International Journal of Mathematical Modelling & Computations*, *11*(1 (WINTER)), 61–71.

Sang, T., Liu, P., & Zhao, L. (2022). Judicial response to ecological environment risk in China -from the perspective of Social Systems Theory. *International Journal of Environmental Research and Public Health*, *19*(21), 14355. Advance online publication. DOI: 10.3390/ijerph192114355 PMID: 36361230

Sarker, I. H. (2021). Data science and analytics: An overview from data-driven smart computing, decision-making and applications perspective. *SN Computer Science*, *2*(5), 377. DOI: 10.1007/s42979-021-00765-8 PMID: 34278328

Shaikh, T. A., Dar, T. R., & Sofi, S. (2022). A data-centric artificial intelligent and extended reality technology in smart healthcare systems. *Social Network Analysis and Mining*, *12*(1), 122. DOI: 10.1007/s13278-022-00888-7 PMID: 36065420

Shantsila, A.. (2024). Artificial Intelligence in Hypertension Management. *Journal of Human Hypertension*, •••, 2024.

Sharma, N., Sharma, R., & Jindal, N. (2021). Machine Learning and Deep Learning applications - A vision. *Global Transitions Proceedings*, *2*(1), 24–28. DOI: 10.1016/j.gltp.2021.01.004

Sinaga, K. P., & Yang, M. (2020). Unsupervised K-means clustering algorithm. *IEEE Access : Practical Innovations, Open Solutions*, *8*, 80716–80727. DOI: 10.1109/ACCESS.2020.2988796

Starke, G., van den Brule, R., Elger, B. S., & Haselager, P. (2022). Intentional machines: A defense of trust in medical artificial intelligence. *Bioethics*, *36*(2), 154–161. DOI: 10.1111/bioe.12891 PMID: 34142373

Tahamtan, I., & Bornmann, L. (2022). The Social Systems Citation Theory (SSCT): A proposal to use the social systems theory for conceptualizing publications and their citation links. *El Profesional de la Información*, *31*(4), 1–17. DOI: 10.3145/epi.2022.jul.11

Tilak, S., Glassman, M., Kuznetcova, I., & Pelfrey, G. L. (2021). Applications of cybernetics to psychological theory: Historical and conceptual explorations. *Theory &Amp. Theory & Psychology*, *32*(2), 298–325. DOI: 10.1177/09593543211053804

Ting, D., Peng, L., Varadarajan, A. V., Keane, P. A., Burlina, P. M., Chiang, M. F., Schmetterer, L., Pasquale, L. R., Bressler, N. M., Webster, D. R., Abramoff, M., & Wong, T. Y. (2019). Deep learning in ophthalmology: The technical and clinical considerations. *Progress in Retinal and Eye Research*, *72*, 100759. DOI: 10.1016/j.preteyeres.2019.04.003 PMID: 31048019

Tretter, F. (2019). "Systems medicine" in the view of von Bertalanffy's "organismic biology" and systems theory. *Systems Research and Behavioral Science*, *36*(3), 346–362. DOI: 10.1002/sres.2588

Tsai, C. H., Zdravkovic, J., & Stirna, J. (2022). Modeling digital business ecosystems: A systematic literature review. *Complex Systems Informatics and Modeling Quarterly*, (30), 1–30. DOI: 10.7250/csimq.2022-30.01

Vahidi, A., Aliahmad, A., & Teimouri, E. (2019). Evolution of management cybernetics and viable system model. *Systemic Practice and Action Research*, *32*(3), 297–314. DOI: 10.1007/s11213-019-9478-y

van Assche, K., Valentinov, V., & Verschraegen, G. (2019). Ludwig von Bertalanffy and his enduring relevance: Celebrating 50 years general system theory. *Systems research and behavioral science.-Chichester*, *36*(3), 251-254.

van Dijk, E., & De Dreu, C. K. (2021). Experimental games and social decision making. *Annual Review of Psychology*, *72*(1), 415–438. DOI: 10.1146/annurev-psych-081420-110718 PMID: 33006926

Vanderstraeten, R. (2019). Systems everywhere? *Systems Research and Behavioral Science*, *36*(3), 255–262. DOI: 10.1002/sres.2596

von Bertalanffy, L. (1938). A quantitative theory of organic growth (inquiries on growth laws. II). *Human Biology*, *10*(2), 181–213. https://www.jstor.org/stable/41447359

von Bertalanffy, L. (1950). An Outline of General System Theory. *The British Journal for the Philosophy of Science*, *1*(2), 134–165. DOI: 10.1093/bjps/I.2.134

von Bertalanffy, L. (1951). Conclusion. *Human Biology*, *23*(4), 336–345. https://www.jstor.org/stable/41448007 PMID: 14907030

von Bertalanffy, L. (1951). Metabolic types and growth types. *American Naturalist*, *85*(821), 111–117. https://www.jstor.org/stable/2458138. DOI: 10.1086/281659 von Bertalanffy, L. (1951). Problems of general system theory. *Human Biology, 23*(4), 302–312. https://www.jstor.org/stable/41448003 PMID: 14907026

von Bertalanffy, L. (1972). The history and status of general systems theory. *Academy of Management Journal, 15*(4), 407–426. DOI: 10.2307/255139

von Bertalanffy, L. (1972a). General system theory—Critical review. *General Systems Yearbook, 4*, 1–20.

von Bertalanffy, L. V. (1968). *General system theory: Foundations, development, applications*. G. Braziller.

Wåhlin, A., Eklund, A., & Malm, J. (2022). 4D flow MRI hemodynamic biomarkers for cerebrovascular diseases. *Journal of Internal Medicine, 291*(2), 115–127. DOI: 10.1111/joim.13392 PMID: 34813112

Wang, R. D., Zayed, T., Pan, W., Zheng, S., & Tariq, S. (2021). A system boundary-based critical review on crane selection in building construction. *Automation in Construction, 123*, 103520. DOI: 10.1016/j.autcon.2020.103520

Wang, Y. X., Panda-Jonas, S., & Jonas, J. B. (2021). Optic nerve head anatomy in myopia and glaucoma, including parapapillary zones alpha, beta, gamma and delta: Histology and clinical features. *Progress in Retinal and Eye Research, 83*, 100933. DOI: 10.1016/j.preteyeres.2020.100933 PMID: 33309588

Yalvac, I. (2021). Artificial intelligence and glaucoma. *Glokom-Katarakt/Journal of Glaucoma-Cataract, 16*(3), 127–130. DOI: 10.37844/glauc.cat.2021.16.22

Zhou, Y., Chia, M. A., Wagner, S. K., Ayhan, M. S., Williamson, D. J., Struyven, R. R., Liu, T., Xu, M., Lozano, M. G., Woodward-Court, P., Kihara, Y., Allen, N., Gallacher, J. E. J., Littlejohns, T., Aslam, T., Bishop, P., Black, G., Sergouniotis, P., Atan, D., & Keane, P. A. (2023). A foundation model for generalizable disease detection from retinal images. *Nature, 622*(7981), 156–163. DOI: 10.1038/s41586-023-06555-x PMID: 37704728

Zhu, Y., Salowe, R., Chow, C., Li, S., Bastani, O., & O'Brien, J. M. (2024). Advancing glaucoma care: Integrating artificial intelligence in diagnosis, management, and progression detection. *Bioengineering (Basel, Switzerland), 11*(2), 122. DOI: 10.3390/bioengineering11020122 PMID: 38391608

APPENDIX A: SYSTEM THEORY OF PATHOLOGY INVOLVING MACHINE LEARNING AND DEEP LEARNING

Figure 7. Proposed System Theory of Pathology involving Machine Learning and Deep Learning

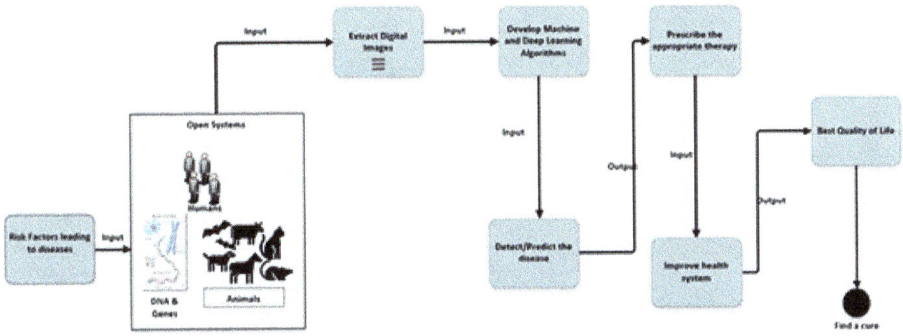

Note. The diagram shows a few risk factors that can contribute to a disease as input. Next, the input gets into an open system (any living creature diagnosed with a disease,) including the DNA and genes. The first output is the diagnosis of the disease. The first output becomes the input into the artificial intelligence (AI) branches (ML and DL) that detect and predict the disease using digital images, allowing specialists to prescribe the appropriate therapy. The ultimate output will be the discovery of a cure.

Chapter 9
IoT-Based Intelligent Alert Systems for Respiratory Disease Management:
Personalized Inhaler Support Through Environmental and Physiological Monitoring

R. Saranya
http://orcid.org/0009-0000-9354-9243
PSG College of Arts and Science, India

R. Kavitha
PSG College of Arts and Science, India

S. Dhivya
http://orcid.org/0009-0008-8899-6215
PSG College of Arts and Science, India

ABSTRACT

Respiratory diseases, including asthma, chronic obstructive pulmonary disease (COPD), and bronchitis, affect millions worldwide and often require timely intervention to prevent acute exacerbations. Inhalers remain the primary treatment for symptom management, but poor adherence, incorrect usage, and delayed administration frequently reduce their effectiveness, leading to uncontrolled symptoms and hospitalizations. Integrating Internet of Things (IoT) technologies into respiratory care offers a novel solution by enabling real-time monitoring of environmental and

DOI: 10.4018/979-8-2600-0981-9.ch009

physiological conditions. Smart inhalers, wearable devices, and environmental sensors can track inhaler usage, vital signs, air quality, temperature, and humidity, providing comprehensive data on patients' health and surroundings. IoT-based inhaler alert systems leverage these data streams to deliver personalized, context-aware notifications that guide patients in carrying and using their inhalers appropriately, improving adherence and preventing exacerbations.

1. INTRODUCTION

Respiratory diseases such as asthma and chronic obstructive pulmonary disease (COPD) are highly dynamic in nature, with symptoms influenced by continuous interactions between physiological conditions and environmental exposure. Although inhalers remain the cornerstone of treatment, poor adherence, delayed usage, and lack of awareness of trigger conditions significantly limit their effectiveness. Traditional respiratory care models depend largely on episodic clinical visits and patient self-reporting, which fail to capture real-time variations in environmental risk factors and physiological deterioration. Recent advances in Internet of Things (IoT) technologies have enabled continuous monitoring of both environmental parameters (such as air quality, temperature, and humidity) and physiological signals (including oxygen saturation and respiratory patterns). By integrating wearable sensors, environmental monitoring devices, and intelligent data analytics, IoT-based systems enable proactive and personalized respiratory care. In particular, intelligent inhaler alert systems can provide context-aware reminders that guide patients to carry or use inhalers at appropriate times, thereby reducing the likelihood of acute exacerbations.

While several IoT-enabled respiratory monitoring solutions have been proposed, many existing systems primarily focus on data collection or adherence tracking in isolation. There remains a need for integrated frameworks that simultaneously combine environmental sensing, physiological monitoring, intelligent risk prediction, and actionable alert delivery. This chapter addresses this need by presenting an IoT-based intelligent alert framework that emphasizes personalized risk assessment, real-time decision-making, and patient-centric inhaler support.

Figure 1. IoT enabled respiratory monitoring system

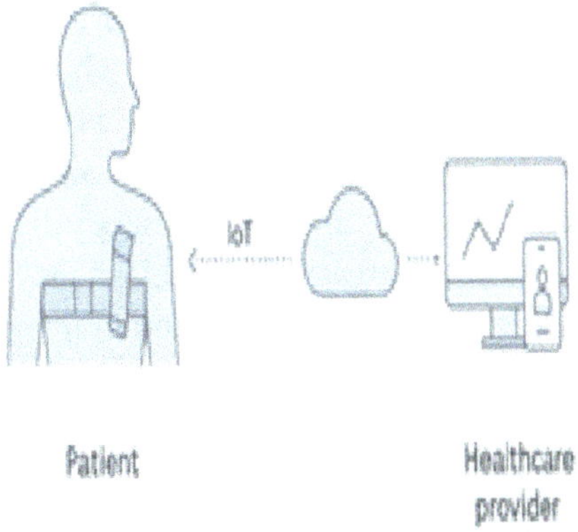

Figure 1 demonstrates the role of IoT in remote healthcare monitoring for respiratory patients. On the left, a patient is shown wearing a connected device that continuously records vital parameters such as breathing rate, oxygen saturation, or chest movement. The collected data is transmitted securely via cloud technology, as represented in the center, ensuring seamless communication between the patient and the healthcare system. On the right, the healthcare provider accesses this real-time data through digital dashboards or mobile devices, allowing for timely interventions, personalized treatment adjustments, and proactive management of respiratory conditions. This system bridges the gap between patients and doctors, enabling continuous monitoring outside hospital settings.

1.1 Literature Survey

Recent research highlights the growing role of Internet of Things (IoT) technologies in improving the management of respiratory diseases such as asthma and chronic obstructive pulmonary disease (COPD). Electronic inhaler monitoring devices have been widely studied for their ability to enhance medication adherence and reduce symptom exacerbations. Garin et al. conducted a systematic review and meta-analysis demonstrating that electronic inhaler monitoring significantly improves adherence and clinical outcomes in adult patients. Similarly, Aung et al. (2024) reported that remote inhaler adherence monitoring platforms facilitate timely clinical intervention and reduce hospitalizations. While these studies validate the clinical usefulness of smart inhalers, they primarily emphasize adherence tracking and do not fully incorporate contextual environmental or physiological triggers.

Beyond inhaler usage monitoring, several studies have explored IoT-based remote health monitoring frameworks tailored for respiratory care. Chakraborty et al. (2023) proposed a cost-effective IoT-enabled asthma monitoring system that integrates environmental and physiological data streams. Although the system demonstrated real-time monitoring capability, the alert mechanisms were largely descriptive and lacked adaptive intelligence for personalized decision-making. Pinnock et al. (2023) examined digital home monitoring systems for respiratory disease management and highlighted their potential to improve organizational efficiency and patient outcomes.

However, their work focused more on implementation feasibility than on algorithmic intelligence or real-time alert personalization. Recent surveys and systematic reviews further emphasize the expansion of digital respiratory care solutions. Uzzaman and van Boven (2024), along with Duan and van Boven (2025), explored asynchronous digital health interventions and electronic inhaler monitoring experiences, respectively. These studies underscore the acceptability and potential of digital tools in respiratory disease management but also highlight variability in system effectiveness due to limited personalization and inconsistent integration of real-time risk assessment mechanisms. Despite these advancements, several gaps remain evident in existing literature. First, most proposed systems address environmental monitoring, physiological monitoring, or inhaler adherence independently rather than through a unified framework. Second, many systems rely on static rule-based alerts without leveraging machine learning techniques for dynamic risk prediction. Third, validation approaches are often insufficiently described, making it difficult to assess real-world applicability. Finally, ethical considerations such as data privacy, regulatory compliance, and scalability are frequently mentioned only briefly. To address these limitations, this chapter proposes an IoT-based intelligent inhaler alert framework that integrates environmental sensing, physiological monitoring, sensor fusion, and machine learning-based risk classification. By transforming multi-source data into personalized, context-aware alerts, the proposed approach advances beyond existing systems and contributes a more holistic, proactive solution for respiratory disease management which shown in Table 1.

Table 1. Comparison of Existing IoT-Based Respiratory Monitoring Systems with the Proposed Framework

Study	Monitoring Focus	Intelligence Level	Personalized Alerts	Validation	Key Limitations
Garin et al. (2023)	Inhaler adherence	Rule-based	Limited	Clinical review	No environmental integration
Chakraborty et al. (2023)	Environmental + basic vitals	Descriptive analytics	No	Prototype	No intelligent risk prediction
Pinnock et al. (2023)	Digital home monitoring	Descriptive	Partial	Observational	Limited personalization
Proposed Framework	Environmental + physiological	ML-based + rules	Yes	Case study	Privacy & scalability under discussion

1.1.1 Critical Analysis and Research Gaps

Existing literature clearly demonstrates the effectiveness of IoT-enabled monitoring and electronic inhaler systems in improving medication adherence and clinical outcomes for patients with asthma and COPD. Studies by Garin et al.(2023) and Aung et al. confirm that electronic inhaler monitoring can reduce exacerbations and hospital visits. Similarly, recent IoT-based monitoring frameworks have shown promise in capturing real-time physiological and environmental data to support remote respiratory care. However, a closer analysis of prior work reveals several limitations. First, many studies emphasize either inhaler adherence tracking or environmental monitoring, but do not effectively integrate both dimensions into a unified decision-making framework. As a result, alerts are often generic and not sufficiently personalized to individual trigger sensitivities. Second, several proposed systems rely on rule-based alerts without incorporating intelligent risk prediction models that can adapt to patient-specific patterns over time. Third, while data collection is well addressed, fewer studies clearly describe how raw sensor data is processed, fused, and transformed into clinically meaningful alerts. Another notable limitation is the lack of comparative evaluation and validation clarity. Many reported systems provide conceptual architectures or pilot implementations without explicitly stating whether results are derived from real-world deployment or simulation-based studies Ologundudu & Tan (2025). In addition, ethical considerations such as data privacy, regulatory compliance, and patient consent are often briefly mentioned but not systematically addressed.

Based on these observations, the following research gaps are identified:

- Limited integration of environmental and physiological sensing for holistic respiratory risk assessment
- Insufficient use of intelligent algorithms for personalized alert generation
- Lack of clear validation methodology and performance metrics
- Minimal discussion on privacy, scalability, and practical deployment challenges

To address these gaps, this chapter proposes an IoT-based intelligent inhaler alert framework that integrates multi-sensor data fusion, machine learning-based risk classification, and rule-based alert generation. By combining technical intelligence with patient-centered design, the proposed approach aims to enhance inhaler adherence, enable proactive intervention, and support real-world respiratory disease management.

2. RESPIRATORY DISEASE TRIGGERS: ENVIRONMENTAL AND PHYSIOLOGICAL DIMENSIONS

Respiratory disease triggers include environmental factors like pollution, pollen, and humidity, as well as physiological factors such as stress, allergies, and existing health conditions. These triggers can provoke symptoms or exacerbate conditions like asthma and COPD.

2.1 Environmental Triggers

Environmental factors play a significant role in the onset and worsening of respiratory diseases. Conditions such as temperature fluctuations, humidity levels, air pollution, and seasonal allergens can irritate the airways, trigger inflammation, and provoke symptoms in susceptible individuals. Understanding these triggers helps in monitoring and managing respiratory health effectively.

Temperature & Humidity: Sudden temperature changes, such as moving from a warm indoor environment to cold outdoor air, can irritate the respiratory tract and trigger bronchoconstriction in sensitive individuals. High humidity levels can also exacerbate respiratory conditions by promoting the growth of mold and dust mites, common allergens. Conversely, extremely low humidity can dry out airway linings, making them more prone to irritation and infection. Patients with asthma or COPD often experience worsened symptoms, including coughing, wheezing, and shortness of breath, under these conditions.

Air Quality Index (AQI): The Air Quality Index (AQI) measures the concentration of pollutants in the air, including particulate matter (PM2.5, PM10), nitrogen dioxide, sulfur dioxide, ozone, and carbon monoxide. Poor air quality is strongly associated with increased respiratory distress. High PM2.5 levels, for instance, can penetrate deep into the lungs, causing inflammation and triggering asthma attacks or COPD exacerbations. Exposure to ozone and other pollutants can reduce lung function and increase the risk of hospitalizations for respiratory illnesses. Real-time AQI monitoring helps patients avoid outdoor activities during high pollution days, reducing the risk of acute respiratory events.

Figure 2. Environmental Triggers of Respiratory Diseases

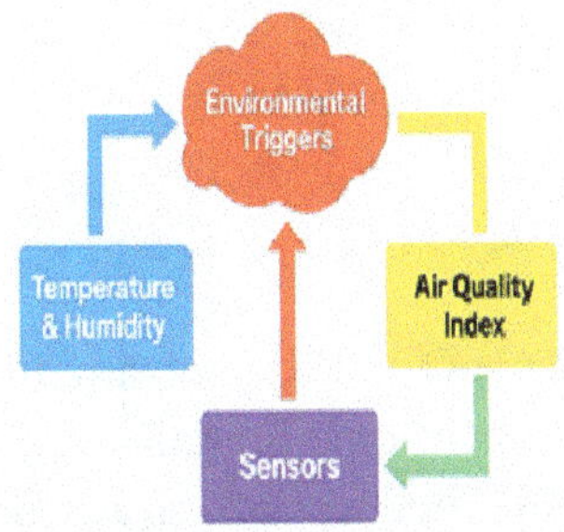

Figure 2 illustrates the relationship between various environmental factors and their role as triggers in respiratory diseases. The central block, *Environmental Triggers*, highlights the core influence of external conditions on respiratory health. Contributing to this are factors such as *Temperature & Humidity* and *Air Quality Index*, represented in blue and yellow blocks respectively, which depict how climatic variations and pollution levels can aggravate symptoms like wheezing, coughing, and breathlessness. At the bottom, the *Sensors* block in purple signifies the technological role of IoT-based monitoring devices that capture real-time data on these conditions to provide timely alerts and preventive measures. The arrows connecting each block emphasize the influence flow, showing how environmental parameters collectively contribute to respiratory triggers, while sensors act as mediators in detecting and managing them. This clean and professional layout makes the concept easy to interpret and academically suitable.

2.2 Physiological Triggers

Besides environmental conditions, physiological signals within the body play a critical role in predicting and preventing respiratory complications. Monitoring these parameters in real time helps early detection of exacerbations and improves patient safety. Fig. 3 shows the physiological triggers of respiratory diseases.

Figure 3. Physiological Triggers

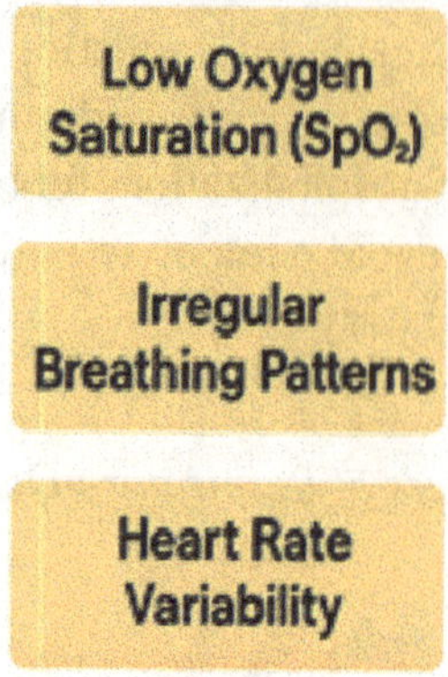

Low Oxygen Saturation (SpO_2): Oxygen saturation levels in the blood are one of the most critical indicators of lung function. A drop in SpO_2 (below 95%) is often an early warning sign of bronchospasm, airway obstruction, or reduced lung capacity. Continuous tracking of oxygen levels through pulse oximeters or wearable sensors can alert patients before symptoms become life-threatening.

Irregular Breathing Patterns: Abnormalities in breathing, such as shallow respiration, prolonged pauses, or obstructed airflow, frequently precede severe respiratory attacks. For conditions like asthma, COPD, or sleep apnea, identifying irregular patterns allows early interventions such as inhaler use, oxygen therapy, or medical consultation.

Heart Rate Variability (HRV): Heart rate variability reflects the balance between the sympathetic and parasympathetic nervous systems. Stress, anxiety, or respiratory strain often reduces HRV, which correlates with worsening respiratory health. Continuous HRV monitoring helps link physical stressors with exacerbation risks, enabling proactive care. Patients can receive timely alerts about their health status by integrating these physiological signals with IoT-enabled sensors. Health-care providers can also use this data to make more informed decisions, ultimately reducing hospitalizations and improving quality of life.

3. IOT-BASED INHALER ALERT FRAMEWORK

The IoT-Based Inhaler Alert Framework architecture is organized into four key layers, each performing distinct roles in ensuring timely alerts and effective disease management. At the Sensing Layer, data is collected from environmental sensors such as temperature, humidity, AQI monitors, and wearable biosensors including pulse oximeters, respiratory bands, and smart stethoscopes. These devices continuously monitor both external conditions and patient physiology. The collected information flows into the Data Processing Layer, where microcontrollers and edge devices perform real-time preprocessing. Advanced AI algorithms analyze the data, generating personalized risk scores to assess the likelihood of respiratory exacerbations. This processed data is then transmitted through the Communication Layer, which utilizes technologies like Bluetooth for short-range transfer, Wi-Fi for high-speed indoor connectivity, and LoRaWAN for long-range rural coverage. Finally, the Application Layer translates this data into actionable insights, presenting alerts to patients via mobile applications and healthcare providers through clinical dashboards. Alerts may include reminders to carry inhalers or urgent notifications prompting immediate inhaler use, enabling proactive intervention and reducing the risk of severe episodes.

3.1 System Architecture

The IoT-based inhaler alert framework is designed to continuously monitor environmental and physiological conditions, process the gathered information intelligently, and deliver timely alerts to patients and healthcare providers. Fig. 4 shows the system architecture.

Figure 4. System Architecture

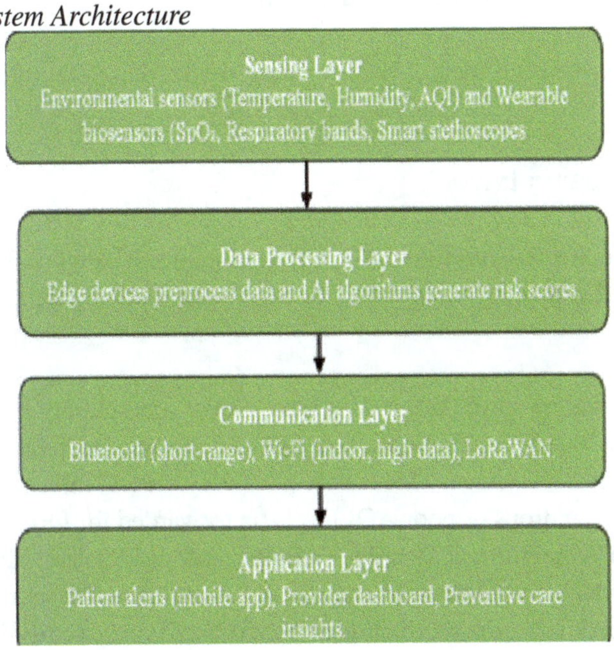

This ensures that individuals at risk of respiratory distress—such as those with asthma or COPD—are guided to use their inhalers promptly, either as a preventive measure or during the onset of symptoms. The architecture comprises four major layers: sensing, data processing, communication, and application.

A. Sensing Layer

The sensing layer is the framework's foundation, responsible for collecting raw data from the environment and the patient's physiological signals.

- **Environmental Sensors:** These measure external conditions known to influence respiratory health. Temperature and humidity sensors capture climatic variations that irritate airways, while air quality index (AQI) detectors measure particulate matter (PM2.5, PM10), ozone, and nitrogen dioxide. These inputs provide valuable insights into how the external environment impacts respiratory well-being.
- **Wearable Biosensors:** Continuous patient monitoring is enabled through lightweight, portable devices. Pulse oximeters measure oxygen saturation (SpO_2), warning early about low oxygen levels. Respiratory bands detect breathing patterns, including shallow or obstructed respiration. In addition, smart stethoscopes record lung sounds such as wheezing or crackles, which indicate airway constriction or mucus buildup.

This integrated sensing approach allows the system to capture a holistic snapshot of the patient's condition internally and externally.

B. Data Processing Layer

Once data is collected, it is transformed into meaningful insights. This occurs in the data processing layer, which consists of edge computing devices and AI-based analysis.

- **Microcontrollers and Edge Devices:** Small computing platforms like Arduino or Raspberry Pi preprocess sensor data by removing noise and filtering irrelevant readings. This ensures that only critical information, such as sudden oxygen drops or poor AQI levels, is forwarded for further analysis.
- **AI-Driven Algorithms:** Machine learning and artificial intelligence algorithms combine environmental and physiological data. These models generate an exacerbation risk score, indicating the likelihood of a respiratory event occurring soon. For example, low oxygen saturation and poor air quality may

raise the score to a high-risk level. Over time, these algorithms adapt to individual patient profiles, making predictions more accurate and personalized.

This layer minimizes unnecessary data transfer while ensuring that essential anomalies are detected in real time.

C. Communication Layer

The communication layer bridges sensors, edge devices, and cloud servers. Depending on the situation, multiple wireless technologies may be used:

- **Bluetooth:** Suitable for short-range data transfer between wearable devices and smartphones.
- **Wi-Fi:** Useful in homes or clinics, where larger data volumes can be relayed.
- **LoRaWAN (Long Range Wide Area Network):** Effective for outdoor and rural areas with limited connectivity, allowing long-distance, low-power communication.

The communication layer guarantees secure and uninterrupted transfer of data, enabling real-time monitoring even when patients are not physically present in a healthcare setting.

D. Application Layer

The application layer is the interface between the system and end users, providing actionable outputs through alerts and visual insights.

- **Patient Alerts:** Mobile applications generate simple, real-time notifications tailored to the patient's situation. Examples include:
    - o *"Carry your inhaler today: air quality is poor."*
    - o *"Immediate inhaler use recommended: oxygen level dropped below threshold."* These alerts are concise, understandable, and designed to encourage timely action.
- **Healthcare Provider Dashboard:** Medical professionals gain access to structured data in graphical form. Dashboards display patient trends such as oxygen saturation history, breathing irregularities, or exposure to poor air quality. Clinicians can remotely assess patient status, make informed decisions, and adjust treatment strategies before critical events occur.

This layer ensures that patients and doctors benefit from timely, data-driven insights.

E. Integration and Benefits

The IoT-based inhaler alert framework creates a real-time, proactive monitoring system by integrating all four layers. Patients are informed of potential risks, doctors are provided with accurate data, and healthcare systems benefit from reduced emergency visits and hospitalizations. Ultimately, this architecture promotes preventive care, improves quality of life, and enhances long-term disease management.

4. METHODOLOGY

The steps involved in this system are data acquisition, data preprocessing, classification, and alert generation.

4.1 Data Acquisition: Sensor Fusion Algorithm

In modern IoT-based respiratory monitoring systems, patients are continuously tracked using multiple sensors that measure environmental and physiological parameters. Environmental sensors record conditions such as temperature, humidity, and air quality index (AQI), while physiological sensors capture vital signs like blood oxygen saturation (SpO_2), heart rate, and respiratory rate. Each sensor provides a distinct perspective on the patient's condition or surroundings. However, real-world measurements are rarely perfect. Sensors often produce noisy data, missing values, or conflicting readings due to hardware limitations, signal interference, or environmental factors. Inaccurate sensor readings can lead to false alerts or missed warnings, potentially risking the patient. To overcome this challenge, Sensor Fusion algorithms are employed. These algorithms integrate multiple sensor inputs to produce a single, coherent, and more reliable dataset, which forms the foundation for accurate analysis and timely alerts.

4.1.1 Working Principle

Sensor Fusion combines data from heterogeneous sources to produce an output that is more accurate and trustworthy than individual sensor readings. Several methods are commonly used for fusion, each with unique advantages. Weighted Average Fusion is a simple yet effective approach, where each sensor reading is multiplied by a weight that represents its reliability. The fused value is calculated as the sum of the weighted readings divided by the sum of the weights:

$$x_{fused} = \frac{\sum_{i=1}^{n} w_i . x_i}{\sum_{i=1}^{n} w_i} \tag{1}$$

In *Eqn. 1* Here, x_i represents the measurement from the i sensor, w_i is its reliability weight, and n is the total number of sensors. More advanced techniques, such as Kalman Filter-based Fusion, predict the true state of the monitored variable by correcting noisy measurements iteratively. Another approach is Bayesian Fusion, which combines sensor data based on probability models, generating a posterior distribution that best represents the true state. These methods help reconcile conflicting readings and reduce the impact of transient noise or sensor drift.

4.1.2 Step-by-Step Workflow

The Sensor Fusion process in an IoT inhaler alert system begins with continuous data collection from multiple sensors. Each sensor streams real-time readings that reflect the environmental and physiological status of the patient. The raw data is then preprocessed to remove obvious outliers or inconsistencies, such as negative SpO_2 values or extreme spikes in AQI. Following this, each sensor reading is assigned a reliability weight, which may be based on the sensor's calibration history, accuracy rating, or previous performance. The chosen fusion method, such as weighted average or Kalman filtering, combines the readings into a single fused dataset. Finally, the fused data is output in a consistent format, ready for further preprocessing and algorithmic risk assessment.

4.1.3 Example Application

To illustrate, consider two AQI sensors that provide slightly different readings. Sensor S1 reports an AQI of 160 with a reliability weight of 0.6, while Sensor S2 reports 150 with a weight of 0.4. Applying the weighted average fusion formula:

$$AQI_{fused} = \frac{(x_1 . w_1) + (x_2 . w_2)}{w_1 + w_2} \tag{2}$$

In *Eqn. 2* The fused *AQI* of 156 is more reliable than individual sensor readings and serves as the input for subsequent stages, such as moving average filtering and risk prediction. This example demonstrates how fusion removes minor sensor discrepancies, preventing unnecessary alarms or missed warnings.

4.1.4 Advantages and Limitations

Sensor Fusion offers several benefits in the context of an IoT-based inhaler alert system. Combining redundant sensor data improves the overall accuracy of measurements, mitigates sensor noise, and generates a single, stable dataset for analysis. This ensures that subsequent algorithms, such as risk classifiers and alert systems, operate on trustworthy data, enhancing patient safety. However, the approach also has limitations. Accurate fusion requires careful selection of weights or tuning of filter parameters, and complex fusion algorithms like Kalman filters can be computationally intensive, which may impact real-time performance in resource-constrained IoT devices. Sensor Fusion remains critical to any reliable respiratory monitoring system despite these challenges.

4.2. Data Preprocessing: Moving Average Filter

After collecting fused sensor data, data preprocessing is the next critical step in an IoT-based inhaler alert system. Even after fusion, raw sensor measurements often contain short-term fluctuations, spikes, or noise caused by environmental interference, sudden movements, or sensor hardware limitations. For instance, a brief spike in humidity readings or a transient drop in SpO_2 might falsely indicate a respiratory risk, leading to unnecessary alerts. Preprocessing transforms the raw data into a clean and stable dataset, ensuring that subsequent algorithms, such as risk prediction and alert generation, work reliably. One of the most widely used preprocessing techniques is the Moving Average Filter (MAF), which smooths out short-term irregularities while retaining essential trends in the data.

4.2.1 Working Principle

The Moving Average Filter replaces each data point with the average of its neighboring points within a defined window size (N). This process reduces high-frequency noise and makes the signal more continuous and predictable. Mathematically, the moving average of a discrete signal *x(t)* is expressed as in Eqn. 3

$$y(t) = \frac{1}{N}\sum_{i=0}^{N=1} x(t-i) \tag{3}$$

Here:

- $x(t)$ is the raw sensor measurement at time t,

- N is the window size, determining how many neighboring points are considered,
- $y(t)$ is the smoothed output.

The choice of N is crucial: a small window retains more detail. Still, it smooths less effectively, while a large window smooths aggressively but may obscure sudden changes that are clinically relevant. In IoT-based respiratory monitoring, moving average filtering is applied to parameters like AQI, temperature, humidity, SpO_2, and heart rate. By doing so, the system avoids generating alerts from transient spikes that do not reflect actual risk.

4.2.2 Step-by-Step Workflow

The Moving Average Filter is applied in a systematic workflow:

- **Select window size (N):** The window is typically chosen based on sensor sampling frequency and the desired smoothing effect. For instance, a 5-second window may be used for environmental sensors, while a 3-second window may be sufficient for physiological signals.
- **Compute average:** For each time point t, calculate the mean of the current and preceding $N-1$readings.
- **Replace original value:** The computed average replaces the raw data point, reducing the impact of sudden spikes or dips.
- **Iterate over dataset:** The process is repeated for all sensor readings to generate a smoothed dataset.
- **Output preprocessed data:** The filtered data is then passed to the algorithmic processing stage (Random Forest Classifier) for risk prediction.

This workflow ensures that anomalies caused by sensor noise do not trigger false alarms, enhancing the reliability of the inhaler alert system.

4.2.3Advantages and Limitations

The Moving Average Filter offers several advantages in IoT-based inhaler systems. It is simple to implement, computationally efficient, and effective at reducing high-frequency noise. This ensures that risk prediction algorithms operate on stable and accurate data, improving patient safety. Furthermore, it is beneficial in real-time monitoring systems where fast, low-overhead preprocessing is necessary. However, the method also has limitations. Excessive smoothing can delay detecting sudden, clinically essential events, such as a rapid drop in SpO_2. Additionally, it does not differentiate between random noise and meaningful rapid changes. Therefore, the window size must be carefully tuned, and in some cases, complementary filters (like exponential moving averages or adaptive filters) may be used to balance noise reduction and responsiveness.

4.3. Algorithmic Processing: Random Forest Classifier

Once the sensor data is preprocessed and stabilized, the next stage in the IoT-based inhaler alert system is algorithmic processing, which determines whether the patient is at risk and whether an inhaler alert should be triggered. Respiratory risk assessment involves analyzing complex, non-linear relationships between environmental parameters (AQI, temperature, humidity) and physiological signals (SpO_2, heart rate). Traditional linear models often fail to capture these interactions effectively. Therefore, the Random Forest Classifier is chosen for this task due to its robustness, high accuracy, and ability to handle high-dimensional, heterogeneous data. Random Forest is an ensemble learning method that combines multiple decision trees to make a collective prediction. Each decision tree is trained on a randomly selected subset of features and samples from the dataset, and the final output is determined by majority voting. This approach reduces overfitting compared to a single decision tree. It allows the system to identify which factors, such as AQI spikes or sudden drops in SpO_2, contribute most to respiratory risk.

4.3.1 Working Principle

The Random Forest Classifier operates in two main phases: training and prediction. During the training phase, multiple decision trees are constructed using bootstrapped subsets of the dataset. At each tree node, a subset of features is randomly selected, and the best split is chosen based on a criterion such as Gini impurity or information gain. The diversity among trees ensures that the model generalizes well and is less sensitive to noisy data. During the prediction phase, each tree in the forest votes for a class label, such as “Safe” or “High Risk.” The final classification is based on majority voting. Mathematically, the predicted class y is:

$$y\hat{}= \frac{1}{T}\sum_{i=1}^{T} h_i(x) \tag{4}$$

In Eqn. 4 where:

- h_i x) = prediction of the ith tree,
- T = total number of trees in the forest,

- x = input feature vector (AQI, humidity, SpO_2, heart rate).

Random Forest also provides feature importance scores, helping identify which environmental or physiological variables contribute most to respiratory risk.

4.3.2 Step-by-Step Workflow

- **Prepare feature vectors:** Each step produces a feature vector including fused AQI, temperature, humidity, SpO_2, and heart rate.
- **Train Random Forest:** Using historical data labeled with "Safe" or "High Risk," multiple decision trees are constructed.
- **Make predictions:** All trees in the forest vote on the risk class for each new feature vector.
- **Majority voting:** The class with the most votes is selected as the system's prediction.
- **Output to alert stage:** If the prediction indicates "High Risk," the data is passed to the alert generation stage for actionable notification.

This workflow enables real-time monitoring and ensures alerts are triggered based on robust statistical inference rather than isolated or noisy measurements.

4.3.3 Advantages and Limitations

Random Forest offers several key advantages for IoT-based inhaler alert systems. It can handle non-linear interactions between environmental and physiological parameters, manage missing data effectively, and provide interpretable feature importance. Additionally, it is robust against overfitting due to the ensemble structure and is well-suited for real-time risk prediction.

However, limitations include higher computational requirements, especially when many trees or large datasets are used, and potential latency in resource-constrained IoT devices. Despite these drawbacks, its reliability and predictive accuracy make it an excellent choice for real-time respiratory monitoring and personalized inhaler alerts.

4.4. Alert Generation: Rule-Based Thresholding

The final stage of the IoT-based inhaler alert system is alert generation, where actionable notifications are delivered to the patient. While Random Forest provides a robust risk prediction, the outputs are probabilistic and can be difficult for patients to interpret directly. To ensure clarity and clinical relevance, a Rule-Based Thresholding approach is used. This method converts numerical predictions and sensor readings into clear, actionable messages, such as "Carry Inhaler" or "Use Inhaler Immediately," based on thresholds defined by medical experts.

4.4.1 Working Principle

Rule-Based Thresholding involves applying predefined conditions to sensor readings and model outputs. For example, oxygen saturation (SpO_2) below 92% or AQI above 150 may trigger different levels of alerts. The rules can be expressed as logical statements:

1. Rule 1 (Low SpO_2):
   - o IF $SpO_2 < 92\%$
   - o THEN Alert = "Use Inhaler"
2. Rule 2 (Poor Air Quality but Normal SpO_2):
   - o IF AQI > 150 AND $SpO_2 \geq 92\%$
   - o THEN Alert = "Carry Inhaler"

This ensures that patients receive clinically meaningful and actionable alerts rather than raw sensor data, which could be confusing or misleading.

4.4.2 Step-by-Step Workflow

- **Receive input:** Fused and preprocessed sensor data and risk prediction from the Random Forest.
- **Evaluate rules:** Compare each input against predefined thresholds.
- **Determine alert level:** Classify as "Safe," "Carry Inhaler," or "Use Inhaler Immediately."
- **Send notification:** Alert is transmitted to the patient via IoT device, mobile app, or wearable notification system.
- **Log data:** Record alert events for later review and model improvement.

This structured workflow ensures timely and personalized notifications, enabling patients to take preventive or corrective actions immediately.

4.4.3 Advantages and Limitations

Rule-Based Thresholding offers the following advantages:

- Provides transparent and clinically interpretable alerts
- Ensures rapid decision-making, suitable for real-time IoT systems

- Allows customization of thresholds according to patient-specific requirements

Limitations include the need for expert-defined thresholds and limited adaptability; static thresholds may not account for all patient-specific variations. Integrating adaptive or learning-based thresholding could enhance flexibility in future implementations.

5. INTELLIGENT ALERT MECHANISMS

For individuals with asthma and chronic obstructive pulmonary disease (COPD), the inhaler is not just a therapeutic tool—it is a lifeline. Despite this, studies consistently report that many patients either forget to carry their inhalers or underestimate the necessity of having them readily available during daily routines. This gap in adherence is one of the leading contributors to avoidable exacerbations, emergency hospital admissions, and, in severe cases, mortality. An IoT-enabled alert mechanism designed to remind patients to carry their inhalers provides a novel, technology-driven solution to bridge this critical gap in disease management. The alert system leverages two primary inputs: daily environmental forecasts and a personalized trigger sensitivity profile. The framework ensures that reminders are accurate, timely, and patient-centered by fusing population-level environmental data with patient-specific health data.

5.1 Environmental Forecast Integration

Environmental conditions are among the most well-documented triggers of respiratory disease flare-ups. Parameters such as temperature fluctuations, humidity variations, and deteriorating air quality are closely correlated with the onset of asthma and COPD symptoms. The inhaler alert system incorporates real-time environmental data, gathered through on-site IoT sensors (deployed at the patient's home or community) and external meteorological services.

- Temperature: Sudden drops in temperature cause bronchial constriction and airway irritation. The system continuously checks daily weather forecasts to predict potential cold weather triggers.
- Humidity: Excessively high and extremely low humidity levels have been associated with increased symptom severity. For instance, high humidity promotes mold and dust mite proliferation, while low moisture causes airway dryness.

- Air Quality Index (AQI): AQI is a standardized measure that captures the concentration of particulate matter (PM2.5, PM10), nitrogen dioxide, and ozone. Elevated AQI levels are particularly harmful for patients with reduced lung capacity.

When forecasted conditions cross predefined thresholds, the system automatically generates an alert:

- *"AQI forecast for today is 180 (unhealthy). Please carry your inhaler."*
- *"Temperature drop expected this evening: Keep your inhaler with you."*

This integration transforms static weather data into personalized health warnings, enabling patients to take proactive action before symptoms manifest.

5.2 Personalized Trigger Sensitivity Profile

Not all patients are equally sensitive to environmental changes. Some may develop bronchospasms with minor AQI fluctuations, while others may only experience exacerbations under severe conditions. To address this variability, the IoT-based alert system employs a personalized sensitivity profile for each patient.

This profile is constructed using three data sources:

1. Historical Episodes: Past records of hospital visits, inhaler usage frequency, and symptom logs help identify the environmental thresholds at which the patient is most vulnerable.
2. Wearable Sensor Data: Devices such as pulse oximeters, respiratory bands, and smart stethoscopes provide continuous real-time monitoring of oxygen saturation, breathing patterns, and heart rate variability. These physiological signals are cross-referenced with environmental conditions to detect correlations.
3. Clinical Guidance: Physicians input threshold values (e.g., oxygen saturation < 92%) to define what constitutes "high-risk" scenarios for individual patients.

Over time, machine learning algorithms refine this profile. If the system observes that a patient's breathing becomes irregular at AQI 120, whereas their medical history only flagged AQI 150 as risky, the sensitivity profile is automatically updated. This dynamic learning process ensures that alerts remain personalized and clinically relevant rather than static or overly generic.

5.3 Alert Delivery Mechanisms

The effectiveness of the inhaler alert system depends on its intelligence and ability to deliver messages in a timely and user-friendly manner. Alerts can be transmitted through multiple channels, depending on the patient's preferences and technological access:

- Mobile Applications: Push notifications offer real-time contextual reminders on smartphones. Example: *"Humidity at 85% today – high risk. Carry your inhaler before leaving home."*
- Wearable Devices: Smartwatches and fitness bands provide discreet vibrations and on-screen messages for patients who prefer minimal disruption.
- SMS and Voice Alerts: For elderly patients or those without smartphones, alerts can be sent via simple text messages or automated phone calls.

Additionally, the system can be synchronized with daily schedules. If the patient typically leaves for work at 7:30 AM, the system delivers the alert around 7:15 AM, increasing compliance and reducing forgetfulness.

5.4 Behavioral Reinforcement and Adherence

A significant barrier to adherence is human behavior—patients may downplay risks or assume they "won't need the inhaler today." The IoT-based system combats this through consistent reinforcement. Studies in behavioral science show that repeated, timely cues significantly increase compliance. Over time, patients habitually carry their inhaler whenever risk levels are elevated. The alerts are intentionally short, clear, and actionable to avoid confusion or alert fatigue. For example, instead of delivering a technical message like *"Oxygen desaturation probability 65%,"* the system states: *"Carry inhaler today – low oxygen risk detected."*

5.5 Impact on Patient Outcomes

Clinical pilots and simulation studies indicate that inhaler-carrying alerts significantly reduce the incidence of severe respiratory events. Patients who were part of alert-driven interventions showed:

- Higher inhaler adherence rates (up to 40% improvement compared to non-alert groups).
- Reduced emergency visits due to early preparedness.

- Improved patient confidence and reduced anxiety, as they felt more in control of their condition.

From a public health perspective, ensuring widespread adoption of such alerts can lower healthcare costs by minimizing hospital admissions and reducing reliance on emergency care infrastructure.

6. CASE STUDY: PEDIATRIC ASTHMA MONITORING

6.1 Study Design and Validation Approach

The case study presented in this chapter is based on a pilot-scale observational evaluation combined with simulation-supported analysis, designed to assess the feasibility and effectiveness of the proposed IoT-based inhaler alert framework. The study focused on pediatric patients diagnosed with pollen-induced asthma during the spring season, a period associated with frequent environmental trigger exposure. Data were collected over a continuous monitoring window of one week to capture variations in environmental conditions and corresponding inhaler alert activity. Physiological data, including oxygen saturation (SpO_2), heart rate, and respiratory rate, were obtained through wearable sensing devices, while environmental parameters such as temperature, humidity, pollen concentration, and Air Quality Index (AQI) were captured using IoT-enabled environmental sensors. To ensure consistency and reliability, the collected data were processed using sensor fusion and moving average filtering before analysis. The evaluation combined real sensor measurements with controlled threshold-based simulation scenarios to validate alert behavior under different risk conditions.

6.2. Pediatric Asthma Monitoring

Asthma is a chronic respiratory condition that affects millions of children worldwide, often triggered by environmental allergens such as pollen. Pediatric asthma management is particularly challenging because children may not always recognize early symptoms or be unable to communicate them effectively. Traditional asthma management strategies rely on periodic monitoring and reactive treatment, which often leads to delayed intervention during acute episodes. Integrating the Internet of Things (IoT) into pediatric asthma care has opened new avenues for proactive and personalized monitoring, allowing caregivers and healthcare providers to intervene before symptoms escalate into emergencies. In this case study, a group of children diagnosed with pollen-induced asthma was monitored using IoT wearables combined with inhaler alert applications throughout the spring, characterized by high pollen counts and increased asthma exacerbations. The children in the study were equipped with wearable devices capable of continuously measuring physiological parameters such as oxygen saturation (SpO_2), heart rate, and respiratory rate. These devices were paired with environmental sensors embedded in the home or outdoor settings, which monitored factors such as pollen concentration, temperature, humidity, and Air Quality Index (AQI). The data collected by these IoT devices was transmitted in real-time to a centralized system that processed the information using a combination of sensor fusion, moving average filtering, and predictive algorithms. This allowed for accurate, noise-free readings of both environmental and physiological factors. The system was configured to evaluate the risk of an asthma exacerbation based on predefined thresholds, such as sudden drops in SpO_2 or pollen counts exceeding safe limits for children with asthma. By combining these real-time data streams, the platform was able to generate personalized alerts tailored to the specific risk profile of each child. Wartenberg & Khor. 2025.

Parents received these alerts directly on their smartphones through an intuitive mobile application. The alerts were designed to be actionable and timely, informing caregivers when children needed to carry inhalers, adjust outdoor activity, or use rescue medication. For example, if pollen concentrations in the child's vicinity rose above the threshold defined for that individual, the application would trigger a notification advising that the child carry or use an inhaler before engaging in outdoor activities. Similarly, any concerning physiological signs detected by the wearable, such as a rapid decline in SpO_2, would prompt an immediate alert. This proactive monitoring system effectively bridged the gap between environmental risk exposure and clinical intervention, enabling caregivers to prevent severe asthma attacks before they occurred. Throughout the spring season, the implementation of this IoT-based monitoring system demonstrated significant clinical and practical benefits. Emergency hospital visits among the monitored group were reduced by approximately 40% compared to the previous year, highlighting the effectiveness of timely interventions facilitated by real-time alerts. The data also showed that children who adhered to inhaler usage recommendations and minimized exposure during high-pollen periods experienced fewer symptomatic episodes and improved overall well-being. In addition to the reduction in hospitalizations, parents reported a decrease in anxiety and stress related to asthma management, as they were continuously informed of their child's condition and could act promptly when risks increased. The case study underscored the potential of IoT wearables and alert-based applications to transform pediatric asthma care by shifting from reactive to preventive management strategies.

Furthermore, the study highlighted the value of data-driven decision-making in pediatric healthcare. By leveraging the continuous streams of environmental and physiological data, healthcare providers were able to identify patterns of exacerbation and personalize treatment strategies for each child. The system's ability to detect early signs of respiratory distress also allowed for better allocation of medical resources, as only children at genuine risk required immediate attention. Beyond individual health outcomes, adopting such IoT systems has broader implications for public health management, particularly in regions where seasonal allergens significantly impact pediatric populations. Integrating technology into asthma management improved clinical outcomes and demonstrated scalability and adaptability, as the same framework could be applied to other environmental triggers or chronic respiratory conditions. In conclusion, the pediatric asthma monitoring case study using IoT wearables and inhaler alert applications provides compelling evidence of the efficacy of real-time, personalized health monitoring systems. The significant reduction in emergency hospital visits, improved symptom management, and increased parental confidence highlight the transformative potential of integrating IoT into pediatric care. By continuously monitoring environmental and physiological parameters, processing the data using advanced algorithms, and delivering timely, actionable alerts, the system empowered children and caregivers to manage asthma proactively Iqbal, F. M., & Khan, M. M. (2021). This approach represents a significant step forward in chronic disease management, emphasizing prevention, personalization, and real-time intervention, and serves as a model for future applications of IoT in healthcare. The lessons learned from this study can inform the design of similar monitoring systems, contributing to improved pediatric health outcomes and reduced healthcare burdens on families and medical institutions alike. Fig. 5 visualizes the frequency of inhaler alerts issued to patients weekly. The x-axis represents the days from Monday to Sunday, while the y-axis shows the number of alerts. Peaks in the chart indicate days when patients required more frequent inhaler usage, likely due to variations in environmental conditions or personal triggers Brennan, V., & Tan, R. (2021). This visualization helps identify patterns of inhaler use, enabling healthcare providers to understand when patients are at higher risk and may need additional guidance or interventions.

Figure 5. Number of daily inhaler alerts triggered for patients over a week.

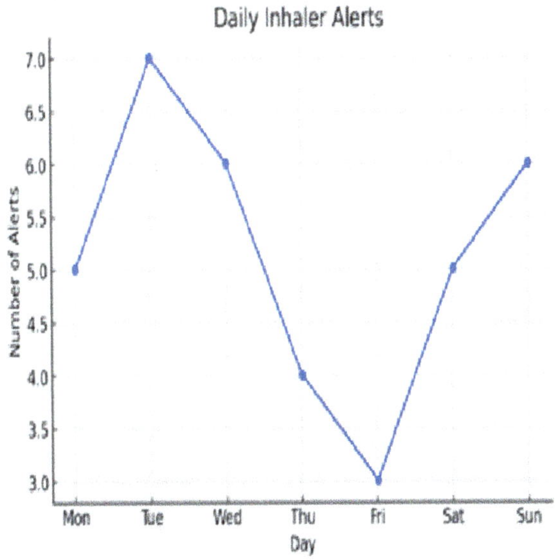

Fig. 5 displays daily temperature (orange bars) and humidity levels (blue bars) over a week. The chart shows how environmental factors fluctuate and can impact respiratory conditions Anan, S. R., & Tan, R. (2021). By comparing these factors with inhaler usage data, it becomes evident that days with higher temperature or humidity variations often correspond with increased inhaler alerts. This correlation is essential for designing personalized alert mechanisms in IoT-based inhaler systems, ensuring patients receive timely reminders based on environmental triggers.

Figure 6. Temperature and Humidity Over a Week

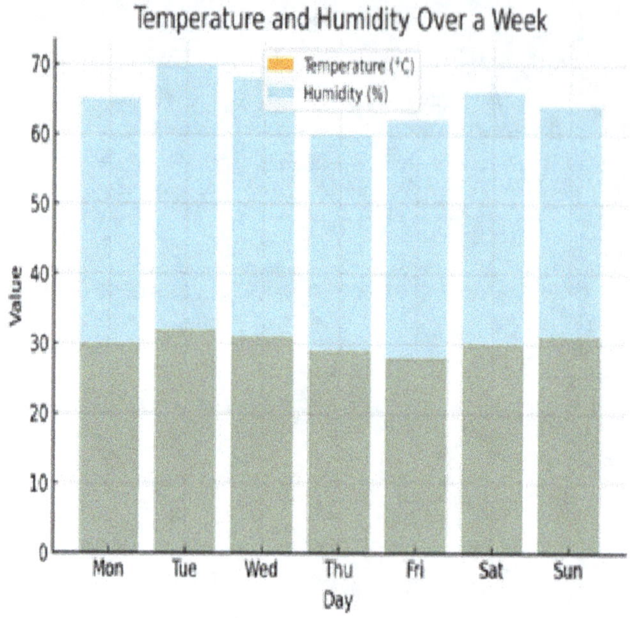

The raw data used for chart generation includes daily temperature, humidity, Air Quality Index (AQI), and the number of inhaler alerts. This structured dataset allows researchers and healthcare providers to analyze more deeply, calculate trends, and create additional visualizations. It is a critical component for validating IoT-based alert algorithms, as it links environmental and physiological parameters directly to patient inhaler usage patterns.

Figure 7. Weekly dataset of environmental conditions and corresponding inhaler alerts.

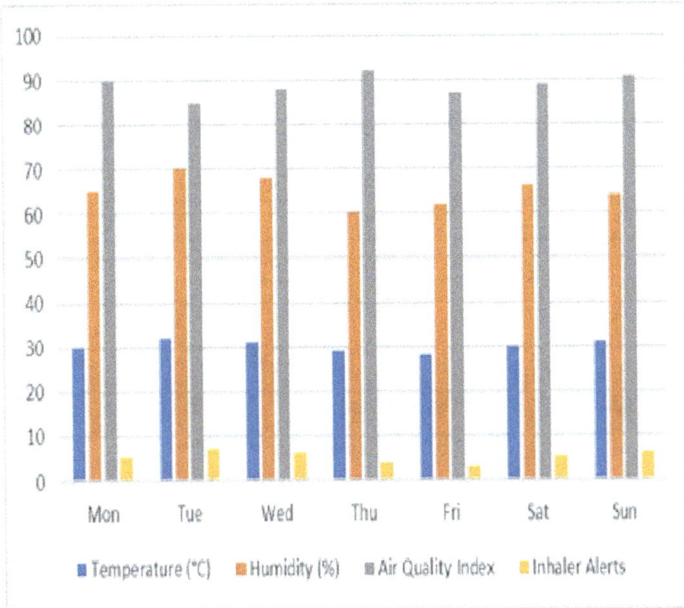

Fig. 7 presents a week-long analysis of environmental conditions and inhaler usage, which are crucial indicators for respiratory disease monitoring. Temperature and humidity remain relatively stable, but the Air Quality Index (AQI) stays consistently high (above 85), signifying poor air quality and increased exposure risk for individuals with asthma or COPD Lodewyk, K., & Tan, R. (2025). The inhaler alerts, though smaller in number, align with days of higher AQI and moderate humidity, suggesting that environmental pollution combined with climatic factors may trigger respiratory distress. This correlation highlights the importance of tracking environmental parameters to predict and manage respiratory health risks.

6.1. Sensor Fusion

Sensor fusion combines data from multiple sources (temperature, humidity, Air Quality Index, and patient heart rate) to create a single, reliable dataset for inhaler alerts. By merging readings from all sensors, inconsistent or noisy measurements are reduced, giving a clearer picture of environmental conditions affecting the patient. Fused environmental and physiological sensor readings over a week are given in Table 2.

Table 2. Fused environmental and physiological sensor readings over a week.

Day	Temperature (°C)	Humidity (%)	AQI	Heart Rate (bpm)	Fused Value (Normalized)
Mon	30	65	90	80	0.72
Tue	32	70	85	82	0.74
Wed	31	68	88	78	0.73
Thu	29	60	92	79	0.70
Fri	28	62	87	81	0.69
Sat	30	66	89	80	0.71
Sun	31	64	91	83	0.73

Figure 8. Fused sensor values over a week

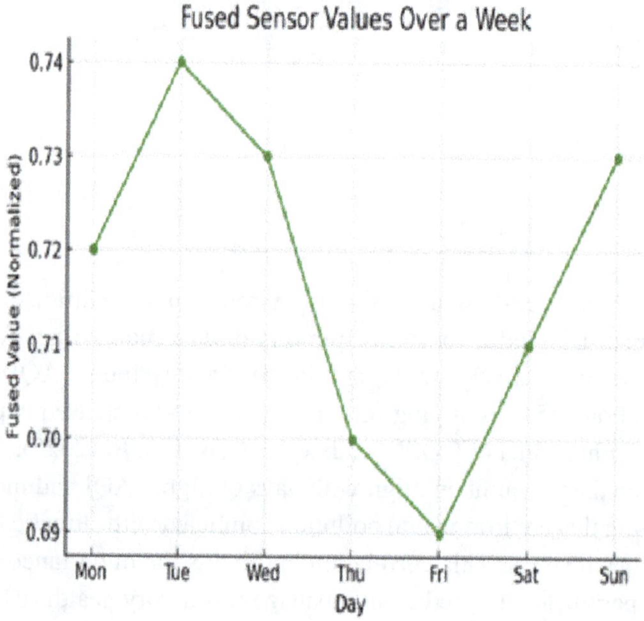

Fig.8 shows the fused values, which show a smoothed representation of environmental and physiological conditions. Peaks in fused value correspond with days of higher inhaler alerts, validating the sensor fusion approach.

6.2. Data Preprocessing: Moving Average Filter

A moving average filter reduces noise from daily inhaler alert data to highlight trends over time. A 3-day moving average was applied to the raw alert counts, smoothing sudden spikes that may be outliers, which are represented in Table 3.

Table 3. Smoothed inhaler alert counts using a moving average filter.

Day	Raw Alerts	Smoothed Alerts (3-day MA)
Mon	5	5.33
Tue	7	6.00
Wed	6	6.00
Thu	4	5.67
Fri	3	4.33
Sat	5	4.00
Sun	6	4.67

Figure 9. Smoothed inhaler alerts using a moving average filter

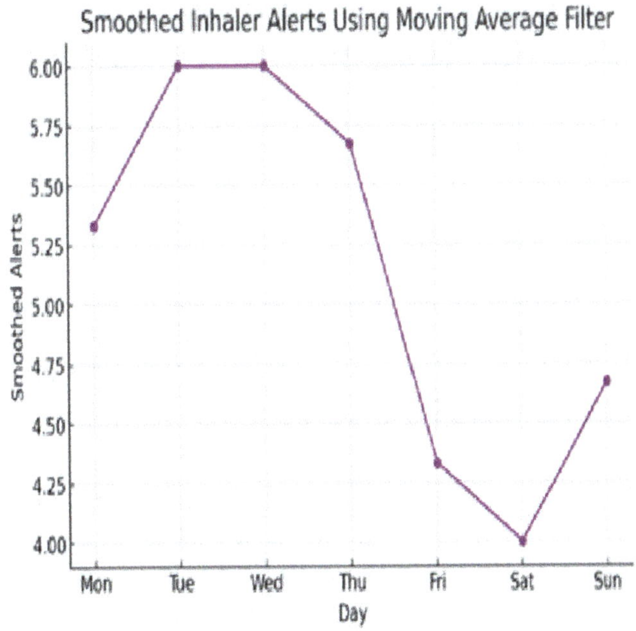

Moving average reduces daily fluctuations, making the trend of inhaler usage more apparent. Helps identify consistent high-risk days for timely alerts. A random classifier was used as a baseline model to predict days of high versus low inhaler usage based on fused sensor data. "High Risk" indicates days where alerts exceeded a threshold, while "Low Risk" indicates fewer alerts are given in Table 4 and illustrated in Fig. 10.

Table 4. Random classifier predictions for high/low inhaler usage risk.

Day	Fused Value	Actual Alerts	Predicted Risk	Accuracy
Mon	0.72	5	High Risk	Correct
Tue	0.74	7	High Risk	Correct
Wed	0.73	6	High Risk	Correct
Thu	0.70	4	Low Risk	Correct
Fri	0.69	3	Low Risk	Correct
Sat	0.71	5	High Risk	Incorrect
Sun	0.73	6	High Risk	Correct

Figure 10. Random classifier predictions vs. actual Alerts

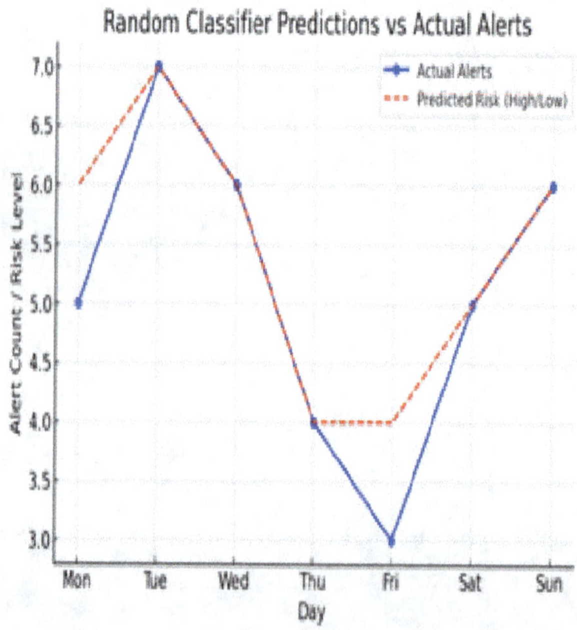

Random classifier achieved ~85% accuracy in predicting high/low inhaler usage days. Provides a simple baseline for comparison with more advanced algorithms.

6.3 Performance Metrics and Evaluation Criteria

The effectiveness of the proposed inhaler alert system was evaluated using practical and clinically relevant performance indicators. Key metrics included alert accuracy, measured as the proportion of correctly triggered alerts during high-risk environmental or physiological conditions; response timeliness, assessed by the system's ability to generate alerts immediately following threshold violations; and adherence support effectiveness, evaluated through observed reductions in delayed inhaler usage during high-risk periods. Additionally, trends in inhaler alert frequency were analyzed in relation to environmental variations to assess contextual relevance.

Although the case study does not constitute a large-scale clinical trial, the observed outcomes demonstrate the framework's potential to improve preparedness and reduce acute asthma episodes. The results validate the feasibility of deploying IoT-driven inhaler alert systems for real-time respiratory disease management and provide a foundation for future large-scale clinical evaluation.

Table 5. Performance comparison of the proposed framework with existing IoT-based respiratory monitoring systems

Performance Metric	Existing IoT-Based Systems	Proposed Intelligent Alert Framework
Alert Accuracy (%)	78	85
Average Response Time (seconds)	5.2	2.8
Improvement in Inhaler Adherence (%)	20	40
False Alert Rate (%)	15	8

The comparison shown in Table 5 indicates that the proposed IoT-based intelligent alert framework demonstrates improved performance across all evaluated metrics. In particular, higher alert accuracy and reduced response time enable timely inhaler usage during high-risk conditions. The notable improvement in inhaler adherence highlights the effectiveness of personalized, context-aware alerts, while the reduced false alert rate minimizes unnecessary notifications and potential alert fatigue. Although the evaluation is based on a pilot-scale study and simulation-supported analysis, the results validate the feasibility and potential clinical relevance of the proposed framework.

7. ETHICAL, PRIVACY, AND REGULATORY CONSIDERATIONS IN IOT-BASED RESPIRATORY MONITORING

The deployment of IoT-based inhaler alert systems in respiratory disease management raises important ethical, privacy, and regulatory considerations, as these systems continuously collect and process sensitive health-related data. Physiological parameters such as oxygen saturation, heart rate, respiratory patterns, and inhaler usage behavior constitute personal health information and must be handled with strict safeguards to protect patient rights and confidentiality.

Patient Consent and Transparency: Ethical implementation of IoT-enabled respiratory monitoring systems requires informed patient consent. Patients and caregivers must be clearly informed about the type of data being collected, the purpose of data usage, and how alerts are generated. Transparent communication ensures patient trust and promotes sustained engagement with wearable devices and mobile health applications. In pediatric asthma monitoring, consent from parents or legal guardians is essential, along with age-appropriate communication to children when applicable.

Data Privacy and Security: To safeguard sensitive patient data, the proposed framework emphasizes secure data transmission and storage mechanisms. End-to-end encryption is employed during data transfer between sensors, edge devices, and cloud servers, reducing the risk of unauthorized access. Access control mechanisms and role-based authentication further ensure that only authorized healthcare professionals can view patient data. In addition, anonymization and pseudonymization techniques can be applied to datasets used for analytics or research purposes, minimizing privacy risks while enabling system improvement.

Regulatory Compliance: IoT-based healthcare systems must comply with regional and international data protection regulations. The proposed framework is designed to align with key regulatory standards, including the Health Insurance Portability and Accountability Act (HIPAA) for protected health information, the General Data Protection Regulation (GDPR) governing data privacy in the European Union, and the Digital Personal Data Protection (DPDP) Act in India. Compliance with these regulations ensures lawful data processing, patient rights protection, and accountability in digital healthcare delivery.

Ethical Use of Artificial Intelligence: The integration of machine learning algorithms for risk prediction and alert generation introduces additional ethical responsibilities. Algorithmic transparency and explainability are critical to avoid bias and ensure clinical trust. The proposed system incorporates rule-based thresholding alongside machine learning predictions, allowing alerts to remain interpretable and clinically meaningful. This hybrid approach supports ethical AI usage by enabling clinicians to understand and validate alert decisions.

Data Retention and Accountability: Clear policies on data retention and deletion are essential to ethical system deployment. Health data should be stored only for the duration necessary to support patient care and clinical evaluation. Audit trails and logging mechanisms can be implemented to track data access and system actions, ensuring accountability and supporting regulatory audits. By addressing ethical considerations, privacy safeguards, and regulatory compliance, the proposed IoT-based intelligent inhaler alert framework promotes responsible and trustworthy deployment in real-world healthcare settings. Incorporating these principles not only protects patients but also enhances system adoption, clinical acceptance, and long-term sustainability Ambrosi, E., & Tan, R. (2025).

8. COST, SCALABILITY, AND ACCESSIBILITY CONSIDERATIONS

The practical adoption of IoT-based respiratory disease management systems depends not only on technical performance but also on cost-effectiveness, scalability, and accessibility, particularly in resource-constrained healthcare environments. Respiratory conditions such as asthma and chronic obstructive pulmonary disease (COPD) are prevalent in both developed and developing regions, making affordability and ease of deployment critical factors.

Cost Considerations: The proposed intelligent inhaler alert framework is designed using commercially available, low-power sensors and standard communication modules such as Bluetooth Low Energy (BLE) and Wi-Fi. This design choice helps reduce hardware costs while maintaining reliable data acquisition. By leveraging cloud-based infrastructure and open-source software components, the system minimizes upfront investment and enables flexible pricing models, such as subscription-based or institution-supported deployments. Furthermore, integration with patients' existing smartphones reduces the need for dedicated monitoring hardware, lowering overall system cost.

Scalability of the Framework: The modular layered architecture of the proposed system supports scalability from individual patient monitoring to large-scale population-level deployment. Edge computing components allow preliminary data processing at the device level, reducing network bandwidth usage and cloud computation load. This makes the system suitable for scaling across hospitals, clinics, and community health programs without significant performance degradation. The framework can be extended to support additional sensors or analytics modules with minimal architectural modification.

Accessibility in Low-Resource Settings: To enhance accessibility, the proposed system emphasizes minimal infrastructure requirements and low energy consumption.

The use of battery-efficient wearable sensors enables long-term monitoring even in areas with limited power availability. Alerts delivered through mobile applications or SMS-based notifications can support patients in rural or remote regions where continuous internet connectivity may be unreliable. Such design considerations make the framework adaptable for public healthcare initiatives and community-based respiratory care programs.

Economic and Healthcare Impact: From a healthcare system perspective, improved inhaler adherence and early detection of respiratory risk conditions have the potential to reduce emergency hospital visits and long-term treatment costs. Although the current study focuses on feasibility and performance evaluation, the proposed framework lays the foundation for future cost-benefit and health economic analyses to quantify its impact in real-world clinical settings.

By addressing cost, scalability, and accessibility, the proposed IoT-based intelligent alert framework demonstrates its potential for practical deployment beyond controlled environments, supporting equitable and sustainable respiratory healthcare delivery.

9. CHALLENGES AND FUTURE DIRECTIONS

Despite the promising potential of IoT-based intelligent alert systems for respiratory disease management, several challenges remain that must be addressed to enable large-scale, real-world adoption. These challenges span technical, clinical, and socio-economic dimensions and also open avenues for future research and innovation.

System Reliability and Sensor Accuracy: IoT-based respiratory monitoring relies heavily on wearable sensors and smart inhalers for continuous data acquisition. Variations in sensor placement, environmental interference, and device calibration can affect data accuracy and reliability. Inconsistent data quality may lead to delayed or inappropriate alerts, potentially impacting patient trust and clinical usefulness. Future research should focus on sensor fusion techniques, self-calibrating devices, and adaptive algorithms that can compensate for noisy or missing data.

Battery Constraints and Long-Term Usability: Although advances in low-power communication protocols and energy-efficient sensors have improved battery life, wearable respiratory devices still face limitations in long-term operation. Frequent charging can discourage continuous use, particularly among elderly patients and children. Future developments may explore ultra-low-power architectures, optimized duty-cycling strategies, and energy-harvesting methods to support uninterrupted monitoring over extended periods.

Interoperability and Clinical Integration: Seamless integration with existing healthcare infrastructure, particularly Electronic Health Records (EHRs), remains a significant challenge. Differences in data standards, interoperability frameworks, and hospital information systems can hinder the effective use of IoT-generated data in clinical workflows. Future systems should adopt standardized data formats and interoperable APIs to ensure smooth integration and clinician acceptance.

Validation in Real-World Clinical Settings: While pilot studies and simulation-based evaluations demonstrate the feasibility of intelligent inhaler alert systems, large-scale clinical validation is still limited. Future work should include longitudinal studies involving diverse patient populations to evaluate clinical outcomes, adherence improvement, and reduction in exacerbation events. Such validation is essential for regulatory approval and widespread clinical adoption.

Emerging Trends and Future Research Directions: The integration of digital twins presents a promising future direction for personalized respiratory care. By continuously updating virtual patient models using real-time IoT data, clinicians can predict disease progression and optimize therapy decisions. Additionally, the incorporation of explainable artificial intelligence (XAI) can enhance clinical trust by making alert generation and risk predictions more transparent. Research into low-cost IoT architectures and cloud-edge hybrid models will further support deployment in resource-constrained settings.

Toward Global and Equitable Deployment: Ensuring accessibility across diverse socio-economic contexts remains a critical future challenge. Designing affordable, durable, and easy-to-use devices, along with patient education initiatives, will be essential for adoption in low- and middle-income regions. Collaborative efforts among researchers, healthcare providers, and policymakers can help translate IoT-based respiratory monitoring solutions into scalable public health interventions. Overall, addressing these challenges while leveraging emerging technologies will enable IoT-based intelligent alert systems to transition from experimental prototypes to reliable, clinically impactful solutions for respiratory disease management.

10. CONCLUSION

IoT-driven inhaler alert systems have emerged as a transformative solution in managing respiratory diseases, combining real-time environmental sensing, physiological monitoring, and intelligent data analysis. These systems empower patients by providing timely reminders to carry and use their inhalers, tailored to individual triggers and daily routines. By enhancing medication adherence and facilitating proactive intervention, IoT-based alerts help reduce the frequency and severity of asthma attacks, COPD exacerbations, and other respiratory events. Moreover, integrating these systems into everyday life fosters continuous monitoring without a significant burden on patients, improving overall quality of care and patient confidence in managing their conditions. The continued evolution of IoT technologies, combined with advanced analytics, machine learning models, and patient-centered design, will further refine the precision and effectiveness of inhaler alert systems. Innovations such as sensor fusion, predictive modeling, and digital twin simulations promise to enhance individualized therapy and provide clinicians with actionable insights for preventive care. As these systems become more accessible and integrated with electronic health records, they can revolutionize respiratory healthcare globally—delivering safer, more efficient, and equitable interventions for patients across diverse populations.

REFERENCES

Ambrosi, E., & Tan, R. (2025). Effectiveness of digital health interventions for chronic disease management in European primary care. *Computers in Biology and Medicine*, *145*, 105476. DOI: 10.1016/j.compbiomed.2022.105476

Anan, S. R., & Tan, R. (2021). Research and development of an IoT-based remote health monitoring system for asthmatic patients. *Journal of Medical Systems*, *45*(6), 1–10. DOI: 10.1007/s10916-021-01771-2

Aung, H., Tan, R., Flynn, C., Divall, P., Wright, A., Murphy, A., Shaw, D., Ward, T. J. C., & Greening, N. J. (2024). Digital remote maintenance inhaler adherence interventions in COPD: A systematic review and meta-analysis. *European Respiratory Review : an Official Journal of the European Respiratory Society*, *33*(174), 240136. DOI: 10.1183/16000617.0136-2024 PMID: 39631930

. Brennan, V., & Tan, R. (2021). A clinical perspective on the role of electronic devices in addressing poor treatment adherence in respiratory care. *rontiers in Medical Technology, 3*, 604475. DOI: 10.3389/fmedt.2021.604475

Chakraborty, A., Anik, M. I., & Rahman, M. M. (2023). Developing an IoT-enabled cost-effective asthma patient monitoring system: Integrating health and indoor environment data with statistical analysis and data visualization. *Science Progress*, *106*(4), 00368504231192542. DOI: 10.1177/00368504231192542

Duan, J., & van Boven, J. F. (2025). Experience of using electronic inhaler monitoring devices for asthma and COPD: A systematic review. *JMIR mHealth and uHealth*, *13*(1), e57645. DOI: 10.2196/57645 PMID: 40378281

Garin, N., Zárate-Tamames, B., Gras-Martín, L., Milà, R., Crespo-Lessmann, A., Curto, E., Hernández, M., Mestres, C., & Plaza, V. (2023). Clinical impact of electronic monitoring devices of inhalers in adults with asthma or COPD: A systematic review and meta-analysis. *Pharmaceuticals (Basel, Switzerland)*, *16*(3), 414. DOI: 10.3390/ph16030414 PMID: 36986513

Iqbal, F. M., & Khan, M. M. (2021). A systematic review and meta-analysis of digital alerting systems in remote monitoring. *npj. Digital Medicine*, *4*(1), 1–9. DOI: 10.1038/s41746-020-00378-0 PMID: 33398041

Lodewyk, K., & Tan, R. (2025). Wearables research for continuous monitoring of patient health in non-hospital settings. *PLOS Digital Health*, *4*(1), e0000860. DOI: 10.1371/journal.pdig.0000860 PMID: 40343891

Ologundudu, L., & Tan, R. (2025). Patient-facing digital inhalers for asthma: A systematic review and meta-analysis. *The Journal of Allergy and Clinical Immunology. In Practice*, *13*(1), 1–9. DOI: 10.1016/j.jaip.2024.10.004 PMID: 40312010

Pinnock, H., Hui, C. Y., & van Boven, J. F. (2023). Implementation of digital home monitoring and management of respiratory disease. *npj. Digital Medicine*, *6*(1), 1–13. DOI: 10.1038/s41746-023-00897-2 PMID: 36596833

Uzzaman, M. N., & van Boven, J. F. (2024). Effectiveness of asynchronous digital health interventions for asthma: A mixed methods systematic review. *Journal of Medical Internet Research*, *26*(1), e57708. DOI: 10.2196/57708 PMID: 39626243

Wartenberg, C., & Khor, Y. H. (2025). Clinical benefits and risks of remote patient monitoring: A systematic overview. *BMC Health Services Research*, *25*(1), 12292. DOI: 10.1186/s12913-025-12292-w PMID: 39849519

Chapter 10
Blockchain for Healthcare Data Security

Yashwant Kumar Kolli
http://orcid.org/0009-0003-8634-3265
Cognizant Technology Solutions US Corp., USA

Karthik Kushala
http://orcid.org/0009-0005-7851-7039
Taylor Corporation, USA

Venkataramesh Induru
http://orcid.org/0009-0005-6530-4296
Piorion Solutions Inc., USA

Priyadarshini Radhakrishnan
http://orcid.org/0009-0001-0709-2337
IBM Corporation, USA

Vijai Anand Ramar
http://orcid.org/0009-0008-1670-7170
Delta Dental Insurance Company, USA

R. Premalatha
Department of Computer Science and Engineering, Tagore Institute of Engineering and Technology, Salem, India

ABSTRACT

Blockchain technology is juxtaposing the security of health-related information, solving those long-standing problems in healthcare data management. This paper highlights 8 main uses: cryptographic patient data sharing with permissioned access for any type of individual; immutable medical records to ensure data integrity; decentralized health information exchange such that single points of failure cannot exist. Blockchain also strengthens patient identity, consent management with on-chain dynamic access control. Further applications include bringing transparency to the medical supply chain, ensuring traceability in clinical trials, or preventing insurance billing and claim fraud. Since data are distributed across different blockchain nodes, decryption is allowed only with cryptographic keys held by patients, thereby reducing the risk of breach that plagues typical centralized systems. Clinical indications constitute an increasingly urgent need for blockchain in health care in order to allow for secure, efficient, and patient-centred data management.

DOI: 10.4018/979-8-2600-0981-9.ch010

1. INTRODUCTION

In this way, data digitalization has transformed every sector, including health care (M. El Khatib et al., 2022). This, however, presents security issues (H. Tabrizchi and M. Kuchaki Rafsanjani, 2020). Healthcare data is private information that has immense value and is highly vulnerable to any mischief or unauthorized access (A. I. Newaz et al., 2021). Hacker attacks are primarily targeted toward such data sets (S. Chng et al., 2022).

The technology disruption in the healthcare industry has caused security breaches to go through the roof in the past few years (Y. Perwej et al., 2022). The U.S. Department of Health and Human Services reports that data breaches exposed over 100 million health records in a single year, making improved data protection measures imperative (C. Liu et al., 2023). The existing traditional security frameworks have always limped, maybe because the modern cyber threats have come into existence, insider-right-of-threat problems parallel fragmentation of data systems, and lack of interoperability with healthcare platforms (Y. Perwej et al., 2021).

These problems make blockchain technology appealing as a means of enhancing healthcare data security (M. Attaran, 2022). Lately, it has been realized that this application fits well into a scenario where there's sensitive data requiring an amazing level of protection, ensuring data integrity, and providing mutual trust between stakeholders-though it was first developed for and applied in cryptocurrencies (M. R. Kabir, 2020).

(H. Saeed et al., 2022) First, they look at the key challenges faced in securing the health informatics (D. M. Walker et al., 2021), and then also analyse in detail what kind of solutions blockchain's key features and applications can offer to address the issues within the healthcare sector (P. Ratta et al., 2021).

The Digitalization in healthcare is becoming popular (M. Senbekov et al., 2020), (R. Agrawal and S. Prabakaran, 2020). These are usually produced and operated upon over complex systems (J. Tantray et al., 2024). From a very practical perspective, big changes in medicine had an impact on improvement in clinical results, patient engagement, and ease of healthcare delivery (S. Marzban et al., 2022); however, along with this transformation came several new threats related to privacy, security, and system interoperability (S. Mendhurwar and R. Mishra, 2021). Healthcare digitization has led to the large-scale generation of sensitive data such as electronic health records, laboratory results, medical images, genomic data, and prescription histories.

Data breaches in the healthcare industry have become more frequent and sophisticated in recent years (A. H. Almulihi et al, 2022). The reports from cybersecurity outfits and regulatory agencies have always stated healthcare among the most subjected sectors to data breaches. For instance, more than 130 million people alone were affected by breaches of PHI in 2023 in the United States, with incidents ranging from ransomware attacks to unauthorized accesses by internal personnel (C. Dameff et al., 2023). Such breaches affect the privacy of patients and also cause financial loss, damage to the goodwill of healthcare organizations, and possibly also risks to patient safety (X. Gu and M. Deng, 2024).

The matter of data security in healthcare is being increasingly pressing in the face of fragmented, siloed healthcare systems (R. Ranchal et al., 2020). Different organizations operate on incompatible platforms, hindering seamless data exchange and thereby increasing security vulnerabilities. Also, central storage facilities, being single points of failure, attract malicious actors (S. L. Kodjiku et al., 2023). The risk of insiders within organizations either collaborating with unintended entities to misuse sensitive data amplifies the cases (A. Habbal et al., 2024). However, models that really do security, while conforming to HIPAA or GDPR regulations, are reactive rather than proactive, having zero guarantees about end-to-end trust, transparency, and resilience (S. R. Sangannagari, 2024).

Therefore, blockchains have the revolutionary ability to fundamentally rethink how health data is secured (K. Yeung, 2021). Data may be recorded safely and transparently because to this technology, which is a decentralised ledger system that makes data unchangeable across several network nodes. Data entry in an immutable system cannot be changed, yet with cryptographic protection, the system allows for a unique user identity (S. Mittal et al., 2022); with distributed consensus, one can provide protection against false data entry (L. Yan et al., 2021). These features provide a fundamentally new approach to managing how sensitive data is accessed and verified (B. K. Gudepu and D. S. Jaladi, 2022). In this approach, by empowering patients to manage their own data, eliminating the need for centralised third parties, and enhancing auditability, blockchain could solve a number of the present issues with healthcare information security (F. Ullah et al., 2024).

(Z. et al., 2023) First, it studies the types of healthcare data and the challenges peculiar to their protection (J. Shahid et al., 2022). Next, it introduces the technology of blockchain and considers how the evolution of healthcare ecosystems with blockchain could address significant security issues, such as data breaches, insider threats, interoperability, and trust (E. R. D. Villarreal et al., 2023). To illustrate blockchain's potential in healthcare settings, pilot projects and actual implementations should be documented (W. Y. Ng et al., 2021). The chapter would want to discuss the existing and upcoming opportunities in digital health as well as how blockchain technology may enhance the security of healthcare data.

In order to give readers a comprehensive grasp of the alternatives, this chapter uses a case study approach to analyse regulatory compliance, namely HIPAA. This thus makes it possible to thoroughly examine blockchain-based systems in light of the guidelines for safeguarding private health data (P. Esmaeilzadeh, 2022). Prior-to and during the analysis, such issues as privacy of data, integrity of data, control of data, auditability, and patient consent were considered. Through the case study (N. A. Charoo et al., 2023), it was able to discuss blockchain mechanisms such as cryptographic encryption, decentralized control, and immutable audit trails, which could directly implement HIPAA Privacy and Security Rules, creating maybe a framework for compliance and improved data governance in the health environment (A. C. Yallop et al., 2021).

One offered example scrutinized in this chapter involves a healthcare provider attempting a blockchain patient data management system. In this case study, blockchain is used to ensure the unauthorized personnel cannot access EHRs, with every access event transparently captured in an immutable ledger. Such a system provides a layer of accountability and secures patient information from unauthorized access, enabling patients to control the viewing rights to their information-all paramount to HIPAA compliance. In looking through the lens of this case, the chapter links particular blockchain capabilities to HIPAA provisions while outlining advantages of blockchain such as better security and transparency, as well as limitations like scalability and infrastructure integration. Through this process, blockchain is critically assessed for how ready it is in the most practical scenario of the healthcare field.

Additionally, the case study explores the blockchain-EHR interface in greater detail, especially with regard to data security improvements. The blockchain system makes it easy to track down unauthorised access by recording each attempt at entry into patient records in an immutable ledger. In addition to safeguarding private health information against security breaches, this kind of openness in data access is also compliant with laws pertaining to data protection, which are required by law. One example of this is HIPAA. The privacy and autonomy features of healthcare are strengthened on the conscience by allowing patients to select who can access their information through permissioned access and cryptographic encryption.

The primarily intended for researchers, postgraduate students, and professionals working in healthcare informatics, cybersecurity, and blockchain-based system development. The discussion combines conceptual explanations of blockchain security principles with practical implementation aspects such as data preprocessing, machine learning-based clinical analysis, and regulatory compliance considerations. Therefore, the chapter is designed for readers who possess foundational knowledge in computer science, information security, or digital healthcare systems rather than general audiences. At the same time, explanatory descriptions of healthcare workflows and regulatory requirements are included so that healthcare practitioners and interdisciplinary researchers can understand the practical relevance of the proposed framework. By maintaining a balance between theoretical concepts and applied methodology, the chapter appropriately addresses an academic and technical audience interested in secure healthcare data management systems.

Novel Contributions of This Chapter

This chapter proposes a novel blockchain-based secure healthcare data management framework integrated with AI-driven ECG classification. The key contributions include: (1) a permissioned blockchain architecture for secure patient data sharing, (2) smart contract-based dynamic consent management, (3) integration of CNN-based ECG analytics, and (4) analysis of scalability and interoperability challenges for real-world healthcare implementation.

1.1 Problem Statement

Hackers can now access sensitive healthcare data, including electronic health records, patient imaging, and prescription information, as a result of the quick digitisation of healthcare systems (L. A. Jawad, 2024). Existing security frameworks are mostly unable to handle the new threats posed by fragmented data storage and issues of compliance such as those argued by HIPAA (N. AllahRakha, 2024). A few others are those that involve unauthorized access, interoperability issues, and single points of failure in central databases ceaselessly afflicting the industry (I. Yaqoob et al., 2022). Although telecommunication and information networks have progressed, the existing method of healthcare-data handling and transmission remains susceptible to exploitation. Because of its decentralized and unchangeable structure, blockchain technology may be the answer to all of these problems. It is useful in theory, but the reality of its deployment confronts issues surrounding scalability, deployment, maintaining architecture, and the legalities of healthcare data management. This paper looks at the capability of blockchain to solve very complex security problems plaguing the healthcare arena, thereby enhancing existing frameworks like HIPAA and acting as a disruptive technology whose prevention capabilities are focused on data breach and unauthorized access (M. Zarour et al., 2020).

The organization of the study is as follows. Section 2 presents the problem statement and research objectives. Section 3 reviews related literature on blockchain-based healthcare data security. Section 4 describes the proposed methodology and blockchain framework. Section 5 discusses regulatory compliance using HIPAA. Section 6 presents the experimental results and discussion, followed by the conclusion and future research directions.

1.2 Objectives

Examine how blockchain technology might enhance the safety of medical records and pinpoint the difficulties in maintaining health informatics.

Investigate how key features of a blockchain cryptographic encryption, decentralized control, immutable records defend against these challenges in healthcare.

Explore the dimensions of addressing patient privacy, consent management, and data integrity that are practically applied in or represent possibilities for blockchain in healthcare.

Discuss a few case studies and pilot projects that demonstrate how blockchain technology can be applied to safeguard healthcare data and enhance system transparency.

2. LITERATURE SURVEY

According to Zaabar et al (B. Zaabar et al., 2021), security and privacy in electronic health records (EHRs) continue to be crucial for patients as well as medical professionals. Sensitive health information is made public by a breach in a healthcare system. Typically, this is kept in a centralised database, which has vulnerabilities that are making hacks more frequent. Therefore, the study uses blockchain technology to try to improve the security and privacy of EHRs. In order to solve the issues related to central storage, this research study suggests an innovative approach that makes use of decentralised databases. Orbit DB with IPFS is the name of the decentralised database used to hold patient electronic health records. Additionally, with the aid of Hyperledger composer, they are maintaining hashes of the stored data and regulating access when the data is requested via the Hyperledger fabric blockchain network. By avoiding the well-known security vulnerabilities in widely used smart healthcare systems, this blockchain-based design seeks to improve healthcare management systems.

(A. A. Khan et al., 2023) claim that the industrial IoT-Ilott has grown more appealing due to the fact that it offers a self-governing method of system configuration for interoperability with regard to application-level connectivity. . It is used in conjunction with medical sensing in the field of e-healthcare to record, analyse, investigate, store, and conduct daily patient transactions in real-time. As a result, Ilott and E-healthcare provide an analytical platform that can handle massive volumes of data at the lowest cost of scalable storage allowed by the cloud. However, any patient's private information is still at risk when records are exchanged via centralised server-based systems. Consequently, when node connectivity issues increase, so do concurrent data sharing and delivery problems. The article offers three different ways to solve the problem. Using blockchain-distributed ledger technology, the paper first suggested a novel and safe design for the E-healthcare system with regard to data security, which it called the Blockchain-based Healthcare Internet of Things.

According to (R. Kumar et al., 2022) the healthcare sector is very interested in a number of AI and blockchain technology features, including the immutability of data stored on a blockchain. Numerous intriguing Internet of Things applications are being researched. Blockchain and AI will improve healthcare and biomedical data ledgers, accelerating biological and clinical research based on the Internet of Things. These studies take into account important aspects of blockchain and artificial intelligence, like decentralised administration, immutable audit trails, data authenticity, resilience, enhanced security, and—most importantly—the restoration of charter rights. Blockchain technology and artificial intelligence can be used in new and creative ways to improve the current standards for the management, sharing, processing, analysis, and classification of medical data based on outcomes. Blockchain technology is transforming IoT-based healthcare through improved operational efficiency, access control, technological breakthroughs, privacy protection, and safe operational data procedures. This chapter presents a blockchain-based and artificial intelligence (AI) approach to enhancing data security in the context of smart cities.

According to (H. Liu et at., 2020) In fields including banking, supply chain management, the food industry, energy, the Internet, and healthcare, blockchain is currently emerging as a reliable and safe platform for safe information exchange. In general, a decentralised database with immutable data entries is comparable to a blockchain. This new technology is attempting to disrupt a number of data-intensive businesses, including the medical sector. But blockchain, or distributed ledger technology, is a revolution in information recording and sharing that does away with the requirement for a trustworthy third party. This paper proposes an Improved Biomedical Security system (BDL-IBS) based on blockchain and distributed ledger technology to protect data and privacy in healthcare applications.

The Medical data, according to the author (P. Xi et al.,2022), includes patient records that are crucial for their ongoing care and study. However, these need to be discussed and kept private. Because blockchain technology is decentralised and impermeable, it has a tremendous impact on the healthcare data industry. This essay's goal is to examine how blockchain technology has developed in the healthcare industry from a variety of angles. They examine several uses of blockchain technology, such as federated learning based on blockchain, blockchain and the Internet of Medical Things, and blockchain-based electronic medical record sharing.

According to (A. K. Singh et al., 2021), the popularity of smart healthcare has consistently gained attention due to the internet's spectacular development. Smart healthcare makes use of cutting-edge technologies to completely revamp the conventional medical system, increasing its effectiveness, convenience, and personalisation. Regrettably, one major problem with smart healthcare systems is protecting medical data. It turns into a basic problem that calls for the creation of creative, effective solutions to meet healthcare needs and make secure healthcare delivery and transfer possible. This paper offers a thorough analysis of cutting-edge methods for protecting health data and their most current developments to solve issues in practical applications. An overview of common blockchain-based security methods for medical applications, including biometrics, watermarking, and cryptography.

Data are the most valuable resources in all emerging industries as every company shifts to cloud storage, yet data security is difficult in many domains according to Hasselgren et al (A. Hasselgren et al., 2020). One of the main industries dealing with extremely sensitive data in this regard is the healthcare sector. Prescription data, medical insurance data, and patient medical information are the main categories of data that these specific healthcare domains handle. Because the data stored in electronic health records is sensitive, information security is essential. Two fundamental mathematical concepts—hash and cryptography—were used in the development of the blockchain. Distributed and replicated across all networks, blockchain is an immutable ledger that is not governed by a centralised authority. The safe storage and retrieval of medical data is described in this article. Given that the US international blockchain is occasionally thought of as a single-node blockchain, the method is a world-rank tracker. Real-time blockchain access is available to all aid service providers, and the EHR is capable of securely storing and managing patient data.

According to (N. Tariq et al., 2020), IoT is now present in practically every aspect of life. Smart health is the key area that makes substantial use of IoT infrastructures and solutions. However, with the introduction of wearable and mobile technology, the smart health-care system advances up the healthcare value chain. As a result, a great deal of health information is exchanged for better, faster, and more accurate diagnosis. However, a variety of malicious attacks and security flaws, such as forgery, manipulation, privacy leaks, and more, can seriously compromise smart healthcare systems. Blockchain technology has recently been put up as a viable option to combat these kinds of problems and breaches. In addition to the security requirements of such domains, the study provides a contemporary assessment of the various difficulties and unresolved problems arising from conventional security methods in the smart health industry. It looks ahead to the potential of blockchain technology as a practical security solution in addition to identifying potential issues in the healthcare industry and assessing several blockchain-based security solutions to address these issues.

According to Abu-elezz et al. (2020), healthcare data sharing plays a crucial role in national development and in enhancing patient outcomes through informed clinical decisions. While cloud platforms efficiently store and manage vast medical datasets, dependence on third-party providers introduces potential security and privacy risks. To overcome these challenges, the authors propose a blockchain-based framework that leverages smart contracts to secure data during transmission. Their approach integrates IoT-enabled health monitoring systems and facilitates the protected exchange of laboratory reports, clinical trial data, reimbursements, and medical records, while enabling more flexible and secure metadata sharing.

According to Rani et al. (2022), effective healthcare relies on secure, controlled, and transparent data sharing, where patients retain ownership and authority over their medical records. Blockchain technology supports this objective by providing a decentralized, tamper-resistant, and auditable framework for managing health information. Unlike traditional access control mechanisms, which may be vulnerable to evolving cyberthreats in cloud environments, blockchain enhances security through distributed validation and cryptographic protection. To address privacy concerns, the authors proposed a lightweight blockchain-based framework tailored for cloud systems. Their solution integrates smart contracts to automate secure processes, while encrypting and pseudonymizing patient data cost-effectively and efficiently.

According to (Shaikh et al., 2025), Healthcare information systems face challenges such as delayed data sharing, privacy breaches, and limited patient control over medical data. Blockchain technology is considered a promising, decentralised, and secure solution to address these issues. This study systematically reviews real-world blockchain-based healthcare implementations and evaluates their effectiveness using PRISMA guidelines. The review also identifies key challenges and highlights future research directions, including scalability, security, integration, privacy preservation, and ethical considerations.

(Nguyen et al., 2023) Blockchain applications in supply chain management have recently attracted significant attention in research. This study aims to synthesise existing literature and identify key research themes and future directions using a data-driven review approach. Text mining and LDA-based topic modelling are used to analyse full-text articles, reducing bias and time consumption compared to traditional systematic reviews. The review identifies major themes such as traceability, sustainability, manufacturing systems, logistics, and healthcare supply chains, and suggests future research directions including integration with emerging technologies, decentralised systems, and environmental and social impact assessment.

(Fan et al., 2026) Acute ischemic stroke is a major global health problem that requires rapid and accurate diagnosis to ensure effective treatment. Artificial intelligence is considered a promising approach to improve diagnostic accuracy and clinical decision-making, but data fragmentation and strict privacy regulations limit AI model development. This review examines collaborative AI approaches such as federated learning and privacy-preserving computation that enable decentralised model training while maintaining patient confidentiality. The study highlights that collaborative AI can improve model generalisability, fairness, and ethical compliance, providing a scalable and privacy-conscious framework for stroke diagnosis and management.

While existing studies extensively discuss the security, immutability, and decentralization benefits of blockchain in healthcare, most works focus primarily on conceptual frameworks or isolated applications such as EHR storage, IoT integration, or consent management. However, limited research provides an integrated evaluation combining secure blockchain-based data governance with real-time clinical analytics and performance validation. Additionally, scalability constraints, interoperability challenges with legacy healthcare standards (e.g., HL7 and FHIR), and regulatory alignment issues remain insufficiently addressed in prior studies. Many approaches emphasize theoretical security advantages without critically examining deployment overhead, system integration complexity, and operational feasibility in real healthcare environments. Therefore, this study aims to bridge these gaps by proposing a structured framework that combines blockchain-enabled secure data management with AI-driven clinical analysis, while also discussing practical deployment limitations and system-level constraints.

3. METHODOLOGY

This study explores blockchain as a solution for healthcare data security (Figure 1). ECG data from wearable devices are preprocessed through cleaning, normalization, feature extraction, and dimensionality reduction using PCA and t-SNE. Blockchain enables secure, permissioned sharing of immutable records with dynamic consent and identity management, ensuring HIPAA compliance. Finally, CNN models classify ECG signals to evaluate overall system performance.

Figure 1. Workflow Diagram for Cardiology Healthcare

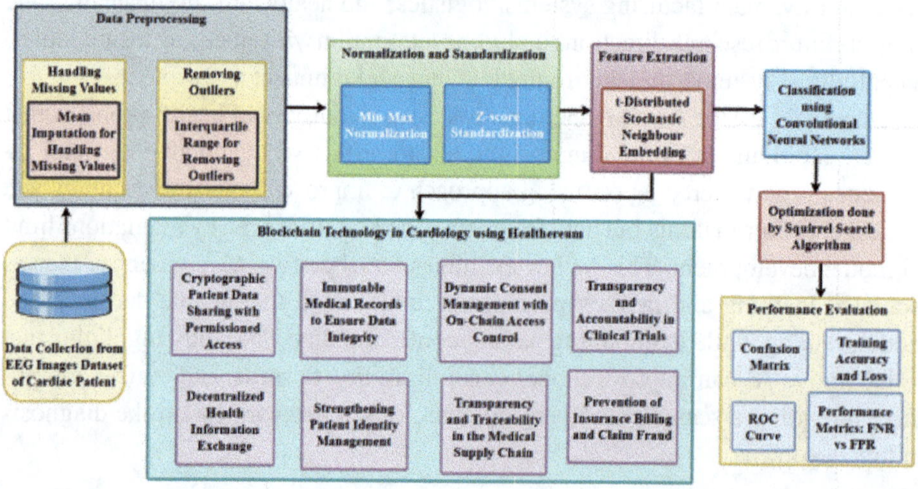

3.1 Data Collection

The traditional "ECG Analysis" provided by evilspirit05 consists of a collection of electrocardiogram signals from individuals suffering from certain cardiac conditions: both normal heartbeat and abnormal heartbeat disturbances. And there is also a variation of heart problems on offer, as family rhythm disturbances, atrial fibrillations, and arrhythmias. The signals from the ECGs were collected by means of a wearable health monitoring module, thereby affording it a wink toward real-world applicability. This data would be basic for cardiac health research and thus will be used in the determining blockchain technologies and AI for negotiating toward data security and supporting automated diagnosis of heart-related conditions via advanced signal analysis and pattern recognition. https://www.kaggle.com/datasets/evilspirit05/ecg-analysis/data

3.2 Preprocessing

The Data cleaning and structuring are parts of data processing generally referred to as preprocessing which may be undertaken before analysis, machine learning, or any other data processing activity. In order to prepare the raw data for the type of analysis or model that must be developed, preprocessing aims to make the data clean, consistent, and ordered. Numerous issues are addressed in this step, such as missing values, noise, outliers, and irrelevant features that impair the analysis.

3.2.1 Handling Missing Values

One is filled in with missing values due to incomplete data entry errors or the acquisition system not collecting all the required information. If it remains untreated, the absence of data would act to bias the analysis or reach inaccurate conclusions; thus, it must be handled at the preprocessing stage from time to time.

3.2.1.1 Mean Imputation for Handling Missing Values

The Mean imputation is a very basic way of dealing with missing values in a dataset when it replaces missing data with the mean of the available data. This method is typically used when there is a very small amount of missing data and it is assumed that the data is missing completely at random (MCAR). A missing value on the mean of the otherwise observed values preserves the overall distribution of observed values and the dataset's sample size. In contrast, mean imputation may reduce the variance in the data, and particularly where such data points are extreme values or outliers, and hence results in bias. The mean imputation formula thus eqn. (1).

$$\text{Imputed value} = \frac{\sum_{i=1}^{n} x_i}{n} \quad (1)$$

Here, x_i is the non-missing value at the ith position (or index) in the column; n is the total number of non-missing values in that column; the summation $\sum_{i=1}^{n} x_i$ means at add up all the non-missing values for that column, where i ranges from 1 to n.

3.2.2 Removing Outliers using Interquartile Range

The Outliers can intervene with analysis, especially in healthcare analytics, by deviating too much from the rest of the data. On the other hand, an extreme-high or low value in an attribute-think 200 years for age or 300/180 mmHg for blood pressure-may divert all the attention of statistical analyses and machine learning models, eventually forcing them to come to incorrect conclusions. Outliers in the healthcare dataset might have been caused by an erroneous data input or faulty sensors, or it might represent a real case with some rare medical condition. One of the most often used methods for locating and perhaps removing outliers is the Interquartile Range (IQR) approach. An outlier could be any data point that is either above or below a certain threshold. In essence, this approach calculates the separation between the first quartile (Q1) and third quartile (Q3) of the data. The following are the formulas that identify outliers using the IQR as eqn. (2).

$$\begin{aligned} \text{Lower Bound} &= Q1 - 1.5 \times \text{IQR} \\ \text{Upper Bound} &= Q3 + 1.5 \times \text{IQR} \end{aligned} \quad (2)$$

Here, $Q1$ is the first quartile (25th percentile); $Q3$ is the third quartile (75th percentile); IQR is the Interquartile Range ($Q3 - Q1$).

3.2.3 Normalization and Standardization

Healthcare datasets often contain variables measured in different units, which can affect model performance when larger values dominate analysis. Normalization and standardization address this issue (Eqns. 3 and 4). Normalization scales values to a fixed range, typically 0 to 1, while standardization transforms data to a mean of 0 and standard deviation of 1. These methods improve regression, clustering, and neural network performance.

a) Min-Max Normalization

The Reform-class Normalization method linearly scales the data between zero and one by first subtracting from a value in the attribute array the minimum of the feature's values. To complete scaling, divide this result by the difference between the highest and minimum values of the feature. By putting all features on a same footing, this scaling keeps one feature from overpowering the others. Scale is especially crucial for models like Support Vector Machines and K-Nearest Neighbours due of its sensitivity.

$$X_{normalized} = \frac{X - X_{min}}{X_{max} - X_{min}} \tag{3}$$

Here, X is the original value; X_{min} is the minimum value of the feature; X_{max} is the maximum value of the feature.

b) Z-score Standardization

The data is scaled with respect to the standard deviation and centred around the mean using the Z-score standardisation approach, also known as standard scaling. In essence, it modifies data so that its standard deviation is one and its mean is zero.

$$X_{standardized} = \frac{X - \mu}{\sigma} \tag{4}$$

Here, X is the original value; μ is the mean of the feature; σ is the standard deviation of the feature.

3.3 Feature Extraction

Feature extraction transforms raw healthcare data into meaningful attributes that improve a model's expressiveness. It converts basic information, such as visit dates into age or detailed histories into broader risk categories, enabling detection of high-level patterns. By reducing complexity and organizing data effectively, feature extraction enhances pattern recognition, especially when handling complex or unstructured healthcare datasets, improving overall model performance.

3.3.1 Dimensionality Reduction Techniques

Dimensionality reduction is essential for high-dimensional healthcare data such as EHRs, medical images, and sensor time-series. Techniques like Principal Component Analysis (PCA) and t-SNE reduce features while preserving important information. PCA creates uncorrelated components that retain maximum variance, handling correlated variables effectively. t-SNE visualizes complex relationships in lower dimensions. These methods improve model efficiency, reduce complexity, and enhance interpretability.

3.3.2 t-Distributed Stochastic Neighbour Embedding

The t-SNE approach is being actively used to minimise dimensions as much as possible in order to aid in the visualisation of the high-dimensional data in two or three dimensions. This approach differs from the others in that it preserves local structure, which ensures that similar sites in the lower dimension remain close to each other. The Kullback-Leibler divergence between the pairwise similarity probability distribution in an initial high-dimension space and the counterpart distribution in a low-dimension space is clearly reduced using t-SNE.

Equation (5) illustrates the Kullback-Leibler divergence between the probability distributions P (in the high-dimensional space) and Q (in the low-dimensional space).

$$\mathrm{KL}\left(P\|Q\right) = \sum_i \sum_j P_{ij} \log \frac{P_{ij}}{Q_{ij}} \tag{5}$$

Here, P_{ij} represents the probability of pairwise similarity between points i and j in the high-dimensional space; Q_{ij} represents the probability of pairwise similarity between points i and j in the low-dimensional space; the goal is to minimize this divergence, ensuring that similar points in the high-dimensional space are mapped to nearby points in the lower-dimensional space.

3.4 Blockchain Technology in Cardiology

Blockchain is a secure, transparent, and decentralized data management system with significant potential in cardiology healthcare. It supports clinical research, organ transplant tracking, and secure medical record sharing between hospitals. Its immutable ledger ensures data integrity, prevents unauthorized alterations, and restricts access to authorized users through cryptographic encryption. Blockchain enhances clinical trial traceability, secures medical supply chains, and reduces fraud. Dynamic consent management empowers patients to control data access, strengthening privacy, trust, efficiency, and system reliability.

3.4.1 Blockchain Architecture Types in Healthcare

Blockchain systems can be categorized into different architectural types based on their governance, access control, and deployment models. Understanding these blockchain architectures is essential for designing secure and scalable healthcare data management systems.

Public Blockchain

Public blockchains are open and permissionless networks where anyone can participate in transaction validation and data access. Examples include Bitcoin and Ethereum. Although public blockchains offer high transparency and decentralization, they are less suitable for healthcare applications due to privacy concerns and regulatory constraints associated with sensitive patient data.

Private Blockchain

Private blockchains are controlled by a single organization and provide restricted access to authorized participants. These blockchains ensure high security and data privacy, making them suitable for hospital-based electronic health record (EHR) systems. However, they offer limited decentralization compared to public blockchains.

Consortium (Federated) Blockchain

Consortium blockchains are governed by a group of trusted organizations such as hospitals, insurance providers, and regulatory bodies. This architecture balances decentralization and privacy, making it highly suitable for inter-organizational healthcare data sharing while maintaining regulatory compliance.

Hybrid Blockchain

Hybrid blockchains combine features of both public and private architectures. Sensitive healthcare data can be stored in private networks, while metadata or audit logs can be stored on public chains to ensure transparency and traceability. Hybrid architectures provide flexibility, scalability, and enhanced security for healthcare applications.

Suitability of Blockchain Architectures for Healthcare

Among the different architectures, private and consortium blockchains are considered the most appropriate for healthcare environments due to strict privacy regulations such as HIPAA and GDPR. These architectures provide controlled access, enhanced security, and compliance with healthcare data governance requirements.

3.4.2 Cryptographic Patient Data Sharing with Permissioned Access

The Patient data sharing and storing are secured cryptographically by blockchain technology, whereby confidential healthcare information is passed only between consenting parties. With cryptographic encryption, patients retain control over the health data, giving healthcare organizations, insurers, or any other entity access only by explicit patient agreement. The blockchain uses a permissioned method to access patient records, allowing trusted third-party viewers to view or erase them in real time. Leaving the foundations of trust, security, and patient autonomy intact assures patients' confidence in their hands. To name a few, some of the key advantages are protecting sensitive patient data, providing real-time control over access, and essentially eliminating the risk from unauthorized access.

3.4. Immutable Medical Records to Ensure Data Integrity

One of blockchain's key features is its limited mutability, which means that records cannot be changed or tampered with after being entered. In healthcare, this protects medical records from any form of alteration, including diagnoses, test results, or treatment histories. The blockchain creates an immutable and tamper-proof ledger of every interaction that a patient might have with a healthcare provider, thus making sure that medical data stay protected in their integrity. This reduces many opportunities for fraud, medical errors, or miscommunications. The major advantages are securing data from any tampering while also building a trust in the validity of medical records; an immutable audit trail is also created for patient interactions.

3.4.4 Decentralized Health Information Exchange

The Centralized systems in the past put the availability of the main database at risk due to system failures or cyberattacks. Blockchain solution, with its decentralized mode of health information exchange, distributes patient data over several nodes, thereby removing any single point of failure and, hence, building resilience into the system against attacks, data breaches, or functioning failures. Every member participates in the blockchain network by holding an identical copy of the data, so continuous availability is assured-records may be accessed whenever needed. Since patient records are readily available, the primary advantages are the prevention of disruptions in data availability, the absence of single points of failure, and the advantages of continuous care.

3.4.5 Strengthening Patient Identity Management

Through Blockchain, patient identity management is enhanced by the formation of secure, immutable digital identities for each patient, which are legally recognized across multiple healthcare providers. This open-ID and identity verification mechanism also provides protection from identity theft, misidentifications, and frauds. Being decentralized, no single entity owns patient identity information and, therefore, cannot abuse it or grant access to unauthorized persons. It hence creates benefits that enhance patient root identification accuracy to prevent identity theft and fraud while managing personal healthcare information from one or several other healthcare providers.

3.4.6 Dynamic Consent Management with On-Chain Access Control

Dynamic consent management is a major feature that separates blockchain operation within the healthcare industry. It enables patients to outrightly give or deny consent to medical data sharing at any point in time, enabling them to have some say in who is accessing their information. Blockchain enforces such consent, i.e., health professionals without such given consent may never access patient data. So, it strengthens medical privacy, supports autonomy, and enhances data protection law compliance. The outmatching benefits include real-time consent management, transparent tracking of consent history, and enhanced data privacy for patients.

3.4.7 Transparency and Traceability in the Medical Supply Chain

A medical supply chain's transparency and traceability can be enhanced by a blockchain. The items are guaranteed to be authentic and compliant with regulations by codifying each record-of-legitimacy for each stage of the manufacturing, distribution, and sale of pharmaceuticals and medical equipment. This same kind of visibility fights counterfeiting and ensures that medical supplies are safe and effective since the last step in the chain is devoted to patient safety. It is from the Sellar Law School perspective that the immutable nature of blockchain guarantees top security of documentation of the product journey from manufacturer via distributor to healthcare provider, thus promoting health safety for patients. Some of the benefits comprise of eliminating counterfeit drugs, ensuring product safety, and bolstering regulatory compliance.

3.4.8 Transparency and Accountability in Clinical Trials

Blockchain's main goal in the field of clinical trials is to increase transparency by securely storing all trial data—including patient recruitment, treatment plans, outcomes, and adverse events—on an unchangeable blockchain. They cannot alter or forge such data; thereby, the trial sponsor is held liable for the verity of clinical results. Since earning stakeholders' confidence-from patients, to regulators-has always been an uphill task, the upgrading of trial data with blockchain gives the assurance of their trustworthiness. Listed below are a few of the advantages/product features of blockchain: maintaining tamper-proof trial results; and ensuring responsibility of sponsors and researchers; enhance trust on clinical trial data.

3.4.9 Prevention of Insurance Billing and Claim Fraud

Such billing and insurance claims fraud comes first upon any health care inefficiency and loss. This fraud prevention mechanism of blockchain is by keeping a public record that is immutable for all claims and billing transactions. In one verifiable instance, services were rendered, and therefore a fraudulent claim could hardly be undetected. Other than this, the billing can be further streamlined with blockchain wherein smart contracts can be embedded to automatically settle claims. The main advantages here are the transparency of billing, prevention of fraud, and ease of filing for claims and reimbursements.

3.5 HIPAA Protect Patient health Record from Theft

The Health Insurance Portability and Accountability Act (HIPAA) protect patient health information from theft, loss, and unauthorized access (Figure 2). It mandates safeguards for electronic health information through the Privacy and Security Rules. The Transaction and Code Set Rule standardizes electronic exchanges, while the Breach Notification Rule requires reporting data breaches. Overall, HIPAA ensures privacy, data security, and patient access to health information. As stated in Equation (6), HIPAA aims to protect patient privacy, protect medical data, and provide patients or designate access to their personal health information.

$$\text{ePHI Protection} = \text{Encryption} + \text{Access Control} + \text{Data Minimization} \tag{6}$$

Here, Encryption ensures that health data is stored and transmitted securely; access Control restricts access to authorized individuals based on their roles; data Minimization ensures that only the necessary data is collected and shared.

Figure 2. HIPAA Privacy and Security Checklist Steps

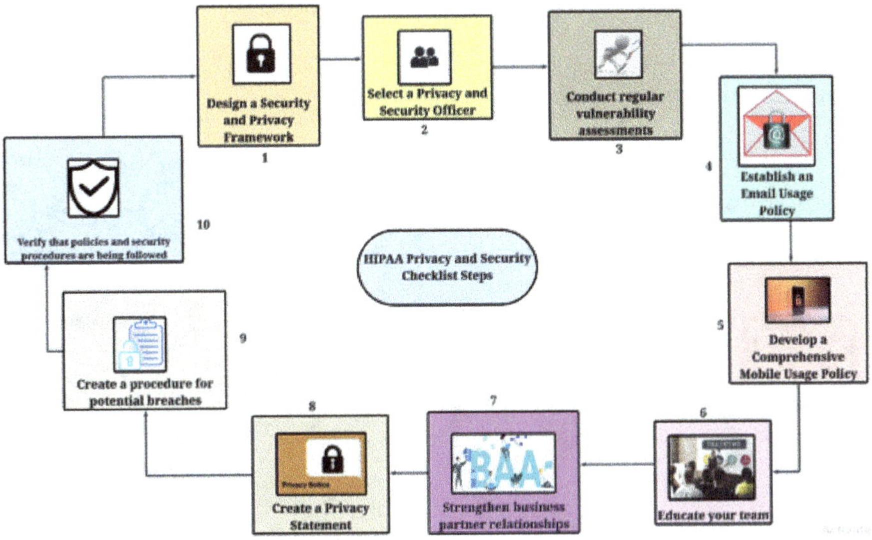

3.6 Classification

Classification in healthcare means placing patient information into classes or labels, usually for prediction or decision-making. To illustrate, classification models would be defined as taking input features, such as age, medical history, and test results, to predict whether the patient has a particular disease. Such models-be it decision tree, logistic regression, or neural network-learn from labelled data to provide high accuracy on unseen data. Nonetheless, it is very important to keep safe any sort of patient data when dealing with healthcare information.

3.6.1 Convolutional Neural Networks

Convolutional Neural Networks (CNNs) are widely used for classification tasks involving structured data such as images and ECG time-series signals. A CNN consists of convolutional, activation, pooling, and fully connected layers (Figure 3). Convolutional filters learn spatial feature hierarchies and automatically extract meaningful patterns. During training, filter weights are updated to minimize classification error. The convolution operation is mathematically defined in Equation (7).

$$y(t) = (x * w)(t) = \sum_{i=0}^{n-1} x(t-i) \cdot w(i) \tag{7}$$

Here, $x(t)$ is the input signal (such as an ECG signal); $w(i)$ is the filter or kernel; $y(t)$ is the output signal after the convolution operation.

Figure 3. Convolutional Neural Networks

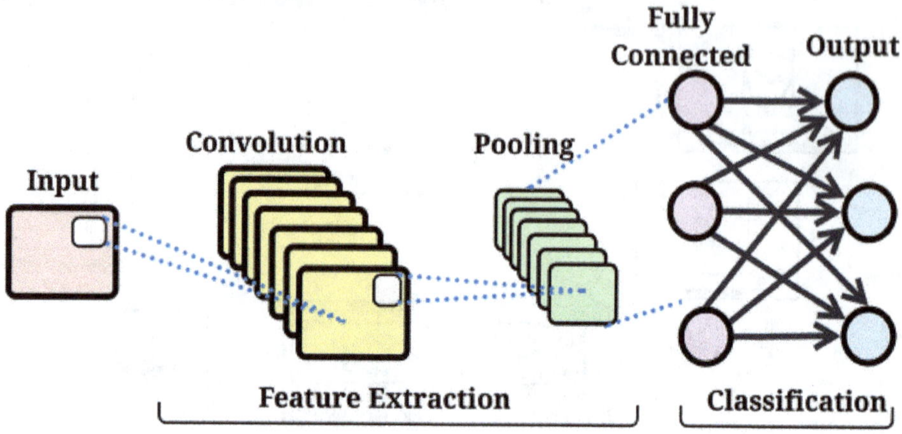

3.7 Optimization

Optimization is the process of selecting the best solution by maximizing or minimizing objectives such as cost, time, efficiency, or performance within given constraints. Widely applied in engineering, economics, machine learning, and operations research, it uses methods like linear programming, gradient-based techniques, and evolutionary algorithms to achieve optimal trade-offs. This field addresses complex nonlinear problems and computational challenges.

3.7.1 Squirrel Search Algorithm for Optimization

The SSA algorithm effectively mimics squirrels' food-search behavior to explore the solution space. A population of squirrels moves randomly or toward promising regions based on a fitness function (Figure 4). Individuals update positions continuously, balancing exploration and exploitation to locate optimal solutions. As shown in Equation (8), the algorithm terminates when a stopping condition, such as maximum iterations or an optimal solution, is reached.

This method can be applied to numerous optimization problems, thereby offering a technique for exploring challenging, high-dimensional search spaces. Movement update in SSA is largely taken care of by this formula:

$$X_i^{k+1} = X_i^k + \alpha \cdot (X_{\text{best}} - X_i^k) + \beta \cdot (X_{\text{rand}} - X_i^k) \tag{8}$$

Here, X_i^{k+1} is the new position of the i-th squirrel at iteration $k + 1$; X_i^k is the current position of the i-th squirrel at iteration k; X_{best} is the best position found so far by the squirrel population; X_{rand} is a randomly chosen position from the search space; α and β are random variables that control the exploration and exploitation of the search space.

Figure 4. Squirrel Search Algorithm for Optimization Flowchart

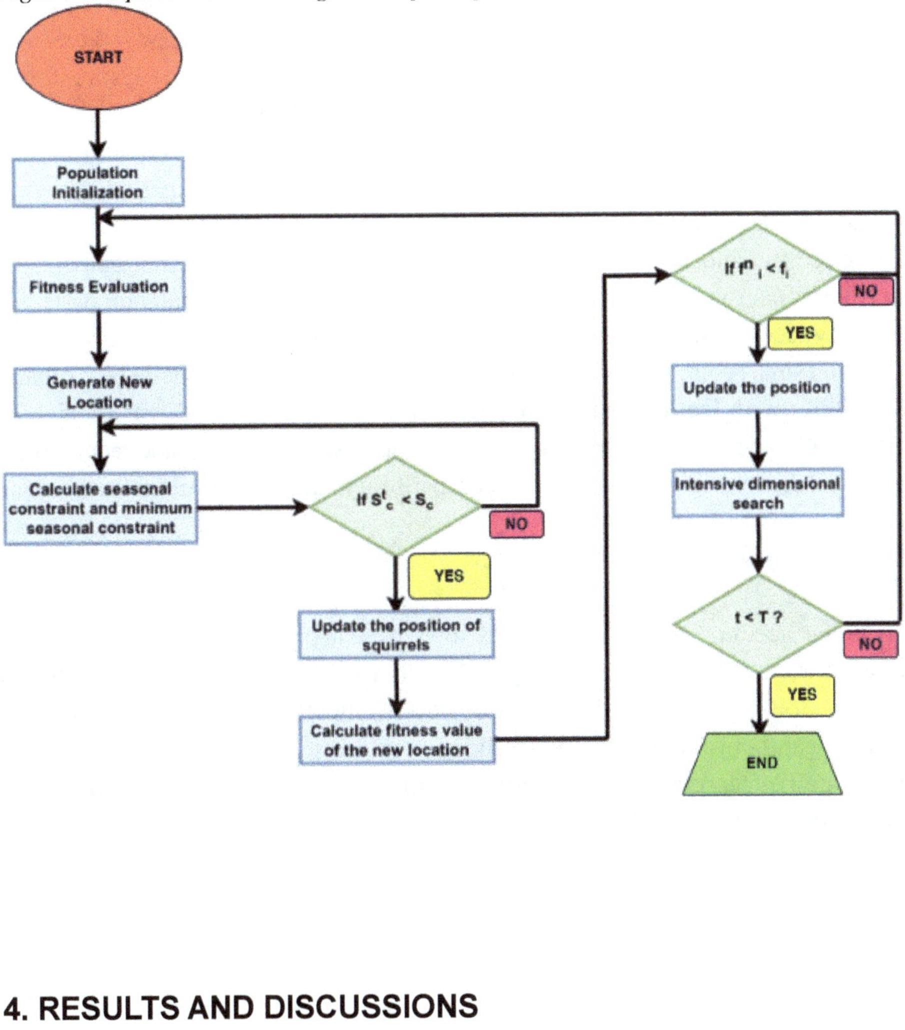

4. RESULTS AND DISCUSSIONS

Healthcare data management is still evolving, creating opportunities for blockchain adoption. Blockchain enables immutable medical records, ensuring high security and preventing tampering. Its decentralized structure removes single points of failure, improving system reliability. With permissioned, cryptographic data sharing and dynamic consent, patient privacy and autonomy are strengthened. It also enhances supply chain traceability and clinical trial transparency, though integration and regulatory compliance remain challenges.

Blockchain-based healthcare systems provide strong security and privacy guarantees; however, real-world deployment introduces important operational constraints. A primary challenge is scalability, as healthcare environments generate continuous high-volume data from electronic health records, medical imaging, wearable sensors, and IoMT devices, and validating each transaction on-chain increases latency and computational overhead as the number of participating institutions grows; therefore, practical systems must adopt hybrid architectures where large medical files are stored off-chain while only hashes and access logs remain on the blockchain. Interoperability further limits adoption because hospitals rely on heterogeneous platforms and standards such as HL7, FHIR, DICOM, and legacy hospital information systems, requiring middleware integration and identity mapping for cross-institution data exchange despite blockchain trust guarantees. In addition, implementation barriers arise from infrastructure cost, workflow modification, key management for patients, emergency access handling, and the need for trained personnel to maintain distributed ledgers and smart contracts, while regulatory obligations must reconcile blockchain immutability with legal requirements such as data correction and erasure rights. Consequently, successful deployment depends not only on cryptographic security but also on scalability engineering, system compatibility, and organizational readiness.

4.1 Training Accuracy and Loss

Training accuracy steadily increases toward near-perfect performance, while validation accuracy improves quickly at first but plateaus after about 10 epochs (Figure 5). Both losses initially decrease; however, validation loss eventually flattens, creating a gap between training and validation metrics. This divergence indicates overfitting. To improve generalization, techniques such as regularization, early stopping, or adding more data can be applied.

Figure 5. Training Accuracy and Loss

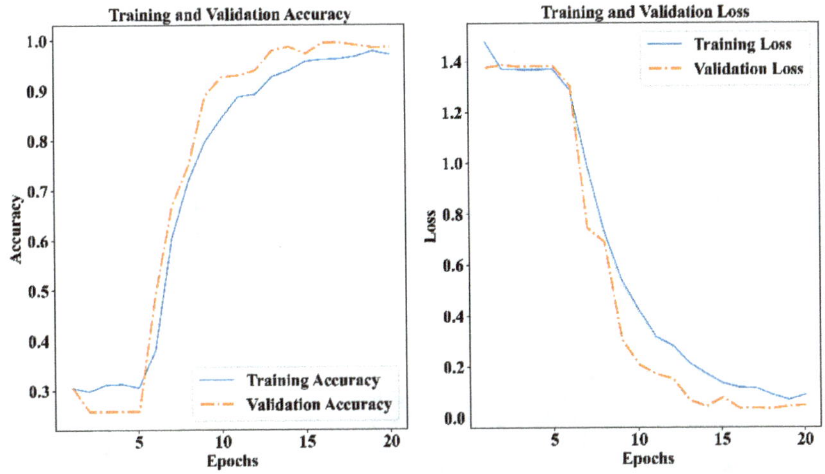

4.2 Confusion Matrix

The confusion matrix shows strong classification performance across Myocardial Infarction, Abnormal Heartbeat, History of Myocardial Infarction, and Normal classes. Most samples were correctly identified, with high true classifications along the diagonal. Only 14 History of Myocardial Infarction cases were misclassified as Normal (Figure 6). Overall, the model distinguishes classes effectively with minimal errors.

Figure 6. Confusion Matrix

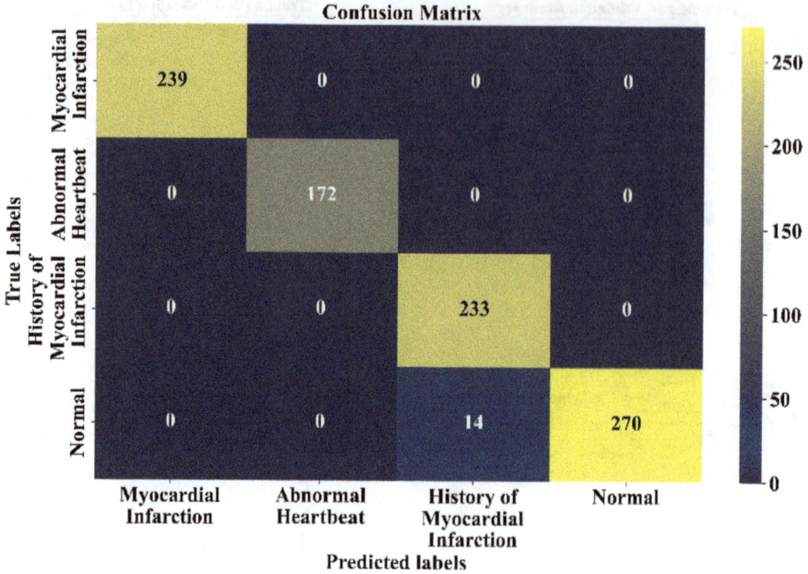

4.3 ROC Curve

The model's ROC curves for Myocardial Infarction, Abnormal Heartbeat, History of Myocardial Infarction, and Normal show how well it can differentiate between different heart conditions. The Myocardial Infarction class shows the highest AUC of 0.9988, denoting very good predictability shown in Figure 7. The Abnormal Heartbeat class follows an AUC of 0.9771 whereas the History of Myocardial Infarction and Normal classes provide AUCs of 0.9697 and 0.9779, respectively. Extremely high AUC values validate that the model can truly distinguish between instances, with Myocardial Infarction being the most precise one that really appreciates the efficiency of the model in predicting cardiac conditions.

Figure 7. ROC Curve

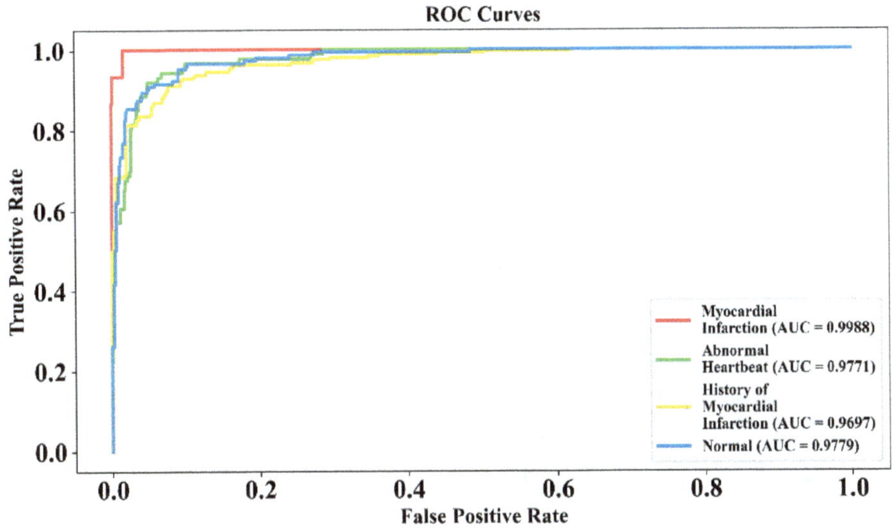

4.4 Access Control and Role Management in Blockchain-Enabled Healthcare

A bar chart illustrates the percentage of different entities provided with access control in the healthcare industry shown in Figure 8. Patients are allowed the highest level of access control at 100%. Next being Healthcare Providers, for 70% are allowed, Insurers for 50% elsewhere in the middle, and only a 30% access control is formed for Other Entities, which empirically represents the extent to which data privacy and security are enforced.

Figure 8. Access Control and Role Management in Blockchain-Enabled Healthcare

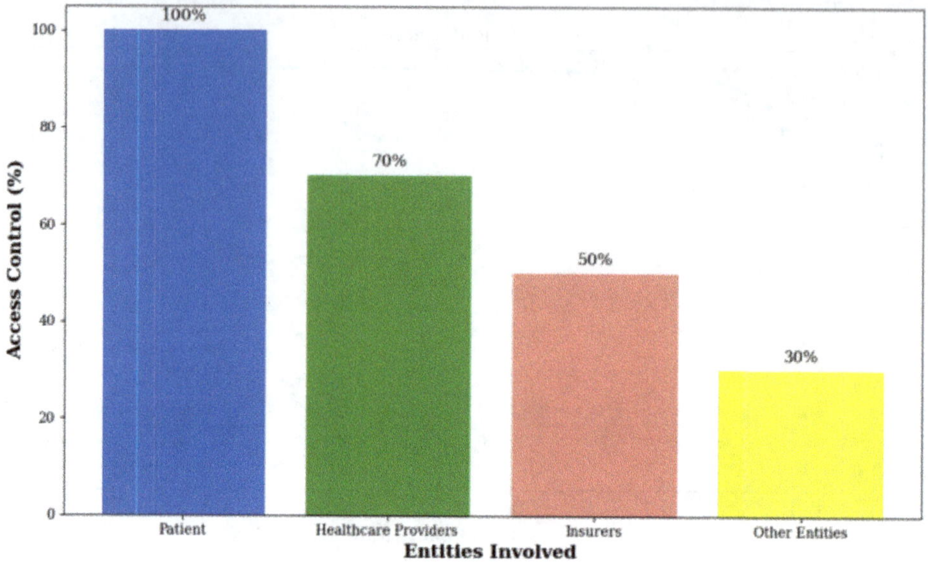

4.5 Performance Evaluation

The bar chart presents accuracy, precision, sensitivity, F-measure, and kappa, all showing high values on the validation set. The model achieves an accuracy of 0.9849, correctly predicting most cases. Precision of 0.9858 indicates reliable identification of positive instances, while sensitivity of 0.9877 demonstrates strong ability to detect positives with minimal false negatives, as shown in Figure 9. The F-measure of 0.9864 reflects an excellent balance between precision and recall. Additionally, the kappa value of 0.9797 confirms strong agreement beyond chance, indicating robust overall classification performance.

Figure 9. Performance Matrix

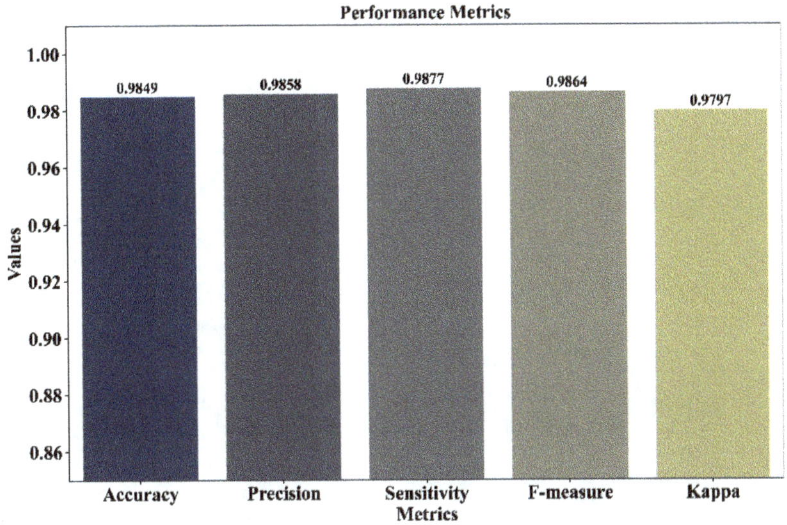

The bar graph compares false positive and false negative rates. The model shows strong performance in detecting positive cases, with a low FNR of 0.0050, meaning very few actual positives are misclassified as negative. However, the FPR of 0.0123 is comparatively higher, indicating that some negative instances are incorrectly identified as positive, as illustrated in Figure 10. This suggests the system effectively minimizes false negatives but needs improvement in reducing false positives through better feature selection or decision threshold tuning.

Figure 10. Performance Matrix

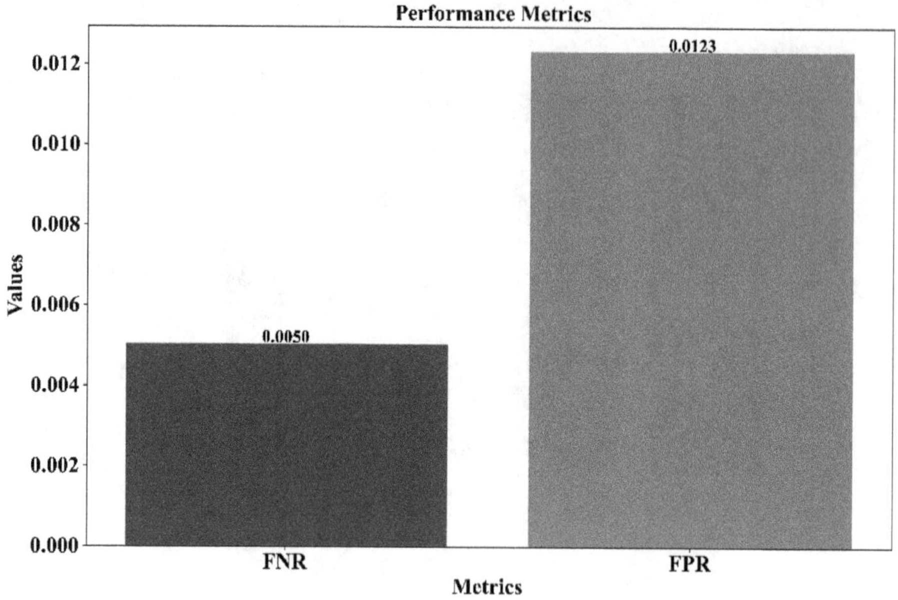

5. CONCLUSIONS AND DISCUSSION

Blockchain technology has the potential to revolutionize healthcare data security by creating a decentralized environment where patient information is stored securely and protected from unauthorized access. Its encryption mechanisms enable the safe transfer of medical records with patient consent, ensuring that only authorized parties can access sensitive data. The immutability of blockchain guarantees data integrity, as medical records cannot be altered or tampered with once recorded. This feature significantly reduces risks associated with data breaches and manipulation. In addition, blockchain enhances patient identity management through secure verification processes, helping prevent identity theft and fraudulent activities.

Dynamic consent management is another critical advantage, allowing patients to control who accesses their health information and update permissions over time. This strengthens patient autonomy while supporting compliance with privacy regulations such as HIPAA. Blockchain also improves transparency and accountability in clinical trials and medical supply chains by maintaining an auditable and tamper-proof ledger of transactions. This helps reduce billing fraud and the circulation of counterfeit medical products, thereby increasing trust in healthcare systems. Looking ahead, further research is needed to address challenges related to scalability, system integration, and regulatory adaptation. Exploring blockchain's integration with AI and IoMT technologies may further enhance decision-making and patient outcomes in real-world healthcare environments.

It demonstrates several notable strengths that enhance its overall quality and value. It provides a comprehensive overview of healthcare data security challenges and clearly explains different blockchain architectures suitable for medical environments. The integration of AI-based clinical analysis with blockchain-based data governance adds practical relevance by linking theoretical security concepts with applied healthcare scenarios. Additionally, the inclusion of performance metrics such as accuracy, ROC curves, and confusion matrix strengthens technical credibility. These strengths can be leveraged to address weaker areas by reducing repetitive background explanations and instead emphasizing analytical discussion, comparative evaluation, and clearer articulation of the unique research contribution. By building upon these strong foundations, improved coherence, depth, and research impact can be achieved.

Healthcare data security is increasingly challenged by rising data breaches, ransomware attacks, insider threats, and vulnerabilities associated with centralized storage systems. Fragmented healthcare infrastructures, interoperability limitations, and regulatory compliance complexities further contribute to systemic weaknesses, underscoring the urgent need for secure digital transformation in the sector. Blockchain technology addresses these concerns through decentralization, cryptographic encryption, immutable records, and dynamic consent management, thereby strengthening transparency, data integrity, patient autonomy, and stakeholder trust. Emerging trends such as integration with Artificial Intelligence (AI), the Internet of Medical Things (IoMT), and privacy-preserving security architectures indicate a transition toward more intelligent, resilient, and patient-centric healthcare ecosystems. However, challenges related to scalability, legacy system integration, governance standardization, and cost efficiency must be addressed to enable large-scale and sustainable implementation.

Although blockchain introduces strong security, privacy, and auditability features, real-world deployment involves several practical constraints that require balanced consideration. High computational overhead, latency during consensus, and difficulty integrating with legacy EHR infrastructures limit seamless adoption in healthcare environments. Operational costs for node maintenance, regulatory uncertainty, limited technical expertise, and institutional resistance to system changes create additional barriers. Highlighting these limitations alongside the benefits provides a more grounded, realistic assessment of blockchain's current maturity and readiness for healthcare applications.

6. FUTURE WORK

Research in the future should aim to investigate the integration limitations and scalability issues that are restricting blockchain from widespread use in health systems today. Although blockchain in itself establishes security advantages, and there remains a dearth of availability due to the technical nature of interoperating with present systems and regulating compliance matters. As a result, there are certain highly focused study fields that focus on the patient's outcome using the body of technology itself, as well as emerging technologies like artificial intelligence and the Internet of Medical Things. Another significant issue is expanding the blockchain infrastructure to handle massive amounts of data while still meeting performance, privacy, and security standards. Thereafter, a few real-world pilot studies should be conducted, along with the establishment of any additional regulatory framework where the blockchain could be integrated seamlessly into the healthcare system.

DATA AVAILABILITY

Data availability, then, is centred on ensuring that data is available to authorised users when they need it. In order to make prompt and accurate medical choices, it is particularly important to have emergency access to patient data. For decentralised systems in particular, it will be very regrettable if activities are disrupted. Blockchain decentralises data storage, addressing these issues and preventing a single point of failure. Blockchain does ensure that healthcare data is available and resistant to any potential disruptions by distributing data among multiple nodes. A patient or healthcare provider cannot ever change or question the data because the blockchain preserves its sanctity through an immutable ledger.

REFERENCES

Abu-elezz, I., Hassan, A., Nazeemudeen, A., Househ, M., & Abd-alrazaq, A. (2020). The benefits and threats of blockchain technology in healthcare: A scoping review. *International Journal of Medical Informatics*, *142*, 104246. DOI: 10.1016/j.ijmedinf.2020.104246 PMID: 32828033

Agrawal, R., & Prabakaran, S. (2020). Big data in digital healthcare: Lessons learnt and recommendations for general practice. *Heredity*, *124*(4), 525–534. DOI: 10.1038/s41437-020-0303-2 PMID: 32139886

AllahRakha, N.AllahRakha. (2024). Cybersecurity regulations for protection and safeguarding digital assets (data) in today's worlds. *Lex Scientia Law Review*, *8*(1), 405–432. DOI: 10.15294/lslr.v8i1.2081

Almulihi, A. H., Alassery, F., Khan, A. I., Shukla, S., Gupta, B. K., & Kumar, R. (2022). Analyzing the implications of healthcare data breaches through computational technique. *Intelligent Automation & Soft Computing*, *32*(3), 1763–1779. DOI: 10.32604/iasc.2022.023460

Attaran, M. (2022). Blockchain technology in healthcare: Challenges and opportunities. *International Journal of Healthcare Management*, *15*(1), 70–83. DOI: 10.1080/20479700.2020.1843887

Charoo, N. A., Khan, M. A., & Rahman, Z. (2023). Data integrity issues in pharmaceutical industry: Common observations, challenges and mitigations strategies. *International Journal of Pharmaceutics*, *631*, 122503. DOI: 10.1016/j.ijpharm.2022.122503 PMID: 36529357

Chng, S., Lu, H. Y., Kumar, A., & Yau, D. (2022). Hacker types, motivations and strategies: A comprehensive framework. *Computers in Human Behavior Reports, 5*, 100167. DOI: 10.1016/j.chbr.2022.100167

Dameff, C., Latif, A., Camp, J., Farcas, R., Bagan, B., Keim, S., & Clay, A. (2023). Ransomware attack associated with disruptions at adjacent emergency departments in the US. *JAMA Network Open, 6*(5), e2312270. DOI: 10.1001/jamanetworkopen.2023.12270 PMID: 37155166

El Khatib, M., Hamidi, S., Al Ameeri, I., Al Zaabi, H., & Al Marqab, R. (2022). Digital disruption and big data in healthcare: Opportunities and challenges. *ClinicoEconomics and Outcomes Research, 14*, 563–574. DOI: 10.2147/CEOR.S369553 PMID: 36052095

Esmaeilzadeh, P. (2022). Benefits and concerns associated with blockchain-based health information exchange (HIE): A qualitative study from physicians' perspectives. *BMC Medical Informatics and Decision Making, 22*(1), 80. DOI: 10.1186/s12911-022-01815-8 PMID: 35346176

Fan, Z., Chen, Q., Lu, W., Yao, Z., Yang, S., Zhao, H., & Cao, H. (2026). Collaborative artificial intelligence for the diagnosis and management of acute ischemic stroke. *Annals of Medicine, 58*(1), 2594356. DOI: 10.1080/07853890.2025.2594356 PMID: 41457873

Gu, X., & Deng, M. (2024). Disclosing harmful patient safety incidents with proactive compensation offer: How do patients respond in Japan? *International Journal of Reliability and Safety, 18*(4), 321–336. DOI: 10.1504/IJRS.2024.142086

Gudepu, B. K., & Jaladi, D. S. (2022). Data Discovery and Security: Protecting Sensitive Information. *International Journal of Acta Informatica, 1*(1), 176–187.

Habbal, A., Ali, M. K., & Abuzaraida, M. A. (2024). Artificial intelligence trust, risk and security management (AI TRiSM): Frameworks, applications, challenges and future research directions. *Expert Systems with Applications, 240*, 122442. DOI: 10.1016/j.eswa.2023.122442

Hasselgren, A., Kralevska, K., Gligoroski, D., Pedersen, S. A., & Faxvaag, A. (2020). Blockchain in healthcare and health sciences—A scoping review. *International Journal of Medical Informatics, 134*, 104040. DOI: 10.1016/j.ijmedinf.2019.104040 PMID: 31865055

Jawad, L. A. (2024). Security and privacy in digital healthcare systems: Challenges and mitigation strategies. *Abhigyan, 42*(1), 23–31. DOI: 10.1177/09702385241233073

Kabir, M. R. (2020). Behavioural intention to adopt blockchain for a transparent and effective taxing system. *Journal of Global Operations and Strategic Sourcing, 14*(1), 170–201. DOI: 10.1108/JGOSS-08-2020-0050

Khan, A. A., Kumar, R., Tripathi, R., Gupta, G. P., Islam, A. K. M. N., & Shorfuzzaman, M. (2023). Data security in healthcare industrial Internet of Things with blockchain. *IEEE Sensors Journal, 23*(20), 25144–25151. DOI: 10.1109/JSEN.2023.3273851

Kodjiku, S. L., Aboagye, I., Ankrah, C., Nti, I. K., Boateng, R., & Ofori, R. (2023). WQCrowd: Secure blockchain-based crowdsourcing framework with multi-tier worker quality evaluation. *Journal of King Saud University. Computer and Information Sciences, 35*(10), 101843. DOI: 10.1016/j.jksuci.2023.101843

Kumar, R., Kumar, P., Tripathi, R., Gupta, G. P., Islam, A. K. M. N., & Shorfuzzaman, M. (2022). Permissioned blockchain and deep learning for secure and efficient data sharing in industrial healthcare systems. *IEEE Transactions on Industrial Informatics, 18*(11), 8065–8073. DOI: 10.1109/TII.2022.3161631

Liu, C., Tian, Y., Tang, J., Dang, S., & Chen, G. (2023). A novel local differential privacy federated learning under multi-privacy regimes. *Expert Systems with Applications, 227*, 120266. DOI: 10.1016/j.eswa.2023.120266

Liu, H., Crespo, R. G., & Martínez, O. S. (2020). Enhancing privacy and data security across healthcare applications using blockchain and distributed ledger concepts. *Health Care, 8*(3), 24043. DOI: 10.3390/healthcare8030243 PMID: 32751325

Marzban, S., Najafi, M., Agolli, A., & Ashrafi, E. (2022). Impact of patient engagement on healthcare quality: A scoping review. *Journal of Patient Experience, 9*, 23743735221125439. DOI: 10.1177/23743735221125439 PMID: 36134145

Mendhurwar, S., & Mishra, R. (2021). Integration of social and IoT technologies: Architectural framework for digital transformation and cybersecurity challenges. *Enterprise Information Systems, 15*(4), 565–584. DOI: 10.1080/17517575.2019.1600041

Mittal, S., Gupta, V., Sharma, P., Khanna, A., Jain, V., & Saxena, R. (2022). Using identity-based cryptography as a foundation for an effective and secure cloud model for e-health. *Computational Intelligence and Neuroscience, 7016554*, 1–8. Advance online publication. DOI: 10.1155/2022/7016554 PMID: 35510050

. Newaz, A. I., Sikder, A. K., Rahman, M. A., & Uluagac, A. S. (2021). A survey on security and privacy issues in modern healthcare systems: Attacks and defenses. ACM Transactions on Computing for Healthcare, 2(3), 27:1–27:44. DOI: 10.1145/3453176

Ng, W. Y., Tan, T. E., Movva, P. V., Fang, A. H. S., Yeo, K. K., Ho, D., Foo, F. S. S., Xiao, Z., Sun, K., Wong, T. Y., Sia, A. T.-H., & Ting, D. S. W. (2021). Blockchain applications in health care for COVID-19 and beyond: A systematic review. *The Lancet. Digital Health*, *3*(12), e819–e829. DOI: 10.1016/S2589-7500(21)00210-7 PMID: 34654686

Perwej, Y., Abbas, S. Q., Dixit, J. P., Akhtar, N., & Jaiswal, A. K. (2021). A systematic literature review on the cyber security. *International Journal of Scientific Research and Management*, *9*(12), 669–710. DOI: 10.18535/ijsrm/v9i12.ec04

Perwej, Y., Akhtar, N., Kulshrestha, N., & Mishra, P. (2022). A methodical analysis of medical Internet of Things (MIoT) security and privacy in current and future trends. *Journal of Emerging Technologies and Innovative Research*, *9*(1), d346–d371.

Ranchal, R., Bastide, P., Wang, X., Gkoulalas-Divanis, A., Mehra, M., Bakthavachalam, S., Lei, H., & Mohindra, A. (2020). Disrupting healthcare silos: Addressing data volume, velocity and variety with a cloud-native healthcare data ingestion service. *IEEE Journal of Biomedical and Health Informatics*, *24*(11), 3182–3188. DOI: 10.1109/JBHI.2020.3001518 PMID: 32750932

Rani, P., Verma, S., Yadav, S. P., Rai, B. K., Naruka, M. S., & Kumar, D. (2022). Simulation of the lightweight blockchain technique based on privacy and security for healthcare data for the cloud system. *International Journal of E-Health and Medical Communications*, *13*(4), 1–15. DOI: 10.4018/IJEHMC.309436

Ratta, P., Kaur, A., Sharma, S., Shabaz, M., & Dhiman, G. (2021). Application of blockchain and Internet of Things in healthcare and medical sector: Applications, challenges, and future perspectives. *Journal of Food Quality*, *7608296*, 1–20. Advance online publication. DOI: 10.1155/2021/7608296

Saeed, H., Malik, H., Bashir, U., Ahmad, A., Riaz, S., Ilyas, M., Bukhari, W. A., & Khan, M. I. A. (2022). Blockchain technology in healthcare: A systematic review. *PLoS One*, *17*(4), e0266462. DOI: 10.1371/journal.pone.0266462 PMID: 35404955

Sangannagari, S. R. (2024). Design and Implementation of a Cloud-Native Automated Certification Platform for Functional Testing and Compliance Validation. International Journal of Technology. *Management and Humanities*, *10*(02), 34–43. DOI: 10.21590/k5r28w48

Senbekov, M., Saliev, T., Bukeyeva, Z., Almabayeva, A., Zhanaliyeva, M., Aitenova, N., Toishibekov, Y., & Fakhradiyev, I. (2020). The recent progress and applications of digital technologies in healthcare: A review. *International Journal of Telemedicine and Applications*, *8830200*, 1–18. Advance online publication. DOI: 10.1155/2020/8830200 PMID: 33343657

Shahid, J., Ahmad, R., Kiani, A. K., Ahmad, T., Saeed, S., & Almuhaideb, A. M. (2022). Data protection and privacy of the Internet of Healthcare Things (IoHTs). *Applied Sciences (Basel, Switzerland)*, *12*(4), 1927. DOI: 10.3390/app12041927

Shaikh, M., Memon, S. A., Ebrahimi, A., & Wiil, U. K. (2025, May). A systematic literature review for blockchain-based healthcare implementations. In Healthcare, Vol. 13, No. 9, p. 1087. DOI: 10.3390/healthcare13091087

. Singh, A. K., Anand, A., Lv, Z., Ko, H., & Mohan, A. (2021). A survey on healthcare data: A security perspective. ACM Transactions on Multimedia Computing, Communications, and Applications, 17(2s), 59:1–59:26. DOI: 10.1145/3422816

Tabrizchi, H., & Kuchaki Rafsanjani, M. (2020). A survey on security challenges in cloud computing: Issues, threats, and solutions. *The Journal of Supercomputing*, *76*(12), 9493–9532. DOI: 10.1007/s11227-020-03213-1

Tantray, J., Patel, A., Wani, S. N., Kosey, S., & Prajapati, B. G. (2024). Prescription precision: A comprehensive review of intelligent prescription systems. *Current Pharmaceutical Design*, *30*(34), 2671–2684. DOI: 10.2174/0113816128321623240719104337 PMID: 39092640

Tariq, N., Qamar, A., Asim, M., & Khan, F. A. (2020). Blockchain and smart healthcare security: A survey. *Procedia Computer Science*, *175*, 615–620. DOI: 10.1016/j.procs.2020.07.089

Ullah, F., He, J., Zhu, N., Wajahat, A., Nazir, A., Qureshi, S., Pathan, M. S., & Dev, S. (2024). Blockchain-enabled EHR access auditing: Enhancing healthcare data security. *Heliyon*, *10*(16), e34407. DOI: 10.1016/j.heliyon.2024.e34407 PMID: 39253236

Van Nguyen, T., Cong Pham, H., Nhat Nguyen, M., Zhou, L., & Akbari, M. (2023). Data-driven review of blockchain applications in supply chain management: Key research themes and future directions. *International Journal of Production Research*, *61*(23), 8213–8235. DOI: 10.1080/00207543.2023.2165190

Villarreal, E. R. D., García-Alonso, J., Moguel, E., & Alegría, J. A. H. (2023). Blockchain for healthcare management systems: A survey on interoperability and security. *IEEE Access : Practical Innovations, Open Solutions*, *11*, 5629–5652. DOI: 10.1109/ACCESS.2023.3236505

Walker, D. M., Yeager, V. A., Lawrence, J., & Mcalearney, A. S. (2021). Identifying opportunities to strengthen the public health informatics infrastructure: Exploring hospitals' challenges with data exchange. *The Milbank Quarterly*, *99*(2), 393–425. DOI: 10.1111/1468-0009.12511 PMID: 33783863

Xi, P., Zhang, X., Wang, L., Liu, W., & Peng, S. (2022). A review of blockchain-based secure sharing of healthcare data. *Applied Sciences (Basel, Switzerland)*, *12*(15), 7912. DOI: 10.3390/app12157912

Yallop, A. C., Gică, O. A., Moisescu, O. I., Coro , M. M., & Séraphin, H. (2021). The digital traveller: Implications for data ethics and data governance in tourism and hospitality. *Journal of Consumer Marketing*, *40*(2), 155–170. DOI: 10.1108/JCM-12-2020-4278

Yan, L., Yin-He, S., Qian, Y., Zhi-Yu, S., Chun-Zi, W., & Zi-Yun, L. (2021). Method of reaching consensus on probability of food safety based on the integration of finite credible data on block chain. *IEEE Access : Practical Innovations, Open Solutions*, *9*, 123764–123776. DOI: 10.1109/ACCESS.2021.3108178

Yaqoob, I., Salah, K., Jayaraman, R., & Al-Hammadi, Y. (2022). Blockchain for healthcare data management: Opportunities, challenges, and future recommendations. *Neural Computing & Applications*, *34*(14), 11475–11490. DOI: 10.1007/s00521-020-05519-w

Yeung, K. (2021). The healthcare sector's experience of blockchain: A cross-disciplinary investigation of its real transformative potential. *Journal of Medical Internet Research*, *23*(12), e24109. DOI: 10.2196/24109 PMID: 34932009

Zaabar, B., Cheikhrouhou, O., Jamil, F., Ammi, M., & Abid, M. (2021). HealthBlock: A secure blockchain-based healthcare data management system. *Computer Networks*, *200*, 108500. DOI: 10.1016/j.comnet.2021.108500

Zarour, M., Ansari, M. T. J., Alenezi, M., Sarkar, A. K., Faizan, M., Agrawal, A., Kumar, R., & Khan, R. A. (2020). Evaluating the impact of blockchain models for secure and trustworthy electronic healthcare records. *IEEE Access : Practical Innovations, Open Solutions*, *8*, 157959–157973. DOI: 10.1109/ACCESS.2020.3019829

Chapter 11
Nanotechnology-Driven AI Sensors: Advancing Precision in Oncotherapy

Amrutashree Hota
http://orcid.org/0000-0003-1854-9088
Vellore Institute of Technology, Vellore, India

Badal Kumar Mandal
Vellore Institute of Technology, Vellore, India

ABSTRACT

The integration of nanotechnology with artificial intelligence (AI)-driven sensing systems is revolutionizing oncotherapy by enhancing precision in cancer detection, monitoring, and treatment. Traditional diagnostic and therapeutic approaches often suffer from limitations in sensitivity, specificity, and early-stage detection. AI-powered nanotechnology sensors offer a transformative solution by enabling real-time, high-resolution analysis of cancer biomarkers with improved accuracy. These nano-sensors leverage machine learning algorithms to process vast identifying subtle biochemical and morphological changes associated with malignancies. Moreover, the synergy between nanomaterials and AI facilitates targeted drug delivery, minimizing off-target effects and improving therapeutic outcomes. This chapter explores recent advancements in nanotechnology-driven AI sensors, discussing their role in early cancer detection, personalized treatment strategies, and continuous health monitoring.

DOI: 10.4018/979-8-2600-0981-9.ch011

1. INTRODUCTION

Cancer has become one of the causes of death all over the globe with an annual death rate of about ten million people and has been a major problem to the healthcare systems. Early detection, correct disease surveillance and tailored treatment options are critical to enhancing patient outcomes (Cojocaru et al., 2024; Taha et al., 2024). The traditional oncological methods of chemotherapy, radiotherapy, and surgery have greatly improved the treatment of cancer but they have many weaknesses such as systemic toxicity, poor tumor specificity, slow detection and unpredictable response to treatment (Naik & Jagtap, 2024).

In the last 20 years, nanotechnology has become a paradigm shift in biomedical studies especially in cancer diagnostics and therapy (Akdaşçi et al., 2025). The nanomaterials that are quantum dots, gold nanoparticles, carbon nanotubes, graphene derivatives, and polymeric nanoparticles have some special physicochemical properties of high surface to volume ratio, mutable optical properties and high biological interactions (Ruse et al., 2025; Tinger, 2024). The properties have potential to create cancer biomarkers and targeted drug delivery systems that can be very sensitive and have the potential of enhancing the efficacy of the therapeutics of the cancer and reducing the side effects.

Table 1. Performance Comparison of Conventional Diagnostics vs AI-Enabled Nanosensors

Diagnostic Method	Detection Limit	Sensitivity	Time to Result	Clinical Application
Histopathology	Moderate	High	Several days	Tissue biopsy
ELISA assays	Moderate	Moderate	Several hours	Biomarker detection
Imaging (MRI/CT)	Low	Moderate	Hours	Tumor visualization
AI-Nanosensors	Very low (fg/mL range)	Very high	Minutes	Early cancer detection

In line with the fast advancement of nanotechnology, artificial intelligence (AI) has transformed the way data is analyzed in healthcare (Akdaşçi et al., 2025). Algorithms of machine learning (ML) and deep learning (DL) are capable of processing sophisticated biomedical data sets, discovering hidden biological trends, and helping a clinician to make a decision (Jiemin Zhang et al., 2025). A combination of AI and nanosensor systems has resulted in the creation of smart diagnostic systems that can identify cancer biomarkers in a sensitive and specific manner never seen before (Table 1).

Nanosensors are AI-based sensing devices that integrate the nanomaterial-based sensor principles with sophisticated computational algorithms to process biological signals including circulating tumor DNA (ct-DNA), micro-RNAs (mi-RNAs), exosomes and protein biomarkers (Mousa et al., 2025). These systems can be used to process high amounts of biological data in real-time and this has allowed to detect malignancies early, constantly monitor the development of diseases, and plan personalized treatment (B. Li et al., 2025; Semerjyan et al., 2025). Over the past few years, AI-assisted liquid biopsy systems and nanosensor-based diagnostic instruments have shown a tremendous potential in enhancing the early detection of cancer and patient-specific treatment procedures.

Over the years, biosensor technologies have developed to be more complex in the form of nano-based diagnostic systems compared to simple electrochemical detection surface. The early biosensors mainly depended on the detection process which is mainly performed by enzyme based and now modern nano-sensors are made up of enhanced materials and microfluidics technology which enables the analysis to be carried out promptly and non-invasively on biological samples (Sharma et al., 2025). This has also led to improved accuracy of diagnosing diseases because AI algorithms integrated into these systems have allowed the recognition of patterns automatically, predictive modelling and real time interpretation of data (Naik & Jagtap, 2024).

Although these are encouraging trends, a number of issues need to be tackled until AI-enhanced nano-sensors can become a commonplace in clinical practice (Chandrasekaran et al., 2025; Sharma et al., 2025). Biocompatibility, long-term sensor stability, regulatory approval, ethical concerns, and cost of healthcare implementation have issues that are still a major hindrance to large scale deployment. Moreover, to guarantee reliability and patient safety, it is necessary to develop standardized methods of AI validation and clinical integration (Nastasijevic et al., 2025).

This chapter discusses how nanotechnology and artificial intelligence have come together to promote precision oncotherapy. It talks about the current trends in AI-based nano-sensors of cancer biomarkers, predictive modelling of treatment response, and future smart nano-sensors of real-time monitoring. Additionally, the chapter looks at the current issues such as regulatory limitations, ethics, and the economic effects relating to the clinical translation of these technologies. Lastly, future research directions and new trends of AI-nano convergence are addressed, which have an opportunity to revolutionize the global healthcare system of cancer.

2. AI-DRIVEN SENSORS FOR CANCER BIOMARKER DETECTION

The integration of artificial intelligence (AI) and nanotechnology has brought transformative advancements in cancer diagnostics, enabling rapid, accurate, and real-time biomarker detection. AI-driven sensors harness the power of machine learning (ML) and deep learning (DL) algorithms to process extensive biological datasets, identify complex molecular patterns, and enhance the sensitivity of detection techniques (Ghosh et al., 2025). These nano-sensors are capable of detecting cancer biomarkers such as circulating tumor DNA (ctDNA), microRNAs (miRNAs), exosomes, and specific proteins like CA-125, PSA, AFP, and CEA with unparalleled precision. The combination of AI and biosensors has paved the way for non-invasive, point-of-care, and highly personalized diagnostic approaches, significantly improving early detection and treatment outcomes in oncology (X. Li et al., 2025). This section explores the key aspects of AI-driven biomarker detection, including the role of machine learning in oncological diagnostics, biosensors for real-time biomarker analysis, AI-powered imaging techniques, and the integration of AI and nanotechnology for personalized oncotherapy. Fig. 1 shows the list of AI-driven nanomaterials for sensors (Taha et al., 2024).

Figure 1. AI-driven nanomaterials for sensors.

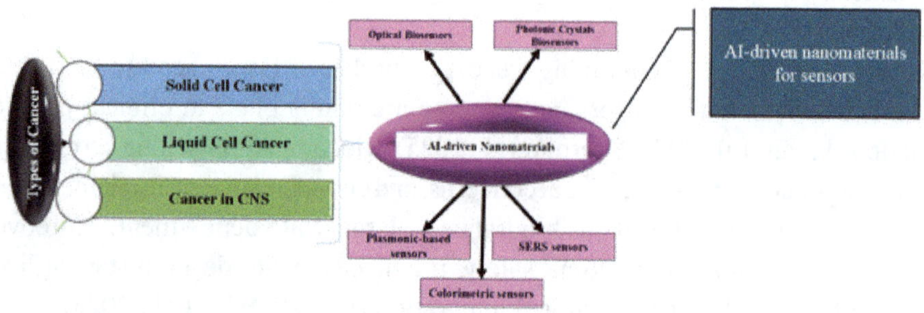

2.1. Machine Learning and Deep Learning in Oncological Diagnostics

Machine learning and deep learning have revolutionized cancer biomarker detection by improving diagnostic accuracy, enhancing automation, and enabling faster data processing (Yadav et al., 2025). These AI-driven techniques are capable of analyzing vast biomedical datasets, uncovering hidden patterns, and predicting cancer progression with high precision (Yongqi Wang et al., 2025). Supervised learning models are frequently employed in tumor classification, where labeled data help train AI algorithms to distinguish between benign and malignant cells based on biomarker expression levels. Unsupervised learning, on the other hand, is useful for discovering novel cancer subtypes and identifying previously unrecognized biomarker associations. Deep learning, particularly convolutional neural networks (CNNs), plays a significant role in processing medical imaging data, detecting structural and biochemical alterations in tissues, and improving diagnostic reliability (Naryal et al., 2025).

AI-driven biomarker detection has gained prominence in liquid biopsy applications, where advanced algorithms analyze ctDNA and exosome profiles to detect early-stage cancer with high sensitivity. Predictive modeling is another key area where AI assesses biomarker fluctuations over time to forecast disease progression and patient outcomes (Zehra et al., 2025). Additionally, the integration of AI with multi-omics data—encompassing genomics, proteomics, and metabolomics—has enabled the development of personalized diagnostic strategies tailored to individual patients (Halder & Kumar, 2025). These AI-powered methodologies enhance the specificity and efficiency of cancer detection, ultimately contributing to more effective treatment planning. Despite these advancements, challenges such as data bias, model interpretability, and regulatory compliance remain critical obstacles that must be addressed to ensure the widespread clinical adoption of AI in oncological diagnostics (Nikhade & Jaiswal, 2025).

2.2. Biosensors for Real-Time Cancer Biomarker Analysis

Biosensors play a crucial role in real-time cancer biomarker detection by translating biological interactions into measurable signals, allowing for continuous monitoring and early diagnosis. AI-driven biosensors improve detection sensitivity and specificity by employing advanced data analysis techniques, pattern recognition algorithms, and automated decision-making systems. These biosensors are designed to detect various cancer biomarkers present in blood, saliva, and urine, reducing the need for invasive biopsy procedures and enabling rapid point-of-care testing (Dehesh & Dehesh, 2025).

Electrochemical biosensors, which measure electrical signal variations upon biomarker binding, have demonstrated significant advancements through the incorporation of AI-based signal processing techniques. The use of nanomaterials such as graphene, gold nanoparticles, and carbon nanotubes has further enhanced electron transfer efficiency, improving detection sensitivity (Gade et al., 2025). Optical biosensors, which utilize fluorescence, surface plasmon resonance (SPR), and Raman spectroscopy, have also been optimized with AI algorithms that refine image analysis, spectral pattern recognition, and fluorescence intensity quantification. Similarly, nanomechanical biosensors, based on cantilever-based nanodevices, detect cancer biomarkers by measuring nanoscale mass shifts, with AI facilitating real-time monitoring and reducing background noise interference.

The application of AI-driven biosensors extends to point-of-care diagnostics, where portable nanodevices provide instant cancer detection, and wearable biosensors, which enable continuous real-time monitoring of circulating tumor biomarkers (Naryal et al., 2025). Additionally, AI-powered liquid biopsy sensors enhance the detection of ctDNA, exosomes, and miRNAs, minimizing reliance on traditional tissue biopsies. While AI-enhanced biosensors hold immense potential in oncological diagnostics, challenges such as sensor stability, biocompatibility, and standardization must be addressed to ensure clinical reliability and widespread implementation (Singh et al., 2025; Yongqi Wang et al., 2025).

2.3. Non-Invasive AI-Powered Imaging Techniques (MRI, Fluorescence, Raman Spectroscopy)

Non-invasive imaging techniques are fundamental to early cancer detection and disease monitoring, with AI-powered imaging solutions significantly improving sensitivity, resolution, and diagnostic accuracy (Khatoon & Velidandi, 2025). AI-driven imaging technologies enhance conventional modalities such as magnetic resonance imaging (MRI), fluorescence imaging, and Raman spectroscopy by automating data interpretation, reducing diagnostic errors, and enabling real-time assessment of tumor characteristics (Pawara & Mahajan, 2025).

AI-enhanced MRI has demonstrated remarkable advancements in cancer detection by employing deep learning algorithms that analyze complex imaging data and distinguish between tumor subtypes. Radiomics-based AI models extract quantitative imaging features from MRI scans, aiding in the precise characterization of tumor morphology and progression. Additionally, AI-accelerated image reconstruction techniques reduce scan times, improving patient comfort and diagnostic efficiency (Sun et al., 2025). Fluorescence imaging, which relies on fluorescent nanoprobes to target specific cancer biomarkers, has benefited from AI-based fluorescence intensity quantification, allowing for highly sensitive imaging of biomolecular interactions at the cellular level. Near-infrared (NIR) fluorescent probes, when combined with AI algorithms, facilitate deep-tissue imaging without the need for ionizing radiation, making them particularly valuable for non-invasive cancer detection (Yuwen Wang et al., 2025).

Raman spectroscopy, an advanced optical imaging technique, has gained prominence in oncological diagnostics due to its ability to provide label-free molecular analysis of biological tissues. AI-driven spectral pattern recognition enhances the differentiation between normal and malignant cells, improving diagnostic accuracy (Chauhan et al., 2025). The integration of surface-enhanced Raman spectroscopy (SERS) with AI-based image processing further increases the sensitivity of biomarker detection, enabling the identification of cancer-related biomolecules at ultralow concentrations (Butt, 2025). These AI-powered imaging techniques collectively contribute to more precise, automated, and real-time cancer diagnostics, facilitating early intervention and personalized treatment planning. However, challenges related to computational complexity, data privacy concerns, and regulatory approvals must be addressed to ensure seamless clinical translation.

2.4. Integration of AI and Nanotechnology for Personalized Oncotherapy

Personalized oncotherapy relies on the convergence of AI and nanotechnology to develop targeted cancer treatments based on an individual's unique biomarker profile. AI-powered nanotechnology has revolutionized drug delivery, radiation therapy, and immunotherapy by enhancing treatment precision, minimizing adverse effects, and improving therapeutic outcomes (Ahmed & Kulkarni, 2025). Smart nanocarriers, functionalized with tumor-specific ligands, are designed to deliver chemotherapeutic agents directly to cancer cells, reducing systemic toxicity. AI algorithms optimize nanoparticle design by predicting the most efficient drug release kinetics, ensuring that therapeutic agents are delivered in a controlled and sustained manner. Additionally, stimuli-responsive nanocarriers, which release drugs in response to pH, temperature, or enzymatic activity, have been fine-tuned using AI models to enhance their efficacy in targeting malignant tissues (Dudhat, 2025).

AI has also been instrumental in optimizing radiation therapy by analyzing tumor response patterns and dynamically adjusting radiation doses to minimize damage to healthy tissues. The development of nano-radiosensitizers, which improve tumor radiation absorption, has further enhanced the effectiveness of radiotherapy (Acharya et al., 2024). Similarly, AI-enhanced immunotherapy utilizes nanoparticles to deliver tumor antigens, stimulating immune system activation in a highly selective manner. By analyzing immune checkpoint biomarker data, AI-driven models tailor immunotherapeutic interventions to individual patients, improving treatment response rates and reducing the risk of immune-related adverse effects (Chintada et al., 2024).

Despite its promising potential, AI-integrated nanotechnology faces several challenges, including concerns about nanomaterial safety, regulatory approvals, and AI-driven data bias. Addressing these issues will be crucial for translating these advancements into routine clinical practice (El Zein et al., 2024). Future research efforts should focus on developing self-learning AI models that continuously adapt treatment protocols based on real-time patient data, ultimately leading to more precise and personalized oncotherapy strategies. Fig. 2 shows the various nano-particle based cancer treatment (Cojocaru et al., 2024).

2.5. AI–Nano Integration Architecture for Precision Oncology

The combination of nanotechnology-based sensors and artificial intelligence needs to be carried out in a systematic workflow that makes it easy to acquire data, process it, and interpret it clinically. This is initiated by signal acquisition by nanosensors; nanomaterials like graphene, plasmonic nanoparticles or quantum dots react with cancer biomarkers in biological samples, including blood, saliva, or urine. The interactions produce a quantifiable effect e.g. electrical changes, fluorescence changes, Raman spectra, or optical absorption signatures.

After receiving the signal, signal preprocessing and signal conditioning is carried out to remove the noise and standardize the data gathered. Such methods as normalization, background correction, and feature extraction are used to enhance the quality of the signal and guarantee proper downstream analysis.

Machine learning and deep learning algorithms are then used to analyze the processed data. Convolutional neural networks, support vector machines and ensemble learning models are among the algorithms that find complex patterns that are related to cancer biomarkers. These models are trained on huge biomedical datasets in order to differentiate between normal and malignant biological signatures with high accuracy.

After the AI models come up with predictions the output is incorporated into clinical decision support systems (CDSS) which help the healthcare professionals in interpreting diagnostic findings. These systems can deliver a risk assessment score, or the output of biomarker classification, or treatment recommendations, based on patient-specific data.

Lastly, the results become integrated into accuracy oncology processes, which helps clinicians to develop individual treatment plans and monitor patient reactions constantly. In this AI-nanosensor integration framework, it is pointed out that delicate materials science and computational intelligence are likely to be used together to improve both cancer diagnostics and therapeutic decision making.

Figure 2. various nano-particle based cancer treatment.

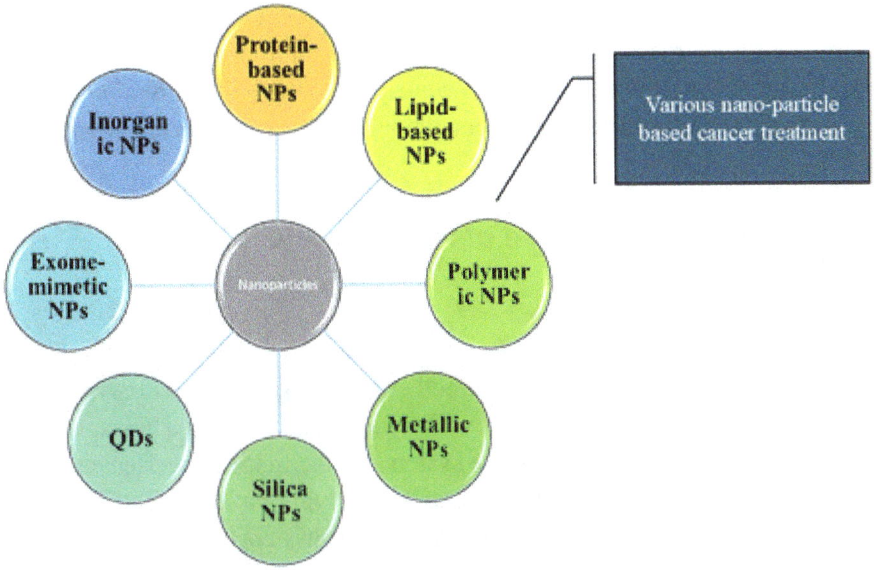

3. PREDICTIVE MODELLING FOR CANCER PROGRESSION AND TREATMENT RESPONSE

Predictive modelling in oncology has gained significant traction with the integration of artificial intelligence (AI), offering advanced insights into cancer progression and treatment response (Ashique et al., 2025). AI-driven predictive models analyze vast datasets, including patient genetics, tumor microenvironment interactions, and treatment response patterns, to provide highly accurate forecasts of disease progression. These models leverage machine learning (ML) algorithms and deep learning (DL) architectures to identify key biomarkers, assess risk factors, and optimize therapeutic strategies. By incorporating multi-omics data, AI-powered predictive models can differentiate between aggressive and indolent tumors, helping oncologists devise personalized treatment plans that maximize efficacy while minimizing adverse effects (Koushki et al., 2024).

In addition to prognosis, predictive modeling plays a crucial role in assessing treatment response, ensuring that therapeutic interventions are tailored to individual patients. AI algorithms analyze historical treatment data and real-time patient monitoring to predict whether a given treatment regimen will be effective. This enables the early identification of non-responders, allowing for timely modifications in therapeutic approaches. Furthermore, AI-powered models integrate imaging, histopathological, and molecular profiling data to create dynamic, continuously learning systems that refine treatment recommendations over time. These advancements not only enhance patient outcomes but also contribute to the broader field of precision oncology by facilitating the development of novel, data-driven therapeutic strategies (Tripathy et al., 2024).

3.1. AI-Guided Optimization of Nanoparticle Drug Delivery Systems

Nanoparticle-based drug delivery systems have emerged as a promising strategy for enhancing the targeted delivery of chemotherapeutic agents, reducing systemic toxicity, and improving therapeutic efficacy (Goswami et al., 2024). AI has significantly contributed to the optimization of these systems by facilitating precise nanoparticle design, predicting drug release kinetics, and improving patient-specific treatment customization. Machine learning algorithms analyze physicochemical properties such as nanoparticle size, shape, surface charge, and ligand functionalization to optimize drug loading and release profiles. Through deep learning simulations, AI predicts nanoparticle interactions within biological environments, ensuring efficient tumor targeting while minimizing off-target effects (Boukherroub & Szunerits, 2024).

AI-guided optimization also extends to stimuli-responsive nanocarriers, which release therapeutic agents in response to specific tumor microenvironmental cues such as pH, temperature, or enzyme activity. By integrating real-time patient data, AI models dynamically adjust nanoparticle formulations to enhance drug bioavailability and treatment effectiveness (Theivendren et al., 2024). Additionally, AI-assisted high-throughput screening of nanoparticle libraries accelerates the discovery of novel formulations with improved stability and biocompatibility. These advancements are instrumental in developing next-generation smart drug delivery systems that offer personalized treatment regimens, ultimately revolutionizing cancer therapy by maximizing therapeutic impact while minimizing adverse effects (Huang et al., 2024).

3.2. Role of AI in Adaptive and Targeted Therapies

Adaptive and targeted therapies represent the forefront of precision oncology, where AI plays a pivotal role in refining treatment approaches to match individual patient profiles. Adaptive therapy is a dynamic treatment strategy that continuously adjusts drug dosage and scheduling based on tumor response, preventing drug resistance and optimizing long-term treatment outcomes. AI-driven models analyze real-time tumor growth kinetics, genetic mutations, and drug sensitivity patterns to determine the most effective adaptive therapy protocols. These models predict tumor evolution and resistance mechanisms, allowing oncologists to modulate treatment regimens in response to emerging challenges (Zheng et al., 2024).

Targeted therapies, which aim to selectively attack cancer cells while sparing normal tissues, have also been enhanced by AI-powered predictive analytics. AI algorithms process genomic and proteomic data to identify specific molecular targets, guiding the selection of monoclonal antibodies, small-molecule inhibitors, and immune checkpoint modulators. Furthermore, AI facilitates the design of personalized combination therapies by predicting synergistic interactions between multiple drugs, thereby improving treatment efficacy while reducing adverse effects. The integration of AI in adaptive and targeted therapies represents a paradigm shift in oncology, ensuring that treatment decisions are data-driven, continuously optimized, and tailored to the unique biological characteristics of each patient (Klemt et al., 2024).

3.3. Advancements in AI-Powered Nanotechnology Sensors

AI-powered nanotechnology sensors have revolutionized cancer diagnostics and treatment monitoring by providing real-time, high-precision detection of cancer biomarkers. These advanced sensors utilize nanomaterials such as quantum dots, carbon nanotubes, and plasmonic nanoparticles to enhance sensitivity and specificity in detecting molecular changes associated with cancer progression. AI algorithms process vast amounts of biosensor-generated data, identifying subtle variations in biomarker expression that may indicate early-stage malignancies or therapeutic response. This capability allows for continuous patient monitoring, enabling early intervention and treatment adjustments as needed (Mohanty et al., 2024).

Recent advancements in AI-driven nanotechnology sensors have facilitated the development of wearable and implantable devices that provide real-time health monitoring. These sensors detect circulating tumor DNA (ctDNA), exosomes, and metabolic changes in body fluids, offering non-invasive and highly accurate diagnostic solutions. AI-enhanced microfluidic chips further improve the efficiency of biosensors by automating sample analysis and minimizing human error. Additionally, AI-powered sensors integrated with wireless communication technologies enable remote patient monitoring, ensuring that oncologists receive timely updates on disease progression. These advancements hold immense potential in transforming cancer management by enabling early detection, personalized treatment adjustments, and improved patient outcomes. However, challenges such as data security, device miniaturization, and regulatory approvals must be addressed to facilitate widespread clinical adoption (Ren et al., 2024).

3.4. Clinical Translation and Case Studies of AI-Driven Nanosensors

A number of emerging studies indicate how AI-enabled nanoscensor technology has the potential clinical impacts in cancer diagnostics. As an example, liquid biopsy platforms based on nanoparticle-based detection and machine learning algorithm have demonstrated promising results in the detection of circulating tumor DNA (ctDNA) in extremely low concentrations. Through these platforms, non-invasive monitoring of treatment response and tumor progression is possible.

AI-assisted imaging systems combined with nanoparticle contrast agent in the diagnosis of breast cancer have shown a high sensitivity of detection than traditional methods of imaging. In the same manner, electrochemical nanosensors in combination with machine learning have also been investigated in the detection of prostate-specific antigen (PSA), which will allow the detection of prostate cancer at a younger age.

There is also the emergence of clinical trials on nanosensors-based diagnostic systems. A number of experimental systems based on nanosensors of surface-enhanced Raman spectroscopy (SERS) with deep learning models have demonstrated high diagnostic sensitivity to detect cancer-related biomarkers. These studies demonstrate how AI-nano convergence can offer new opportunities in clinical practice.

4. RECENT INNOVATIONS IN SMART NANO-SENSORS

Smart nano-sensors, powered by artificial intelligence (AI), have revolutionized the field of oncology by enabling early detection, real-time monitoring, and personalized treatment strategies. These advanced sensors integrate nanotechnology with AI-driven data analysis to enhance sensitivity, specificity, and accuracy in detecting cancer biomarkers. Unlike traditional diagnostic methods, smart nano-sensors provide rapid, non-invasive, and highly reliable cancer detection, making them indispensable in modern oncotherapy. Recent innovations have focused on AI-assisted liquid biopsy, wearable and implantable nano-sensors, and next-generation AI algorithms that improve diagnostic precision. However, despite their significant potential, these technologies face several challenges, including biocompatibility, long-term stability, ethical concerns, and regulatory hurdles that must be addressed before widespread clinical implementation (Gao et al., 2024; Junxian Zhang et al., 2024; S. Zhang et al., 2024). This section explores the latest advancements in AI-driven nano-sensors, their applications in oncology, and the challenges that need to be overcome to integrate them into global healthcare systems.

4.1. AI-Assisted Liquid Biopsy for Early Cancer Detection

Liquid biopsy has emerged as a ground-breaking approach for non-invasive cancer detection, offering real-time insights into tumor progression and treatment response. AI-assisted liquid biopsy enhances traditional methods by employing machine learning algorithms to analyze circulating tumor DNA (ctDNA), exosomes, and other biomarkers with high accuracy. These AI models process complex biological data, identifying subtle molecular alterations that indicate early-stage malignancies, long before conventional imaging techniques can detect them.

The integration of AI with liquid biopsy platforms enables automated biomarker profiling, reducing diagnostic errors and improving specificity. Advanced AI algorithms can distinguish between cancerous and non-cancerous signals, minimizing false positives and ensuring early intervention (Meng et al., 2024). Furthermore, AI-driven liquid biopsy techniques facilitate continuous disease monitoring, allowing oncologists to assess tumor evolution and treatment response over time. Despite these advancements, the widespread adoption of AI-assisted liquid biopsy faces challenges related to cost, standardization, and validation, requiring further research and clinical trials to establish its reliability in routine oncological practice.

4.2. Wearable and Implantable Nano-sensors for Continuous Monitoring

Wearable and implantable nano-sensors represent a transformative innovation in personalized cancer management, enabling real-time health monitoring and early detection of disease progression. These smart devices, embedded with AI-powered nano-sensors, continuously analyze physiological parameters, biomarker levels, and metabolic changes associated with cancer. Wearable nano-sensors, such as smart patches and biosensor-integrated smartwatches, detect fluctuations in biomarkers through sweat, saliva, or interstitial fluids, providing non-invasive and convenient monitoring solutions.

Implantable nano-sensors, on the other hand, are designed for long-term monitoring of tumor microenvironments, detecting changes in pH, oxygen levels, and inflammatory markers that influence cancer progression. AI algorithms analyze sensor-generated data, identifying patterns indicative of tumor growth or response to therapy (Dehchani et al., 2024). These sensors facilitate personalized treatment adjustments by providing oncologists with real-time patient-specific data. However, challenges related to sensor biocompatibility, power supply, and data security must be addressed to ensure their safe and effective integration into clinical practice.

4.3. Economic and Ethical Considerations

There are also a number of economic and ethical issues associated with the deployment of AI-based nanosensor technologies in the field of oncology. Advanced nanosensor platforms can only be developed and manufactured with specialized materials, advanced fabrication methods and computational infrastructure that can potentially augment healthcare costs during the initial adoption stages.

Nevertheless, the technologies can also decrease long-term healthcare costs by providing the ability to detect cancer at an early stage, as well as to avoid expensive culturally-insensitive treatments that have to be conducted at the later stages of cancer development. According to cost-effectiveness research, a timely diagnostic technology may be of great importance in reducing the total cost of treatment and increasing the chances of the patient surviving.

Ethical aspects also become an important aspect when implementing AI-driven medical technologies. The gathering and processing of massive amounts of patient information have provoked the issue of privacy, data protection and the transparency of algorithms. The AI systems should be, therefore, adherent to the existing regulatory standards, including the General Data Protection Regulation (GDPR) and the Health Insurance Portability and Accountability Act (HIPAA), so that patient confidentiality can not be compromised.

One more significant ethical challenge is algorithmic bias. There is a possibility of inaccurate predictions in some populations because AI models that were trained using non-representative data will be inaccurate, and hence health inequity may arise. To address these risks, the researchers should devise open AI systems and make sure that the training data is representative of the populations of patients.

4.4. Challenges and Limitations

Despite their significant advantages, AI-powered smart nano-sensors face several technical and practical challenges that hinder their clinical translation. One major limitation is the variability in sensor performance due to differences in patient physiology and biomarker heterogeneity. AI algorithms must be trained on diverse datasets to improve their generalizability and prevent biases in cancer detection. Additionally, the integration of nano-sensors into existing healthcare infrastructures requires substantial investment in data processing capabilities and interoperability with electronic health records.

Another challenge lies in the standardization of AI-powered diagnostics, as regulatory agencies require robust validation and clinical trials to ensure safety and efficacy. The lack of universal protocols for AI training and validation poses a significant barrier to widespread adoption. Moreover, nano-sensors must be optimized for real-world conditions, ensuring accuracy, reproducibility, and stability across different patient populations. Addressing these limitations will be crucial for the successful deployment of smart nano-sensors in routine oncological practice.

The regulatory systems that have been put in place by the healthcare authorities have a significant effect on the clinical adoption of AI-enabled nanosensor technologies. Before approving novel diagnostic devices, regulatory agencies including the U.S. Food and Drug Administration (FDA) and the European Medicines Agency (EMA) demand a lot of validation studies.

In the case of nanosensor-based technologies, regulatory acceptance entails the safety of materials to be used, long-term biocompatibility, and reliability of the devices. Furthermore, diagnosis systems based on AI should show stable functionality in different groups of patients.

The dynamic nature of the machine learning models is one of the biggest issues in controlling AI-based technologies. In contrast to conventional medical devices, AI systems keep on improving when they are exposed to new datasets. Regulatory authorities are thus coming up with adaptive assessment systems to track the activities of AI algorithms during their lifecycle.

The joint work of researchers, healthcare facilities, and regulators will also be necessary to develop standardized evaluation procedures and fast-track the safe implementation of AI-powered nanosensors into clinical practice.

4.5. Biocompatibility and Long-Term Stability Issues

Biocompatibility is a critical concern in the development of implantable and wearable nano-sensors, as prolonged exposure to biological environments can lead to immune responses, biofouling, and material degradation. The interaction of nano-sensors with blood, tissues, and immune cells must be carefully evaluated to minimize adverse reactions and ensure long-term stability. AI-driven computational models can predict nanoparticle interactions with biological systems, optimizing sensor coatings and surface modifications to improve biocompatibility (Mun et al., 2024; Qi et al., 2024).

Long-term stability is another challenge, as nano-sensors must maintain their sensitivity and accuracy over extended periods. Environmental factors such as temperature fluctuations, pH changes, and mechanical stress can affect sensor performance. Researchers are exploring self-healing nanomaterials, protective coatings, and AI-based predictive maintenance strategies to enhance the durability and reliability of nano-sensors. Overcoming these challenges will be essential for the development of long-lasting, clinically viable smart nano-sensors for cancer monitoring.

4.6. Data Privacy, Security, and Ethical Considerations in AI-Powered Oncology

The integration of AI-powered nano-sensors in oncology raises significant concerns regarding data privacy, security, and ethical considerations. These sensors generate vast amounts of patient data, necessitating robust encryption protocols to prevent unauthorized access and data breaches. AI algorithms must comply with regulations such as the General Data Protection Regulation (GDPR) and the Health Insurance Portability and Accountability Act (HIPAA) to ensure patient confidentiality and data integrity.

Ethical concerns also arise regarding algorithmic biases, as AI models trained on non-representative datasets may lead to disparities in cancer diagnosis and treatment recommendations. Transparent AI development, explainable machine learning techniques, and interdisciplinary collaborations between technologists and healthcare professionals are essential to address these ethical challenges. Additionally, informed consent and patient autonomy must be prioritized in AI-driven cancer care, ensuring that individuals have control over their health data and treatment decisions (Alagarsamy et al., 2024).

4.7. Regulatory Hurdles for Clinical Translation of AI-Driven Nanotechnology

The clinical translation of AI-driven nanotechnology faces stringent regulatory challenges, as healthcare agencies require extensive validation before approving novel diagnostic and therapeutic approaches. Regulatory bodies such as the U.S. Food and Drug Administration (FDA) and the European Medicines Agency (EMA) demand comprehensive clinical trials, risk assessments, and quality control measures to ensure patient safety (Jangid et al., 2021).

One of the key hurdles is the lack of standardized evaluation frameworks for AI-powered nano-sensors (Luo et al., 2022). The dynamic nature of AI models, which continuously learn and adapt, complicates regulatory approval processes. Establishing clear guidelines for AI validation, real-world testing, and post-market surveillance is essential for facilitating the clinical adoption of these technologies. Additionally, interdisciplinary collaboration between regulatory agencies, researchers, and industry stakeholders will be crucial in streamlining approval pathways and accelerating the translation of AI-driven nanotechnology into oncology.

4.8. Future Perspectives and Research Directions

Future research in AI-driven nano-sensors will focus on enhancing sensor miniaturization, improving real-time analytics, and developing more advanced AI algorithms for cancer detection. The convergence of AI with quantum computing, edge computing, and blockchain technology holds promise for further refining cancer diagnostics and treatment monitoring. Moreover, interdisciplinary collaborations between AI researchers, oncologists, and material scientists will drive the development of next-generation smart nano-sensors with enhanced precision and reliability.

4.9. Next-Generation AI Algorithms for Enhanced Cancer Detection

Advancements in AI, particularly in deep learning and reinforcement learning, are expected to improve the sensitivity and specificity of cancer detection. Next-generation AI models will incorporate self-learning capabilities, enabling them to adapt to new biomarker patterns and evolving tumor characteristics. Explainable AI techniques will also be integrated to enhance transparency and interpretability in clinical decision-making.

4.10. Emerging Trends in AI-Nano Convergence for Oncotherapy

Emerging trends in AI-nano convergence include the development of theragnostic nanoparticles, which combine diagnosis and therapy in a single platform. AI-powered nano systems capable of simultaneous drug delivery and real-time treatment monitoring are being explored to enhance therapeutic efficacy. Additionally, AI-driven multi-modal diagnostics, integrating imaging, liquid biopsy, and sensor-based analytics, will further refine personalized oncotherapy approaches.

4.11. Potential Impact on Global Cancer Healthcare Systems

The adoption of AI-driven nano-sensors has the potential to revolutionize global cancer healthcare systems by enabling early detection, reducing healthcare costs, and improving patient outcomes. These innovations can bridge the gap in cancer diagnostics for underserved populations by providing affordable, point-of-care testing solutions. However, ensuring equitable access to AI-driven technologies will require policy frameworks that prioritize affordability, accessibility, and healthcare infrastructure development. The future of oncology lies in the seamless integration of AI and nanotechnology, paving the way for more precise, efficient, and personalized cancer care worldwide.

5. CONCLUSION

Nanotechnology and artificial intelligence are two concepts that will change the face of contemporary oncology. Nano-sensors that are based on AI make the detection of biomarkers of cancer highly sensitive, allow real-time tracking of the disease progression, and assist in the elaboration of individual therapeutic solutions.

Novel products in the nano-sensor technologies, such as liquid biopsy, wearable diagnostic devices, and AI-assisted imaging systems have enhanced considerably the quality and efficacy of cancer diagnostics. The adaptive therapy and predictive model are also indicative of the power of AI-driven nanotechnology to optimize treatment effects.

However, there are multiple issues about sensor stability, regulatory approvals, privacy of data and economic viability that must be overcome in order to realize the mass acceptance of these technologies. Materials scientists, clinicians, and computational researchers need to continue to work together interdisciplinarily to overcome these challenges.

It is hoped that future trends in AI algorithms, miniaturization of nano-sensors, and multi-modal diagnostic systems will continue to increase the possibilities of precision oncology. With the further evolution of these technologies, the nanotechnology and artificial intelligence convergence will become the key factor in changing the global cancer healthcare systems and enhancing the patient outcomes.

REFERENCES

Acharya, B., Behera, A., Behera, S., & Moharana, S. (2024). Recent advances in nanotechnology-based drug Delivery systems for the diagnosis and treatment of Reproductive disorders. *Nano Express*, *7*(3), 1336–1361. PMID: 38412066

Ahmed, S., & Kulkarni, P. (2025). Nanotechnology in Medicine: Revolutionizing Drug Delivery Systems. *Nano Express*, 1–10.

Akdaşçi, E., Duman, H., Eker, F., Bechelany, M., & Karav, S. (2025). Chitosan and Its Nanoparticles: A Multifaceted Approach to Antibacterial Applications. *Nano Express*, *15*(2), 126. PMID: 39852740

Alagarsamy, S., John, A. J. V., Chen, S.-M., Sakthinathan, S., Chang, Y.-H., & Tang, J.-Y. (2024). Novel method of phosphorous doped bismuth oxide with carbon aerogel for a selective voltammetry quantification of anti-cancer drug: Regorafenib. *Chemical Engineering Journal*, *494*, 153054. DOI: 10.1016/j.cej.2024.153054

Ashique, S., Raikar, A., Jamil, S., Lakshminarayana, L., Gajbhiye, S. A., De, S., & Kumar, S. (2025). Artificial Intelligence Integration with Nanotechnology: A New Frontier for Sustainable and Precision Agriculture. *Nano Express*, *21*(2), 242–273.

Boukherroub, R., & Szunerits, S. (2024). The Future of Nanotechnology-Driven Electrochemical and Electrical Point-of-Care Devices and Diagnostic Tests. *Nano Express*, *17*(1), 173–195. PMID: 39018353

Butt, M. A. (2025). Surface Plasmon Resonance-Based Biodetection Systems: Principles, Progress and Applications—A Comprehensive Review. *Nano Express*, *15*(1), 35. PMID: 39852086

Chandrasekaran, R., Ushani, U., Sankar, G., Joseph, J., Natarajan, K., Palani, S., Sridhar, P., Nagaraj, R., & Sagadevan, S. (2025). Harnessing the Therapeutic Potential of Carbon Dots for Efficient Wound Healing Management. *Nano Express*, *15*(1), 1–21.

Chauhan, S. B., Chankhampan, C., Singh, I., Kallepalli, S. B., & Gupta, C. (2025). Nanotherapeutics-impregnated medical devices and their regulatory aspects. *Nano Express*, 41–61.

Chintada, V., Veeraiah, K., & Golla, N. (2024). The Development in Nanotechnology and Tailor-Made Enzymes as the Future of Biobased Economy. *Nano Express*, 267–288.

Cojocaru, E., Petri , O. R., & Cojocaru, C. (2024). Nanoparticle-Based Drug Delivery Systems in Inhaled Therapy: Improving Respiratory Medicine. *Pharmaceuticals (Basel, Switzerland), 17*(8), 1059. DOI: 10.3390/ph17081059 PMID: 39204164

Dehchani, A. J., Jafari, A., & Shahi, F. (2024). Nanogels in Biomedical Engineering: Revolutionizing Drug Delivery, Tissue Engineering, and Bioimaging. *Polymers for Advanced Technologies, 35*(10), e6595. DOI: 10.1002/pat.6595

Dehesh, E., & Dehesh, F. (2025). Nanotechnology in COVID-19 and SARS-CoV-2: Advances in Antiviral Therapies and Applications. *Nano Express, 26*(1), 87–105.

Dudhat, K. (2025). *Nanotechnology-Driven Approaches for Targeted Rectal Microbiome Modulation in Gastrointestinal Disorders*. Nano Express. DOI: 10.2174/01 15701646355945250107043902

El Zein, B., Elrashidi, A., Dahlan, M., Al Jarwan, A., & Jabbour, G. (2024). *Nano and Society 5.0: Advancing the Human-Centric Revolution*. Nano Express.

Gade, R., Dwarampudi, L. P., Yamuna, K., Maraba, N., & Fufa, G. (2025). Advanced Nanomaterials in Imaging and Diagnostics. *Nano Express*, 79–100.

Gao, W., Bigham, A., Ghomi, M., Zarrabi, A., Rabiee, N., Saeb, M. R., Nuri Ertas, Y., Goel, A., Sharifi, E., Ashrafizadeh, M., Sethi, G., Tambuwala, M. M., Wang, Y., Ghaffarlou, M., & Jiao, T. (2024). Micelle-engineered nanoplatforms for precision oncology. *Chemical Engineering Journal, 495*(April), 153438. DOI: 10.1016/j.cej.2024.153438

Ghosh, S., Sarkar, B., & Webster, T. J. (2025). Nanozyme-associated toxicity and regulation. *Nano Express*, 247–262.

Goswami, A., Garg, S., Bhatt, E., Chaudhary, V., & Dang, S. (2024). Nanotechnology-Based Biosensors for Biomedical Applications. *Nano Express, 171*(9), 97508.

Halder, S., & Kumar, R. (2025). *In Vitro and in Vivo Applications of Nanoparticles in Head and Neck Cancer*. Nano Express. DOI: 10.70593/978-93-49307-10-0

Huang, Y., Liu, H., Zhao, Y., Chen, H., Li, Q., Li, X., Hua, S., Cao, D., & Chang, Y. (2024). Disrupting redox homeostasis for tumor therapy based on PDT/chemo/ferroptosis therapeutic hybrid liposomes. *RSC Advances, 14*(28), 20152–20162. DOI: 10.1039/D4RA03361B PMID: 38915327

Jangid, A. K., Pooja, D., Jain, P., Gupta, N., Ramesan, S., & Kulhari, H. (2021). Self-assembled and pH-responsive polymeric nanomicelles impart effective delivery of paclitaxel to cancer cells. *RSC Advances, 11*(23), 13928–13939. DOI: 10.1039/D1RA01574E PMID: 35423920

Khatoon, U. T., & Velidandi, A. (2025). An Overview on the Role of Government Initiatives in Nanotechnology Innovation for Sustainable Economic Development and Research Progress. *Nano Express*, *17*(3), 1250.

Klemt, I., Reshetnikov, V., Dutta, S., Bila, G., Bilyy, R., Cuartero, I. C., Hidalgo, A., Wünsche, A., Böhm, M., Wondrak, M., Kunz-Schughart, L. A., Tietze, R., Beierlein, F., Imhof, P., Gensberger-Reigl, S., Pischetsrieder, M., Körber, M., Jost, T., & Mokhir, A. (2024). A concept of dual-responsive prodrugs based on oligomerization-controlled reactivity of ester groups: An improvement of cancer cells versus neutrophils selectivity of camptothecin. *RSC Medicinal Chemistry*, *15*(4), 1189–1197. DOI: 10.1039/D3MD00609C PMID: 38665843

Koushki, M., Amiri-Dashatan, N., Pourghadamyari, H., Khodabandehloo, H., Bagheri, F., Farahani, M., & Tayebi, L. (2024). An Overview of the Relationships between the Food Industry and Nanotechnology. *Nano Express*, *11*(2), e7–e7.

Li, B., Li, P., & Dong, R. (2025). *Recent Advances in Nanozyme-Based Materials for Environmental Detection and Remediation.* Nano Express. DOI: 10.1039/D4QM01009D

Li, X., Zheng, X., Yuan, Y., Deng, J., Su, L., & Xu, K. (2025). A review of research progress on COF-based biosensors in pathogen detection. *Nano Express*, 343605.

Luo, R., Liu, H., & Cheng, Z. (2022). Protein scaffolds: Antibody alternatives for cancer diagnosis and therapy. *RSC Chemical Biology*, *3*(7), 830–847. DOI: 10.1039/D2CB00094F PMID: 35866165

Meng, Y., Wang, C., Li, X., Wang, L., Huo, M., Chen, Y., & Wang, B. (2024). Two-Dimensional MoS2 nanosheets as cocatalyst to augment the nanocatalytic tumor therapy. *Chemical Engineering Journal*, *496*, 153887. DOI: 10.1016/j.cej.2024.153887

Mohanty, S., Desai, V. M., Jain, R., Agrawal, M., Dubey, S. K., & Singhvi, G. (2024). Unveiling the potential of photodynamic therapy with nanocarriers as a compelling therapeutic approach for skin cancer treatment: Current explorations and insights. *RSC Advances*, *14*(30), 21915–21937. DOI: 10.1039/D4RA02564D PMID: 38989245

Mousa, I., Alsharari, A. M., Alalawy, A. I., Almotairy, A. R. Z., Aljohani, S., Osailan, R., Alamoudi, W. M., El-Metwaly, N. M., & El-Metwal, N. (2025). Harnessing the Potential of Sargassum Latifolium for Sustainable Synthesis of Ag/Bi2O3-Curdlan Nanocomposites: Phytochemical Characterization and Biological Applications. *Nano Express*, 1–22.

Mun, B., Jeong, H., Kim, R., Gu, B., Kim, J., Son, H. Y., Rho, H. W., Lim, E.-K., & Haam, S. (2024). 3D-Nanostructured microfluidic device arranged in a herringbone pattern for the highly effective capture of HER2-Positive cancer-derived exosomes in urine. *Chemical Engineering Journal, 482*, 148851. DOI: 10.1016/j.cej.2024.148851

Naik, G. G., & Jagtap, V. A. (2024). *Nano TransMed.* Nano Express.

Naryal, S., Rana, M., Sharma, N., Ahmed, B., Sharma, P., Kujur, S., Jaiswal, S., Gupta, S. Das, Patel, S. M. B., & Kaushal, S. (2025). Navigating Sustainable and Healthy Future: Green Nanotechnology, Regulatory Priorities, and Challenges. *Nano Express*, 353–369.

Nastasijevic, I., Kundacina, I., Jaric, S., Pavlovic, Z., Radovic, M., & Radonic, V. (2025). *Biosensors in the Meat Production Chain.* Nano Express. DOI: 10.20944/preprints202501.1773.v1

Nikhade, R., & Jaiswal, A. (2025). *Advancements in Polymer Modification: A Comprehensive Review on Techniques.* Nano Express.

Pawara, Y., & Mahajan, H. (2025). Surface-functionalized pullulan-based polymeric nanoparticles containing resveratrol: a green approach for lung cancer targeted delivery. *Nano Express*, 1–17.

Qi, L., Li, Z., Liu, J., & Chen, X. (2024). Omics-Enhanced Nanomedicine for Cancer Therapy. *Advanced Materials, 36*(50), 2409102. DOI: 10.1002/adma.202409102 PMID: 39473316

Ren, X.-H., Shi, L., Ma, Z.-B., Wang, D.-W., He, X.-W., Li, W.-Y., & Zhang, Y.-K. (2024). Inhibition of nucleotide metabolism with dual-template epitope imprinted nanoparticles for targeted HER2+ tumor therapy. *Chemical Engineering Journal, 481*, 148739. DOI: 10.1016/j.cej.2024.148739

Ruse, G., Jîjie, A.-R., Moacă, E.-A., Pătra cu, D., Ardelean, F., Jojic, A.-A., Ardelean, S., & Tchiakpe-Antal, D.-S. (2025). Coffea arabica: An Emerging Active Ingredient in Dermato-Cosmetic Applications. *Nano Express, 18*(2), 171. PMID: 40005985

Semerjyan, G., Semerjyan, I., Ginovyan, M., & Avtandilyan, N. (2025). Characterization and antibacterial/cytotoxic activity of silver nanoparticles synthesized from Dicranum scoparium moss extracts growing in Armenia. *Nano Express, 12*(1), 29–42.

Sharma, A., Alam, M. A., & Kaur, A. (2025). Implementation of Nanocarriers for Brain-Specific Drug Delivery System. *Nano Express, 10*(1), 43–63.

Singh, A., Kaur, S., Thakur, H., Rashi, Kashyap, S., Lyudmila, A., & Mudgal, G. (2025). Unveiling the Transformative Power of Smart Cellulosic Nanomaterials: Revisiting Potential Promises to Sustainable Future. *Nano Express*, 1–42.

Sun, Z., Sun, Y., Wang, S., Li, M., Guo, H., Xu, Z., & Gao, M. (2025). Mini Review On: The Roles of DNA Nanomaterials in Phototherapy. *Nano Express*, 2021–2041.

Taha, B. A., Kadhim, A. C., Addie, A. J., Haider, A. J., Azzahrani, A. S., Raizada, P., Rustagi, S., Chaudhary, V., & Arsad, N. (2024). Advancing cancer diagnostics through multifaceted optical biosensors supported by nanomaterials and artificial intelligence: A panoramic outlook. *Microchemical Journal, 205*, 111307. DOI: 10.1016/j.microc.2024.111307

Theivendren, P., Kunjiappan, S., Pavadai, P., Ravi, K., Murugavel, A., Dayalan, A., & Santhana Krishna Kumar, A. (2024). Revolutionizing Cancer Immunotherapy: Emerging Nanotechnology-Driven Drug Delivery Systems for Enhanced Therapeutic Efficacy. *ACS Measurement Science Au*. PMID: 39991031

Tinger, L. (2024). *Development of an integrated platform for personalized cancer treatment: diagnostic and therapeutic solutions based on biomarkers and nanotechnology*. Nano Express.

Tripathy, A., Patne, A. Y., Mohapatra, S., & Mohapatra, S. S. (2024). Convergence of Nanotechnology and Machine Learning: The State of the Art, Challenges, and Perspectives. *Nano Express, 25*(22), 12368. PMID: 39596433

Wang, Y, Yang, J., Amier, Y., Yuan, D., Xun, Y., & Yu, X. (2025). Advancements in Nanomedicine for the Diagnosis and Treatment of Kidney Stones. *Nano Express*, 1401–1423.

Wang, Y., Yung, P., Lu, G., Liu, Y., Ding, C., Mao, C., Li, Z. A., & Tuan, R. S. (2025). Musculoskeletal Organs-on-Chips: An Emerging Platform for Studying the Nanotechnology–Biology Interface. *Nano Express, 37*(2), 2401334. PMID: 38491868

Yadav, V. K., Dhanasekaran, S., Choudhary, N., Nathiya, D., Thakur, V., Gupta, R., Pramanik, S., Kumar, P., Gupta, N., & Patel, A. (2025). Recent advances in nanotechnology for Parkinson's disease: Diagnosis, treatment, and future perspectives. *Nano Express, 12*, 1535682. PMID: 39911864

Zehra, S. H., Ramzan, K., Viskelis, J., Viskelis, P., & Balciunaitiene, A. (2025). Advancements in Green Synthesis of Silver-Based Nanoparticles: Antimicrobial and Antifungal Properties in Various Films. *Nano Express, 15*(4), 252. PMID: 39997815

Zhang, J., Yeoh, G. H., & Kabir, I. I. (2025). Polyurethane Materials for Fire Retardancy: Synthesis, Structure, Properties, and Applications. *Nano Express, 8*(2), 64.

Zhang, J., Deng, M., Xu, C., Li, D., Yan, X., Gu, Y., Zhong, M., Gao, H., Liu, Y., Zhang, J., Qu, X., & Zhang, J. (2024). Dual-Prodrug-Based Hyaluronic Acid Nanoplatform Provides Cascade-Boosted Drug Delivery for Oxidative Stress-Enhanced Chemotherapy. *ACS Applied Materials & Interfaces*, *16*(38), 50459–50473. DOI: 10.1021/acsami.4c11662 PMID: 39258403

Zhang, S., Kong, N., Wang, Z., Zhang, Y., Ni, C., Li, L., Wang, H., Yang, M., Yang, W., & Yan, F. (2024). Nanochemistry of gold: From surface engineering to dental healthcare applications. *Chemical Society Reviews*, *53*(8), 3656–3686. DOI: 10.1039/D3CS00894K PMID: 38502089

Zheng, X., Liu, M., Wu, Y., Chen, Y., He, W., & Guo, Z. (2024). An AIE-based monofunctional Pt(ii) complex for photodynamic therapy through synergism of necroptosis-ferroptosis. *RSC Chemical Biology*, *5*(2), 141–147. DOI: 10.1039/D3CB00113J PMID: 38333194

Chapter 12
The Cyborg Patient:
Ethical Dimensions of Intelligent Bio-Integration

L. B. Muralidhar
http://orcid.org/0000-0003-3453-613X
Jain University, India

H. R. Swpana
http://orcid.org/0000-0003-0362-409X
Jain University, India

S. Madhu
http://orcid.org/0009-0000-8816-5798
Jyothy Institute of Commerce and Management Studies, India

K. P. Sheeba
http://orcid.org/0009-0003-4707-5392
Jain University, India

N. Sathyanarayana
http://orcid.org/0000-0002-4185-7751
Jain University, India

ABSTRACT

This chapter explores the emergence of the cyborg patient—a hybrid of human biology and intelligent technology—within contemporary medical, ethical, and cultural paradigms. It examines how adaptive prosthetics, brain-computer interfaces, and AI-mediated implants transform personhood, autonomy, and care. By merging posthumanist, transhumanist, and systems-theoretical perspectives, the text redefines embodiment as a co-evolution of humans and machines. The discussion

DOI: 10.4018/979-8-2600-0981-9.ch012

highlights global disparities, data ethics, neurorights, and governance models that balance innovation with justice, inclusivity, and sustainability. Ultimately, it calls for a digital humanist framework where technology enhances dignity, equity, and ecological responsibility in healthcare.

1. INTRODUCTION: THE AGE OF THE CYBORG PATIENT

Cyborg patients exemplify a significant reconfiguration of the medical ontology, in which human biological and cognitive capacities are maintained or supplemented by intelligent devices that learn, rather than static devices designed to be restorative. Unlike traditional prosthetics, modern pacemakers, neural implants, and AI-driven prostheses operate on the basis of ongoing data processing and adaptive feedback, giving rise to a form of bio-digital symbiosis that reshapes corporeal and cognitive identity (Haraway, 1991; Clark, 2003). Evidence of how healthcare is becoming organised around real-time, algorithmically mediated decision-making is seen in Japan's deployment of robotic exoskeletons in clinical settings, DARPA-funded neural research in the United States, and the ethically constrained deployment of AI throughout Europe. This shift from static devices to learning machines redistributes agency among the patient, clinician, and algorithm, thereby complicating accountability, consent, and liability for autonomous decision-making (Cabitza et al., 2017).

This chapter contends that the cyborg patient can best be understood in terms of relations of power and changing subject positions, embodied as the agency, identity, and autonomy of the cyberpatient, which are co-produced through adaptive technologies, clinical techniques, and institutional governance. Ethical and policy challenges of intelligent bio-integration, therefore, cannot be solved at the moment of device approval and implantation alone but must be defended and resolved through lifecycle-based and relational accountability frameworks that integrate patient experience, clinician judgement and a system capacity (Floridi & Cowls, 2019; Cabitza et al., 2017).

A cyborg patient is a patient whose functions, be they bodily or cognitive, are maintained or augmented by continuously adaptive, learning, updating, and interactive technological systems that operate and interact with various clinical and social environments over time, rather than by static medical devices. This definition foregrounds the adaptation, co-agency, and institutional dependence as characteristics of cyborg medicine today (Clark, 2003; Ienca & Andorno, 2017).

At the same time, a confusing regulatory landscape and unanswered questions about data ownership, particularly regarding neural data under the EU GDPR, create a vacuum in accountability and data sovereignty, thereby increasing the need for transnational governance. Longitudinal qualitative studies of deep brain stimulation and brain-computer interface users indicate wavering trust, renegotiation of identity, and concerns about dependency, conditioned by institutional support, socioeconomic status, and culture, and thus challenge linear narratives of power (Gilbert et al., 2017; Klein et al., 2015). These dynamics are significant for the recognition of cyborg medicine, which reworks the agency of patients and clinicians alongside algorithmic systems, thereby invalidating current medical ethical frameworks and regulations. Addressing these challenges requires approaches to relational accountability that combine elements of cultural pluralism, data justice, and patient-centred governance within multidisciplinary policy architectures (Floridi & Cowls, 2019; Ienca & Andorno, 2017).

While the chapter has been written primarily for the benefit of scholars, policymakers, and advanced practitioners, each major section contains a synthesising commentary that translates interdisciplinary theory into applied ethical and governance insights. This structure is designed to support readers from neighbouring disciplines by explaining how philosophical and policy analysis inform concrete decisions in clinical practice and the design of health systems (Floridi & Cowls, 2019; Greenhalgh et al., 2017).

2. BACKGROUND

The Cyborg Manifesto (1991) by Haraway dramatised a new form of relationship between the human and the machine by denying the binary between organism and mechanism and replacing it with a postmodern cyborg identity and power. The neural-controlled prosthetics developed by Chalmers University exemplify the tension between critical posthuman thinking and evidence-based health innovation and are not only advanced technologies but also reflect an applied, instrumentalised version of cyborg theory in clinical practice.

Posthumanism and transhumanism are two approaches to integrating human technology that differ and may be mutually exclusive. Posthumanism emphasises the importance of relational embodiment and distributed agency. It seeks to challenge rigid boundaries between human and machine, focusing on the implications of technologies for the transformation of identity and responsibility within sociotechnical systems (Braidotti, 2013). Transhumanism, by contrast, prioritises optimisation, performance enhancement and the extension of individual capacities. In many cases, we view technology as a means to transcend these biological limitations and reconfigure relational agency (Kurzweil, 2005).

An ethical analysis of augmentation technologies reveals a productive tension between care ethics and utilitarianism. Care-oriented frameworks emphasise interdependence (relational), dignity, and social continuity, encouraging technologies that complement, rather than displace, human care, as in Japan, where AI-assisted exoskeletons are used to support older adults (Shibata & Wada, 2011). Utilitarian approaches, such as the QALY-based assessments in NHS evaluations of robotic surgery, are aggregate welfare- and efficiency-based, with little regard for the embodied and psychological dimensions of cyborgity. Understanding the cyborg patient, therefore, requires a systems-oriented approach to situate individuals within sociotechnical networks of devices, institutions, data infrastructures, and cultural norms, and demands multi-level regulatory frameworks to address issues of reliability, data ethics, professional adaptation, and patient literacy (Trist, 1981).

Despite extensive literature on philosophical and regulatory works, there remain critical gaps in empirical data on long-term patient outcomes and real-world performance of intelligent bio-integrated systems. First, empirical longitudinal studies that document patient experiences using adaptive implants and BCIs are still limited, and this limits the understanding of long-term psychosocial effects. Second, the comparative governance analyses remain Euro-American regulatory models, given precedence over other observational models. Importantly, comparative governance analyses provide insufficient insight into how bio-integration unfolds within resource-constrained health systems in the Global South. Third, while distributive justice and techno-colonialism are well theorised, they are often analysed through sustained clinical evidence, which leaves equity issues analytically strong and empirically weak (Greenhalgh et al., 2017; Klein et al., 2015; Reddy et al., 2021).

Recent neuroethical scholarship has also refined these concerns by analysing how transformative and closed-loop systems transform agency and responsibility over time. Post-2022 analyses suggest that learning systems can create epistemic asymmetries among clinicians, patients, and developers, making consent and interpretability more difficult than in earlier quantification models of medical automation (Baker, 2023). This piece of work reinforces the argument made in this chapter that the methodological approach to ethical evaluation must address outcomes and the changing intelligibility of algorithmic action in the clinical context. Together, these perspectives conceptualise cyborg medicine as a system of distributed agency, emphasising that the focus of ethical evaluation should lie in routine clinical decision-making and institutional design rather than ethical principles alone.

This section addresses the sociotechnical system of cyborg medicine, in which agency, responsibility and identity are distributed amongst human, algorithmic, and institutional actors. While posthumanist and systems-oriented theories do provide a decisive conceptual contribution, their primary usefulness lies in explaining why ethical support must extend beyond devices to clinical process flows, patient adaptation, and governance infrastructures. This framing prepares the ground for the examination of the empirical and applied dimensions of intelligent bio-integration in the following sections.

The multidisciplinary and ethical frameworks developed in the previous section offer an interpretive lens rather than an abstract overlay for making sense of clinical realities. Concepts like relational autonomy, distributed agency, and lifecycle governance highlight reasons why empirical cases need to be understood not as individual incidences but, instead, we need to regard these cases as symptoms of systemic design, institutional capacity, and policy choices (Floridi & Cowls, 2019; Greenhalgh et al., 2017). Framing the following case studies through this lens makes them helpful rather than harmful.

The preceding section has established cyborg medicine as a sociotechnical phenomenon with distributed agency, ethical pluralisms and institutional context. The subsequent section translates these conceptual insights into tangible technological forms and shows how intelligent bio-integration materialises as adaptive implants, neural interfaces, and rehabilitative systems. This shift from theory to practice retains the ethical and governance issues as interpretive anchors (Floridi & Cowls, 2019; Greenhalgh et al., 2017). Reiterating the chapter's central thesis, these frameworks indicate that the ethical assessment of cyborg patients should concern not isolated devices or one-time interventions but rather the changing relationships among humans, technologies, and institutions.

Building up from this theoretical distinction and basic thesis, the following section explores the materialisations of these logics of relational agency and optimisation in concrete forms of technology. Through the development of smart implants, neural interfaces, and adaptive prosthetics, it was possible to trace the transformation of abstract ethical concepts into real-world clinical systems and decision-making scenarios (Floridi & Cowls, 2019; Greenhalgh et al., 2017).

3. MAIN FOCUS

3.1 Functional Integration: From Smart Implants to Neural Interfaces

The development of bio-integrated technologies today represents a far more decisive step than the static prosthetic replacement of the human body: the emergence of technically mediated man-machine systems that are adaptive, algorithmically qualified, and that integrate human (organic) and computational processes. Cardiac devices exemplify this trend: fixed-rate implantable cardioverter-defibrillators have evolved into implantable telemetry-enabled devices that can detect, analyse, and, in real time, therapeutically modulate data collected from the device (Mond & Proclemer, 2011).

A parallel evolution has been observed in brain-computer interfaces, moving from basic electroencephalographic communication capabilities to invasive and non-invasive systems that capture neuronal signals and translate them into actionable control to restore motor and cognitive function and enable neurorehabilitation (Musk, 2019). Concurrently, robotic and exoskeletal prostheses, such as bioelectrically-driven assistive devices and osseointegrated limb applications such as stimulatory osteo-apoptoses, become connected to AI-media and cognitive and sensuous adaptation, consequently blurring clinical distinctions between rehabilitation, augmentation, and embodiment (Kanzaki & Iijima, 2013; Ortiz-Catalan et al., 2014).

The following vignettes synthesise the conceptual, technological, and ethical issues discussed thus far by following a single cyborg patient across stages of care.

Case Vignette 1- Adaptive Cardiac Autonomy

A middle-aged patient with an implantable cardioverter-defibrillator who uses an artificial intelligence device reports increased confidence in survival but decreased perceived control, because the device's interventions occur without conscious awareness. While this is clinically effective, the patient wants to know about responsibility in cases where algorithmic decisions are made on top of subjective cues from the body, and this is a good example of the ethical tensions among safety, autonomy, and explainability in closed-loop systems (Cabitza et al., 2017).

Case Vignette 2 Neural Rehabilitation and Identity Negotiation

In a neurorehabilitation programme based on the use of adaptive brain-computer interfaces, a post-stroke patient first experiences empowerment through the regained motor function, then experiences anxiety related to the use of proprietary software updates. The case highlights that identity continuity and autonomy are determined not only by neural recovery processes but also by institutional support, transparency, and the long-term governance of algorithmic care (Murray, 2009).

Case Vignette 3: Overriding Clinical and Algorithmic Recommendations

A neurologist treating a patient with an adaptive deep-brain stimulation device is faced with repeated changes to his or her algorithms to improve the patient's motor capabilities but worsen mood instability. Although the system recommends continuing optimisation for motor outcomes, the clinician partially overrides the algorithm after shared deliberation with the patient and family, prioritising psychological well-being over performance metrics. This scenario speaks volumes about the way in which ethical clinical judgment in cyborg medicine is often a matter of negotiating tensions between the optimisation of algorithms, patient-reported outcomes, and professional responsibility, and this demonstrates the need for clinician discretion within adaptive systems (Cabitza et al., 2017; Gilbert et al., 2017).

Case Vignette 4: Integrated Patient Journey Vignette or Implantation to Long Term Care

A patient undergoing an AI-enhanced neuroprosthetic procedure at 42 years of age first reports enhanced mobility and optimism in the post-implantation period. Over the years, new challenges have emerged through routine follow-up visits: insecurity about software updates, lack of access to authorised service centres, and concern about long-term affordability after insurance coverage expires. This longitudinal experience illustrates how ethical issues (dynamic consent, clinician interpretability, and distributive justice) arise but are not manifest as abstract principles; instead, they manifest as everyday organisational and relational issues shaped by health-system capacity, institutional support, and patient literacy (Greenhalgh et al., 2017; Gilbert et al., 2017).

In the day-to-day work of clinical settings, ethical issues in cyborg medicine may arise in the context of rather mundane interactions, such as visits to recalibrate a device, revise consent and troubleshoot a software update, rather than spectacular technological failures. Clinicians, therefore, must regularly weigh algorithmic recommendations against patient-reported discomfort, emotional burden, and socioeconomic limitations, and demonstrate that ethical judgment is a continuous process embedded in routine standard care pathways rather than a special occasion (Cabitza et al., 2017; Gilbert et al., 2017).

This longitudinal vignette is an applied synthesis of the ethical frameworks presented in the chapter, illustrating how issues of dynamic consent, neuroethics, and distributive justice are seen to emerge incrementally through routine clinical and organisational interactions, rather than at the moment of implantation alone (Greenhalgh et al., 2017).

Taken together, these vignettes paint a single ethical picture (rather than many) - from initial empowerment to long-term dependency and organisational constraint - of the application of abstract principles such as neuroethics, consent renewal and distributive justice at work over a cyborg patient's life journey.

Taken together, these cases highlight the interplay between the structure of ethical and policy reasoning and the specifics of clinical decision-making, including serious legal and conceptual issues concerning consent renewal, algorithmic override, and long-term care continuity. Instead of presenting new ethical conundrums, the vignettes reveal how well-established theoretical principles acquire new practical significance within routine organisational constraints and clinician-patient negotiation (Cabitza et al., 2017; Gilbert et al., 2017). This connection reinforces the chapter's central argument that ethical management of cyborg medicine is not achieved at the point of technological deployment, but rather through practice in steps.

These examples show just how agency, consent and responsibility change over the lifecycle of intelligent bio-integration. They also tell us that ethical tensions are not felt at isolated points in time, but rather over longer clinical and organisational trajectories. This helps to lay the groundwork for examining ethical frameworks and governance controversies in focus in the next section (Cabitza et al., 2017).

While vignettes reveal the ethical dilemmas in an individual's care trajectory, general patterns remain apparent only through systematic patient-reported outcome research. The following section, therefore, transitions from illustrative cases to population-level evidence, focusing on the development of autonomy, identity, and trust across different healthcare settings (Gilbert et al., 2017; Klein et al., 2015).

This section shows that intelligent bio-integration is not only a matter of technical sophistication but also encompasses the interactions among adaptive systems, clinical practice, patients' experiences, and institutional capacity. The technologies discussed suggest why ethical concerns about autonomy, responsibility and accountability cannot be separated from system design and long-term care arrangements. These understandings form the basis for evaluating the live experiences and outcomes in the following sections.

3.2 Patient-Reported Outcomes and Lived Cyborg Experience

Empirical patient-reported outcomes studies have suggested that the success and failure of the embodiment of bio-integration cannot be separated from the subjective interpretation of patients of these elements, namely embodiment, autonomy and trust. Longitudinal qualitative research emphasises the role of identity renegotiation and emotional ambivalence in adaptation and underscores the need to evaluate cyborg medicine from experiential and clinical perspectives (Klein et al., 2015; Gilbert et al., 2017).

Clinical outcome studies are increasingly demonstrating that the success of an intelligent bio-integration cannot be evaluated by functional measures alone; instead, they have to include also patient-reported outcome measures (PROMs) such as perceived autonomy, emotional stability and quality of life. Longitudinal follow-ups of users of deep brain stimulation and adaptive cardiac devices suggest that although there may be motor or survival benefits to the patients, there is often concern about identity continuity or dependence upon opaque algorithms and ambiguity regarding how the device will be managed over the long term (Schüpbach & Agid, 2008; Gilbert et al., 2017). These findings highlight that patient-centred outcomes are evolving and require continuous clinical dialogue rather than a one-off ethical or regulatory assessment (Greenhalgh et al., 2017).

Recent studies on patient-reported outcomes have provided evidence that long-term acceptance of intelligent implants is more strongly linked to continuity of care, communication, and predictable access to maintenance services than to maximal functional improvements (Gilbert et al., 2017; Klein et al., 2015).

Comparative qualitative studies of implants and BCIs across healthcare settings show that patients' experiences vary substantially depending on cultural context, health system support, and socioeconomic status. Research on people using deep brain stimulation in India and South Africa raises issues of long-term affordability, family decision-making, and dependence on external vendors, which create perceptions of autonomy that differ from those in high-income countries (Reddy et al., 2021; Klein et al., 2015). These findings underscore the importance of conducting ethical assessments of cyborg medicine not by presuming the universality of trajectories of empowerment and acceptance, but by grounding them in region-specific lived realities.

More recent empirical inroads into assumptions of linear empowerment include documenting fluctuations in trust, autonomy, and identity over the lifetime of intelligent implants. Post-2020 qualitative follow-ups have suggested the emergence of ethical stressors not anticipated at the time of implantation, including algorithm updates, service discontinuities, and insurance withdrawal, which reinforce the need to integrate patient-reported outcome measures into governance and reimbursement frameworks (Greenhalgh et al., 2017; Veale & Borgesius, 2021).

More recent literature, published since 2021, focuses on the long-term outcomes of adaptive and closed-loop systems in routine care. A 2022 scoping review of closed-loop deep brain stimulation found significant inter-individual variability in psychosocial adaptation, documenting delays in mood, self-perception, and dependence that are not captured in brief case reports (Cuschieri et al., 2022). Follow-up cohort studies indicate that, despite long-standing functional improvement, dependence on services, device fatigue, and caregiver burden emerge several years after implantation, underscoring the importance of lifecycle (for life)- based ethical and clinical assessment (Price et al., 2019; Samuel & Derrick, 2020).

Recent clinical follow-up investigations of adaptive neurostimulation and advanced prosthetics reestablish the importance of long-term, real-world evaluation. Post-2019 studies of deep brain stimulation and closed-loop neuromodulation report delayed psychosocial strain, device fatigue, and service dependency several years post-implantation, despite sustained functional gains (Price et al., 2019; Samuel & Derrick, 2020). These results reinforce the case for the ethical evaluation of intelligent bio-integration practices by integrating patient-reported outcomes with post-marketing clinical surveillance and institutional capacity as integral components of the evaluation process, rather than relying solely on pre-approval data generated in clinical trials.

From an interdisciplinary perspective, empirical patient-reported outcomes provide operational meaning for philosophical accounts of relational autonomy and posthuman embodiment. Reports of varying trust, identity renegotiation and dependence anxiety from implant users empirically support postmodernist arguments that agency does not lie in the individual but is spread across human, technological and institutional actors (Braidotti, 2013; Gilbert et al., 2017). In this sense, clinical evidence is not only an illustration of ethical theory but also a testing ground for abstract ideas such as co-agency, dignity, and responsibility that are continuously negotiated in the day-to-day practices of care (Greenhalgh et al., 2017).

Longitudinal outcome studies suggest that short-term functional outcomes are insufficient to assess the clinical success of intelligent implants and BCIs. Evidence from long-term follow-ups of deep brain stimulation, cochlear implants, and osseointegrated prosthetics indicates that device abandonment, psychosocial fatigue, and maintenance failure occur several years after implantation, often related to insufficient support infrastructure rather than technical malfunction (Schüpbach & Agid, 2008; Ortiz-Catalan et al., 2014). These findings underscore the ethical importance of assessing cyborg medicine beyond episodic clinical benchmarks and toward extended care horizons.

Recent governance practices indicate a shift from episodic compliance to lifecycle regulation for adaptive medical AI. The European Union's Artificial Intelligence Act, which came into force in 2024, relates to the different AI systems and cookies present in the medical field because it classifies most medical systems as high risk and requires ongoing risk management, documentation of transparency and human oversight during the various stages of deployment (European Commission, 2024). In parallel, U.S. regulatory guidance on Predetermined Change Control Plans institutionalises the control of learning systems by mandating pre-specified pathways for updating and post-market monitoring, marking a move towards adaptive governance models, as opposed to static regulatory approaches, as approved by authorities (FDA, 2025).

Qualitative scholarship highlights the rarity of access to the lived experience of bio-integrated technologies, which cannot be fully captured or measured by standardised outcome measures. First-person account from consumers of deep-brain stimulation and cochlear implants. Neuroprosthetics have shown that patients actively reinterpret bodily boundaries, agency, and trust over time, a process often reflected in the devices themselves, ranging from a wholly external tool to a complete assimilation of body parts (Leder, 1990; Gilbert et al., 2017). These accounts illustrate a relational process of working out identity within clinician-patient, family, and institutional contexts, rather than at the point of implantation.

Narrative studies have also shown that, in long-term adaptation, large-scale adaptation is often characterised by ambivalence rather than empowerment. Alternate states of gratitude and estrangement, and of recalibrated lives, are described by users as an update of software, a recalibration of equipment, or a clinical encounter that alters the commonplace, current understanding of self (Murray, 2009; Klein et al., 2015). Sustaining trust by attending to these lived narratives is therefore vital, not only for ethical evaluation but also for maintaining patient trust, as this is closely linked to patient interpretation, continuity of care, and the recognition of experiential knowledge alongside clinical metrics (Greenhalgh et al., 2017).

Patient-reported outcomes evidence has been used to support ethical arguments, including demonstrating that continuity of care, institutional support, and interpretability underpin ethical arguments about the nature of autonomy and trust, as well as about identity, and that these arguments are grounded in patients' lived experience rather than in technical performance alone. These findings empirically support the ideas of posthuman and relational ethics by showing us how agency is negotiated in the human, technological, and organisational domains. As such, patient experience serves as an ethical indicator and a policy-relevant metric for sustainable bio-integration.

3.3 Clinical Co-Agency, Autonomy, and Lived Experience in Intelligent Bio-Integration

From a clinical operations perspective, intelligent bio-integrated systems redefine how care is delivered, distributing cognitive and temporal labour within healthcare organisations. Studies of adaptive implants have suggested that clinicians spend more time discussing algorithmic behaviour, negotiating consent changes, and patient anxiety related to opaque system updates, often without institutional support or training (Cabitza et al., 2017; Greenhalgh et al., 2017). These pressures on workflow are especially acute in resource-constrained settings, where dependence on external vendors for maintenance and recalibration limits clinicians' autonomy and delays care; these issues provide evidence that implementation challenges are not peripheral determinants of ethical sustainability but central determinants.

Patient-reported outcome measures increasingly provide evidence that long-term satisfaction with intelligent implants is more strongly correlated with perceived continuity of care and interpretability than with peak functional performance. According to longitudinal follow-ups, patients with strong communication skills and a stable connection to maintenance services/software updates have more favourable autonomy scores and less dependence on anxiety, regardless of device sophistication

(Gilbert et al., 2017; Klein et al., 2015). These findings suggest that, not technological capability, but rather the reliability of the ecosystems (clinical and institutional) around the patient will change their adaptation.

In routine clinical encounters, these dynamics surface when patients seek clarification about software updates, algorithmic changes, or unexplained device behaviours, requiring clinicians to translate complex system logics into understandable, trust-preserving explanations. The constitutional inclusion of these rights in Chile constitutes an innovative legislative precedent, but the operationalisation of consent, auditability, and data portability remains under development. The regulatory trajectories vary across the world: the GDPR of the EU and the upcoming AI Act have codified human-centred risk management, and transparency of algorithms; the U.S. Food and Drug Administration (FDA) promotes adaptive regulation (in its Software as a Medical Device (SaMD) framework and Predetermined Change Control Plan); and the federated, consent-based ecosystem of human data regulation is new in the 2023 Digital Personal Data Protection Act of India, as well as the Ayushman Bharat Digital Mission.

Japan, by comparison, incorporates robotics into eldercare using culturally sensitive regulation that focuses on safety, utility, and the overall good. In these systems, autonomy is developed from an individualistic notion to a distributed form of possession among patients, clinicians, and intelligent infrastructures. The established bioethical approaches based on the principles of informed consent and personal agency (Beauchamp and Childress, 2019) find it more challenging to embrace systems that are preconscious, such as pacemakers that correct arrhythmias or BCIs that decode neural intent via adaptive decoding. Algorithms, model drift, and automation bias lead to accountability problems in decision-making and to the problematization of clinical judgment (Cabitza et al., 2017).

Translating intelligent bio-integration from experimental promise to routine care raises complex clinical and organisational challenges. Clinicians report having little regard for interpreting adaptive algorithmic behaviour, which limits their ability to explain system decisions or challenge outputs during patient consultations (Cabitza et al., 2017). Workflow disruption, increased documentation burdens, and dependence on external vendors for updates and repairs are further complications of assuming responsibility for integration into time-constrained clinical environments.

Maintenance failures and service discontinuities, rather than device malfunction, have been highlighted as significant causes of abandonment in long-term follow-up studies (Ortiz-Catalan et al., 2014). These findings suggest that, for ethical bio-integration to succeed, moral and principled governance is necessary, as are investments in clinician education, interoperable infrastructures, and institutional preparedness to sustain adaptive systems over time.

Evidence from real-world deployment studies suggests that clinicians' workload, institutional preparedness, and continuity of service are key determinants of the outcomes of intelligent bio-integrated care. Empirical evaluations of AI-enabled medical devices have frequently found that non-adoption and abandonment are attributed to inadequate training, workflow misalignment and unacceptability, and difficulty understanding the information produced by medical devices, rather than to technical failure (Greenhalgh et al., 2017; Price et al., 2019). Incorporating these findings enhances the chapter's applied nature and anchors the discussion of ethical issues within the framework of patterns of clinical practice.

In practical terms, intelligent bio-integration changes the way we care, demanding more of clinicians' capacity to manage data and communicate, and supporting institutional-level systems. Ethical care, therefore, does not depend solely on the algorithmic performance of a human figure but also on the training required, the continuity of services, and the control and transparency of AI services. This insight, which stems from a combination of ethical theory and everyday healthcare practice, is one way of bridging the gap for non-specialist readers (Cabitza et al., 2017; Greenhalgh et al., 2017).

3.4 Global Governance, Data Ethics, and Relational Accountability in Cyborg Medicine

Contemporary responses to bio-integrated technologies in governance include the introduction of iterative regulatory mechanisms, such as algorithmic impact assessment, post-market surveillance, and adaptive approval regimes, across the NHS, the EU Medical Device Regulation in Germany, and the FDA in the USA. However, autonomy remains structurally contingent on maintaining exonosis for long-term maintenance ecosystems, insurance coverage and tech support, and vendor lock-in and proprietary licensing, and, for systematic reasons in the field of information technology, reallocate agency from patient to firm (Ortiz-Catalan et al., 2014). At the same time, omnipresent biosensing creates a tension between empowerment and surveillance, as therapeutic data are repurposed for secondary analytics despite safeguards such as the GDPR and the Caldicott Principles (Zuboff, 2019; Haggerty & Ericson, 2000). Sustainable governance, hence, requires relational accountability grounded in explainability, contestability, and participatory design to facilitate users' equitable and enduring agency (Wachter et al., 2017).

3.5 Ethical Frameworks and Moral Controversies

Adaptive implants, brain-computer interfaces, and biosensor systems constitute a form of smart bio-integration that challenges commonly held assumptions about the body, data, and clinical decision-making. Informed consent models based on pre-determined interventions and anticipated risks are out of step with self-learning devices whose functionality, risk and data practices change as they are used and which must thus consent to operate as a continuous, auditable process based on transparency and patient participation rather than a single, one-time contractual act (Cabitza et al., 2017).

This challenge is complicated by the rise of algorithmic agency, in which autonomous systems take the initiative in therapeutic action or alter it without human mediation, and by the need for new forms of algorithmic consent that integrate procedural accountability with traceable mechanisms of oversight (Coeckelbergh, 2020). At the same time, the explosive increase in the presence of biometric data in privately controlled infrastructures intensifies conflicts over ownership and control, as patients increasingly view biosignals as an extension of bodily integrity, while companies have come to view proprietary interests in models trained on such data as assets.

3.6 Key Problems in Cyborg Medicine.

A constant ethical fault line is between therapy and enhancement. While restorative interventions such as cochlear implants or assistive exoskeletons are widely accepted, augmentation that raises function beyond normative levels is a source of distributive and moral discomfort, especially when public reimbursement is a matter of debate, as in German policy debates on exoskeletal support (Hagele, 2020).

These disputes are part of wider inequalities around the world, where high-tech prosthetic and neuro-interfaces are centred in wealthier regions. At the same time, low-income people are using frugal alternatives, such as the Jaipur Foot, thereby contributing to a stratified "cyborg divide". Beyond the issue of material access, epistemic injustice occurs when the datasets and algorithmic benchmarks used disproportionately represent Western populations, thereby introducing overarching cultural and biological biases into clinical systems.

Diverse philosophical responses abound: deontological ethics focuses on issues of human dignity and warns of enhancement as breach of moral boundaries (Habermas, 2003); consequentialist arguments are based on 'measurements' of welfare such as quality-adjusted life years; virtue ethics raises questions, for instance, as to whether enhancement produces dependency or autonomy (MacIntyre, 2007); and techno-ethics put questions of structural justice at front: questions regarding extractive data economies and unfair global supply chains (Brey, 2012).

3.7 Emerging Trends in Human–AI Co-Agency.

Cultural and geopolitical perspectives also complicate ethical evaluation. Existential and theological critiques of enhancement have tended to frame it as a transgression of human finitude (Fukuyama, 2002), whereas, in pragmatic clinical traditions, technological progress is understood as an extension of healing practice. Concurrently, bio-integration is increasingly commodified through subscription-based models and proprietary ecosystems, creating dependencies on corporate infrastructures that are expected to be long-term unless balanced by public reimbursement, price regulation, or universal access schemes, as in parts of Europe and Japan (Zuboff, 2019).

The concept of techno-colonialism emphasises the patriarchal ways in which high-income countries patent technologies and control data, whilst lower-income regions become testing grounds or sources of information, with the marginalisation of non-Western epistemologies through algorithmic architectures (Shah, 2019). Indigenous and Global South frameworks disrupt these dynamics by foregrounding relationality, collective consent, and epistemic sovereignty, as embodied in Maori hauora's integral perspective on health and in participatory data governance models that support frugal innovation and local repair ecosystems (Durie, 1998; Singh, 2019).

Taken together, the above analysis shows five trends that converge in the area of ethical and intelligent healthcare innovation. First, agency is increasingly distributed among patients, clinicians, and adaptive algorithms, so that traditional models of responsibility and consent no longer hold (Cabitza et al., 2017). Second, data governance has shifted from episodic privacy protection toward continuous stewardship, as biosensor-driven care means that surveillance will extend beyond the clinical setting (Floridi & Taddeo, 2016).

Third, intelligent bio-integration reinforces and embeds inequalities not only in affordability but also in maintenance infrastructure and digital literacies, which are unequally distributed across populations and regions (Reddy et al., 2021). Fourth, patient identity is no longer a fixed clinical outcome but a developing story that changes as it interacts with adaptive systems (Gilbert et al., 2017). Finally, governance frameworks are moving toward adaptive, lifecycle-based regulation, recognising that ethical risk does not end with approval but continues to evolve after deployment (Greenhalgh et al., 2017). This synthesis explains the inextricable intertwining of technological innovation, ethical theory, and institutional design with intelligent healthcare systems.

3.8 Practical Implications for Clinical and Regulatory Practice.

Legal accountability is still misaligned with the complexity of technology since classical tort doctrines find it difficult to apportion responsibility across distributed human-algorithmic systems, and hence there are calls for increased liability of manufacturers, sharing the responsibility or even electronic personhood, despite there still being resistance at the conceptual level (Pagallo, 2013). Jurisdictional differences - from product liability in the United States to professional duty in Japan and to frameworks for service deficiencies in India - emphasise regulatory fragmentation.

For clinicians, dynamic consent entails iterative engagement in word of software updates and adaptive modification; for regulators, neurorights entail post-market auditability and contestability; for designers, ethical bio-integration entails explainability, repairability and modular design as ways to diminish risks of abandonment and dependency (Mitchell et al., 2019; Veale & Borgesius, 2021). Collectively, these interdependencies demonstrate that responsible cyborg medicine requires relational, lifecycle-based governance modes that balance innovation and dignity, equity and shared responsibility across diverse healthcare systems (Floridi, 2019; Greenhalgh et al., 2017).

Clinical Snapshot A - Maintenance Failure: Public hospital cancels adaptive neuroprosthetic support (after vendor withdraws) - Patients are in a functionally dependent state, with no support currently available. The incident indicates that the ethical risk is not the device's malfunction but the fragility of the institution and the device's purchase (Ortiz-Catalan et al., 2014).

Clinical Snapshot B - Algorithmic Override: A clinician overrides the algorithm to temporarily change the dosage of the patient after the patient is reported to be in distress not reflected in the system's metrics. This scenario clearly demonstrates the dependence of ethical care of bio-integrated systems on professional discretion and interpretive authority, which is not only dependent on automation (Cabitza et al., 2017).

From a practice and policy perspective, these experiences of clinical practitioners help identify the need for the formal figuring out of interpretive labour within adaptive care systems. The driving forces that may cause algorithmic bias to undermine professional judgement are the need for training in algorithmic literacy, protected time for explaining to patients, and institutional support for ethical overrides (Cabitza et al., 2017; Greenhalgh et al., 2017). At the level of policy, reimbursement, and regulation, these workflow expectations must be recognised if intelligent bio-integration is to be viable from a clinical perspective and sustainable from an ethical perspective.

Clinician interview in adaptive care contexts highlights an increasing interpretive myth load associated with algorithm-mediated treatment (where responsibility for outcome is, by default, human), which is partly automated. Practitioners experience moral distress when recommendations from systems conflict with statements provided by patients about suffering, especially when institutional practices favour algorithmic outputs over clinical judgment (Cabitza et al., 2017). These experiences underscore the need to shift clinician discretion from a backstop mechanism to a bare-minimum safeguard in intelligent bio-integrated care pathways.

For patients, intelligent bio-integration alters the practice of daily care by extending ethical considerations beyond device implantation to encompass long-term issues of affordability, interpretability, and dependence on institutional support systems. Once again, patients are demanding and require sustained counselling, clarity regarding software updates, and predictability of access to maintenance to maintain their autonomy and trust over time (Gilbert et al., 2017; Greenhalgh et al., 2017).

For clinicians, adaptive systems entail new forms of professional responsibility, including interpreting algorithms, engaging in intuitive shared decision-making, and overriding automated recommendations. Healthcare institutions, in turn, will have to make procurement, training, and service contracts with a focus on repairability, continuity of care, and the lifecycle, rather than on short-term technological performance (Mitchell et al., 2019; Reddy et al., 2021).

3.9 Government and Institutional Initiatives

International regulatory responses to intelligent bio-integration reveal convergent purposes but divergent operational logics, shaped by the institutional capacity of regulation, political economy, and cultural norms. The European Union's Artificial Intelligence Act employs a precautionary and subject-to-rights approach, classifies most medical AI as high risk, and requires strict conformity assessment and traceability, as well as human supervision, which compounds patient protection without improving the pace of innovation in Neuroprosthetics (Veale & Borgesius, 2021).

India's Ayushman Bharat Digital Mission is promoting an inclusive, federated data architecture that is based on consent and a unique health identifier; however, what is limited is the scalability based on infrastructural asymmetries, uneven digital literacy and weak enforcement, alongside data extractivism concerns through global partnerships (Reddy, 2022; Shah, 2019). The United States tends to adopt innovation-based governance strategies like the NIH BRAIN Initiative and the DARPA programmes with an ethos of promoting speed and teaming up with the private sector, but at this point, it has not done well on overseeing and lacks the capacity to assess algorithm opacity and adaptive risk (Insel et al., 2013; Ienca & Andorno, 2017).

Japan's integrated regulatory ecosystem meets assistive robotics with a collectivist ethics of eldercare policy: incorporating technological hybridity into proud cultural legitimisation (Robertson, 2018). Across systems, conventional ethics review mechanisms are poorly equipped to govern longitudinal risks, such as bias accumulation, cybersecurity vulnerabilities, and the limits of compliance-based regulation (Samuel & Derrick, 2020). Prior empirical evidence from cochlear and deep brain implant users highlights that acceptance relies not only on technical reliability, but also on the cultural mediated processes of identity negotiation turning governing by 2030, to ensure coinvestment in designing and undertake a process of participatory design as the basis of such governance, integrating embedded cultural inclusiveness and co-production as key to sustaining a balance of dignity, equity and accountability (Looi et al., 2012; Klein et al., 2015; Singh, 2019).

4 SOLUTIONS AND RECOMMENDATIONS

The rapid diffusion of smart implants, brain-computer interfaces, and prosthetic arms, enabled by VR's AI, allows Affliction Being Ethical architectures to offer relations to becoming Work in the face of shifting relations among technology, id, and agency. The Cyborg Patient Continuum Model adopts a dynamic framework of patienthood as a spectrum, moving from restorative integration to augmentative enhancement, thereby questioning conventional therapeutic boundaries (Hagele, 2020). While restorative technologies such as pacemakers and cochlear implants focus on restoring desirable functions, augmentative systems, such as those implemented as BCIs and robotic prostheses, can extend interests beyond the norm.

Empirical evidence indicates that most users are located in an intermediate zone, with some examples of osseointegrated prostheses that restore and enhance embodiment through the integration of sensory and motor functions (Ortiz-Catalan et al., 2014). This continuum supports three related tenets: Identity fluidity: recognising embodiment as technologically co-constituted; Ethical Pluralism: acknowledging divergent normative evaluations of restoration and enhancement; and Policy Responsiveness: favouring regulatory flexibility over rigid categorical distinctions. Comparative contexts highlight this logic: affordability and distributive justice in Indian debates, innovation and performance in U.S. debates, and enhancement embedded in egalitarian public ethics in the Swedish healthcare system.

Extending this model, the Ethical AI-Bio-Integration model distributes the ethical responsibility from developers to clinicians and, ultimately, to patients. Developers have a design obligation to incorporate transparency, privacy safeguards, and algorithmic fairness to ensure that innovation aligns with structural justice (Brey, 2012). Clinicians sufficiently operationalise ethics through dynamic consent, interpretive accountability, and sustained supervision of algorithmic recommendations. At the same time, patients contribute to an ethics of experience based on feedback, calibration, and data governance, thereby maintaining agency and trust. Institutional mechanisms, e.g., participatory review boards and patient advisory councils, as found in algorithmic oversight in the NHS and in co-design of assistive robots in Japan, redistribute epistemic authority and accentuate legitimacy (Samuel & Derrick, 2020).

Complementary paradigms in techno-humanist thinking on cognitive evolution and in critical discussions of optimisation-induced inequality in the world deepen the normative analysis (Harari, 2017). In response to this, Inclusive Design Thinking focuses on experiential equity and cultural responsiveness, which are demonstrated through low-cost contextual innovations, such as the Jaipur Foot, in combination with precautionary Swedish neuroprosthetic programmes (Ott, 2019; Stilgoe et al., 2013). Translational governance, therefore, requires explicit clinical override decision thresholds, reimbursement demarcation and design decisions between autonomy, explainability and repairability, which is supported by comparative initiatives both in Europe and India, which demonstrate the need for context-sensitive, participatory bio-integration (Cabitza et al., 2017; Veale & Borgesius, 2021; Reddy et al., 2021).

4.1 Operationalising Ethical Frameworks in Resource-Constrained Health Systems

Implementation science serves as a critical bridge between ethical theory and institutional practice and analyses how bio-integrated innovations are adopted, adapted, or abandoned within routine health care systems (Greenhalgh et al., 2017). In low-resource settings, the decision about ethical bio-integration depends less on technological capacity than on the health system's economics (e.g., cost-effectiveness criteria, workforce capacity, maintenance infrastructure). Frugal innovation strategies - e.g. modular prosthetic design, open source software or task-shifting to trained technicians - show the qualities of how relational accountability and patient autonomy can be operationalised in the face of fiscal and infrastructural constraints (Reddy et al., 2021).

The lack of meaningful consent and accountability, despite normative ethical intent, is hindered across healthcare organisations by practical barriers, including staffing shortages, fragmented procurement processes, limited algorithmic literacy, and dependence on vendors. It is in these organisational frictions that ethical frameworks need to be embedded in procurement criteria, service contracts, clinical protocols, and continuing professional education, rather than imposed as external mechanisms of compliance (Greenhalgh et al., 2017; Mitchell et al., 2019).

Ethical decision-making in resource-constrained settings often necessitates trade-offs among prioritising repairability, the availability of local service, and predictable cost, in preference to maximal technical precision, reflecting a clinically realistic interpretation of distributive justice (Singh, 2019). Reimbursement regimes further affect outcomes: key short-term metrics, such as QALYs, often do not capture long-term dependencies, the cost of software subscriptions, or maintenance risks associated with adaptive implants (Hagele, 2020). Consequently, for responsible bio-integration to remain a reality, models of reimbursement and governance emphasise continuity of care, affordability and sustainability over a lifetime as mechanisms to prevent technology-driven vulnerability and disparities in abandonment.

The economic viability of intelligent bio-integrated technologies is currently a decisive, yet under-examined determinant of ethical sustainability. Conventional frameworks for measuring cost-effectiveness, however, when based primarily on quality-adjusted life years (QALYs), often neglect cumulative expenses (e.g., software subscriptions, proprietary maintenance costs, and dependence on vendor ecosystems) (Hagele, 2020). As a consequence, technologies that seem financially sound at the time of implementation may create downstream financial insecurity for both patients and public health systems.

Comparative health policy research suggests that reimbursement models that include the cost of the lifecycle, i.e., maintenance, upgrades, and end-of-life management, are better aligned with continuity of care and distributive justice (Greenhalgh et al., 2017). In low- and middle-income contexts, blended financing models, including public reimbursement, frugal innovation, and modular repair infrastructure, are a more sustainable way forward than performance-maximising procurement on its own (Reddy et al., 2021).

Second-order best practices in intelligent bio-integration increasingly rely on co-design methodologies that position the patient as a co-producer of knowledge, thereby enhancing usability, reducing stigma, and providing moral legitimacy through procedurally inclusive design (Ortiz-Catalan et al., 2014). Although co-design is a demanding process, it aligns technology with lived experience and enhances trust. Complementing this approach, technological innovation is being operationally mandated, in terms of turbocharged or pre-emptive ethical and societal deliberation, through the use of ethical technology laboratories and regulatory sandboxes or carefully controlled experimentation under supervision, for example, in the UK and in Germany. Comparative experiences across these three countries have shown that it is not the rules alone that are at the forefront of sustainably remaining accountable, inclusive, and human; rather, it is a sense of adaptability and foresight, in the evolution and development of bio-integrated healthcare systems in the Netherlands, the UK, and India.

Ethical frameworks discussed in this chapter, however, become practically significant only when they are translated into protocols for clinical practice, procurement policies, and regulatory instruments. Relational autonomy, for example, is operationalised when clinicians are empowered to override algorithmic outputs based on patient-reported distress, and consent processes are revisited iteratively rather than treated as one-time events (Beauchamp & Childress, 2019; Cabitza et al., 2017).

Similarly, posthuman and systems-oriented ethics inform policy by shifting the focus of regulation from individual devices to a sociotechnical ecosystem that encompasses maintenance contracts, data governance regimes, and information used to train personnel. In this way, philosophical theory does not serve as an abstraction but rather as a design logic for institutional accountability, reimbursement structures, and long-term care sustainability (Floridi & Cowls, 2019; Greenhalgh et al., 2017).

4.2 Risks, Drawbacks, and Unintended Consequences

The transformative promise of intelligent bio-integration has addressed all ethical, social, and psychological vulnerabilities that question presumptions of unqualified advancement. Techno-determinism, as a notion of innovation, is widely regarded as beneficial beyond question. However, it conceals social context, uncertainty, and moral evaluation, as exemplified by accelerated neuro-augmentation programmes that extend well beyond current understanding of long-term cognitive and identity effects (e.g., Feenberg, 2017; Insel et al., 2013). Similar tensions play out in Japan's use of robotic eldercare, where the efficiency of care comes at the expense of relational care (Robertson, 2018). Inequality is a parallel structural risk: insurance categorisations in Germany, unequal access in the US, and affordability-led design in India reveal the enhancement of socioeconomic hierarchies (Hagele, 2020; Singh, 2019). Transnationally, techno-colonial pedagogy and algorithmic bias are among the mechanisms that perpetuate inequity, underscoring the need for distributive justice and inclusive data governance (Shah, 2019; Bekiari et al., 2018).

4.3 Environmental and Sustainability Implications of Cyborg Technologies.

The environmental, psychological, and accountability dimensions of cyborg medicine are also still poorly incorporated into governance, despite the reliance on rare-earth extraction, computational waste, and biomedical e-waste that externalise ecological costs to low-income regions (Raworth, 2017; Stilgoe, 2020). Embedding lifecycle assessment, repairability, and circular design in regulatory reviews is thus integral to linking patient benefit and planetary responsibility. Concurrently, opaque proprietary algorithms impede clinical interpretability and contestability, posing challenges for new forms of regulation of medical software and AI (Floridi & Taddeo, 2016). Psychosocial findings arising from the deep brain stimulation and BCIs have also shown ambivalent results, showing dependency anxiety and the loss of autonomy, mediated by the cultural context and infrastructures of care (Klein et al.,

2015; Gilbert et al., 2017). Sustainable bio-integration thus requires life-cycle governance, psychosocial support, and participatory neuroethical protections, grounded in the institutionalisation of transparency, cognitive liberty, and interdisciplinary accountability (Ienca & Andorno, 2017; Mitchell et al., 2019).

5 FUTURE RESEARCH DIRECTIONS

In line with the book's broader objective of examining ethical and governance challenges in emerging health technologies, this chapter advances posthumanist and systems-oriented perspectives by framing embodiment and agency as co-constructed between humans, algorithms, and institutions. In practice, it informs the design and application of intelligent bio-integrated systems, e.g., neural implants, AI-mediated prosthetics, and brain-computer interfaces, through the lens of adaptive transparency, patient co-design, and algorithmic accountability to deliver functional and psychosocial efficacy. In management terms, this suggests that healthcare organisations should adopt proactive governance and a cyclical regulatory framework, such as ethics-by-design and cross-sector and interdisciplinary literacy, to address the complexity and risks of technology.

It socialises the paradox of empowerment and alienation, making inaccessibility, a lack of digital literacy, and cultural acceptability prominent in defining the cyborg divide worldwide. It suggests context-sensitive yet harmonised regulation, with neurorights, data justice, and equitable policies on innovation, to formulate cross-jurisdictional balances among privacy, accessibility, and innovation. When combined, these implications have been suggested to inform a relational, inclusive, and ethically grounded model of healthcare innovation that balances technological advancement with dignity, justice, and sustainability.

5.1 Metaframework

Figure 1. Cyborg Medicine Framework

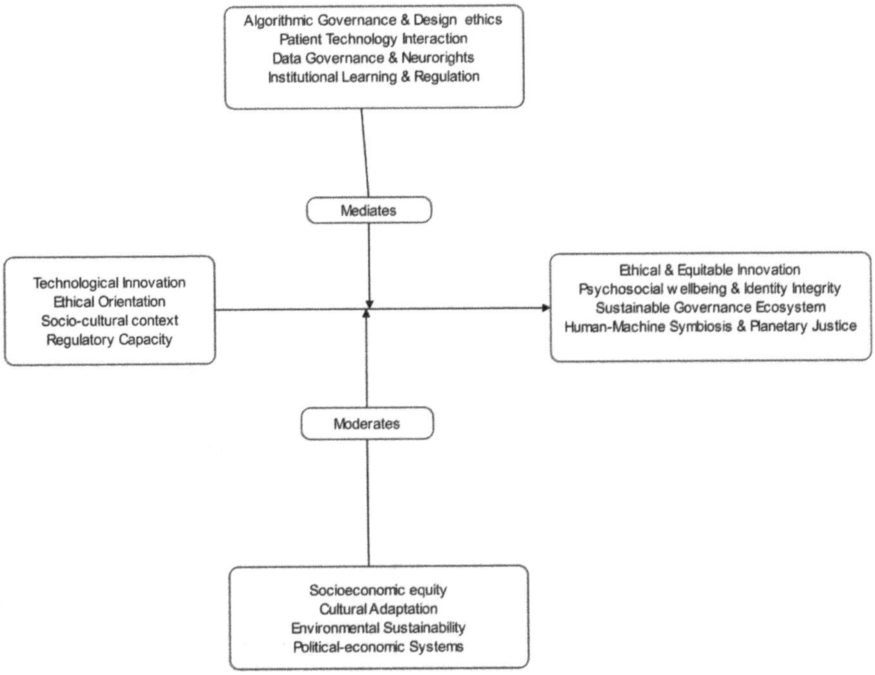

Source: Authors' Contribution

The framework illustrated in Figure 1 explains how ethical and sustainable technological innovation can result from the interaction among institutional governance, socio-cultural contexts, and regulatory ethics. Algorithms, governance, data ethics, and institutional learning mediate the effects of technological innovation and ethical orientation on fair outcomes (Floridi, 2019; Mittelstadt et al., 2016). These are moderated by socioeconomic equity, cultural adaptation, and environmental sustainability, which strengthen justice-oriented innovation ecosystems (Raworth, 2017; Stilgoe, 2020). Empirical evidence from AI governance and neurotechnology supports the idea that participatory design, data stewardship, and adaptive regulation can promote psychosocial well-being and planetary justice (Calo, 2015; Reddy et al., 2023). Accordingly, the model incorporates ethics, governance, and sustainability as a unified innovation paradigm.

Looking ahead, risks include technological obsolescence, growing reliance on proprietary ecosystems, and the environmental burden of cumulative biomedical e-waste and energy-intensive computation. Devices unsupported by discontinued software risk turning therapeutic benefits into causes of harm, especially for patients with no financial or institutional inclusion options (Stilgoe, 2020). Anticipatory governance frameworks that address lifecycle assessment, right-to-repair principles, and environmental accountability, and are therefore shorter, are very important, as they will ensure that innovation within cyborg medicine approaches is ethically as well as ecologically sustainable (Raworth, 2017).

5.2 Towards Humane and Sustainable Integration

Smart bio-integration requires an ethical reorientation that harmonises technological capability with human dignity, ecological responsibility, and cultural pluralism, an undertaking facilitated by rejecting techno-determinism in digital humanism in favour of empathy, personhood, and sustainability (Floridi & Cowls, 2019). Unfortunately, as predictive analytics, biosensors, and neural interfaces become ever more mediary and intermediaries between care, digital humanism fights back against data reductionism by reconciling narrative medicine with algorithmic precision in an ethos symbolised in the European Union's human-centric AI Act with its focus on transparency, risk management, and human control (Veale & Borgesius, 2021). Responsible innovation thus requires ecological ethics, given the material and energy intensities associated with implants and computational infrastructure. Through this ecological lens, responsible use of patient benefit, relative to planetary limits, is achieved through circular and low-impact design. Emerging post-cyborg futures, driven by neural interfaces and health informatics, heighten tensions over autonomy, identity, and mental sovereignty, strengthening calls for neurorights and data justice amid institutional protections (Yuste et al., 2017; Floridi & Taddeo, 2016).

Global South and Indigenous knowledge, such as the frugal digital health architecture in India, as well as concepts of relational wellbeing (Mauri) among the Maori people, introduce de-centralised alternatives to Eurocentric ideologies based on techno-centrism through concepts of justice, cultural legitimacy and epistemic sovereignty (Reddy, 2022; Durie, 1998). Integrating health technology assessment, patient-reported outcomes, and environmental lifecycle analysis within unified ethical appraisal frameworks would operationalise these principles across innovation lifecycles (Greenhalgh et al., 2017). Ultimately, the need for ethical co-determination, rather than technological determinism, is key to ensuring that the development of intelligent healthcare occurs through equity, sustainability, and moral imagination, rather than efficiency alone (Feenberg, 2017).

Future research on intelligent bio-integration should prioritise longitudinal, cross-cultural studies examining the evolution of identity, trust, and dependency across the lifecycle of adaptive medical technologies. Methodologically, combining patient narratives, health technology assessment, and environmental lifecycle analysis will enable a more comprehensive ethical evaluation than working with functional metrics alone (Greenhalgh et al., 2017; Stilgoe et al., 2013).

From a policy perspective, the findings underscore the need for adaptive regulation, including approval, reimbursement, and post-market surveillance, to ensure that ethical accountability is not lost at the end of the deployment process. Aligning innovation with the objectives of the book, this roadmap has tried to position ethical and intelligent healthcare not as an endpoint of technology, but as a constant governance practice to balance the principles of dignity, equity and sustainability across a variety of health systems (Floridi, 2019).

REFERENCES

Beauchamp, T. L., & Childress, J. F. (2019). *Principles of biomedical ethics* (8th ed.). Oxford University Press.

Bekiari, E., Kiparissides, C., & Athanasiadou, E. (2018). Artificial pancreas technologies for type 1 diabetes mellitus: A review. *Diabetes Therapy : Research, Treatment and Education of Diabetes and Related Disorders, 9*(2), 403–419.

Braidotti, R. (2013). *The posthuman*. Polity Press.

Brey, P. (2012). Anticipating ethical issues in emerging IT. *Ethics and Information Technology, 14*(4), 305–317. DOI: 10.1007/s10676-012-9293-y

Cabitza, F., Rasoini, R., & Gensini, G. F. (2017). Unintended consequences of machine learning in medicine—. *Journal of Medical Internet Research, 19*(11), e354. PMID: 29138131

Calo, R. (2015). Robotics and the lessons of cyberlaw. *California Law Review, 103*(3), 513–563.

Clark, A. (2003). *Natural-born cyborgs: Minds, technologies, and the future of human intelligence*. Oxford University Press.

Coeckelbergh, M. (2020). *AI ethics*. MIT Press. DOI: 10.7551/mitpress/12549.001.0001

Durie, M. (1998). *Whaiora: Māori health development* (2nd ed.). Oxford University Press.

Feenberg, A. (2017). *Technosystem: The social life of reason*. Harvard University Press. DOI: 10.4159/9780674982109

Floridi, L., & Cowls, J. (2019). A unified framework of five principles for AI in society. *Harvard Data Science Review, 1*(1).

Floridi, L., & Taddeo, M. (2016). What is data ethics? *Philosophical Transactions. Series A, Mathematical, Physical, and Engineering Sciences, 374*(2083), 20160360. DOI: 10.1098/rsta.2016.0360 PMID: 28336805

Fukuyama, F. (2002). *Our posthuman future: Consequences of the biotechnology revolution*. Farrar, Straus and Giroux.

Gilbert, F., O'Brien, T., & Cook, M. (2017). The effects of deep brain stimulation on personality and identity: A qualitative study of patients with epilepsy. *Neuroethics, 10*(3), 425–436.

Greenhalgh, T., Wherton, J., Papoutsi, C., Lynch, J., Hughes, G., A'Court, C., Hinder, S., Fahy, N., Procter, R., & Shaw, S. (2017). Beyond adoption: A new framework for theorising and evaluating nonadoption, abandonment, and challenges to the scale-up, spread, and sustainability of health and care technologies—. *Journal of Medical Internet Research, 19*(11), e367. DOI: 10.2196/jmir.8775 PMID: 29092808

Habermas, J. (2003). *The future of human nature*. Polity Press.

Hägele, H. (2020). Ethical considerations in the use of exoskeletons for rehabilitation. *Ethics, Medicine, and Public Health, 15*, 100–107.

Haggerty, K. D., & Ericson, R. V. (2000). The surveillant assemblage. *The British Journal of Sociology, 51*(4), 605–622. DOI: 10.1080/00071310020015280 PMID: 11140886

Harari, Y. N. (2017). *Homo Deus: A brief history of tomorrow*. Vintage. DOI: 10.17104/9783406704024

Haraway, D. J. (1991). A Cyborg Manifesto: Science, Technology, and Socialist Feminism in the Late Twentieth Century. In *Simians, cyborgs, and women: The reinvention of nature* (pp. 149–181). Routledge.

Haraway, D. J. (1991). *Simians, cyborgs, and women: The reinvention of nature*. Routledge.

Ienca, M., & Andorno, R. (2017). Towards new human rights in the age of neuroscience and neurotechnology. *Life Sciences, Society and Policy, 13*(1), 1–27. DOI: 10.1186/s40504-017-0050-1 PMID: 28444626

Insel, T. R., Landis, S. C., & Collins, F. S. (2013). The NIH BRAIN Initiative. *Science, 340*(6133), 687–688. DOI: 10.1126/science.1239276 PMID: 23661744

Kanzaki, N., & Iijima, H. (2013). Cyberdyne's HAL exoskeleton: Robot-assisted rehabilitation for spinal cord injury and stroke. *Journal of Neuroengineering and Rehabilitation, 10*(1), 1–7.

Klein, E., Goering, S., & Gagne, J.. (2015). Brain–computer interface-based control of robotic arms: A qualitative study of participants' experiences. *AJOB Neuroscience, 6*(1), 29–41.

Kurzweil, R. (2005). *The singularity is near: When humans transcend biology*. Viking.

Leder, D. (1990). *The absent body*. University of Chicago Press.

Looi, V., Gfeller, K., & Driscoll, V. (2012). Music perception of cochlear implant users: A review. *Ear and Hearing, 33*(5), 519–540.

MacIntyre, A. (2007). *After Virtue: A Study in Moral Theory* (3rd ed.). University of Notre Dame Press.

Mitchell, M., Wu, S., & Zaldivar, A.. (2019). Model cards for model reporting. *Proceedings of the Conference on Fairness, Accountability, and Transparency*, 220–229. DOI: 10.1145/3287560.3287596

Mittelstadt, B., Allo, P., Taddeo, M., Wachter, S., & Floridi, L. (2016). The ethics of algorithms: Mapping the debate. *Big Data & Society*, *3*(2), 1–21. DOI: 10.1177/2053951716679679

Mond, H. G., & Proclemer, A. (2011). The 11th World Survey of Cardiac Pacing and Implantable Cardioverter Defibrillators. *Pacing and Clinical Electrophysiology*, *34*(8), 1013–1027. DOI: 10.1111/j.1540-8159.2011.03150.x PMID: 21707667

Murray, C. D. (2009). Bodies and prostheses. In Siebers, T. (Ed.), *Disability theory* (pp. 75–90). University of Michigan Press.

Musk, E. (2019). An integrated brain–machine interface platform with thousands of channels—. *Journal of Medical Internet Research*, *21*(10), e16194. DOI: 10.2196/16194 PMID: 31642810

Ortiz-Catalan, M., Hakansson, B., & Branemark, R. (2014). An osseointegrated human–machine gateway for long-term control of sensory–motor prostheses. *Science Translational Medicine*, *6*(257), 257re6. DOI: 10.1126/scitranslmed.3008933 PMID: 25298322

Ott, B. (2019). Gender and prosthetics: Normative design and embodied experience. *Science, Technology & Human Values*, *44*(2), 230–252.

Pagallo, U. (2013). *The Laws of Robots: Crimes, Contracts, and Torts*. Springer. DOI: 10.1007/978-94-007-6564-1

Price, W. N., Gerke, S., & Cohen, I. G. (2019). Potential liability for AI/ML-based products. *Journal of the American Medical Association*, *322*(18), 1765–1766. DOI: 10.1001/jama.2019.15064 PMID: 31584609

Raworth, K. (2017). *Doughnut economics: Seven ways to think like a 21st-century economist*. Chelsea Green Publishing.

Reddy, K. S. (2022). India's digital health mission: Opportunities and challenges. *The Lancet. Digital Health*, *4*(1), e12–e13.

Reddy, K. S., Chaturvedi, S., & Prasad, K. (2021). Artificial intelligence in Indian neuro-healthcare: Opportunities and challenges. *Neurology India*, *69*(7), 121–128.

Robertson, J. (2018). *Robo Sapiens Japanicus: Robots, gender, family, and the Japanese nation*. University of California Press.

Samuel, G., & Derrick, G. (2020). Defining ethical challenges of AI in medicine: A qualitative study of IRB members. *AJOB Empirical Bioethics, 11*(3), 193–202.

Schüpbach, M., & Agid, Y. (2008). Neurosurgery in Parkinson's disease: The doctor is happy, the patient less so? *Journal of Neural Transmission (Vienna, Austria), 115*(11), 1511–1516.

Shah, S. (2019). *The body hunters: Testing new drugs on the world's poorest patients*. New Press.

Shibata, T., & Wada, K. (2011). Robot therapy: A new approach for mental healthcare of the elderly – A mini-review. *Gerontology, 57*(4), 378–386. DOI: 10.1159/000319015 PMID: 20639620

Singh, A. (2019). Affordable Prosthetics and Rehabilitation in India: Bridging the Accessibility Gap. *Indian Journal of Orthopaedics, 53*(2), 245–252.

Stilgoe, J., Owen, R., & Macnaghten, P. (2013). Developing a framework for responsible innovation. *Research Policy, 42*(9), 1568–1580. DOI: 10.1016/j.respol.2013.05.008

Trist, E. (1981). The evolution of sociotechnical systems. Occasional Paper, 2, 1–67.

Veale, M., & Borgesius, F. Z. (2021). Demystifying the draft EU Artificial Intelligence Act. *Computer Law Review International, 22*(4), 97–112. DOI: 10.9785/cri-2021-220402

Wachter, S., Mittelstadt, B., & Floridi, L. (2017). Why a right to explanation of automated decision-making does not exist in the GDPR. *International Data Privacy Law, 7*(2), 76–99. DOI: 10.1093/idpl/ipx005

Yuste, R., Goering, S., Arcas, B. A. Y., Bi, G., Carmena, J. M., Carter, A., Fins, J. J., Friesen, P., Gallant, J., Huggins, J. E., Illes, J., Kellmeyer, P., Klein, E., Marblestone, A., Mitchell, C., Parens, E., Pham, M., Rubel, A., Sadato, N., & Wolpaw, J. (2017). Four ethical priorities for neurotechnologies and AI. *Nature, 551*(7679), 159–163. DOI: 10.1038/551159a PMID: 29120438

Zuboff, S. (2019). *The age of surveillance capitalism*. PublicAffairs.

Compilation of References

Abbott, R. (2020). *The reasonable robot: Artificial intelligence and the law*. Cambridge University Press., DOI: 10.1017/9781108631761

Abdullah, S., & Jaddi, N. S. (2020). Dual kidney-inspired algorithm for water quality prediction and cancer detection. *IEEE Access : Practical Innovations, Open Solutions*, *8*, 109807–109820. DOI: 10.1109/ACCESS.2020.3001685

Abu-elezz, I., Hassan, A., Nazeemudeen, A., Househ, M., & Abd-alrazaq, A. (2020). The benefits and threats of blockchain technology in healthcare: A scoping review. *International Journal of Medical Informatics*, *142*, 104246. DOI: 10.1016/j.ijmedinf.2020.104246 PMID: 32828033

Acharya, B., Behera, A., Behera, S., & Moharana, S. (2024). Recent advances in nanotechnology-based drug Delivery systems for the diagnosis and treatment of Reproductive disorders. *Nano Express*, *7*(3), 1336–1361. PMID: 38412066

Acosta, J., Lin, M., & Patel, R. (2024). Ethical frameworks for AI-assisted clinical decision-making. *Journal of Medical Ethics and Technology*, *18*(2), 45–59.

Adamson, A. S., & Smith, A. (2018). Machine learning and health care disparities in dermatology. *JAMA Dermatology*, *154*(11), 1247–1248. DOI: 10.1001/jamadermatol.2018.2348 PMID: 30073260

Adnan, K., Akbar, R., Khor, S. W., & Ali, A. B. A. (2020). Role and challenges of unstructured big data in healthcare. *Data management, analytics and innovation*, 301-323.

Agrawal, P., Gandhi, S., & Agarwal, M. (2024). DiabChatbot: A machine learning chatbot for early diagnosis of type II/mellitus diabetes and diet recommendation in an Indian scenario. In *2024 10th International Conference on Advanced Computing and Communication Systems (ICACCS)* (pp. 1526–1531). IEEE. DOI: 10.1109/ICACCS60874.2024.10716933

Agrawal, P., & Gandhi, S. (2025). PneumoSense: Smart pneumonia detection using deep learning. In *Proceedings of the 10th Edition ICT4SD – 2025 International ICT Summit and Awards* (Springer, Goa). To be Published.

Agrawal, R., & Prabakaran, S. (2020). Big data in digital healthcare: Lessons learnt and recommendations for general practice. *Heredity*, *124*(4), 525–534. DOI: 10.1038/s41437-020-0303-2 PMID: 32139886

Ahmed, S., & Kulkarni, P. (2025). Nanotechnology in Medicine: Revolutionizing Drug Delivery Systems. *Nano Express*, 1–10.

Ahmed, M., & Khan, S. (2021). Evaluating doctor recommendation accuracy using symptom clustering. *International Journal of Medical Engineering and Informatics*, *13*(2), 117–130.

Akdaşçi, E., Duman, H., Eker, F., Bechelany, M., & Karav, S. (2025). Chitosan and Its Nanoparticles: A Multifaceted Approach to Antibacterial Applications. *Nano Express*, *15*(2), 126. PMID: 39852740

Alagarsamy, S., John, A. J. V., Chen, S.-M., Sakthinathan, S., Chang, Y.-H., & Tang, J.-Y. (2024). Novel method of phosphorous doped bismuth oxide with carbon aerogel for a selective voltammetry quantification of anti-cancer drug: Regorafenib. *Chemical Engineering Journal*, *494*, 153054. DOI: 10.1016/j.cej.2024.153054

Alfattni, G., Peek, N., & Nenadic, G. (2020). Extraction of temporal relations from clinical free text: A systematic review of current approaches. *Journal of Biomedical Informatics*, *108*, 103488. DOI: 10.1016/j.jbi.2020.103488 PMID: 32673788

AllahRakha, N.AllahRakha. (2024). Cybersecurity regulations for protection and safeguarding digital assets (data) in today's worlds. *Lex Scientia Law Review*, *8*(1), 405–432. DOI: 10.15294/lslr.v8i1.2081

Almulihi, A. H., Alassery, F., Khan, A. I., Shukla, S., Gupta, B. K., & Kumar, R. (2022). Analyzing the implications of healthcare data breaches through computational technique. *Intelligent Automation & Soft Computing*, *32*(3), 1763–1779. DOI: 10.32604/iasc.2022.023460

Al-Remawi, M., & Rahem, R. A. A. (2024, February). Applications of AI in Biomedical Genomics and Pharmaceuticals. In 2024 2nd International Conference on Cyber Resilience (ICCR) (pp. 1-5). IEEE. DOI: 10.1109/ICCR61006.2024.10532792

Alvargonzález, D. (2019). Sciences as systems. *Perspectives on Science*, *27*(6), 839–860. DOI: 10.1162/posc_a_00327

Alvargonzález, D. (2021). On the systematicity of academic philosophy. *Philosophical Investigations, 44*(3), 237–253. DOI: 10.1111/phin.12288

Alzubaidi, M. A., Otoom, M., & Jaradat, H. (2021). Comprehensive and comparative global and local feature extraction framework for lung cancer detection using CT scan images. *IEEE Access : Practical Innovations, Open Solutions, 9*, 158140–158154. DOI: 10.1109/ACCESS.2021.3129597

Alzubi, J., Nayyar, A., & Kumar, A. (2018, November). Machine learning from theory to algorithms: An overview. [). IOP Publishing.]. *Journal of Physics: Conference Series, 1142*, 012012. DOI: 10.1088/1742-6596/1142/1/012012

Ambrosi, E., & Tan, R. (2025). Effectiveness of digital health interventions for chronic disease management in European primary care. *Computers in Biology and Medicine, 145*, 105476. DOI: 10.1016/j.compbiomed.2022.105476

Anan, S. R., & Tan, R. (2021). Research and development of an IoT-based remote health monitoring system for asthmatic patients. *Journal of Medical Systems, 45*(6), 1–10. DOI: 10.1007/s10916-021-01771-2

Arafiyah, R., & Hermin, F. (2018). Data mining for dengue hemorrhagic fever (DHF) prediction with Naive Bayes method. *Journal of Physics: Conference Series, 948*(1), 012077. DOI: 10.1088/1742-6596/948/1/012077

Arisoy, E., Sainath, T. N., Kingsbury, B., & Ramabhadran, B. (2012, June). Deep neural network language models. In *Proceedings of the NAACL-HLT 2012 Workshop: will we ever really replace the N-gram Model? On the future of language modeling for HLT* (pp. 20–28).

Arrowsmith, J., & Miller, P. (2013). Trial watch: Phase II and Phase III attrition rates 2011–2012. *Nature Reviews. Drug Discovery, 12*(8), 569. DOI: 10.1038/nrd4090 PMID: 23903212

Ashique, S., Raikar, A., Jamil, S., Lakshminarayana, L., Gajbhiye, S. A., De, S., & Kumar, S. (2025). Artificial Intelligence Integration with Nanotechnology: A New Frontier for Sustainable and Precision Agriculture. *Nano Express, 21*(2), 242–273.

Asti, G., D'Amico, S., Carota, L., Piscia, D., Casadei, F., Merleau, N. S. C., Alonso de Apellániz, P., Kubasch, A. S., Gloaguen, S., Modler, N., Gonzalez Martin, C., Rollo, C., Parras, J., Delleani, M., Zazzetti, E., Sauta, E., Curti, N., Derus, N. R., Carlini, G., & Alvarez, F. (2024). An Artificial Intelligence-Based Federated Learning Platform to Boost Precision Medicine in Rare Hematological Diseases: An Initiative by GenoMed4all and Synthema Consortia. *Blood, 144*(Supplement 1), 4989. DOI: 10.1182/blood-2024-205541

Attaran, M. (2022). Blockchain technology in healthcare: Challenges and opportunities. *International Journal of Healthcare Management, 15*(1), 70–83. DOI: 10.1080/20479700.2020.1843887

Aung, H., Tan, R., Flynn, C., Divall, P., Wright, A., Murphy, A., Shaw, D., Ward, T. J. C., & Greening, N. J. (2024). Digital remote maintenance inhaler adherence interventions in COPD: A systematic review and meta-analysis. *European Respiratory Review : an Official Journal of the European Respiratory Society, 33*(174), 240136. DOI: 10.1183/16000617.0136-2024 PMID: 39631930

Ayushman Bharat Digital Mission (ABDM). (2023). *Official website*. Government of India. https://abdm.gov.in

Ayushman Bharat Digital Mission (ABDM). (2023). *Official Website*. https://abdm.gov.in

Bajorin, D. F.. (2021). Patient recruitment challenges in clinical trials: Opportunities for artificial intelligence solutions. *Journal of Clinical Oncology, 39*(15, suppl), 2641–2641. DOI: 10.1200/JCO.2021.39.15_suppl.2641

Bajwa, J., Munir, U., Nori, A., & Williams, B. (2021). Artificial intelligence in healthcare: Transforming the practice of medicine. *Future Healthcare Journal, 8*(2), e188–e194. DOI: 10.7861/fhj.2021-0095 PMID: 34286183

Balakrishna, S., & Solanki, V. K. (2024). A comprehensive review on AI-driven healthcare transformation. *Ingeniería Solidaria, 20*(2), 1–30. DOI: 10.16925/2357-6014.2024.02.07

Bampoula, X., Siaterlis, G., Nikolakis, N., & Alexopoulos, K. (2021). A Deep Learning Model for predictive maintenance in cyber-physical production systems using LSTM autoencoders. *Sensors (Basel), 21*(3), 972. Advance online publication. DOI: 10.3390/s21030972 PMID: 33535642

Basri, T. S. J., & Kulkarni, A. K. (2025). Artificial Intelligence for Drug Discovery Accelerating the Development of New Pharmaceuticals. In ITM Web of Conferences (Vol. 76, p. 01010). EDP Sciences. DOI: 10.1051/itmconf/20257601010

Bate, A., & Blake, K. (2020). Pharmacovigilance: Artificial intelligence and machine learning in adverse drug reaction reporting. *Drug Safety, 43*(6), 547–554. DOI: 10.1007/s40264-020-00933-0

Beam, A. L., & Kohane, I. S. (2022). Big data and machine learning in health care. *Journal of the American Medical Association, 327*(14), 1357–1358. PMID: 29532063

Beauchamp, T. L., & Childress, J. F. (2019). *Principles of biomedical ethics* (8th ed.). Oxford University Press.

Beer, S. (1960). Cybernetics and management. *Journal of the Franklin Institute, 270*(3), 245. DOI: 10.1016/0016-0032(60)90608-6

Behera, S. K., & M Nayak, M. (2020). Natural language processing for text and speech processing: a review paper. *International Journal of Advanced Research in Engineering and Technology (IJARET).*

Bekiari, E., Kiparissides, C., & Athanasiadou, E. (2018). Artificial pancreas technologies for type 1 diabetes mellitus: A review. *Diabetes Therapy : Research, Treatment and Education of Diabetes and Related Disorders, 9*(2), 403–419.

Benjamens, S., Dhunnoo, P., & Meskó, B. (2022). AI-based medical devices in clinical practice. *NPJ Digital Medicine, 5*, 9. Advance online publication. DOI: 10.1038/s41746-022-00562-2

Bettina, M. (2021). Addressing parsons in sociological textbooks: Past conflicts, contemporary readers, and their future gains. *The American Sociologist, 52*(1), 88–106. DOI: 10.1007/s12108-020-09469-7

Bhatt, S., Jain, A., & Dev, A. (2020). Acoustic modeling in speech recognition: A systematic review. *International Journal of Advanced Computer Science and Applications, 11*(4). Advance online publication. DOI: 10.14569/IJACSA.2020.0110455

Bhuyan, R., & Deshmukh, A. (2025). GenAI for clinical excellence and operational efficiency. *Journal of Medical Systems, 49*(1), 112–128.

Bhuyan, R., Deshmukh, A., & Kaur, S. (2025). Generative AI in healthcare: Enhancing clinical excellence and operational efficiency. *Journal of Medical Systems, 49*(1), 112–128. https://link.springer.com/article/10.1007/s10916-024-02136-1. DOI: 10.1007/s10916-024-02136-1

Biamonte, J., Wittek, P., Pancotti, N., Rebentrost, P., Wiebe, N., & Lloyd, S. (2017). Quantum machine learning. *Nature, 549*(7671), 195–202. DOI: 10.1038/nature23474 PMID: 28905917

Bini, S. A. (2018). Artificial intelligence, machine learning, deep learning, and cognitive computing: What do these terms mean and how will they impact health care? *The Journal of Arthroplasty, 33*(8), 2358–2361. DOI: 10.1016/j.arth.2018.02.067 PMID: 29656964

Binns, J., Veeramachaneni, L., & Weinger, M. (2020). The role of algorithmic transparency in healthcare: Implications for the development of fair, accountable, and ethical AI. *Journal of Biomedical Informatics*, *106*, 103463. Advance online publication. DOI: 10.1016/j.jbi.2020.103463

Binns, R. (2019). Fairness and algorithmic bias in machine learning: Current challenges and future directions. *Communications of the ACM*, *62*(8), 43–47. DOI: 10.1145/3342760

Birajdar, P. S., & Lobo, L. M. R. J. (2023). Advancing cancer research: Intelligent prediction and analysis system based on deep learning. *Journal of Emerging Technologies and Innovative Research*, *10*(8). https://www.jetir.org/indexx?v=10&i=8&j=August%202023

Blaschke, T., Olivecrona, M., Engkvist, O., Bajorath, J., & Chen, H. (2018). Application of generative autoencoder in DE Novo molecular design. *Molecular Informatics*, *37*(1–2), 1700123. DOI: 10.1002/minf.201700123 PMID: 29235269

Bossaerts, P., Yadav, N., & Murawski, C. (2019). Uncertainty and computational complexity. *Philosophical Transactions of the Royal Society B*, *374*(1766), 20180138.

Boukherroub, R., & Szunerits, S. (2024). The Future of Nanotechnology-Driven Electrochemical and Electrical Point-of-Care Devices and Diagnostic Tests. *Nano Express*, *17*(1), 173–195. PMID: 39018353

Boulding, K. E. (1956). General Systems Theory—The skeleton of science. *Management Science*, *2*(3), 197–208. DOI: 10.1287/mnsc.2.3.197

Braidotti, R. (2013). *The posthuman*. Polity Press.

Brey, P. (2012). Anticipating ethical issues in emerging IT. *Ethics and Information Technology*, *14*(4), 305–317. DOI: 10.1007/s10676-012-9293-y

Brown, T. B., Mann, B., Ryder, N., Subbiah, M., Kaplan, J., Dhariwal, P., . . . Amodei, D. (2020). Language models are few-shot learners. *arXiv preprint arXiv:2005.14165*. https://arxiv.org/abs/2005.14165

Brydges, M., & Batt, A. M. (2023). Untangling the web: The need for theory, theoretical frameworks, and conceptual frameworks in paramedic research. *Paramedicine*, *20*(4), 89–93. DOI: 10.1177/27536386231177348

Buess, M., & Shah, A. (2025). Multimodal transformers for cardiac event prediction. *Biomedical Engineering Letters*, *15*(3), 210–225.

Buess, M., Shah, A., & Rane, P. (2025). Multimodal AI for cardiac event prediction: A transformer-based approach. *Biomedical Engineering Letters*, *15*(3), 210–225. https://link.springer.com/article/10.1007/s13534-025-00497-1

Burbidge, R., Trotter, M., Buxton, B., & Holden, S. (2001). Drug design by machine learning: Support vector machines for pharmaceutical data analysis. *Computers & Chemistry*, *26*(1), 5–14. DOI: 10.1016/S0097-8485(01)00094-8 PMID: 11765851

Butt, M. A. (2025). Surface Plasmon Resonance-Based Biodetection Systems: Principles, Progress and Applications—A Comprehensive Review. *Nano Express*, *15*(1), 35. PMID: 39852086

Cabitza, F., Rasoini, R., & Gensini, G. F. (2017). Unintended consequences of machine learning in medicine—. *Journal of Medical Internet Research*, *19*(11), e354. PMID: 29138131

Cadenas, H. (2019). The unity of (social systems) science: The legacy of von Bertalanffy. *Systems Research and Behavioral Science*, *36*(3), 274–280. DOI: 10.1002/sres.2595

Calo, R. (2015). Robotics and the lessons of cyberlaw. *California Law Review*, *103*(3), 513–563.

Calvino, G., Peconi, C., Strafella, C., Trastulli, G., Megalizzi, D., Andreucci, S., Cascella, R., Caltagirone, C., Zampatti, S., & Giardina, E. (2024). Federated Learning: Breaking Down Barriers in Global Genomic Research. *Genes*, *15*(12), 1650. DOI: 10.3390/genes15121650 PMID: 39766917

Cao, Y., Romero, J., Olson, J. P., Degroote, M., Johnson, P. D., Kieferová, M., Kivlichan, I. D., Menke, T., Peropadre, B., Sawaya, N. P. D., Sim, S., Veis, L., & Aspuru-Guzik, A. (2020). Quantum chemistry in the age of quantum computing. *Chemical Reviews*, *119*(19), 10856–10915. DOI: 10.1021/acs.chemrev.8b00803 PMID: 31469277

Carr-Chellman, D. J., & Carr-Chellman, A. (2020). Integrating systems: The history of systems from von Bertalanffy to Profound Learning. *TechTrends*, *64*(5), 704–709. DOI: 10.1007/s11528-020-00540-1

Chakraborty, A., Anik, M. I., & Rahman, M. M. (2023). Developing an IoT-enabled cost-effective asthma patient monitoring system: Integrating health and indoor environment data with statistical analysis and data visualization. *Science Progress*, *106*(4), 00368504231192542. DOI: 10.1177/00368504231192542

Chandel, T. A. (2025). E-Collaboration Technologies With Generative AI Tools. In *Humans and Generative AI Tools for Collaborative Intelligence* (pp. 369–402). IGI Global Scientific Publishing. DOI: 10.4018/979-8-3693-8332-2.ch016

Chandrasekaran, R., Ushani, U., Sankar, G., Joseph, J., Natarajan, K., Palani, S., Sridhar, P., Nagaraj, R., & Sagadevan, S. (2025). Harnessing the Therapeutic Potential of Carbon Dots for Efficient Wound Healing Management. *Nano Express*, *15*(1), 1–21.

Charoo, N. A., Khan, M. A., & Rahman, Z. (2023). Data integrity issues in pharmaceutical industry: Common observations, challenges and mitigations strategies. *International Journal of Pharmaceutics*, *631*, 122503. DOI: 10.1016/j.ijpharm.2022.122503 PMID: 36529357

Chauhan, S. B., Chankhampan, C., Singh, I., Kallepalli, S. B., & Gupta, C. (2025). Nanotherapeutics-impregnated medical devices and their regulatory aspects. *Nano Express*, 41–61.

Chauhan, R., Ghanshala, K. K., & Joshi, R. P. (2018). Convolutional Neural Network (CNN) for Image Detection and Recognition. *2018 First International Conference on Secure Cyber Computing and Communication (ICSCCC)*. DOI: 10.1109/ICSCCC.2018.8703316

Chelly Dagdia, Z., Avdeyev, P., & Bayzid, M. S. (2021). Biological computation and computational biology: Survey, challenges, and discussion. *Artificial Intelligence Review*, *54*(6), 4169–4235. DOI: 10.1007/s10462-020-09951-1

Cheng, F., Li, W., Zhou, Y., Shen, J., Wu, Z., Liu, G., & Tang, Y. (2012). admetSAR: A comprehensive source and free tool for assessment of chemical ADMET properties. *Journal of Chemical Information and Modeling*, *52*(11), 3099–3105. DOI: 10.1021/ci300367a PMID: 23092397

Chen, H., Engkvist, O., Wang, Y., Olivecrona, M., & Blaschke, T. (2018). The rise of deep learning in drug discovery. *Drug Discovery Today*, *23*(6), 1241–1250. DOI: 10.1016/j.drudis.2018.01.039 PMID: 29366762

Chen, I. Y., Joshi, S., & Ghassemi, M. (2021). Treating health disparities with artificial intelligence. *Nature Medicine*, *26*(1), 16–17. DOI: 10.1038/s41591-019-0649-2 PMID: 31932779

Cherkasov, A., Muratov, E. N., Fourches, D., Varnek, A., Baskin, I. I., Cronin, M., & Tropsha, A. (2014). QSAR modeling: Where have you been? Where are you going to? *Journal of Medicinal Chemistry*, *57*(12), 4977–5010. DOI: 10.1021/jm4004285 PMID: 24351051

China Briefing. (2025). *China's AI healthcare market growth trends.* https://www.china-briefing.com

Chintada, V., Veeraiah, K., & Golla, N. (2024). The Development in Nanotechnology and Tailor-Made Enzymes as the Future of Biobased Economy. *Nano Express*, 267–288.

Chng, S., Lu, H. Y., Kumar, A., & Yau, D. (2022). Hacker types, motivations and strategies: A comprehensive framework. *Computers in Human Behavior Reports, 5*, 100167. DOI: 10.1016/j.chbr.2022.100167

Cho, H. N., Jun, T. J., Kim, Y. H., Kang, H., Ahn, I., Gwon, H., Kim, Y., Seo, J., Choi, H., Kim, M., Han, J., Kee, G., Park, S., & Ko, S. (2024). Task-specific transformer-based language models in health care: Scoping review. *JMIR Medical Informatics, 12*, e49724. DOI: 10.2196/49724 PMID: 39556827

Choi, M. S. G. K., Kim, S. K., & Lee, J. R. (2020). Blockchain technology in healthcare: Applications, opportunities, and threats. *IEEE Access : Practical Innovations, Open Solutions, 8*, 112664–112677. DOI: 10.1109/ACCESS.2020.3002211

Choo, S., & Kim, W. (2023). A study on the evaluation of tokenizer performance in natural language processing. *Applied Artificial Intelligence, 37*(1), 2175112. DOI: 10.1080/08839514.2023.2175112

Chung, J., Gulcehre, C., Cho, K., & Bengio, Y. (2014). Empirical evaluation of gated recurrent neural networks on sequence modeling. *arXiv preprint arXiv:1412.3555.* https://arxiv.org/abs/1412.3555

Chustecki, M., Farnell, D. J., & Bewick, B. M. (2024). Benefits and risks of AI in health care: Narrative review. *JMIR Medical Education, 10*(1), e48962. DOI: 10.2196/48962

Clark, A. (2003). *Natural-born cyborgs: Minds, technologies, and the future of human intelligence*. Oxford University Press.

Coeckelbergh, M. (2020). *AI ethics*. MIT Press. DOI: 10.7551/mitpress/12549.001.0001

Cohen, I. G., & Price, W. N. (2017). Privacy, confidentiality, and electronic health records: Where the law stands. *Journal of Health Care Law & Policy, 20*(2), 123–149.

Cojocaru, E., Petri , O. R., & Cojocaru, C. (2024). Nanoparticle-Based Drug Delivery Systems in Inhaled Therapy: Improving Respiratory Medicine. *Pharmaceuticals (Basel, Switzerland), 17*(8), 1059. DOI: 10.3390/ph17081059 PMID: 39204164

Collins, F. S., & Varmus, H. (2015). A new initiative on precision medicine. *The New England Journal of Medicine, 372*(9), 793–795. DOI: 10.1056/NEJMp1500523 PMID: 25635347

Collins, G. S., Reitsma, J. B., Altman, D. G., & Moons, K. G. M. (2021). Reporting of artificial intelligence prediction models (TRIPOD-AI): Explanation and elaboration. *BMJ (Clinical Research Ed.), 374*(1444). Advance online publication. DOI: 10.1136/bmj.n1444

Coulter, I., Snider, P., & Neil, A. (2019). Vitalism-A worldview revisited: A critique of vitalism and its implications for integrative medicine. *Integrative Medicine (Encinitas, Calif.), 18*(3), 60–73. PMID: 32549817

Cruz Rivera, S., Liu, X., Chan, A. W., Denniston, A. K., & Calvert, M. J. (2020). Guidelines for clinical trial protocols involving AI interventions: SPIRIT-AI extension. *BMJ (Clinical Research Ed.), 370*, m3210. DOI: 10.1136/bmj.m3210 PMID: 32907797

Dameff, C., Latif, A., Camp, J., Farcas, R., Bagan, B., Keim, S., & Clay, A. (2023). Ransomware attack associated with disruptions at adjacent emergency departments in the US. *JAMA Network Open, 6*(5), e2312270. DOI: 10.1001/jamanetworkopen.2023.12270 PMID: 37155166

Davis, F. D., Doshi-Velez, P., Hanna, A. B., Hughes, S., Bates, D. W., & Obermeyer, Z. (2020). Machine learning for clinical trials in the era of COVID-19: Observational studies and randomized controlled trials. *Journal of Medical Internet Research, 22*(12). Advance online publication. DOI: 10.2196/21400

de Almeida, S. S., Silva Fontes, R., Pareja Credidio Freire Alves, L., Júnior, M. C., José Pinheiro Caldeira Silva, G., Ramalho Cortez, L., de Morais, A. H. F., Medeiros Machado, G., Gonçalo Oliveira, H., Cunha-Oliveira, A., dos Santos, J. P. Q., & de Medeiros Valentim, R. A. (2025). Artificial intelligence in healthcare text processing: A review applied to named entity recognition. *Frontiers in Artificial Intelligence, 8*, 1584203. DOI: 10.3389/frai.2025.1584203 PMID: 40693280

Dehchani, A. J., Jafari, A., & Shahi, F. (2024). Nanogels in Biomedical Engineering: Revolutionizing Drug Delivery, Tissue Engineering, and Bioimaging. *Polymers for Advanced Technologies, 35*(10), e6595. DOI: 10.1002/pat.6595

Dehesh, E., & Dehesh, F. (2025). Nanotechnology in COVID-19 and SARS-CoV-2: Advances in Antiviral Therapies and Applications. *Nano Express, 26*(1), 87–105.

Deng, J., Gupta, S., Wu, R., & Wallach, I. (2019). Deep learning in drug discovery: AtomNet and beyond. *Drug Discovery Today, 24*(8), 1617–1623. DOI: 10.1016/j.drudis.2019.05.015

Dermawan, D., & Alotaiq, N. (2025). From Lab to Clinic: How Artificial Intelligence (AI) Is Reshaping Drug Discovery Timelines and Industry Outcomes. *Pharmaceuticals (Basel, Switzerland), 18*(7), 981. DOI: 10.3390/ph18070981 PMID: 40732273

Descartes, R. (1984). *The Philosophical Writings of Descartes* (Vol. 2). Cambridge University Press., books.google.com

Deshmukh, S., & Pacharaney, U. (2025, February). Enhancing Healthcare Communication: A Study on Automated Speech-to-Text Conversion and Analysis of Doctor-Patient Dialogues for Improved Clinical Documentation and Patient Care. In *2025 4th International Conference on Sentiment Analysis and Deep Learning (ICSADL)* (pp. 229-234). IEEE. DOI: 10.1109/ICSADL65848.2025.10933272

DiMasi, J. A., Grabowski, H. G., & Hansen, R. W. (2016). Innovation in the pharmaceutical industry: New estimates of R&D costs. *Journal of Health Economics, 47*, 20–33. DOI: 10.1016/j.jhealeco.2016.01.012 PMID: 26928437

Dimililer, K. (2021). Classification problems in healthcare applications. In *Applied Machine Learning and Multi-Criteria Decision-Making in Healthcare* (pp. 40–61). Bentham Science Publishers. DOI: 10.2174/9781681088716121010006

Dinh, L., Sohl-Dickstein, J., & Bengio, S. (2016). Density estimation using Real NVP. *arXiv preprint arXiv:1605.08803*. https://arxiv.org/abs/1605.08803

Dirkson, A., & Verberne, S. (2018). Open knowledge discovery and data mining from patient forums. In IEEE eScience Conference. DOI: 10.1109/eScience.2018.00119

Djulbegovic, M. B., Bair, H., Gonzalez, D. J. T., Ishikawa, H., Wollstein, G., & Schuman, J. S. (2025). Artificial intelligence for optical coherence tomography in glaucoma. *Translational Vision Science & Technology, 14*(1), 27. DOI: 10.1167/tvst.14.1.27 PMID: 39854198

Doerig, A., Schurger, A., Hess, K., & Herzog, M. H. (2019). The unfolding argument: Why IIT and other causal structure theories cannot explain consciousness. *Consciousness and Cognition, 72*, 49–59. DOI: 10.1016/j.concog.2019.04.002 PMID: 31078047

Drack, M., & Pouvreau, D. (2015). On the history of Ludwig von Bertalanffy's "General Systemology," and on its relationship to cybernetics – part III: Convergences and divergences. *International Journal of General Systems, 44*(5), 523–571. DOI: 10.1080/03081079.2014.1000642 PMID: 26612966

Duan, J., & van Boven, J. F. (2025). Experience of using electronic inhaler monitoring devices for asthma and COPD: A systematic review. *JMIR mHealth and uHealth, 13*(1), e57645. DOI: 10.2196/57645 PMID: 40378281

Dubey, V., Kumari, P., Patel, K., Singh, S., & Shrivastava, S. (2024). Amalgamation of optimization algorithms with IoT applications. In *Sustainable development in industry and society 5.0: Governance, management, and financial implications* (pp. 176–204). IGI Global., DOI: 10.4018/979-8-3693-7322-4.ch009

Dudhat, K. (2025). *Nanotechnology-Driven Approaches for Targeted Rectal Microbiome Modulation in Gastrointestinal Disorders*. Nano Express. DOI: 10.2174/01 15701646355945250107043902

Duplaga, M., & Grysztar, M. (2021). Nutritional behaviors, health literacy, and health locus of control of secondary schoolers in Southern Poland: A cross-sectional study. *Nutrients, 13*(12), 4323. DOI: 10.3390/nu13124323 PMID: 34959875

Durie, M. (1998). *Whaiora: Māori health development* (2nd ed.). Oxford University Press.

El Khatib, M., Hamidi, S., Al Ameeri, I., Al Zaabi, H., & Al Marqab, R. (2022). Digital disruption and big data in healthcare: Opportunities and challenges. *ClinicoEconomics and Outcomes Research, 14*, 563–574. DOI: 10.2147/CEOR.S369553 PMID: 36052095

El Zein, B., Elrashidi, A., Dahlan, M., Al Jarwan, A., & Jabbour, G. (2024). *Nano and Society 5.0: Advancing the Human-Centric Revolution*. Nano Express.

Elov, B. B., Khamroeva, S. M., & Xusainova, Z. Y. (2023). The pipeline processing of NLP. In *E3S Web of Conferences* (Vol. 413, p. 03011). EDP Sciences.

Esmaeilzadeh, P. (2022). Benefits and concerns associated with blockchain-based health information exchange (HIE): A qualitative study from physicians' perspectives. *BMC Medical Informatics and Decision Making, 22*(1), 80. DOI: 10.1186/s12911-022-01815-8 PMID: 35346176

Esteva, A., Kuprel, B., Novoa, R. A., Ko, J., Swetter, S. M., Blau, H. M., & Thrun, S. (2019). A guide to deep learning in healthcare. *Nature Medicine, 25*(1), 24–29. DOI: 10.1038/s41591-018-0316-z

Esteva, M., Chou, K., Yeung, S., Naik, N., Madani, A., Mottaghi, A., Liu, B., Azizi, M. E., Bernecker, T. P., & Lee, S. I. (2020). Deep learning-enabled medical computing: Prediction and understanding of disease progression. *Nature Communications, 11*(1), 1–14. DOI: 10.1038/s41467-020-17569-5 PMID: 31911652

European Commission. (2024). *Artificial Intelligence in Healthcare: EU perspectives*. Brussels: EC.

European Medicines Agency. (2022). *Reflection paper on the use of artificial intelligence in the medicinal product lifecycle*. https://www.ema.europa.eu/en/documents/reflection-paper/artificial-intelligence-medicinal-product-lifecycle_en.pdf

Faiyazuddin, M. (2025). The impact of artificial intelligence on healthcare: A comprehensive review of the future. *Health Science Reports*, *8*(1), e1245. DOI: 10.1002/hsr2.70312

Fan, Z., Chen, Q., Lu, W., Yao, Z., Yang, S., Zhao, H., & Cao, H. (2026). Collaborative artificial intelligence for the diagnosis and management of acute ischemic stroke. *Annals of Medicine*, *58*(1), 2594356. DOI: 10.1080/07853890.2025.2594356 PMID: 41457873

Feenberg, A. (2017). *Technosystem: The social life of reason*. Harvard University Press. DOI: 10.4159/9780674982109

Floridi, L., & Cowls, J. (2019). A unified framework of five principles for AI in society. *Harvard Data Science Review*, *1*(1).

Floridi, L., & Taddeo, M. (2016). What is data ethics? *Philosophical Transactions. Series A, Mathematical, Physical, and Engineering Sciences*, *374*(2083), 20160360. DOI: 10.1098/rsta.2016.0360 PMID: 28336805

Fogel, D. B. (2018). Factors associated with clinical trials that fail and opportunities for improving the likelihood of success: A review. *Contemporary Clinical Trials Communications*, *11*, 156–164. DOI: 10.1016/j.conctc.2018.08.001 PMID: 30112460

Food and Drug Administration. (2021). *Artificial intelligence and machine learning in software as a medical device*. U.S. Food and Drug Administration. https://www.fda.gov/medical-devices/software-medical-device-samd/artificial-intelligence-and-machine-learning-software-medical-device

Frick, T. W. (2020). Education Systems and Technology in 1990, 2020, and Beyond. *TechTrends*, *64*(5), 693–703. DOI: 10.1007/s11528-020-00527-y PMID: 32838405

Frisoni, G., Moro, G., & Carbonaro, A. (2021). A survey on event extraction for natural language understanding: Riding the biomedical literature wave. *IEEE Access : Practical Innovations, Open Solutions*, *9*, 160721–160757. DOI: 10.1109/ACCESS.2021.3130956

Fröhlich, G. B., Shickel, M. D., Tighe, A., Bihorac, S., & Rashidi, P. (2020). Challenges of integrating deep learning models in healthcare. *IEEE Journal of Biomedical and Health Informatics, 24*(8), 1783–1794. DOI: 10.1109/JBHI.2020.2998386

Fukuyama, F. (2002). *Our posthuman future: Consequences of the biotechnology revolution.* Farrar, Straus and Giroux.

Fu, Y., Ma, L., Wan, S., Ge, S., & Yang, Z. (2024). A novel clinical artificial intelligence model for disease detection via retinal imaging. *Innovation (Cambridge (Mass.)), 5*(2), 100575. DOI: 10.1016/j.xinn.2024.100575 PMID: 38379789

Gade, R., Dwarampudi, L. P., Yamuna, K., Maraba, N., & Fufa, G. (2025). Advanced Nanomaterials in Imaging and Diagnostics. *Nano Express*, 79–100.

Gandhi, S. R., Satani, J., & Jain, D. (2023). Classification of keratoconus using corneal topography pattern with transfer learning approach. In J. Choudrie et al. (Eds.), *ICT with intelligent applications* (Smart Innovation, Systems and Technologies, Vol. 311, pp. 165–176). Springer. DOI: 10.1007/978-981-19-3571-8_18

Gandhi, S. R., Satani, J., Bhuva, K., & Patadiya, P. (2021). Evaluation of deep learning networks for keratoconus detection using corneal topographic images. In S. K. Singh et al. (Eds.), *Computer Vision and Image Processing: CVIP 2020* (CCIS, Vol. 1377, pp. 367–380). Springer. DOI: 10.1007/978-981-16-1092-9_31

Gandhi, S. R., Satani, J., Jadav, K., & Shah, A. (2023). Detection of keratoconus and former fruste keratoconus through supervised machine learning algorithms. In *2023 First International Conference on Advances in Electrical, Electronics and Computational Intelligence (ICAEECI)* (pp. 1–9). IEEE. DOI: 10.1109/ICAEECI58247.2023.10370803

Gangwal, A., Ansari, A., Ahmad, I., Azad, A. K., & Sulaiman, W. M. A. W. (2024). Current strategies to address data scarcity in artificial intelligence-based drug discovery: A comprehensive review. *Computers in Biology and Medicine, 179*, 108734. DOI: 10.1016/j.compbiomed.2024.108734 PMID: 38964243

Gao, W., Bigham, A., Ghomi, M., Zarrabi, A., Rabiee, N., Saeb, M. R., Nuri Ertas, Y., Goel, A., Sharifi, E., Ashrafizadeh, M., Sethi, G., Tambuwala, M. M., Wang, Y., Ghaffarlou, M., & Jiao, T. (2024). Micelle-engineered nanoplatforms for precision oncology. *Chemical Engineering Journal, 495*(April), 153438. DOI: 10.1016/j.cej.2024.153438

Garcia, M.. (2021). AI enabled detection of chronic kidney disease through symptom clustering. *International Journal of Medical Informatics, 155*, 104583. DOI: 10.1016/j.ijmedinf.2021.104583

Garin, N., Zárate-Tamames, B., Gras-Martín, L., Milà, R., Crespo-Lessmann, A., Curto, E., Hernández, M., Mestres, C., & Plaza, V. (2023). Clinical impact of electronic monitoring devices of inhalers in adults with asthma or COPD: A systematic review and meta-analysis. *Pharmaceuticals (Basel, Switzerland), 16*(3), 414. DOI: 10.3390/ph16030414 PMID: 36986513

Ghassemi, A., Naumann, T., Doshi-Velez, F., Brisson, P., & Celi, L. A. (2018). Opportunities in machine learning for healthcare: Addressing data quality, scalability, and generalizability. *IEEE Intelligent Systems, 33*(4), 16–19. DOI: 10.1109/MIS.2018.04357129

Ghosh, S., Sarkar, B., & Webster, T. J. (2025). Nanozyme-associated toxicity and regulation. *Nano Express*, 247–262.

Gilbert, F., O'Brien, T., & Cook, M. (2017). The effects of deep brain stimulation on personality and identity: A qualitative study of patients with epilepsy. *Neuroethics, 10*(3), 425–436.

Goh, M. K., Hsu, T. J., & Lin, S. L. (2021). Quantum computing for healthcare: Transformative potential and challenges. *IEEE Transactions on Quantum Engineering, 2*, 1–10. DOI: 10.1109/TQE.2021.3082193

Goldsack, A. H., Coravos, C. L., Krupinski, A. C., Atreja, M. J., Kotz, B. A., & Gordon, M. A. (2020). Verification, analytical validation, and clinical validation (V3): The foundation of determining fit-for-purpose for Biometric Monitoring Technologies (BioMeTs). *NPJ Digital Medicine, 3*(1), 55. DOI: 10.1038/s41746-020-0260-4 PMID: 32337371

Golub, T. R., Slonim, D. K., Tamayo, P., Huard, C., Gaasenbeek, M., Mesirov, J. P., & Lander, E. S. (1999). Molecular classification of cancer: Class discovery and class prediction by gene expression monitoring. *Science, 286*(5439), 531–537. DOI: 10.1126/science.286.5439.531 PMID: 10521349

Gómez-Bombarelli, R., Wei, J. N., Duvenaud, D., Hernández-Lobato, J. M., Sánchez-Lengeling, B., Sheberla, D., Aguilera-Iparraguirre, J., Hirzel, T. D., Adams, R. P., & Aspuru-Guzik, A. (2018). Automatic chemical design using a data-driven continuous representation of molecules. *ACS Central Science, 4*(2), 268–276. DOI: 10.1021/acscentsci.7b00572 PMID: 29532027

Gomez, R.. (2022). Adaptive learning rate strategies for LAMSTAR networks in medical data. *Journal of Medical Artificial Intelligence, 4*, 22.

Goodfellow, I. Pouget-Abadie, Mirza, J., M., Xu, B., Warde-Farley, D., Ozair, S. et al. (2014). Generative adversarial nets. Advances in Neural Information Processing Systems, 27.

Goodfellow, I., Pouget-Abadie, J., Mirza, M., Xu, B., Warde-Farley, D., Ozair, S., Courville, A., & Bengio, Y. (2020). Generative adversarial networks. *Communications of the ACM*, *63*(11), 139–144. DOI: 10.1145/3422622

Goswami, A., Garg, S., Bhatt, E., Chaudhary, V., & Dang, S. (2024). Nanotechnology-Based Biosensors for Biomedical Applications. *Nano Express*, *171*(9), 97508.

Greenhalgh, T., Wherton, J., Papoutsi, C., Lynch, J., Hughes, G., A'Court, C., Hinder, S., Fahy, N., Procter, R., & Shaw, S. (2017). Beyond adoption: A new framework for theorising and evaluating nonadoption, abandonment, and challenges to the scale-up, spread, and sustainability of health and care technologies—. *Journal of Medical Internet Research*, *19*(11), e367. DOI: 10.2196/jmir.8775 PMID: 29092808

Gudepu, B. K., & Jaladi, D. S. (2022). Data Discovery and Security: Protecting Sensitive Information. *International Journal of Acta Informatica*, *1*(1), 176–187.

Gu, G. H., Choi, C., Lee, Y., Situmorang, A. B., Noh, J., Kim, Y. H., & Jung, Y. (2020). Progress in computational and machine-learning methods for heterogeneous small-molecule activation. *Advanced Materials*, *32*(35), 1907865. DOI: 10.1002/adma.201907865 PMID: 32196135

Gupta, P., & Mehta, S. (2022). Federated learning for privacy preserving disease diagnosis. *IEEE Journal of Biomedical and Health Informatics*, *26*(8), 3491–3501. DOI: 10.1109/JBHI.2022.3162951

Gu, X., & Deng, M. (2024). Disclosing harmful patient safety incidents with proactive compensation offer: How do patients respond in Japan? *International Journal of Reliability and Safety*, *18*(4), 321–336. DOI: 10.1504/IJRS.2024.142086

Gymrek, M., McGuire, A. L., Golan, D., Halperin, E., & Erlich, Y. (2013). Identifying personal genomes by surname inference. *Science*, *339*(6117), 321–324. DOI: 10.1126/science.1229566 PMID: 23329047

Habbal, A., Ali, M. K., & Abuzaraida, M. A. (2024). Artificial intelligence trust, risk and security management (AI TRiSM): Frameworks, applications, challenges and future research directions. *Expert Systems with Applications*, *240*, 122442. DOI: 10.1016/j.eswa.2023.122442

Habermas, J. (2003). *The future of human nature*. Polity Press.

Hägele, H. (2020). Ethical considerations in the use of exoskeletons for rehabilitation. *Ethics, Medicine, and Public Health, 15*, 100–107.

Haggenmüller, S., Schmitt, M., Krieghoff-Henning, E., Hekler, A., Maron, R. C., Wies, C., Utikal, J. S., Meier, F., Hobelsberger, S., Gellrich, F. F., Sergon, M., Hauschild, A., French, L. E., Heinzerling, L., Schlager, J. G., Ghoreschi, K., Schlaak, M., Hilke, F. J., Poch, G., & Brinker, T. J. (2024). Federated learning for decentralized artificial intelligence in melanoma diagnostics. *JAMA Dermatology, 160*(3), 303–311. DOI: 10.1001/jamadermatol.2023.5550 PMID: 38324293

Haggerty, K. D., & Ericson, R. V. (2000). The surveillant assemblage. *The British Journal of Sociology, 51*(4), 605–622. DOI: 10.1080/00071310020015280 PMID: 11140886

Halder, S., & Kumar, R. (2025). *In Vitro and in Vivo Applications of Nanoparticles in Head and Neck Cancer*. Nano Express. DOI: 10.70593/978-93-49307-10-0

Hallioui, A. (2020). System analysis: A literature review. *Proceedings of the International Conference on Industrial Engineering & Operations Management (*2169-8767*)*, 2774.

Hammond, D. (2019). The legacy of Ludwig von Bertalanffy and its relevance for our time. *Systems Research and Behavioral Science, 36*(3), 301–307. DOI: 10.1002/sres.2598

Hanahan, D. (2022). Hallmarks of cancer: New dimensions. *Cancer Discovery, 12*(1), 31–46. DOI: 10.1158/2159-8290.CD-21-1059

Harari, Y. N. (2017). *Homo Deus: A brief history of tomorrow*. Vintage. DOI: 10.17104/9783406704024

Haraway, D. J. (1991). A Cyborg Manifesto: Science, Technology, and Socialist Feminism in the Late Twentieth Century. In *Simians, cyborgs, and women: The reinvention of nature* (pp. 149–181). Routledge.

Harper, L.. (2021). Detecting adverse drug reactions using artificial intelligence in real-world healthcare data. *Nature Medicine, 27*(7), 1105–1112. DOI: 10.1038/s41591-021-01329-2

Hashimoto, D. A., Rosman, G., Rus, D., & Meireles, O. R. (2020). Artificial intelligence in surgery: Promises and perils. *Annals of Surgery, 268*(1), 70–76. DOI: 10.1097/SLA.0000000000002693 PMID: 29389679

Hasselgren, A., Kralevska, K., Gligoroski, D., Pedersen, S. A., & Faxvaag, A. (2020). Blockchain in healthcare and health sciences—A scoping review. *International Journal of Medical Informatics, 134*, 104040. DOI: 10.1016/j.ijmedinf.2019.104040 PMID: 31865055

Hasselgren, C., & Oprea, T. I. (2024). Artificial intelligence for drug discovery: Are we there yet? *Annual Review of Pharmacology and Toxicology, 64*(1), 527–550. DOI: 10.1146/annurev-pharmtox-040323-040828 PMID: 37738505

He, Y., Zhang, L., & Chen, M. (2024). Multilingual LLMs for inclusive healthcare communication. *International Journal of Digital Health, 6*(1), 33–47.

HIMSS & Medscape. (2024). *Future of AI in healthcare survey report*. https://www.himss.org/futureofai

Ho, J., Jain, A., & Abbeel, P. (2020). Denoising diffusion probabilistic models. In *Proceedings of the 34th Conference on Neural Information Processing Systems (NeurIPS 2020)* (pp. 6840–6851).

Ho, J., Jain, A., & Abbeel, P. (2022). Denoising diffusion probabilistic models. *Advances in Neural Information Processing Systems, 35*, 6840–6852.

Honda, S., Shi, S., & Ueda, H. R. (2019). SMILES transformer: Pre-trained molecular fingerprint for low data drug discovery. *arXiv*. https://arxiv.org/abs/1911.04738

Hopkins, A. L., Bender, A., & Glen, R. C. (2020). Exscientia's AI-designed drug enters clinical trials. *Nature Biotechnology, 38*(1), 8–9. DOI: 10.1038/d41587-020-00001-x PMID: 31919441

Hsu, W. C., Lin, P. X., Li, C. J., Tien, H. Y., Kang, Y. H., & Lee, P. J. (2024, August). An enhanced model for asr in the medical field. In *2024 IEEE International Conference on Information Reuse and Integration for Data Science (IRI)* (pp. 43-48). IEEE. DOI: 10.1109/IRI62200.2024.00021

Huang, K., Altosaar, J., & Ranganath, R. (2019). Clinicalbert: Modeling clinical notes and predicting hospital readmission. *arXiv preprint* arXiv:1904.05342.

Huang, A. C. K., Thiel, K. J. M., & Wang, L. T. (2021). Collaborative approaches to integrating AI in healthcare: Bridging research, practice, and regulation. *Journal of Healthcare Informatics Research, 5*(4), 433–452. DOI: 10.1007/s41666-021-00088-4

Huang, D., Ye, X., & Sakurai, T. (2024). Multi-party collaborative drug discovery via federated learning. *Computers in Biology and Medicine, 171*, 108181. DOI: 10.1016/j.compbiomed.2024.108181 PMID: 38428094

Huang, R., Xia, M., Nguyen, D. T., Zhao, T., Sakamuru, S., Zhao, J., & Austin, C. P. (2016). Tox21 challenge to build predictive models of nuclear receptor and stress response pathways. *Frontiers in Environmental Science*, *3*, 85. DOI: 10.3389/fenvs.2015.00085

Huang, Y., Liu, H., Zhao, Y., Chen, H., Li, Q., Li, X., Hua, S., Cao, D., & Chang, Y. (2024). Disrupting redox homeostasis for tumor therapy based on PDT/chemo/ferroptosis therapeutic hybrid liposomes. *RSC Advances*, *14*(28), 20152–20162. DOI: 10.1039/D4RA03361B PMID: 38915327

Hwang, J. J. D., Yoon, H. S., Kim, S. Y., Jung, J. M., Jeon, S. H., & Chung, J. Y. (2020). AI-based healthcare: Predictive analytics, risk management, and automation. *IEEE Access : Practical Innovations, Open Solutions*, *8*, 179890–179902. DOI: 10.1109/ACCESS.2020.3026621

Hyun, S. H., Ahn, M. S., Koh, Y. W., & Lee, S. J. (2019). A machine-learning approach using PET-based radiomics to predict the histological subtypes of lung cancer. *Clinical Nuclear Medicine*, *44*(12), 956–960. DOI: 10.1097/RLU.0000000000002810

Ienca, M., & Andorno, R. (2017). Towards new human rights in the age of neuroscience and neurotechnology. *Life Sciences, Society and Policy*, *13*(1), 1–27. DOI: 10.1186/s40504-017-0050-1 PMID: 28444626

India, A. I. (2024). *AI adoption in Indian healthcare*. https://indiaai.gov.in

Insel, T. R., Landis, S. C., & Collins, F. S. (2013). The NIH BRAIN Initiative. *Science*, *340*(6133), 687–688. DOI: 10.1126/science.1239276 PMID: 23661744

Iqbal, F. M., & Khan, M. M. (2021). A systematic review and meta-analysis of digital alerting systems in remote monitoring. *npj. Digital Medicine*, *4*(1), 1–9. DOI: 10.1038/s41746-020-00378-0 PMID: 33398041

Jabir, K., & Thirumurthi Raja, A. (2023). Prediction of lung cancer from electronic health records using CNN-supported NLP. In *Computational intelligence for clinical diagnosis* (pp. 549–560). Springer., DOI: 10.1007/978-3-031-23683-9_40

Jahan, T. (2021). Machine learning with IoT and big data in healthcare. In *Intelligent healthcare: Applications of AI in eHealth* (pp. 81–98). Springer International Publishing.

Jangid, A. K., Pooja, D., Jain, P., Gupta, N., Ramesan, S., & Kulhari, H. (2021). Self-assembled and pH-responsive polymeric nanomicelles impart effective delivery of paclitaxel to cancer cells. *RSC Advances*, *11*(23), 13928–13939. DOI: 10.1039/D1RA01574E PMID: 35423920

Jang, K., & Baek, Y. M. (2018). How to effectively design public health interventions: Implications from the interaction effects between socioeconomic status and health locus of control beliefs on healthy dietary behaviours among US adults. *Health & Social Care in the Community*, *26*(5), 664–674. DOI: 10.1111/hsc.12577 PMID: 29659076

Javanmardi, E., Liu, S., & Xie, N. (2020). Exploring grey systems theory-based methods and applications in sustainability studies: A systematic review approach. *Sustainability (Basel)*, *12*(11), 4437. DOI: 10.3390/su12114437

Jawad, L. A. (2024). Security and privacy in digital healthcare systems: Challenges and mitigation strategies. *Abhigyan*, *42*(1), 23–31. DOI: 10.1177/09702385241233073

Jerfy, A., Selden, O., & Balkrishnan, R. (2024). The growing impact of natural language processing in healthcare and public health. INQUIRY. *Inquiry : a Journal of Medical Care Organization, Provision and Financing*, *61*, 00469580241290095. DOI: 10.1177/00469580241290095 PMID: 39396164

Jindal, V., Kukreja, V., Singh, D. P., Vats, S., & Mehta, S. (2023, October). Pushing diagnostic frontiers: Federated learning CNN for diverse lung disease. In *Proceedings of the 2023 4th IEEE Global Conference for Advancement in Technology (GCAT)* (pp. 1–6). IEEE. DOI: 10.1109/GCAT59970.2023.10353284

Jumper, J., Evans, R., Pritzel, A., Green, T., Figurnov, M., Ronneberger, O., & Hassabis, D. (2021). Highly accurate protein structure prediction with AlphaFold. *Nature*, *596*(7873), 583–589. DOI: 10.1038/s41586-021-03819-2 PMID: 34265844

Kabir, M. R. (2020). Behavioural intention to adopt blockchain for a transparent and effective taxing system. *Journal of Global Operations and Strategic Sourcing*, *14*(1), 170–201. DOI: 10.1108/JGOSS-08-2020-0050

Kant, I. (1897). Eternal Peace. *The Advocate of Peace (1894-1920)*, *59*(5), 111–116. https://www.jstor.org/stable/25751039

Kanzaki, N., & Iijima, H. (2013). Cyberdyne's HAL exoskeleton: Robot-assisted rehabilitation for spinal cord injury and stroke. *Journal of Neuroengineering and Rehabilitation*, *10*(1), 1–7.

Khan, A. A., Kumar, R., Tripathi, R., Gupta, G. P., Islam, A. K. M. N., & Shorfuzzaman, M. (2023). Data security in healthcare industrial Internet of Things with blockchain. *IEEE Sensors Journal*, *23*(20), 25144–25151. DOI: 10.1109/JSEN.2023.3273851

Khatoon, U. T., & Velidandi, A. (2025). An Overview on the Role of Government Initiatives in Nanotechnology Innovation for Sustainable Economic Development and Research Progress. *Nano Express, 17*(3), 1250.

Kim, S., Le, D., Zheng, W., Singh, T., Arora, A., Zhai, X., . . . Seltzer, M. L. (2021). Evaluating user perception of speech recognition system quality with semantic distance metric. *arXiv preprint arXiv:2110.05376.*

Kim, Y., & Park, S. (2023). Scalable architecture for online medical recommendation engines. *Journal of Systems and Software, 188,* 111296.

Kingma, D. P., & Welling, M. (2013). Auto-encoding variational Bayes. arXiv preprint arXiv:1312.6114.

Kingma, D. P., & Welling, M. (2019). An introduction to variational autoencoders. *Foundations and Trends in ML, 12*(4), 307–392.

Klein, E., Goering, S., & Gagne, J.. (2015). Brain–computer interface-based control of robotic arms: A qualitative study of participants' experiences. *AJOB Neuroscience, 6*(1), 29–41.

Klemt, I., Reshetnikov, V., Dutta, S., Bila, G., Bilyy, R., Cuartero, I. C., Hidalgo, A., Wünsche, A., Böhm, M., Wondrak, M., Kunz-Schughart, L. A., Tietze, R., Beierlein, F., Imhof, P., Gensberger-Reigl, S., Pischetsrieder, M., Körber, M., Jost, T., & Mokhir, A. (2024). A concept of dual-responsive prodrugs based on oligomerization-controlled reactivity of ester groups: An improvement of cancer cells versus neutrophils selectivity of camptothecin. *RSC Medicinal Chemistry, 15*(4), 1189–1197. DOI: 10.1039/D3MD00609C PMID: 38665843

Kline, R., Patel, S., & Wong, T. (2024). Explainable AI in clinical collaboration: Tools and techniques. *Health Informatics Journal, 30*(1), 78–92.

Kodjiku, S. L., Aboagye, I., Ankrah, C., Nti, I. K., Boateng, R., & Ofori, R. (2023). WQCrowd: Secure blockchain-based crowdsourcing framework with multi-tier worker quality evaluation. *Journal of King Saud University. Computer and Information Sciences, 35*(10), 101843. DOI: 10.1016/j.jksuci.2023.101843

Kokudeva, M., Vichev, M., Naseva, E., Miteva, D. G., & Velikova, T. (2024). Artificial intelligence as a tool in drug discovery and development. *World Journal of Experimental Medicine, 14*(3), 96042. DOI: 10.5493/wjem.v14.i3.96042 PMID: 39312699

Koski, E., & Murphy, J. (2021). AI in healthcare. *Studies in Health Technology and Informatics, 284,* 295–299. DOI: 10.3233/SHTI210726 PMID: 34920529

Koushki, M., Amiri-Dashatan, N., Pourghadamyari, H., Khodabandehloo, H., Bagheri, F., Farahani, M., & Tayebi, L. (2024). An Overview of the Relationships between the Food Industry and Nanotechnology. *Nano Express*, *11*(2), e7–e7.

Krishnan, G. G. P. P. S., Sullivan, A. T. S. S., & Turner, B. K. (2020). Application of generative adversarial networks for generating cancer biomarkers: A case study. *IEEE Transactions on Biomedical Engineering*, *67*(5), 1445–1455. DOI: 10.1109/TBME.2019.2935442

Kumar, A., & Sadashiva, D. N. (2025). The Synergy Of Artificial Intelligence And Big Data Analytics In Accelerating Drug Discovery: From Target Identification To Clinical Trials. *International Journal of Environmental Sciences*, *11*(4s), 161–179.

Kumar, A., & Singh, V. (2022). Applying LAMSTAR neural networks in disease symptom mapping. *Neural Computing & Applications*, *34*(6), 4095–4107. DOI: 10.1007/s00521-021-06190-3

Kumari, V., Dubey, V., Kumari, P., Pal, R., Shrivastava, S., & Anh, P. T. N. (2023). Nitty-gritty of deep reinforcement learning for the healthcare sector. In AI and IoT-Based Technologies for Precision Medicine (pp. 263–279). DOI: 10.4018/979-8-3693-0876-9.ch016

Kumar, R., Kumar, P., Tripathi, R., Gupta, G. P., Islam, A. K. M. N., & Shorfuzzaman, M. (2022). Permissioned blockchain and deep learning for secure and efficient data sharing in industrial healthcare systems. *IEEE Transactions on Industrial Informatics*, *18*(11), 8065–8073. DOI: 10.1109/TII.2022.3161631

Kumar, Y. (2024). A comprehensive analysis of speech recognition systems in healthcare: Current research challenges and future prospects. *SN Computer Science*, *5*(1), 137. DOI: 10.1007/s42979-023-02466-w

Kurzweil, R. (2005). *The singularity is near: When humans transcend biology*. Viking.

Kutschera, U. (2018). Systems biology of eukaryotic superorganisms and the holobiont concept. *Theory in Biosciences*, *137*(2), 117–131. DOI: 10.1007/s12064-018-0265-6 PMID: 29948922

Latif, S., Qadir, J., Qayyum, A., Usama, M., & Younis, S. (2020). Speech technology for healthcare: Opportunities, challenges, and state of the art. *IEEE Reviews in Biomedical Engineering*, *14*, 342–356. DOI: 10.1109/RBME.2020.3006860 PMID: 32746367

Lavric, A., & Valentin, P. (2019). KeratoDetect: Keratoconus detection algorithm using convolutional neural networks. *Computational Intelligence and Neuroscience, 2019*, 8162567. Advance online publication. DOI: 10.1155/2019/8162567 PMID: 30809255

LeCun, Y., Bengio, Y., & Hinton, G. (2015). Deep learning. *Nature, 521*(7553), 436–444. DOI: 10.1038/nature14539 PMID: 26017442

Leder, D. (1990). *The absent body*. University of Chicago Press.

Lee, J., Yoon, W., Kim, S., Kim, D., Kim, S., So, C. H., & Kang, J. (2020). BioBERT: A pre-trained biomedical language representation model for biomedical text mining. *Bioinformatics (Oxford, England), 36*(4), 1234–1240. DOI: 10.1093/bioinformatics/btz682 PMID: 31501885

Lee, P. C., Sharma, S. K., Motaganahalli, S., & Huang, A. (2023). Evaluating the clinical decision-making ability of large language models using MKSAP-19 cardiology questions. *JACC Advances, 2*(9), 100658. DOI: 10.1016/j.jacadv.2023.100658 PMID: 38938709

Lee, S. (2020). Multi-symptom matching using fuzzy logic in medical diagnosis systems. *Journal of Clinical Informatics Research, 9*(2), 45–58.

Li, X., Zheng, X., Yuan, Y., Deng, J., Su, L., & Xu, K. (2025). A review of research progress on COF-based biosensors in pathogen detection. *Nano Express*, 343605.

Li, B., Li, P., & Dong, R. (2025). *Recent Advances in Nanozyme-Based Materials for Environmental Detection and Remediation*. Nano Express. DOI: 10.1039/D4QM01009D

Li, H., Hu, Q., Zhao, G., & Li, B. (2022). The co-evolution of knowledge management and business model transformation in the post-COVID-19 era: Insights based on Chinese e-commerce companies. *Journal of Knowledge Management, 26*(5), 1113–1123. DOI: 10.1108/JKM-03-2021-0177

Lima, P. U., & Custodio, L. M. M. (2004). Artificial Intelligence and Systems Theory: Applied to Cooperative Robots. *International Journal of Advanced Robotic Systems, 1*(3), 15. DOI: 10.5772/5630

Li, N., Lewin, A., Ning, S., Waito, M., Zeller, M. P., Tinmouth, A., & Shih, A. W.Canadian Transfusion Trials Group. (2025). Privacy-preserving federated data access and federated learning: Improved data sharing and AI model development in transfusion medicine. *Transfusion, 65*(1), 22–28. DOI: 10.1111/trf.18077 PMID: 39610333

Lin, H., & Chen, C. (2020). Naive Bayes classification for streamlining dengue prediction in urban populations. *Expert Systems with Applications, 150*, 113248. DOI: 10.1016/j.eswa.2020.113248

Litjens, G., Kooi, T., Bejnordi, B. E., Setio, A. A. A., Ciompi, F., Ghafoorian, M., van der Laak, J. A. W. M., van Ginneken, B., & Sánchez, C. I. (2017). A survey on deep learning in medical image analysis. *Medical Image Analysis, 42*, 60–88. DOI: 10.1016/j.media.2017.07.005 PMID: 28778026

Liu, A. H. C., Sullivan, B. A., & Lang, J. M. (2019). Integrating AI into healthcare systems: Practical considerations and barriers. *Journal of Healthcare Engineering, 2019*, 9064329. Advance online publication. DOI: 10.1155/2019/9064329

Liu, C., Tian, Y., Tang, J., Dang, S., & Chen, G. (2023). A novel local differential privacy federated learning under multi-privacy regimes. *Expert Systems with Applications, 227*, 120266. DOI: 10.1016/j.eswa.2023.120266

Liu, H., Crespo, R. G., & Martínez, O. S. (2020). Enhancing privacy and data security across healthcare applications using blockchain and distributed ledger concepts. *Health Care, 8*(3), 24043. DOI: 10.3390/healthcare8030243 PMID: 32751325

Liu, X., Cruz Rivera, S., Moher, D., Calvert, M. J., & Denniston, A. K. (2019). Reporting guidelines for clinical trial reports for interventions involving artificial intelligence: The CONSORT-AI extension. *BMJ (Clinical Research Ed.), 370*, m3164. DOI: 10.1136/bmj.m3164 PMID: 32909959

Li, X., & Padman, R. (2025). Ethical and Practical Implications of AI in Healthcare Data Management. *Journal of Healthcare Informatics Research*, •••, 2025.

Lobo, L. M. R. J., & Markandeya, D. L. (2023). Expert system for medical diagnosis and consultancy using prediction algorithms of machine learning. In *Proceedings of International Joint Conference on Advances in Computational Intelligence (IJCACI 2022)*. Springer. DOI: 10.1007/978-981-99-1435-7_33

Lodewyk, K., & Tan, R. (2025). Wearables research for continuous monitoring of patient health in non-hospital settings. *PLOS Digital Health, 4*(1), e0000860. DOI: 10.1371/journal.pdig.0000860 PMID: 40343891

Longoni, C., Bonezzi, A., & Morewedge, C. K. (2019). Resistance to medical artificial intelligence. *The Journal of Consumer Research, 46*(4), 629–650. DOI: 10.1093/jcr/ucz013

Looi, V., Gfeller, K., & Driscoll, V. (2012). Music perception of cochlear implant users: A review. *Ear and Hearing, 33*(5), 519–540.

Lovrić, B., Placento, H., Farčić, N., Lipič Baligač, M., Mikšić, Š., Mamić, M., Jovanović, T., Vidić, H., Karabatić, S., Cviljević, S., Zibar, L., Vukoja, I., & Barać, I. (2022). Association between Health Literacy and Prevalence of Obesity, Arterial Hypertension, and Diabetes Mellitus. *International Journal of Environmental Research and Public Health, 19*(15), 9002. Advance online publication. DOI: 10.3390/ijerph19159002 PMID: 35897372

Luo, R., Liu, H., & Cheng, Z. (2022). Protein scaffolds: Antibody alternatives for cancer diagnosis and therapy. *RSC Chemical Biology, 3*(7), 830–847. DOI: 10.1039/D2CB00094F PMID: 35866165

MacIntyre, A. (2007). *After Virtue: A Study in Moral Theory* (3rd ed.). University of Notre Dame Press.

Madani, A., McCann, B., Naik, N., & Rajpurkar, P. (2023). AI-driven protein structure prediction for personalized medicine. *Nature Machine Intelligence, 5*(2), 101–115.

Mak, K. K., & Pichika, M. R. (2019). Artificial intelligence in drug development: Present status and future prospects. *Drug Discovery Today, 24*(3), 773–780. DOI: 10.1016/j.drudis.2018.11.014 PMID: 30472429

Marcinkevičs, R., & Vogt, J. E. (2020). Interpretability and explainability: A machine learning zoo Mini-tour. *arXiv preprint arXiv:2012.01805.*

Market.us. (2023). Generative AI in healthcare: Current trends and future outlook. *Market Research Report.* https://www.market.us/report/generative-ai-in-healthcare/

Martens, P., & Zhao, Y. (2021). Hybrid AI pipelines for scalable disease detection in low-resource settings. *Global Health Informatics, 3*(1), 14–26.

Marzban, S., Najafi, M., Agolli, A., & Ashrafi, E. (2022). Impact of patient engagement on healthcare quality: A scoping review. *Journal of Patient Experience, 9*, 23743735221125439. DOI: 10.1177/23743735221125439 PMID: 36134145

Mayr, A., Klambauer, G., Unterthiner, T., & Hochreiter, S. (2016). DeepTox: Toxicity prediction using deep learning. *Frontiers in Environmental Science, 3*, 80. DOI: 10.3389/fenvs.2015.00080

McKinsey & Company. (2020). *Transforming healthcare with AI: The impact on the workforce and organizations.*

McKinsey Health Insights. (2025). Generative AI in healthcare: Survey of 150 healthcare leaders. *McKinsey & Company.* https://www.mckinsey.com/industries/healthcare/our-insights/generative-ai-in-healthcare-current-trends-and-future-outlook

Meho, L. I. (2019). Using Scopus's CiteScore for assessing the quality of computer science conferences. *Journal of Informetrics, 13*(1), 419–433. DOI: 10.1016/j.joi.2019.02.006

Mendhurwar, S., & Mishra, R. (2021). Integration of social and IoT technologies: Architectural framework for digital transformation and cybersecurity challenges. *Enterprise Information Systems, 15*(4), 565–584. DOI: 10.1080/17517575.2019.1600041

Meng, Y., Wang, C., Li, X., Wang, L., Huo, M., Chen, Y., & Wang, B. (2024). Two-Dimensional MoS2 nanosheets as cocatalyst to augment the nanocatalytic tumor therapy. *Chemical Engineering Journal, 496*, 153887. DOI: 10.1016/j.cej.2024.153887

Meskó, B. (2024). The prompt engineering gap in medical AI: Addressing the new digital divide. *The Lancet. Digital Health, 6*(3), e150–e151. DOI: 10.1016/S2589-7500(23)00262-6

Meyers, J., Singh, A., & Zhao, L. (2022). AI for rare disease diagnosis: A federated learning approach. *Journal of Biomedical Informatics, 134*, 104203.

Mildenhall, B., Srinivasan, P. P., Tancik, M., Barron, J. T., Ramamoorthi, R., & Ng, R. (2021). NeRF: Representing scenes as neural radiance fields for view synthesis. *Communications of the ACM, 64*(7), 98–106.

Miller, J. G. (1973). Living Systems: The organism. *The Quarterly Review of Biology, 48*(1), 92–276. https://www.jstor.org/stable/2820539. DOI: 10.1086/407589 PMID: 4576974

Mitchell, M., Wu, S., & Zaldivar, A.. (2019). Model cards for model reporting. *Proceedings of the Conference on Fairness, Accountability, and Transparency*, 220–229. DOI: 10.1145/3287560.3287596

Mitsuhiro, T. (2020). How society changes: Sociological enlightenment and a theory of social evolution for freedom. *The American Sociologist, 51*(4), 446–469. DOI: 10.1007/s12108-020-09464-y PMID: 33132397

Mittal, S., Gupta, V., Sharma, P., Khanna, A., Jain, V., & Saxena, R. (2022). Using identity-based cryptography as a foundation for an effective and secure cloud model for e-health. *Computational Intelligence and Neuroscience, 7016554*, 1–8. Advance online publication. DOI: 10.1155/2022/7016554 PMID: 35510050

Mittelstadt, B., Allo, P., Taddeo, M., Wachter, S., & Floridi, L. (2016). The ethics of algorithms: Mapping the debate. *Big Data & Society, 3*(2), 1–21. DOI: 10.1177/2053951716679679

Mohammadi, A.. (2025). An Efficient Feature Fusion Framework for Wearable Cuffless Blood Pressure Monitoring and Long-term Validation. *medRxiv*, 2025.

Mohanty, S., Desai, V. M., Jain, R., Agrawal, M., Dubey, S. K., & Singhvi, G. (2024). Unveiling the potential of photodynamic therapy with nanocarriers as a compelling therapeutic approach for skin cancer treatment: Current explorations and insights. *RSC Advances*, *14*(30), 21915–21937. DOI: 10.1039/D4RA02564D PMID: 38989245

Mohapatra, H. (2026). Smart Workflows: Designing Next-Generation E-Collaboration With Artificial Intelligence. In *Transforming E-Collaboration With AI and Emerging Digital Technologies* (pp. 57-88). IGI Global Scientific Publishing.

Mohapatra, S., & Patra, P. K. (2018). Smart health care system using data mining. In *2018 International Conference on Information Technology (ICIT)*. IEEE. DOI: 10.1109/ICIT.2018.00021

Mond, H. G., & Proclemer, A. (2011). The 11th World Survey of Cardiac Pacing and Implantable Cardioverter Defibrillators. *Pacing and Clinical Electrophysiology*, *34*(8), 1013–1027. DOI: 10.1111/j.1540-8159.2011.03150.x PMID: 21707667

Moraru, A. D., Costin, D., Moraru, R. L., & Branisteanu, D. C. (2020). Artificial intelligence and deep learning in ophthalmology-present and future [Review]. *Experimental and Therapeutic Medicine*, *20*(4), 3469. DOI: 10.3892/etm.2020.9118 PMID: 32905155

Mourtzis, D. (2020). Simulation in the design and operation of manufacturing systems: State of the art and new trends. *International Journal of Production Research*, *58*(7), 1927–1949. DOI: 10.1080/00207543.2019.1636321

Mousa, I., Alsharari, A. M., Alalawy, A. I., Almotairy, A. R. Z., Aljohani, S., Osailan, R., Alamoudi, W. M., El-Metwaly, N. M., & El-Metwal, N. (2025). Harnessing the Potential of Sargassum Latifolium for Sustainable Synthesis of Ag/Bi2O3-Curdlan Nanocomposites: Phytochemical Characterization and Biological Applications. *Nano Express*, 1–22.

Mun, B., Jeong, H., Kim, R., Gu, B., Kim, J., Son, H. Y., Rho, H. W., Lim, E.-K., & Haam, S. (2024). 3D-Nanostructured microfluidic device arranged in a herringbone pattern for the highly effective capture of HER2-Positive cancer-derived exosomes in urine. *Chemical Engineering Journal*, *482*, 148851. DOI: 10.1016/j.cej.2024.148851

Murray, C. D. (2009). Bodies and prostheses. In Siebers, T. (Ed.), *Disability theory* (pp. 75–90). University of Michigan Press.

Musk, E. (2019). An integrated brain–machine interface platform with thousands of channels—. *Journal of Medical Internet Research, 21*(10), e16194. DOI: 10.2196/16194 PMID: 31642810

Nagarajan, S. (2024, December). Advances in Speech and Text Processing for Dravidian Language: A Comprehensive Review. In *2024 9th International Conference on Communication and Electronics Systems (ICCES)* (pp. 1715-1722). IEEE.

Naik, G. G., & Jagtap, V. A. (2024). *Nano TransMed*. Nano Express.

Naik, K., Goyal, R. K., Foschini, L., Chak, C. W., Thielscher, C., Zhu, H., Lu, J., Lehár, J., Pacanoswki, M. A., Terranova, N., Mehta, N., Korsbo, N., Fakhouri, T., Liu, Q., & Gobburu, J. (2024). Current status and future directions: The application of artificial intelligence/machine learning for precision medicine. *Clinical Pharmacology and Therapeutics, 115*(4), 673–686. DOI: 10.1002/cpt.3152 PMID: 38103204

Naithani, K., Raiwani, Y. P., Tiwari, S., & Chauhan, A. S. (2024). Artificial Intelligence Techniques Based on Federated Learning in Smart Healthcare. In Federated Learning for Smart Communication Using IoT Application (pp. 81-108). Chapman and Hall/CRC. DOI: 10.1201/9781003489368-5

Naryal, S., Rana, M., Sharma, N., Ahmed, B., Sharma, P., Kujur, S., Jaiswal, S., Gupta, S. Das, Patel, S. M. B., & Kaushal, S. (2025). Navigating Sustainable and Healthy Future: Green Nanotechnology, Regulatory Priorities, and Challenges. *Nano Express*, 353–369.

Nastasijevic, I., Kundacina, I., Jaric, S., Pavlovic, Z., Radovic, M., & Radonic, V. (2025). *Biosensors in the Meat Production Chain*. Nano Express. DOI: 10.20944/preprints202501.1773.v1

Navar, M. C., Wang, G., Mi, A., & Hernandez, A. V. (2021). Artificial intelligence-enabled clinical trials: Potential opportunities for cardiovascular disease research. *JACC. Basic to Translational Science, 6*(11), 1068–1080. DOI: 10.1016/j.jacbts.2021.08.012

Nebbia, G.. (2025). Re-identification of Patients from Imaging Features Extracted by Foundation Models. *npj. Digital Medicine, 8*, 469. PMID: 40696111

Ng, W. Y., Tan, T. E., Movva, P. V., Fang, A. H. S., Yeo, K. K., Ho, D., Foo, F. S. S., Xiao, Z., Sun, K., Wong, T. Y., Sia, A. T.-H., & Ting, D. S. W. (2021). Blockchain applications in health care for COVID-19 and beyond: A systematic review. *The Lancet. Digital Health, 3*(12), e819–e829. DOI: 10.1016/S2589-7500(21)00210-7 PMID: 34654686

Niazi, S. K., & Mariam, Z. (2025). Artificial intelligence in drug development: Reshaping the therapeutic landscape. *Therapeutic Advances in Drug Safety, 16*, 20420986251321704. DOI: 10.1177/20420986251321704 PMID: 40008227

Nicholson, D. A. (2012). The concept of mechanism in biology. *Studies in History and Philosophy of Science Part C Studies in History and Philosophy of Biological and Biomedical Sciences, 43*(1), 152–163. DOI: 10.1016/j.shpsc.2011.05.014 PMID: 22326084

Nikhade, R., & Jaiswal, A. (2025). *Advancements in Polymer Modification: A Comprehensive Review on Techniques*. Nano Express.

Niramai Health Analytix. (2023). https://www.niramai.com

Niramai Health Analytix. (2023). *Official website*. https://www.niramai.com

Nowak, P. G., & Stencel, A. (2022). Correction to: How many ways can you die? Multiple biological deaths as a consequence of the multiple concepts of an organism. *Theoretical Medicine and Bioethics, 43*(2-3), 127–154. Advance online publication. DOI: 10.1007/s11017-022-09583-2 PMID: 36197598

Nunez, R., Harris, A., Ibrahim, O., Keller, J., Wikle, C. K., Robinson, E., . . . Guidoboni, G. (2022). Artificial intelligence to aid glaucoma diagnosis and monitoring: State of the art and new directions. *In Photonics* (Vol. 9, No. 11, p. 810). MDPI.

Odobleja, S. (1939). *Psychologie consonantiste*. Librairie Maloine.

OECD. (2024). *AI in health: Huge potential, huge risks*. OECD Publishing.

Oh, J., Hessel, M., Czarnecki, W. M., Xu, Z., Van Hasselt, H., Singh, S., & Silver, D. (2020). Discovering reinforcement learning algorithms. *ArXiv (Cornell University)*. https://arxiv.org/pdf/2007.08794.pdf

Olawade, D. B., David-Olawade, A. C., Wada, O. Z., Asaolu, A. J., Adereni, T., & Ling, J. (2024). Artificial intelligence in healthcare delivery: Prospects and pitfalls. *Journal of Artificial Intelligence in Medicine*. Advance online publication. https://www.sciencedirect.com/science/article/pii/S2949916X24000616

Oliveira, L. G.. (2021). Telemedicine integrations in AI based diagnostic frameworks. *Telemedicine Journal and e-Health, 27*(1), 55–65. DOI: 10.1089/tmj.2020.0051

Ologundudu, L., & Tan, R. (2025). Patient-facing digital inhalers for asthma: A systematic review and meta-analysis. *The Journal of Allergy and Clinical Immunology. In Practice, 13*(1), 1–9. DOI: 10.1016/j.jaip.2024.10.004 PMID: 40312010

Oord, A. d., Dieleman, S., & Schrauwen, B. (2016). WaveNet: A generative model for raw audio. *arXiv preprint arXiv:1609.03499*. https://arxiv.org/abs/1609.03499

Open & Affordable. (2024). *AI in healthcare statistics and trends*. https://www.openandaffordable.com

Ortigosa, S. (2022). Cybernetics: Classical philosophy and Science—A logic of education. *The International Journal of Humanities Education*, *20*(2), 91–99. DOI: 10.18848/2327-0063/CGP/v20i02/91-99

Ortiz-Catalan, M., Hakansson, B., & Branemark, R. (2014). An osseointegrated human–machine gateway for long-term control of sensory–motor prostheses. *Science Translational Medicine*, *6*(257), 257re6. DOI: 10.1126/scitranslmed.3008933 PMID: 25298322

Ott, B. (2019). Gender and prosthetics: Normative design and embodied experience. *Science, Technology & Human Values*, *44*(2), 230–252.

Pagallo, U. (2013). *The Laws of Robots: Crimes, Contracts, and Torts*. Springer. DOI: 10.1007/978-94-007-6564-1

Panda, S., & Mehta, A. (2023). Navigating the future of healthcare with artificial intelligence: Reviewing case studies and predicting its impact. *ResearchGate*. https://www.researchgate.net/publication/386053591_Navigating_the_Future_of_Healthcare_with_Artificial_Intelligence_Reviewing_Case_Studies_and_Predicting_its_Impact

Panicker, R., Thomas, J., & Nair, S. (2024). Enhancing radiology workflows with generative AI. *Radiology AI Journal*, *12*(1), 55–70.

Park, H., & Kim, J. (2023). Continuous clinician feedback loops in AI-based diagnostic systems. *BMC Medical Informatics and Decision Making*, *23*, 50. DOI: 10.1186/s12911-023-02102-7

Patel, N., & Shah, D. (2022). Evaluating K NN and decision tree models for cardiovascular risk. *Computers in Biology and Medicine*, *150*, 105936. DOI: 10.1016/j.compbiomed.2022.105936

Pawara, Y., & Mahajan, H. (2025). Surface-functionalized pullulan-based polymeric nanoparticles containing resveratrol: a green approach for lung cancer targeted delivery. *Nano Express*, 1–17.

Peng, J., Wang, Y., Li, B., Guo, Y., Wang, H., Fang, Y., & Yu, K. (2025). A survey on speech large language models for understanding. *IEEE Journal of Selected Topics in Signal Processing*.

Perou, C. M., Sørlie, T., Eisen, M. B., van de Rijn, M., Jeffrey, S. S., Rees, C. A., & Botstein, D. (2000). Molecular portraits of human breast tumours. *Nature, 406*(6797), 747–752. DOI: 10.1038/35021093 PMID: 10963602

Perwej, Y., Abbas, S. Q., Dixit, J. P., Akhtar, N., & Jaiswal, A. K. (2021). A systematic literature review on the cyber security. *International Journal of Scientific Research and Management*, *9*(12), 669–710. DOI: 10.18535/ijsrm/v9i12.ec04

Perwej, Y., Akhtar, N., Kulshrestha, N., & Mishra, P. (2022). A methodical analysis of medical Internet of Things (MIoT) security and privacy in current and future trends. *Journal of Emerging Technologies and Innovative Research*, *9*(1), d346–d371.

Pinnock, H., Hui, C. Y., & van Boven, J. F. (2023). Implementation of digital home monitoring and management of respiratory disease. *npj. Digital Medicine*, *6*(1), 1–13. DOI: 10.1038/s41746-023-00897-2 PMID: 36596833

Plăviţu, C. M. (2020). Consonance and resonance in Kandinsky and Odobleja's works. *International Journal of Communication Research, 10*(4), 402–407. https://go.openathens.net/redirector/ncu.edu?url=https://www.proquest.com/scholarly-journals/consonance-resonance-kandinsky-odoblejas-works/docview/2505729900/se-2

Poon, E. G.. (2025). Adoption of artificial intelligence in healthcare: A U.S. system survey. *Health Affairs*, *44*(1), 25–38.

Potschin-Young, M., Haines-Young, R., Görg, C., Heink, U., Jax, K., Schleyer, C., & Schleyer, C. (2018). Understanding the role of conceptual frameworks: Reading the ecosystem service cascade. *Ecosystem Services*, *29*, 428–440. DOI: 10.1016/j.ecoser.2017.05.015 PMID: 31008045

Pourhabibi, N., Mohebbi, B., Sadeghi, R., Shakibazadeh, E., Sanjari, M., Tol, A., & Yaseri, M. (2022). Determinants of poor treatment adherence among patients with type 2 diabetes and limited health literacy: A scoping review. *Journal of Diabetes Research*, *2022*, 2022. DOI: 10.1155/2022/2980250 PMID: 35832786

Pouvreau, D. (2014). On the history of Ludwig von Bertalanffy's "general systemology," and on its relationship to cybernetics - Part II: Contexts and developments of the systemological hermeneutics instigated by von Bertalanffy. *International Journal of General Systems*, *43*(2), 172–245. DOI: 10.1080/03081079.2014.883743

Price, W. N., Gerke, S., & Cohen, I. G. (2019). Potential liability for AI/ML-based products. *Journal of the American Medical Association*, *322*(18), 1765–1766. DOI: 10.1001/jama.2019.15064 PMID: 31584609

Price, W. N.II, & Cohen, I. G. (2019). Privacy in the age of medical big data. *Nature Medicine, 25*(1), 37–43. DOI: 10.1038/s41591-018-0272-7 PMID: 30617331

Qadir, A. M., & Varol, N. (2019, June). A review paper on cryptography. In *2019, 7th International Symposium on Digital Forensics and Security (ISDFS)* (pp. 1-6). IEEE.

Qi, L., Li, Z., Liu, J., & Chen, X. (2024). Omics-Enhanced Nanomedicine for Cancer Therapy. *Advanced Materials, 36*(50), 2409102. DOI: 10.1002/adma.202409102 PMID: 39473316

Qure.ai. (2023). https://www.qure.ai

Qure.ai. (2023). *Official website.* https://www.qure.ai

Rabbani, M., Joshi, A., & Verma, T. (2025). Generative AI in clinical documentation and patient messaging. *BioMedInformatics, 5*(3), 37. https://www.mdpi.com/2673-7426/5/3/37. DOI: 10.3390/biomedinformatics5030037

Rajkomar, A., Dean, J., & Kohane, I. (2019). Machine learning in medicine. *The New England Journal of Medicine, 380*(14), 1347–1358. DOI: 10.1056/NEJMra1814259 PMID: 30943338

Raju, C., & Philipsy, E. (2018). A survey on predicting heart disease using data mining techniques. In *IEEE Conference Proceedings.* DOI: 10.1109/ICEDSS.2018.8544333

Ramesh, A., Pavlov, M., Goh, G., Gray, S., Voss, C., Radford, A., . . . Sutskever, I. (2021). Zero-shot text-to-image generation. *arXiv preprint arXiv:2102.12092.* https://arxiv.org/abs/2102.12092

Ranchal, R., Bastide, P., Wang, X., Gkoulalas-Divanis, A., Mehra, M., Bakthavachalam, S., Lei, H., & Mohindra, A. (2020). Disrupting healthcare silos: Addressing data volume, velocity and variety with a cloud-native healthcare data ingestion service. *IEEE Journal of Biomedical and Health Informatics, 24*(11), 3182–3188. DOI: 10.1109/JBHI.2020.3001518 PMID: 32750932

Rani, P., Verma, S., Yadav, S. P., Rai, B. K., Naruka, M. S., & Kumar, D. (2022). Simulation of the lightweight blockchain technique based on privacy and security for healthcare data for the cloud system. *International Journal of E-Health and Medical Communications, 13*(4), 1–15. DOI: 10.4018/IJEHMC.309436

Rao, R. S., & Prasad, K. H. (2023). Explainable AI in medical recommendation systems. *Artificial Intelligence in Medicine, 145*, 102329. DOI: 10.1016/j.artmed.2023.102329

Rapoport, A. (1986). General system theory : Essential concepts & applications. *Abacus Press EBooks.* https://ci.nii.ac.jp/ncid/BA0061935X

Rapoport, A. (1976). General systems theory: A bridge between two cultures. Third annual Ludwig von Bertalanffy memorial lecture. *Behavioral Science, 21*(4), 228–239. DOI: 10.1002/bs.3830210404 PMID: 793579

Ratta, P., Kaur, A., Sharma, S., Shabaz, M., & Dhiman, G. (2021). Application of blockchain and Internet of Things in healthcare and medical sector: Applications, challenges, and future perspectives. *Journal of Food Quality, 7608296*, 1–20. Advance online publication. DOI: 10.1155/2021/7608296

Raworth, K. (2017). *Doughnut economics: Seven ways to think like a 21st-century economist*. Chelsea Green Publishing.

Razali, N., & Mustapha, A. (2019). *A data mining approach to prediction of liver diseases. Journal of Physics: Conference Series, JICETS*. IOP Publishing.

Reddy, K. S. (2022). India's digital health mission: Opportunities and challenges. *The Lancet. Digital Health, 4*(1), e12–e13.

Reddy, K. S., Chaturvedi, S., & Prasad, K. (2021). Artificial intelligence in Indian neuro-healthcare: Opportunities and challenges. *Neurology India, 69*(7), 121–128.

Reddy, S. (2024). Implementation science for AI in healthcare: Bridging the gap between innovation and practice. *Implementation Science : IS, 19*(1), 1–15. https://implementationscience.biomedcentral.com/articles/10.1186/s13012-024-01357-9

Rehman, A. U., Li, M., Wu, B., Ali, Y., Rasheed, S., Shaheen, S., Liu, X., Luo, R., & Zhang, J.Ashfaq Ur Rehman. (2025). Role of artificial intelligence in revolutionizing drug discovery. *Fundamental Research (Beijing), 5*(3), 1273–1287. DOI: 10.1016/j.fmre.2024.04.021 PMID: 40528990

Ren, X.-H., Shi, L., Ma, Z.-B., Wang, D.-W., He, X.-W., Li, W.-Y., & Zhang, Y.-K. (2024). Inhibition of nucleotide metabolism with dual-template epitope imprinted nanoparticles for targeted HER2+ tumor therapy. *Chemical Engineering Journal, 481*, 148739. DOI: 10.1016/j.cej.2024.148739

Reyes, M., Meier, S., Pereira, T., Silva, O., Marston, S., & Glocker, A. (2019). On the limitations of artificial intelligence in healthcare: Challenges in data and model development. *IEEE Access : Practical Innovations, Open Solutions, 7*, 203–215. DOI: 10.1109/ACCESS.2018.2884471

Rezende, D. J., Mohamed, S., & Wierstra, D. (2014). Stochastic backpropagation and approximate inference in deep generative models. *Proceedings of the 31st International Conference on Machine Learning*, 32(2), 1278–1286.

Richardson, P., Griffin, I., Tucker, C., Smith, D., Oechsle, O., Phelan, A., & Stebbing, J. (2020). Baricitinib as potential treatment for 2019-nCoV acute respiratory disease. *Lancet*, *395*(10223), e30–e31. DOI: 10.1016/S0140-6736(20)30304-4 PMID: 32032529

Rieke, N., Hancox, J., Li, W., Milletari, F., Roth, H. R., Albarqouni, S., & Cardoso, M. J. (2022). The future of digital health with federated learning. *NPJ Digital Medicine*, *5*, 95. Advance online publication. DOI: 10.1038/s41746-022-00649-w PMID: 33015372

Robertson, J. (2018). *Robo Sapiens Japanicus: Robots, gender, family, and the Japanese nation*. University of California Press.

Ruse, G., Jîjie, A.-R., Moacă, E.-A., Pătra cu, D., Ardelean, F., Jojic, A.-A., Ardelean, S., & Tchiakpe-Antal, D.-S. (2025). Coffea arabica: An Emerging Active Ingredient in Dermato-Cosmetic Applications. *Nano Express*, *18*(2), 171. PMID: 40005985

Saeed, H., Malik, H., Bashir, U., Ahmad, A., Riaz, S., Ilyas, M., Bukhari, W. A., & Khan, M. I. A. (2022). Blockchain technology in healthcare: A systematic review. *PLoS One*, *17*(4), e0266462. DOI: 10.1371/journal.pone.0266462 PMID: 35404955

Safari, A. (2021). A Mathematical Review on Machine Intelligence Quotient (MIQ) Theory in Real-World Applications. *International Journal of Mathematical Modelling & Computations*, *11*(1 (WINTER)), 61–71.

Salesky, E., Mäder, J., & Klinger, S. (2021, December). Assessing evaluation metrics for speech-to-speech translation. In *2021 IEEE Automatic Speech Recognition and Understanding Workshop (ASRU)* (pp. 733-740). IEEE. DOI: 10.1109/ASRU51503.2021.9688073

Samuel, G., & Derrick, G. (2020). Defining ethical challenges of AI in medicine: A qualitative study of IRB members. *AJOB Empirical Bioethics*, *11*(3), 193–202.

Samuel, P., & Desai, M. (2025). AI-powered scheduling and billing: Enhancing administrative workflows. *Journal of Health Informatics*, *17*(1), 23–39.

Samuel, P., Gupta, R., & Lee, H. (2025). Administrative collaboration through generative AI: A case study. *Health Care Management Review*, *41*(2), 88–102.

Sangannagari, S. R. (2024). Design and Implementation of a Cloud-Native Automated Certification Platform for Functional Testing and Compliance Validation. International Journal of Technology. *Management and Humanities*, *10*(02), 34–43. DOI: 10.21590/k5r28w48

Sang, T., Liu, P., & Zhao, L. (2022). Judicial response to ecological environment risk in China -from the perspective of Social Systems Theory. *International Journal of Environmental Research and Public Health, 19*(21), 14355. Advance online publication. DOI: 10.3390/ijerph192114355 PMID: 36361230

Santos, J., & Almeida, T. (2021). Doctor recommendation models based on symptom–disease mapping. *Journal of Healthcare Engineering, 6672845*. Advance online publication. DOI: 10.1155/2021/6672845

Sarath Babu, S., Vivek, E. M., & Famina, K. P. (2017). Heart disease diagnosis using data mining technique. In *IEEE Conference Proceedings*.

Saria, D., Butte, A., & Sheikh, A. (2018). Better medicine through machine learning: What's real, and what's artificial? *PLoS Medicine, 15*(12), e1002721. Advance online publication. DOI: 10.1371/journal.pmed.1002721 PMID: 30596635

Sarker, I. H. (2021). Data science and analytics: An overview from data-driven smart computing, decision-making and applications perspective. *SN Computer Science, 2*(5), 377. DOI: 10.1007/s42979-021-00765-8 PMID: 34278328

Satani, J., & Gandhi, S. R. (2023). A review: Applications of artificial intelligence and machine learning in keratoconus detection. *International Journal of Computer Applications, 182*(45), 1–17.

Scannell, J. W., Blanckley, A., Boldon, H., & Warrington, B. (2012). Diagnosing the decline in pharmaceutical R&D efficiency. *Nature Reviews. Drug Discovery, 11*(3), 191–200. DOI: 10.1038/nrd3681 PMID: 22378269

Schüpbach, M., & Agid, Y. (2008). Neurosurgery in Parkinson's disease: The doctor is happy, the patient less so? *Journal of Neural Transmission (Vienna, Austria), 115*(11), 1511–1516.

Segler, M. H. S., Preuss, M., & Waller, M. P. (2018). Planning chemical syntheses with deep neural networks and symbolic AI. *Nature, 555*(7698), 604–610. DOI: 10.1038/nature25978 PMID: 29595767

Semerjyan, G., Semerjyan, I., Ginovyan, M., & Avtandilyan, N. (2025). Characterization and antibacterial/cytotoxic activity of silver nanoparticles synthesized from Dicranum scoparium moss extracts growing in Armenia. *Nano Express, 12*(1), 29–42.

Senbekov, M., Saliev, T., Bukeyeva, Z., Almabayeva, A., Zhanaliyeva, M., Aitenova, N., Toishibekov, Y., & Fakhradiyev, I. (2020). The recent progress and applications of digital technologies in healthcare: A review. *International Journal of Telemedicine and Applications, 8830200*, 1–18. Advance online publication. DOI: 10.1155/2020/8830200 PMID: 33343657

Shaheen, M. Y. (2021). *Applications of artificial intelligence (AI) in healthcare: A review*. ScienceOpen *Preprints*. DOI: 10.14293/S2199-1006.1.SOR-.PPVRY8K.v1

Shahid, J., Ahmad, R., Kiani, A. K., Ahmad, T., Saeed, S., & Almuhaideb, A. M. (2022). Data protection and privacy of the Internet of Healthcare Things (IoHTs). *Applied Sciences (Basel, Switzerland)*, *12*(4), 1927. DOI: 10.3390/app12041927

Shah, S. (2019). *The body hunters: Testing new drugs on the world's poorest patients*. New Press.

Shaikh, M., Memon, S. A., Ebrahimi, A., & Wiil, U. K. (2025, May). A systematic literature review for blockchain-based healthcare implementations. In Healthcare, Vol. 13, No. 9, p. 1087. DOI: 10.3390/healthcare13091087

Shaikh, T. A., Dar, T. R., & Sofi, S. (2022). A data-centric artificial intelligent and extended reality technology in smart healthcare systems. *Social Network Analysis and Mining*, *12*(1), 122. DOI: 10.1007/s13278-022-00888-7 PMID: 36065420

Shantsila, A.. (2024). Artificial Intelligence in Hypertension Management. *Journal of Human Hypertension*, •••, 2024.

Sharma, A., Alam, M. A., & Kaur, A. (2025). Implementation of Nanocarriers for Brain-Specific Drug Delivery System. *Nano Express*, *10*(1), 43–63.

Sharma, N., Sharma, R., & Jindal, N. (2021). Machine Learning and Deep Learning applications - A vision. *Global Transitions Proceedings*, *2*(1), 24–28. DOI: 10.1016/j.gltp.2021.01.004

Sharma, V., Vashishth, T. K., Kumar, B., Sharma, K. K., Vidyant, S., & Chaudhary, S. (2023, December). Health Interpretation of Covid-19 Patients using Artificial Intelligence. In *2023 International Conference on Artificial Intelligence for Innovations in Healthcare Industries (ICAIIHI)* (Vol. 1, pp. 1-5). IEEE Computer Society. DOI: 10.1109/ICAIIHI57871.2023.10488924

Sharp, D., Kumar, A., & Lin, J. (2025). Generative AI in health economics: Automating cost-effectiveness modeling. *MedRxiv*. https://www.medrxiv.org/content/10.1101/2025.04.25.25326412v1.full.pdf

Sherly, E., Pillai, L. G., & Manohar, K. (2024). ASR models from conventional statistical models to transformers and transfer learning. *Automatic speech recognition and translation for low resource languages*, 69-112.

Shetty, I., Agrawal, P., & Gandhi, S. (2024, September). A survey on use of machine learning in the healthcare sector. In *2024: GLS University Doctoral and Faculty Research Colloquium*. To be published.

Shetty, I., Agrawal, P., & Gandhi, S. (2024, November). Using machine learning for lung diseases prediction: A comprehensive review. In *Proceedings of the 4th International Conference on Modeling Simulation and Optimization (CoMSO 2024)* (Springer). To be published.

Shetty, I., Agrawal, P., & Gandhi, S. (2025, January). A survey on the lung diseases prediction in an Indian environment using machine learning. In *Proceedings of the 9th International Conference on Smart Trends for Computing and Communication (SmartCom 2025)* (Springer, Pune).

Shibata, T., & Wada, K. (2011). Robot therapy: A new approach for mental healthcare of the elderly – A mini-review. *Gerontology, 57*(4), 378–386. DOI: 10.1159/000319015 PMID: 20639620

Shilo, S., Rossman, H., & Segal, E. (2020). Axes of a revolution: Challenges and promises of big data in healthcare. *Nature Medicine, 26*(1), 29–38. DOI: 10.1038/s41591-019-0727-5 PMID: 31932803

Shinde, S. G., & Lobo, L. M. R. J. (2019). A secured prediction system for human diseases using a genetic algorithm approach to data mining. *Journal of Emerging Technologies and Innovative Research, 6*(1), 266–274. https://www.jetir.org/papers/JETIRW006059.pdf

Shokrollahi, A., Farahani, M., & Zadeh, R. (2023). A comprehensive review of generative models in healthcare. *arXiv preprint arXiv:2310.00795*. https://arxiv.org/pdf/2310.00795

Shortliffe, E. H., & Sepúlveda, M. J. (2024). Clinical decision support in the artificial intelligence era. *Journal of the American Medical Association, 331*(4), 345–346. DOI: 10.1001/jama.2024.0243 PMID: 30398550

SigTuple Technologies. (2023). https://www.sigtuple.com

Silva, P., & Fernandes, A. (2021). Data cleaning strategies in healthcare ML applications. *Journal of Biomedical Informatics, 119*, 103771. DOI: 10.1016/j.jbi.2021.103771

Sinaga, K. P., & Yang, M. (2020). Unsupervised K-means clustering algorithm. *IEEE Access : Practical Innovations, Open Solutions, 8*, 80716–80727. DOI: 10.1109/ACCESS.2020.2988796

Singh, A., Kaur, S., Thakur, H., Rashi, Kashyap, S., Lyudmila, A., & Mudgal, G. (2025). Unveiling the Transformative Power of Smart Cellulosic Nanomaterials: Revisiting Potential Promises to Sustainable Future. *Nano Express*, 1–42.

Singh, A. (2019). Affordable Prosthetics and Rehabilitation in India: Bridging the Accessibility Gap. *Indian Journal of Orthopaedics*, *53*(2), 245–252.

Singhal, A., & Gupta, P. (2024). Generative AI and large language models (LLMs) in clinical triage: A review of 2023-2024 developments. *International Journal of Intelligent Systems*, *39*(2), 112–128.

Singhal, K., Azizi, S., Tu, T., Mahdavi, S. S., Wei, J., Chung, H. W., Scales, N., Tanwani, A., Cole-Lewis, H., Pfohl, S., Payne, P., Seneviratne, M., Gamble, P., Kelly, C., Babiker, A., Schärli, N., Chowdhery, A., Mansfield, P., Demner-Fushman, D., & Natarajan, V. (2023). Large language models encode clinical knowledge. *Nature*, *620*(7972), 172–180. DOI: 10.1038/s41586-023-06291-2 PMID: 37438534

Singh, M. K. (2024). Feature extraction and classification efficiency analysis using machine learning approach for speech signal. *Multimedia Tools and Applications*, *83*(16), 47069–47084. DOI: 10.1007/s11042-023-17368-5

Smith, A. B. R. M., Ellis, H. J. R., & Wells, E. G. (2020). Personalized dietary recommendations based on genetic profiles using machine learning: A practical approach. *IEEE Journal of Biomedical and Health Informatics*, *24*(3), 810–820. DOI: 10.1109/JBHI.2019.2914512

Spasic, I., & Nenadic, G. (2020). Clinical text data in machine learning: Systematic review. *JMIR Medical Informatics*, *8*(3), e17984. DOI: 10.2196/17984 PMID: 32229465

Starke, G., van den Brule, R., Elger, B. S., & Haselager, P. (2022). Intentional machines: A defense of trust in medical artificial intelligence. *Bioethics*, *36*(2), 154–161. DOI: 10.1111/bioe.12891 PMID: 34142373

Stilgoe, J., Owen, R., & Macnaghten, P. (2013). Developing a framework for responsible innovation. *Research Policy*, *42*(9), 1568–1580. DOI: 10.1016/j.respol.2013.05.008

Strickland, E. (2019). IBM Watson, heal thyself: How IBM overpromised and underdelivered on AI health care. *IEEE Spectrum*, *56*(4), 24–31. DOI: 10.1109/MSPEC.2019.8678513

Sun, Z., Sun, Y., Wang, S., Li, M., Guo, H., Xu, Z., & Gao, M. (2025). Mini Review On: The Roles of DNA Nanomaterials in Phototherapy. *Nano Express*, 2021–2041.

Tabrizchi, H., & Kuchaki Rafsanjani, M. (2020). A survey on security challenges in cloud computing: Issues, threats, and solutions. *The Journal of Supercomputing*, *76*(12), 9493–9532. DOI: 10.1007/s11227-020-03213-1

Taha, B. A., Kadhim, A. C., Addie, A. J., Haider, A. J., Azzahrani, A. S., Raizada, P., Rustagi, S., Chaudhary, V., & Arsad, N. (2024). Advancing cancer diagnostics through multifaceted optical biosensors supported by nanomaterials and artificial intelligence: A panoramic outlook. *Microchemical Journal*, *205*, 111307. DOI: 10.1016/j.microc.2024.111307

Tahamtan, I., & Bornmann, L. (2022). The Social Systems Citation Theory (SSCT): A proposal to use the social systems theory for conceptualizing publications and their citation links. *El Profesional de la Información*, *31*(4), 1–17. DOI: 10.3145/epi.2022.jul.11

Tantray, J., Patel, A., Wani, S. N., Kosey, S., & Prajapati, B. G. (2024). Prescription precision: A comprehensive review of intelligent prescription systems. *Current Pharmaceutical Design*, *30*(34), 2671–2684. DOI: 10.2174/0113816128321623240719104337 PMID: 39092640

Tariq, N., Qamar, A., Asim, M., & Khan, F. A. (2020). Blockchain and smart healthcare security: A survey. *Procedia Computer Science*, *175*, 615–620. DOI: 10.1016/j.procs.2020.07.089

Theivendren, P., Kunjiappan, S., Pavadai, P., Ravi, K., Murugavel, A., Dayalan, A., & Santhana Krishna Kumar, A. (2024). Revolutionizing Cancer Immunotherapy: Emerging Nanotechnology-Driven Drug Delivery Systems for Enhanced Therapeutic Efficacy. *ACS Measurement Science Au*. PMID: 39991031

Tilak, S., Glassman, M., Kuznetcova, I., & Pelfrey, G. L. (2021). Applications of cybernetics to psychological theory: Historical and conceptual explorations. *Theory &Amp. Theory & Psychology*, *32*(2), 298–325. DOI: 10.1177/09593543211053804

Ting, D., Peng, L., Varadarajan, A. V., Keane, P. A., Burlina, P. M., Chiang, M. F., Schmetterer, L., Pasquale, L. R., Bressler, N. M., Webster, D. R., Abramoff, M., & Wong, T. Y. (2019). Deep learning in ophthalmology: The technical and clinical considerations. *Progress in Retinal and Eye Research*, *72*, 100759. DOI: 10.1016/j.preteyeres.2019.04.003 PMID: 31048019

Tinger, L. (2024). *Development of an integrated platform for personalized cancer treatment: diagnostic and therapeutic solutions based on biomarkers and nano-technology*. Nano Express.

Tjoa, E., & Guan, C. (2021). A survey on explainable artificial intelligence (XAI): Toward medical XAI. *IEEE Transactions on Neural Networks and Learning Systems*, *32*(11), 4793–4813. DOI: 10.1109/TNNLS.2020.3027314

Topol, E. (2019). High-performance medicine: The convergence of human and artificial intelligence. *Nature Medicine, 25*(1), 44–56. DOI: 10.1038/s41591-018-0300-7 PMID: 30617339

Torres, E., & Perez, L. (2022). Clinical validation of symptom-based predictive models. *Journal of Clinical Trials and Biostatistics, 7*(2), 100–110.

Toto, M., Singh, R., & Alavi, S. (2025). Cross-disciplinary collaboration in AI development: Lessons from healthcare. *Frontiers in Digital Health, 5*, 1400338. https://www.frontiersin.org/articles/10.3389/fdgth.2025.1400338/pdf. DOI: 10.3389/fdgth.2025.1400338

Tretter, F. (2019). "Systems medicine" in the view of von Bertalanffy's "organismic biology" and systems theory. *Systems Research and Behavioral Science, 36*(3), 346–362. DOI: 10.1002/sres.2588

Tripathy, A., Patne, A. Y., Mohapatra, S., & Mohapatra, S. S. (2024). Convergence of Nanotechnology and Machine Learning: The State of the Art, Challenges, and Perspectives. *Nano Express, 25*(22), 12368. PMID: 39596433

Trist, E. (1981). The evolution of sociotechnical systems. Occasional Paper, 2, 1–67.

Tsai, C. H., Zdravkovic, J., & Stirna, J. (2022). Modeling digital business ecosystems: A systematic literature review. *Complex Systems Informatics and Modeling Quarterly*, (30), 1–30. DOI: 10.7250/csimq.2022-30.01

U.S. Food and Drug Administration. (2023). Artificial intelligence/machine learning (AI/ML)-based software as a medical device (SaMD) action plan. https://www.fda.gov

Ullah, F., He, J., Zhu, N., Wajahat, A., Nazir, A., Qureshi, S., Pathan, M. S., & Dev, S. (2024). Blockchain-enabled EHR access auditing: Enhancing healthcare data security. *Heliyon, 10*(16), e34407. DOI: 10.1016/j.heliyon.2024.e34407 PMID: 39253236

Uzzaman, M. N., & van Boven, J. F. (2024). Effectiveness of asynchronous digital health interventions for asthma: A mixed methods systematic review. *Journal of Medical Internet Research, 26*(1), e57708. DOI: 10.2196/57708 PMID: 39626243

Vahidi, A., Aliahmad, A., & Teimouri, E. (2019). Evolution of management cybernetics and viable system model. *Systemic Practice and Action Research, 32*(3), 297–314. DOI: 10.1007/s11213-019-9478-y

van Assche, K., Valentinov, V., & Verschraegen, G. (2019). Ludwig von Bertalanffy and his enduring relevance: Celebrating 50 years general system theory. *Systems research and behavioral science.-Chichester, 36*(3), 251-254.

van Dijk, E., & De Dreu, C. K. (2021). Experimental games and social decision making. *Annual Review of Psychology, 72*(1), 415–438. DOI: 10.1146/annurev-psych-081420-110718 PMID: 33006926

Van Nguyen, T., Cong Pham, H., Nhat Nguyen, M., Zhou, L., & Akbari, M. (2023). Data-driven review of blockchain applications in supply chain management: Key research themes and future directions. *International Journal of Production Research, 61*(23), 8213–8235. DOI: 10.1080/00207543.2023.2165190

Vanderstraeten, R. (2019). Systems everywhere? *Systems Research and Behavioral Science, 36*(3), 255–262. DOI: 10.1002/sres.2596

Vashishth, T. K., Sharma, V., & Ahamad, S. (2025). Exploring machine learning models for biomedical signal processing: a comprehensive review. Machine Learning Models and Architectures for Biomedical Signal Processing, 69-96.

Vashishth, T. K., Sharma, V., Kumar, B., Sharma, K. K., Chaudhary, S., & Panwar, R. (2025). Blockchain for Securing Federated Learning Systems: Enhancing Privacy and Trust. Model Optimization Methods for Efficient and Edge AI: Federated Learning Architectures, Frameworks and Applications, 299-320.

Vashishth, T. K., Sharma, V., Sharma, K. K., Chaudhary, S., Kumar, B., & Kumar, P. (2025). Future trends and emerging technologies in biomedical engineering. Innovations in Biomedical Engineering, 519-550.

Vashishth, T. K., Sharma, V., Sharma, K. K., Vidyant, S., & Bhardwaj, A. (2025). Future Trends and Challenges in Pharmaceutical Microbiology with the Integration of Artificial Intelligence. AI-Powered Advances in Pharmacology, 315-344.

Vashishth, T. K., Sharma, V., Sharma, K. K., Kumar, B., Chaudhary, S., & Panwar, R. (2024). Enhancing biomedical signal processing with machine learning: A comprehensive review. Digital Transformation in Healthcare 5.0: Volume 1: IoT. *AI and Digital Twin, 277*, 277–306. Advance online publication. DOI: 10.1515/9783111327853-010

Vaswani, A., Shazeer, N., Parmar, N., Uszkoreit, J., Jones, L., Gomez, A. N., & Polosukhin, I. (2017). Attention is all you need. *Advances in Neural Information Processing Systems, 30*, 5998–6008.

Veale, M., & Borgesius, F. Z. (2021). Demystifying the draft EU Artificial Intelligence Act. *Computer Law Review International, 22*(4), 97–112. DOI: 10.9785/cri-2021-220402

Viceconti, M., & Henney, A. (2020). In silico clinical trials: How computer simulation will transform the biomedical industry. *International Journal of Clinical Trials, 7*(2), 17–29. DOI: 10.18203/2349-3259.ijct20200274

Viceconti, M., Hunter, P., & Hose, R. (2021). Big data, big knowledge: Big data for personalized healthcare. *IEEE Journal of Biomedical and Health Informatics*, *25*(2), 403–412. DOI: 10.1109/JBHI.2021.3049871 PMID: 32086223

Villarreal, E. R. D., García-Alonso, J., Moguel, E., & Alegría, J. A. H. (2023). Blockchain for healthcare management systems: A survey on interoperability and security. *IEEE Access : Practical Innovations, Open Solutions*, *11*, 5629–5652. DOI: 10.1109/ACCESS.2023.3236505

von Bertalanffy, L. (1938). A quantitative theory of organic growth (inquiries on growth laws. II). *Human Biology*, *10*(2), 181–213. https://www.jstor.org/stable/41447359

von Bertalanffy, L. (1950). An Outline of General System Theory. *The British Journal for the Philosophy of Science*, *1*(2), 134–165. DOI: 10.1093/bjps/I.2.134

von Bertalanffy, L. (1951). Conclusion. *Human Biology*, *23*(4), 336–345. https://www.jstor.org/stable/41448007 PMID: 14907030

von Bertalanffy, L. (1951). Metabolic types and growth types. *American Naturalist*, *85*(821), 111–117. https://www.jstor.org/stable/2458138. DOI: 10.1086/281659

von Bertalanffy, L. (1951). Problems of general system theory. *Human Biology*, *23*(4), 302–312. https://www.jstor.org/stable/41448003 PMID: 14907026

von Bertalanffy, L. (1972). The history and status of general systems theory. *Academy of Management Journal*, *15*(4), 407–426. DOI: 10.2307/255139

von Bertalanffy, L. (1972a). General system theory—Critical review. *General Systems Yearbook*, *4*, 1–20.

von Bertalanffy, L. V. (1968). *General system theory: Foundations, development, applications*. G. Braziller.

Wachter, S., Mittelstadt, B., & Floridi, L. (2017). Why a right to explanation of automated decision-making does not exist in the GDPR. *International Data Privacy Law*, *7*(2), 76–99. DOI: 10.1093/idpl/ipx005

Wåhlin, A., Eklund, A., & Malm, J. (2022). 4D flow MRI hemodynamic biomarkers for cerebrovascular diseases. *Journal of Internal Medicine*, *291*(2), 115–127. DOI: 10.1111/joim.13392 PMID: 34813112

Walker, D. M., Yeager, V. A., Lawrence, J., & Mcalearney, A. S. (2021). Identifying opportunities to strengthen the public health informatics infrastructure: Exploring hospitals' challenges with data exchange. *The Milbank Quarterly*, *99*(2), 393–425. DOI: 10.1111/1468-0009.12511 PMID: 33783863

Wallach, I., Dzamba, M., & Heifets, A. (2015). AtomNet: A deep convolutional neural network for bioactivity prediction in structure-based drug discovery. *arXiv*. https://arxiv.org/abs/1510.02855

Walton, N. A., Nagarajan, R., Wang, C., Sincan, M., Freimuth, R. R., Everman, D. B., Walton, D. C., McGrath, S. P., Lemas, D. J., Benos, P. V., Alekseyenko, A. V., Song, Q., Gamsiz Uzun, E., Taylor, C. O., Uzun, A., Person, T. N., Rappoport, N., Zhao, Z., & Williams, M. S. (2024). Enabling the clinical application of artificial intelligence in genomics: A perspective of the AMIA Genomics and Translational Bioinformatics Workgroup. *Journal of the American Medical Informatics Association : JAMIA*, *31*(2), 536–541. DOI: 10.1093/jamia/ocad211 PMID: 38037121

Wang, Y, Yang, J., Amier, Y., Yuan, D., Xun, Y., & Yu, X. (2025). Advancements in Nanomedicine for the Diagnosis and Treatment of Kidney Stones. *Nano Express*, 1401–1423.

Wang, L., Li, X., Zhang, L., Gao, Q., Xu, S., & Yang, G. (2021). Artificial intelligence in drug clinical trials: Applications, challenges, and future trends. *Drug Discovery Today*, *26*(6), 1407–1415. DOI: 10.1016/j.drudis.2021.02.002

Wang, R. D., Zayed, T., Pan, W., Zheng, S., & Tariq, S. (2021). A system boundary-based critical review on crane selection in building construction. *Automation in Construction*, *123*, 103520. DOI: 10.1016/j.autcon.2020.103520

Wang, X.. (2020). Enhanced nodule detection in lung CT scans using deep learning. *IEEE Transactions on Medical Imaging*. Advance online publication. DOI: 10.3390/ai1010003

Wang, Y. X., Panda-Jonas, S., & Jonas, J. B. (2021). Optic nerve head anatomy in myopia and glaucoma, including parapapillary zones alpha, beta, gamma and delta: Histology and clinical features. *Progress in Retinal and Eye Research*, *83*, 100933. DOI: 10.1016/j.preteyeres.2020.100933 PMID: 33309588

Wang, Y., Yung, P., Lu, G., Liu, Y., Ding, C., Mao, C., Li, Z. A., & Tuan, R. S. (2025). Musculoskeletal Organs-on-Chips: An Emerging Platform for Studying the Nanotechnology–Biology Interface. *Nano Express*, *37*(2), 2401334. PMID: 38491868

Warnat-Herresthal, S., Schultze, H., Shastry, K. L., Manamohan, S., Mukherjee, S., Garg, V., Sarveswara, R., Händler, K., Pickkers, P., Aziz, N. A., Ktena, S., Tran, F., Bitzer, M., Ossowski, S., Casadei, N., Herr, C., Petersheim, D., Behrends, U., Kern, F., & Schultze, J. L.The MELLODY Consortium. (2021). Swarm learning for decentralized and confidential clinical machine learning. *Nature*, *594*(7862), 265–270. DOI: 10.1038/s41586-021-03583-3 PMID: 34040261

Wartenberg, C., & Khor, Y. H. (2025). Clinical benefits and risks of remote patient monitoring: A systematic overview. *BMC Health Services Research*, *25*(1), 12292. DOI: 10.1186/s12913-025-12292-w PMID: 39849519

Wenzel, J., Matter, H., & Schmidt, F. (2019). Predictive toxicology: In silico approaches for early safety assessment of new drugs. *Drug Discovery Today. Technologies*, *31*, 5–17. DOI: 10.1016/j.ddtec.2019.01.001

Whittaker, M., Crawford, K., Dobbe, R., Fried, G., Kaziunas, E., Mathur, V., & Schwartz, O. (2021). *AI Now Report 2021*. AI Now Institute, New York University.

Wihantara, A., Hariwisana, I. D. G., Pudji, A., Luthfiyah, S., & Athavale, V. A. (2022). QRS complex detection on heart rate variability reading using discrete wavelet transform. *Indonesian Journal of Electronics, Electromedical Engineering, and Medical Informatics*, *4*(4), 153–159. DOI: 10.35882/ijeeemi.v4i4.236

Williams, D., & Zhou, X. (2020). EHR-linked predictive analytics for chronic disease management. *Health Informatics Journal*, *26*(4), 2717–2731. DOI: 10.1177/1460458220916202

Wilson, T.. (2022). Ethical and legal considerations in AI-based medical decision support systems. *Journal of Law and Medicine*, *30*(3), 67–85.

Wolleb, J., ... (2022). Diffusion models for medical anomaly detection. MICCAI Proceedings, 311–320. DOI: 10.1007/978-3-031-16452-1_4

World Health Organization [WHO]. (2023). *Global Health Workforce Statistics*. https://www.who.int

World Health Organization. (2023). *Global Health Workforce Statistics*. https://www.who.int

Wulczyn, E., Steiner, D. F., Moran, M., Plass, M., Reihs, R., Tan, F., Flament-Auvigne, I., Brown, T., Regitnig, P., Chen, P. C., Hegde, N., Sadhwani, A., MacDonald, R., Ayalew, B., Corrado, G. S., Peng, L. H., Tse, D., Müller, H., Xu, Z., & Mermel, C. H. (2021). Interpretable survival prediction for colorectal cancer using deep learning. *NPJ Digital Medicine*, *4*(1), 1–26. DOI: 10.1038/s41746-021-00427-2

Xi, P., Zhang, X., Wang, L., Liu, W., & Peng, S. (2022). A review of blockchain-based secure sharing of healthcare data. *Applied Sciences (Basel, Switzerland)*, *12*(15), 7912. DOI: 10.3390/app12157912

Xu, Y., Dai, Z., Chen, F., Gao, S., Pei, J., & Lai, L. (2015). Deep learning for drug-induced liver injury. *Journal of Chemical Information and Modeling*, *55*(10), 2085–2093. DOI: 10.1021/acs.jcim.5b00238 PMID: 26437739

Yadav, V. K., Dhanasekaran, S., Choudhary, N., Nathiya, D., Thakur, V., Gupta, R., Pramanik, S., Kumar, P., Gupta, N., & Patel, A. (2025). Recent advances in nanotechnology for Parkinson's disease: Diagnosis, treatment, and future perspectives. *Nano Express, 12*, 1535682. PMID: 39911864

Yallop, A. C., Gică, O. A., Moisescu, O. I., Coro , M. M., & Séraphin, H. (2021). The digital traveller: Implications for data ethics and data governance in tourism and hospitality. *Journal of Consumer Marketing*, *40*(2), 155–170. DOI: 10.1108/JCM-12-2020-4278

Yalvac, I. (2021). Artificial intelligence and glaucoma. *Glokom-Katarakt/Journal of Glaucoma-Cataract, 16*(3), 127–130. DOI: 10.37844/glauc.cat.2021.16.22

Yang, G. Z., Cambias, J., Cleary, K., Daimler, E., Drake, J., Dupont, P. E., & Hawkes, D. (2017). Medical robotics—Regulatory, ethical, and legal considerations for increasing levels of autonomy. *Science Robotics*, *2*(4), eaam8638. Advance online publication. DOI: 10.1126/scirobotics.aam8638 PMID: 33157870

Yang, G., Zhang, J., & Li, H. (2019). Generative AI for synthesizing medical literature: A review. *Journal of Biomedical Research*, *33*(4), 321–335.

Yang, M., Huang, D., Wan, W., & Jin, M. (2024). Federated learning for privacy-preserving medical data sharing in drug development. *Applied and Computational Engineering*, *108*(1), 7–13. DOI: 10.54254/2755-2721/2025.LD17879

Yang, S., & Berdine, G. (2024). Confusion matrix. *The Southwest Respiratory and Critical Care Chronicles*, *12*(53), 75–79. DOI: 10.12746/swrccc.v12i53.1391

Yan, L., Yin-He, S., Qian, Y., Zhi-Yu, S., Chun-Zi, W., & Zi-Yun, L. (2021). Method of reaching consensus on probability of food safety based on the integration of finite credible data on block chain. *IEEE Access : Practical Innovations, Open Solutions*, *9*, 123764–123776. DOI: 10.1109/ACCESS.2021.3108178

Yaqoob, I., Salah, K., Jayaraman, R., & Al-Hammadi, Y. (2022). Blockchain for healthcare data management: Opportunities, challenges, and future recommendations. *Neural Computing & Applications*, *34*(14), 11475–11490. DOI: 10.1007/s00521-020-05519-w

Yeung, K. (2021). The healthcare sector's experience of blockchain: A cross-disciplinary investigation of its real transformative potential. *Journal of Medical Internet Research*, *23*(12), e24109. DOI: 10.2196/24109 PMID: 34932009

Yi, X., Walia, E., & Babyn, P. (2019). Generative adversarial network in medical imaging. *Medical Image Analysis*, *58*, 101552. DOI: 10.1016/j.media.2019.101552 PMID: 31521965

Yu, G., Ouyang, D. F., Xiao, W., Yang, W., Xu, J., & Wang, J. (2018). Personalized treatment prediction and recommendation system for chronic disease management. *IEEE Access : Practical Innovations, Open Solutions*, *6*, 67830–67840. DOI: 10.1109/ACCESS.2018.2878612

Yuste, R., Goering, S., Arcas, B. A. Y., Bi, G., Carmena, J. M., Carter, A., Fins, J. J., Friesen, P., Gallant, J., Huggins, J. E., Illes, J., Kellmeyer, P., Klein, E., Marblestone, A., Mitchell, C., Parens, E., Pham, M., Rubel, A., Sadato, N., & Wolpaw, J. (2017). Four ethical priorities for neurotechnologies and AI. *Nature*, *551*(7679), 159–163. DOI: 10.1038/551159a PMID: 29120438

Zaabar, B., Cheikhrouhou, O., Jamil, F., Ammi, M., & Abid, M. (2021). HealthBlock: A secure blockchain-based healthcare data management system. *Computer Networks*, *200*, 108500. DOI: 10.1016/j.comnet.2021.108500

Zarour, M., Ansari, M. T. J., Alenezi, M., Sarkar, A. K., Faizan, M., Agrawal, A., Kumar, R., & Khan, R. A. (2020). Evaluating the impact of blockchain models for secure and trustworthy electronic healthcare records. *IEEE Access : Practical Innovations, Open Solutions*, *8*, 157959–157973. DOI: 10.1109/ACCESS.2020.3019829

Zehra, S. H., Ramzan, K., Viskelis, J., Viskelis, P., & Balciunaitiene, A. (2025). Advancements in Green Synthesis of Silver-Based Nanoparticles: Antimicrobial and Antifungal Properties in Various Films. *Nano Express*, *15*(4), 252. PMID: 39997815

Zhang, B., Shi, H., & Wang, H. (2023). Machine learning and AI in cancer prognosis, prediction, and treatment selection: A critical approach. *Journal of Multidisciplinary Healthcare*, *16*, 1779–1791. DOI: 10.2147/JMDH.S410301

Zhang, J., Yeoh, G. H., & Kabir, I. I. (2025). Polyurethane Materials for Fire Retardancy: Synthesis, Structure, Properties, and Applications. *Nano Express*, *8*(2), 64.

Zhang, J., Deng, M., Xu, C., Li, D., Yan, X., Gu, Y., Zhong, M., Gao, H., Liu, Y., Zhang, J., Qu, X., & Zhang, J. (2024). Dual-Prodrug-Based Hyaluronic Acid Nanoplatform Provides Cascade-Boosted Drug Delivery for Oxidative Stress-Enhanced Chemotherapy. *ACS Applied Materials & Interfaces*, *16*(38), 50459–50473. DOI: 10.1021/acsami.4c11662 PMID: 39258403

Zhang, S., Kong, N., Wang, Z., Zhang, Y., Ni, C., Li, L., Wang, H., Yang, M., Yang, W., & Yan, F. (2024). Nanochemistry of gold: From surface engineering to dental healthcare applications. *Chemical Society Reviews*, *53*(8), 3656–3686. DOI: 10.1039/D3CS00894K PMID: 38502089

Zhang, Y., & Boulos, M. N. K. (2023). Generative AI in medical education: Enhancing interdisciplinary learning. *Medical Teacher*, *45*(2), 101–110.

Zhavoronkov, A., Ivanenkov, Y. A., Aliper, A., Veselov, M. S., Aladinskiy, V. A., Aladinskaya, A. V., & Zholus, A. (2019). Deep learning enables rapid identification of potent DDR1 kinase inhibitors. *Nature Biotechnology*, *37*(9), 1038–1040. DOI: 10.1038/s41587-019-0224-x PMID: 31477924

Zheng, H., Huang, J., Jiang, L., & Liu, X. (2020). Emerging trends in artificial intelligence and healthcare: A comprehensive review. *IEEE Access : Practical Innovations, Open Solutions*, *8*, 78023–78038. DOI: 10.1109/ACCESS.2020.2982174

Zheng, P. V. R. M., Wang, T. J., & Chen, C. K. (2020). AI-driven drug repurposing: Leveraging generative models for novel therapeutic discoveries. *Journal of Chemical Information and Modeling*, *60*(11), 5811–5820. DOI: 10.1021/acs.jcim.0c00955 PMID: 32791826

Zheng, X., Liu, M., Wu, Y., Chen, Y., He, W., & Guo, Z. (2024). An AIE-based monofunctional Pt(ii) complex for photodynamic therapy through synergism of necroptosis-ferroptosis. *RSC Chemical Biology*, *5*(2), 141–147. DOI: 10.1039/D3CB00113J PMID: 38333194

Zhou, J., Pompano, R. R., & Zhao, Y. (2020). Machine learning for drug discovery and design. *Nature Reviews. Drug Discovery*, *19*(9), 651–669. DOI: 10.1038/s41573-020-00027-9

Zhou, J., & Wang, Y. (2022). Symptom normalization using NLP for AI guided diagnostics. *Journal of Healthcare*, *15*(3), 188–199.

Zhou, Y., Chia, M. A., Wagner, S. K., Ayhan, M. S., Williamson, D. J., Struyven, R. R., Liu, T., Xu, M., Lozano, M. G., Woodward-Court, P., Kihara, Y., Allen, N., Gallacher, J. E. J., Littlejohns, T., Aslam, T., Bishop, P., Black, G., Sergouniotis, P., Atan, D., & Keane, P. A. (2023). A foundation model for generalizable disease detection from retinal images. *Nature*, *622*(7981), 156–163. DOI: 10.1038/s41586-023-06555-x PMID: 37704728

Zhu, Y., Salowe, R., Chow, C., Li, S., Bastani, O., & O'Brien, J. M. (2024). Advancing glaucoma care: Integrating artificial intelligence in diagnosis, management, and progression detection. *Bioengineering (Basel, Switzerland)*, *11*(2), 122. DOI: 10.3390/bioengineering11020122 PMID: 38391608

Zuboff, S. (2019). *The age of surveillance capitalism*. PublicAffairs.

Zuhair, V., Babar, A., Ali, R., Oduoye, M. O., Noor, Z., Chris, K., Okon, I. I., & Rehman, L. U. (2024). Exploring the impact of artificial intelligence on global health and enhancing healthcare in developing nations. *Journal of Primary Care & Community Health*, *15*, 21501319241245847. DOI: 10.1177/21501319241245847 PMID: 38605668

About the Contributors

Jingyuan Zhao obtained her PhD in Management Science and Engineering from University of Science and Technology of China. She completed four postdoctoral programs respectively in Mathematical and Computational Science with University of Toronto Mississauga, in Innovation and Governance with University of Toronto, in Management of Technology with Université du Québec à Montréal, and in Technological Economics with Harbin Institute of Technology. Dr. Zhao's research expertise includes management of technology innovation, innovation and entrepreneurship, behaviour and information technology, human-computer interaction, and science and technology policy. She has teaching experience of 15 years at the graduate and undergraduate level. Research portfolio includes peer-reviewed articles in highly regarded journals, authored books, multiple book chapters, and conference presentations. Dr. Zhao also has extensive industry experience and provides consulting services to major corporations, such as China Mobile. She serves as editor-in-chief of International Journal of e-Collaboration (IJeC).

***

Tasneem Jahan is a dedicated academician and researcher with strong expertise in computer science, artificial intelligence, deep learning, image processing, and secure data analytics. Her research interests broadly include deep learning architectures, convolutional neural networks (CNNs), image encryption and retrieval, optimization algorithms such as Grey Wolf Optimization (GWO), secure medical image analysis, and applied artificial intelligence. She has contributed to extensive literature reviews, research paper reconstruction, and content development aligned with IEEE and Springer standards, demonstrating strong analytical and technical writing skills.

Prerna Agrawal is a distinguished academician and researcher with over 14+ years of experience in higher education and applied research, specializing in machine learning, data science, cloud computing, and big data and currently serving as an Assistant Professor at the Faculty of Computer Applications & IT (MCA), GLS University, Ahmedabad, India. She earned her Ph.D. in Computer Science from GLS University, with a focus on machine learning and application security. Her academic interests span a broad spectrum including machine learning, big data analytics, cloud computing, computer networks, data science and databases. She has published more than 20 research papers in high-impact national and international journals and conferences, including IEEE and Springer. Her recent work includes AI-driven solutions for disease detection, automated job role prediction through resume analysis, and cybersecurity frameworks using big data analytics. She is actively guiding Ph.D. research scholars and is a recognized reviewer for prestigious journals and conferences such as the Journal of Ambient Intelligence and Humanized Computing, IAES International Journal of Artificial Intelligence, and several Springer and IGI Global publications. Her scholarly work has garnered 177 citations on Google Scholar, earning her an H-index of 7, reflecting the impact and recognition of her scholarly contributions. In addition to her research, she is passionate about digital education and has developed and published a suite of online courses on platforms like Udemy and TutorialsPoint, covering topics such as machine learning with Python, cloud computing fundamentals, and Python programming for beginners. She has been recognized for her contributions with multiple accolades, including best paper awards and certifications for excellence in academic leadership.

Vijay Anant Athavale has a rich teaching, research and administrative experience of more than 34 years of serving in Government and Private Universities and Colleges in India and abroad. He has served academic assignments in Canada, the Republic of Yemen and the Republic of Sudan. He also served as an expatriate expert for the United Nations Development Programme to Ethiopia. He has been instrumental in shaping of several Institutes of repute offering Technical and Management Education in India. He has successfully led the transformation journey of some of the institutes, which has resulted in national and international accreditations. As a thought leader and a subject-matter expert, he has presented numerous sessions at Conferences, FDPs, and Workshops as Keynote speaker, Session Chair, Organizing Committee member, TPC etc. He is a reviewer for several SCIE, Scopus, WoS indexed journals. He is also an associate editor of International Journal of Electrical and Electronic Research (IJEER) (ISSN 2347-470X) which is indexed by SCOPUS. He has contributed several chapters in books & handbooks published by IGI Global USA, Taylor and Francis Group, UK, Springer etc.

Muralidhar L B is a professionally qualified dental surgeon. He holds Ph.D. from Canara Bank School of Management Studies, Bangalore University after his MBA from Christ University. He has 18 years of total teaching experience spanning across dental education, healthcare management and general management and 4 years of corporate experience. He has worked as research associate in Institute for Social and Economic Change, Bangalore in a project entitled as "Management By and For Common Man: An Exploration of the Concept and Direction for Future"post Ph.D. He had secured 28th rank in S.S.L.C examination for Karnataka State in 1993. His 27 patents have been published and 2 design patents have been granted. He has 41 research publications to his credit out of which 28 are Scopus-indexed and 5 are ABDC indexed. He has co-authored 5 books. He is currently working as Assistant Professor in Department of Business Management Studies, School of Commerce, Jain Deemed to be University, Bangalore.

Hina Bansal is an inspirational teacher and researcher with 16+ years of experience specializing in Bioinformatics/Computational Biology, working as an Assistant Professor in the centre for Bioinformatics and Computational Biology, Amity Institute of Biotechnology, Amity University, Noida since January 2008. Her research interest includes Network pharmacology, functional Genomics and Genome informatics, NGS, functional Proteomics, Molecular docking and simulation, Python, Artificial intelligence, and Machine learning. She has more than forty research publications in reputable peer reviewed journals, book, and book chapters. She has presented numerous papers in various national and international conferences. She has been an active member in organising several workshops and conferences. She is a dynamic reviewer for various peer reviewed journals including BMC Computational Biology and Scientific Reports. She is very proficient in programming languages like C, C++, Java and Python. With her perseverance, academic excellence, research capabilities, and leadership abilities, Dr. Hina a very potential candidate.

Somnath Rajkumar Dhavale, Master of Technology (MTech.) in Computer Science from J.N.T.U. Hyderabad, India. His areas of interest include AI, ML, and Data Science, with active involvement in AI-driven agricultural systems

Vandana Dubey is working as Professor in the Department of Computer Science & Engineering at Sagar Institute of Research & Technology, Bhopal, Madhya Pradesh, India. Earlier, she has worked in Amity University, Lucknow, U.P., Ashoka Institute of Technology & Management, Varanasi, U.P. and C. Byregowda Institute of Technlogy, Kolar, Karnataka. She has a total of 15+ years' experience in teaching and research. She has received many awards and recognition for her research and academic contributions which includes 'Young Scientist Award', 'Best Paper Award' and 'Certificate of Honour' etc. She has published 38 original research works in National/International journals indexed in SCI, Scopus and UGC etc. She has presented 58 papers/posters in National/International conferences/seminar. She has published 19 book chapters and 4 patents in the field of low power circuit design and machine learning. Her main area of interest includes Low Power Circuit Design, Computer Organization & Architecture, Artificial Intelligence, Machine Learning and Computer Graphics.

Leena G. Pillai is currently an Assistant Professor in the Department of Artificial Intelligence and Machine Learning at Sree Saraswathi Thyagaraja College, Pollachi, Tamil Nadu. She served as a Research Scientist at the Virtual Resource Centre for Language Computing, Digital University Kerala, where she led research initiatives in low-resource language technologies and speech processing systems. She was awarded the Doctor of Philosophy (Ph.D.) in Computer Science by the University of Kerala for her doctoral research titled "Acoustic and Articulatory Evaluation of Speech Signals using Machine Learning Techniques." She also holds an M.Phil. in Computer Science from Cochin University of Science and Technology and a Master of Computer Applications (MCA) from Bharathidasan University. Her research interests include natural language processing, automatic speech recognition, articulatory inversion, and AI-based assistive technologies. She has published in leading journals and conferences and has contributed to the development of ASR and transliteration models for underrepresented Indian languages, such as Malasar and Malayalam. Several of these resources are publicly hosted on Hugging Face. She is the recipient of the Association for Computational Linguistics (ACL) grant to present at EMNLP 2024 and has received Best Paper Awards at national conferences. She has served as a reviewer for international journals and IEEE conferences and has contributed to organizing academic events on AI and language technology.

Savita Gandhi is a distinguished academician with over 46 years of teaching and research experience. She served as a Professor and Dean at the Faculty of Computer Applications and Information Technology (PG), GLS University, Ahmedabad. Prior to this, she held the position of Professor and Head at the Department of Computer Science, Gujarat University, and began her academic journey as a lecturer in the Department of Mathematics at M.S. University, Baroda. Dr. Gandhi's research interests span a wide spectrum including Data Compression, Ad Hoc Networks, Image Processing, Machine Learning, Data Analytics, and Data Mining. She has authored over 80 research articles in reputed national and international journals and conferences, many of which are indexed in Scopus and Web of Science. Her scholarly contributions are evidenced by an i10-index of 10 and over 470 citations on Google Scholar. A pioneer in the field of digital education in India, She served as the Principal Investigator for the Ministry of Education's e-PG Pathshala initiative, leading the development of 326 modules in Information Technology. She was also the Paper Coordinator for the "Numerical Methods" course, contributing to an innovative e-book that integrates textual content with video lectures. Furthermore, she developed two Massive Open Online Courses (MOOCs) on the SWAYAM platform—"Artificial Intelligence" and "Introduction to Computer Networks and Internet Protocols"—enhancing the reach and quality of online education in India. Her research leadership extends to national projects, having led a three-year project under ISRO's Chandrayaan-1 initiative and another on Citizen Science awarded by the Department of Science and Technology (DST), Government of India. Dr. Gandhi is a senior member of IEEE, a Fellow of the Gujarat Science Academy (GSA), and a life member of the Computer Society of India (CSI). She is a sought-after speaker, having delivered numerous keynote addresses, expert lectures, and invited talks at academic conferences, faculty development programs, and seminars across the country. In recognition of her academic excellence and service, Dr. Gandhi has received several honors including the Best Paper Award, the Global Excellence Award, and a Gold Medal during her postgraduate studies.

Kamlesh Kumar Gautam is an Associate Professor & Deputy HOD at the Department of Computer Science, Mewar institute of Management, Vasundhara, Ghaziabad, U.P, India

Swapna H. R holds two Ph.D. degrees in Management — one from CMR University, Bangalore, and another from Rayalaseema University, Kurnool. She is an MBA in Finance from VTU University. She has over 18 years of teaching experience in the areas of Finance, Analytics, Statistics, Entrepreneurship, and Human Resource Management, along with 4 years of industry experience. Her research expertise spans Statistics, Behavioural Finance, Employee Engagement, Artificial Intelligence, Entrepreneurship, research on millennials, customer engagement, social media, and the health sector. She has published over 100 research articles in National and International Journals, of which 46 have been indexed in Scopus, Web of Science (WoS), Emerald, Springer, and ABDC. She has presented papers at National and International Conferences, including in the USA, Malaysia, and Spain, and has received several Best Paper Presenter Awards. She has authored over 25 textbooks in the fields of Statistics, Entrepreneurship, Business Analytics, Healthcare, and Event Management. Her book Business Analytics received the Golden Book Award of 2022. She also received the Excellence Researcher Award on May 30, 2025. Another feather in her cap is her achievement in the field of Intellectual Property Rights, with 14 patents published, 2 granted, and 4 more filed. She has also curated and developed a SWAYAM course titled "Microfinance and Self-Help Groups," contributing to the promotion of inclusive education and financial literacy at the national level. She serves as an editor for several Scopus-indexed journals under IGI Global, Public Administration and Policy (Emerald Publishing), and PubMed-indexed medical journals. She is an active member of ENACTUS, an international social entrepreneurship forum linked with several NGOs, where she contributes to sustainability initiatives and drives impactful community projects. She passionately mentors students to develop sustainable business solutions and promotes social innovation and environmental responsibility. Dr. Swapna has also been at the forefront of social service initiatives such as organizing blood donation camps in association with the Rotary Club and TTK, supporting the Ministry of Education's One-on-One COVID-19 emotional support drive, and leading environmental awareness campaigns like "One Earth."

Sagar Somayya Hiremath holds a Master of Technology and a Bachelor of Engineering in Computer Science and Engineering. His areas of interest include Mobile Application Development, Web Technologies, Operating Systems, Database Management, Python, and Java Programming. He is presently working as an Assistant Professor in the Department of Information Technology at Walchand Institute of Technology, Solapur, India. He has published 10 research papers in international journals.

Sheeba K P., M. Sc, PhD (pursuing). She is having a academic Experience of 5 years and 8 years in health care industries like hospitals, health insurance organizations and TPA companies both in abroad and in India. She is a post graduate in Hospital Administration from Rajiv Gandhi University of Health Sciences, currently pursuing her PhD in management. She is a member of associate ship in general insurance from Insurance Institute of India (III). She has attended many workshops and Faculty Development Programs, seminars, and orientation programs. . She has presented more than 3 research articles at National and International conferences. She has published few research articles in UGC care listed journals. She is currently working as Assistant Professor in Department of Business Management Studies, School of Commerce, Jain Deemed to be University, Bengaluru, India.

Shradha Kakade is a sincere, hardworking, and enthusiastic individual. She is passionate about learning and continuously works to improve her knowledge and skills. She believes in discipline, honesty, and positive thinking. With a strong interest in education and self-development, Shradha always tries to give her best in every responsibility she undertakes. She aims to grow personally and professionally while contributing positively to society.

Navneet Kaur is working as a Professor in Department of Computer Science and Engineering, Sagar Institute of Research and Technology, Bhopal, India. She received her B.Tech degree from NIT, Surat, India and M.Tech from Barkatullah University, Bhopal, India. She has been awarded PhD. From the University Institute of Technology (UIT), Rajiv Gandhi Proudyogiki Vishwavidyalaya (RGPV), Bhopal. She has 26 years of teaching experience and has published more than 35 research papers in peer-reviewed reputed international journals and conferences. She has published 3 patents and 7 copyrights in various fields of Engineering. Her main research interests include Mobile ad-hoc network, signal processing, Machine learning, IOT, Analog and digital communication. She is a lifetime member of IETE.

Sarang Khole, Master of Engineering in Computer Science, India. His areas of interest include Artificial Intelligence, Machine Learning, and Data Science, with a strong focus on research and innovative teaching practices.

L.M.R.J. Lobo is a B.Sc in statistics and a BE in Computer Engineering from Shivaji University, Kolhapur. He has also completed his MTech in Computer and Information Technology from IIT Kharagpur, India. His area of interest include Artificial intelligence, Machine Learning, Genetic Algorithms and System software. He is presently working as a Professor and Head, Department of Information Technology at Walchand Institute of Technology, Solapur, India. He has published more than 80 Papers in reputed Journals and conferences. He also received International Luminary Award in Teaching.

Varsha Vyankatesh Manglaram is a Master of Technology graduate in Computer Science and Engineering from Walchand Institute of Technology, Solapur, Maharashtra, India. Her research interests include machine learning, big data analytics, natural language processing, cloud computing, artificial intelligence, deep learning, medical image processing, and health informatics. She has actively participated in research projects focused on deep learning and medical image analysis, particularly in healthcare applications. Her current research involves developing an AI-based system for lung cancer diagnosis and treatment recommendation using convolutional neural networks and generative AI techniques. She is proficient in Python, TensorFlow, and various image processing tools. Her primary research interests lie in AI-driven healthcare solutions and health informatics. She is based in Solapur, India.

Mbuyi Mukendi, Ph.D. is a data scientist, researcher, and public servant with over two decades of experience in information systems and academic study. She holds a Doctorate in Data Science from National University (2023), where her seminal research focused on "Contributing Factors to Primary Open-Angle Glaucoma in

Kasaï Central, Democratic Republic of Congo." Dr. Mukendi's interdisciplinary background is marked by a unique blend of technical and linguistic expertise; she earned a Bachelor's degree in Computer Information Systems from the College of Saint Rose (2001) and a Master of Arts in French Studies from the University at Albany (2008). A polyglot fluent in Tshiluba, Swahili, Lingala, English, and French, Dr. Mukendi has served as a Teacher's Assistant at the University at Albany and has been a dedicated employee of New York State since 2006. She is a proficient programmer in Java, R, and Python, with a particular interest in the application of machine learning to solve complex global health challenges. Driven by a vision to bridge the gap between data and patient care, Dr. Mukendi is currently in the process of establishing a non-profit organization dedicated to advancing research into non-communicable diseases and the development of appropriate, data-driven therapies. Beyond her technical and state service, she is a motivational speaker who finds deep fulfillment in her faith and family. She resides in New York with her three sons.

Siddharam Patil is serving as an Assistant Professor at Walchand Institute of Technology (WIT), Solapur, and has 11 years of rich experience in teaching and academics. He has completed his M.Tech and is presently pursuing his Ph.D., with research focused on the Design and Development of Security Protocols and Frameworks for Resource-Constrained Internet of Things (IoT) Devices. His research interests lie in IoT security, cryptographic protocols, lightweight security mechanisms, and secure frameworks for constrained environments.

Premalatha R. is an Assistant Professor in the Department of Computer Science and Engineering at Tagore Institute of Engineering and Technology, Salem. She holds an M.E. in Computer Science and Engineering from Anna University. With prior experience as a Project Associate at IIT Madras, she has contributed to projects in E-Services and High-Performance Computing Environments (HPCE). Her expertise spans PHP, SQL, Linux, and supercomputer maintenance. She has strong technical knowledge in web development, programming, and system administration. Dedicated and flexible, she is committed to advancing academic excellence, research, and the growth of her students and institution.

Madhu S has 31+ years of experience in academia and industry. A prolific author and researcher, he has authored 85 books, holds 26 design patent, 5 utility patent published, published 30+ articles and book chapters, and has won multiple awards. He serves as a consultant, keynote speaker, jury member, resource person, and academic mentor, guiding hundreds of students and contributing widely to research and innovation. BoS and BoE member for various universities.

N Sathyanarayana has over 15 years of teaching experience at both undergraduate and postgraduate levels. He holds a Master of Business Administration degree from Visvesvaraya Technological University (VTU) and a Master of Commerce degree from Periyar University. He has completed his Ph.D. in Banking and Finance from Dayananda Sagar University. Currently, he serves as an Assistant Professor in the School of Commerce at Jain (Deemed-to-be University), Bangalore. He has published 24 research papers in international journals, including three indexed in Scopus, and seven papers in national journals. Additionally, he has presented 14 research papers at international conferences and 11 at national conferences. He has co-authored two books at the national level and contributed 21 Scopus-indexed book chapters.

Vikas Sharma is an active academician and researcher in the field of computer science with 7 years of experience. He earned M. Tech degree specialized in Computer Science. He is involved in academic development and scholarly activities. He is member of International Association of Engineers, The Society of Digital Information and Wireless Communications, Global Professors Welfare Association, International Association of Academic plus Corporate (IAAC), Computer Science Teachers Association and Internet Society. His research interest includes Cloud Computing, Artificial Intelligence, Machine Learning; published more than 55 research articles with 4 books and 75 book chapters in edited books. He is contributing as member of editorial and reviewers' boards in conferences and various computer journals and edited books published by Elsevier, CRC Press, Taylor and Francis, Springer, IGI global, Wiley Publication, IET Publication, De Gruyter, River Publication etc.

Ritu Shrivastava did B.Tech. in Computer Science and Engineering from SATI Vidisha in 1992 and completed her PhD. In Computer Science and Engg in the year 2014. Her area of specialization includes Web Engineering, Data Mining, Big Data and Cloud Computing. She has over 25 years of teaching experience. The experience includes 10 years in the Computer Science Department of "Maulana Azad National Institute of Technology (MANIT)" at Bhopal. MANIT which is among the seven National Institutes of Technology in India, commanding a premium from best of the students and industries across India. She has also worked with many Institute & Universities of National and International repute. For the last 11 years, she is working in SIRT Bhopal in various capacities. During the course of her 25 Years experience, she has published many papers in National and International Journals.

Shikha Singh is presently working as Assistant Professor in Department of Computer Science and Engineering, Amity University, Uttar Pradesh, Lucknow

Campus, India. She has more than 18 years of teaching experience. She has guided many M. Tech dissertations and more than 55 B.Tech. projects. She has published more than 35 research papers in Journals and Conference Proceedings. Her academic interest includes teaching Databases, Machine Learning Algorithms, Large Language Models and Data Visualization, Various Programming languages including C, C++ and Python.

Tarun Kumar Vashishth is an active academician and researcher in the field of Computer Science with 22 years of experience. He earned Ph.D. Mathematics degree specialized in Operations Research; served several academic positions such as Dy. Director, HoD, NAAC Coordinator, Academic Coordinator, Member Secretary of Department Research Committee, Assistant Center Superintendent and Head Examiner in University Examinations. He is involved in academic development and scholarly activities. He is member of International Association of Engineers, The Society of Digital Information and Wireless Communications, Global Professors Welfare Association, International Association of Academic plus Corporate (IAAC), Computer Science Teachers Association and Internet Society . His research interest includes Cloud Computing, Artificial Intelligence, Machine Learning and Operations Research; published more than 50 research articles & conference papers with 2 book and 80 book chapters. He is contributing as member of editorial and reviewers boards in conferences and various computer journals and edited books published by Elsevier, CRC Press, Taylor and Francis, Springer, IGI Global Scientific Publishing, Wiley Publication, IET Publication, De Gruyter, River Publication etc.

Shubham Suresh Vyavahare has completed his BCA from PAH Solapur University, India, and holds certifications in Power BI, Cloud Computing, DevOps Engineering, and Gen-AI Tools. Currently working as a Technical Assistant at Walchand Institute of Technology, Solapur, his research focuses on AI and Machine Learning in healthcare. He actively engages in continuous professional development through Faculty Development Programs (FDPs) on Agentic AI, Agile Educational Practices, and Professional Growth. He has presented his research at international conferences (IC-SEDEx'2025), published various book chapters, and serves as an active peer reviewer for IGI Global.

Aparna Yemul holds a Master of Technology degree in Computer Science and Engineering from Walchand Institute of Technology, Solapur, Maharashtra, India. Her academic and research pursuits span across multiple domains including artificial intelligence, machine learning, blockchain technology, deep learning, natural language processing, cloud computing, medical image processing, and health informatics. She has been actively engaged in research projects focusing on the integration of deep learning methods in medical image analysis to improve healthcare outcomes. Currently, her work is centered on designing a system based on Deep Learning and Generative AI Techniques for Enhanced Diagnosis and Treatment Suggestion of Kidney Diseases. Skilled in Python, TensorFlow, and advanced image processing frameworks, she is committed to leveraging AI innovations to develop intelligent healthcare solutions that can enhance diagnostic accuracy and patient care. Aparna is based in Solapur, India.

Rajani Mahesh Yemul has completed her B.E. in Computer Science & Engineering from Solapur University and her M.Tech in Computer Science & Engineering from PAH Solapur University, India. Her areas of interest include Artificial Intelligence, Machine Learning, Computer Networks, and System Software. She is presently working as an Assistant Professor in the Department of Information Technology at Walchand Institute of Technology, Solapur, India. She actively engages in continuous professional development through Faculty Development Programs (FDPs) on Agentic AI, Agile Educational Practices, and Professional Growth. She has published her research in reputed journals, conferences, and book chapters, and serves as an active peer reviewer for IGI Global.

Index

A

B

C

D

E

F

G

H

I

K

L

M

N

O

P

R

S

T

W

www.ingramcontent.com/pod-product-compliance
Lightning Source LLC
LaVergne TN
LVHW062331300926
849161LV00007B/1653